SOCIETY

This book is dedicated to all teachers of sociology who are devoting their lives to helping others understand their place in American society and in the larger world.

John J Macionis

SOCIETY
The Basics

John J. Macionis
Kenyon College

Prentice Hall, Englewood Cliffs, New Jersey 07632

Library of Congress Cataloging-in-Publication Data

MACIONIS, JOHN J.
    Society: the basics/John J. Macionis.
      p. cm.
    Includes bibliographical references and index.
    ISBN 0-13-817222-6
    1. Sociology. I. Title.
    HM51.M1657 1992
    301—dc20   91–10075
                             CIP

Acquisitions Editor: Nancy Roberts
Editor-in-Chief: Charlyce Jones Owen
Development Editor: Susanna Lesan and Diana Drew
Production Editor: Marianne Peters
Marketing Manager: Roland Hernandez
Designers: Meryl Poweski, Lee Cohen, and Amy Rosen
Cover Designer: Bruce Kenselaar
Prepress Buyer: Debbie Kesar
Manufacturing Buyer: Mary Ann Gloriande
Photo Editor: Lorinda Morris-Nantz
Photo Researcher: June Whitworth
Supplements Editor: Sharon Chambliss
Editorial Assistant: Pat Naturale
Page Layout: Charles Pelletreau and Karen Noferi
Cover Art: *Crowd* by Diana Ong. Photo by Superstock, Inc.

© 1992 by Prentice-Hall, Inc.
A Simon & Schuster Company
Englewood Cliffs, New Jersey 07632

Printed in the United States of America
10 9 8 7 6 5 4 3 2 1

ISBN   0-13-817222-6

Prentice-Hall International (UK) Limited, *London*
Prentice-Hall of Australia Pty. Limited, *Sydney*
Prentice-Hall Canada Inc., *Toronto*
Prentice-Hall Hispanoamericana, S.A., *Mexico*
Prentice-Hall of India Private Limited, *New Delhi*
Prentice-Hall of Japan, Inc., *Tokyo*
Simon & Schuster Asia Pte. Ltd., *Singapore*
Editora Prentice-Hall do Brasil, Ltda., *Rio de Janeiro*

Brief Contents

Contents

4

Social Interaction in Everyday Life 77

5

Groups and Organizations 99

6

Deviance 123

10
Sex and Gender   229

11
Economics and Politics   255

12
Family and Religion 287

13
Education and Medicine 317

14
Population and Urbanization   347

15
Social Change and Modernity   373

Boxes

CRITICAL THINKING

CROSS-CULTURAL COMPARISON

SOCIOLOGY OF EVERYDAY LIFE

Preface

A distinctive introductory sociology text appeared in 1987 inviting students in community colleges, state universities, and private liberal arts institutions to discover a fresh and exciting way to see the world and themselves. A major challenge in writing *Sociology* was to address the interests of the diversity of America's students—African-American, white, Hispanic American and Asian American; male and female; traditional younger students as well as non-traditional older learners. My motivation to create a broadly inclusive text is the product of twenty years' teaching in a wide range of academic settings, including large universities, small colleges, community colleges, and even a prison and a police academy. From these experiences, I have learned that inclusiveness is good sociology, because a text that is inviting to *all* categories of students provides more learning for *each* by portraying the rich variety of American society.

The swelling popularity of the subsequent editions of *Sociology* has been most gratifying. At this point, the text has been used at more than 500 colleges and universities in the United States and around the world. Despite the enthusiastic reception—or perhaps because of it—a number of instructors have expressed an interest in a brief version of the book. The result is *Society: The Basics*, a fifteen-chapter paperbound text that provides the essentials of sociological insight in a trim and inexpensive format.

Society: The Basics is not the first text of its kind, but it is distinctive. Authors (or sometimes editors) have produced brief texts simply by cutting down a longer manuscript. Such cut-and-paste texts may be attractively priced, but typically they do not earn the loyalty of instructors, who try them for a term only to return to more comprehensive books. By contrast, *Society: The Basics* has been thoroughly *rewritten*. It reads seamlessly because it has been planned and prepared to be a short text. Just as important, this brief book contains each and every major topic found in the hardback version. There are no holes in the coverage; the presentations are simply more focused and direct, providing fundamentals without frills. I hope that short-text users will conclude, in this case, that less is truly more.

CONTENT

The crafting of *Society: The Basics* has been guided by research as to what instructors wish to include in their classes. Simply put, we offer the greatest coverage to the topics that most people define as basic to the introductory course. Chapter 1 ("Sociology: Perspective, Theory, and Method") illuminates the discipline's special point of view that so often transforms the world of beginning students. In addition, this first chapter presents all the major theoretical approaches of the discipline, and explains how sociologists use methods of scientific research to test their insights.

The next five chapters present core sociological concepts. Chapter 2 ("Culture") explains how and why our unique species has created fascinating and variable ways of life around the world. Chapter 3 ("Socialization: From Infancy to Aging") investigates how humans everywhere cultivate their humanity as they learn to participate in society. While highlighting the importance of the early years to the socialization process, this chapter also describes significant transformations that occur throughout the life course, including old age. Chapter 4 ("Social Interaction in Everyday Life") outlines how humans construct the daily realities that we often take for granted. Chapter 5 ("Groups and Organizations") focuses on the source of perhaps the most meaningful experiences—social groups. This chapter also investigates the expansion of formal organizations and suggests some of the problems of living in a bureaucratic age. Chapter 6 ("Deviance") analyzes how the routine operation of society promotes both deviance as well as conformity.

The next four chapters provide broader coverage of social inequality than is available in any other brief text. Chapter 7 ("Social Stratification") presents basic concepts that introduce students to the variety of human hierarchy throughout history and around the world. The chapter then focuses on dimensions of social difference in American society. Chapter 8 ("Global Inequality") is a unique chapter that demonstrates this text's commitment to global education by analyzing social stratification in the world as a whole. This chapter reveals the extent of differences in wealth and power between rich and poor societies and suggests how the regions of our world are becoming increasingly interdependent.

Society: The Basics is also unique among short texts in providing full-chapter coverage of two vital issues for the 1990s. Chapter 9 ("Race and Ethnicity") explores the racial and ethnic diversity of American society, as well as differences in social standing among various categories of Americans. Chapter 10 ("Sex and Gender") describes patterns of human sexuality and explains how societies transform the biological facts of sex into systems of gender stratification.

Next are three chapters that survey American social institutions. Society: The Basics first considers "Economics and Politics" (Chapter 11), describing how the Industrial Revolution transformed the Western world, contrasting capitalist and socialist economic models, and explaining how economic systems are linked to a society's distribution of power. This chapter also contains coverage of the important issues of war and peace.

Chapter 12 ("Family and Religion") investigates two institutions central to the organization and symbolism of social life. The chapter begins by focusing on the variety of American families, while making frequent comparisons to kinship systems in other parts of the world. The basic elements of religious life are discussed next, with an overview of religious trends in the United States.

Chapter 13 ("Education and Medicine") examines two institutions that have gained importance in the modern world. The historical emergence of schooling is discussed first, in the context of the many ways in which educational systems are linked to other social institutions. Like education, medicine has become a central institution during the last century. The chapter concludes by explaining how and why this has occurred, showing how various societies have devised distinctive strategies for promoting public health.

The final two chapters of the text focus on important dimensions of social change. Chapter 14 spotlights *population growth and urbanization* in the United States and throughout the world. The reasons for the increase in size of the human community are presented, along with an historical account of the invention and dispersion of cities. As in other chapters, the discussion of American trends is supplemented with material about poor societies where cities are reaching unprecedented size. Chapter 15 offers an analysis of *social change and modernity*. This chapter explains why societies change, how people forge social movements to encourage or to resist change, and the benefits and liabilities of modern social patterns.

THEMATIC FEATURES OF THE TEXT

Many of the features that have made the longer version of the text, *Sociology*, so popular are also found in *Society: The Basics*.

Placing American society in global perspective. Sociology reveals the links between individuals and their society. In the 1990s, sociology is extending its reach by showing how American society is itself shaped by its placement in the world community. Currently, only about 50,000 of some 12 million American college students have firsthand experience studying abroad, far fewer than the 350,000 foreign students in the United States. Including global material in an introductory sociology course is a sensible and significant way to help prepare our students for living in a world that is becoming increasingly interdependent. One very practical reason to do so: Eight of every ten new jobs created in the 1990s will be linked to the international economy.

Global material is found throughout *Society: The Basics*. For example, students appreciate that casual communication among Americans is easily misread by people elsewhere, they discover how American crime rates compare with those of other nations, and they learn what the expansion of multinational corporations is doing to the class structure here at home. The text also highlights the dramatic economic development of the "Pacific Rim" (including Japan, North and South Korea, Taiwan—Republic of China, Hong Kong, and the Peoples Republic of China), as well as the vexing lack of development in much of Latin America and Africa. The dramatic economic and political changes that have rippled across Eastern Europe and the ongoing reorganization of Soviet society are also included in many of the chapters of this text.

In addition, this brief version includes the new "Global Inequality" chapter that won widespread praise when it appeared in the third edition of *Sociology*. This unique chapter presents American society's position in the world's hierarchy of nations, and offers various explanations of the origins of global inequality, what that means for Americans, and what trends are likely in the coming century. Taken together, these global insights in no way lessen—but *strengthen*—the text's focus on American society.

Highlighting social diversity. American college students have never been as socially diverse as in the 1990s. This diversity has brought change to many disciplines, especially to sociology. *Society: The Basics* is a celebration of human variety. In part, this text recognizes human diversity by including full chapters on race and ethnicity and on sex and gender. In addition, the text "mainstreams" the variables of sex, race, ethnicity, and social class in each and every chapter.

Surprisingly, perhaps, many sociology texts speak only of "generic" Americans, which is, at best, a shorthand fiction. *Society: The Basics* is stronger for continuously showing how topics have different significance to various categories of readers, and for encouraging students to intellectually reach beyond their own lives.

Focus on women and men. *Society: The Basics* provides a full chapter on the important concepts of sex and gender. And rather than limiting the discussion of gender to one part of the book, this text incorporates gender into *every* chapter, showing how the topic at hand differently affects the lives of men and women. This is done by incorporating recent sociological research concerned with gender throughout the text.

Emphasis on critical thinking. Today's sociology courses are no longer designed merely to convey facts; instructors wish to stimulate students to actively learn for themselves. This text develops specific critical thinking skills: the ability to challenge common assumptions, to formulate questions, to identify and weigh appropriate evidence, and to reach reasoned conclusions.

By encouraging critical thinking skills, *Society: The Basics* empowers students to discover as well as to learn, to seek out contradictions as well as to recognize consistent arguments, and to make connections among the various dimensions of social life. These goals have guided the line-by-line rewriting of this brief edition, and are reflected in features such as the *Critical Thinking* boxes that appear in each chapter.

Theoretically clear and balanced. *Society: The Basics* makes theory easy. The discipline's major theoretical

approaches are clearly set forward in Chapter 1 and are systematically integrated in subsequent chapters. In addition to the social-conflict, structural-functional, and symbolic-interaction paradigms, various chapters employ social-exchange analysis, ethnomethodology, cultural ecology, and sociobiology.

Recent sociological research. Ongoing research continuously renews the discipline of sociology. This text blends classical sociological statements with the latest research, as reported in the leading publications in the field. About two-thirds of the research that supports this text has been published since 1980. In addition, this book contains the very latest statistical data, including some material from the 1990 census.

TEACHING FEATURES OF THE TEXT

Society: The Basics offers many class-tested features that motivate students and enhance their comprehension.

Writing style. Perhaps most important, *Society: The Basics* offers a writing style praised by students and faculty alike as elegant and engaging. This inviting text encourages students to read—even beyond their assignments. This brief edition is not a cut-down version of a longer book; it is a carefully planned and extensively rewritten book in its own right.

American sociologist George Herbert Mead once described the ideal teacher as a person able to transform simple information into real knowledge. *Society: The Basics* embodies Mead's insight by including on virtually every page illuminating illustrations that demonstrate the power of applying sociology to our everyday lives.

Engaging chapter introductions. One of the most popular features of the long version of this text is the engaging vignettes that begin each chapter. In this brief edition, as well, chapter openings spark the interest of the reader and introduce important themes that are carried through the chapter.

Topic outlines. To assist student readers, each chapter begins with a topic outline. Referring to this plan, readers can see at a glance the content and organization of each chapter.

Key concepts. Each chapter identifies key concepts with **boldfaced type** followed by *a precise, italicized definition*. An alphabetical listing of key concepts with definitions appears at the end of the chapter, and again in a glossary at the end of the book.

Chapter summaries.   Each chapter concludes with a numbered summary to aid students in reviewing material and in assessing their understanding.

Illustrations.   *Society: The Basics* has been produced with a rich program of photography, fine art, and colorful graphics to enhance learning and to make reading more fun. Each illustration has been carefully selected by the author, not simply to increase the book's visual appeal, but to enhance its teaching effectiveness. Like the writing, the illustration program incorporates work by Americans of diverse social backgrounds, and reflects the variety of the world's cultures.

Boxes.   Although boxes are found in many introductory texts, *Society: The Basics* includes two or three outstanding boxes in every chapter. Boxes are never distracting or confusing; unlike most other texts, this book links each box directly to the textual material. The boxes are of three kinds, each highlighting a central theme of the book. *Cross-Cultural Comparison* boxes invite students to compare their own way of life to other fascinating cultural patterns found around the world. *Critical Thinking* boxes provoke students to ask sociological questions, to evaluate their assumptions about the world, and to assess competing sides of controversial issues. Finally, *Sociology of Everyday Life* boxes show how many of sociology's most important insights involve new ways of thinking about familiar, everyday experiences.

UNPARALLELED COVERAGE

Society: The Basics has been designed to support discussion of *all* important topics in the field. Despite its trim dimensions, it includes coverage of dozens of issues not found in other brief texts or in many full-sized books.

Included as examples are how gender affects sociological research (Chapter 1), the controversy over making English the official language of the United States (Chapter 2), the continuing presence of stereotypes in American advertising (Chapter 3), how people are sometimes defined in terms of their physical disabilities (Chapter 4), reasons that many American workers resist Japanese organizational practices (Chapter 5), why crime

rates in the United States are so high by world standards (Chapter 6), how wealthy black Americans differ from their white counterparts (Chapter 7), how modernization can undermine the economic security of women (Chapter 8), the relative social standing of various categories of Americans (Chapter 9), the "mommy-track" controversy involving women in corporate America (Chapter 10), economic and political transformation in Eastern Europe and the Soviet Union, as well as the reasons behind the continuing arms race (Chapter 11), why some people oppose "high-tech" reproduction (Chapter 12), the development of urban magnet schools (Chapter 13), the coming super-cities of the Third World (Chapter 14), and why economic development threatens the culture of many of the world's traditional societies (Chapter 15).

SUPPLEMENTS

This text is the heart of an unsurpassed learning package that includes a wide range of proven instructional aids. John Macionis has supervised the development of all of the supplements, ensuring their quality and compatibility with the text. The goal has been to avoid gimmicks or gadgets in favor of high-quality material that truly enhances teaching.

The Annotated Instructor's Edition.   Instructors receive *Society: The Basics* in an annotated instructor's edition (AIE). The AIE is a complete student text that has been enriched by the author with additional material on every page. Annotations include summaries of research findings, statistics that allow comparisons between American society and other nations of the world, insightful quotations, and high-quality survey data from the National Opinion Research Center's (NORC) General Social Survey.

Data File.   This is an "instructor's manual" that will interest seasoned sociologists who have never used one before. Beyond chapter outlines and discussion questions, the *Data File* contains statistical data about American society and other nations of the world, brief summaries of important developments and significant research, and "briefs" on topics that expand every chapter of the text. The *Data File* has been prepared by Stephen W. Beach (Avila College) and John Macionis.

Social Survey.   *Social Survey* is a software program that allows instructors and students alike to investigate American society with the best source of survey data available, the General Social Survey from the National Opinion Research Center. Jere Bruner (Oberlin College) and John Macionis have prepared several data sets for each chapter of *Society: The Basics*; Jere Bruner has written an easy-to-understand student manual and instructor's manual to accompany the software. *Social Survey* allows multivariate analysis of survey responses by sex, race, income, education, and a host of other variables. *Social Survey* is executed on the CHIPendale 1 microcomputer program developed by James A. Davis (Harvard University) and is available to operate on IBM and Macintosh personal computers.

Seeing Ourselves: Classic, Contemporary, and Cross-Cultural Readings in Sociology.   A powerful and affordable teaching package can be created by combining this brief text with its best-selling companion reader. The second edition of *Seeing Ourselves* contains sixty-six readings edited by John J. Macionis and Nijole V. Benokraitis (University of Baltimore). *Seeing Ourselves* presents a unique combination of good sociology—classic sociological statements (by Emile Durkheim, Karl Marx, George Herbert Mead, Max Weber, and others), contemporary research findings, and cross-cultural inquiry—to provide exceptional flexibility for instructors who wish to supplement the text with primary sources. Classic, contemporary, and cross-cultural articles are provided for each of the major topics covered in the introductory sociology course.

Test Item File.   The test item file for this text contains 100 questions per chapter—1500 in all—in multiple-choice, true-false, and essay formats. Questions are page-referenced to the text. *Prentice-Hall Data Manager* is a test generator and classroom management system designed to provide maximum flexibility in producing and grading tests and quizzes. Micro Test III, Macintosh Version, is available for Macintosh users.

Prentice Hall Color Transparencies: Sociology Series I and II.   The 93 transparencies in these two series are taken from illustrations and charts in the text and other sources. The transparencies are accompanied by the *Instructor's Guide to Prentice Hall Color Transparencies: Sociology Series I and II*, a guide giving background information and suggestions for using the transparencies.

Film/Video Guide: Prentice Hall Introductory Sociology.   Prepared by Peter Remender, University of Wis-

consin of Oshkosh, the guide describes films and videos appropriate for classroom viewing for each text chapter (more than 160 films and videos are included). Summaries, discussion questions, and rental sources are provided for each film and video. Half of the entries are new to this edition of the text.

Study Guide.   Prepared by Henry Borne for this edition, each chapter in this new study guide offers a topical outline, a chapter summary, learning objectives, and chapter review questions with an answer key.

Critical Thinking Audiocassette Tape.   This 60-minute cassette shows students how to develop their critical thinking and study skills, with an emphasis on how to ask the right questions and how to analyze what is read.

ABC News/Prentice Hall Video Library for Sociology.   Video is the most dynamic supplement you can use to enhance a class. But the quality of the video material and how well it relates to your course still makes all the difference. Prentice Hall and ABC News are now working together to bring you the best and most comprehensive video ancillaries available in the college market.

   Through its wide variety of award-winning programs—*Nightline, Business World, On Business, This Week with David Brinkley, World News Tonight,* and *The Health Show*—ABC offers a resource for feature and documentary-style videos related to the chapters in *Society: The Basics*. The programs have extremely high production quality, present substantial content, and are hosted by well-versed, well-known anchors.

   Prentice Hall and its authors and editors provide the benefit of having selected videos on topics that will work well with this course and text and include notes on how to use them in the classroom. An excellent video guide in the *Data File* carefully and completely integrates the videos into your lecture. The guide has a synopsis of each video showing its relation to the chapter and discussion questions to help students focus on how concepts and theories apply to real-life situations.

A Contemporary View.   *The New York Times* and Prentice Hall are sponsoring *A Contemporary View*, a program designed to enhance student access to current information of relevance in the classroom. Through this program, the core subject matter provided in the text is supplemented by a collection of current articles from one of the world's most distinguished newspapers, *The New York Times*. These articles demonstrate the vital, ongoing connection between what is learned in the classroom and what is happening in the world around us. To enjoy the wealth of information of *The New York Times* daily, a reduced subscription rate is available. For information, call toll-free 1–800–631–1222.

Prentice Hall and *The New York Times* are proud to co-sponsor A *Contemporary View*. We hope it will make the reading of both textbooks and newspapers a more dynamic, involving process.

A Year That Changed the World.   *The New York Times* and Prentice Hall are also sponsoring *A Year That Changed the World*, a collection of articles from *The New York Times* covering the dramatic changes in China, the Soviet Union, Eastern Europe, and South Africa from May 1989 to July 1990. The implications of these changes are covered in specific chapters in *Society: The Basics*, but it was also thought helpful to gather together in one place the headline articles that chronicled the events of this amazing year.

ACKNOWLEDGMENTS

The conventional practice of designating a single author obscures the efforts of dozens of women and men that have resulted in *Sociology* as well as *Society: The Basics*. Nancy Roberts, sociology editor at Prentice Hall, is an energetic colleague and valued friend who has provided spirit, support, and sound advice. Susanna Lesan has played a major part in the development of all my texts at Prentice Hall, and her exceptional editorial eye is once again evident here. I am grateful to John Paul Jones, national sales manager, and all the Prentice Hall sales representatives for their enthusiastic efforts on behalf of the various editions of *Sociology* and for their support of this brief text.

The production of *Society: The Basics* was supervised by Marianne Peters. She expended extraordinary time and energy, kept track of countless details, and was relentless in the pursuit of excellence. Books of this quality are simply not possible without the talent and dedication of people such as she. The interior design of the book is the creative work of Meryl Poweski, Lee Cohen, and Amy Rosen. Charles Pelletreau and Karen Noferi created each of the pages with exceptional skill. Copyediting of the manuscript was provided by Diana Drew and Amy Marsh Macionis. Lorinda Morris-Nantz, June Whitworth, and Chris Pullo served as photography researchers; Joelle Burroughs assisted in securing the fine art. Special thanks is due to my friend Paul Liebhart for allowing us to use many of his stunning photographs in this text.

The marketing program for this book is the work of Roland Hernandez. I also wish to extend my sincere gratitude to Bill Webber, Susan Willig, Charlyce Jones Owen, Will Ethridge, and Ed Stanford for all that they have done to make this text what it is today.

The various editions of *Sociology*, on which this text is based, have benefited from the critical evaluation of many of my colleagues. The following people have reviewed at least some part of the manuscript: David Ashley, University of Wyoming; Morita Bailey, Oakton Community College; Lee Braude, State University of New York at Fredonia; William J. Brindle, Monroe Community College; Carol Copp, California State University-Fullerton; John Curra, Eastern Kentucky University; G. Elsewiersma, Salem State College; Michael P. Farrell, SUNY-Buffalo; Herbert Haines, SUNY Cortland; Patricia Johnson, Houston Community College; Allan O. KirkPatrick, Riverside Community College; Jerome Krase, Brooklyn College; Charles A. Malesky, Jr., San Antonio College; Maureen Mullinax, University of Kentucky; James H. Parker, Long Island University; Susan R. Takata, University of Wisconsin-Parkside; and Andrew M. Weber, Catonsville Community College.

These additional colleagues have shared ideas that have improved this book: David Adams, The Ohio State University; Kip Armstrong, Bloomsburg State College; Rose Arnault, Fort Hays State University; Philip Berg, University of Wisconsin, La Crosse; Karen Campbell, Vanderbilt University; Gerry Cox, Fort Hays State University; Harrold Curl, Mount Vernon Nazarene College; James A. Davis, Harvard University; Helen Rose Fuchs Ebaugh, University of Houston; Heather Fitz Gibbon, The College of Wooster; Kevin Fitzpatrick, University of Alabama-Birmingham; Andrew Foster, Kenyon College; Charles Frazier, University of Florida; Karen Lynch Frederick, Saint Anselm College; Steven Goldberg, City College, City University of New York; Jeffrey Hahn, Mount Union College; Peter Hruschka, Ohio Northern University; Glenna Huls, Camden County College; Harry Humphries, Pittsburg State University; Cynthia Imanaka, Seattle Central Community College; Patricia Johnson, Houston Community College; Ed Kain, Southwestern University; Irwin Kantor, Middlesex County College; Thomas Korllos, Kent State University; Michael Levine, Kenyon College; Don Luidens, Hope College; Larry Lyon, Baylor University; Li-Chen Ma, Lamar University; Alan Mazur, Syracuse University; Jack Melhorn,

Emporia State University; Meredith McGuire, Trinity University; Daniel Quinn, Adrian College; Toby Parcel, The Ohio State University; Nevel Razak, Fort Hays State College; Virginia Reynolds, Indiana University of Pennsylvania; Laurel Richardson, The Ohio State University; Howard Schneiderman, Lafayette College; Ray Scupin, Linderwood College; Harry Sherer, Irvine Valley College; Timothy Shutt, Kenyon College; Glen Sims, Glendale Community College; Len Tompos, Lorain County Community College; Christopher Vanderpool, Michigan State University; Marilyn Wilmeth, Iowa University; Stuart Wright, Lamar University; and Frank Zulke, Harold Washington College.

I also wish to thank members of my department at Kenyon College—Nick Kardulias, Rita Kipp, George McCarthy, Howard Sacks, Ric Sheffield, J. Kenneth Smail, David Suggs, Edward Schortman, and Patricia Urban—for maintaining a daily environment of intellectual stimulation. Sharon Duchesne, a valued member of our department family for over a decade, provided skillful editorial and secretarial help with this revision.

Carol Singer, Government Documents Librarian at Kenyon College, has served as a consultant and researcher. I am grateful to her for providing the latest statistical data for this book.

Finally, I wish to thank Amy Marsh Macionis for contributing her editorial skills to the development and production of this text.

JJM

About the Author

John J. Macionis (pronounced ma-SHOW-nis) is a native of Philadelphia, Pennsylvania. He received his bachelor's degree from Cornell University and his doctorate in sociology from the University of Pennsylvania. He is the author of articles and papers on topics such as community life in the United States, interpersonal relationships in families, effective teaching, and humor. An area of particular interest is urban sociology; he is coauthor of a well-received text, *The Sociology of Cities*. He has also coedited the new companion volume to this text: *Seeing Ourselves: Classic, Contemporary, and Cross-Cultural Readings in Sociology.*

John Macionis is currently professor of sociology at Kenyon College in Gambier, Ohio. He recently served as chair of the Anthropology-Sociology Department, as director of Kenyon's multidisciplinary program in humane studies, and as chair of Kenyon's faculty.

Professor Macionis teaches a wide range of upper-level courses, but his favorite course is Introduction to Sociology, which he teaches every semester. He enjoys extensive contact with students on his home campus, as a frequent visitor to other campuses, and as a regular participant in teaching programs abroad.

SOCIETY

Sociology: Perspective, Theory, and Method

Chapter Outline

One way to grasp the power that society has in shaping the lives of individuals is to imagine how your life would be different had you been born in the place of one of these children.

On a spring evening in New York's Central Park in 1989, a twenty-eight-year-old woman was jogging after a day of work in the city's financial district. As she passed a grove of sycamore trees, the quiet setting suddenly exploded into a chase as a gang of more than twenty teenage boys pursued her. Flushed with terror, the woman stumbled into a gully where she fought off her attackers while being battered with a pipe and a rock and stabbed with a knife. Overpowered and seriously wounded, she was then repeatedly raped. The attackers left her for dead, and she collapsed helpless and broken until she was found three hours later. Having lost most of her blood, she reached a local hospital in a coma. After months of intensive medical care, she has made a courageous physical recovery.

Many Americans reacted to this incident with disbelief. Partly, this was because of the brutality of the attack, and partly because the attackers were so young—fourteen to sixteen years of age. But most curiously, the boys offered no sensible explanation for their crime beyond seeking the excitement of what they called a night of "wilding." Thus this terrible event provoked people everywhere to confront the basic question: *What makes people do the things they do?*

There are, of course, many ways to look at human events. The *perspective*—or point of view—that is used determines which facts become important and suggests how these facts can be woven together into patterns of meaning. The police officers investigating the "wilding" case used one perspective. They focused on piecing together who did what to whom and apprehending the individuals responsible. From the point of view of the police, determining the sequence of events and establishing a course of legal action take on paramount importance.

A psychiatrist approaches the behavior of the young attackers from a different perspective. For a psychiatrist, the important issue is the state of mind that could lead an individual to commit an act of such wanton violence. In this case, the psychiatric perspective would identify a different set of facts and prescribe a response based on appropriate medical principles.

A sociologist brings yet another perspective to understanding human behavior. A sociologist attempting to make sense of this incident might note that the offenders were males, that they were teenagers, and that they were members of an economically disadvantaged minority. Notice that the facts highlighted by the sociological perspective differ markedly from those noted by law enforcement officials or psychiatrists. The police are concerned with facts that pertain to this one, specific crime. Knowing that an offender is male is useful only insofar as it leads to identifying *which* male was involved. Likewise, psychiatrists seek out the personal traumas that may have contributed to an explosive outburst by a particular person. Both police and psychiatrists share the assumption that, in important respects at least, every crime—and every person—is unique. By contrast, a sociologist organizes unique individuals into general categories and seeks to understand how and why their behavior is much the same.

This chapter introduces the sociological perspective and explains how sociologists make use of theory and scientific methods in their study of human behavior.

THE SOCIOLOGICAL PERSPECTIVE

The discipline of **sociology** is defined as *the scientific study of human social activity*. All sociologists use one basic point of view in their efforts to understand the social world.

Seeing the General in the Particular

Peter Berger (1963) describes the sociological perspective as *seeing the general in the particular*. This means that sociologists see general social patterns in the behavior

of particular individuals. While acknowledging that each individual has unique qualities, we also recognize that general social forces shape us into various *kinds* of people. In the Central Park jogger case, the sociological perspective leads us to wonder, for example, if violent crime may be more common among males, the young, and the disadvantaged than among females, older people, and the more privileged. Sociological research confirms that this is actually so.

Social forces also affect victimization. Figure 1–1 provides several sociological insights about the chances of becoming a victim of homicide. First, *blacks* are more likely than *whites* to become victims of homicide. The overall rate of victimization for blacks (31.9 cases for every 100,000 people in this category in 1987) is almost six times higher than the rate for whites (5.4 per 100,000). Also notice that for both races, *males* are more likely than *females* to become homicide victims. Among whites, males (7.9) are almost three times more likely than females (3.0) to fall victim to homicide. For blacks, males (53.3) have a rate more than four times higher

Figure 1–1 Rate of Death by Homicide, by Race and Sex, for Americans

Rates indicate the number of deaths by homicide for every 100,000 people in each category for 1987.

(National Center for Health Statistics, 1990.)

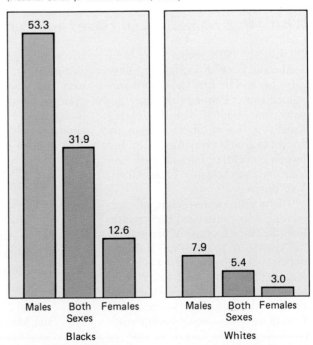

than that for females (12.6). As we shall see in Chapter 6 ("Deviance"), disadvantaged, black males are involved in violent crime as victims and as offenders in disproportionately high numbers. Clearly, then, our particular life experiences are shaped by the general categories of society into which we fall.

Seeing the Strange in the Familiar

The sociological perspective also allows us to *see the strange in the familiar*. This does not mean that sociologists focus on the bizarre elements of society. Rather, sociological observation involves stepping back from familiar ways of thinking in order to gain new insights that at first may seem strange. Using the sociological perspective leads us to conclude that, in the words of Peter Berger (1963:23), "things are not what they seem."

Because Americans are taught that individual choices shape our world, learning to "see" how society affects us may take a bit of practice. Consider the seemingly personal matter of peoples' names. Historically,

many American celebrities changed their names as they began their careers. But are the names they use simply a matter of personal choice or are social forces at work? The box takes a critical look at what's in a name.

Individuality in Social Context

Sociological insights often challenge our common sense, suggesting that human behavior is not as individualistic as we may think. Learning to place individual behavior in a social context takes a leap of imagination, especially for North Americans, who learn to view their lives in very personal terms. Our everyday awareness carries a heavy load of personal responsibility: We pat ourselves on the back when we succeed in our endeavors and kick ourselves when things go wrong. Proud of our individuality, we resist the idea that we or others act in socially patterned ways.

For this reason, a crime like the Central Park attack, described at the beginning of this chapter, provokes controversy about how much blame the offenders themselves

CRITICAL THINKING

What's in a Name? Social Forces and Personal Choice

On July 4, 1918, twins were born to Abe and Becky Friedman in Sioux City, Iowa. The first to be born was named Esther Pauline Friedman; her sister was named Pauline Esther Friedman. Today, these women are known to almost every American, but by new names they later adopted: Ann Landers and Abigail ("Dear Abby") Van Buren.

Many Americans—especially celebrities—have changed their names to further their careers. At first glance, this may seem to be simply a matter of personal preference. However, examining the name list from a sociological perspective uncovers a general pattern. Historically, women and men of various national backgrounds

have adopted *English-sounding* names. Why? Because American society has long accorded high social prestige to those of Anglo-Saxon background. How many of these well-known people can you identify from their original names?

1. Michael James Vijencio Gubitosi
2. Cherilyn Sarkisian
3. Cheryl Stoppelmoor
4. Robert Allen Zimmerman
5. Margarita Carmen Cansino
6. John Bongiovi
7. Frederick Austerlitz
8. George Kyriakou Panayiotou
9. Ana Mae Bullock

10. Issur Danielovitch Demsky
11. Mladen Sekulovich
12. Gerald Silberman
13. Bernadette Lazzarra
14. Karen Ziegler
15. Ramon Estevez
16. Henry John Deutschendorf, Jr.
17. Allan Stewart Konigsberg
18. Judy Cohen
19. Eugene Maurice Orowitz
20. William Claude Dukenfield

1. Robert Blake; 2. Cher; 3. Cheryl Ladd; 4. Bob Dylan; 5. Rita Hayworth; 6. Jon Bon Jovi; 7. Fred Astaire; 8. George Michael; 9. Tina Turner; 10. Kirk Douglas; 11. Karl Malden; 12. Gene Wilder; 13. Bernadette Peters; 14. Karen Black; 15. Martin Sheen; 16. John Denver; 17. Woody Allen; 18. Juice Newton; 19. Michael Landon; 20. W. C. Fields

deserve and how much stems from societal forces at work in their lives. In the weeks following the "wilding" incident in New York's Central Park, the American press presented divergent views about how much personal responsibility should be assigned to the boys who carried out the attack.

On one side of the controversy, a number of social scientists pointed out that a wide range of social factors—including gender, youth, race, and social background—had to be considered in accurately assigning responsibility. Taking an opposing view, several nationally known commentators claimed simply that these were bad kids who alone were to blame for a morally repulsive act. Sociology, they maintained, sides with the offenders when it argues that society contributes to such an attack (Will, 1989).

Such criticism of sociology tells us something about the United States. When a particular event causes pain and anguish, Americans want to know who is to blame and want to see the guilty punished. In this case, six teenage boys (of the total who participated) were arrested and charged with the crime. This action addresses the perceived evil and at least partially satisfies people's passionate sense of anger and injustice. But is this the whole picture?

Sociologists would have to say no. To begin, sociological analysis does *not* advocate turning loose people who commit violent crimes. But in truth, no human behavior is solely the product of what philosophers call simple "free will" or "personal choice." All human action involves decisions, but choices are made within a constellation of powerful social forces (not to mention whatever biological and psychological forces may also be at work).

Gender is one such social force. Would anyone imagine that teenage girls would be as likely as teenage boys to commit this kind of crime? In fact, American males engage in nine times as many violent crimes as females do, as Chapter 6 ("Deviance") explains. And what about age? Are middle-aged people as likely as teenagers to "choose" to attack innocent people? Hardly, as evidenced by the fact that Americans between the ages of fifteen and twenty-four represent only one-sixth of the population but account for almost half of all violent crimes. Likewise, we know that categories of Americans who are poor—white and black alike—experience more violence in their lives, both as victims and offenders, than more affluent people do. Finally, crimes such as the Central Park attack are also remarkably *American*. More assaults and murders occur in New York and other American cities in a typical week than occur in most large, European cities in a year. In fact, more people die from stray bullets in New York than die from deliberate attacks in the major cities of Europe.

No society can exist without demanding that people take at least some personal responsibility for their actions. Americans respond to morally outrageous behavior by seeking to attach blame to specific people. To blame "society" is to blame everyone—and no one. But in our cultural climate of individualism, sociology provides a needed dose of realism. Embedded in society from the moment of our birth, we learn to think, feel, and act as products of a larger social world. To think sociologically, therefore, does not mean we become "bleeding hearts." Rather, thinking sociologically helps us understand ourselves and the world around us more fully and accurately.

Suicide: The most individual act. There is no more compelling demonstration of how social forces affect human behavior than the study of suicide. What, after all, is more personal than taking one's own life? Perhaps this is why Emile Durkheim, a pioneer of sociology writing a century ago, chose this as a topic of study. He was able to show that social forces are at work even in the apparent isolation of a self-destructive act.

Durkheim, who lived in France, examined records of suicide in various regions of Central Europe.[1] These records clearly showed that some categories of people are much more likely than others to commit suicide. Specifically, Durkheim found, males, Protestants, wealthy people, and the unmarried all had significantly higher suicide rates than did females, Catholics and Jews, the poor, and married people. Durkheim explained these differences in terms of the varying degree of *social integration* linking people in each category. Low suicide rates characterized those types of people who commonly have stronger bonds to others. On the other hand, high suicide rates were found among those categories of people who are typically more individualistic and autonomous.

In the patriarchal societies studied by Durkheim, males certainly had more autonomy than females. Whatever its advantages, reasoned Durkheim, this freedom also contributes to a higher suicide rate among men. Likewise, Catholic and Jewish practices foster stronger social ties and greater conformity than do individualistic Protestant beliefs. The result is that Protestants have a

---

[1] This discussion is a much-abbreviated account of Durkheim's (1966; orig. 1897) considerably more complex analysis of suicide.

higher suicide rate than Catholics or Jews. The wealthy clearly have much more freedom than the poor, but with a predictably higher suicide rate. Finally, single people have fewer social bonds than married people, which, consistent with Durkheim's theory, explains their greater likelihood of suicide.

A century later, statistical evidence still supports Durkheim's analysis (Pescosolido & Georgianna, 1989). Figure 1–2 shows suicide rates for four categories of Americans. Whites had 13.7 recorded instances of suicide for every 100,000 people in 1987, a rate twice as high as that of blacks (6.6). Also, for each racial category, suicide is more common among males than females. White males (22.1) are almost four times more likely than white females to take their own lives. Among African-Americans, males (11.6) are about five times more likely than females to do so. Following Durkheim's argument, we conclude that the higher suicide rate among whites, males, and especially white males is due to their greater affluence and autonomy in American society. By contrast, poorer people and those with limited choices are more socially rooted and have correspondingly lower rates of self-destruction.

Through these statistics on suicide, then, we see how even the most personal actions of individuals are guided by the impersonal operation of society. In comparing Figure 1–1 and Figure 1–2, we can see that complex social forces linked to race produce distinctive patterns with regard to death from homicide and suicide. Blacks and other disadvantaged categories of Americans suffer disproportionately from homicide; whites, as a privileged

category, suffer disproportionately from suicide. For both races, however, males are more prone to homicide and suicide than females. By revealing such patterns—the general in the particular—the sociological perspective shows how social forces affect our individual lives.

The Sociological Perspective in Everyday Life

Although Americans often overlook the power of social forces, certain kinds of situations prompt us to view the world sociologically even before we take a first course in sociology.

Encountering social diversity. Experiencing—and even thinking about—other cultures stimulates the sociological perspective. Imagine how different our lives would be had we been born in ancient China, medieval England, Hitler's Germany, or contemporary Bangladesh. Foreign students who arrive on an American college campus are likely to notice social patterns that Americans take for granted. The strangeness of the surroundings helps foreigners see that both individual choice and the operation of society guide people's behavior. In the same way, visiting other countries makes Americans think sociologically. Cross-cultural experiences also encourage us to look at our own society with new eyes when we return home.

Marginality: Race, gender, and age. Sociologists use the term *social marginality* to refer to a condition of being excluded that makes someone an "outsider." All people experience social marginality from time to time; for some categories of Americans, however, standing apart from the mainstream is an everyday occurrence. The more intense peoples' social marginality, the more likely they are to embrace the sociological perspective.

No African-American, for example, could live very long in the United States without being aware of how much race affects personal experiences. But because whites constitute the dominant majority of American society, whites think about race only from time to time. When they do, they may consider race an issue that affects only African-Americans rather than one that has an impact on themselves as well.

In a similar way, women of all races tend to see the world sociologically more than men do. During recent decades, women who have personally encountered some of the limitations of being female in American society have come to realize that their individual problems constitute patterns within our way of life. Some

Figure 1–2 Rate of Death by Suicide, by Race and Sex, for Americans

Rates indicate the number of deaths by suicide for every 100,000 people in each category for 1987.

(*National Center for Health Statistics, 1990.*)

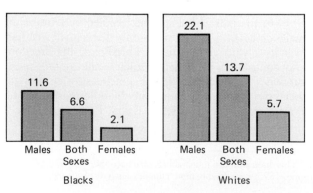

Because elderly Americans are often viewed as social outsiders, they tend to be more sociological in their outlook than younger people. In Japan, however, the elderly play a central part in social life; as a result, they probably adopt a sociological perspective less readily.

men, because of their dominant social position, reveal a form of "social blindness" on this issue, failing to recognize societal patterns of sexual inequality.

The elderly often perceive social patterns more acutely than young people. While this may be partly due to wisdom gained over a lifetime, it also stems from elderly Americans' considerable social marginality. As Chapter 3 ("Socialization: From Infancy to Aging") explains, Americans tend to define growing old as the loss of the capacity to engage in many important human activities, including physical recreation, work, and even sex. Since most elderly people are physically and mentally capable of all these activities, they understand more clearly than the young the degree to which society defines what individuals are and how they should think and act.

In short, people who are relegated to the outskirts of social life—because of their race, sex, age, or a host of other factors—generally recognize social patterns that others take for granted. They have stepped back from society (perhaps more accurately, society has stepped back from them) and therefore take a more sociological view of the world.

Social crisis. American sociologist C. Wright Mills (1959) suggested that times of social disruption foster widespread sociological thinking. In this century, the 1930s stand out as a decade of heightened sociological awareness. During the Great Depression, one-fourth of the labor force was out of work. In this catastrophic situation, unemployed workers could not help but see general social forces at work in their particular lives.

To American sociologist C. Wright Mills (1916–1962), the "sociological imagination" empowers individuals to understand more about how their lives are shaped by the larger society. An outspoken critic of the American way of life, Mills envisioned a central role for sociological thinking in the effort to forge a more gentle and just existence.

Rather than claiming, "Something is wrong with me; I can't find a job," they were likely to say, "The economy has collapsed; there are no jobs to be found!"

People develop a sociological perspective very quickly when the established patterns of society begin to shake and crumble. The decade of the 1960s, for example, enhanced the sociological awareness of Americans because the civil rights, women's liberation, and anti–Vietnam War movements all challenged accepted social patterns. This social climate highlighted the ways in which personal experiences were being shaped by forces beyond individuals themselves—the political, economic, military, and technological elements of "the system" (dubbed by some the "military-industrial complex"). Although the merits of these movements may be debated, the movements did call attention to the sociological perspective by pointing to social forces that affect the lives of all Americans.

While people adopt a sociological perspective when society becomes unstable, the converse also holds true: Sociological thinking sometimes fosters social disruption. In other words, the more we concentrate on the operation of "the system," the more we may wish to change it in some way. Some thirty years ago, C. Wright Mills (1959) cited the importance of what he called the "sociological imagination" in prompting people to actively engage their surroundings. An introduction to sociology, then, magnifies our ability to reshape the world around us.

THE ORIGINS OF SOCIOLOGY

Like individual "choices," historical events rarely "just happen"; they are usually products of powerful social forces. So it was with sociology itself.

Although people have thought about society since the beginning of human history, sociology is one of the youngest academic disciplines—far younger than history, physics, or economics, for example. It was only in 1838 that the French social thinker Auguste Comte coined the term *sociology* to describe a new way of looking at the world.

Science and Sociology

The nature of society constituted a major area of inquiry for the brilliant thinkers of the ancient world, including

Raised in the shadow of the French Revolution, Auguste Comte (1798–1857) was stimulated to investigate society by the momentous social changes swirling around him. The breakdown of traditional social patterns disturbed Comte, but he hoped that the scientific study of society would improve the human condition.

the Greek philosophers Plato (427–347 B.C.E.) and Aristotle (384–322 B.C.E.).[2] Similarly, the Roman emperor Marcus Aurelius (121–180), the medieval theologian St. Thomas Aquinas (c. 1225–1274), the great English playwright William Shakespeare (1564–1616), and a host of others reflected on human society in their writings. Yet, as Emile Durkheim explained toward the end of the last century, none of these social thinkers approached society from a sociological point of view.

> Looking back in history . . . we find that no philosophers ever viewed matters [with a sociological perspective] until quite recently. . . . It seemed to them sufficient to ascertain what the human will should strive for and what it should avoid in established societies. . . . Their aim was not to offer us as valid a description of nature as possible, but

---

[2] Throughout this text, the abbreviation B.C.E. designates "before the common era." This terminology is used in place of the traditional B.C. ("before Christ") in recognition of the religious plurality of American society. Similarly, in place of the traditional A.D. (anno Domini, or "in the year of our Lord"), the abbreviation C.E. ("common era") is employed.

In other words, before the birth of sociology, philosophers and theologians concentrated their energies on imagining the "ideal" society. None attempted to analyze "real" society, as it actually was. In creating the discipline of sociology, pioneers such as Auguste Comte and Emile Durkheim reversed these priorities. Although they were certainly concerned with how human society could be improved, the major goal of early sociologists was to understand how society actually operates.

Comte (1975; orig. 1851–1854) identified three historical stages in the emergence of scientific sociology. During the earliest stage, encompassing the medieval period in Europe, people's view of the world around them was rooted in religion. Society was widely held to be an expression of God's will. Comte called this the *theological stage* in humanity's understanding of society.

With the Renaissance, this theological approach to society gave way to what Comte called the *metaphysical stage*. During this period, people were less likely to see society as the work of supernatural forces and placed more emphasis on the forces of nature. For instance, the English philosopher Thomas Hobbes (1588–1679) suggested that society was guided less by God than by a rather selfish human nature.

What Comte heralded as the final, *scientific stage* in the long quest to understand society began with the work of natural scientists like the Polish astonomer Copernicus (1473–1543), the Italian astronomer and physicist Galileo (1564–1642), and the English physicist and mathematician Isaac Newton (1642–1727). Following their lead, Comte applied this new scientific approach to the study of society itself.

This approach is often called **positivism,** meaning *a path to understanding the world based on science.* As a positivist, Comte believed that society had an inherent, underlying order that could be studied and understood, much as the physical world operates according to gravity and other laws of nature.

When sociology became established as an academic discipline in the United States at the beginning of this century, early sociologists such as Lester Ward (1841–1913) were strongly influenced by Comte's ideas. Even today, most sociologists continue to view science as a crucial element of sociology. But since Comte's time, sociologists have learned that the causes of human behavior are often far more complex than the causes of events in the natural world. In other words, human beings are not just physical objects but creatures with considerable imagination and spontaneity. Therefore, our behavior can never be fully explained by any rigid "laws of society."

This drawing suggests the apprehension as well as the excitement of early scientists breaking away from conventional understandings of the universe. Pioneering sociologists set out to explore the operation of human society, generating new and often controversial ideas.

Social Change and Sociology

Sociology emerged in the wake of striking transformations in the societies of seventeenth- and eighteenth-century Europe. As the social ground trembled under their feet, people understandably focused more of their attention on society.

This sociological perspective was sparked by three basic and interrelated changes. First, rapid technological innovation in eighteenth-century Europe gave rise to factories and an industrial economy. During the Middle Ages, most people in Europe tilled fields near their homes or engaged in small-scale *manufacturing* (a word derived from Latin words meaning "to make by hand"). Thus, most people worked where they lived, and homes were often centers of commercial endeavors such as baking, making furniture, and sewing garments.

By the middle of the eighteenth century, factories began to appear as people applied new sources of energy—including steam power—to the operation of large machines. Now, instead of laboring at home or in tightly knit communities, workers became part of a large and anonymous industrial labor force, toiling for strangers who owned and controlled the factories. This rising industrial economy prompted the rapid breakdown of long-established ways of life in countless small communities.

Cities also grew as the factories that sprouted across England and the European continent attracted people in need of work. Unemployment in the English countryside increased as textile industrialists transformed farmland into grazing land to raise sheep—the source of wool. In the process known as the Enclosure Movement, countless people who were pushed from the countryside set out to find work in the new factories.

Industrialization swelled the populations of cities. During the Middle Ages, settlements had been small, self-contained worlds, often within defensive walls. As late as 1700, the dawning of the industrial era, London was the largest city in Europe, with only 500,000 people. Two centuries later, London's population had increased thirteen times over to 6.5 million (Chandler & Fox, 1974).

Urban growth of this kind took place all across the European continent, dramatically changing people's lives. Cities filled with strangers, in some cases overwhelming available resources. Widespread social problems—including pollution, crime, and inadequate housing—soon stimulated the development of the sociological perspective.

A transformed economy and the rapid growth of cities soon brought changes in political thought. By the seventeenth century, every kind of tradition came under spirited attack, especially the notion that society was an expression of divine will. In the writings of Thomas Hobbes, John Locke (1632–1704), and Adam Smith (1723–1790), we find less concern with the moral obligations of people to society and more support for the idea that society is the product of self-interest. Indeed, the key phrases in the new political climate—*liberty* and *rights*—highlighted not the group but the individual. Echoing the thoughts of John Locke, the American Declaration of Independence, which celebrated the separation of the American colonies from England, clearly spells out these new political ideas. Here we read that all people have "certain inalienable rights," including "life, liberty, and the pursuit of happiness." The political revolution in France that began soon afterward in 1789—under the banner of "liberty, equality, fraternity"—was an even more dramatic effort to break with political and social traditions.

Karl Marx maintained that ideas about the world should be linked to action intended to improve the human condition.

As he surveyed his own country after the French Revolution, the French social and political thinker Alexis de Tocqueville exaggerated only slightly when he asserted that the changes wreaked by the French Revolution amounted to "nothing short of the regeneration of the whole human race" (1955:13; orig. 1856). The new industrial economy, enormous cities, and fresh political ideas combined to foster the development of the discipline of sociology. Sociology soon flowered in precisely those countries—France, Germany, and England—that had experienced the most pronounced social changes.

Individual sociologists reacted differently to the emerging social order, just as they respond differently to society today. Auguste Comte found the dawning modern world deeply disturbing. He feared that people would be overpowered by change and uprooted from long-established local communities. As a conservative, he sought a rebirth of traditional family, community, and morality. In stark contrast, the German social critic Karl Marx (1818–1883) despised traditional social patterns and celebrated their demise. But he equally detested the concentration of the great wealth produced by industrial technology in the hands of a small elite, while the masses faced only hunger and misery.

Comte and Marx differed in their prescriptions for alleviating social conditions, yet they shared the conviction that society cannot be understood simply in terms of individual choice. Rather, the sociological perspective that animates the work of each reveals that the fundamental issues in sociology involve not particular people but general social patterns that influence us all even today.

SOCIOLOGICAL THEORY

Linking observations to generate meaning brings us to another dimension of sociology: theory. A **theory** is *an explanation of the relationship between two or more specific facts*. Emile Durkheim's study of suicide exemplifies sociological theory. Durkheim found meaning in the variations of suicide rates as he observed that categories of people with high suicide rates (including males, Protestants, the wealthy, and the unmarried) were those with low social integration.

In developing theories about human society, sociologists face a wide range of choices. What issues should they choose to study? How should facts be linked together? In making sense of society, sociologists are guided by one or more general frameworks, or theoretical paradigms (Kuhn, 1970). As applied to sociology, a **theoretical paradigm** constitutes *a set of fundamental assumptions about society that guides sociological thinking*. There are three major paradigms in sociology: the structural-functional paradigm, the social-conflict paradigm, and the symbolic-interaction paradigm.

The Structural-Functional Paradigm

The **structural-functional paradigm** is *a theoretical framework based on the assumption that society is a complex system whose parts work together to promote stability*. As its name suggests, the structural-functional paradigm has two components. First, society is composed of various kinds of **social structure,** defined as *a relatively stable pattern of social behavior*. Social structure ranges from broad patterns, including the family and religious systems, to greetings and other forms of face-to-face behavior. Second, all structures are related in terms of their **social function,** which refers to *consequences for the operation of society as a whole*. Thus all the elements of society—from religious beliefs to a simple handshake—have a part in perpetuating society, at least in its present form.

The structural-functional paradigm owes much to the ideas of Auguste Comte, whose work focused on how his own society managed to remain unified while undergoing massive changes. Another architect of this theoretical approach was the English sociologist Herbert Spencer (1820–1903). A student of both the human body and society, Spencer asserted that the two have much in common. The structural parts of the human body include the skeleton, muscles, and various internal organs. All these body parts are interdependent, and each one contributes to the survival of the overall human organism. Likewise, reasoned Spencer, the elements of human society are interdependent and work to keep society operating. This approach, then, leads sociologists to identify the various structures of society, asking what part each plays in the operation of the whole.

Several decades after the death of Comte, Emile Durkheim advanced the development of the structural-functional paradigm. Like Spencer, Durkheim investigated ways in which modern societies maintain their social integration. A number of later chapters will detail Durkheim's ideas and research.

Robert K. Merton (1968), a contemporary American sociologist whose work follows the structural-functional approach, has shown that any single part of society usually has many functions, although some are more obvious than others. The **manifest functions** of any element of social structure are *consequences that are recognized and intended by people in the society.* **Latent functions,** on the other hand, are *consequences that are largely unrecognized and unintended.* The rapid proliferation of automobiles during the twentieth century illustrates this distinction. The manifest functions of cars range from transporting people and goods from one place to another to serving as *status symbols,* indicating something about a person's taste and bank account. Automobiles also have latent functions. Because they allow people to travel in relative isolation, cars reinforce the American emphasis on privacy and personal autonomy. This is one reason that automobiles have long been favored by Americans over public transit systems.

Merton also explains that every element of social structure has both desirable and harmful consequences. He uses the term **social dysfunction** to designate *undesirable effects on the operation of society.* One of the dysfunctions of the American reliance on private motor vehicles is that, with more than 180 million of them, air quality has become poor, especially in large cities. No doubt, too, the easy travel made possible by cars has contributed to a decline in the strength of traditional families and local neighborhoods, changes lamented by many Americans.

Critical evaluation. The structural-functional paradigm has long been influential in sociology, although in recent decades critics have revealed limitations of this approach. By focusing attention on the ways in which society is unified, critics point out, structural-functionalism tends to overlook powerful divisions based on social class, race, ethnicity, and sex, and to ignore how such divisions can generate tension and conflict. In addition, the structural-functional emphasis on social stability tends to downplay important processes of conflict and social change. Overall, then, this paradigm takes a conservative stance toward society. As a critical response to this approach, another theoretical orientation in sociology has developed: the social-conflict paradigm.

The Social-Conflict Paradigm

The **social-conflict paradigm** is *a theoretical framework based on the assumption that society is a complex system characterized by inequality and conflict that generate social change.* This orientation complements the structural-functional paradigm by highlighting not social integration but social inequality. Guided by this paradigm, sociologists investigate how factors such as social class, race, ethnicity, gender, and age are linked to unequal distribution of valuable resources, including wealth, power, education, and social prestige. Therefore, rather than identifying how social patterns work to promote society as a whole, this approach concentrates on how they benefit some people at the expense of others.

Social-conflict theorists view society as an arena in which conflict arises from the incompatible interests of various categories of people. Not surprisingly, dominant categories—the rich in relation to the poor, whites in relation to nonwhites, and males in relation to females—typically try to protect their privileges by supporting the status quo. Those with fewer advantages commonly counter these efforts by attempting to bring about a more equitable distribution of social resources.

To illustrate, Chapter 13 ("Education and Medicine") details how American secondary schools prepare some students for college and emphasize vocational training for others. A structural-functional analysis might lead us to ask how society as a whole would benefit from "tracking" that provided different types of education to students according to their academic abilities. The social-conflict paradigm offers a contrasting insight: that this practice confers privileges on some that it denies to others, thereby perpetuating social inequality and promoting conflict between favored and disadvantaged categories of people.

Research has shown that American students are placed in college-preparatory tracks not just because of their intelligence but due to the privileged backgrounds of their families. Virtually ensured of becoming part of the minority of Americans with a college education, most will enter occupations that confer both prestige and a high income. In the process, the privileges of one generation are passed on to another. By contrast, schools generally fill vocational tracks with students from less privileged backgrounds, sometimes with little regard for their academic potential. They receive no preparation for college, and thus, like their parents before them, they typically enter occupations that offer little prestige and low income. So while tracking is presumably based on students' academic abilities, in practice, social background also plays a pivotal role (Bowles & Gintis, 1976; Oakes, 1982, 1985).

Social conflict appears in American society in a host of other guises, including strikes, the civil rights movement, and the drive for social equality by women. Overall, then, rather than viewing society as relatively stable, the social-conflict paradigm points up how social structure fosters continual conflict between the forces of change and those resistant to change.

Finally, many sociologists who embrace the social-conflict paradigm attempt not only to understand society as it is but also to reduce social inequality. This was the central goal of Karl Marx, the social thinker who had a singularly important influence on the development of the social-conflict paradigm in sociology. Marx had little patience with those who sought to use science only to understand how society works. In a well-known declaration (inscribed on his monument in London's Highgate Cemetery), Marx charged: "The philosophers have only interpreted the world, in various ways; the point, however, is to change it."

Critical evaluation. In recent decades, the social-conflict paradigm has developed rapidly, becoming a major force in American sociology. Yet, like other approaches, it has come in for its share of criticism. Because this paradigm highlights the domination by elites as the primary way in which society is held together, it sheds little light on how social unity can be forged from shared values or functional interdependence. In addition, the social-conflict approach is often criticized for advocating explicitly political goals in its drive for a more egalitarian society, thereby giving up some claim to scientific objectivity. Supporters of this paradigm respond that *all* social approaches have political consequences, albeit different ones.

Both the structural-functional and the social-conflict paradigms envision society in broad, abstract terms, which sometimes seem quite distant from the way we experience society in our everyday lives. Thus, sociologists also employ a third theoretical paradigm, which views society more in terms of face-to-face social interaction. We now turn to this third approach.

The Symbolic-Interaction Paradigm

Both the structural-functional and social-conflict paradigms share a **macro-level orientation,** meaning *a concern with large-scale patterns that characterize society as a whole.* They approach society from afar, as you might investigate a city from the vantage point of a helicopter, noting, for example, that highways facilitate traffic flow from one place to another, or that there are striking contrasts between the neighborhoods of the rich and the poor. The symbolic-interaction paradigm differs by providing a **micro-level orientation,** meaning *a concern with small-scale patterns of social interaction in specific settings.* Exploring urban life in this way means being at street level, observing face-to-face interaction in public parks or how people respond to a homeless person they pass on the street. The **symbolic-interaction paradigm,** then, is *a theoretical framework based on the view that society emerges from the construction of reality by individuals in everyday life.*

How are the lives of millions of distinct individuals woven together into the drama of society? One answer, examined in detail in Chapter 2 ("Culture"), is that people interact in terms of shared symbols and meanings. Only in rare situations do we respond to each other in direct, physical terms, as when someone ducks to avoid a punch. Mostly, we react to the meanings we attach to human actions. For example, if we define a homeless man on a city street as "just a bum looking for a handout," we may ignore him. If, on the contrary, we consider him a "fellow human being in need," he becomes the target of our active interest. Sociologists guided by the symbolic-interaction approach view society as a complex mosaic of subjective perceptions and responses.

The development of the symbolic-interaction paradigm was greatly influenced by Max Weber (1864–1920), a German sociologist who emphasized the importance of understanding society as it is subjectively perceived by individuals. From this foundation, others have developed a number of related approaches to understanding society. Chapter 3 ("Socialization: From Infancy to Aging") discusses the ideas of American sociologist George Herbert Mead (1863–1931), who explored how the human personality gradually emerges as a result of social experience. Chapter 4 ("Social Interaction in Everyday Life") presents the work of American sociologist Erving Goffman (1922–1982), whose approach to understanding society, known as *dramaturgical analysis,* emphasizes how human beings resemble actors on a stage as they deliberately foster certain impressions in the minds of others. Other contemporary sociologists, including George Homans and Peter Blau, have developed *social-exchange analysis.* In their view, social interaction is often guided by what each person stands to gain and lose from others. In the process of courtship, for example, individuals seek mates who offer them at least as much— in terms of physical attractiveness, intelligence, and social background—as they offer in return.

Critical evaluation. The symbolic-interaction paradigm helps to overcome a limitation typical of macro-level approaches to understanding society. Society is in-

Sports: An Illustration of Sociological Theory

Sports is a multibillion-dollar industry, one in which almost every American has participated to some degree. What insights can the sociological perspective provide about this important and familiar element of American society?

A structural-functional approach directs attention to the functions of sports for society as a whole. Manifest functions include providing both recreation and a relatively harmless way to "let off steam," and contributing to the physical fitness of the population. Sports has important latent functions as well, from fostering social relationships to generating tens of thousands of jobs. Perhaps the most important latent function of sports is celebrating competition, achievement, and success—all central to America's way of life (Spates, 1976a; Coakley, 1990). When he said, "Winning is not everything, but making the effort to win is," Vince Lombardi was speaking not only as a football coach; he was also speaking as a typical American.

Sports has dysfunctional consequences as well. For example, colleges and universities intent on having winning teams may recruit students whose athletic ability far outshines their academic aptitude. This can adversely affect the academic standards of the school and may leave the athletes themselves little time to concentrate on anything but their athletic pursuits. In general, however, sports is an important ritual that helps to define the American way of life.

A social-conflict analysis of sports would begin by pointing out that sports closely mirrors patterns of American social inequality. Some sports, such as tennis, swimming, golf, and skiing, require large outlays of money, so participation is largely limited to the well-to-do. The sports with mass appeal, including football, baseball, and basketball, are accessible to people of modest means. In other words, the games people play reflect broader patterns of economic inequality.

In the United States, boys and men participate in sports in much greater proportions than their female counterparts. Sexual discrimination has traditionally limited the opportunities of females to take part in most sports, even when they have the talent, interest, and economic means to do so. The first modern Olympic Games held in 1896, for example, excluded women from all competition (Mangan & Park, 1987). Until quite recently, girls were also barred from Little League teams in most parts of the country. Such discrimination has been defended by ungrounded sexual stereotypes holding that women lack the ability to engage in sports and by assertions that they risk losing their femininity by engaging in athletic competition. Thus American males are encouraged to be athletes while females are expected to be attentive observers and cheerleaders. More American women now take part in professional sports than ever before, yet they continue to take a back seat to men, particularly in sports that provide the most earnings and social prestige.

Nonwhites in American society enjoy greater opportunities in professional sports than in many other occupations. Jackie Robinson broke the "color line" in 1947, making professional baseball the first of the major American sports to include nonwhite players. By the mid-1980s, African-Americans accounted for one in five professional baseball players, just over half of all football players, and three-fourths of all basketball players (Coakley, 1986:145).

According to Harry Edwards (1973), African-Americans are represented in increasing proportions in professional sports because individual athletic achievement is easily demonstrated, even in the presence of racial prejudice. For this reason, faced with discrimination in many areas of life, some blacks look to careers in athletics as a chance to escape disadvantage. Nonetheless, racial discrimination still marks professional sports in the United States. For example, although black and Hispanic players are now common in the 1990s, almost all managers, head coaches, and owners of sports teams are still white. Furthermore, nonwhite players generally do not hold starring positions in professional sports: About 70 percent of African-American players in major-league baseball play the outfield (Staples, 1987; Coakley, 1990). In football and basketball, as well, whites predominate in central positions.

A social-conflict analysis might also investigate sports in America as a business—one that is immensely profitable for a small number of "owners." Thus, the social-conflict paradigm suggests that sports in the

United States is bound up with extensive inequalities based on gender, race, and economic power.

According to the symbolic-interaction paradigm, sports forms a complex and changing pattern of social interaction. Players are guided in their actions by their assigned positions and by formal and informal rules of the game. But like all patterns of human behavior, sports is also partly spontaneous; each game unfolds in ways that cannot be predicted and each player looks at the game from a unique perspective. Some people, for example, thrive in competitive situations. Others love the game more than winning, and may actually play badly when under pressure. Still others turn to sports as a means of building personal friendships (Coakley, 1986).

Team members, each distinct human beings, tend to "shape their own realities" as they perceive one another in terms of particular prejudices and jealousies, admiration and respect. In addition, the behavior of any single player generally changes over time. A rookie, for example, may feel quite self-conscious during the first few games in the big leagues. In time, however, the player develops a more comfortable sense of team membership. This process of coming to feel at home in professional sports was slow and agonizing for Jackie Robinson, who recognized early on that many white players, and millions of white baseball fans, resented his presence in major-league baseball (Tygiel, 1983). Eventually, however, his outstanding performance as a player

The painting *Pastime* by Gerald Garston suggests that baseball—the Great American Pastime—is more than mere diversion and entertainment. In addition, it provides valuable lessons about how we as Americans are expected to think and behave.

and his confident and cooperative manner off the field won him the respect of the entire nation.

By noting how each of these paradigms differs in its approach to any issue, we do not mean to imply that one is more correct than another. Applied to various social issues, the different theoretical paradigms spark fascinating debates and controversies; the richest sociology, therefore, is produced by utilizing all three.

Table 1–1   THE THREE MAJOR THEORETICAL PARADIGMS: A SUMMARY

Theoretical Paradigm	Orientation	Image of Society	Illustrative Questions
Structural-functional	Macro-level	A system of interrelated parts that is relatively stable based on widespread consensus as to what is morally desirable; each part has functional consequences for the operation of society as a whole	How is society integrated? What are the major parts of society? How are these parts interrelated? What are the consequences of each for the operation of society?
Social-conflict	Macro-level	A system characterized by social inequality; any part of society benefits some categories of people more than others; conflict-based social inequality promotes social change	How is society divided? What are major patterns of social inequality? How do some categories of people attempt to protect their privileges? How do other categories of people challenge the status quo?
Symbolic-interaction	Micro-level	An ongoing process of social interaction in specific settings based on symbolic communications; individual perceptions of reality are variable and changing	How is society experienced? How do human beings interact to create, sustain, and change social patterns? How do individuals attempt to shape the reality perceived by others? How does individual behavior change from one situation to another?

deed composed of broad social patterns, such as "the family" and "social inequality." But we must remember that the foundation of society is people engaging in social interaction. Put another way, as a micro-approach, this paradigm attempts to convey more of how we as individuals actually *experience* society.

The box on pages 14–15 illustrates how the structural-functional paradigm, the social-conflict paradigm, and the symbolic-interaction paradigm can be combined to produce a comprehensive analysis of American sports. Sometimes, of course, one paradigm may be more useful than the others, since each one is suitable for asking different kinds of questions. Table 1–1 summarizes the distinctive features of the three theoretical paradigms. society operates as it does. To answer such questions,

SCIENTIFIC SOCIOLOGY

Refinements in sociological theory come as a result of research. Spurred on by curiosity about the surrounding world, sociologists ask questions about how and why

researchers rely on **science,** *a logical system that bases knowledge on direct, systematic observation.* Scientific knowledge is based on **empirical evidence,** *evidence we are able to verify with our senses.*

Sociological research often reveals that what we accept as "common sense" is not entirely true. Here are three examples of widely held attitudes that are contradicted by scientific evidence.

1. **Differences in the social behavior of males and females is "human nature."** Sociological investigation shows us that what we call "human nature" is largely the product of the society in which we are raised; Chapter 2 ("Culture") explores this issue in detail. Further, researchers have discovered that definitions of "masculine" and "feminine" vary significantly from one society to another (see Chapter 10, "Sex and Gender").

2. **The United States and Canada are middle-class societies in which most people are more or less equal.** Research reveals that the richest 5 percent of North Americans control half of the continent's total wealth. Chapter 7 ("Social Stratification") provides details.

Artist Roxanne Swentzell depicts the story of creation according to the Santa Clara Pueblo in her painting, *The Emergence of the Clowns*. The Pueblo believe that life began when four clowns ascended to the earth's surface, and each set out in a different direction. All societies have beliefs of this kind, although such beliefs are sometimes dismissed as mere myth. But these accounts express the very real human need to comprehend our origins and some larger order to the universe. Science does investigate human history, but can offer no account of the ultimate meaning of human existence.

3. **Most people marry because they are in love.** It may come as a surprise to most Americans, but researchers have discovered that most marriages among humans have little to do with love. In addition, as Chapter 12 ("Family and Religion") explains, Americans typically fall in love with someone who is a socially suitable marriage partner.

As these examples indicate, the sociological perspective—linked to scientific research—can help us to evaluate with a critical eye a wide range of information we encounter every day.

Concepts, Variables, and Measurement

All disciplines make use of concepts. A **concept** is *an abstract idea that represents an aspect of the world, inevitably in a somewhat ideal and simplified form*. Sociologists use concepts to describe dimensions of social life, including "religion" and "the economy," and to identify individuals in terms of their "gender," "race," or "social class."

A **variable** is *a concept with a value that changes from case to case*. The familiar variable known as "price" varies from item to item in a supermarket. In a similar way, the concept of "social class" varies as we describe people as "upper class," "middle class," "working class," and "lower class."

Measurement is *the process of determining the value of a variable in a specific case*. Scientists can measure some variables easily, just as we determine our weight by stepping on a scale. Measuring sociological variables, however, is often more difficult than taking physical measurements. A sociologist could make an assessment of social class, for example, based on income, occupation, or education; which variable is used has a significant effect on what the measurement turns out to be.

An important rule of research states that how a variable is defined affects what its value is. Therefore, researchers must spell out definitions carefully. **Operationalizing a variable** means *specifying exactly what is to be measured when assigning a value to a variable*. In measuring social class, for example, researchers must decide precisely what aspects of social class are being measured and report this decision along with their findings.

A related issue arises when sociologists seek to describe all Americans in terms of a variable like income. Because it is impractical to provide a measurement of the income of *every* person, sociologists make use of one or more numerical measures often called *descriptive statistics*. The box explains how this is done.

Reliability and validity. Beyond carefully operationalizing each variable, useful measurement involves two other considerations—reliability and validity. **Reliability** is *the quality of consistency in measurement*. If, for exam-

What's Average? Three Statistical Measures

We often describe people, things, or numbers in terms of averages: the average price of a gallon of gasoline or the average income of Americans, for example. Sociologists use three different statistical measures to describe what is average or typical.

Assume that we wish to statistically describe the annual incomes of seven individuals in a night-school course:

$24,250	$27,000
$76,000	$15,500
$21,750	$18,500
$27,000	

The simplest of the three statistical measures is the **mode,** defined as *the value that occurs most often in a series of numbers.* In this example, the mode is $27,000, since that value occurs twice, while the others occur only once. If each value were to occur only once, there would be no mode; if two values each occurred twice, there would be two modes.

A more common statistical measure, the **mean,** is calculated by taking *the arithmetic average of a series of numbers.* To find the mean, add all the values and divide by the number of cases. The sum of the seven incomes here is $210,000 which, divided by 7, results in a mean income of $30,000. Notice that the mean income is actually higher than the in-come of six of the seven individuals; this shows how the mean is influenced by any extremely high or low value (in this case, the $76,000 income).

The **median** is *the value that occurs midway in a series of numbers or, simply, the middle case.* Here the median income for the seven people is $24,250, since three incomes are higher and three are lower. (With an even number of cases, the median would be halfway between the two middle cases.) Typically, the median gives the best picture of the income of the entire group because it is not affected by extreme scores.

---

ple, repeated measurements of a community's religious attitudes produce very different values, the measurements are not reliable.

Even consistent results, however, may not be valid. **Validity** is *the quality of measurement gained by actually measuring what one intends to measure.* Say that you are interested in assessing how religious people are. You decide to do this by asking how often your respondents attend religious services. But does measuring attendance at services *really* measure religiosity? People may, after all, engage in religious rituals for any number of reasons, not all of them religious; some devout believers, on the other hand, avoid organized religion altogether. Thus, even when yielding consistent results (and thus having reliability), any measurement can still miss the real, intended target (and therefore lack validity). Poor mea-surement undermines scientific precision; therefore, re-searchers must always pay close attention to reliability and validity in any research.

Correlation and Cause

Insights about the social world are based on linking vari-ables together. **Correlation** refers to *a relationship be-tween two (or more) variables*; in simple terms, when one variable changes, so does the other. Ideally, sociolog-ical research seeks to understand not only *what* changes but *why*. Relationships of **cause and effect** mean that *change in one variable is explained by change in another.* As we noted earlier, Emile Durkheim concluded that the degree of social integration explained change in an-other variable, the suicide rate for a particular category of people. In cause-and-effect relationships, the **inde-pendent variable** (in this example, the degree of social integration) is *the variable that causes the change.* The **dependent variable** (here, the suicide rate) is *the variable that is changed.* Information about cause allows research-ers to engage in *prediction* based on available knowledge. However, few dimensions of social life are likely to have a single cause.

Just because two variables change together does not necessarily mean they are linked by a cause-and-effect relationship. To take a simple case, more cars are stolen during months when the consumption of ice cream rises, but there is no direct link between the two. Sociologists use the term **spurious correlation** to refer to *a "false" relationship between variables that is not based on direct cause and effect.* Variables that display spurious correlation are typically both caused by some third variable. In this case, rising temperatures increase auto thefts because people leave car windows open, just as warm weather encourages people to indulge in ice cream.

Researchers unmask cases of spurious correlation by utilizing scientific **control,** *the ability to neutralize the effect of one variable so that the relationships among other variables can be more precisely determined.* The effects of temperature might be controlled, in our example, by studying auto thefts and ice cream sales that occurred only on very hot days; doing so would no doubt reveal little of the original correlation.

In summary, correlation means that two variables change together. Cause and effect implies correlation and something more: that change in one variable actually causes change in another. To conclude that variables are linked by cause and effect, three factors must be demonstrated: (1) the two variables are correlated; (2) the independent (or causal) variable precedes the dependent variable in time; and (3) no evidence suggests that the correlation is spurious due to the effects of some third variable.

The Ideal of Objectivity

A traditional goal of scientific research is **objectivity,** *a state of complete personal neutrality in conducting re-* *search.* Objective research allows the facts to speak for themselves rather than being filtered through the personal values and biases of the researcher. Objective research stands as an ideal rather than a reality, however, because achieving complete neutrality is impossible for any researcher. Carefully adhering to the logic of scientific research enhances objectivity; researchers should also look inward to discover any personal biases and state them explicitly along with their findings. In this way, readers of the research can evaluate conclusions in the appropriate context.

The influential German sociologist Max Weber conceded that the personal values of sociologists play a part in the selection of topics they study. In this way, Weber argues, investigations are often *value-relevant.* Yet, he maintained, research should be carried out dispassionately, with the goal of discovering truth *as it is* rather than as we think *it should be.* This, for Weber, exemplifies the essential difference between science and politics. Weber urged researchers, whatever the political implications of their work, to strive to be *value-free.* This means having an open-minded readiness to accept the results of an investigation, no matter what those results might be.

Although widely supported, Weber's views have been criticized in two ways. First, *researchers must always make some interpretation of their data.* No scientist's data speak for themselves; sociologists always face the

A basic lesson of social research is that being observed affects human behavior. Researchers can never be sure precisely how this will occur: Some people become shy as the subject of attention, while others become highly animated. In neither case does the researcher witness natural behavior.

task of creating meaning from the facts that confront them. Moreover, the best research springs from a lively sociological imagination as well as careful attention to scientific procedures. Science, after all, is basically a series of procedures, like a recipe used in cooking. Just as something more than a good recipe is needed to make a great chef, so scientific procedures never, in and of themselves, create a great sociologist. In this sense, sociology is an art as well as a science (Nisbet, 1970).

A second criticism of Max Weber's goal of value-free research comes from those who claim that *any and all research is inevitably political* (Gouldner, 1970a, 1970b). From this point of view, all knowledge has implications for the distribution of power in society. Sociologists, therefore, must accept that their work is political, although they *do* have a choice about *which* values are worth supporting. Although this viewpoint is not limited to sociologists of any one political orientation, it predominates among those influenced by the ideas of Karl Marx, who asserted that while there is merit in understanding the world, the crucial task is to change it (1972:109; orig. 1845).

Research and Gender

In recent years, sociologists have become increasingly aware that research is also affected by gender—the ways in which males and females are socially defined. In the view of Margrit Eichler (1988), sound research can fall victim to four elements involving gender.

1. **Androcentricity.** Androcentricity (*andro* is the Greek word for "male"; *centricity* means "being centered on") refers to approaching any issue from a male perspective. This problem arises, for instance, when a researcher assumes that a man is the head of a household and directs questions to him, thereby excluding the views of a woman. The parallel problem, *gynocentricity*—seeing the world from a female perspective—limits sociological investigation as well. However, this occurs less commonly than androcentricity in male-dominated American society.

2. **Overgeneralizing.** Historically, sociologists have used data obtained from males as the basis for claims about all people. In an example of overgeneralizing, researchers may gather information about a corporation from male officials and use this as the basis for conclusions about the corpora-

tion in general. This problem can also occur in reverse. In a study of childrearing practices, collecting data only from women would support conclusions about "motherhood" but not about the more general issue of "parenthood."

3. **Gender insensitivity.** This problem occurs when research completely overlooks the variable of gender. As we shall see throughout this book, social forces often affect males and females quite differently. For example, researchers who fail to consider the importance of gender in a study of growing old in America would overlook important information, such as the fact that the majority of elderly males live with spouses while elderly females are most likely to live alone.

4. **Double standards.** Researchers must avoid evaluating the attitudes or behaviors of each sex in different terms. A double standard emerges when researchers describe a household as composed of a "man and wife," or systematically evaluate the work of one sex as more significant than that of the other.

5. **Interference.** Beyond Eichler's four ways that gender may affect research, the attitudes of *subjects* concerning gender also shape any study. The problem of "interference" arises as subjects react to the sex of the researcher rather than to the research itself. For instance, while conducting research in Sicily, Maureen Giovannini (1989) reported that many males, guided by local traditions, responded to her as a *woman* rather than in the sex-neutral sense of a *researcher*. Their response prevented her from engaging in activities (such as private conversations with men) that were deemed inappropriate for single women.

Nothing stated here is intended to discourage researchers from focusing on one sex or the other. Indeed, the pervasive attention to males at the expense of females in the past has led many of today's researchers to make special efforts to investigate the lives of women. But researchers—and others who read their work—must think critically about how gender can, and often does, shape the process of sociological investigation.

Research Ethics

Sociologists must be mindful of how their research affects their subjects. The American Sociological Association—the major professional association of sociologists in North

America—has established formal guidelines for the conduct of research (1984). These include protecting the rights, privacy, and safety of anyone involved in a research project. Sociologists are obligated to terminate any research, however valuable its possible results, if they become aware of any potential danger to participants.

Sociologists should accurately present the purpose of their research to subjects, especially if it involves working for a particular political organization or a business. Such affiliations must also be disclosed in the publication of the research. All subjects in research are also entitled to full anonymity, even if sociologists come under legal pressure to release confidential information. After completing their research, sociologists should report their findings in full, with a complete description of how the study was conducted. Researchers should also clearly indicate their organizational affiliations and sources of funding, attempt to provide all possible interpretations of their data, and point out the limitations of their conclusions (American Sociological Association, 1984).

MAJOR RESEARCH METHODS

A **research method** is *a systematic strategy for carrying out research*. Here we introduce four commonly used methods of sociological investigation: experiments, surveys, participant observation, and existing sources. None is better or worse than any other. Just as a carpenter selects a particular tool for a particular task, distinctive strengths and weaknesses make each method suitable for specific kinds of research.

Experiments

Research conducted by **experiment** *investigates cause-and-effect relationships under highly controlled conditions*. Experiments are typically devised to test a specific **hypothesis,** *an unverified statement of a relationship between two (or more) variables*. In everyday language, a hypothesis is a hunch or an educated guess about how variables are linked. An experiment provides the empirical evidence needed to accept or reject the hypothesis by carrying out three steps: (1) the dependent variable is measured; (2) the independent variable is altered; and (3) the dependent variable is measured again to see what, if any, change has taken place.

Successful experiments depend on careful control of all factors that might affect what is being measured. This is easiest in a laboratory, an artificial setting specially constructed for this purpose. But experiments in an everyday location—"in the field" as sociologists say—have the advantage of allowing researchers to observe subjects in their natural settings.

Surveys

A **survey** is *a research method in which subjects respond to a series of items or questions in a questionnaire or an interview*. Perhaps the most widely used of all research methods, surveys are particularly well suited to studying what cannot be observed directly, such as political attitudes or religious beliefs.

Surveys are directed at a **population,** *the people about whom a researcher seeks knowledge*. We might wish, for example, to determine the average years of schooling of adults living in a particular city; all the city's adult residents would then be the survey population. Sometimes every adult in the country can be the survey population, as in the familiar polls taken during political campaigns. Since contacting each of a vast number of people is all but impossible, researchers often study a **sample,** meaning *a relatively small number of cases selected to be representative of an entire population*. National surveys commonly provide accurate estimates based on samples of only about fifteen hundred people.

Selecting the subjects, however, is only the first step in carrying out a survey. The next stage involves implementing a specific plan for asking questions and recording answers. The most common way to do this is through a **questionnaire,** *a series of written questions or items to which subjects are asked to respond*. Usually the researcher provides possible responses to each item and asks the subject to select only one (similar to a multiple-choice examination). Sometimes, though, a researcher may want subjects to respond in an entirely free way, in an effort to discover subtle shades of opinion. Of course, the researcher later has to make sense out of what can be a bewildering array of answers.

In an **interview,** *a series of questions or items administered personally by a researcher to respondents*, subjects have considerable freedom to respond as they wish. Researchers often ask follow-up questions, both to probe a bit more deeply and to clarify the subject's responses. In doing this, however, a researcher must avoid influencing the subject even in subtle ways, such as raising an eyebrow when the subject begins to answer.

Table Reading: An Important Skill

A table provides a great deal of information in a small amount of space, so learning to read tables can increase your reading efficiency. Table 1–2 provides data from a survey of sexual activity among American couples (Blumstein & Schwartz, 1983). Look first at the title to see what variables are used. This table describes sexual patterns in terms of three additional variables: (1) the type of relationship involved (married couples, cohabiting heterosexual couples, and homosexual couples); (2) the duration of the relationship (under 2 years, 2 to 10 years, over 10 years); and (3) the sex of the respondent (male or female).

These three variables divide the table into three major parts, and six categories of people are found in each part. For each category, the proportion that reportedly did and did not engage in sexual activity outside of the relationship is presented; the two percentages add up to 100 percent.

The first part of the table shows that 13 percent of females married for less than two years reported having sexual activity outside of their relationship, while 87 percent reported not doing so. For women married between two and ten years, the corresponding figures are 22 percent and 78 percent. The same percentages hold for women married for more than ten years. Comparable information is provided for all the other categories of people.

What do these data tell us? First, for all types of relationships, the longer the couple has been together, the more likely a partner is to engage in sexual activity with someone else (which the researchers describe using the morally neutral term, "nonmo-

nogamy"). Second, men are more likely than women to be nonmonogamous. Third, married couples are less likely to be nonmonogamous than cohabiting heterosexual couples are. Note, too, that the pattern among homosexual couples differs sharply by sex: Gay men are far more likely to be nonmonogamous than are lesbian couples.

Finally, a critical reader should try to assess the overall quality of the research. Important clues include the identity and background of the researchers themselves (are they sociologists? newspaper reporters?), as well as bibliographical information (was the research published by an established journal? a group with some vested interest in the topic?). The research presented here is sound on both counts.

Table 1–2 SEXUAL ACTIVITY AMONG AMERICAN COUPLES, BY TYPE OF RELATIONSHIP, DURATION OF RELATIONSHIP, AND SEX OF RESPONDENT

Married Couples					Cohabiting Heterosexual Couples					Homosexual Couples				
	Reported Sexual Activity outside Relationship					Reported Sexual Activity outside Relationship					Reported Sexual Activity outside Relationship			
	Females		Males			Females		Males			Females		Males	
Years Together	Yes	No	Yes	No	Years Together	Yes	No	Yes	No	Years Together	Yes	No	Yes	No
Under 2	13%	87%	15%	85%	Under 2	20%	80%	21%	79%	Under 2	15%	85%	66%	34%
2–10	22	78	23	77	2–10	42	58	47	53	2–10	38	62	89	11
Over 10	22	78	30	70	Over 10*		no data			Over 10	43	57	94	6

* Too few cohabiting couples had been together for more than ten years.

SOURCE: Adapted from Philip Blumstein and Pepper Schwartz, *American Couples* (New York: William Morrow, 1983), p. 276. © 1983 by Philip Blumstein and Pepper W. Schwartz. Adapted by permission of William Morrow & Co.

Participant Observation

Participant observation is *a method in which researchers systematically observe people while joining in their routine activities.* This method works especially well in studying social life in a wide range of settings, from gambling casinos to religious seminaries. Cultural anthropologists, who make wide use of participant observation to study other societies, call this approach "fieldwork."

Researchers are likely to choose participant observation when they have a limited understanding of the social patterns they wish to investigate. They often begin with few, if any, specific hypotheses to test, since researchers may not be sure what the important questions will turn out to be. Compared to experiments and survey research, then, participant observation has fewer hard and fast rules. Flexibility can be an advantage, however, since researchers frequently must adapt to unexpected circumstances in an unfamiliar environment. Initially, the researcher concentrates on gaining entry into the setting without intruding on—and thereby changing—the routine behavior of others. In time, general observations give rise to specific questions that are answered as the research generates a detailed account of a way of life.

As its name suggests, participant observation has two dimensions. On the one hand, gaining an insider's viewpoint depends on becoming a participant in the setting—"hanging out" with others, attempting to act, think, and even feel the way they do. In contrast to other research methods, participant observation requires a personal immersion in a social setting, not for a week or two, but for months or even years. Even so, the researcher must also maintain the role of "observer," standing back from the action and applying the sociological perspective to social patterns that others take for granted.

Because the personal impressions of individual researchers play such a central role in participant observation, this method is sometimes criticized as lacking scientific rigor. Yet its personal approach is also a strength; while a highly visible team of sociologists administering formal surveys may disrupt many social settings, a sensitive participant-observer can often gain considerable insight into people's natural behavior.

Participant-observation research is well suited for exploring an unfamiliar setting. Doing so, however, usually requires extensive preparation, as anthropologists who routinely study other cultures know well. Before entering this urban community in Bombay, India, a researcher would need new language skills and at least a basic understanding of a complex and distinctive culture. To minimize these difficulties, researchers usually study communities with which they have at least some previous experience.

Table 1–3 FOUR RESEARCH METHODS: A SUMMARY

Method	Application	Advantages	Limitations
Experiment	For explanatory research that specifies relationships among variables; generates quantitative data	Provides greatest ability to specify cause-and-effect relationships; replication of research is relatively easy	Laboratory settings have artificial quality; unless research environment is carefully controlled, result may be biased
Survey	For gathering information about issues that cannot be directly observed, such as attitudes and values; useful for descriptive and explanatory research; generates quantitative or qualitative data	Sampling allows surveys of large populations using questionnaires; interviews provide indepth responses	Questionnaires must be carefully prepared and may produce low return rate; interviews are expensive and time-consuming
Participant observation	For exploratory and descriptive study of people in a "natural" setting; generates qualitative data	Allows study of "natural" behavior; usually inexpensive	Time-consuming; replication of research is difficult; researcher must balance roles of participant and observer
Existing sources	For exploratory, descriptive, or explanatory research whenever suitable data are available	Saves time and expense of data collection; makes historical research possible	Researcher has no control over possible bias in data; data may not be suitable for current research needs

Existing Sources

Each of the methods of conducting sociological investigation described so far involves researchers collecting their own data. Sometimes, however, this is not possible; often, it is not necessary. In many cases, sociologists draw from existing sources, analyzing data originally collected by others.

The data most widely used in this way are gathered by government agencies such as the Bureau of the Census. Data about other societies in the world are found in various publications of the United Nations and the World Bank. A wide range of such information is as near as the college library.

The obvious advantage of using available data—whether government statistics or the result of other research studies—is the savings in time and money that would otherwise be needed to assemble the information from scratch. Using data collected by others is especially appealing to sociologists with low budgets, who can undertake research that might otherwise be impossible. Moreover, the quality of data available from government agencies is generally better than what even well-funded researchers could hope to obtain on their own.

Still, the use of existing sources can create problems. For one thing, although government data are generally quite precise, the accuracy of much existing data may be difficult to assess. Using data collected by others thus sometimes parallels the experience of buying a used car: Although the savings are appealing, the potential for error and distortion means that "what you see may not be what you get."

Emile Durkheim's nineteenth-century study of suicide, described earlier, is a well-known study that made use of existing records. But Durkheim's research also illustrates some of the pitfalls of this approach. Whether a recorded death was actually a suicide is uncertain; accidents may be incorrectly classified as suicides just as actual suicides may be recorded as deaths due to other causes.

Characteristics of the four major methods of sociological investigation we have introduced are summarized in Table 1–3.

Ten Steps in Sociological Research

The following ten steps can serve as guidelines for carrying out research projects in sociology.

1. **Define the topic you wish to investigate.** Ideas for social research arise easily if you remain curious and observe the world around you from the sociological perspective.

2. **Find out what has already been written about the topic.** You are probably not the first person to have an interest in a particular issue. Spend enough time in the library to learn what theories and methods of sociological investigation have been applied to your topic. In looking over earlier research on the topic, be especially mindful of problems that may have come up before.

3. **Assess the requirements for carrying out the research.** What resources are necessary to support your research? How much time will you need? Can you do the work yourself? What sources of funding might be available to support your research? You must be able to answer all these questions before you actually begin to design a research project.

4. **Specify the questions you are going to ask.** Is your plan to explore an unfamiliar social setting? To describe some category of people? To investigate cause-and-effect links among several variables? If your study is exploratory, identify general questions that will guide your work. If it is descriptive, specify the population and the characteristics of interest. If your study is explanatory, state the hypothesis to be tested and carefully operationalize each variable.

5. **Consider the ethical issues involved in the research.** Be alert for ethical concerns throughout the research. Can you promise anonymity to the subjects? If so, how can you ensure that anonymity will be maintained? Could the research harm anyone? How could you design the study to minimize the chances for such harm?

6. **Choose the research method.** Consider all major research strategies—as well as innovative combinations of approaches—before deciding how to proceed. Which method is best depends on the kinds of questions you are asking as well as the resources available to support your research.

7. **Put the method to work to gather data.** Assess the reliability and validity of all measurements. Be sure to record all information accurately and in a way that will make sense to you later (it may be some time before you actually write up the results of your work). Be aware that various sources of bias can weaken the research.

8. **Interpret the findings.** What answers to the initial questions do the data suggest? Remember that there may be several ways to interpret the results of your study, consistent with different theoretical paradigms, and you should consider them all. Be alert to your own personal values or initial expectations, which affect how you make sense out of the data you have collected.

9. **State the conclusions based on your findings.** Prepare a final report indicating what you have learned from the research. Consider how your work contributes both to sociological theory and to improving sociological methods of research. Finally, evaluate your own work. What problems arose during the research process? What questions were left unanswered? How might your own biases have affected your conclusions?

10. **Publish your research!**

SUMMARY

1. The sociological perspective enables us to recognize that the lives of individuals are shaped by the forces of society. Because Americans tend to see events as the product of individual choice, the impact of social forces on people's lives goes largely unrecognized.

2. Auguste Comte gave sociology its name in 1838. Earlier social thought focused on what society ought to be; sociology was based on the use of scientific methods to understand society as it is.

3. Sociology emerged as a reaction to the rapid transformation of European society during the eighteenth and nineteenth centuries. The rise of an industrial economy, the explosive growth of cities, and the emergence of new political ideas combined to stimulate the development of the sociological perspective.

4. Sociological insights are linked together in meaningful ways by sociological theory. Theory building is guided by one or more theoretical paradigms.

5. The structural-functional paradigm is a framework for exploring how social structures promote the operation of society. This approach tends to minimize conflict and views societies as typically stable.

6. The social-conflict paradigm suggests that the conflict generated by social inequality promotes change. This approach downplays the extent of social integration and social stability.

7. In contrast to these two macro-level approaches, the symbolic-interaction paradigm offers a micro-level framework for studying patterns of social interaction in specific situations. At this level of analysis, society is seen as subjective, highly variable, and at least somewhat unpredictable.

8. Sociological research applies the logic of science to the study of the social world. Scientific facts are based on empirical evidence and often reveal the limitations of common sense.

9. Measurement is the process of determining the value of a variable in any specific case. Sound measurement is both reliable and valid.

10. Science seeks to specify the relationship among variables. Ideally, researchers try to identify relationships of cause and effect in which change in an independent variable can be used to predict change in a dependent variable.

11. The scientific ideal is objectivity. Although the issues studied typically reflect personal interests, value-free research depends on suspending personal values and biases as much as possible. However, some sociologists argue that all research involves political values, and that sociologists should use their work to promote desirable social change.

12. Because research can affect the well-being of subjects, sociological investigation must observe ethical guidelines.

13. Experiments investigate the relationship between two (or more) variables under controlled, laboratory conditions.

14. Surveys study attitudes and behavior by soliciting subject responses to items in questionnaires and interviews.

15. Participant observation involves direct observation of a social setting for an extended period of time. The researcher is both a participant in the setting and a careful observer of it.

16. The use of existing sources is often preferable to collecting one's own data; this method is of special interest to sociologists with limited research budgets.

KEY CONCEPTS

cause and effect a relationship between two variables in which change in one (the independent variable) causes change in another (the dependent variable)

concept an abstract idea that represents some aspect of the world, inevitably in a somewhat ideal and simplified form

control the ability to neutralize the effect of one variable so that the relationships among other variables can be more precisely determined

correlation a relationship between two (or more) variables

dependent variable a variable that is changed by another (independent) variable

empirical evidence evidence we are able to verify with our senses

experiment a research method that investigates cause-and-effect relationships under highly controlled conditions

hypothesis an unverified statement of a relationship between two (or more) variables

independent variable a variable that causes change in another (dependent) variable

interview a series of items or questions administered personally by a researcher to respondents

latent functions the unrecognized and unintended consequences of any social pattern

macro-level orientation a concern with large-scale patterns that characterize society as a whole

manifest functions the recognized and intended consequences of any social pattern

mean the arithmetic average of a series of numbers

measurement the process of determining the value of a variable in a specific case

median the value that occurs midway in a series of numbers or, simply, the middle case

micro-level orientation a concern with small-scale patterns of social interaction in specific settings

mode the value that occurs most often in a series of numbers

objectivity the state of complete personal neutrality in conducting research

operationalizing a variable specifying exactly what is to be measured when assigning a value to a variable

participant observation a method in which researchers systematically observe people while joining in their routine activities

population the people about whom a researcher seeks knowledge

positivism a path to understanding the world based on science

questionnaire a series of written questions or items to which subjects are asked to respond

reliability the quality of consistency in measurement

research method a systematic strategy for carrying out research

sample a relatively small number of cases selected to be representative of the entire population

science a logical system that bases knowledge on direct, systematic observation

social-conflict paradigm a theoretical framework based on the assumption that society is a complex system characterized by inequality and conflict that generate social change

social dysfunction the undesirable consequences of any social pattern for the operation of society

social function the consequences of any social pattern for the operation of society

social structure a relatively stable pattern of social behavior

sociology the scientific study of human social activity

spurious correlation a "false" relationship between two (or more) variables not based on direct cause and effect

structural-functional paradigm a theoretical framework based on the assumption that society is a complex system whose parts work together to promote stability

survey a research method in which subjects respond to a series of items or questions in a questionnaire or interview

symbolic-interaction paradigm a theoretical framework based on the view that society emerges from the construction of reality by individuals in everyday life

theoretical paradigm a set of fundamental assumptions that guides thinking and research

theory an explanation of the relationship between two or more specific facts

validity the quality of measurement gained by actually measuring what one intends to measure

variable a concept with a value that changes from case to case

Culture

2

A small aluminum motorboat chugged steadily along the muddy Orinoco River, deep in the vast tropical rain forest of southern Venezuela. American anthropologist Napoleon Chagnon was nearing the end of a three-day journey to the home territory of the Yąnomamö, one of the few technologically primitive societies remaining on earth.

Some twelve thousand Yąnomamö live in scattered villages along the border between Venezuela and Brazil. Their way of life contrasts sharply with our own. The Yąnomamö are spirit worshippers who have no form of writing. Until recent contact with outsiders, they used only handcrafted weapons like the bow and arrow to hunt for food. Thus Chagnon would be as strange to them as they were to him.

By two o'clock in the afternoon, Chagnon had almost reached his destination. Under the hot sun, the anthropologist's clothes were soaked with perspiration; his face and hands were swollen from the bites of gnats that swarmed around him.

Chagnon's heart pounded as the boat slid onto the riverbank near a Yąnomamö village. Voices could be heard nearby. Chagnon and his guide climbed from the boat and walked toward the sounds, stooping as they pushed their way through the dense undergrowth. Chagnon describes what happened next:

> I looked up and gasped when I saw a dozen burly, naked, sweaty, hideous men staring at us down the shafts of their drawn arrows! Immense wads of green tobacco were stuck between their lower teeth and lips making them look even more hideous, and strands of dark green slime dripped or hung from their nostrils—strands so long that they clung to their [chests] or drizzled down their chins.
>
> My next discovery was that there were a dozen or so vicious, underfed dogs snapping at my legs, circling me as if I were to be their next meal. I just stood there holding my notebook, helpless and pathetic. Then the stench of the decaying vegetation and filth hit me and I almost got sick. I was horrified. What kind of welcome was this for the person who came here to live with you and learn your way of life, to become friends with you? (1983:10)

Fortunately for Chagnon, the Yąnomamö villagers recognized his guide and withdrew their weapons. Reassured that he would at least survive the afternoon, Chagnon was still shaken by his inability to make any sense of the people surrounding him. And this was to be his home for a year and a half! He wondered why he had forsaken physics to study human culture in the first place.

All 5 billion people living on our planet are members of a single biological species: *Homo sapiens*. Even so, humans can be overwhelmed by how different we are from one another, differences not of biology but of culture. His journey to the Yąnomamö village brought Chagnon the first-hand experience of **culture shock,** *the personal disorientation that may accompany exposure to an unfamiliar way of life.* Like most of us, Chagnon had been raised to keep his clothes on, even in hot weather, and to use a handkerchief when his nose was running, especially in front of others. The Yąnomamö clearly had other ideas about how to live. The nudity that embarrassed Chagnon was customary to the Yąnomamö. The green slime hanging from their nostrils was caused by inhaling a hallucinogenic drug, a practice common among friends. The "stench" from which Chagnon recoiled in disgust no doubt smelled like "Home Sweet Home" to the inhabitants of that Yąnomamö village.

Human beings the world over have very different ideas about what is pleasant and unpleasant, polite and rude, true and false, right and wrong. This capacity for startling diversity is a wonder of our species: the expression of human culture.

CULTURE AND SOCIETY

Culture may be defined as *the beliefs, values, behavior, and material objects shared by a particular people.* Sociologists distinguish between *nonmaterial culture,* which includes intangible human creations ranging from altruism to zen, and *material culture,* the tangible products of human society, everything from armaments to zippers. *Culture* and *society* have much in common, but they are distinct concepts. Culture is a way of life or social heritage that certain people have in common. **Society** refers to *people interacting in a limited territory on the basis of shared culture.* Neither society nor culture can exist without the other.

Culture is expressed in everyday life in what we wear to work, when and what we eat, and how we enjoy spending our free time. Culture infuses life with meaning, by providing standards of success, beauty, and goodness, and reverence for a divine power, the forces of nature, or long-dead ancestors. Culture also shapes our personalities, creating many variations of what we commonly (yet inaccurately) describe as "human nature." The Yąnomamö are fierce and warlike, and they strive to develop these "natural" qualities in their children.

People around the world have created highly diverse ways of life. This is evident in outward differences of appearance: Compare the women shown here from Iran, Kenya, Greece, and Egypt and the men from Taiwan, Peru, India, and Indonesia. Less obvious, but of even greater importance, are the internal differences, since culture also shapes our self-concept and innermost personal feelings.

The Tasaday of the Philippines, by contrast, have been described as so peace-loving that their language has no word for violence. Both the American and Japanese cultures stress achievement and hard work; but Americans value competition and individualism, while the Japanese place great emphasis on cooperation and self-denying obedience to authority. In short, our culture affects virtually every dimension of social life, from the power of enormous corporations to the subtle action of raising an eyebrow.

In everyday conversation, "culture" usually refers to art forms associated with elites, such as classical literature, music, dance, and painting. Sociologists, however, use the term to refer to *everything* that makes up a people's way of life—Motown as well as Mozart, fish sticks as well as fine cuisine, ping pong as well as polo.

Culture is distinctively human. Every other species of living creatures—from ants to antelopes—behaves in uniform ways. To a world traveler, the enormous diversity of humanity contrasts sharply with, say, cats, which behave the same everywhere. The way of life of most living things is largely determined by biological forces we call *instincts*, strategies for survival that change only over long periods of time. A few animals—notably chimpanzees and other related primates—have a limited cultural capacity to use simple tools, and to teach these skills to their offspring. But our creative ability to shape the world far exceeds that of any other form of life, so that *only humans depend on culture rather than instinct to ensure the survival of their kind* (Harris, 1987).

To understand how this came to be, we must briefly review the history of our species on earth.

Culture and Human Intelligence

In a universe scientists estimate to be 15 billion years old, our planet is a relatively young 4.5 billion years of age, and the human species is a wide-eyed infant of only 40,000. We can trace our ancestry to the first forms of life that emerged a billion years after the earth was formed. One crucial turn in human history was the development of primates some 65 million years ago.

Early primates gradually evolved into highly intelligent life forms, with the largest brains relative to body weight of all living creatures. The human line diverged from that of our closest primate relatives, the great apes, some 12 million years ago. Our common lineage remains apparent, however, in traits that humans share today with chimpanzees, gorillas, and orangutans: great socia-

bility; affectionate and long-lasting bonds; the ability to walk upright (normal in humans, but less common among other primates); and hands that manipulate objects with great precision.

Studying fossil records, scientists have concluded that creatures displaying some human characteristics existed about 2 million years ago. The mental capacity of these distant ancestors allowed them to use fire, tools, and weapons, and to build simple shelters. Such "stone age" achievements may seem modest, but they signify the point at which our ancestors embarked on an evolutionary course by which culture—made possible as the human brain grew larger—became the primary strategy for survival. This extraordinary mental capacity has made us the only species that names itself, and we are appropriately termed *homo sapiens*, Latin for "thinking person."

Culture, therefore, progressed with the biological evolution of the human animal. It is a strategy for survival that began as our ancestors gradually moved from the trees to the ground and started walking upright. Culture emerged as biological instincts were gradually replaced by a more efficient survival strategy: *Human beings gained the mental power to actively fashion the natural environment for themselves.* That is, human nature was no longer grounded in instinct but rather in culture (Barash, 1981). Ever since, humans have made and remade their worlds in countless ways, which explains today's fascinating (and, as Napoleon Chagnon's experiences show, sometimes disturbing) cultural diversity around the world.

THE COMPONENTS OF CULTURE

Although cultures vary greatly, they all have components in common, including symbols, language, values, and norms. We shall begin with the one that underlies the rest: symbols.

Symbols

Human beings live in a world not just of objects and action, but of *meaning*. The human world, in short, is *symbolic*. A **symbol** is *anything that carries a particular meaning recognized by members of a culture.* A whistle, a wall of graffiti, a flashing red light, a fist raised in the air are all symbolic. The human capacity to create and manipulate symbols comes through in the various

All animals are expressive. Only to humans, however, do facial gestures have symbolic meaning.

ways a simple wink of the eye can convey interest, understanding, or insult.

As the basis of culture, symbols form the foundation of everyday reality. We become so familiar with the symbols of our own culture that we usually take them for granted. Often, however, we gain a heightened sense of the importance of our symbolic world when a symbol (such as the flag) is used in an unconventional way (set ablaze as an act of political protest).

Confronting an unfamiliar culture also makes us recognize the power of symbols. Culture shock looms large when we are unable to properly attach meaning to what is happening around us. Like Napoleon Chagnon confronting the Yąnomamö, we feel lost, unsure of how to act, and sometimes frightened—a consequence of being outside the symbolic web of culture.

Meanings vary from culture to culture; any action or object with a particular meaning in one culture may have a very different significance in another. To people in North America, a baseball bat symbolizes sport and relaxation, but the Yąnomamö would probably see it as a well-carved club that arouses thoughts of hunting or war. A dog is a beloved household pet to millions of Americans but a regular meal to millions of Chinese. Likewise, the cows that are sacred to Hindus in India are routinely consumed in the form of "quarter-pounders" by hungry Americans. Thus symbols that bind together people of one society can also separate people who live in the various societies of the world.

Some behavior that seems trivial to Americans gives offense to people in other societies. Counting one's change may make sense to us, yet it is considered insulting to people in Japan. Similarly, sitting with one leg draped casually across the other is simply a relaxed pose to Americans, but the same posture prompts Iranians to take offense because, as Muslims, they define the bottom of the foot as unclean.

Symbolic meanings also vary within a single society. The fur coat, a prized symbol of success to one person, may exemplify the inhumane treatment of animals to another. Opening a door for a woman may signify a common courtesy in the minds of some men yet symbolize male condescension and dominance to some women.

Language

The most important symbols in a culture are those that form language. **Language** is defined as *a system of symbols with standard meanings that allows members of a society to communicate with one another.* All societies have a spoken language; some, including the Yąnomamö, lack a written language and communicate entirely through speech.

Language not only facilitates communication, but it also ensures the continuity of culture. As a means of perpetuating cultural heritage in coded form, language is the key to **cultural transmission,** *the process by which culture is passed from one generation to the next.* Just as our bodies contain the genes of our ancestors, so our words and ideas are rooted in the lives of those who came before us. Language, then, gives us enormous power by providing access to the accumulated knowledge of centuries.

For most of human history, culture has been transmitted through speech alone, often called the *oral tradition.* Writing was devised only about five thousand years ago, but until recent times few people learned to read and write. In America, only a small elite was literate a century ago. Even today, perhaps 25 million adults in the United States cannot read and write very well. Many economically disadvantaged Americans, in particular, rely on the oral tradition in a society that increasingly demands the symbolic skills of written language. Perpetuating the cycle of disadvantage, this situation has been called a national tragedy.

Language skills unlock the human imagination. By connecting symbols in virtually infinite combinations, we can conceive of life other than as it is. In this way, language distinguishes human beings as creatures who dream and hope, able to imagine a future better than the present and, unique among all creatures, aware of our own mortality.

Language shapes the reality we experience. To Americans, whose symbolic system is the English language, crystals of frozen water that fall from the sky register simply as *snow.* Eskimos, by contrast, have twenty specific words for particular kinds of snow—falling snow, drifting snow, damp snow, dry snow, and so on.

Two anthropologists who specialized in linguistic studies, Edward Sapir and Benjamin Whorf, claimed that language amounts to more than simply attaching labels to the "real world" (Sapir, 1929, 1949; Whorf, 1956). Standing between us and the world, language *becomes* our reality. Sapir and Whorf therefore suggested that, rather than describing a single reality, the thousands of human languages give rise to differing truths. This occurs because every language includes words or expressions that have no precise counterpart in another symbolic system. In addition, each language fuses symbols with particular emotions. Thus, as multilingual people can attest, a single idea may "feel" different if spoken in Spanish rather than in English or German (Falk, 1987). Formally, then, the **Sapir-Whorf hypothesis,** as this insight has come to be called, holds that *we know the world only in terms of our language.* Making use of different symbolic systems, a Turk, a Brazilian, and a

Filipino actually experience "distinct worlds, not merely the same world with different labels attached" (Sapir, 1949:162).

Of course, the Sapir-Whorf hypothesis still allows for the human capacity to generate new symbols as well as to employ familiar symbols in novel ways. Technological advances such as the invention of computers led to new words and phrases, including *bytes, interface,* and *random access memory.* Political controversy, too, can force changes in language. The desire for greater equality in America, a predominantly white society, led African-Americans to replace the word *Negro* with the term *black* or *person of color.* After more than twenty years of increasing usage, this symbolic change has helped improve white people's perceptions of African-Americans. If language shapes reality, then, humans also retain the capacity to alter their language, and the corresponding reality it evokes.

Values

What accounts for the popularity among Americans of films featuring characters like James Bond, Dirty Harry, and Rambo? Each is based on a rugged individual, suspicious of "the system," who relies primarily on his own skill and initiative. Together, they suggest that Americans celebrate an ideal of sturdy individualism, especially among men. Such patterns reflect **values,** *standards by which members of a culture define what is desirable or undesirable, good or bad, beautiful or ugly* (Williams, 1970:27). Values are evaluations and judgments, from the standpoint of a particular culture, of what ought to be. Such broad principles touch most facets of a people's way of life.

Because the United States is a nation of immigrants, few American values are shared by everyone. Even so, a number of dominant values have emerged. Sociologist Robin Williams (1970) suggests that the following ten values stand at the core of American culture.

1. **Equal opportunity.** Americans believe everyone should have the opportunity to get ahead, although, due to varying talents and efforts, people are not expected to end up in the same situation. In other words, while not endorsing *equality of condition,* Americans do embrace *equality of opportunity.*

2. **Achievement and success.** American culture encourages competition. In this way, we believe, each person reaps a share of success based on personal

merit. Succeeding in one's endeavors thus implies a measure of personal worth—that one is a "winner."

3. **Activity and work.** American heroes, from Olympic track star Jackie Joyner-Kersee to film's famed archaeologist Indiana Jones, are "doers," people who get the job done. Americans prefer *action* to *reflection*, and through hard work seek to control events rather than passively accepting "fate."

4. **Material comfort.** Activity defined as worthwhile generally brings money and all it will buy. Americans may quip that "money won't buy happiness," but most eagerly pursue wealth and its trappings all the same.

5. **Practicality and efficiency.** Americans value activity that solves problems and produces the greatest results in the least amount of time. "Building a better mousetrap" is praiseworthy in our culture, especially when done in the most cost-effective way.

6. **Progress.** Americans have traditionally believed that the present is better than the past, and that the future is likely to be better still. In the United States, advertising continually sparks sales with claims that the "very latest" constitutes the "very best."

7. **Science.** Most Americans are confident that science can effectively address problems and improve our lives. We think of ourselves as rational people, which probably explains our cultural tendency (among men more than women) to devalue emotions and intuition as sources of truth.

8. **Democracy.** Americans recognize individual rights that cannot be overridden by government. Our political system is based on the ideal of free elections in which all adults exercise their right to vote.

9. **Freedom.** Closely related to democracy, this cultural value suggests that individual initiative is more desirable than collective conformity. While recognizing many responsibilities and obligations to others, Americans endorse the belief that individuals should pursue personal goals without unreasonable interference from anyone else.

10. **Racism and group superiority.** While expressing a commitment to the values of equality and freedom, Americans often link personal worth to categories based on social class, race, ethnicity, and sex. Many Americans value males above females, whites above nonwhites, and more privileged peo-

Artist Sally Swain alters Degas' famous painting of a ballerina to make fun of our culture's tendency to ignore the everday lives of most women.

Sally Swain, Mrs. Degas Vacuums the Floor. *From* °Great Housewives in Modern Art, *Penguin Books, 1988.*

ple above those who are disadvantaged. Thus, although Americans often describe theirs as a nation of equals, there is little doubt that some of us are thought to be "more equal than others."

By carefully examining this listing, we discover that dominant cultural values are likely to contain certain contradictions (Lynd, 1967; Bellah et al., 1985). For example, Americans frequently find themselves torn between the "me first" attitude of an individualistic, success-at-all-costs orientation and the contradictory need to be part of a community. In addition, the value Americans place on equality of opportunity for all has long conflicted with a tendency to promote or degrade others because of their race, sex, or social background. Such value conflicts inevitably cause strain, leading to awkward balancing acts in our views of the world. Sometimes we decide that one value is more important than another; in other cases, we may simply learn to live with such contradictions.

Norms

Through values, cultures give shape to our lives. **Norms,** or *rules that guide behavior*, also provide meaning to individuals. William Graham Sumner (1959; orig. 1906), an early American sociologist, coined the term **mores** (pronounced MORE-ays; the rarely used singular form is *mos*) to refer to *norms that have great moral significance*. Mores, which are often called *taboos*, are exemplified by the American expectation that adults not engage in sexual relations with children.

Sumner used the term **folkways** to designate *norms that have little moral significance*. Examples include norms involving dress and polite behavior. Considered less important than mores, folkways deal with matters about which we tend to allow people considerable personal discretion. Because their significance is rather minor, violations of folkways typically result in mild penalties. A man who does not wear a tie to a formal dinner party is violating folkways or "etiquette"; he might be the subject of some derisive comments, but little more. By contrast, were he to arrive at the dinner party wearing *only* a tie, he would be violating cultural mores and inviting far more serious sanctions.

Cultural norms, then, steer our behavior by defining what is right and wrong, proper and improper. Although we sometimes object to the conformity norms demand, norms are the shared expectations that make possible a sense of security and trust in our personal interactions. Norms thus form part of the symbolic road map of culture, guiding us through sometimes confusing social situations.

Violations of norms typically elicit criticism from others, just as conforming to norms is likely to be met with praise. Once we learn the norms of our culture, we usually respond to ourselves just as someone else observing our behavior would. In short, we *internalize* cultural norms, building them into our own personalities. Our experience of *guilt*—the negative judgment we make of ourselves for having violated a norm—and *shame*—the painful acknowledgment of others' disapproval—

proves that we have incorporated cultural norms into our own view of the world. This is no doubt what writer Mark Twain had in mind when he quipped that human beings "are the only animals that blush . . . or need to."

"Ideal" and "Real" Culture

Values and norms do not describe actual behavior as much as prescribe how we *should* act as members of a particular culture. Members of every culture recognize some difference between *ideal culture*, expectations embodied in values and norms, and *real culture*, social patterns that actually occur in everyday life. For example, the vast majority of Americans acknowledge the importance of sexual fidelity in marriage; however, roughly one-third of married people are sexually unfaithful to their spouses at some point in their marriages. These discrepancies are common to all cultural systems, as suggested by the adage "Do as I say, not as I do."

TECHNOLOGY AND CULTURE

In addition to intangible cultural elements such as values and norms, every culture encompasses a wide range of tangible (from Latin meaning "touchable") human creations that sociologists refer to as *artifacts*. The Yąnomamö gather material from the forest to build huts and make hammocks. They craft bows and arrows to hunt and defend themselves, fashion tools for raising crops, and use pigments to paint their bodies.

Examining a society's artifacts reveals that the things people create often express their cultural values; that is, material and nonmaterial elements of culture are closely related. Because warfare is central to their lives, the Yąnomamö value militaristic skills, devote great care to making weapons, and prize the poison tips on their arrows. In the same way, the material elements of American culture reflect distinctive values. Individuality and independence, for instance, are expressed in the production of a vast number of automobiles, which Americans prefer to public, mass transportation. Some 140 million automobiles are registered in the United States, a number sufficient to accommodate every American at one time—with no one sitting in back!

Cultural patterns also reflect a society's **technology,** *the application of cultural knowledge to the task of living* *in a physical environment.* In simple terms, technology links the world of nature and the world of culture. The more complex a society's level of technology, the more its members are able to shape their world for themselves, for better or worse. Gerhard and Jean Lenski (1987) have explored what they call **sociocultural evolution,** *the historical process of cultural change that has accompanied technological innovation.* They identify four major levels of technological development, explaining how each generates distinctive cultural patterns.[1]

Hunting and Gathering

The most basic productive technology is **hunting and gathering,** *the use of simple tools to hunt animals and gather vegetation.* From the emergence of our species, this way of life characterized most of human existence until several centuries ago. Now hunting and gathering can be found in only a few societies, including the Pygmies of central Africa, the Bushmen of southwestern Africa, the Aborigines of Australia, the Kaska Indians of northwest Canada, and the Tasaday of the Philippines.

Because food production in these societies is inefficient, their cultures focus on the search for game and edible plants. The societies remain small—generally only several dozen people in a family-like group. Hunting and gathering bands distance themselves from one another since food production requires a large amount of land. They are typically nomadic, moving on as they deplete the vegetation in one area, or as they pursue migratory animals.

Most activities center on seeking out the next meal, and everyone takes part. The very young and the very old are expected to contribute only what they can, while healthy adults secure most of what is consumed. The gathering of vegetation—the primary food source—is typically carried out by women, while men do most of the hunting. Males and females thus have somewhat different positions, but most hunters and gatherers view men and women as generally equal in social importance (Leacock, 1978).

Hunting and gathering peoples have few formal leaders. One person may be recognized as a *shaman,* who presides over spiritual concerns. However, this position provides added prestige rather than wealth, with

no release from the duty to help procure food. Overall, hunting and gathering is a relatively simple and equitable way of life.

With such limited technology, hunters and gatherers are vulnerable to the forces of nature. Storms and droughts can easily destroy their food supply, and they have few effective ways to deal with accident and disease. Such high risks encourage a cooperative orientation, a strategy that enhances the odds of survival. Nonetheless, many members do not outlive childhood, and perhaps half die before reaching the age of twenty (Lenski & Lenski, 1987:105).

Because hunters and gatherers now face depletion of game and vegetation and the encroachment of technologically advanced people, the Lenskis suggest that the 1990s may bring an end to this way of life. Fortunately, study of hunters and gatherers has already produced valuable information about humanity's sociocultural history and our fundamental ties to the natural world.

Horticulture and Pastoralism

Between ten and twelve thousand years ago, **horticulture,** or *the use of hand tools to raise crops,* slowly began to transform the way of life of many hunters and gatherers. The hoe and the digging stick (used to punch holes in the ground for seeds) first appeared in fertile regions of the Middle East and Southeast Asia and had altered life from Western Europe to China by about six thousand years ago. Central and South Americans devised the cultivation of plants independently, but rocky soil and mountainous terrain encouraged many societies—including the Yąnomamö—to combine this new technology with traditional hunting and gathering (Fisher, 1979; Chagnon, 1983).

In particularly arid regions, horticulture had little impact. There, another type of culture emerged based on **pastoralism,** *the domestication of animals.* Horticulture and pastoralism are often combined; numerous societies of this kind are found in South America, Africa, the Middle East, and Asia.

The domestication of plants and animals had a marked effect on cultural patterns. First, greater productivity allowed societies to expand to hundreds of members. While pastoral peoples remained nomadic, horticulturalists formed settlements that were linked by trade, sometimes encompassing thousands of people.

Second, a material surplus freed some of the population from food production. Thus, cultures became

---

[1] This account examines only the major types of societies described by the Lenskis.

The members of hunting and gathering societies are dependent on nature to provide basic foods. Pastoral societies have a somewhat higher standard of living based on the capacity to domesticate animals. In agrarian societies, animal power is used to plow land and for a host of other tasks. Industrial societies are the most productive of all, making use of vastly more powerful energy sources. This allows people far greater choice in how they earn a livelihood.

more internally complex, as some individuals created crafts, engaged in trade, or served as full-time priests. In comparison to hunters and gatherers, pastoral and horticultural people are also more hierarchical. Wealth becomes concentrated in the hands of some families, fostering a rudimentary government partly concerned with protecting the privileges of these elites.

Hunters and gatherers, who have little control over

nature, generally believe that the world is inhabited by numerous spirits. Once humans gain control over plants and animals, however, they tend to conceive of God as the creator of the world. The pastoral roots of Judaism and Christianity are evident in the term "pastor" for some members of the clergy and the common view of God as "shepherd," overseeing the well-being of the world.

Agriculture

About five thousand years ago, further technological advances led to the emergence of **agriculture**, *large-scale cultivation using plows drawn by animals*. Agrarian technology first appeared in the Middle East and gradually spread throughout the world. So important to human culture was the invention of the animal-drawn plow and related advances including the wheel, writing, numbers, and the expanding use of metals, that this era is widely regarded as "the dawn of civilization" (Lenski & Lenski, 1987:166).

The animal-drawn plow further increased food production. By turning the soil, plows allowed land to be farmed for decades, encouraging permanent settlements. Large food surpluses, combined with the use of animals and wagons for transportation, allowed agrarian societies to reach unprecedented size—in some places more than 1 million people spread over vast regions.

Advancing technology also promoted productive specialization. Distinct occupations emerged, part of an economy based on money rather than simple barter. Expanding trade and the growth of cities generated a wider range of human opportunities, but also rendered social life increasingly individualistic and impersonal.

Agriculture also fostered a dramatic increase in social inequality. In many cases, portions of the population became slaves or serfs who labored for elites. As a result, sharply different cultural patterns emerged within a single society. Freed from the need to work, elites cultivated a "refined culture" based on the study of philosophy, art, and literature. Commoners, by contrast, generally remained illiterate and centered their lives on their work. At all levels of society, the lives of the two sexes also became distinct: Agrarian societies typically conferred pronounced power and privilege on males and placed females in a clear position of social subordination.

Technologically simple people tend to be similar the world over; differences in their ways of life are mostly due to variations in the natural environment. The Lenskis explain that agrarian technology provided sufficient control over the natural world to allow extensive use of the creative elements of human culture.

Industrialization

Industrialization, explored in detail in Chapter 11 ("Economics and Politics"), occurred as societies replaced the muscle power of animals and humans with advanced sources of energy. Formally, an **industrial society** is *a society that produces goods using sophisticated machinery powered by advanced fuels*. The introduction of large machines, first powered by steam engines in England in 1765, greatly expanded productivity, transforming cultural patterns in the process.

Agrarian people typically work in or near the home; industry, however, is based on the creation of factories where people work in the company of strangers, to whom they are linked only by economic necessity. Lost in the process of European industrialization were many traditional cultural values and customs that had guided agrarian life for centuries.

Industry vastly enlarged the scope of social experience. During the nineteenth century, railroads and steamships revolutionized transportation, moving people farther in less time than ever before. During the twentieth century, automobiles further expanded the familiar world, just as the telephone, radio, and television gradually made the globe seem smaller and smaller.

Industrial technology has raised the living standards and extended the lives of millions of the world's people. An increasing proportion of people also benefit from schooling, because industrial production requires an increasingly literate and skilled labor force. Further, as Chapter 7 ("Social Stratification") explains, industrial societies gradually extended political rights to the population and achieved some lessening of economic inequality.

Simultaneously, however, industry was eroding most traditional cultural patterns. Consequently, work, learning, and even worship are now carried out in a largely impersonal environment in most industrialized nations. People gain greater privacy and a wider range of choices, but, as Chapter 15 ("Social Change and Modernity") shows, such individualism is often experienced as bewildering social isolation.

Whatever the drawbacks of our own way of life, Americans tend to judge cultures based on simpler technology as less advanced. Some facts support such a judgment. The average life expectancy of Americans, for example, now stands at more than seventy-one years for males and exceeds seventy-eight years for females. In contrast, Napoleon Chagnon estimated the life expectancy of the Yąnomamö to be only about forty years.

We must take care, however, to avoid self-serving judgments about cultures different from our own. Although the Yąnomamö are quite eager to gain some of the advantages of modern technology (such as steel tools and shotguns), they are generally well fed by world standards and most are quite satisfied with their lives (Chagnon, 1983). Like other technologically simple societies, the Yąnomamö adapt well to their surroundings. We, on the other hand, manipulate the natural world to suit ourselves. Driven by a sophisticated technology, our culture has had an enormous impact on the natural world—for better and worse. Advanced technology has produced work-reducing devices and seemingly miraculous forms of medical treatment, but it has also contributed to unhealthy levels of stress, opened threatening holes in the planet's ozone layer, and created weapons capable of destroying in a flash everything that humankind has managed to achieve in its entire history.

CULTURAL DIVERSITY

The blend of complex technology and high immigration produces remarkably diverse cultural patterns. Perhaps no society illustrates this fact better than the United States.

Over the last 150 years, more than 55 million immigrants have come to America. Earlier in this century, most came from Europe; by the 1980s, the majority were immigrating from Asia and Latin America (Fallows, 1983; U.S. Bureau of the Census, 1989). This large-scale immigration has made the United States truly a cultural kaleidoscope. Although sociologists sometimes speak of the "cloth of culture," a more accurate description of American culture might be a "patchwork quilt."

Subcultures

A **subculture** is *a cultural pattern that differs from the dominant culture in some distinctive way.* Teenagers, Korean-Americans, homeless people, and "southerners" all display subcultural attitudes and behavior. Particular occupations also foster subcultures, which are often marked by distinctive speech, as anyone who has ever spent time with race-car drivers, jazz musicians, or even sociologists can attest. Residents of rural areas sometimes mock the ways of "city slickers," who may, in turn, deride their "country cousins." Sexual orientation generates yet another subculture, especially in San Francisco and New York, where large gay communities are found.

In many societies of the world, subcultures reflect ethnic differences. Yugoslavia, a nation in southeastern Europe, presents a rather extreme case. This *one* small country (roughly the size of the state of Wyoming, with a population of about 25 million) makes use of *two* alphabets, has *three* religions, speaks *four* languages, includes *five* nationalities, is divided into *six* separate republics, and absorbs cultural influences from *seven* other nations with which it shares borders. How does American culture compare to Yugoslavia's?

A widespread view holds that the United States is a "melting pot" that blends people of many nationalities into a single "American" culture. This belief greatly underestimates the social differences—and conflicts—that historically stem from ethnicity and race. Even so, in recent decades cultural distinctiveness has become a source of pride, leading many new and not-so-new immigrants to maintain at least some of their traditions.

In 1990, perhaps 30 million people—more than one in ten Americans—spoke a language other than English at home. This number is growing rapidly, and will reach 40 million by the beginning of the next century. Spanish will gain in importance as America's "second language," and Italian, German, and French will continue to be widely used, reflecting the historical immigration of Europeans to North America. Immigration from other world regions—notably Asia—has greatly multiplied the number of native speakers of Filipino, Japanese, Korean, and Vietnamese. Sensing the controversy this heightened cultural diversity has sparked, in 1981 Congress first considered legislation that would make English the official language of the United States. The box focuses on this national debate.

Countercultures

Cultural differences within a society may also represent active opposition to some aspects of the dominant culture. A **counterculture** is defined as *cultural patterns strongly at odds with the dominant culture.* People who embrace a counterculture may question the morality of the majority. Not surprisingly, the majority may be swift to condemn them in response, at times imposing the power of the law.

In many societies, counterculture has been linked to youth (Spates, 1976b, 1982, 1983). During the 1960s, youthful hippies criticized American culture as overly competitive, individualistic, and materialistic. Instead, they favored a collective and cooperative lifestyle in which "being" took precedence over "doing," and personal qualities such as "expanded consciousness" were prized over the drive for material objects and money. These differences prompted many hippies to "drop out" of the larger

An Official American Language? The Diversity Debate

To some, designating English as the official language of the United States seems a bit silly—after all, doesn't almost everybody speak English? The answer, in a word, is *no*. Some 30 million Americans now speak a language other than English at home, and an increasing number of Americans use *only* a language other than English.

Behind these facts lies rising immigration, examined in Chapter 9 ("Race and Ethnicity"). Not since the early decades of this century have Americans confronted such cultural diversity. According to some, this threatens to undermine America's way of life. Consider the experience of Emmy Schafer. In 1978, seeking assistance at a government office in southern Florida, Schafer could not find a single employee who understood English. Outraged by this, she started the drive for official recognition of English.

Those favoring an official American language point out, first, that our cultural diversity demands that Americans have something as basic as language in common. Government policy should support what *unites* all people rather than what *divides* us.

Second, they believe that declaring English as the official language would ensure that young people of all cultural backgrounds learn English in school, giving them a fair chance for higher education and a good job. By 1990, some 6 million schoolchildren in the United States were native speakers of a language other than English. Unless they know the language of the majority, it is argued, these children risk becoming second-class citizens.

Opponents view the idea of "official English" as little more than a backlash against rising immigration. First, they condemn the movement as an expression of *xenophobia*, a word derived from the Greek for "fear of what is strange." Forcing all Americans to speak English, opponents claim, amounts to an effort to stamp out cultural diversity. Second, they cite support for diversity in law. The 1968 Bilingual Education Act mandates that children who do not speak English at home can request to be educated in their own language as they simultaneously learn to speak English. While conceding the difficulty of securing teachers able to converse in 125 different languages—in-

cluding not only Spanish, but Haitian, Creole, Hmong, Khmer, and Ulithian—proponents of bilingualism maintain that only in this way will all Americans value their cultural heritage.

By 1990, one-third of the states had made English the official language, and a national campaign was under way to officially designate the United States as an English-speaking country. Many Americans are wary, the sentiments of United States Senator John McCain, Republican of Arizona: "Our nation and the English language have done quite well with Chinese spoken in California, German in Pennsylvania, Italian in New York, Swedish in Minnesota, and Spanish in New York. I fail to see the cause for alarm now." But, in a nation of intense cultural diversity, the debate is likely to continue.

SOURCE: Based on Edward B. Fiske, "One Language or Two? The Controversy over Bilingual Education in America's Schools," *The New York Times*, November 10, 1985, Sect. 12, pp. 1, 45; also, Margaret Carlson, "Only English Spoken Here," *Time*, December 5, 1988:30.

---

society, often forming countercultural communities of their own.

Countercultures involve not only political principles but distinctive folkways, in the form of greetings, dress, and music. To many members of the 1960s countercultures, for instance, blue jeans and "ethnic" clothing symbolized identification with the common people. Rock and roll music flourished as a countercultural anthem, with little of the middle-class respectability it enjoys today.

Countercultures still exist, although they maintain a lower profile than in the 1960s. In the United States, the Ku Klux Klan and other white supremacist groups promote violence and racial hatred to protect what they see as "real American values." In Europe, young "punks" express their contempt for established culture through styles of music and appearance—shaved heads or multicolored hairstyles, black leather, and chains—intended to challenge and offend more conventional members of their societies.

Cultural Change

The Greek philosopher Aristotle stated that "There is nothing permanent except change." Caught up in day-to-day concerns, we may not notice changes going on around us because we are busy living our lives, not observing them. Cultural change proceeds continuously, however, although it is sometimes evident only after a period of years. Consider, for example, changes in the American family over the past half-century. Government records show that the divorce rate now stands more than twice as high as it did in 1940. A half-century ago, the family norm was a bread-winning father, a homemaking mother, and their children. Since then, the number of single-parent households has increased so that now a majority of children in the United States live for some time with only one parent before they reach the age of eighteen. Moreover, as increasing numbers of women pursue careers outside the home, they are delaying marriage and children, or remaining single yet having children all the same.

Table 2–1 compares attitudes among students entering college in 1968 and those matriculating in 1987. The figures in the table indicate that about the same proportion of students come to college to "gain a general education" and to "learn more about things." But today's students clearly appear more interested in gaining skills that will lead to a high-paying job. In addition, the political activism of the 1960s has declined in favor of pursuing personal success. Note that changes generally have been greater among women than among men. This, no doubt, reflects the women's movement for social equality, which intensified after 1968.

Change in one part of a cultural system typically sparks other changes as well. Arlie Hochschild (1988:258) has commented that "The gender revolution is primarily *caused* by changes in the economy, but people *feel* it in marriage." Such a linkage illustrates the principle of **cultural integration**, which holds that *the various parts of a cultural system are linked together.* Even so, some parts of a cultural system change more quickly than others. William Ogburn (1964) observed that technological advances tend to create new elements of material culture ("test-tube babies," for example) faster than new nonmaterial elements (such as ideas about parenthood). Ogburn used the term **cultural lag** to refer to *inconsistencies in a cultural system resulting from the unequal rates at which different cultural elements change.* In a culture that now has the technical ability to allow one woman to give birth to a child by using another woman's egg,

Table 2–1 ATTITUDES AMONG STUDENTS ENTERING AMERICAN COLLEGES, 1968 AND 1987

		1968	1987	Change
REASONS TO GO TO COLLEGE (Very Important)				
Gain a general	male	60	61	+1
education	female	67	67	0
Learn more about	male	69	72	+3
things	female	74	76	+2
Improve reading	male	22	36	+14
and writing skills	female	23	43	+20
Get a better job	male	74	83	+9
	female	70	83	+13
Prepare for gradu-	male	39	44	+5
ate or profes-	female	29	50	+21
sional school				
Make more money	male	57	75	+18
	female	42	68	+26
LIFE OBJECTIVES (Essential or Very Important)				
Develop a philoso-	male	79	40	−39
phy of life	female	87	39	−48
Keep up with po-	male	52	43	−9
litical affairs	female	52	33	−19
Raise a family	male	64	56	−8
	female	72	60	−12
Help others in	male	50	50	0
difficulty	female	71	67	−4
Be successful in	male	55	55	0
my own business	female	32	46	+14
Be well off finan-	male	51	80	+29
cially	female	27	72	+45

Note: To allow comparisons, data from early 1970s rather than 1968 are used for some items.

SOURCE: Richard G. Braungart and Margaret M. Braungart, "From Yippies to Yuppies: Twenty Years of Freshman Attitudes," *Public Opinion*, Vol. 11, No. 3 (September–October 1988):53–56.

which has been fertilized in a laboratory with the sperm of a total stranger, what do the traditional terms *motherhood* and *fatherhood* mean?

Finally, it is worth asking how cultural changes are set in motion in the first place. Cultural change has three general sources. The first is *invention*, the process of creating new cultural elements such as the telephone (1876), the airplane (1903), and the aerosol spray can (1941). The process of invention is going on constantly, as indicated by the thousands of applications received by the United States Patent Office each year.

Discovery, a second, closely related cause of cultural change, involves recognizing and understanding something already in existence—from a distant star, to the foods of a foreign culture, to the muscle power of American women. Discovery often results from scientific research; many medical breakthroughs happen this way. Yet discovery can also occur quite by accident, as when Marie Curie unintentionally left a "rock" on a piece of photographic paper in 1898 and discovered radium.

The third cause of cultural change is *diffusion*, the spread of both material and nonmaterial elements from one cultural system to another. Missionaries and anthropologists like Napoleon Chagnon have introduced many cultural elements to the Yąnomamö. Elements of American culture have spread throughout the world through diffusion: jazz, with its roots deep in the culture of African-Americans; computers, first built in the mid-1940s in a Philadelphia laboratory; and even the United States Constitution, on which several other countries have modeled their own political systems. Conversely, much of what we assume is "American" is actually borrowed from other cultures. Ralph Linton (1937) has pointed out that commonplace elements of our way of life—most of our clothing and furniture, clocks, newspapers, money, and even the English language—are all imports, derived from other cultures. Obviously, as the technology of travel and communication makes the world smaller, the rate of cultural diffusion will increase.

Ethnocentrism and Cultural Relativity

A question in the popular game Trivial Pursuit asks which beverage is most popular among Americans. Milk? Soft drinks? Coffee? The answer is actually soft drinks, but all the beverages mentioned are favored by members of our culture.

If the Masai of eastern Africa were to join the game, however, their answer might well be "blood." To us, of course, the idea of drinking blood is revolting, if not downright unnatural. On the other hand, milk, which Americans consider "nature's perfect food," is actually detested by billions of people in the world, including the Chinese (Harris, 1985).

In a world of many cultures, how do we come to terms with other people's ways of living when they offend our own notions of what is proper? Anthropologists and sociologists caution us against **ethnocentrism,** *the practice of judging another culture by the standards of our own culture*. A tendency toward ethnocentrism arises inevitably because our understanding of the world is closely tied to one particular way of life. Yet evaluating any unfamiliar practice outside its own cultural context can lead to misunderstanding and conflict. Ethnocentrism is a two-way street, of course. Just as we tend to dismiss those who differ from us, so others may judge us in the same way. Anthropologist Napoleon Chagnon was initially appalled at the behavior of the Yąnomamö

In outdoor markets throughout the southern region of the People's Republic of China, dogs are a prized food. To an American observer, selecting a puppy for dinner may well seem cruel and inhumane. From the Chinese point of view, however, the common American practice of drinking milk provokes disgust.

CRITICAL THINKING

"The Traveler's Dilemma": How Should You Judge Another Culture?

Being receptive to another culture requires resisting the temptation to judge another way of life by our own standards. This is easier said than done, as a traveler might discover in many parts of the world.

Taipei is the capital city of Taiwan, in the Republic of China. This island nation, about the size of the states of Maryland and Delaware combined, lies 150 miles off the shore of the Chinese mainland. Although a rapidly developing nation, Taiwan's way of life is shaped by distinctive cultural traditions and a history of great poverty.

A visitor quickly discovers that the streets of Taipei are teeming with people and motor scooters. Drivers show little concern for pedestrians, making moves that Americans may perceive as intentional efforts to run them down. The pace of life becomes more frenzied after dark, when people flood into the city's vast "night market." Here, thousands of outdoor vendors offer just about everything for sale. Merchants hawk familiar items of clothing, fruits, and jewelry but also "snacks" such as chicken feet and cooked dogs. Children with withered limbs lie on the ground, begging from the people who swarm around them.

Wandering into the night market's infamous "Snake Alley," Americans are likely to have their sensibilities pushed to the limit. Here—from an outsider's point of view, at least—cruelty and violence are elevated to the level of a sport. A crowd forms in a stall, drawn by a man beckoning over a loudspeaker. At the back of the stall several televisions "warm up" the crowd by displaying dog fights, bringing cheers and whistles from some in the audience. The real show, however, is not televised but live and begins as the master of ceremonies displays dozens of huge snakes. "Who will drink the venom?" he asks once in Chinese, once in Japanese, and then in English. One or two young men, eager to show courage to their comrades, push forward. To capture everyone's attention, one of the snakes is raised overhead while being poked and taunted. Suddenly, the snake's head is punctured by a hook suspended from the ceiling and—as it lashes back and forth—its skin is torn from its body and fingered eagerly by members of the audience. Then, the man in the stall skillfully squeezes venom from the body of the snake into a small glass. A spectator pays for the prize, to be promptly consumed like so much whiskey as the crowd cheers. The process is repeated.

Looking away from this display, the American's eyes settle on a small monkey caged at the back of the stall.

who, in return, looked at him as a "subhuman foreigner" (Chagnon, 1983:14).

An alternative to ethnocentrism is **cultural relativism**, *the practice of judging any culture by its own standards.* Cultural relativism is often a difficult attitude to achieve, since it requires not only understanding unfamiliar values and norms but also suspending those of the culture we have known all our lives. Still, the attempt is worth making for reasons of goodwill and self-interest, as people the world over come into greater contact with one another. As American business reaches out to the global economy, for instance, people are learning that economic success depends on cultural sensitivity and sophistication. When Coors first translated their slogan "Get loose with Coors" into Spanish, would-be customers were startled by words that meant "Get the runs with Coors." Similarly, Kentucky Fried Chicken was dismayed to learn that the Chinese viewed "licking one's fingers" as rude table manners. And Coca-Cola's early attempts to expand sales of their soft drink to the Far East stumbled on a translation of "Coke adds life" that Japanese people took to mean "Coke brings your ancestors back from the dead" (Westerman, 1989:32).

Cultural awareness, a keen sense of how the world's peoples differ, promotes successful business and helps generate a fair and just world order. *Cultural relativity*, on the other hand, can pose problems. Are any and all cultural practices morally right simply because someone, somewhere endorses them? Consider the custom among Yąnomamö men of routinely offering their wives

Soon snatched from its cage, the monkey is thrust into the center of attention. "Pay to see him die!" the man shrieks. "See *real* blood now!" More cash is passed forward, and the monkey is struck dead. Although a few turn and walk off in shock, others continue to shout their approval, encouraging more of the same.

Incidents like this, in which the values of cultures collide, reveal two kinds of dangers. On the one hand, ethnocentrism closes off insight and understanding by leading us to condemn others simplistically and often unfairly. On the other hand, complete cultural relativism defends any human behavior to the extent that right and wrong become simple matters of convention that, in the end, are arbitrary and meaningless.

There may be a resolution to "the traveler's dilemma," however. Consider the following strategies. First,

we can try to suspend judgment and confront the unfamiliar with an *open mind*. To learn, after all, we must be receptive to others' ways of life. Second, we can try to imagine events from *their* standpoint rather than

ours. Witnessing the events of the night market, for instance, one might wonder if animals have a different significance in a society in which human poverty, hunger, and suffering are commonplace. Third, after a period of careful and critical thinking, we should form a judgment of an unfamiliar cultural practice. After all, a world in which everyone observed but no one evaluated or attempted to right a wrong would be frightening. But bear in mind that, unable to "stand in the shoes" of other people, we can never experience the world as they do. Fourth, and finally, learning to take the perspective of others also helps us to evaluate our own way of life more critically. Would an experience in the night market of Taipei change an American's view of fox hunts or boxing in the United States?

SOURCE: Based on the author's personal experiences in Taipei.

to other men, and reacting violently to women who allegedly commit a social impropriety. Sometimes, Chagnon reports, this goes as far as men shooting women with arrows or otherwise mutilating them. Even in the unlikely event that Yąnomamö women accept this sort of treatment, should we adopt the culturally relative view that these practices are morally right simply because the Yąnomamö themselves accept them?

As members of one human species, we might imagine that some universal standards of conduct are "fair" for people everywhere. But what are they? How can we resist the tendency to impose our own standards of fair play on everyone else? Sociologists have no simple answers to this dilemma, yet in a world where societies confront each other amid ever-present problems like hun-

ger and war, this issue demands careful thought. The box explores how this dilemma affects travelers abroad.

THEORETICAL ANALYSIS OF CULTURE

Drawing on our culture, we are able to make sense of our lives and the world around us. Sociologists, however, have the special task of understanding culture itself. To comprehend something as complex as culture, we will present several widely used approaches.

Structural-Functional Analysis

The structural-functional paradigm depicts culture as a complex and relatively stable way of meeting various human needs. Any part of this system—or *cultural trait*—has one or more functions that help to maintain the way of life.

Core values stabilize every culture, as we explained earlier in the case of American society (Parsons, 1966; Williams, 1970). Thus this approach is akin to the philosophical doctrine of *idealism*, claiming that ideas (rather than material production) guide human activity. A culture's core values, as expressed in everyday routines, make life meaningful and bind people together.

From this point of view, how are we to make sense of unfamiliar cultural patterns? Consider the Amish, who live in farming communities across Pennsylvania, Ohio, and Indiana. The outsider is likely to be puzzled by an Amish farmer tilling hundreds of acres

Funerals are often defined as a form of respect for the deceased. The social function of funerals, however, has much more to do with the living. For survivors, funerals reaffirm their sense of unity and continuity in the face of separation and disruption.

with a horse and plow rather than a tractor, and living without electricity and other modern conveniences. Within the Amish cultural system, however, rejection of complex technology and hard work function to maintain the Amish value of discipline. Long days of shared labor, along with meals and recreation at home, also bind family members together (Hostetler, 1980). In short, cultural patterns form an integrated system that constitutes a distinctive way of life; the sociologist's job is to identify the various pieces and eventually gain an appreciation for the culture as a whole.

As we noted in Chapter 1 ("Sociology: Perspective, Theory, and Method"), cultural elements also have *dysfunctional* consequences. The Amish practice of "shunning," by which people ignore anyone judged to have violated Amish mores, functions to enhance conformity but can also divide the community. In the extreme case, a cultural practice may even lead to a community's demise. The Shakers, another countercultural religious group that flourished in the nineteenth century, prohibited sexual relations among its members. Although they survived for decades by assimilating new members from the outside world, the Shakers' failure to reproduce themselves ultimately led to their extinction.

Since the structural-functional paradigm holds that cultures are devised to meet human needs, we might expect to find that all world cultures have some patterns in common. The term **cultural universals** refers to *traits found in every culture of the world*. Comparing hundreds of different cultures, George Murdock (1945) found dozens of universal patterns. One important example is the family, which functions everywhere to control sexual reproduction and to oversee the care and upbringing of children. Funeral rites is another example, responding to the universal human need to confront the disruption of death. Jokes, too, exist in all cultures, at least partly because they provide a relatively safe means of relieving stress.

Critical evaluation. Structural-functional analysis presents cultures as organized systems attempting to meet human needs. Created by a single species, all cultures have much in common. At the same time, since there are many ways to meet almost any human need, cultures around the world reveal striking diversity. One limitation of structural-functional thinking is its tendency to stress a society's dominant cultural patterns, while directing less attention to cultural diversity. This is especially true with regard to cultural differences that arise from social inequality. By emphasizing cultural stability, in addition, this paradigm downplays the importance of change.

Social-Conflict Analysis

The social-conflict paradigm suggests that many cultural traits function to the advantage of some and the disadvantage of others. Thus, according to this view, a culture operates as a dynamic arena where social conflicts involving inequality among categories of people take the form of a continual power struggle.

The social-conflict paradigm also critically asks why certain values gain dominance in a society. What forces generate one set of values rather than another? How are these values linked to social inequality? Many who make use of this paradigm, especially sociologists influenced by the work of Karl Marx, argue that values are shaped by a society's system of economic production. "It is not the consciousness of men that determines their existence," Marx asserted, "it is their social existence that determines their consciousness" (1977:4; orig. 1859). In this way, the social-conflict paradigm draws on the philosophical doctrine of *materialism*, the argument that how people deal with the material world (in the American case, an industrial-capitalist economy) has a powerful effect on all other dimensions of their culture. Philosophically speaking, this materialist approach contrasts with the idealist leanings of structural-functionalism.

Social-conflict analysis, then, holds that America's competitive and individualistic values reflect our capitalist economy, in which factories and other productive enterprises are privately owned. In a culture of capitalism, for instance, people are likely to believe that the rich and powerful have more talent and discipline than other people, and therefore deserve greater wealth and privileges. Such a culture also encourages the view that capitalism reflects the "natural" order of things and fosters distrust of any change that would lessen the great economic disparities found in American society.

Eventually, however, conflict analysts claim, the strains created by social inequality are likely to transform the cultural system. Of course, changes sought by people with few social resources will certainly provoke resistance from those with much to lose. Both the civil rights movement and the women's movement exemplify the process of change generated by disadvantaged segments of American society; both have met with opposition from defenders of the status quo.

Critical evaluation. The strength of the social-conflict paradigm lies in its suggestion that if cultural systems address human needs they do so unequally. Just as important, this orientation asserts that cultural elements serve to maintain the dominance of some people over others.

This inequity, in turn, generates conflict that promotes change. However, the social-conflict paradigm falls short in stressing the divisiveness of culture, minimizing ways in which cultural patterns integrate members of a society. Thus students of culture should consider both social-conflict and structural-functional insights to gain a fuller understanding of culture.

Cultural Ecology

Ecology is a branch of the natural sciences that explores the relationship between a living organism and its natural environment. **Cultural ecology,** then, forms *a theoretical paradigm that explores the relationship of human culture and the physical environment.* This paradigm investigates how ecological factors, such as climate and the availability of food, water, and other natural resources, shape cultural patterns.

Consider the case of India, a nation with widespread hunger and malnutrition. The norms of India's predominantly Hindu culture prohibit the killing of cows, which are considered sacred animals. To North Americans who consume so much beef, this is puzzling. What accounts for the prohibition against killing cows?

Marvin Harris (1975) claims that the cow's importance to India's ecology greatly exceeds its value as a source of food. Harris points out that cows consume grasses of little value to humans to produce two vital resources: oxen (the neutered offspring of cows) and manure. Unable to afford the high costs of machinery, Indian farmers depend on oxen to power their plows. From their point of view, killing cows makes as much sense as destroying factories that build tractors would to American farmers. Millions of tons of cow manure is also processed annually into building material and burned as fuel (India has little oil, coal, or wood). To kill cows, then, would deprive millions of Indians of homes and a source of heat. In terms of this country's ecology, the destruction of cows would be a calamity.

Critical evaluation. Cultural ecology adds to our understanding of the interplay between culture and the natural environment. This approach can reveal how and why specific patterns arise as human beings try to survive in a particular physical environment. However, because the physical environment rarely shapes cultural patterns in any simple or direct way, this paradigm limits our understanding to some extent. More correctly, the cultural and physical worlds interact, each shaping the other.

Visitors to the cities of India are often puzzled by how cows wander the streets. Americans, accustomed to eating beef, may wonder why the animals are not used as a source of food. To Indians, however, cows are defined as sacred. Marvin Harris suggests that the veneration of cows is a way of protecting a resource vital to the nation's survival.

Sociobiology

Since its origin in the nineteenth century, sociology has maintained a rather uneasy relationship with biology. In part, this stems from rivalry between two disciplines that study human life. A more important source of friction, however, lies deep in the past: Biological interpretations—for example, that some categories of people are inherently "better" than others—were expressions of historical racism and ethnocentrism rather than legitimate science. Early sociologists provided evidence to refute such thinking.

By the middle of this century, sociologists had demonstrated that culture rather than biology was the major force shaping human behavior. In recent decades, however, new ideas linking culture to the principles of biological evolution have revived old debates. This research has created **sociobiology**, *a theoretical paradigm that seeks to explain cultural patterns as the product, at least in part, of biological forces.* Not surprisingly, some sociologists are skeptical of this new paradigm; others, however, think that it may provide useful insights into human culture.

The scientific theory of evolution was presented by Charles Darwin (1859) in his book *The Origin of Species.* The theory states that living organisms change over long periods of time as a result of *natural selection,* a four-stage process. First, all living organisms live and reproduce within a natural environment. Second, each species exhibits random variability in genes, the basic units of life that carry characteristics of one generation into the next. This genetic variation allows species to "try out" new life patterns in a particular environment. Third, this variation enables some organisms to survive better than others; survivors then pass on their advantageous genetic variant to their offspring. Fourth and finally, over thousands of generations, genetic traits that do not promote survival disappear while those associated with greater survival and reproduction become dominant. In this way, a species *adapts* to its environment, and dominant traits represent the "nature" of the organism.

Although Darwin's insights revolutionized the study of living things, his work cannot readily be applied to human beings because human behavior, unlike that of other living things, is not rigidly regulated by encoded genetic programs. The behavior of all ants and bees reveals considerable uniformity, making them prisoners of their own biology (Berger, 1967). Humans, however, are freed from the tyranny of biology; we have the capacity to create diverse and changing cultures. But sociobiologists point out that the cultures of the world are not nearly as different as they *could be*, and display a surprising number of universal traits. Why, sociobiologists ask, would creative human beings, in remote corners of the world, devise so many of the same cultural patterns? The answer may lie in the fact that all people belong to a single biological species. Perhaps, then, our biological characteristics influence the cultures we create.

Why is sugar sweet? With this question, David Barash reminds us that human beings everywhere favor foods that taste sweet over those that taste sour. Chemically, the answer is that sugar tastes sweet because it contains sucrose. From the sociobiological point of view, a deeper process unfolds:

What is the evolutionary explanation for sugar's sweetness? Clearly, just as beauty is in the eye of the beholder, sweetness is in the mouth of the taster. To anteaters, ants are "sweet"; anteaters may even find sugar bitter—certainly they don't like it as much as we do. The reason is clear enough: we are primates, and some of our ancestors spent a great deal of time in trees, where they ate a great deal of fruit. Ripe fruit is more nutritious than unripe, and one thing about ripe fruit is that it contains sugars. It doesn't take much imagination to reconstruct the evolutionary sequence that selected for a strong preference among our distant ancestors for the taste that characterized ripe fruit. Genes that influenced their carriers to eat ripe fruit and reject the unripe ultimately made more copies of themselves than did those that were less discriminating. (1981:39)

Sociobiologists extend this argument to some forms of human behavior. Sex, for example, is "sweet" to human beings, as to all forms of life, because it is vital to the process of reproducing our genes. But the two sexes favor somewhat different sexual patterns. According to what has been widely termed the "double standard," men engage in sexual activity more freely than women do. Sex researcher Alfred Kinsey once commented, "Among all people everywhere in the world, the male is more likely than the female to desire sex with a variety of partners" (cited in Barash, 1981:49). Like people of other nations, Americans often encourage men to "sow their wild oats," while cautioning women to be far more discriminating in their sexual relationships.

Following the sociobiological argument, nature has assigned different reproductive roles to the two sexes. Females bear children that result from the joining of a woman's egg with a man's sperm. But there are striking differences in the value of a single sperm to the man and a single egg to the woman. For healthy men, sperm represents a "renewable resource" produced regularly by the testes throughout most of life. A male releases hundreds of millions of sperm in a single ejaculation— technically speaking, enough "to fertilize every woman in North America," according to Barash (1981:47). A newborn female's ovaries, however, contain her entire lifetime allotment of follicles or immature eggs. Women commonly release just one mature egg cell from their ovaries each month. So, while men are biologically capable of fathering thousands of offspring, women are able to bear only a relatively small number of children. From a strictly biological point of view, then, men reproduce their genes most efficiently through a strategy of sexual promiscuity. This strategy, however, opposes the reproductive interests of women. Each of a woman's relatively few pregnancies demands that she carry the child for the duration of the pregnancy, give birth, and perhaps nurse the child afterward. Thus, efficient reproduction on the part of the female depends on selecting a male whose qualities will contribute to her child's survival and successful reproduction (Remoff, 1984). No one doubts that the double standard represents a pattern linked to the historical domination of females by males (Barry, 1983). But sociobiology suggests that this cultural pattern, like many others, has an underlying bio-logic. Simply put, it has developed widely around the world because males and females everywhere benefit from distinctive reproductive strategies.

Critical evaluation. Because sociobiology is a new approach, its significance is not yet entirely clear. Poten-

tially, this paradigm offers insights about the biological roots of some cultural patterns, especially those that are universal. At present, however, sociobiology remains controversial.

The controversy over sociobiology springs from several sources. First, because so-called biological facts historically have been used (or more precisely, *mis*used) to justify oppression of one race or sex, critics of sociobiology suspect that this new paradigm may follow the same path. Defenders respond, however, that sociobiology has no connection to the past pseudoscience of racial superiority. On the contrary, sociobiology serves to unite rather than divide humanity by asserting that all humanity shares a single evolutionary history.

Sexism—the assertion that males are inherently superior to females and are therefore justified in wielding greater social power—also has no place in sociobiological thinking. Sociobiology does rest on the assumption that, from a biological standpoint, men and women differ in specific ways, and that no culture is ever likely to eliminate these differences completely—if, in fact, any culture intended to. Barash points out that, far from asserting that males are somehow better or more worthy than females, sociobiology emphasizes that both sexes are vital to the reproduction of the human species.

A second issue involves scientific evidence. Some sociobiologists, including Edward O. Wilson (1975, 1978), who is generally credited as the founder of this field of study, believe that future research will demonstrate the biological roots of human culture. It is highly doubtful, however, that research will ever show that biological forces *determine* human behavior; abundant evidence supports the conclusion that human behavior is *learned* within a cultural system. Perhaps, however, biological forces may turn out to make some cultural patterns more common than others among humanity as a whole.

As biological creatures, our large brains allow us to create the survival strategy we call culture. In this sense, the forces of "nature" (our biological being) and "nurture" (what we learn) are more intertwined than in opposition. As noted earlier, *culture is our nature* (Berger, 1967; Lewontin et al., 1984).

CULTURE AND HUMAN FREEDOM

The final task of this chapter is to consider the individual in the midst of culture. Does the power of culture always benefit human beings?

Always powerful, culture sometimes is experienced as an alien force that overwhelms individuals. This is vividly evident in Tom Lea's portrayal of a marine caught up in the agony of war.

Humanity could hardly live without culture. Yet, experiencing the world through symbols and meaning makes possible the experience of alienation, which is unknown to other forms of life. Cultural systems can also weigh heavily on us: A form of social inertia often carries forward from generation to generation, making us relive troubling patterns from the past. Then, too, American culture promotes widespread social inequality, conferring great privilege on some and consigning others to poverty. Women of all social classes, too, have often felt powerless in the face of cultural patterns that reinforce the dominance of men.

The value American culture places on competitive achievement encourages us to strive for excellence, yet it also isolates us from one another and discourages cooperation. Material plenty may add comfort to our lives, yet a preoccupation with acquiring objects may divert us from the security and satisfaction that come from close relationships with others or a strong religious faith. Our emphasis on personal freedom ensures a great deal of privacy and autonomy, but this focus on individuality may deny us the support of a human community in which the problems of life are shared among many people (Slater, 1976; Bellah et al., 1985).

In the end, human beings appear to be prisoners of culture, just as other animals are prisoners of biology. But there is a crucial difference. The burden of culture is *freedom*; the human condition is to shape the world for ourselves. The human capacity to create shines through in the cultural diversity of our own society, and the even richer human variety found around the world. Furthermore, far from static, culture is constantly changing. And although it sometimes takes the form of constraint, culture also provides a continual source of human opportunity. The more we discover about the workings of our culture, the greater will be our ability to use the freedom it offers us.

SUMMARY

1. Culture refers to the patterned ways in which humans live together; although some animals display limited culture, only human beings rely on culture for survival.

2. Culture emerged over the long course of human evolution as the human brain gradually grew larger. Although basic elements of culture appeared some 2 million years ago, complex human civilization emerged only within the last 10,000 years.

3. Culture is based on the use of symbols. The most important symbolism is language, by which culture is passed from generation to generation.

4. An important cultural element is values, standards that shape our orientation to the surrounding world.

5. Cultural norms guide human behavior. Mores have great moral significance; folkways have little moral importance.

6. Material creations reflect cultural values. Cultural patterns are also shaped by a culture's technology.

7. Technological innovation can be traced through four stages of sociocultural evolution: hunting and gathering, horticulturalism and pastoralism, agriculture, and industry.

8. Cultural patterns vary in industrial societies. Subcultures are cultural patterns that differ from the dominant culture; countercultures are strongly at odds with the dominant culture.

9. Invention, discovery, and diffusion all generate cultural change. Not all parts of a cultural system change at the same rate, however; this difference causes cultural lag.

10. Ethnocentrism results from basing judgments on the standards of our own culture. The alternative to ethnocentrism is cultural relativism, by which different cultures are understood in terms of their own standards.

11. Structural-functional analysis emphasizes that cultures are relatively stable systems of related parts. In this theoretical paradigm, any cultural trait is understood in terms of its function in maintaining the entire cultural system.

12. The social-conflict paradigm draws attention to cultural systems as dynamic arenas of social inequality and conflict.

13. Cultural ecology explores ways in which cultural patterns are shaped by the natural environment.

14. Sociobiology investigates links between human culture and the human species' evolutionary past.

15. Culture can be a constraint on needs and ambitions, yet it provides human beings with the capacity to shape and reshape their world.

KEY CONCEPTS

agriculture a way of life based on large-scale cultivation using plows drawn by animals

counterculture cultural patterns that are strongly at odds with the dominant culture

cultural ecology a theoretical paradigm that explores the relationship of human culture and the physical environment

cultural integration the close relationship among various parts of a cultural system

cultural lag inconsistencies within a cultural system resulting from the unequal rates at which different cultural elements change

cultural relativism the practice of judging any culture by its own standards

cultural transmission the process by which culture is passed from one generation to the next

cultural universals traits found in every culture

culture the beliefs, values, behavior, and material objects shared by a particular people

culture shock the personal disorientation that may accompany exposure to an unfamiliar way of life

ethnocentrism the practice of judging another culture by the standards of our own culture

folkways norms that have little moral significance

horticulture a way of life based on the use of hand tools to raise crops

hunting and gathering a way of life based on the use of simple tools to hunt animals and gather vegetation

industrial society a society that produces goods using sophisticated machinery powered by advanced fuels

language a system of symbols with standard meanings that allows members of a society to communicate with one another

mores norms that have great moral significance

norms rules by which a society guides the behavior of its members

pastoralism a way of life based on the domestication of animals

Sapir-Whorf hypothesis the assertion that people perceive the world only in terms of the symbols provided by their language

society people interacting in a limited territory on the basis of shared culture

sociobiology a theoretical paradigm that seeks to explain cultural patterns as a product, at least in part, of biological forces

sociocultural evolution the historical process of cultural change that accompanies technological innovation

subculture a cultural pattern that differs from the dominant culture in some distinctive way

symbol anything that carries a particular meaning recognized by members of a culture

technology the application of cultural knowledge to the task of living in a physical environment

values culturally defined standards of desirability, goodness, and beauty that serve as broad guidelines for social life

Socialization: From Infancy to Aging

3

Chapter Outline

On a cold winter day in 1938, a concerned social worker drove to a farmhouse in rural Pennsylvania and found a five-year-old girl hidden in a second-floor storage room. Anna was in a chair with her arms tied above her head. Unable to move, her limbs had become like matchsticks—so thin and frail that she could not use them (Davis, 1940:554).

Anna had been born to an unmarried woman of twenty-six who lived with her father. Enraged by his daughter's "illegitimate" motherhood, at first he refused to even have the child in his house. Anna therefore spent the early months of her life in the custody of various welfare agencies. Finally, because her mother was unable to pay for such care, and her grandfather was unwilling to do so, Anna was returned to a home where she was not wanted.

At this point, her ordeal intensified. The grandfather's hostility and the mother's indifference caused Anna to be kept in a room where she received little attention and just enough milk to keep her alive. There she stayed, with virtually no human contact, for five years.

Upon reading of the discovery of Anna, sociologist Kingsley Davis traveled immediately to see the child, who had been taken by local authorities to a county home. He was appalled by her condition. Emaciated and devoid of strength, Anna could not laugh, show anger, speak, or even smile. She was completely apathetic, as if alone in an empty world (Davis, 1940).

THE IMPORTANCE OF SOCIAL EXPERIENCE

Here is a case, at once deplorable and instructive, of a human being deprived of social contact. Although Anna was physically alive, she had none of the abilities and responsiveness associated with full humanity. Anna's story illustrates that social experience is vital in order to gain the capacity for thought, emotion, and meaningful action. Without such experience humans remain, like Anna, more *objects* than *people*.

Sociologists use the term **socialization** to refer to *the lifelong process of social experience by which individuals develop their human potential and learn the patterns of their culture.* As Chapter 2 ("Culture") explained, the behavior of other species of life is biologically determined; only humans depend on culture for survival.

Common and unique social experiences blend together to form **personality,** *a person's fairly consistent pattern of thinking, feeling, and acting.* In the absence of social experience, as the case of Anna shows, personality simply does not develop.

Socialization ensures the survival of both the individual and society. A society has a history and a future that extends far beyond the life span of any individual. Through the complex and lifelong process of socialization, culture links generation after generation of people in an ongoing way of life (Elkin & Handel, 1984).

Nature and Nurture

Charles Darwin's ground-breaking work in the mid-nineteenth century, described in the last chapter, led most people to believe that human behavior was instinctive, simply expressing the "nature" of our species. Such notions are still with us. People sometimes claim, for example, that our economic system reflects "instinctive human competitiveness," that particular individuals are "born criminals," or that females are emotional while males are rational (Witkin-Lanoil, 1984).

This naturalist view of human behavior was also adapted to explain how entire societies differed from one another. Centuries of world exploration and empire building brought Western Europeans into contact with people whose customs, manners, and mores differed markedly from their own. They readily attributed these differences to biological characteristics rather than to cultural diversity. Thus Europeans and North Americans viewed the members of technologically simple societies as biologically less evolved and, thus, less human. This self-serving and ethnocentric view justified colonial practices. It presents no ethical dilemmas to enter another society, exploit its resources, and perhaps enslave its people if you believe they are not truly human in the same sense you are.

In the twentieth century, naturalistic explanations of human behavior came under criticism. Psychologist John B. Watson (1878–1958) founded an approach called *behaviorism* on the claim that human behavior is not instinctive but, rather, socially learned. Arguing that all the world's cultures have the same biological foundation, Watson rejected the notion that cultural diversity reflects any evolutionary distinctions. Rather, Watson argued, human behavior is malleable, and will respond to virtually any imaginable environment.

Watson, therefore, explained human behavior in

 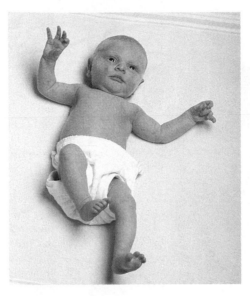

Present at birth, reflexes are behavioral patterns that enhance the likelihood of survival. The grasping reflex can be demonstrated by placing a finger in the infant's palm, causing the hand to close. This reflex helps the infant to maintain contact with a parent as well as to grasp objects. The Moro reflex, which occurs when an infant is startled, causes the arms to spread outward and then come together on the chest. This grasping action, which disappears after several months, probably developed among our evolutionary ancestors so that a falling baby would grasp the body hair of a parent.

terms of *nurture* rather than nature. Endorsing this view, anthropologist Margaret Mead summed up the evidence: "The differences between individuals who are members of different cultures, like the differences between individuals within a culture, are almost entirely to be laid to differences in conditioning, especially during early childhood, and this conditioning is culturally determined" (1963:280; orig. 1935).

Today, social scientists are cautious about describing *any* human behavioral trait as instinctive. This does not mean that biology plays no part in human behavior. Obviously, all life depends on the functioning of the human body. We also know that children share some of the biological traits of their parents, especially physical characteristics such as height, weight, hair and eye color, and facial features. Heredity also plays a role in the transmission of intelligence and personality characteristics (such as how one reacts to stimulation). The potential to excel in such activities as art and music also has a genetic component. However, whether or not any inherited potential reaches full flower still depends on social experiences (Plomin & Foch, 1980; Goldsmith, 1983).

Overall, then, nurture has much more influence than nature in shaping human behavior. But are nature and nurture really in opposition? As suggested in Chapter 2 ("Culture"), what we call human nature is the creation, learning, and modification of culture. Thus, the constant interplay of nature and nurture makes them inseparable.

Social Isolation

For obvious ethical reasons, researchers cannot conduct experiments involving the social isolation of human beings. Consequently, much research on the effects of social isolation has involved nonhuman primates.

Psychologists Harry and Margaret Harlow (1962) placed rhesus monkeys—whose behavior is in some ways surprisingly similar to that of human beings—in various conditions of social isolation to observe the consequences. They found that complete social isolation for a period of even six months (while ensuring adequate nutrition) was sufficient to produce serious developmental disturbances. When subsequently introduced to others

The research of Harry and Margaret Harlow demonstrates the importance of physical contact to emotional development. The Harlows found that the infant monkey's opportunity to hug even a soft artificial "mother" lessened the detrimental effects of social isolation.

of their kind, these monkeys were fearful and defenseless against aggression.

The Harlows also placed infant rhesus monkeys in cages with an artificial mother constructed of wire mesh and a wooden head, with the nipple of a feeding tube where the breast would be. These monkeys were also subsequently unable to interact with other monkeys. However, when the artificial mother was covered with soft terry cloth, the infant monkeys clung to it and appeared to derive some emotional benefit from the closeness, resulting in less developmental harm. The Harlows concluded that emotional development depends on affectionate cradling as part of mother-infant interaction.

The Harlows also made two other discoveries. First, even deprived of mother-infant contact, monkeys surrounded by other infant monkeys did not suffer adversely. This shows that it is the lack of all social experience, rather than the specific absence of maternal contact,

that produces devastating effects. Second, the Harlows found that infant monkeys socially isolated for shorter periods of time (about three months) became emotionally disturbed, but would eventually regain normal emotional patterns once social contact was restored. Thus the effects of short-term isolation can be overcome, although longer-term isolation appears to cause irreversible emotional and behavioral damage to the monkeys.

The later development of Anna seems roughly consistent with the research by the Harlows. Her discovery led to extensive social contact, and Anna soon began to show some improvement. When Kingsley Davis (1940) visited her in the county home after ten days, he noted that she was more alert and displayed some human expression, even smiling with obvious pleasure. During the next year, Anna made slow but steady progress, as she experienced the humanizing effects of socialization, showing increasing interest in other people and gradually gaining the ability to walk. After a year and a half, she was able to feed herself, walk alone for short distances, and play with toys.

Yet it was becoming apparent that Anna's five years of social isolation may have left her permanently damaged. At the age of eight she had the mental and social development of a typical child of a year and a half. Only as she approached the age of ten did she begin to use language. Complicating the problem, Anna's mother was thought to be mentally retarded, so that Anna's progress may have been similarly delayed. The puzzle was never solved, however, because Anna died at age ten of a blood disorder, possibly related to her long years of abuse (Davis, 1940).

A second, quite similar case reveals more about the long-range effects of social isolation. At the same time that Anna was discovered, another girl of about the same age was found under strikingly similar circumstances. After more than six years of virtual isolation, this girl—known as Isabelle—revealed the same lack of human responsiveness that had characterized Anna (Davis, 1947). Isabelle made more rapid progress than Anna, however. One week after an intensive program was begun, Isabelle was attempting to speak, and a year and a half later, her vocabulary was almost two thousand words. Psychologists concluded that Isabelle had managed to progress through what is normally about six years of development during two years of intensive effort. By the time she was fourteen, Isabelle was attending sixth-grade classes in school, apparently well on her way to at least an approximately normal life.

A final case of childhood isolation involves a thirteen-year-old girl in California who was isolated in a small room from the age of about two. Upon discovery, her condition was similar to that of the other children. She weighed only fifty-nine pounds, and had the mental development of a one-year-old. Genie, as she came to be known, was afforded intensive treatment under the direction of specialists and is alive today. Yet even after years of care, her ability to use language is no better than that of a young child (Pines, 1981).

Taken together, the evidence demonstrates that social experience is crucial for the development of human personality. Human beings are resilient creatures, sometimes able to recover from even the crushing ordeal of prolonged isolation. But, consistent with the Harlows' research with rhesus monkeys, there may be a point at which isolation in infancy results in developmental damage that cannot be fully repaired, including a loss of capacity for language. Precisely what this point is, however, remains unclear from the small number of cases that have been studied.

UNDERSTANDING SOCIALIZATION

The complex process of socialization has been explored by many notable thinkers. Three of the most important contributions to our understanding of human development are presented here.

Sigmund Freud: The Elements of Personality

Sigmund Freud (1856–1939) lived in Vienna at a time when most Europeans viewed human behavior as a reflection of biological forces. Freud began his career as a physician but soon dedicated himself to analyzing human personality. Increasingly drawn to the study and treatment of psychological problems, Freud eventually accomplished a towering achievement, the development of psychoanalysis.

Freud's work in psychoanalysis led him to believe that biological factors play an important part in the human personality, not as specific instincts, but as general human needs in the form of *urges* or *drives*. First, he claimed, humans have a basic need for bonding, which he described as the life instinct, or *eros* (ancient Greece's god of love). Second, he postulated the existence of an aggressive drive or a death instinct that he termed *thana-*

tos (derived from Greek meaning "death"). Freud asserted that these opposing forces generate tension within us, both at the conscious and the unconscious level.

Freud incorporated both basic human needs and the influence of society into an overall model of personality. The model has three parts: id, ego, and superego. Freud claimed that the **id** represents *the human being's basic needs*, which are unconscious and demand immediate satisfaction. (The word *id* is Latin for "it," suggesting Freud's tentative conception of the unconscious mind; it also derives from the Greek word *es*, meaning "primal urge.") Rooted in the biological organism, the id is present at birth. In Freud's view, a newborn infant is basically a bundle of needs—for attention, touching, food, and so on. Since society does not allow unlimited physical satisfaction, the id's desires inevitably encounter resistance, which is why the first word many children learn is "no."

In learning to accept certain societal constraints, the child develops a more realistic approach to the world. In the process, a second part of the personality emerges, gradually becoming differentiated from the id. The **ego** (Latin for "I") represents *the conscious attempt to balance the innate pleasure-seeking drives of the human organism and the demands of society*. The ego arises as children learn that they cannot have everything they want. In the process, they realize that they are distinct entities, existing apart from others.

Finally, the human personality develops the **superego** (Latin meaning "above" or "beyond" the ego), which is *the presence of culture within the individual*. Through the superego, we understand *why* we cannot have everything we want. It comprises internalized values and norms and is experienced as human conscience. Initially, the superego is an awareness of parental demands but its scope expands as the child learns that parental control is itself a response to the moral mandates of the larger cultural system.

A child first experiences the world as a jumble of physical sensations comprehended only as pain and pleasure. As personality develops, however, human comprehension reaches beyond physical perceptions to encompass moral ideas of right and wrong. In other words, initially an infant feels good only as a physical sensation. Later the child gains the capacity to feel good for behaving in culturally appropriate ways and, conversely, to feel bad (the experience of guilt) for breaking the rules.

If the ego successfully manages the opposing forces of the id and the superego, the personality is considered to be well adjusted. If this conflict is not successfully

Sigmund Freud is one of the pioneers who explored the complexities of the human personality. His daughter Anna Freud, also shown here in this 1913 photograph, further developed another of her father's achievements: the theory of psychoanalysis.

resolved, personality disorders can result. Freud viewed childhood as the critical period for the formation of an individual's basic personality, and he believed that conflicts experienced during this stage of life often linger as an unconscious source of personality problems later on.

Freud termed society's control over the drives of each individual *repression.* Some repression is inevitable, he claimed, since society cannot permit all of an individual's urges to be met without compromise. This mediation, which Freud called *sublimation,* transforms fundamentally selfish drives into more socially acceptable behavior. For example, the sexual urges of the individual may lead to marriage, or aggressive impulses may be expressed in the form of competitive sports.

Critical evaluation. Freud's work was controversial in his own lifetime, and some elements of his theory remain so today. His own society vigorously repressed human sexuality, and few of his contemporaries were prepared to confront this dimension of life, much less to acknowledge it as a basic drive. More recent critics of Freud's work argue that his thinking depicts humanity strictly

in male terms, presenting a distorted view of women (Donovan & Littenberg, 1982). In any case, Freud provided a foundation that has influenced virtually all who subsequently examined the human personality. Of special importance to sociology is his notion that we internalize social norms, and that childhood experiences have lasting importance in the socialization process.

Jean Piaget: Cognitive Development

Swiss psychologist Jean Piaget (1896–1980) was one of the foremost thinkers of this century. Much of his theory and research centered on human *cognition*—the process of thought and understanding. Early in his career, Piaget became fascinated with the behavior of his own three children, wondering not only *what* they knew, but *how* they understood the world. He gradually identified four age-linked stages of cognitive development that reflected biological maturation as well as increasing social experience.

The first stage of human development in Piaget's model is the **sensorimotor stage,** *in which a child experiences the world only through sensory contact.* In this stage, roughly corresponding to the first two years of life, the infant explores the world by touching, looking, sucking, and listening. Only as children reach the end of this stage do they understand what Piaget called the concept of *object permanence,* the realization that existence does not depend on direct, sensory contact. Earlier, for example, infants may react with despair when an adult leaves the room (moving beyond their senses) because they conclude that the person has ceased to exist. In time, as children learn that adults leave the room only to return, they gain greater confidence and comprehend the world more accurately.

The second stage, from about age two to seven, is called the **preoperational stage,** *in which language and other symbols are first used.* Symbols are the doorway into a vast world of meanings extending beyond the immediate senses. In addition, children gain an appreciation of fantasy and fairy tales (Kohlberg & Gilligan, 1971; Skolnick, 1986). They still do not think as adults do, however. Names and meanings are attached only to specific objects; children may describe a particular toy, for example, but are unable to describe toys in general. Put another way, they cannot yet grasp abstract concepts such as beauty, size, or weight.

One of Piaget's best-known experiments illustrates this distinction. He placed two identical glasses filled

In his well-known experiment, Piaget demonstrated that children over the age of seven entered the concrete operational stage of development as they were able to recognize that the quantity of liquid remained the same when poured from a wide beaker into a tall beaker.

with the same amount of water on a table and asked several five- and six-year-olds if the amount in each was the same. They acknowledged that it was. The children then watched Piaget take one of the glasses and pour its contents into a much taller, narrower glass, so that the level of water was now higher. He asked again if each glass held the same amount. The typical child claimed that the taller glass held more water. But children over the age of seven are able to think in abstract terms. Therefore, seven-year-olds confronted with the same experiment could comprehend that the amount of water in the two different-shaped glasses remained the same. Piaget called this concept *conservation of matter*.

In the third stage in Piaget's model, the **concrete operational stage,** *logic is used to link objects or events.* During this stage, typically corresponding to the years between about seven and eleven, children begin to connect events in terms of cause and effect. They also learn that more than one symbol can be attached to a single event or object; "my birthday," for instance, can also be "Wednesday." However, the thinking of children remains centered on concrete objects and events. They may understand that hitting their brothers without provocation will bring punishment, but they are generally unable to conceive of situations in which hitting a brother would be fair.

The fourth stage in Piaget's model is the **formal operational stage,** *in which people engage in highly abstract thought and imagine alternatives to reality.* Beginning at about the age of twelve, children start to think of themselves and the world in abstract terms rather than solely in terms of concrete situations. They may

not only imagine growing up to become a doctor, for example, but can also describe their aspirations abstractly, hoping to do work that is "challenging" or that "contributes to others." This capacity for abstract thought also allows the child to comprehend metaphors. Hearing the phrase "A penny for your thoughts" might prompt a younger child to think of money, but an older child will recognize a gentle invitation to intimacy.

Critical evaluation.   More than Freud, who viewed human beings as torn by the opposing forces of biology and society, Piaget envisioned the human mind as active and creative. In other words, Piaget believed that people have considerable ability to shape their own social world, an assertion supported by other research (Corsaro & Rizzo, 1988). His contribution to understanding socialization lies in showing that this capacity unfolds gradually as the result of both biological maturation and increasing social experience.

Some critics question whether Piaget's developmental stages apply to people in every culture. For instance, living in a traditional society that changes very slowly generally inhibits the ability to imagine one's life or an entire world apart from what actually exists. In addition, Carol Gilligan (1982) has suggested that we have yet to examine adequately how being male or female affects the process of social development. Finally, among both males and females, a substantial proportion of American adults never reach the formal operational stage (Kohlberg & Gilligan, 1971). Regardless of biological maturity, people who are not exposed to highly creative and imaginative thinking rarely develop this capacity in themselves.

George Herbert Mead: The Social Self

George Herbert Mead (1863–1931) spent much of his life exploring the character of social experience and its relationship to our humanity. Mead's approach (1962; orig. 1934) has often been described as *social behaviorism,* which suggests a connection with the behaviorist ideas of psychologist John B. Watson, described earlier. Mead agreed that the environment exerts a powerful influence on human behavior, but he believed that symbols rather than mere action constitute the essence of social behavior.

Mead saw the basis of humanity as the **self,** *the individual's active self-awareness.* Mead's genius lay in seeing the self as inseparable from society, a connection that can be explained in a series of steps. First, Mead asserted, the self emerges as a result of social experience.

George Herbert Mead, a pioneer of social psychology, devoted much of his life to the investigation of social experience. Although Mead believed humans to be spontaneous and creative, he argued that our thoughts, feelings, and actions are shaped by the surrounding social world.

In his view, the self has no biological component and does not exist at birth. Mead rejected the view that human personality and behavior reflect biological drives (as Freud asserted) or biological maturation (as Piaget claimed). For Mead, the self gradually develops as the individual comes into contact with others. In the absence of social experience—as demonstrated by cases of isolated children—the body may grow but no self will emerge.

Second, Mead viewed social experience as the exchange of symbols or *symbolic interaction.* A wave of the hand, a word, or a smile are all symbolic. Thus, while Mead agreed with Watson that human behavior can be shaped through manipulating the environment, he maintained that symbolic capacity alone is the distinctively human trait. A dog, for example, can be trained to respond to a specific stimulus; but the dog attaches no meaning to this behavior. Human beings, on the other hand, perceive behavior in terms of meanings and are as sensitive to intention as to action. In short, a dog responds to *what you do,* but a human being responds to *what you have in mind* as you do it. Thus one can train a dog to walk out on the porch and bring back an umbrella. But, grasping no intention behind the command, a dog unable to find an umbrella would never look for a raincoat instead, as a human being would.

"Peek-a-boo" reveals the inability of very young children to accomplish what Mead calls taking the role of the other. Children assume that, "since I cannot see you, you cannot see me." Once this ability is gained, play such as "dress up" is common. This involves assuming the role of one other person, often a parent. Complex team sports require children to imaginatively take the role of many other people. Thus, games such as soccer can be played only by children who have had considerable social experience.

Only humans understand actions in terms of underlying intentions.

Third, humans understand intention by learning to *take the role of the other*. Imaginatively putting ourselves in another person's place, we can anticipate the other person's response to us. This mental process precedes even a simple act such as throwing a ball. We imagine the other's response to us—in this case, the act of catching the ball—and this directs our throw. Thus society exists not only in the interaction of many, but in the mind of each person alone.

Charles Horton Cooley, one of Mead's colleagues, offered the useful insight that other people serve as a social mirror or looking glass in which we imagine ourselves as they see us. Cooley (1964; orig. 1902) used the phrase **looking-glass self** to capture his idea that *a person's self conception is based on the responses of others*. The basic social experience of imaginatively "putting ourselves in their shoes," in short, is the foundation of self-concept.

The notion that *the self thinks about itself* suggests an important dualism. First, there is *self as subject*, by which we initiate any social action. Mead claimed that humans are innately active and spontaneous in their environment, initiating social interaction with others. For simplicity, he dubbed this subjective element of the self the *I* (the subjective form of the personal pronoun). Second, there is *self as object*, how we imagine ourselves using the perspective of others. Mead called this objective element of the self the *me* (the objective form of the personal pronoun). In other words, the self initiates interaction (as the I) which is guided through taking the role of the other as the self becomes an object to itself (the me). All social experience involves a continuous interplay between the I and the me: Our behavior emerges and is subsequently guided by how we imagine others will respond to us.

The key to developing the self, then, is gaining sophistication in taking the role of the other. Like Freud and Piaget, Mead believed early childhood was crucial to this process. He did not, however, link the development of the self closely to age. Mead consistently minimized the importance of biological forces, claiming that the complexity of the self simply derived from amassing social experience.

Mead explained that infants with limited social experience respond to others only in terms of *imitation*. That is, they mimic behavior without understanding underlying intentions. Without the ability to use symbols and to take the role of the other, Mead concluded, there

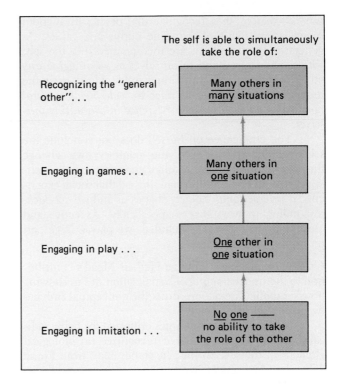

The self is able to simultaneously take the role of:

Recognizing the "general other"... — Many others in <u>many</u> situations

Engaging in games... — Many others in <u>one</u> situation

Engaging in play... — <u>One</u> other in <u>one</u> situation

Engaging in imitation... — <u>No one</u> —— no ability to take the role of the other

Figure 3–1 Building on Social Experience
George Herbert Mead described the development of self as the process of gaining social experience. This is largely a matter of taking the role of the other with increasing sophistication.

is as yet no self. Only as children learn to use language and other symbols does the self appear, first in the form of *play*. Play involves assuming roles modeled on significant people—such as parents—who are sometimes termed *significant others*. Playing "Mommy" or "Daddy," for instance, helps children imagine the world and themselves from one of their parents' point of view. Further social experience teaches children to take the roles of several others simultaneously. Able to initiate different actions in response to different others, children move from simple play involving one role to more complex *games* involving many roles at one time. As this occurs, the self-concept becomes more complex, making use of numerous "looking-glasses."

A final step in the development of the self depends on children acquiring the ability to see themselves as society in general does. Figure 3–1 shows how this works as an extension of the ability to engage in play and games. Individuals learn to take the role of others *in general*; that is, they recognize that people throughout society share many of the same norms and values. As general cultural patterns are incorporated into the self, we are able to respond to ourselves as we imagine *any* other person in *any* situation would. Mead used the term **generalized other** to refer to *widespread cultural norms and values used as a reference in evaluating ourselves*.

The emergence of the self does not conclude the socialization process. On the contrary, we change throughout our lives as a result of changing social experiences. Just as important, Mead stressed that social experience is *interactional*: Society shapes us and we *act back*, responding in ways that shape society. As active and creative beings, Mead concluded, we play a large part in our own socialization.

Critical evaluation. George Herbert Mead's contribution to the understanding of socialization lies in showing how symbolic interaction forms the conceptual link between the self and society.

Mead's view is sometimes criticized for being radically social—meaning that it recognizes no biological element in the self. In this, he stands apart from Freud (who identified general drives in the organism) and Piaget (whose stages of development are tied to biological maturation).

Mead's concepts of the I and the me bear an interesting resemblance to Freud's terms id and superego; the two approaches are different in two respects, however. First, Freud rooted the id in the biological organism, while Mead rejected any link between the self and biology (although he never clearly spelled out the origin of the "I"). Second, although Freud's concept of the superego and Mead's concept of the me both reflect the power society wields over our lives, Freud's superego is locked in continual combat with the id. Mead's concept of the me, by contrast, operates in concert with the I (Meltzer, 1978).

AGENTS OF SOCIALIZATION

We are affected in at least some small way by every social experience we have. However, several agents of socialization have pronounced importance, as we shall now explain.

The Family

For most of the world's people, the family has the greatest impact on socialization. Infants are almost entirely dependent on others, and this responsibility typically falls on family members. The family is the center of a child's world, at least until the onset of schooling, and continues to shape our social experiences throughout the life course (Riley, Foner, & Waring, 1988).

Parents serve as vital "looking-glasses" for children who are developing a self-concept. Not all socialization in the family is intentional, however. Children also learn constantly from the environment adults unconsciously create. Whether children believe they are strong or weak, smart or stupid, loved or simply tolerated—and whether they believe the world around them is trustworthy or dangerous—largely stems from early family experiences.

Although parenting styles obviously vary, research

Family members, who usually provide the earliest social experiences to children, remain important in the socialization process for much of life. A growing child's self-image, her degree of self-esteem, as well as her understanding of cultural norms and values, are strongly influenced by parents.

suggests that paying attention to children encourages their social development. Physical contact, verbal stimulation, and responsiveness from parents all foster intellectual growth (Belsky, Lerner, & Spanier, 1984).

Socialization within the family also means that children gain the social position of their parents. That is, parents not only bring children into the physical world, they place them in a social world in terms of social class, religion, race, and ethnicity. In time, all these elements of social identity are incorporated into the self. Melvin Kohn (1977) compared the socialization practices of working-class and middle-class parents in the United States. He found that working-class parents stress behavioral conformity in rearing their children. Middle-class parents, by contrast, tolerate a wider range of behavior and show greater concern for the intentions and motivations that underlie their children's actions. Kohn explained that working-class parents usually lack higher education and often hold jobs in which they are closely supervised and expected to do as they are told. They, in turn, demand similar obedience and conformity in their children. With more formal education, middle-class people usually have jobs that provide more autonomy and encourage the use of imagination. As parents, then, they are likely to inspire creativity in their children. In many ways, parents teach children to follow in their footsteps, adapting to the constraints or privileges of their inherited social positions.

Schooling

Schooling introduces children to unfamiliar people and new experiences. In school, children learn to interact with others who are initially strangers and who may have social backgrounds that differ from their own. Encountering social diversity also heightens children's awareness of their own social identities. For example, one study of kindergarten children showed that, once in school, whites and blacks tended to form same-race play groups (Finkelstein & Haskins, 1983). Similarly, boys and girls form distinct groups, a process that teaches the importance that our culture attaches to gender (Lever, 1978).

The most widely recognized task of schooling is to teach children a range of knowledge and skills. Basic skills such as reading, writing, and arithmetic gradually give way to advanced material students will need eventually to assume a specialized productive role in a complex industrial society. Beyond formal lessons, however, the school's so-called *hidden curriculum* inculcates important cultural values. School activities such as spelling bees and sports encourage competition and the pursuit of success. Children also receive countless subtle and not-so-subtle messages that their society's way of life is both practically and morally good. Raphaela Best (1983) adds that instructional activities for boys and girls often differ; boys engage in more physical activities and spend more time outdoors, while girls tend to be more sedentary, often helping the teacher with various housekeeping chores. Such distinctions involving gender follow students through school, so that college women may be steered toward the arts or humanities, while college men may be encouraged to study the physical sciences.

For most youngsters, school introduces the new learning experience of being evaluated in tasks such as reading and athletic performance according to universal standards rather than on the basis of personal relationships, as is often the case in families. Finally, school is generally children's first experience with rigid formality. The school day follows a strict time schedule, subjecting students to impersonal regimentation and fostering traits, such as punctuality, that are required for success in many large organizations where students will work later in life.

Peer Groups

In school, children discover another new setting for social activity, the **peer group,** defined as *people in regular interaction who share common interests and social position and are of similar age.*

The peer group differs from the family and the school by allowing children an escape from the direct supervision of adults. This, of course, constitutes the primary appeal of peer groups for their members. Among their peers, children have considerable independence, and gain valuable experience in forging social relationships on their own. Peer groups also provide a forum for discussion of interests that may not be shared by adults (such as styles of dress and popular music) as well as topics young people may wish to avoid in the presence of parents and teachers (such as drugs and sex).

The autonomy of the peer group, with the ever-present possibility of activity that would not be condoned by adults, accounts for parents' deep concern about who their children's friends are. Especially in a rapidly changing society, the influence of peer groups rivals that of parents. After all, the interests and attitudes of parents and children may differ considerably—as suggested by the familiar phrase "the generation gap." The support of peer groups plays an especially important part in the lives of adolescents, as they begin to break away from their families and to think of themselves as responsible adults.

Even during adolescence, however, parental influence remains paramount in the lives of children. While peers may guide such short-term concerns as style of dress and musical taste, parents retain more sway over long-term aspirations. For example, one study found that parents had more influence than even best friends on young people's educational aspirations (Davies & Kandel, 1981).

Finally, a neighborhood or school is typically a social mosaic of many peer groups. As we shall see in Chapter 5 ("Groups and Organizations"), members often perceive their own peer group in positive terms while viewing others negatively. Many peer groups, therefore, contribute to the socialization process as individuals form identities as they conform to their own groups while opposing others. In some cases, too, people are strongly influenced by peer groups they would like to join. For example, upon entering a new school, a young man with a desire to excel at basketball may wish to become part of the basketball players' social crowd. He is likely to adopt what he sees as the social patterns of this group in the hope of eventual acceptance. This represents what sociologists call **anticipatory socialization,** *the process of social learning directed toward gaining a desired position.* Later in life, career development is also likely to involve anticipatory socialization. For instance, a young lawyer who hopes to become a partner in her law firm may conform to the attitudes and behavior of other partners to encourage her acceptance into this exclusive group.

The Mass Media

The **mass media** are *impersonal communications directed to a vast audience.* Common to industrial societies, the mass media include television, radio, newspapers, and magazines. Because public exposure to the mass media is extensive, they have an enormous effect on our attitudes and behavior. Television, in particular, has become a powerful arbiter of taste, style, and sophistication.

Television was rapidly incorporated into the American way of life after 1950. Back then, only about 9 percent of American households had one or more television sets; by the late 1980s, this proportion had soared to 98 percent (while only 92 percent had telephones), and surveys indicate that the average household has a television turned on for seven hours a day (U.S. Bureau of the Census, 1989). Children watch television before they learn to read, and they actually spend more hours in front of a television than they do in school (Anderson & Lorch, 1983; Singer, 1983). Television consumes more of many children's time than interacting with parents does. Overall, television is now the most powerful mass medium, with enormous influence on socialization (Singer & Singer, 1983).

Television does more than entertain us; it also programs many of our attitudes and beliefs. Television has traditionally portrayed men and women according to cultural stereotypes, showing, for instance, males in positions of power and women only as mothers or subordinates (Cantor & Pingree, 1983; Ang, 1985). As Chapter 10 ("Sex and Gender") describes in detail, advertising further contributes to sex stereotyping (Courtney & Whipple, 1983). Similarly, television shows have long presented affluent people in favorable terms, while depicting less affluent people (Archie Bunker is the classic example) as ignorant and wrongheaded (Gans, 1980). In addition, although racial and ethnic minorities tend to watch more television than others, until recently they have been all but absent from programming. The successful 1950s comedy *I Love Lucy,* for example, was shunned by all the major television producers because it featured Desi Arnaz—a Cuban—in a starring role. Even now, minorities often appear on television in ways attractive to white middle-class Americans (as in the affluent black family on *The Cosby Show*). This situation improved during the 1980s as advertisers recognized the marketing advantages of appealing to diverse segments of American society (Wilson & Gutierrez, 1985). The box offers a critical look at how mass media advertising has historically portrayed minorities in terms of negative stereotypes.

Just as important as what television portrays is what it ignores, such as the lives of poor or homosexual people. In this way, television sends a message that these categories of people do not matter or—even more incorrectly—that they do not exist at all.

Television has unquestionably enriched American culture in many respects, bringing into our homes a wide range of entertaining and educational programming. Furthermore, this "window on the world" has increased our awareness of diverse cultures and provided a means of addressing current public issues. At the same

When Advertising Offends: The Death of the Frito Bandito

Commercial advertising obviously attempts to sell products. Some ad campaigns, however, offend many Americans by portraying particular categories of people in inaccurate and negative ways.

A century ago, the vast majority of consumers in the United States were white Anglos, and many were uncomfortable with the growing racial and cultural diversity of American society. Businesses commonly exploited this discomfort, depicting racial and cultural minorities in ways that were condescending at best. In 1889, for example, a package of pancake mix appeared on the market featuring a servant mammy named "Aunt Jemima." Although modified in recent years, this logo is still widely seen in the mass media, largely because the product continues to hold a commanding share of the market. Likewise, the hot cereal "Cream of Wheat" continues to be symbolized by the black chef Rastus, just as "Uncle Ben" remains familiar to millions of Americans as a brand name for rice. To many Americans, use of such caricatures—which, after all, originally depicted the black slaves of white people—is socially offensive.

However, changes in advertising have gradually occurred in all the mass media. The stereotypical Frito Bandito, long familiar to older television viewers, was abandoned in 1971 by Frito-Lay (a company whose first product was a corn chip ironically invented by a Hispanic in San Antonio). A host of other such images have also disappeared as American businesses confront a new reality: the growing voice and financial power of minorities. Taken together, African-Americans, Hispanics, and Asians now represent 20 percent of Americans, and will constitute a majority during the next century. Even now, these segments of society comprise a commercial market worth almost half a trillion dollars. As immigrants, many minorities rely heavily on television to learn about their new society. This obviously makes them especially accessible to advertisers. At the same time, however, all categories of Americans are increasingly voicing a simple demand: that no product be marketed at the expense of human dignity.

Source: Based on Marty Westerman, "Death of the Frito Bandito," *American Demographics*, Vol. 11, No. 3 (March 1989):28–32.

time, the power of television has made this medium controversial, especially in cases where it supports traditional stereotypes.

Public Opinion

Public opinion refers to *the attitudes of people about one or more controversial issues*. Although family and peer groups exert the greatest influence in the process of socialization, our attitudes and behavior are also shaped by what we perceive to be the opinions held by others in our society. The mass media cover the latest trends, prompting many Americans to conform to such patterns. For example, the clothing industry's success in marketing changing fashions several times a year illustrates people's tendency to adopt, within their budgets, a look that trend makers define as desirable.

As we have explained, what others think—or what we *think* they think—affects how we perceive ourselves. Because public opinion tends to reflect the dominant values and norms of a society, widespread attitudes may devalue people who differ in some way from the majority. Popular beliefs hold that people who are homosexual are "bad," that men who are noncompetitive "lack character," and that women who are assertive are "pushy." Thus people who do not conform to cultural patterns may be viewed as social outsiders. No one, of course, ever conforms completely to dominant values and norms. Even public conformists often experience private anxiety about their failure to live up to ideal cultural expectations.

Complex, industrial societies encompass numerous agents of socialization in addition to those described here. Religious organizations, the workplace, the military, and social clubs all affect our thoughts and actions. Amid this bewildering array of often-contradictory forces, socialization inevitably proceeds inconsistently; we pick up different information from various kinds of social experiences. Thus socialization does not involve a simple, straightforward process of learning, but rather a complex balancing act in which individuals encounter a wide range of ideas in the process of forming their own distinctive personalities.

SOCIALIZATION AND THE LIFE COURSE

Socialization continues throughout our lives. Our experiences are shaped during different stages of the life course, including childhood, adolescence, adulthood, and, as a final stage of adulthood, old age. Each stage has distinctive characteristics, which we now examine.

Childhood

In American culture today, *childhood*—roughly the first twelve years of life—is a time of freedom from the responsibilities of the adult world. During the Middle Ages in Europe, however, children's lives were very much like those of adults. Historian Philippe Ariès (1965) explains that for medieval Europeans, childhood as we know it did not exist at all; as soon as children were able to survive without constant care, they were expected to fend for themselves just like everyone else. Children therefore worked long hours, and were the objects of no special concern. Although "child labor" is now scorned in American society, this pattern persists in preindustrial societies throughout Latin America, Africa, and Asia.

Expecting youngsters to take charge of their lives may seem startling because our common sense suggests that children are biologically immature and inexperienced in the ways of the world. Technologically complex societies define children as incapable because so much must be learned before assuming adult activities. This encourages opposing views of children and adults, the former "irresponsible" and "dependent," the latter "responsible" and "independent" (Benedict, 1938). Anthropologist Ruth Benedict discovered that various cultures define childhood in quite different ways, however, suggesting that this stage of life is no simple expression of biological forces. Many characteristics of childhood—and even whether it exists at all—are embedded in culture.

Among a growing number of American families today, childhood as a stage of life is again changing. The "hurried child" pattern encourages children still in elementary school to look and act like adults.

More recently, researchers have found that—especially in relatively affluent families—childhood is changing once again, this time becoming shorter. So-called "hurried children" are subjected to mounting pressures to dress, speak, and act like adults at a young age (Elkind, 1981; Winn, 1983). The mass media now introduce sexuality, violence, and a host of other issues into the child's world that were considered to be strictly adult topics only a generation ago. Young children may routinely watch films that graphically depict violence and listen to rock music that contains sexually explicit lyrics. Pressure to grow up quickly also comes from the home because greater numbers of mothers work, requiring children to fend more for themselves and perhaps care for younger sisters and brothers. For their part, many of today's parents are delighted if their children read, spell, or discuss world events before their peers do, believing that this indicates greater intelligence. Schools also encourage rapid maturation by emphasizing achievement; this reflects positively on both the child and the school. In the view of child psychologist David Elkind (1981), however, the recent—and controversial—"hurried child" pattern raises serious concerns. This change in American society's conception of childhood, Elkind contends, results in children being confronted with issues they have little basis for understanding, let alone successfully resolving.

Adolescence

As childhood became defined as a distinct stage of life in industrial societies, adolescence—corresponding roughly to the teenage years—emerged as a buffer stage between childhood and adulthood. This period of life is marked by transition, offering teenagers the opportunity to make early efforts at some of the specialized activities of adult life.

We generally associate adolescence with emotional and social turmoil as young people spar with their parents and grapple with their own identities. Since adolescence commonly accompanies the onset of puberty, we often attribute the turbulence of this stage of life to physiological changes. However, the instability of adolescence also reflects inconsistencies in the socialization process. For example, teens are expected to be increasingly self-reliant, yet they are considered unequipped for the adult occupations that would give them financial independence. They also receive mixed signals about sexuality—encouragement by the mass media to be sexually active and messages of restraint from adults. Consider, also, that eighteen-year-olds may have the adult responsibility of going to war thrust on them while simultaneously being denied the adult right to toast their victory. By the end of the 1980s, the federal government had pressured states to raise the legal drinking age to twenty-one even though, in 1971, the Twenty-sixth Amendment to the United States Constitution gave eighteen-year-olds of both sexes the right to vote. Without denying that biological changes mark the onset of adolescence, we must also recognize that marked contradictions characterize a stage of life when people are no longer children but not yet adults.

Like all periods of the life course, adolescence varies according to social background. Young people

from working-class families often move directly into the adult world of work and parenthood after completing high school. Those from wealthier families, by contrast, have the resources to attend college and sometimes graduate school, perhaps extending adolescence into the later twenties and even the thirties (Skolnick, 1986). Some of the poorest Americans also experience an extended adolescence, but for a different reason. Especially in the inner cities, many young minorities cannot attain full adult standing bcause there are few jobs available to them.

Adulthood

Adulthood, which begins at some point between the late teens and the early thirties depending on social background, is the period during which most of life's accomplishments typically occur. Having amassed considerable learning, people embark on careers and raise families of their own. Personalities are largely formed by the onset of adulthood, although marked changes in an individual's social environment—brought on by unemployment, divorce, or serious illness, for example—may cause significant personality modifications (Dannefer, 1984).

Early adulthood—until about age forty—is generally a time of working toward many goals set earlier in life. Young adults learn to manage for themselves a host of day-to-day responsibilities that had been taken care of by parents or others. In addition, early adulthood typically involves establishing intimacy with another person who may have just as much to learn. This is also a period of juggling conflicting priorities and demands on time: parents, spouse, children, and work (Levinson et al., 1978). Women, especially, face the realization that "doing it all" creates tremendous pressure, because our culture expects them to assume primary responsibility for childrearing and household chores, even as they maintain demanding careers outside the home. Today's women often feel trapped between the traditional femi*nine* ideals they learned as children and the more contemporary femin*ist* ideals they embraced as adults (Sexton, 1980; cited in Giele, 1982:121).

By middle adulthood—roughly the years between the ages of forty and sixty—people begin to feel that marked improvements in their life circumstances are less likely to occur in the future. The distinctive character of middle adulthood thus involves greater reflection, as people gain a more realistic sense of what their life accomplishments are likely to be. Often, among ambitious

Americans, real achievements are disappointing when compared to the standard of earlier expectations. People also become more aware of the fragility of health at this age—not typically a major concern in youth. Women who have spent the first part of their adulthood raising a family can find middle adulthood especially trying. Children have grown up and require less attention, husbands are absorbed in their careers, and women may therefore find spaces in their lives that are difficult to fill. Women who are divorced during middle adulthood may confront serious economic problems (Weitzman, 1985). For all these reasons, many middle-aged women return to school as they set off on new careers. During the 1980s, women between thirty-five and forty-four years of age were the fastest growing segment of the American labor force (U.S. Bureau of the Census, 1989). But neither education nor a career comes easily after several decades of working primarily in the home.

The traditional notion of femininity also stresses physical attractiveness. Both older men and older women face the reality of physical decline, but our society's traditional socialization of women has made good looks crucial, so that wrinkles, weight gain, and loss of hair are generally more traumatic for women than for men. Men, of course, have their own characteristic difficulties. Some face disillusionment over their limited achievements; others, realizing that the price of career success has been neglect of family or personal health, harbor deep uncertainties about their accomplishments even in the face of praise from others (Farrell & Rosenberg, 1981).

Socialization in America's youth-oriented culture has convinced many people that life ends at forty. As the life expectancy of Americans increases, however, such limiting opinions are changing. Major life transformations may become less likely, but, for many Americans, the greatest personal satisfaction may occur after the midpoint in the life course.

Old Age

Old age constitutes the later years of adulthood and the final stage of life, beginning in about the mid-sixties. As Figure 3–2 shows, about one in eight Americans is now over the age of sixty-five, a proportion meaning that the elderly now outnumber teenagers. By the middle of the next century, one-fourth of Americans will be over sixty-five, and half of Americans will be over forty-five. In the coming decades, the Census Bureau (1989b) predicts that the fastest-growing segment of Americans will be those over eighty-five. According to government projections, we can expect almost six times as many people to live to eighty-five a century from now as reach that age today.

This "graying of America" will have profound consequences for everyone. More and more people will depend on Social Security and other pension programs, medical facilities will be increasingly taxed, and elderly people will be commonplace in everyday life. Today's adult women will spend as much time caring for aging parents and in-laws as they have for young children; in the next century, this balance will shift even further, making the elderly ever more the center of American life.

The graying of America has sparked the development of a relatively new field of social science called **gerontology** (a term derived from the Greek word *geron*, meaning "an old person"), *the study of aging and the elderly*. In addition to investigating the physical transitions of growing old, gerontologists have found that aging is also a matter of cultural definitions.

For most Americans, gray hair, wrinkles, loss of height, weight gain, and an overall decline in strength and vitality begin in middle age (Colloway & Dollevoet, 1977). After about the age of fifty, bones become brittle, and falls that would be of little consequence earlier in life can result in disabling injuries. Physical damage to older bodies also takes longer to heal. In addition, a substantial proportion of the elderly suffer from chronic illnesses, including arthritis, that limit physical activity and life-threatening conditions like heart disease and cancer. Sensory abilities tend to diminish with age. While only about 5 percent of middle-aged people have visual impairments, about 10 percent of the elderly do. Hearing problems are more common, increasing in frequency from about 15 percent of middle-aged people to about 30 percent of the elderly. Both impairments are more common among men than women (U.S. National Center for Health Statistics, 1989). Declining ability to taste and smell are also widespread and can affect eating habits, resulting in health problems stemming from poor nutrition (Eckholm, 1985).

Although advancing age increases the likelihood of a wide range of diseases, the vast majority of the elderly are not disabled by physical illnesses. Only about one in ten reports having trouble walking, and roughly one in twenty requires the intensive care provided by a hospital or nursing home. No more than 1 percent of the elderly are bedridden. Overall, about 70 percent of

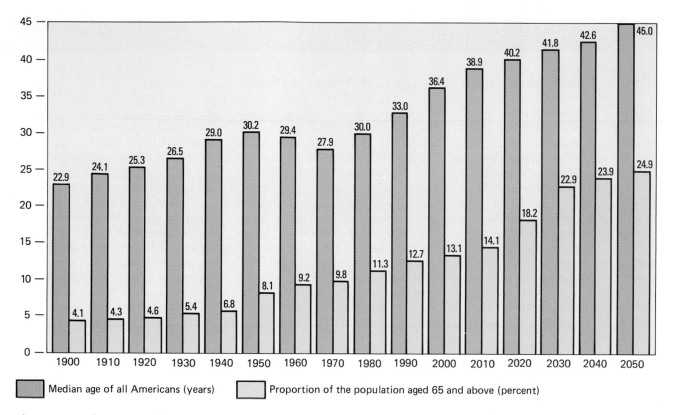

Figure 3–2 The Graying of American Society
(*Spencer, 1989*)

people over the age of sixty-five assess their health as "good" to "excellent," while 30 percent characterize their overall condition as "fair" or "poor" (U.S. National Center for Health Statistics, 1989).

The experience of growing old, like other stages of life, involves more than biological change; it is also a matter of culture. In preindustrial societies, old age typically confers great influence and respect because the elderly control most land and other wealth, and, based on wisdom gained over a lifetime, make important decisions for younger family members (Sheehan, 1976; Hareven, 1982). A preindustrial society, therefore, can be described as a **gerontocracy,** *a form of social organization in which the elderly have the most wealth, power, and privileges.*

Industrialization, however, diminishes the social standing of the elderly. Younger people typically work and live apart from their parents, and rapid social change renders some of what older people learn obsolete, from

the point of view of the young. Thus members of industrial societies may come to think that the elderly have little to contribute to others. **Ageism,** *prejudice and discrimination against the elderly,* becomes common.

For all these reasons, growing old in America today fosters uncertainty about oneself and the future. For children, adolescents, and younger adults, advancing age typically means entering new roles and taking on fresh and exciting responsibilities. Old age, however, follows the opposite path: leaving roles that have long provided social identity and meaningful activity and often losing value in the eyes of others. Retirement serves as a clear example of this process. Although retirement sometimes fits the common image of being a period of restful activity after years of work, it often means abandoning familiar routines, losing the self-worth derived from work, and sometimes suffering from outright boredom. Like any life transition, retirement demands that a person learn new and different ways of living while simultane-

Setting Limits: How Much Old Age Can America Afford?

For most of human history, people contended with life-threatening accidents and illnesses at every age; thus the question "Can people live *too long?*" would have seemed absurd. In recent decades, however, an explosion of the elderly population, widespread support for using medical technology to prolong life, and a dizzying increase in medical resources directed toward diseases of old age have forced Americans to begin asking such questions.

The graying of America, Daniel Callahan suggests, will eventually force us to critically consider what proportion of finite resources should be allocated to the needs of older people. To even raise this issue, he concedes, may seem uncaring. But ignoring it poses an increasing threat to the well-being of the majority. Some $80 billion was spent on health care for the elderly in 1981; the figure will soar to over $200 billion by 2000. This increase is not just due to rising medical costs; it also reflects the recent trend of directing a growing *proportion* of medical expenditures to combat diseases and disabilities common to old age. Callahan asks, first, if we can continue to increase spending on behalf of the elderly, when doing so means spending less on others, especially children. At some point, he concludes, American society will have to set limits. Such standards will be difficult to devise, but the need to do so appears inescapable.

Second, Callahan urges Americans to recognize that using medical technology to produce *longer* life does

ously *un*learning patterns and routines of earlier stages in life. A nearly equal transition is required of the non-working wife or husband who must accommodate a spouse now spending more time at home.

Until recently, poverty was common among elderly Americans. In 1960, more than one-third of all Americans over the age of sixty-five were officially poor; today, however, the proportion is only one in eight (U.S. Bureau

The power and prestige of elders in preindustrial societies is based on wisdom accumulated over a lifetime. Rituals such as community storytelling provide occasions both to celebrate old people and to transmit a society's way of life to the young.

not necessarily provide *better* life. Costs aside, does expensive and stressful heart surgery that may prolong the life of an 84-year-old woman for two years truly improve the quality of her life? Costs considered, would the resources involved produce more "quality of life" if used, say, to provide a kidney transplant for a 10-year-old boy?

Third, Callahan urges Americans to reconsider our conception of death. Death is now widely viewed as an unnatural enemy to be conquered at all costs. Yet, he suggests, any sensible health-care program in an aging society requires that we recognize death as a natural end to the life span. If we cannot make peace with death for our own benefit, limited resources demand that we do so for the benefit of our children. Callahan concludes that an aging America must pursue an understanding of the process of aging and death that looks to our obligations to the young and to the future, that sees old age as a source of knowledge and insight of value to other age groups, that recognizes the necessity of limits and the acceptance of decline and death, and that values the old for their age and not their continuing youthful vitality. (1987:223)

SOURCE: Daniel Callahan, *Setting Limits: Medical Goals in an Aging Society*, New York: Simon and Schuster, 1987.

of the Census, 1990). This improving situation stems from expanding pension programs won by many workers and increases in Social Security benefits. As Chapter 7 ("Social Stratification") explains, children rather than old people now form the "new poor" in the United States. Despite the growing affluence of elderly Americans, however, a debate has developed about whether our society can afford to allow older people to purchase as much health care as they may wish. The box provides details.

Death and Dying

Throughout human history, a low standard of living and simple medical technology made death from disease and accident common for people in all stages of life. In industrial societies, however, although death can still occur at any time (especially among the poor), about 70 percent of people die after reaching the age of sixty-five. Therefore, even though most senior citizens can look forward to decades of life, patterns of socialization in old age cannot be separated from the ultimate recognition of impending death.

After observing many dying people, Elisabeth Kübler-Ross (1969) described death as an orderly transition involving five distinct stages. Because American culture tends to ignore the reality of death, people's first reaction to the prospect of their own demise is usually *denial*. This involves avoiding anything that might suggest the inevitability of death. The second stage is *anger*; the person has begun to accept the fact of impending death but only as a gross injustice. In the third stage, anger gives way to *negotiation*, the attitude that death may not be inevitable and that a bargain might be struck with God to prolong life. The fourth stage is *resignation*, often accompanied by psychological depression. Finally, adjustment to death is complete in the fifth stage, *acceptance*. At this point, rather than being paralyzed by fear and anxiety, the person sets out to constructively make use of whatever time remains.

As the proportion of older Americans increases, we can expect attitudes toward death to change. Today, death is physically removed from public life. The clearest evidence of this is that many Americans have never seen a person die. While our ancestors typically died at home, death today usually occurs in unfamiliar and impersonal settings such as hospitals and rest homes (Ariès, 1974). Even in hospitals, dying patients are commonly kept in a special part of the building, and hospital morgues are located well out of sight of patients and visitors (Sudnow, 1967). Thus the historical acceptance of death has now been largely replaced by fear and anxiety about dying. This accounts, in part, for the increase in medical research aimed at prolonging the life of the elderly. However, the fear of death may loom larger for the young than the old. For elderly people who suffer from severe and painful disabilities, the end of life may not be feared as much as welcomed as a release from suffering. Enduring the death of a spouse, other family members, and friends is traumatic, but it also helps many elderly people come to accept death as a natural closure to the life course (Kalish, 1976, cited in Atchley, 1983). Because younger Americans tend to avoid even the mention of death, they effectively isolate dying people from friends and relatives at a time when relationships may take on a special meaning.

Critical evaluation. This brief examination of the life course leads to two general conclusions. First and most important, although linked to the biological process of aging, essential characteristics of each stage of the life course are constructed by society. For this reason, particular periods of life may be experienced differently in various cultures. Second, each stage presents characteristic problems and transitions that involve learning something new and, in many cases, unlearning what has become familiar.

A final point. The fact that societies organize social experience according to age in no way negates the effects of other social forces, such as those based on social background, race, ethnicity, and sex. Thus, the general patterns described here are all subject to further refinement and modification as they apply to various categories of people.

RESOCIALIZATION: TOTAL INSTITUTIONS

To this point, we have focused on socialization as it applies to the vast majority of Americans. For almost 1 million Americans, however, a special type of socialization takes place because they are confined—often against their will—in prisons, mental hospitals, and other restricted places. The term **total institution** refers to *a setting in which individuals are isolated from the rest of society and manipulated by an administrative staff.*

According to Erving Goffman (1961), total institutions have three distinctive characteristics. First, they control all aspects of the daily lives of their residents (often called "inmates"), including eating, sleeping,

working, and playing. Second, they subject residents to standardized activities, food, and living quarters. Third, they apply formal rules and rigid scheduling to all events from walking to retiring. Throughout the day and night, inmates are supervised by the administrative staff, which wields complete power over them, much as adults in our society monitor the activities of young children.

This rigid control supports a policy of **resocialization:** *deliberate socialization intended to radically alter the individual's personality.* Total institutions reshape personality by depriving inmates of any other source of social experience. This isolation is achieved through physical barriers such as walls and fences, barred windows, locked doors, and control of the telephone, mail, and visitors. Cut off from the outside world, the inmates' environment is manipulated by the administrative staff in an attempt to produce change—or at least compliance.

Resocialization is a two-part process. First, the staff attempts to destroy the new inmate's established conception of self. Inmates are subjected to what Goffman (1961:14) describes as "abasements, degradations, humiliations, and profanations of self." For example, they are required to surrender personal possessions, including the clothing and grooming articles that are normally used to maintain a distinctive appearance. In their place, inmates receive standard-issue items that make everyone look alike. In addition, inmates are typically given "regulation" haircuts, so that, once again, what was personalized becomes standardized. The staff also uniformly processes new inmates by searching, weighing, fingerprinting, and photographing them, and by issuing them a serial number. Individuals also surrender the right to privacy; oftentimes they are forced to undress publicly as part of the admission procedure, and surveillance and searches of their living quarters are conducted on a routine basis. These "mortifications of self" undermine the identity and autonomy that the inmate brings to the total institution from the outside world.

Once they have "stripped" the inmate of an old self, the staff begins the second phase of resocialization: rebuilding a new self. They do this by manipulating inmates with rewards and punishments. Being allowed to keep a book, receive a visitor, or have extra cigarettes may seem trivial from the vantage point of outsiders, but in the rigidly controlled total institution, such privileges are powerful motivations toward conformity. Noncompliance, however, means that privileges can quickly be withdrawn or, in serious cases, the inmate can be subjected to physical pain or solitary confinement. Furthermore, the duration of incarceration in a prison or mental hospital is typically related to the extent of cooperation with the staff. Goffman emphasizes that even a person who displays no outward violation of the rules may be subject to punishment for having "an attitude problem."

Resocialization in a total institution often effects considerable change in an inmate's personality. The rebuilding of a person's self is extremely difficult, however, and no two people are likely to respond to the environment of any total institution in precisely the same way (Irwin, 1980). Therefore, while some inmates may experience "rehabilitation" or "recovery" (meaning change that is officially approved), others may gradually sink into an embittered state because of the perceived injustice of their situation. Sometimes, over a long period of time, the rigidly controlled environment of a total institution renders people completely *institutionalized*, incapable of the independence required for living in the outside world.

SOCIALIZATION AND HUMAN FREEDOM

This chapter has explored how society, through the process of socialization, shapes how we think, feel, and act. If society has this power over us, do we have any meaningful freedom? Is all of society one vast "total institution"?

One way to answer this question is to recall the Muppets, stars of television and film. Observing the expressive antics of Kermit the Frog, Miss Piggy, and the rest of the troupe, we almost believe that these puppets have minds of their own, even though we know they are merely passive objects animated by movements that originate backstage. The sociological perspective suggests that human beings are like puppets in that we respond to the backstage guidance of society. Indeed, more so, in that society affects not just our outward behavior but our innermost feelings.

But our analysis of socialization also reveals that the puppet analogy ultimately breaks down. Viewing human beings as the puppets of society leads to a trap that Dennis Wrong (1961) has called an "oversocialized" conception of the human being. In part, Wrong reminds us that we are biological as well as social creatures—a point that was emphasized by Sigmund Freud, who identified a general tendency in the human species to resist the demands of society. To the extent that any biological force motivates our being, we can never be entirely shaped by society.

The fact that we may be subject to *both* biological and social influences, however, hardly supports the notion of human freedom. Here the ideas of George Herbert Mead come into play. Mead recognized the power of society to act on us, but he argued that human spontaneity and creativity (conceptualized in the "I") allow us to continually *act back* on and perhaps change society. In this way, the process of socialization affirms the capacity for choice. As human beings, we continually engage in reflection, evaluation, and action. Therefore, while the process of socialization may initially suggest that we resemble puppets whose strings are pulled by society, Peter Berger points out that "unlike . . . puppets, we have the possibility of stopping in our movements, looking up, and perceiving the machinery by which we have been moved" (1963:176). In doing so, we can act to change society—to pull back on the strings if we wish. This reaffirms our individual autonomy. And the more we utilize the sociological perspective to recognize how the machinery of our society works, the freer we are.

SUMMARY

1. Socialization is the process by which social experience renders individuals fully human. For society as a whole, socialization perpetuates culture by teaching norms and values to each new generation.

2. A century ago, human behavior was widely thought to reflect an instinctive human nature. Today, however, we recognize that human behavior primarily stems from nurture rather than nature.

3. The observed and damaging effects of social isolation in humans and other primates reveal the importance of social experience to human development.

4. Sigmund Freud conceived of the human personality in terms of three parts. The id represents general human drives, which Freud claimed were innate. The superego embodies cultural values and norms

internalized by the individual. The needs of the id and the cultural restraints of the superego are mediated by the ego.

5. Jean Piaget believed that human development reflects both biological maturation and increasing social experience. His analysis of socialization identified four major stages of development: sensorimotor, preoperational, concrete operational, and formal operational.

6. To George Herbert Mead, the process of socialization promotes the emergence of the self. Mead characterized the self as partly autonomous (the "I") and partly guided by society (the "me").

7. Charles Horton Cooley used the term looking-glass self to describe how our self-image is influenced by perceptions of how others respond to us.

8. Commonly the first setting of socialization, the family has the greatest influence in shaping a child's attitudes and behavior.

9. School exposes children to greater social diversity and introduces them to evaluation using impersonal standards of performance. In addition to formal lessons, school's hidden curriculum teaches cultural definitions of race and gender and fosters support for the political and economic status quo.

10. Peer groups free children from much adult supervision in the family and in school. Peer groups take on increasing significance in adolescence.

11. The mass media, especially television, have a considerable impact on the socialization process. The average American child now spends more time watching television than attending school.

12. Public opinion is important to the socialization process because Americans are influenced by popular attitudes and values.

13. As in all stages of the life course, the characteristics of childhood are socially constructed. During the Middle Ages, European societies did not recognize childhood as a stage of life. In industrial societies, including the United States, childhood is defined in opposing terms to adulthood.

14. Americans define adolescence as the transition between childhood and adulthood. Adolescence is often a difficult period for today's Americans; however, this pattern does not hold in all times and places.

15. During early adulthood, socialization includes settling into careers and raising families. Later adulthood is often marked by considerable reflection about earlier goals in light of actual achievements.

16. Old age involves many transitions, including retirement and accompanying new patterns of social life. While the elderly typically enjoy high prestige in preindustrial societies, industrial societies are more youth-oriented.

17. Death usually occurs in old age; adjustment to the death of others and acceptance of the inevitability of one's own death are part of socialization in old age.

18. Total institutions such as prisons and mental hospitals strive for resocialization—radically changing each inmate's personality.

19. Socialization demonstrates the power of society to shape our thoughts, feelings, and actions. Yet, self and society shape each other as part of ongoing social interaction.

KEY CONCEPTS

ageism prejudice and discrimination against the elderly

anticipatory socialization the process of social learning directed toward gaining a desired position

concrete operational stage Piaget's term for the level of human development characterized by the use of logic to link objects or events

ego Freud's designation of the conscious attempt to balance the pleasure-seeking drives of the human organism and the demands of society

formal operational stage Piaget's term for the level of human development characterized by highly abstract thought and the ability to imagine alternatives to reality

generalized other George Herbert Mead's term for widespread cultural norms and values used as a reference in evaluating ourselves

gerontocracy a form of social organization in which the elderly have the most wealth, power, and privileges

gerontology the study of aging and the elderly

id Freud's designation of the human being's basic needs

looking-glass self Cooley's term meaning a conception of self derived from the responses of others

mass media impersonal communications directed to a vast audience

peer group people in regular interaction who share common interests and social position and are of similar age

personality a person's fairly consistent pattern of thinking, feeling, and acting

preoperational stage Piaget's term for the level of human development in which language and other symbols are first used

public opinion the attitudes of people throughout a society about one or more controversial issues

resocialization deliberate socialization intended to radically alter the individual's personality

self George Herbert Mead's term for the individual's active self-awareness

sensorimotor stage Piaget's term for the level of human development in which the world is experienced only through the senses in terms of physical contact

socialization the lifelong process of social experience by which individuals develop their human potential and learn the patterns of their culture

superego Freud's designation of the presence of culture within the individual in the form of internalized values and norms

total institution a setting in which individuals are isolated from the rest of society and manipulated by an administrative staff

Social Interaction in Everyday Life

4

The automobile roared down the mountain road, tearing through sheets of windblown rain. Two people, a man and his young son, peered intently through the windshield, keeping a close eye on the edge of the road; beyond that, there was only a black void. Suddenly, as the car rounded a bend, the headlights shone on a large tree that had fallen across the roadway. The man swerved and braked but, unable to stop, the car skidded wildly, crashed through some brush, and turned end over end, finally coming to rest on its roof. The noise of the crash was heard at a nearby hunting lodge, and a telephone call from the lodge soon brought police and a rescue crew to the accident site. The driver, beyond help, was pronounced dead at the scene. The boy was still alive, though badly hurt and unconscious. Rushed by ambulance to a hospital at the foot of the mountain, he was taken immediately into emergency surgery.

Alerted in advance, the medical team burst through the swinging doors ready to try to save the boy's life. Then, with a single look at his face, the surgeon abruptly exclaimed: "Oh, no! Get someone to take over for me—I can't operate on this boy. *He's my son!*"

Can you explain the surgeon's reaction?

This situation contains an apparent contradiction: If the boy's father died in the crash, how could the boy be the surgeon's son? The contradiction, however, exists only in the reader's *assumption* that the surgeon is male. If, on the other hand, we conclude that the surgeon is the boy's *mother*, the apparent contradiction disappears.

This chapter explores **social interaction,** *the process by which people act and react in relation to others.* Through social interaction, human beings create meaning in any situation. Every setting and every social interaction that occurs, however, are also shaped by assumptions and expectations rooted in the larger society.

SOCIAL STRUCTURE: A GUIDE TO EVERYDAY LIVING

In earlier chapters, we noted that social life functions as an organized system in which we all participate. Chapter 2 ("Culture") examined the symbolic web that unites members of society into a culture, guiding everyday interaction with norms and values. Chapter 3 ("Socialization: From Infancy to Aging") showed that we are creatures who gain our humanity only with social experience.

Even so, we tend to resist the idea that human behavior follows specific social patterns. Living in a culture that prizes autonomy, few Americans readily see the social constraints that affect our behavior. Instead, we prefer to believe in individual responsibility for what we do and to play up the unique elements of our personalities. But behaving in patterned ways does not threaten our individuality. Quite the contrary: Individuality *depends on* the structure of society.

Social structure enhances our lives in two key ways. First, as Chapter 3 explained, our humanity develops only through social life. Distinct personalities emerge as people blend their unique qualities with the values and norms of the larger culture. Second, in the absence of social structure, we would have no way of making sense out of any social situation. The world would become disorienting and frightening. Even entering an unfamiliar setting inhibits us from freely expressing ourselves. Joining strangers at a party, for example, we feel understandable anxiety at not knowing quite what to expect. We look, therefore, to others for clues about what sort of behavior is appropriate. Only after we have established some behavioral standards for the situation do we begin to relax and "act like ourselves."

This is not to deny that social structure places some constraints on everyday life: Established social patterns inevitably discourage the unconventional. Traditional values and norms in North America, for example, still hold that males should be dominant and assertive, and that females should be deferential and supportive. Because Americans do not readily associate a powerful and prestigious occupation like that of a surgeon with being female, the opening of this chapter causes confusion. By pressuring each of us to fit neatly into "feminine" or "masculine" categories, social structure limits any individual's freedom to think and act according to personal preference.

Yet social structure *guides* rather than *determines* human behavior. A cello and a saxophone are each designed to make only certain kinds of sounds. Similarly, "fatherhood" or any other social role carries with it certain expectations about behavior. Like musical instruments, however, any social arrangement can be "played" in a wide range of creative ways.

STATUS

Among the most important components of social interaction is **status,** *a recognized social position that an individual occupies in society.* Every status involves various rights, duties, and expectations. This sociological use of the word "status" obviously differs from its everyday meaning of "prestige." In common usage, a bank president has "more status" than a bank teller; sociologically, however, both "bank president" and "bank teller" are statuses because they each represent socially defined (if unequal) positions.

Statuses guide social interaction in any setting. In the college classroom, for example, the two major statuses of professor and student have distinct, well-defined rights and duties. Similarly, interaction within families also reflects the statuses of mother, father, son, and daughter. As these examples suggest, statuses often form reciprocal pairs, defining relationships between individuals. We can consider a status, then, as a social definition of who and what we are in relation to specific others.

We each hold many statuses simultaneously. The term **status set** refers to *all the statuses a particular person holds at a given time.* A teenage girl is a *daughter* in relation to her parents, a *sister* to her younger brother, a *friend* to others in her social circle, and a *goalie* to members of her hockey team. Status sets are complex as well as changeable. A child becomes an adult, a student becomes a lawyer, and people marry to become husbands and wives, sometimes becoming single again as a result of divorce or the death of a spouse. Joining an organization or finding a job enlarges our status set; withdrawing from activities diminishes it. Individuals gain and lose many statuses over a lifetime.

Statuses also play an important part in how we define ourselves. Occupational status, for example, is an integral element of the self-concept of most Americans. Long after retirement, for instance, a man may still think of himself as a professor, continue to engage in many academic routines on campus, and be defined in those terms by others.

Ascribed and Achieved Status

Sociologists have devised a useful distinction between two general kinds of statuses. An **ascribed status** refers to *a social position attached to a person at birth or one that is involuntarily assumed later in life.* Statuses that are commonly ascribed at birth include being a daughter, a Hispanic, a Canadian, or the Prince of Wales. Statuses ascribed as part of the aging process range from becoming a teenager to joining the ranks of senior citizens. All ascribed statuses are matters about which people have little or no personal choice.

In rigidly hierarchical societies, such as traditional villages in India, social interaction cannot proceed unless everyone clearly understands each other's social position. This problem is solved by a highly visible "status symbol," a mark on the forehead indicating to which caste group a person belongs.

In contrast, an **achieved status** refers to *a social position that people assume voluntarily and that reflects a significant measure of personal ability and effort.* Examples of achieved statuses include becoming an honors student, an Olympic athlete, a husband or wife, a gambler, or a computer programmer. In each case, the individual has a definite choice in the matter.

Most statuses actually derive from some combination of ascription and achievement. That is, people's ascribed statuses influence the statuses they are likely to achieve. Adults who complete law school are likely to have been born into relatively privileged families. Although the status of lawyer is widely viewed as an

SOCIOLOGY OF EVERYDAY LIFE

Physical Disability as Master Status

In the following excerpts, three people describe how a physical disability can shape a person's life, because others perceive the individual as different or incomplete.

Now in his late thirties, David Clark was stricken with polio when he was ten months old. He lives and works in Corning, New York.

All the stares you get from the public used to really bother me when I was younger. But either it doesn't happen as much nowadays, or parents have taught their children better about disabilities, or else I'm older and more immune to it, I don't know. It doesn't bother me now like it used to; it used to really bother me. But I really think people are better educated now about disabilities and they don't look as much and make you feel like you're a freak, which is the way I felt when I was younger and they were looking at you like you didn't belong there, what's your problem?

At twenty-nine years old, Donna Finch holds a master's degree in social work, and lives with her husband and son in Muskogee, Oklahoma. She is also blind.

Most people don't expect handicapped people to grow up, they are always supposed to be children. . . . [Y]ou aren't supposed to date, you aren't supposed to have a job, somehow you're just supposed to disappear. I'm not saying this is true of anyone else, but in my own case I think I was more intellectually mature than most children, and more emotionally immature. I'd say that not until the last four or five years have I felt really whole.

Rose Helman is an elderly woman living near New York City. She suffers from spinal meningitis and is also blind.

You ask me if people are really different today than in the '20s and '30s.

Not too much. They are still fearful of the handicapped. I don't know if fearful is the right word, but uncomfortable at least. But I can understand it somewhat; it happened to me. I once asked a man to tell me which staircase to use to get from the subway out to the street. He started giving me directions that were confusing, and I said, "Do you mind taking me?" He said, "Not at all." He grabbed me on the side with my dog on it, so I asked him to take my other arm. And he said, "I'm sorry, I have no other arm." And I said, "That's all right, I'll hold onto the jacket." It felt funny hanging onto the sleeve without the arm in it.

SOURCE: Michael D. Orlansky and William L. Heward, *Voices: Interviews with Handicapped People* (Columbus, OH: Charles E. Merrill, 1981), pp. 85, 92, 133–134, 172. Reprinted by permission of the publisher.

---

achieved one, then, it also reflects a substantial element of ascription. As a general rule, any person of a privileged sex, race, ethnic background, or age has more opportunity to achieve desirable statuses than does someone without such advantages. By contrast, many less desirable statuses, such as criminal, welfare recipient, or drug addict, are more easily "achieved" by people disadvantaged by ascription.

Master Status

Among the many statuses a person holds at any time, one often has overarching significance to everyday life. Called a **master status,** it serves as *the focal point of an individual's social identity, often shaping that person's entire life*. A master status, which usually forms a core element of one's self-concept, may stem from any combination of ascription and achievement. In American society, a person's occupation—largely due to achievement—often acts as a master status because it reflects a person's education, income, and family background. This accounts for the widespread practice among adults of introducing themselves by stating their occupations along with their names. Other master statuses, however, are based on ascription. For a Rockefeller or a Kennedy, family name stands out in the minds of others.

Serious disease can also form the basis of a master status. For people with cancer or acquired immune deficiency syndrome (AIDS), disease may become a master status, frequently resulting in social isolation. Most societies of the world also limit the opportunities of women, whatever their abilities, so that sex, too, can function as a master status. Additionally, the physically disabled may feel dehumanized because others perceive them as little more than the sum of their handicaps. In the box, several people with physical disabilities describe this problem.

Race also has traditionally served as a master status in American society. Consider the life and death of Dr. Charles Drew, a surgeon largely responsible for the establishment of blood banks—lifesaving supplies of blood available to hospitals across the United States. In 1950, while driving to a medical conference in Alabama, Dr. Drew was critically injured in an automobile accident. Arriving at a local hospital that was then restricted to white patients, Dr. Drew, who was renowned as a distinguished physician and scientist, was initially denied admission to the hospital because he was black. In the end, the hospital did treat Dr. Drew. (Ironically, however, the hospital lacked the blood plasma that might have saved his life.) This incident suggests how some people overlook substantial personal accomplishments simply because of a person's race (Low & Clift, 1981; Logan, 1982).

ROLE

Besides status, a second major component of social interaction is **role**, *the patterns of expected behavior attached to a particular status.* Ralph Linton (1937) described a role as the dynamic expression of a status. Every status confers various privileges and obligations that shape the role. The student role, for example, entails responsibilities to professors and other students, as well as entitling the student to devote much time to personal enrichment through academic study. Thus, individuals *hold a status* and *perform a role.* Cultural norms suggest how a person with a particular status ought to act; this is often called a *role expectation.* As noted in Chapter 2 ("Culture"), however, real culture only approximates ideal culture, so that actual *role performance* varies according to each individual's unique personality. In addition, because values and norms differ throughout a society, people holding different statuses may perform comparable roles quite differently.

Like a status, a role is *relational*, organizing our behavior toward some other person. The parent's role, for example, centers on responsibilities toward a child. Correspondingly, the role of son or daughter consists largely of obligations toward a parent. Other examples

of such role pairs include wives and husbands, baseball pitchers and catchers, physicians and patients, and performers and members of the audience.

Because individuals hold many statuses simultaneously—a status set—they perform multiple roles. The total number of roles usually exceeds the number of statuses because each status can require an individual to carry out several roles in relation to various other people. Robert Merton (1968) introduced the term **role set** to identify *a number of roles attached to a single status.* Figure 4–1 depicts four statuses of one individual, each linked to a different role set. First, the woman holds the status of "wife," with corresponding roles toward her husband ("conjugal roles" such as confidant and sexual partner), with whom she would share a "domestic role" in the household. Second, she also has the status of "mother," with routine responsibilities toward her children (the "maternal role") and activities in various organizations like the PTA (the "civic role"). Third, as a professor, she interacts with students (the "teaching role") as well as with other academics (the "colleague role"). Fourth, her work in a laboratory (the "researcher

Figure 4–1 Status Set and Role Set

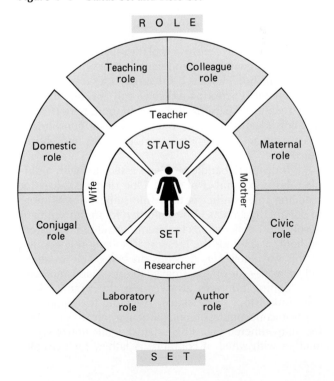

role") provides the data she uses in her publications (the "author role"). Of course, Figure 4–1 offers only a partial listing of status and role sets, since everyone generally occupies dozens of statuses at one time, each linked to a role set.

Conflict and Strain

The personal performance required by an array of role sets often makes heavy demands on an individual's time and energy. This holds especially true for members of industrial societies in which people routinely assume many statuses and an even greater number of roles. As mothers who work outside the home can testify, carrying out the role of parent as well as the role of breadwinner taxes both their physical and their emotional strength. Sociologists define such **role conflict** as *the incompatibility among the roles corresponding to two or more statuses*. We experience role conflict when we find ourselves pulled in various directions as we try to respond to the many statuses we hold at the same time. A surgeon might well choose not to operate on her own son because her personal involvement as a mother could impair her professional objectivity as a physician.

Even the many roles linked to a single status may make competing demands on us. The concept of **role strain** refers to *incompatibility among the roles corresponding to a single status*. A plant supervisor may wish to become a good friend and confidant of other workers. At the same time, however, the supervisor's responsibility for everyone's performance may call for maintaining some measure of personal distance. In short, performance of roles attached to even one status may constitute a "balancing act" as we juggle various duties and obligations.

Individuals handle problems associated with multiple roles in a number of ways. One simple strategy for reducing role conflict is to define some roles as more important than others. A new mother, for instance, might devote most of her efforts to parenting and put her career on hold, at least for the present. Resolving role conflict in this way, however, depends on being able to afford not to work—an option unavailable to many mothers.

Setting priorities also reduces the strain among roles linked to a single status. Adopting this approach, a person concentrates on one particular role (from among the many inherent in a single status), while downplaying another with which it conflicts. A father, for example, may decide that maintaining a close and trusting relationship with his child takes precedence over enforcing cultural norms as a disciplinarian.

Some people minimize role conflict by "insulating" roles from one another (Merton, 1968). Instead of ignoring or downplaying the importance of a particular role, people "compartmentalize" their lives so that they perform roles linked to one status in one place for part of the day, while roles corresponding to another status dominate activity elsewhere or at some other time. For example, people usually try to leave the pressures and concerns of their jobs behind when they go home to assume the responsibilities of spouse or parent.

Role Exit

Recent research has focused on *role exit*, the process by which people disengage from social roles that have been central to their lives. Helen Rose Fuchs Ebaugh (1988) began to study role exit when she herself left the life of a Catholic nun to become a university sociologist. Interviewing a range of "exes," including ex-nuns, ex-doctors, ex-husbands, and ex-alcoholics, Ebaugh identified elements common to the process of "becoming an ex."

According to Ebaugh, people considering role exit typically begin by reflecting critically on their existing lives, entertaining doubts about their ability or willingness to carry out that role. As they focus on alternative roles, they may ultimately reach a turning point and decide to pursue a new life. In the subsequent "ex-role," they disengage from the previous role, building a new sense of self, which is evident in changes in outward appearance and behavior (an ex-nun, for example, begins to wear stylish clothing and make-up). "Exes" must also grapple with changing responses from those who may have known them in their earlier role, as well as those who do not realize how new and unfamiliar their present role may be. Forming new relationships is especially challenging for an "ex," since many new social skills must be learned. Ebaugh reports, for example, that nuns who begin dating after decades in the church are often startled to learn that sexual norms are now vastly different from those they knew as teenagers.

In modern society, fewer and fewer people expect to hold one job or stay married to one person their entire lives. The study of role exit, therefore, will no doubt gain in importance.

THE SOCIAL CONSTRUCTION OF REALITY

Over fifty years ago, the Italian playwright Luigi Pirandello skillfully applied the sociological perspective to social interaction. In *The Pleasure of Honesty*, Angelo Baldovino—a brilliant man with a checkered past—enters the fashionable home of the Renni family and introduces himself in a most peculiar way:

> Inevitably we construct ourselves. Let me explain. I enter this house and immediately I become what I have to become, what I can become: I construct myself. That is, I present myself to you in a form suitable to the relationship I wish to achieve with you. And of course, you do the same with me. . . . (1962:157–158)

This curious statement suggests that, while social interaction is guided by status and role, each human being has considerable freedom to shape what happens next. This means that the "reality" of society is not as fixed as we might think it is. The social world does have an objective existence, of course; it existed long before we were born, affects us throughout our lives, and is likely to continue long after we die. But society still encompasses the behavior of countless creative people. If society affects individuals, then individuals also shape society (Berger & Luckmann, 1967).

The phrase **social construction of reality** refers to *the process by which individuals creatively build reality through social interaction.* This idea stands at the root of the symbolic-interaction paradigm in sociology, detailed in Chapter 1 ("Sociology: Perspective, Theory, and Method"). In this context, Angelo Baldovino's remark suggests that, especially in an unfamiliar situation, quite a bit of "reality" remains unclear in everyone's mind. Pirandello's character will simply use his ability to "present himself" in terms that he thinks suit his purposes. As others do the same, a complex reality emerges.

Social interaction, then, amounts to a process of negotiating reality. Usually, interaction yields at least some agreement about how to define a situation. But participants rarely share precisely the same perception of events. Impressions vary because social interaction brings together people with different purposes, interests, and hidden agendas, each of whom is seeking a somewhat different shaping of reality.

Steering reality in this way is sometimes referred to as "street smarts." In his biography *Down These Mean Streets*, Piri Thomas recalls moving to a new apartment in New York City's Spanish Harlem, which soon brought him in contact with the local street gang. Returning home one evening, young Piri found himself cut off by Waneko, the gang's leader, and a dozen others.

> "Whatta ya say, Mr. Johnny Gringo," drawled Waneko.
>
> *Think man*, I told myself, *think your way out of a stomping. Make it good.* "I hear you 104th street coolies are supposed to have heart," I said. "I don't know this for sure. You know there's a lot of streets where a whole 'click' is made out of punks who can't fight one guy unless they all jump him for the stomp." I hoped this would push Waneko into giving me a fair one. His expression didn't change.
>
> "Maybe we don't look at it that way."
>
> *Crazy, man. I cheer inwardly, the* cabron *is falling into my setup.* . . . "I wasn't talking to you," I said. "Where I come from, the pres is president 'cause he got heart when it comes to dealing."
>
> Waneko was starting to look uneasy. He had bit on my worm and felt like a sucker fish. His boys were now light on me. They were no longer so much interested in stomping me as seeing the outcome between Waneko and me. "Yeah," was his reply. . . .
>
> I knew I'd won. Sure, I'd have to fight; but one guy, not ten or fifteen. If I lost, I might still get stomped, and if I won I might get stomped. I took care of this with my next sentence. "I don't know you or your boys," I said, "but they look cool to me. They don't feature as punks."
>
> I had left him out purposefully when I said "they." Now his boys were in a separate class. I had cut him off. He would have to fight me on his own, to prove his heart to himself, to his boys, and most important, to his turf. He got away from the stoop and asked, "Fair one, Gringo?" (1967:56–57)

This situation reveals the drama—sometimes subtle, sometimes savage—by which human beings creatively build reality. There are limits, of course, to what even the most skillful and persuasive personality can achieve. Should the police have happened on the fight that ensued between Piri and Waneko, both young men might well have ended up in jail. Obviously, not everyone enters a negotiation with equal standing; the police would almost certainly have had the last word simply because their status holds greater power (Molotch & Boden, 1985).

The Thomas Theorem

Piri Thomas won acceptance that evening. Having been defined as worthy, he was now one of the group, and from that moment on his social identity was changed. W. I. Thomas (1966:301; orig. 1931) (no relation to Piri Thomas) succinctly explained such events in what has come to be known as the **Thomas theorem:** *Situations that are defined as real are real in their consequences.* Applied to social interaction, his insight means that although reality is initially "soft" and undefined, it becomes "hard" in its effects. In other words, now that he has been accepted by gang members, Piri Thomas will be treated with respect in subsequent interaction.

Culture and Reality Construction

Human beings do not construct everyday experience "out of thin air"; we creatively manipulate elements in the surrounding culture. This means, for example, that the construction of social experience in Spanish Harlem differs markedly from the way residents of the affluent East Side of Manhattan construct social interaction. More broadly, the world familiar to those living in ancient Greece was significantly different from that of contemporary Saudi Arabia; both would seem foreign to most Americans.

Grounded in culture, socially constructed realities typically come to be regarded as "given" or "natural." This is one way of understanding the Thomas theorem, which claims that the emerging social world is real to those who fashion it. The sociological perspective constantly reminds us that humans have made—and can remake—the surrounding social world, perhaps altogether differently than we initially imagine.

Any object or human action is subject to distinctive interpretation, depending on its cultural context. The meanings attached to the two sexes, stages of the life course, or even the days of the week vary according to cultural setting. In a recent study, for example, Wendy Griswold (1987) asked respondents from the West Indies, Great Britain, and the United States to interpret several novels. She found that the messages her respondents drew from the novels differed along the lines of the basic "blueprint" of their culture. What people see in a book—or anything else—then, is guided by their social world.

Ethnomethodology

Not surprisingly, we take for granted most of the reality we create. Practically speaking, how could we negotiate everyday life if we questioned every situation we encountered? Some sociologists, however, attempt to learn about

Cultures frame reality differently. This man collapsed on the street in Bombay, India, and, after two hours, died. In the United States, such an event would probably have provoked someone to call the rescue squad. In a poor society where encountering death on the streets is part of everyday life, some Indians responded with simple decency by pausing to place flowers and incense on the body.

social patterns precisely by challenging conventional behavior.

One way sociologists do this is through *ethnomethodology*, a specialized approach within the symbolic-interaction paradigm. The term itself has two parts: The Greek *ethno* refers to shared culture, and "methodology" designates a system of methods or principles. Combining them, we define **ethnomethodology** as *the study of the everyday, common-sense understandings that people within a culture have of the world around them.*

Ethnomethodology was developed in the 1950s by Harold Garfinkel, a sociologist who was dissatisfied with the then-widespread view of society as a broad "system" with a life of its own. Instead, Garfinkel explored how we constantly engage in building understandings of familiar, everyday experiences (Heritage, 1984). For example, people readily expect certain behavior when sitting down to dinner in a restaurant, when beginning to take a final examination, or when driving onto a freeway. Although such conventional understandings enable us to manage the tasks of day-to-day living, Garfinkel (1967) maintained that few of us ever think much about them.

In the rebellious social climate of the 1960s, Garfinkel devised a distinctive technique for exposing the typically unacknowledged patterns of everyday life: *Break the rules.* There is no better way to tease out the conventional realities, he reasoned, than to deliberately ignore them. In a series of experiments, Garfinkel (1967) had his students map patterns of everyday life by deliberately refusing to "play the game." Some entered stores and insisted on bargaining for standard-priced items, others recruited people into simple games (like tic-tac-toe) only to intentionally flout the rules, still others initiated conversations and slowly moved closer and closer until they were almost nose to nose with their quarry. At the very least, intentional rule violation provoked bewilderment; oftentimes "victims" responded with anger. One of Garfinkel's students reported, for example, the following exchange (1967:44):

Acquaintance: "How are you?"

Student: "How am I in regard to what? My health, my finances, my school work, my peace of mind, my . . ."

Acquaintance (now red in the face and suddenly out of control): "Look! I was just trying to be polite. Frankly, I don't give a damn how you are."

In each case, Garfinkel maintained, a deliberate lack of social cooperation enabled the researcher to perceive more clearly the unspoken rules of everyday life. Researchers gauge the importance of these rules by how strongly people react to their violation.

The provocative character of ethnomethodology, coupled with its focus on commonplace experiences, has led some sociologists to view it as less-than-serious research. Even so, ethnomethodology has heightened awareness of many unnoticed patterns of everyday life.

DRAMATURGICAL ANALYSIS: "THE PRESENTATION OF SELF"

Erving Goffman (1922–1982) shared with Garfinkel an interest in the patterned character of everyday life. Goffman agreed that people socially construct reality, and he showed that this process parallels the work of actors performing on stage. Calling to mind a director scrutinizing the drama of the theater, Goffman termed his approach **dramaturgical analysis,** *the investigation of social interaction in terms of theatrical performance.*

Dramaturgical analysis offers a fresh look at two now-familiar concepts. In this theoretical scheme, a status mirrors a part in a play, and a role serves as a script, supplying dialogue and action for each of the characters. In every setting, then, each of us plays a role, like an actor, just as we also form part of the audience. Goffman, then, called the intricate social interaction that makes up everyday life the **presentation of self,** *ways in which individuals, in various settings, attempt to create specific impressions in the minds of others.* This process, sometimes termed *impression management*, contains several distinctive elements (Goffman, 1959, 1967), which we turn to now.

Performances

As individuals present themselves to others, they convey information—consciously and unconsciously—about how they wish to be understood. Goffman called these efforts, taken together, a *performance*. Dress (costume), the objects people carry with them (props), and their tone of voice and gestures all make up a performance. In addition, just as any performance varies according to its physical location, many cultural norms change depending on the setting. Thus, performance responds to the social context in which it occurs. People may joke loudly on the sidewalk, for example, but assume a more reverent manner when they enter a church. Equally important, individuals often design settings, such as their home or office, to evoke desired reactions in others. A setting, then, is a stage that enhances an individual's performance by providing numerous specific pieces of information.

Consider, for example, how a physician's office guides social interaction and conveys appropriate information to the audience of patients. Physicians enjoy considerable prestige and power in American society, and as soon as patients enter a doctor's office, they pick up clues to the physician's high status. First, the physician is nowhere to be seen. Instead, in what Goffman describes as the "front region" of the setting, the patient encounters a receptionist, who functions as a gatekeeper, deciding if and when the patient can meet the physician. A simple survey of the doctor's waiting room, with patients (often impatiently) waiting to gain entry to the inner sanctum, leaves little doubt that the medical team controls events.

The physician's private office and examination room constitute the "back region" of the setting. Here the patient encounters a wide range of props, such as medical books and framed degrees, that reinforce the impression that the physician, not the patient, has the specialized knowledge necessary to guide their social interaction. In the office, the physician usually remains seated behind a large desk—a symbol of power—while the patient is provided with only a chair.

The physician's appearance and manner convey still more information. The usual costume of white lab coat may have the practical function of keeping clothes from becoming soiled, but its primary function is to let others know at a glance the physician's status. A stethoscope around the neck has the same purpose. The doctor's use of highly technical terminology—occasionally necessary, but frequently mystifying—also emphasizes the hierarchy in the situation. The use of the title "Doctor" by patients who, in turn, are commonly addressed by only their first names also underscores the physician's dominant position. The overall message of a doctor's performance is clear: "I can help you, but you must acknowledge that I am in charge."

Joan P. Emerson (1970) adds that some medical situations are especially prone to ambiguity; in such cases, physicians and their staff conduct their performances with great care. Emerson systematically observed seventy-five gynecological examinations, concluding that this situation is open to dangerous misinterpretation in cases when a male physician must touch the genitals of a female patient. In other settings, of course, such behavior would constitute a sexual act and possibly a sexual assault. The medical staff, therefore, removes sexual connotations as completely as possible so the patient will define the situation as a medical procedure in which her dignity is fully respected.

To accomplish this, the examination occurs in a specific setting used for no other purpose—a room whose plain decor and professional equipment enhance a medical definition of the situation. Each staff member wears a medical uniform, never clothing that could be worn

Professionals often carry out their personal performances in carefully crafted settings. The prominent display of numerous degrees behind this physician's desk informs her patients that she expects to take charge of the interaction.

in other, nonmedical situations. Staff members also try to make the patient feel that such examinations are simply routine, although, from the patient's point of view, they are actually highly unusual.

Once the examination begins, the performance of a male physician must be extremely matter-of-fact, suggesting to the patient that examining the genitals is no different from examining any other part of the body. A female nurse is usually present during the examination. Her manifest role is to assist the physician, but she also plays an important part in dispelling any impression that the situation involves a man and woman "alone in a room" (Emerson, 1970:81). The nurse may initiate the procedure with a soothing phrase such as "The doctor wants to take a peek at you now." After the examination has begun, though, all members of the medical staff are careful to use only technical and impersonal language. Moreover, the staff members address the patient solely in terms reflecting her status as patient. Instead of mentioning "*your* vagina," for example, the physician refers, more technically, to "*the* vagina." Similarly, phrases such as "let your knees fall apart" are used in place of such sexually loaded language as "spread your legs" (Emerson, 1970:81–82). Finally, physical contact between the physician and the patient is limited to what is medically necessary.

Emerson's analysis shows that physicians must understand the social dimensions of medicine as well as mastering the medical skills involved. Fortunately, medical professionals are beginning to recognize the importance of sociological insights.

Nonverbal Communication

Novelist William Sansom describes the performance of a fictional Mr. Preedy—an English vacationer on a beach in Spain:

> He took care to avoid catching anyone's eye. First, he had to make it clear to those potential companions of his holiday that they were of no concern to him whatsoever. He stared through them, round them, over them—eyes lost in space. The beach might have been empty. If by chance a ball was thrown his way, he looked surprised; then let a smile of amusement light his face (Kindly Preedy), looked around dazed to see that there were people on the beach, tossed it back with a smile to himself and not a smile *at* the people. . . .
>
> . . . (He) then gathered together his beach-wrap and bag into a neat sand-resistant pile (Methodical and Sensible Preedy), rose slowly to stretch his huge frame (Big-Cat Preedy), and tossed aside his sandals (Carefree Preedy, after all). (1956; cited in Goffman, 1959:4–5)

Through his conduct, Mr. Preedy offers a great deal of information about himself to anyone caring to observe him. Notice that it is conveyed without his uttering a single word. This illustrates the process of **nonverbal communication,** *communication using body movements, gestures, and facial expressions rather than spoken words.*

Nonverbal communication occurs when the body conveys information to others, as suggested by the more common phrase *body language.* Facial expressions form the most significant element of nonverbal communication. Smiling, for example, symbolizes pleasure, although we distinguish between the casual, lighthearted smile of Kindly Preedy on the beach, a smile of embarrassment, and the full, unrestrained smile of self-satisfaction we often associate with the "cat who ate the canary." Other facial expressions convey an almost limitless range of human emotions, from anger, confusion, and disgust to pain, sadness, and indifference.

Eye contact is another important element of nonverbal communication. Generally, eye contact precedes social interaction. Someone across the room "catches our eye," for example, sparking a conversation. Avoiding the eyes of another, by contrast, discourages communication. Hands, too, speak for us. Common hand gestures in our culture convey, among other things, an insult, a request for a ride, an invitation for someone to join us, or a demand that others stop in their tracks. Gestures also supplement spoken words. Pointing in a menacing way to someone, for example, gives greater emphasis to a word of warning, as shrugging the shoulders adds an air of indifference to the phrase "I don't know," and rapidly waving arms lends urgency to the single word "Hurry!"

Like all symbols, nonverbal communication is largely culture-specific. Few gestures have uniform meaning among all humanity, and many significant gestures in North American culture mean nothing—or something very different—to members of other cultures. For instance, what Americans call the "A-Okay" gesture with thumb touching forefinger means "You're a zero" to the French, and symbolizes a crude word for "rectum" to many Italians (Ekman, 1984).

The examples of nonverbal communication presented so far typically refer to intentional behavior. Sometimes, however, the information we unintentionally give off contradicts our intended performance. Listening to

Telling Lies: Clues to Deceit

On September 15, 1938, Germany's chancellor Adolf Hitler and Britain's prime minister Neville Chamberlain met for the first time, as the world looked on in hopes of avoiding war.

Telling lies is difficult because few people can skillfully manipulate their facial gestures. The grief in Figure A is probably genuine, since most people cannot intentionally lift the upper eyelids and inner corners of the eyebrows in this way. Likewise, the apprehension in Figure B appears genuine; raising and pulling together the eyebrows as in the example is also extremely difficult. In contrast, the asymmetrical smile in Figure C is probably a phony expression of pleasure since, for most people, genuine pleasure is expressed by a "balanced" smile.

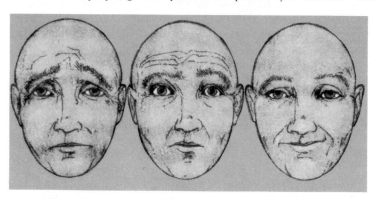

| Figure A | Figure B | Figure C |

Although his plans for war were already well under way, Hitler assured Chamberlain that peace could be preserved. Chamberlain believed what he heard, writing soon afterward, "In spite of the hardness and ruthlessness I thought I saw in his face, I got the impression that here was a man who could be relied upon when he had given his word" (Ekman, 1985:15–16). In retrospect, Chamberlain should have paid less attention to the message Hitler *gave* and more to the contradictory nonverbal signals he *gave off*.

Detecting lies is a difficult task, because no single bodily gesture directly indicates deceit in the same way a smile, for example, conveys pleasure. Even so, because each performance draws on a complex web of elements, few people can lie without allowing some piece of contradictory information to arouse the suspicions of a careful observer. The key, therefore, to identifying deceit is to scan a person's complete performance looking for discrepancies in the information that is conveyed.

Specifically, Ekman suggests scrutinizing four types of information provided by a performer—language,

---

her teenage son's explanation for returning home at a late hour, for example, a mother begins to doubt his words because he is unable to maintain eye contact. The guest on a television talk show asserts that her recent divorce is "the best thing that ever happened to me," but the nervous swing of her leg suggests otherwise. Such nonverbal communication may provide clues to deception, in much the same way that a lie detector measures the subtle physical changes in breathing, pulse rate, perspiration, and blood pressure that signal the stress involved in telling lies. Does this mean that careful observers can detect dishonesty in someone else's performance? Paul Ekman believes they can, as the box explains.

Gender and Personal Performances

Because females are socialized to be less assertive than males, they tend to be especially sensitive to nonverbal communication. In fact, society prompts us to make assumptions about performances simply on the basis of a person's sex. Based on the work of Nancy Henley, Mykol Hamilton, and Barrie Thorne (1989), we can extend the conventional discussion of personal performances to spotlight the importance of *gender*, the differing social patterns expected of males and females.

Demeanor. Goffman (1967) links *demeanor*—general conduct or deportment—to social power. Simply put, voice, body language, and facial expression. *Language* serves as the major channel of communication in social interaction. People manipulate words relatively easily because they can be mentally rehearsed prior to presentation. One clue to deception, however, lies in a simple slip of the tongue—something the performer did not mean to say in quite that way. For example, a young man who is deceiving his parents by claiming that his roommate is a male friend rather than a female lover might inadvertently use the word *she* rather than *he* to refer to the roommate in the course of a discussion. The more complicated the deception, the more likely a performer will introduce odd contradictions in conversation.

Voice—meaning all the qualities of speech other than words—also conveys important information. Tone and patterns of speech often contain clues to deception because they are hard to control. In attempting to mask powerful emotion, for example, a person's voice is likely to tremble or break. Similarly, the rate of speech may become unusually fast (suggesting anger) or slow (suggesting sadness). In other cases, inappropriate pauses between words—or nonwords, such as *ah* and *ummm*—hint at discomfort.

A "leak" of *body language* that a performer is unable to conceal may tip off an observer to deception as well. Subtle body movements, for example, given the impression of nervousness, as do sudden swallowing or rapid breathing. These are especially good clues to deception because few people can control them. Sometimes, *not* using the body in a particular way to enhance words—as, for instance, when a person faking excitement remains unanimated—may also suggest deception.

Uncontrollable *facial expressions* can also reveal deception. A sad person feigning happiness, for example, generally "flashes" momentary frowns while trying to smile. In this case, the concealed emotion leaks through the performance. Raising and drawing together the eyebrows signals fear or worry, a movement virtually impossible for most people to make voluntarily. Should this expression cross the face of a person who claims to be at ease, deception is likely.

In sum, lies are detectable but the ability to notice relevant clues usually requires training. Knowing the other person well makes detecting deception much easier; parents, for example, can usually spot deception in their children. Clues to deception also appear more obvious when a person is trying to contain strong emotions. Even so, some people have (or develop) the unusual ability to carefully manage their verbal and nonverbal performances. There are, in short, both good and bad liars.

SOURCE: Adapted from Paul Ekman, *Telling Lies: Clues to Deceit in the Marketplace, Politics, and Marriage* (New York: W. W. Norton, 1985).

people in positions of power have far greater personal discretion in how they act; those subject to supervision act more self-consciously and formally. Office behavior such as swearing, removing shoes, or putting feet up on the desk may well be considered acceptable for the boss, but not for subordinates (Henley, Hamilton, & Thorne, 1989). Similarly, people in positions of dominance can interrupt the performances of others with impunity, while the people who were interrupted are expected to display deference by becoming silent (Smith-Lovin & Brody, 1989).

For women, who generally occupy positions of low power, demeanor is a matter of particular concern. As Chapter 10 ("Sex and Gender") explains, about half of all working women in the United States hold clerical or service jobs that place them under the control of supervisors, who are usually male. American women, therefore, generally craft their personal performances more formally than men, and tend to display a greater degree of deference in social interaction.

Use of space. How much space do personal performances require? Here again, power plays a key role because using more space conveys a nonverbal message of personal importance. According to Henley, Hamilton, and Thorne (1989), men use significantly more space than women do. Traditionally, our society has measured femininity by how little space women occupy (the standard of "daintiness"), while men enhance their masculinity by controlling as much territory as possible.

The concept of **personal space** refers to *the surrounding area over which a person makes some claim to privacy*. In the United States, we maintain somewhat larger personal space than people in more densely populated societies such as Japan; Americans typically remain at least several feet from others. But this distance varies significantly by sex. In social interactions, men readily intrude on the personal space of women. A woman's intrusion into a man's personal space, however, is likely to be construed as a sexual overture. Here again, women have less power to define a specific reality than men do.

Staring, smiling, and touching. Eye contact encourages interaction. Women more than men actively maintain interaction, generally sustaining eye contact longer. One exception is *staring*. Women often find themselves the objects of men's stares; this reflects both the dominance of males in American society and their tendency to define women as sexual objects.

Although frequently conveying pleasure, *smiling* can also project a wide range of meaning. In a male-dominated world, women often smile to indicate appeasement, or acceptance of submission. For this reason, Henley, Hamilton, and Thorne maintain, women smile more than men; in extreme cases, smiling may reach the level of nervous habit.

Finally, *touching* reveals an intriguing social pattern. Mutual touching generally conveys intimacy and caring. Apart from close relationships, however, touching is something men generally do to women. A male physician touches the shoulder of his female nurse as they examine a report, a young man who has just begun dating touches the back of his woman friend as he guides her across the street, or a male skiing instructor unnecessarily touches his female students. In such cases, the touching may prompt little response. But it amounts to a subtle ritual by which males express their dominant position in an assumed hierarchy that subordinates women (Henley, Hamilton, & Thorne, 1989:108–110).

Idealization

Complex motives underlie all human behavior. Even so, Goffman suggests, performances tend to *idealize* our intentions. That is, we try to convince others that what we do reflects ideal cultural standards rather than less virtuous motives.

We can illustrate idealization by returning to the world of physicians and patients. In a hospital, physicians engage in a performance commonly called "making rounds." Entering the room of a patient, a doctor often stops at the foot of the bed and silently examines the patient's chart. Afterwards, physician and patient briefly converse. In culturally ideal terms, this routine involves

In private interactions involving the two sexes, women tend to maintain more eye contact than men do. In public places, however, eye contact in the form of staring is common behavior among males. This reflects male dominance and the tendency of men to view women as sexual objects.

Gestures vary widely from one culture to another. Yet a chuckle, grin, or smirk in response to someone's personal performance is a universal sign of not taking the person seriously. Therefore, people the world over tactfully cover their faces in such situations.

a physician making a personal visit to inquire about a patient's condition.

In reality, something less ideal is usually going on. A physician who sees perhaps thirty-five patients a day may remember little about most of them. Reading the chart gives the physician an opportunity to rediscover the patient's identity and medical problems. Openly revealing the actual impersonality of much medical care would undermine the culturally ideal perception of the physician as deeply concerned about the welfare of others. Idealizing the behavior of physicians also encourages patients to "follow doctor's orders," which, they assume, is in their own best interest. No doubt this is often the case. But, as Chapter 13 ("Education and Medicine") suggests, physicians sometimes prescribe drugs, admit patients to hospitals, and perform surgery with a keen awareness of what's in it for themselves (Kaplan et al., 1985).

Idealization is woven into the fabric of everyday life in countless ways. Physicians and other professionals idealize their motives for entering their chosen careers. They describe their work as "making a contribution to science," perhaps "answering a calling from God," or "serving the community." Rarely do people concede the less honorable, although common, motives of seeking the income, power, and prestige these occupations confer. More generally, we all smile and make polite remarks to people we do not like. Such small hypocrisies ease our way through social interactions. Even when we suspect that others are putting on an act, we rarely challenge their performances openly, for reasons we shall explain next.

Embarrassment and Tact

The presidential candidate enters the room and stumbles over the rug; the eminent professor consistently mispronounces a simple word; the visiting dignitary rises from the table to speak, oblivious to the napkin that still hangs from her neck. As carefully as individuals may craft their performances, slipups of this kind frequently occur. The result is *embarrassment*, which in a dramaturgical analysis means recognizing that a performance has failed to have the intended effect on an audience. Goffman describes embarrassment simply as "losing face."

Embarrassment looms as an ever-present danger because, first, idealized performances typically contain some deception. Second, since most performances involve a complex network of elements, any inconsistent piece of information threatens to shatter the illusion of an entire performance.

Curiously, an audience often overlooks flaws in a person's performance, thereby allowing the person to avoid embarrassment. Generally, we point out, in hushed tones, that a man's zipper is open (thus limiting his embarrassment) only if doing so will spare him even greater embarrassment. In Hans Christian Andersen's classic fable "The Emperor's New Clothes," the child who blurts out that the emperor is naked tells the truth, but is scolded for being rude.

Members of an audience not only ignore flaws in a performance, Goffman explains, they often help the performer recover from them by means of *tact*, or enabling another person to "save face." After hearing a supposed expert make an embarrassingly inaccurate remark, for example, people may handle the situation in a variety of tactful ways. No response at all may signal the pretense that the statement was never made. Mild laughter may indicate that others wish to dismiss what they have heard as a joke. Or a listener may simply respond, "I'm sure you don't mean that," suggesting that one part of a performance will not destroy the actor's overall social image.

Why is tact such a common response? Simply because embarrassment provokes discomfort not simply for one person but for *everyone*. Just as members of a theater audience feel uneasy when an actor forgets a line, people who observe another lose face are reminded of how fragile their own performances are. Socially constructed reality thus functions like a dam holding back a sea of chaotic alternatives. Should one person's performance spring a leak, others tactfully assist in making repairs. Everyone, after all, is engaged in jointly building reality, and no one wants it suddenly to be swept away.

Goffman's research shows that while individuals interact with a considerable degree of individuality and spontaneity, everyone's social interactions are constructed out of similar patterned elements. Almost four hundred years ago, Shakespeare wrote:

> All the world's a stage,
> And all the men and women are merely players.
> They have their exits and their entrances,
> And one man in his time plays many parts.
> (*As You Like It*, V)

Of course, human behavior is never as rigidly scripted as a stage performance. In a lifetime, though, each of us does play many parts as we perform social roles with our own unique personality. Yet though human behavior does not consist simply of stage and script, Shakespeare's observation still contains a good measure of truth.

INTERACTION IN EVERYDAY LIFE: TWO ILLUSTRATIONS

We have examined a number of dimensions of social interaction. In the final sections of this chapter, we shall focus on two important, yet quite different, elements of everyday life.

Language: The Gender Issue

As we noted in Chapter 2 ("Culture"), language is the means by which members of a society weave the symbolic web we call culture. In everyday life, language conveys meaning on more than one level. Besides the *manifest* content, or what is explicitly stated, the *latent* content conveys various additional assumptions about reality. One latent message involves gender. Language defines the two sexes differently in at least three key ways (Henley, Hamilton, & Thorne, 1989).[1]

The control function of language. A young man drives into the gas station, eager to display his new motorcycle, and proudly asks, "Isn't she a beauty?" On the surface, the question has nothing to do with people. Yet, why does the young man use the female "she," rather than the male "he," to refer to his prized motorcycle?

Language helps males establish control over their surroundings. That is, a man attaches a female pronoun to a motorcycle, car, yacht, or any other admired object because it reflects *possession*. Conversely, use of a male pronoun in such cases (by either a male or a female owner) sounds awkward.

A more obvious control function of language relates to people's names. Traditionally in American society, and elsewhere in the world, women take the family name of the men they marry. While few today consider this an explicit statement of male ownership of a female, many believe it suggests male dominance. For this reason, an increasing proportion of women have retained their own name (more precisely, the family name obtained from their father) or, more equitably, merged two family names.

The value function of language. Language tends to attach greater value to what is defined as masculine. This pattern is deeply rooted in the English language, in ways that few men or women realize. For instance, the positive adjective "virtuous," meaning "morally worthy" or "excellent," stems from the Latin word *vir* meaning "man." By contrast, the disparaging adjective "hysterical" is derived from the Greek word *hyster*, meaning "uterus."

In numerous, more familiar ways, language also

---

[1] The following sections draw primarily on Henley, Hamilton, and Thorne, 1989. Additional material comes from Thorne, Kramarae, and Henley, 1983, and MacKay, 1983, and others as noted.

confers different value on the two sexes. Traditional masculine terms such as "king" or "lord" have retained their positive meaning, while some comparable terms, such as "queen," "madam," or "dame" have acquired negative connotations in contemporary usage. Language thus both mirrors social attitudes and serves as a means by which they are perpetuated.

Similarly, use of the suffixes "ette" and "ess" to denote femininity generally devalue the words to which they are added. For example, a *major* has higher standing than a *majorette*, as does a *host* in relation to a *hostess*. And, certainly, male groups with names like the Los Angeles Rams carry more stature than female groups bearing names such as the Radio City Music Hall Rockettes.

The attention function of language. Language also shapes reality by directing greater attention to masculine endeavors. The most obvious example appears in our use of personal pronouns. In the English language, the plural pronoun "they" is neutral as it refers to both sexes. But the corresponding singular pronouns "he" and "she" are sex linked. According to traditional grammatical practice, "he" along with the possessive "his" and the objective "him" have been used to refer to *all people*. Thus, we assume that the masculine pronoun in the bit of wisdom "He who hesitates is lost" refers to women as well as men. But some research suggests that people tend to respond to generic male pronouns as if only males were involved (Martyna, 1978, 1980; MacKay 1983). To many female readers, especially those who embrace feminism, encountering male pronouns carries the message that females are of only peripheral importance (MacKay, 1983).

For a century, advocates of gender equality have urged the creation of a gender-neutral, singular personal pronoun. In 1984, one language critic offered the new word "thon" (from "that" + "one") to solve the pronoun problem, as in "the confident person is thon who is well-prepared" (Converse, 1884; cited in Kramarae, Thorne, & Henley, 1983:175). The awkward sound of this phrasing suggests how firmly entrenched traditional patterns are in our everyday lives. More recently, the plural pronoun "they" increasingly has been employed as a singular pronoun ("*Everyone* should do as *they* please"). This usage remains controversial because it violates grammatical rules. Yet, in an age of growing concern over gender-linked bias, the English language may be evolving in a way that responds to this growing concern.

Humor: Playing with Reality

Humor plays an important part in our everyday lives. Comedians are among our favorite entertainers, most newspapers contain cartoon pages, and even professors and members of the clergy include humor in their performances. Like many aspects of everyday life, humor is largely taken for granted. While everyone laughs at a joke, few people think about what makes something funny or why humor appears as a universal element of social life. Many of the ideas developed in this chapter provide insights into the character of humor, as we shall now see.[2]

The foundation of humor. Humor stems from the contrast between two incongruous realities. Generally, one socially constructed reality can be termed *conventional* because it describes what people expect in a specific situation. The other reality, dubbed *unconventional*, represents a significant violation of cultural patterns. Humor arises from ambiguity and "double meanings" involving two differing definitions of the same situation. Note how this principle works in these simple pieces of humor:

> Steve Martin muses: "I like a woman with a head on her shoulders. *I hate necks!*"
>
> A bumper sticker reads: "Insanity is hereditary—you get it from your kids!"

In each of these examples, the first sentence presents a conventional reality. A man seeks a woman with common sense and intelligence. Mental illness can be inherited. There is nothing startling here. The second sentence in each example, however, offers an unconventional meaning that collides with the conventional understanding we take for granted. Steve Martin's assertion "I hate necks!" suddenly transforms the entire statement into an unexpectedly grotesque image. Similarly, the line ". . . you get it from your kids!" presents an absurd reversal of the hereditary process. All humor rests on such contrasting realities.

The same simple pattern appears in the humor of other well-known comedians:

> Groucho Marx, trying to sound manly: "This morning, I shot a lion in my pajamas." He then turns to the camera

---

[2] The ideas contained in this discussion are those of the author (1987), except as otherwise noted. The general approach draws on work presented earlier in this chapter, especially on the ideas of Erving Goffman.

and adds, "What the lion was doing in my pajamas I'll *never* know . . ."

On the television show "M*A*S*H," Hawkeye Pierce observed Colonel Henry Blake gallivanting around with a young woman half his age and dryly responds, "There's an age problem there; she's twenty-two and his wife's forty-eight."

Like the previous two examples, each of these jokes contains two major elements—a conventional assertion followed by an unconventional one. The greater the opposition, or incongruity, between the two definitions of reality, the funnier the joke. When telling jokes, people therefore try to strengthen this opposition in subtle ways. One technique, often used by Groucho Marx, George Burns, and other comedians of the screen, involves presenting the first, or conventional, remark in conversation with another actor, then turning toward the audience (or the camera) when delivering the second, or unconventional, line. This "shift of channel" underscores the incongruity of the two parts. To fashion the strongest incongruity, comedians pay careful attention to their performances: the precise words they use, as well as the timing of each part of the delivery. A joke is "well told" by creating the sharpest possible contrast between the realities, just as the humor falls flat in a careless performance. Since the key to humor lies in this opposition of realities, it follows that the climax of a joke has come to be known as the *punch line*.

The dynamics of humor: "Getting it."   Someone who does not understand both the conventional and unconventional realities embedded in a joke offers the typical complaint: "I don't get it." To "get" the humor, then, listeners must understand the two realities involved well enough to perceive their incongruity.

But there is something more to getting a joke, because some of the information listeners must grasp is usually left unstated. The audience, therefore, must pay attention to the stated elements of the joke and then inferentially complete the joke in their own minds. Consider the following exchange, from the well-known television show "Cheers":

Sam: "Diane, you're drunk."

Diane: "Yes, Sam, and you're stupid, but I'll be sober in the morning."

In this case, "getting" the joke depends on following the logic well enough to mentally complete Diane's line with the words ". . . and you'll *still* be stupid."

A more complex joke, written on the wall of a college rest room, states:

Dyslexics of the World, Untie!

This joke demands much more of the audience. We must know, first, that dyslexia is a condition in which people routinely reverse letters; second, we must identify the line as an adaptation of Karl Marx's call to the world's workers to unite; third and finally, we must recognize "untie" as an anagram of "unite," as we might imagine a disgruntled dyslexic person would write it.

Why would an audience make this sort of effort to understand a joke? Simply because our reaction to a joke is heightened by the pleasure of having completed the puzzle necessary to "get it." This pleasure derives partly from satisfaction at our own mental abilities. Additionally, "getting" the joke confers a favored status as an "insider" in the larger audience. Conversely, not getting a joke gives rise to frustration, based on perceived mental inadequacy coupled with a sense of being socially excluded from the insights shared by others. Not surprisingly, "outsiders" in such a situation may fake "getting" the joke; others may also tactfully explain a joke to them to end their sense of being left out.

But, as the old saying goes, if a joke has to be explained, it won't be very funny. Besides taking the edge off the language and timing on which the *punch* depends, an explanation completely relieves the audience of any mental involvement, substantially reducing their pleasure.

The topics of humor.   Since people throughout the world live in diverse cultures, they differ in what they find funny. Musicians perform for receptive audiences around the world, suggesting that music may be the "universal language" of humanity. Comedians rarely do this, demonstrating that humor does not travel well.

What is humorous to the Chinese, then, may be lost on most Americans. To some degree, too, different categories of people in one society find humor in different situations. In the United States, New Englanders, southerners, and westerners have their own brands of humor, as do Hispanics and Anglos, fifteen- and forty-year-olds, bankers and construction workers.

In all cases, however, humor deals with topics that lend themselves to double meanings. One trait of humorous material everywhere, in other words, is *controversy*. For example, the first jokes many of us learned as children concerned what American culture defines as a childhood taboo: sex. The mere mention of "unmentionable acts" or even certain parts of the body can dissolve young faces in laughter.

The controversy inherent in humor often walks a fine line between what is funny and what is considered "sick." During the Middle Ages, the word *humors* (derived from the Latin *humidus*, meaning "moist") referred to a balance of bodily fluids that determined a person's health or sickness. Most cultures value the ability to take conventional definitions of reality lightly (in other words, having a "sense of humor"). Evidence also suggests that maintaining a sense of humor contributes to physical health (Robinson, 1983). At the other extreme, however, people who always take conventional reality lightly risk being defined as deviant or even mentally ill (mental hospitals have long been dubbed "funny farms").

Every social group considers some topics too sensitive for humorous treatment. A violation may result in the comic being admonished for telling a "sick" joke, one that pokes fun at a situation that is expected to be handled with reverence. Some topics, in other words, are "off limits," because they are expected to be under-

Because humor involves challenging social realities, "outsiders"—particularly ethnic and racial minorities—have always been disproportionately represented among America's comedians. The Marx Brothers, sons of Jewish immigrants, delighted in revealing the pretensions of the Protestant upper class. A half-century later, black comedian Eddie Murphy employed a similar pattern, as suggested in this movie role as he is arrested for trespassing on a millionaire's estate in Beverly Hills.

stood in only one way. People's religious beliefs, or tragic accidents, for example, are the stuff of "sick" jokes.

The functions of humor. As a means of expressing opposition to cultural convention, humor enhances any social system. A structural-functional analysis suggests that the universality of humor reflects its function as a social "safety valve," allowing potentially disruptive sentiments to be released with little consequence. Put another way, jokes express sentiments that might be dangerous if taken seriously, as in the case of racial and ethnic jokes. Called to account for a remark that could be defined as offensive, a person may defuse the situation by simply stating, "I didn't mean anything by what I said; it was just a joke!" Likewise, rather than taking offense at another's behavior, a person might use humor as a form of tact, smiling, as if to say, "I could be angry at this, but I'll assume you were only kidding."

Like theater and art, humor allows a society to safely explore alternatives to the status quo. Sometimes, in fact, humor actually promotes social change.

Humor and conflict. Through humor, conflict among various categories of people bubbles to the surface. Men and women, blacks and whites, rich and poor tend to endorse somewhat different definitions of reality. Conse-quently, members of one category generally use humor to challenge others they oppose. Men who tell jokes about feminists, for example, typically are voicing some measure of hostility to the interests of women (Benokraitis & Feagin, 1986; Powell & Paton, 1988). Similarly, jokes at the expense of homosexuals reveal the tensions surrounding sexual orientation in American society.

The significance of humor looms large in everyday life. Michael Flaherty (1984, 1990) points out that socially constructing reality takes constant work. Furthermore, the reality that emerges may suffer by comparison to what we are able to imagine. As long as we maintain a sense of humor, however, we are never prisoners of the present. Indeed, we can fight back at the world and in doing so, perhaps, change it (and ourselves) just a little.

These very different issues—the significance of gender in our language and the way humor plays with reality—are but two of the countless dimensions of everyday life. These issues each grow out of people's social interaction, as they construct a world of meaning and then react to the world they have made. They also demonstrate the value of sociological thinking for understanding—and more actively participating in—this process.

SUMMARY

1. Social life is patterned in various ways. By guiding behavior within culturally approved bounds, social structure helps to make situations more understandable and predictable.

2. A major component of social structure is status. Within an entire status set, a master status has particular significance.

3. Ascribed statuses are essentially involuntary, while achieved statuses are largely earned. In practice, however, many statuses incorporate elements of both ascription and achievement.

4. Role is the dynamic expression of a status. Like statuses, roles are relational, guiding people as they interact.

5. When roles corresponding to two or more statuses are incompatible, role conflict results. Likewise, incompatibility among various roles linked to a single status (the role set) can generate role strain.

6. The phrase "social construction of reality" conveys the important idea that people build the social world as they interact.

7. According to the Thomas theorem, reality is a human creation that is real in its consequences for those involved.

8. Ethnomethodology refers to a means of discovering the structure of everyday social situations by violating patterns of expected behavior.

9. Dramaturgical analysis explores everyday life in terms of theatrical performances.

10. People make use of language, nonverbal behavior, and physical settings in their performances. The situational behavior of males and females differs in various ways.

11. All social behavior carries the ever-present danger of embarrassment. Tact is a common response to a "loss of face" by others.

12. Language constitutes a major element in forming social reality. In various ways, language defines males and females in different terms, generally to the advantage of males.

13. Humor stems from the contrast between conventional and unconventional social realities. Because comedy is framed by a specific culture, people throughout the world find humor in very different situations.

KEY CONCEPTS

achieved status a social position that people assume voluntarily and that reflects a significant measure of personal ability and effort

ascribed status a social position attached to a person at birth or one that is involuntarily assumed later in life

dramaturgical analysis the investigation of social interaction in terms of theatrical performance

ethnomethodology the study of the everyday, common-sense understandings that people within a culture have of the world around them

master status a status that serves as the focal point of an individual's social identity, often shaping that person's entire life

nonverbal communication communication using body movements, gestures, and facial expressions rather than spoken words

personal space the surrounding area over which a person makes some claim to privacy

presentation of self the ways in which individuals, in various settings, attempt to create specific impressions in the minds of others

role patterns of expected behavior attached to a particular status

role conflict incompatibility among the roles corresponding to two or more statuses

role set a number of roles attached to a single status

role strain incompatibility among roles corresponding to a single status

social construction of reality the process by which individuals creatively build reality through social interaction

social interaction the process by which people act and react in relation to others

status a recognized social position that an individual occupies in society

status set all the statuses a particular person holds at a given time

Thomas theorem the assertion that situations that are defined as real are real in their consequences

Groups
and
Organizations

5

Chapter Outline

On March 8, 1965, a young marine named Philip Caputo landed in Danang, Vietnam. Sixteen months later, his tour of duty completed, he came home. He had endured a living hell. He had made it. But he would never be the same. A decade later, telling the story of his time in Vietnam, Caputo (1977:xiv–xv) wrote:

> . . . an honorable discharge released me from the Marines and the chance of dying an early death in Asia. I felt as happy as a condemned man whose sentence has been commuted, but within a year I began growing nostalgic for the war.
>
> Other veterans I knew confessed to the same emotion. In spite of everything, we felt a strange attachment to Vietnam and, even stranger, a longing to return. The war was still being fought, but this desire to go back did not spring from any patriotic ideas about duty, honor, and sacrifice, the myths with which old men send young men off to get killed or maimed. It arose, rather, from a recognition of how deeply we had been changed, how different we were from everyone who had not shared with us the miseries of the monsoon, the exhausting patrols, the fear of a combat assault on a hot landing zone. We had very little in common with them. Though we were civilians again, the civilian world seemed alien. We did not belong to it as much as we did to that other world, where we had fought and our friends had died. . . .
>
> . . . [I also want] to describe the intimacy of life in infantry battalions, where the communion between men is as profound as any between lovers. Actually, it is more so. It does not demand for its sustenance the reciprocity, the pledges of affection, the endless reassurances required by the love of men and women. It is, unlike marriage, a bond that cannot be broken by a word, by boredom or divorce, or by anything other than death. Sometimes even that is not strong enough. Two friends of mine died trying to save the corpses of their men from the battlefield. Such devotion, simple and selfless, the sentiment of belonging to each other, was the one decent thing we found in a conflict otherwise notable for its monstrosities.

These words reveal the power of social experience—even in the midst of violence—to fuse human beings into something greater than themselves. Notice how Caputo writes of *we* contrasted to *them*; how he stresses the sense of *belonging* shared with his fellow soldiers, and a collective *intimacy*, *bonding*, and *devotion*.

Chapter 4 ("Social Interaction in Everyday Life") examined how individuals organize their daily routines in relation to others. These others often take the form of *social groups*, illustrated by countless soldiers who forge a common identity on the battlefield. Much of

modern social life also revolves around *formal organizations*, including the Marine Corps, corporations, universities, and volunteer associations such as the American Red Cross. This chapter explores both social groups and formal organizations.

SOCIAL GROUPS

Virtually everyone lives with a sense of belonging, which is the experience of group life. A **social group** is defined as *two or more people who identify with one another and have a distinctive pattern of interaction*. As human beings, we continually join together in couples, families, circles of friends, platoons, teams, churches, businesses, clubs, and numerous large organizations. Whatever the form, groups encompass people with shared experiences, loyalties, and interests. In short, while maintaining their individuality, the members of social groups also think of themselves as a special "we."

Not every collection of people is a social group. The term *aggregate* refers to people who are in the same place at the same time but who interact little, if at all, and have no sense of belonging together. People riding together on a subway, for example, form an aggregate, not a social group. People who have some status in common, such as "mother," "corporal," "homeowner," or "Roman Catholic," are considered a *category*. They do not constitute a social group because, while they may be aware of others like themselves, most are strangers who never socially interact.

People in some aggregates and categories *could* become a social group if the right circumstances gave them a common identity and produced interaction over a period of time. If, for example, a subway train stalled beneath the streets of New York City, passengers might be prompted by their common plight to generate some group awareness. Similarly, combat soldiers assigned to the same unit quickly develop a distinctive set of social patterns.

Primary and Secondary Groups

People commonly greet one another with a smile and a simple "Hi! How are you?" The response is usually a well-scripted "Just fine, thanks. How about you?" This answer, of course, is often far from truthful: In most cases, providing a detailed account of how you *really*

Reacting to the expansion of industry and the growth of cities early in this century, Charles Horton Cooley (1864–1929) expressed concern that primary groups—which he deemed vital to human development—might be weakened.

are doing would prompt the other person to make a hasty and awkward exit.

Types of social groups can be distinguished by the degree of personal concern for others in social interaction. According to Charles Horton Cooley, a **primary group** typically refers to *a small social group in which relationships are both personal and enduring*. Bound together by strong and lasting loyalties that Cooley termed *primary relationships*, people in primary groups share many activities, spend a great deal of time together, and feel that they know one another well. As a consequence, they typically display genuine concern for one another's welfare. The family is generally the most important primary group in any society.

Cooley called social groups of this kind *primary* because they are among the first groups we experience in life. In addition, the family and peer groups also hold primary importance in the socialization process, shaping personal attitudes and behavior. We look to members of our primary groups for clues to social identity as well, which is why members of any primary group almost always think of themselves as "we."

The strength of primary relationships gives individuals considerable comfort and security, as shown in their

personal performances, described in Chapter 4 ("Social Interaction in Everyday Life"). Within the familiar social circles of family or friends, people tend to feel they can "be themselves" without constantly worrying about the impressions they are making.

Members of primary groups generally provide one another with many forms of personal, financial, and emotional support. But people tend to think of the primary group as an end in itself rather than as a means to other ends. For example, we readily call on family members or close friends to help us move into a new apartment, without expecting to pay for their services. And we would do the same for them. If we consistently help a friend who never returns the favor, however, we are likely to feel "used" and to question the depth of the friendship.

Members of primary groups are considered unique and not interchangeable with others. We usually do not care who cashes our check or approves a loan for us at the bank. Yet in primary groups—especially the family—we are bound to others by emotion and loyalty. Although brothers and sisters may experience periodic conflict, they always remain siblings.

In contrast to the primary group, the **secondary group** is *a large and impersonal social group usually based on a specific interest or activity*. Secondary groups are generally larger than primary groups. For example, people who work together in an office, enroll in the same college course, live in the same city neighborhood, or belong to a particular political organization all form secondary groups.

In most respects, secondary groups have precisely the opposite characteristics of primary groups. *Secondary relationships* typically involve little personal knowledge of one another and weak emotional ties. Groups built on secondary relationships vary in duration, but they are frequently of short term, beginning and ending without particular significance. Students in a college course, who may not see one another after the semester ends, exemplify the secondary group. Because secondary groups are formed around a single activity or interest, members have little chance to develop a deep concern for one another's overall welfare. In some cases, such as co-workers who share an office for many years, secondary relationships may become more primary with the passing of time. Generally, however, although people in a secondary group sometimes think of themselves as "we," the boundary that distinguishes members from nonmembers is usually far less clear than it is in primary groups.

Americans tend to define business ties as secondary relationships in which little personal knowledge is necessary or even desirable. In many traditional societies, however, people routinely conduct business with others they know well. This pattern is still evident in Turkey, where a ritual of exchanging greetings and news and sharing refreshments precedes business dealings.

While secondary relationships are less intense than primary ties, they are valued as a means of achieving specific ends. Primary relationships have a *personal orientation*, while secondary ties have a *goal orientation*. This does not mean that secondary bonds are necessarily formal and unemotional. On the contrary, social interactions with fellow students, co-workers, and business contacts can be enjoyable even if they are rather impersonal.

In primary groups, people define one another according to *who* they are; members of secondary groups look to each other for *what* they are, that is, what they can do. In secondary groups, in other words, we remain mindful of what we offer others and what we receive in return. This comes through most clearly in business relationships. Likewise, secondary ties among neighbors are based on the expectation that a neighborly favor will be reciprocated.

The goal orientation of secondary groups encourages members to craft personal performances carefully, and to expect others to do the same. In these roles, we remain characteristically impersonal and polite. The secondary relationship, therefore, is one in which the question "How are you?" may be asked with no real concern for a truthful answer.

The characteristics of primary and secondary groups are summarized in Table 5–1. Because these two types of social groups are presented in ideal terms, neither concept precisely describes most actual social

groups in our lives. Some family relationships, for example, are more primary than others, and not all business relationships are equally secondary. Thus, these concepts form a continuum on which any group can be placed.

Historically, the balance between primary and secondary groups tends to shift as traditional societies undergo industrialization. In general, primary relationships dominate family and local village life in preindustrial societies. Strangers stand out in the social landscape. By contrast, secondary ties take precedence in modern, industrial societies, where people assume highly specialized roles. In today's world, we routinely experience impersonal, secondary relationships with strangers—people about whom we know very little and whom we may never meet again (Wirth, 1938).

Group Leadership

Social groups vary in the extent to which they designate one or more persons as leaders, with responsibility to direct the activities of all members. Some friendship groups grant someone the clear status of leader; others do not. Within families, parents traditionally share leadership responsibilities, although husband and wife may disagree about who is really in charge. In many secondary groups, such as corporations, leadership is likely to involve a formal chain of command with clearly defined roles.

Leaders are commonly thought to possess extraordinary personal abilities, but research over several decades has failed to produce convincing evidence of so-called "natural leaders." Group members, in fact, often discourage an individual who tries to assume a dominant position in the group. Instead of reflecting individual traits, researchers conclude that leadership has more to do with the needs of the group itself (Ridgeway, 1983; Ridgeway & Diekema, 1989).

Two different leadership roles, usually held by different individuals, often emerge in groups (Bales, 1953; Bales & Slater, 1955). **Instrumental leadership** refers to *group leadership that emphasizes the completion of tasks.* Group members look to instrumental leaders to "get things done." **Expressive leadership,** in contrast, *emphasizes collective well-being.* Expressive leaders take less of an interest in the performance goals of a group than in providing emotional support to group members and minimizing tension and conflict among them.

Because they concentrate on performance, instrumental leaders usually have secondary relationships with other group members. Instrumental leaders give orders and punish those who hold back the group's efforts. Expressive leaders cultivate more personal or primary relationships. They offer sympathy when a member is going through a difficult time, work to keep the group united, and lighten serious moments with humor. Expressive leaders generally receive more *affection* from members, while successful instrumental leaders enjoy a more distant *respect.*

This differentiation of leadership is sometimes linked to gender. Consider, for example, the traditional American family (Parsons & Bales, 1955). For generations, cultural norms have bestowed instrumental leadership on men, as fathers and husbands. In this traditional pattern, men assume primary responsibility for providing family income, making major family decisions, and disciplining children. By contrast, expressive leadership has traditionally been assigned to women. Within the family, mothers and wives have been expected to lend emotional support and to maintain peaceful relationships among all family members. In this context, it is not surprising that children may have greater respect for their fathers, but closer personal relationships with their mothers (Macionis, 1978). As gender roles in the family have been changing in recent decades (see Chapter 12, "Family and Religion"), the assignment of instrumental and expressive leadership roles has become less rigid. In other group settings, women and men are both assuming leadership roles.

Decision-making styles also distinguish leaders from one another. *Authoritarian leaders* focus on instrumental concerns, make decisions on their own, and demand strict compliance from subordinates. This leadership style rarely wins personal affection from group members. However, the authoritarian leader may be highly effective in crisis situations requiring immediate decisions and in maintaining strong group discipline. *Democratic leaders* take a more expressive approach to leadership, seeking the participation of everyone in decision making. Although less successful during crises, when there is little time for discussion, democratic leaders can otherwise draw on the ideas of all group members to forge reflective and imaginative responses to the tasks at hand. *Laissez-faire leaders* (from the French phrase meaning roughly "to leave alone") tend to downplay their position and power, allowing the group to function more or less on its own. Laissez-faire leaders generally are the least effective in promoting group goals. Clearly, the leadership style of the person who guides a social group is closely linked to the character and the needs of the group itself (White & Lippitt, 1953; Ridgeway, 1983).

Group Conformity

How do groups influence the behavior of their members? Among friends, some amount of *group conformity* may

Table 5–1 PRIMARY GROUPS AND SECONDARY GROUPS: A SUMMARY

	Primary Group	Secondary Group
Quality of relationships	Personal orientation	Goal orientation
Duration of relationships	Usually long term	Variable; often short term
Breadth of relationships	Broad; usually involving many activities	Narrow; usually involving few activities
Subjective perception of relationships	As an end in itself	As a means to an end
Typical examples	Families; close friendships	Co-workers; political organizations

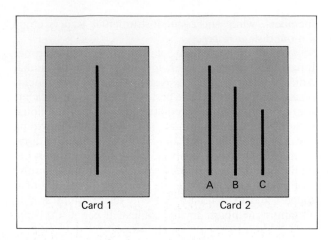

Figure 5–1 The Cards Used in Asch's Experiment in Group Conformity

(Asch, 1952:452–453)

offer a secure feeling of belonging. In other groups, such as families, some members may demand considerable conformity from others. Even interaction with strangers can result in conformity, as shown by a classic experiment conducted some forty years ago by Solomon Asch.

Asch (1952) formed groups of six to eight people, allegedly to study visual perception. He arranged with all but one member of the group to create a situation in which the remaining subject would be pressured to accept conclusions that were quite unreasonable. Sitting around a table, group members were asked to match a "standard" line, as shown in Figure 5–1 on the left card, to one of three lines on the right card. Anyone with normal vision could easily see that the line marked "A" on the second card would be the correct choice. Initially, everyone gave correct answers. Then, Asch's secret accomplices began answering incorrectly, causing the naïve subject to become bewildered and uncomfortable. Asch found that more than one-third of individuals placed in such a situation conformed to the others by answering incorrectly. Many of us are apparently willing to compromise our own judgment to avoid the discomfort of being different from others, even from people we do not know.

In the early 1960s, Stanley Milgram (who had been a student of Solomon Asch) conducted a controversial conformity experiment of his own. In his initial study (Milgram 1963, 1965; Miller, 1986), a "researcher" explained to pairs of subjects that they were about to engage in a study of memory. One subject was assigned

the role of "teacher" and the other the role of "learner." Actually, the person assigned to be the learner was an "insider" to the study; only the subject assigned to the position of teacher was unaware of what was really going on.

The learner was placed in a contraption resembling an electric chair with electrodes attached to one arm. The researcher then instructed the teacher to read aloud pairs of words. In subsequent trials, the teacher repeated the first word of each pair and asked the learner to respond with the corresponding second word. As mistakes occurred, the researcher instructed the teacher to administer a shock to the learner using a formidable-looking device marked to indicate shocks ranging from 15 volts (labeled "mild shock") to 450 volts (marked "Danger: Severe Shock" and "XXX"). Beginning at the lowest level, the teachers were told to increase the shock by 15 volts every time a mistake was made. The experimenter claimed that the shocks were "extremely painful" but caused "no permanent tissue damage."

The results were striking evidence of the ability of leaders to obtain compliance. None of the forty subjects assigned to the role of teacher during the initial research even questioned the procedure before 300 volts had been applied, and twenty-six of the subjects—almost two-thirds—went all the way to 450 volts.

In later research, although the proportion who applied the maximum shock varied, Milgram's subjects administered shocks to people who verbally objected; many shocked others who protested that they had heart conditions; and some even increased the voltage as accomplices screamed and then feigned unconsciousness. Not surprisingly, most subjects found the experiment extremely stressful, the source of the controversy ever since. But many followed orders all the same.

Milgram (1964) then modified his research to see if Solomon Asch had found a high degree of group conformity only because the task of matching lines seemed trivial. What if groups pressured people to administer electrical shocks? To investigate, Milgram set up groups of three "teachers," two of whom were his accomplices. Milgram asked each of the three teachers to suggest a shock level when an error was made, explaining that the shock actually given would be the *lowest* of the three suggestions. This gave the naïve subject the power to set the shock level regardless of what the other two subjects suggested. The accomplices recommended increasing the shock level with each error, placing group pressure on the third member to do the same. Under these conditions, subjects applied voltages three to four times higher than in experiments with a subject acting alone. Milgram's research shows that people are surprisingly likely to follow the directions of "legitimate authority figures," and are also influenced by groups made up of "ordinary people."

Even the experts succumb to pressure for group conformity, according to Irving L. Janis (1972, 1989). Janis contends that a number of American foreign policy errors, including the failure to foresee the Japanese attack on Pearl Harbor in World War II, the disastrous U.S. attempt to invade Cuba in 1961, and our ill-fated involvement in the Vietnam War, were the result of group conformity among our highest-ranking political leaders.

We often think that "brainstorming" in groups improves decision making. However, Janis showed that group thinking sometimes backfires. First, rather than examining a problem from many points of view, groups often seek consensus, thereby *narrowing* the range of options. Second, groups may develop a distinctive language, adopting terms that favor a single interpretation of events. Third, having settled on a position, members of the group may come to see anyone with another view as the "opposition." Janis called this process **"groupthink,"** *a reduced capacity for critical thinking caused by group conformity.*

Janis claims that "groupthink" led the Kennedy administration to invade Cuba—a plan that failed and provided international criticism of the United States. Arthur Schlesinger, Jr., former adviser to President John Kennedy, confessed guilt "for having kept so quiet during those crucial discussions in the Cabinet Room," but added that the group discouraged anyone from challenging what, in retrospect, appeared to be "nonsense" (Janis,

1972:30, 40). More recently, "groupthink" probably contributed to the Iran-contra affair. Some officials of the Reagan administration secretly planned to sell weapons to Iran, hoping to win the release of American hostages held by pro-Iranian groups in Lebanon, and to direct proceeds from the weapons sales to the contras, soldiers opposed to the Sandinista government in Nicaragua. Congressional hearings in 1987 revealed that some of the officials, including Lieutenant Colonel Oliver North, became so committed to the plan that they disregarded the law. Further, those involved in the decision developed a language that supported only one interpretation of events. For example, they never called the plan a strategy of "trading arms for hostages" but rather one of "opening relations with moderates in Iran." Likewise, those they supported were dubbed not Nicaraguan rebels or "guerilla insurgents," but "freedom fighters."

Reference Groups

How do we assess a decision's merits? Frequently, we evaluate our views in relation to those of others, often using **reference groups,** *social groups that serve as points of reference for people making evaluations and decisions.*

A young man who imagines his family's response to a woman he is dating is using his family as a reference group. Similarly, a banker who assesses her colleagues' reactions to a new loan policy is using her co-workers as a standard of reference. As these examples suggest, reference groups can be both primary and secondary. The desire to conform often means that the perceived attitudes of a group greatly affect personal evaluations.

Reference groups are not only important for making specific evaluations; such groups also serve as role models, guiding the personality development of a society's young people.

This is true both of groups we belong to and those we would like to join, as the discussion of *anticipatory socialization* in Chapter 3 ("Socialization: From Infancy to Aging") suggests.

Samuel A. Stoufer (1949) and his associates conducted a classic study of reference group dynamics during World War II. In a survey, researchers asked soldiers to evaluate the chances of promotion for a competent person in their branch of the service. Common sense suggests that soldiers serving in outfits with a relatively high promotion rate would be optimistic about their future advancement. Yet survey responses revealed just the opposite: Soldiers in branches of the service with low promotion rates were actually more optimistic about their own chances for advancement.

The key to this paradox was in identifying the groups against which the soldiers measured their progress. Those in branches with lower promotion rates compared their advancement with people like themselves; therefore, although they had not been promoted, neither had many others, so they did not feel deprived and expressed favorable attitudes about their chances for promotion. Soldiers in a service branch with a higher promotion rate, however, could easily think of people who had been promoted sooner or more often than they had. Using these people as a reference group, even individuals who had been promoted were likely to feel they had come up short. These were the soldiers who voiced more negative attitudes in their evaluations.

Stouffer's research demonstrates that we do not make judgments in isolation, nor do we compare ourselves with just anyone. Instead, we use specific social groups as standards in developing individual attitudes. Regardless of our situation in *absolute* terms, then, we perceive well-being subjectively, *relative* to some specific reference group (Merton, 1968; Mirowsky, 1987).

Ingroups and Outgroups

Differences among groups, in political outlook, social status, even manner of dress, may lead us to embrace one while avoiding others. Across the United States, for example, students wear high-school jackets and place school decals on car windows to indicate that, to them, school serves as an important social group. Students attending another school may become the targets of derision simply because they belong to a rival group.

This illustrates an important process of group dynamics: the opposition of ingroups and outgroups. An **ingroup** constitutes *an esteemed social group commanding a member's loyalty*. An ingroup exists in relation to an **outgroup,** *a scorned social group toward which one feels competition or opposition*. A sports team, for instance, is both an ingroup to its members and an outgroup for members of opposing teams. A town's Democrats generally think of themselves as an ingroup in relation to the local Republicans. All ingroups and outgroups work on the principle that "we" have valued traits that "they" lack.

The ingroup/outgroup dynamic establishes the boundaries that define many social groups. Joining together with some people while simultaneously avoiding others gives us a clearer identity in a world of diversity.

The popularity of "celebrity" clothing among young people is partly explained by the desire to display ingroup solidarity.

However, this process also promotes self-serving distortions of reality. Research has shown that members of ingroups hold unrealistically positive views of themselves and unfairly negative views of various outgroups (Tajfel, 1982). Ethnocentrism, for example, grows out of the tendency to overvalue one's own "group," while undervaluing other cultures as outgroups.

When an ingroup has greater social power than an outgroup it opposes, serious personal and social problems may result. For example, whites have historically viewed nonwhites in negative terms and subjected them to certain social, political, and economic disadvantages. Internalizing these negative attitudes, African-Americans, Hispanics, Asians, and Native Americans often struggle to overcome negative self-images based on stereotypes held by the larger society. The operation of individual ingroups and outgroups often mirrors patterns of social inequality in the larger society. Clarifying group boundaries, then, may foster both loyalty (to the ingroup) as well as social tension and conflict (with the outgroup).

Group Size

If you are among the first to arrive at a party, you can observe a fascinating process in group dynamics. Until about six people enter the room, everyone generally shares a single conversation. But as more people arrive, the group divides into two or more smaller clusters. The number of members in a group therefore influences how members socially interact.

To understand why, consider the mathematical connection between the number of people in a social group and the number of relationships among them, as shown in Figure 5–2. Two people create one relationship; adding a third person generates three relationships; a fourth person yields six. Adding people one at a time— a process mathematicians describe as an *arithmetic* increase—causes the number of relationships to increase rapidly—in what is called a *geometric progression*. By the time six people join one conversation, fifteen different relationships connect them, so the group usually divides at that point.

German sociologist Georg Simmel (1858–1918) explored the social dynamics of the smallest social groups. Simmel (1950; orig. 1902) used the term **dyad** (from the Greek word for "pair") to designate *a social group with two members*. In American society, love affairs, marriages, and the closest friendships are dyadic. Simmel identified two special qualities of the dyad. First, they

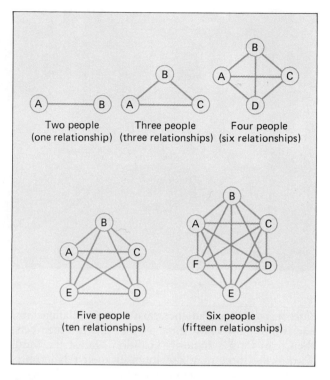

Figure 5–2 Group Size and Relationships

are typically less stable than groups with many members. Both members of a dyad must actively participate in the relationship; if either withdraws, the group dissipates. Because the stability of marriages is important to society, the potentially fragile bond between two spouses is reinforced with legal and often religious ties. In contrast, a large group is inherently more stable. A volunteer fire company, for example, does not collapse if a few members drop out.

Second, social interaction in a dyad is typically more intense than in other groups. In a one-to-one relationship, neither member shares the other's attention with anyone else. For this reason, dyads have the potential to be the most meaningful social bonds we ever experience. Because marriage in our culture is dyadic, powerful emotional ties generally unite wives and husbands. As we shall see in Chapter 12 ("Family and Religion"), however, marriage in many other societies involves more than two people. In such cases, the marriage is more stable although the strength of any one of the marital relationships may or may not be very strong.

Simmel also probed the **triad**—*a social group with*

A distinctive characteristic of a triad is that the social bond between two of the members can intensify, excluding the third.

three members. A triad encompasses three relationships, each uniting two of the three people. Any two members, then, can form a majority coalition against the third. Two of the three may also intensify their relationship, transforming the group into a dyad with a "third wheel." For example, two members of a triad who develop a romantic interest in each other are likely to understand the old saying "Two's company, three's a crowd."

A triad, however, is more stable than a dyad. If the relationship between any two of the group's members becomes strained, the third can act as a mediator to restore the group's vitality. Similarly, members of a dyad (such as a married couple) often seek out a third person (a trusted friend or counselor) to resolve tensions between them.

Social groups with more than three members allow for greater stability than triads, because even the loss of several members does not threaten the group's existence. Larger social groups usually develop formal rules and regulations that stabilize their operation. Yet, larger groups inevitably lack the intense personal interaction that is possible only in the smallest groups.

Does a social group have an ideal size? That depends on the group's purpose. A dyad offers unsurpassed emotional intensity, while a group of several dozen people will be more stable and capable of accomplishing larger, more complex tasks. In general, research suggests that moderate-sized groups of about five people are the most satisfying to group members. Smaller groups require much more effort from each person, and larger ones

are typically too impersonal (Slater, 1958; Ridgeway, 1983).

Networks

The term **network** refers to *a web of social ties that links people, often with little common identity and social interaction.* Like a social group, a network joins people in relationships. Unlike a social group, network members usually feel little sense of membership and have only occasional contact. The boundaries of networks are also less clear than those of groups. If a group can be thought of as a "circle of friends," then a network is better described as a "social web" expanding outward, with most members connected indirectly through others.

The social ties within networks may be close, as among people who attended college together and have since maintained friendships by mail and telephone. More commonly, networks involve secondary relationships. A social network may include people we *know of*—or who *know of us*—but with whom we interact infrequently, if at all. As one woman with a widespread reputation as a community organizer explains, "I get calls at home. Someone says, 'Are you Roseann Navarro? Somebody told me to call you. I have this problem . . .'" (Kaminer, 1984:94). For this reason, social networks have been described as "clusters of weak ties" (Granovetter, 1973).

A network serves as a resource. For example, many

people rely on networks to find jobs. Even the scientific genius Albert Einstein needed a hand in landing his first job. After a year of interviewing, he succeeded in obtaining employment only when the father of one of his classmates put him in touch with an office manager who hired him (Clark, 1971; cited in Fischer, 1977:19). As the saying goes, *who you know* is often just as important as *what you know*.

A survey by Nan Lin (1981) determined that almost 60 percent of 399 men in an urban area of the United States had used networks to find a job—more than any other single resource. He also found that networks do not provide equal advantages to everyone. Men whose fathers held important occupational positions gained the greatest advantages from networks. This finding underscores the commonly held belief that networks tend to link people of similar social background, thereby perpetuating social privilege.

Peter Marsden (1987) discovered that the most extensive social networks are maintained by those who are young, well educated, and living in urban areas. The networks of women and men tend to be the same size, although women include more relatives in their networks. Women's networks, as a result, may not carry the clout that the "old-boy" networks do. Therefore, women who work in settings where men outnumber them have begun to pay more attention to building occupational networks. Women's networks provide the support, camaraderie, and business contacts that women might otherwise lack (Speizer, 1983; Coppock, 1987).

FORMAL ORGANIZATIONS

A century ago, social life was centered in small groups— the family, friendship and working groups, and the local neighborhood. Today, our lives revolve far more around **formal organizations,** *large, secondary groups organized to achieve their goals efficiently.* Formal organizations, such as corporations or branches of government, differ from small family or friendship groups in more than simply their numbers. Their greater size makes social relationships less personal, and also fosters a planned or formal atmosphere. Formal organizations are designed to accomplish specific tasks, rather than to meet personal needs.

With a population exceeding 250 million, American society performs countless, complicated tasks ranging

from educating expectant parents to delivering the mail. Most of these are carried out by large, formal organizations. The United States government, the largest formal organization in America, employs more than 5 million people in various agencies and the armed forces. Each government agency includes many smaller organizations with specific goals. Such large groups develop lives and cultures of their own; as members come and go, then, the statuses they fill and the roles they perform remain unchanged over the years.

Types of Formal Organizations

Amitai Etzioni (1975) has identified three types of formal organizations, distinguished by the type of member affiliation—normative organizations, coercive organizations, and utilitarian organizations. *Normative organizations* pursue goals that their members consider morally worthwhile, offering personal satisfaction, perhaps social prestige, but no monetary reward to members. Sometimes called *voluntary associations*, these include community service groups (such as the PTA, the Lions Club, the League of Women Voters, and the Red Cross), political parties, religious organizations, and numerous other confederations concerned with specific social issues. Because women have historically been excluded from much of the paid labor force, they have traditionally played a greater part than men in civic and charitable organizations.

In Etzioni's typology, *coercive organizations* are distinguished by involuntary members (that is, members have no choice in the matter) who are subjected to punishment (a prison) or treatment (a psychiatric hospital). Coercive organizations have extraordinary physical features, such as locked doors, barred windows, and security personnel (Goffman, 1961). They are designed to segregate people as "inmates" or "patients" for a period of time, and sometimes radically alter people's attitudes and behavior. Recall from Chapter 3 ("Socialization: From Infancy to Aging") the power of coercive total institutions to transform a human being's overall sense of self.

According to Etzioni, *utilitarian organizations* bestow material benefits on their members. Large business enterprises, for example, generate profits for their owners and income in the form of salaries and wages for their employees. Joining utilitarian organizations is usually a matter of individual choice, although, obviously, most people must join one utilitarian organization or another

Although formal organization is a central part of modern societies, it is far from new. Twenty-five centuries ago, the Chinese philosopher and teacher K'ung Fu-tzu (known to Westerners as Confucius) endorsed the notion that government offices should be staffed by the most talented young men. This led to a system of civil service examinations. Here, would-be bureaucrats compose essays to demonstrate their knowledge of Confucian texts.

to make a living. While utilitarian organizations offer greater individual freedom than coercive organizations, they provide less autonomy than normative organizations. Membership in utilitarian organizations is generally full time and may last for many years, sometimes for a person's entire working life.

From differing vantage points, a formal organization may fall into *all* of these categories. A psychiatric hospital, for example, serves as a coercive organization for a patient, a utilitarian organization for a psychiatrist, and a normative organization for a part-time hospital volunteer.

Origins of Bureaucracy

Formal organizations date back thousands of years. Religious and political administration was used to extend the control of elites over millions of people living in vast areas. Formal organizations also allowed rulers to undertake monumental tasks never before possible, such as building the Great Wall that stretches for some three thousand miles across China.

The effectiveness of these early organizations was limited, however. This was not because elites lacked ambition; rather, it was due to the traditional character of preindustrial societies. The influential German sociologist Max Weber claimed that **tradition,** referring to *sentiments and beliefs about the world that are passed from generation to generation,* guided the world view of preindustrial societies. In a traditional society, human thought and action strongly reflected the past. Therefore, people in the preindustrial world tended to believe a social pattern was right and proper precisely because it had existed for so long. Under such circumstances, Weber reasoned, organizational efficiency was a minor concern.

Modern society, by contrast, encourages the expansion of formal organization. Weber described the contemporary world view as one guided by **rationality,** *deliberate, matter-of-fact calculation of the most efficient means to accomplish any particular task.* In a rational world view, which takes a largely indifferent stance toward the past, tradition tends to be simply a form of information without any special claims on individuals. Patterns of traditional thought and behavior are adopted only on the basis of their utility in the present. As members of modern societies, we tend to evaluate our jobs, our schooling, and even our relationships by means of a "cost-benefit" analysis that weighs what we contribute to them in relation to what we hope they provide us in return.

Thus the key to the "organizational society" lies in the process Weber termed **rationalization,** *the change from tradition to rationality as the dominant mode of human thought.* Modern society, he contended, became "disenchanted" as sentimental ties to the past gave way to greater reliance on scientific thinking and advancing technology. In response to this profound change in cultural patterns, and further sparked by technological innovations associated with the Industrial Revolution, the form of organizational structure called *bureaucracy* rapidly developed in Europe and North America during the last several centuries.

Characteristics of Bureaucracy

Bureaucracy is *an organizational model rationally designed to perform complex tasks efficiently.* Through bureaucratic organization, officials formulate and modify policy to make the organization as efficient as possible. To appreciate the power and scope of bureaucratic organization, consider the telephone system in the United States. Each of over 150 million telephones can be used to reach any other telephone (and millions more through-

out the entire world) at any time within seconds. This major technological feat reaches far beyond the imagination of the ancient world. We cannot overlook technological developments such as electricity on which the telephone system depends. But equally important is the organizational capacity to keep track of every telephone call—noting which phone was used to call which other phone, when, and for how long—and presenting all this information to millions of telephone users in the form of a monthly bill. A task of this kind clearly requires a complex form of organizational structure.

What characteristics promote organizational efficiency? Max Weber (1978; orig. 1921) identified six elements of the ideal bureaucratic organization.

1. **Specialization.** Through most of human history, people's lives centered on securing food and shelter. Bureaucracy differs by assigning people highly specialized tasks that correspond to organizational offices.

2. **Hierarchy of offices.** Bureaucratic offices are arranged vertically to form a hierarchy, according to their responsibilities. Each person is thus supervised by "higher-ups" in the organization while, in turn, supervising others in lower positions.

3. **Rules and regulations.** Tradition plays little part in bureaucracy. Instead, operations are guided by rationally enacted rules and regulations. These guide not only the organization's own functioning but, as much as possible, seek to control its larger environment. Ideally, a bureaucracy seeks to operate in a completely predictable fashion.

4. **Technical competence.** Bureaucratic officials are expected to have the technical competence needed to carry out the duties of their offices. Bureaucracies typically evaluate new staff members according to set criteria and subsequently monitor their performance. This practice of impersonal evaluation based on performance contrasts sharply with the custom, followed through most of human history, of favoring relatives—whatever their talents—over strangers.

5. **Impersonality.** In bureaucratic organizations, rules take precedence over personal feelings. Ideally, this ensures the uniform treatment of each client, supervisor, or subordinate. From this detached approach stems the notion of the "faceless bureaucrat."

6. **Formal, written communications.** An old adage

suggests that the heart of bureaucracy is not people but paperwork. Rather than casual, verbal communication, bureaucracy demands formal, written letters, memos, and reports. Over time, this correspondence accumulates into vast *files*. Such documents guide an organization in roughly the same way that personality guides an individual.

Bureaucracy versus Small Groups

Small groups, especially primary groups like the family, are valuable for what they *are*. By contrast, the value of bureaucratic organizations lies in what they *do*. As a path of efficient performance, bureaucracy serves as a means to an end.

Bureaucratic organization works to promote effi-

ciency by carefully recruiting personnel and limiting the variable and unpredictable effects of personal tastes and opinions. In smaller, informal groups, members have considerable discretion in their personal behavior, respond to each other personally, and are more or less equal in rank. Weber believed, however, that such traits compromised organizational efficiency; thus he advocated in their place a rigid and impersonal organizational system. Table 5–2 summarizes differences between small social groups and large formal organizations.

The Informal Side of Bureaucracy

In Weber's ideal bureaucracy, every activity is deliberately regulated. In actual organizations, however, human behavior often diverges from organizational rules. Sometimes informality helps to meet a legitimate need overlooked by regulations. In other situations, such as cutting corners in one's job, informal behavior undermines organizational operation (Scott, 1981). In any case, bureaucratic blueprints are not always observed in actual operations; large organizations, therefore, can also be viewed as *natural systems* responsive to their members and the larger environment.

Personality, for example, greatly affects patterns of organizational leadership. Formally, power resides in offices, not with the people who occupy them. Studies of American corporations reveal, however, that the qualities and quirks of individuals—including their charisma or skill in interpersonal relations—have a tremendous impact on organizational outcomes (Halberstam, 1986). Although many have held the post of president of the Soviet Union, Mikhail Gorbachev's personal leadership skills—his ability to manage (or manipulate) others—clearly have led to significant restructuring of Soviet society.

Authoritarian, democratic, and laissez-faire types of leadership—described earlier in this chapter—also reflect individual personality as much as any organizational plan. Then, too, decision making in an organization does not always conform to the defined hierarchy and the official regulations. As the recent savings and loan scandal reveals, officials and their friends may personally benefit from abuse of organizational power. In the "real world" of organizational life, officials who attempt to operate strictly by the book may even find themselves denied promotions and power, which are often based on informal alliances. In many organizations, too, people

Table 5–2 SMALL GROUPS AND FORMAL ORGANIZATIONS: A COMPARISON

	Small Groups	Formal Organizations
Activities	Members typically engage in many of the same activities	Members typically engage in various highly specialized activities
Hierarchy	Often informal or nonexistent	Clearly defined, corresponding to offices
Norms	Informal application of general norms	Clearly defined rules and regulations
Criteria for membership	Variable, often based on personal affection or kinship	Technical competence to carry out assigned tasks
Relationships	Variable; typically primary	Typically secondary, with selective primary ties
Communications	Typically casual and face to face	Typically formal and in writing
Focus	Person oriented	Task oriented

An organization's formal hierarchy is often modified according to personal preferences and abilities. In the popular television show *M*A*S*H*, Radar O'Reilly was only an army corporal, but he was largely responsible for keeping the outfit running smoothly.

in leadership positions rely on subordinates to handle much of their own work. Many secretaries, for example, have more authority and responsibility than their official job titles and salaries suggest.

Communication offers another example of organizational informality. Formally, memos and other written communications disseminate information through the hierarchy. Typically, however, individuals cultivate informal networks or "grapevines" that spread information much faster, if not always as accurately. Grapevines are particularly important to subordinates because executives often attempt to conceal important information from them.

Sometimes employees of formal organizations modify or ignore rigid bureaucratic structures to assert their individuality or to advance their own interests. A classic study of the Western Electric factory in Chicago revealed that few workers reported fellow workers who violated rules, as they were required to (Roethlisberger & Dickson, 1939). On the contrary, those who *did* were socially isolated, labeled by other workers as "squealers" who could not be trusted. Although the company formally set productivity standards, workers also informally created their own definition of a fair day's work, criticizing those who exceeded it as "rate-busters" and others who fell short as "chiselers."

Such informal social structures suggest that many people reject the dehumanizing aspects of bureaucratic organization. But these informal structures also show that human beings have the creative capacity to humanize even the most rigidly defined social situations.

Limitations of Bureaucracy

Weber touted the ideal bureaucracy as a model of efficiency. Still, real-life formal organizations certainly have their limitations, even when it comes to task performance. Anyone who has ever tried to replace a lost driver's license, return defective merchandise to a discount chain store, or change an address on a magazine subscription knows that large organizations can be maddeningly unresponsive to individual needs.

Some of these problems occur because organizations are *not* truly bureaucratic. Furthermore, no organizational system will ever completely eradicate human failings. But, as Weber himself recognized, the pure form of bureaucracy has inherent limitations. Perhaps the most serious problem is bureaucracy's potential to *dehumanize* those it purports to serve. To operate efficiently, each client must be treated impersonally as a standard "case." In other words, in striving for efficiency, organization members lose the ability to really *know* their clients or customers by providing individual attention.

Weber also feared that bureaucratic impersonality would *alienate* those who worked in large organizations. He described the bureaucrat as "a small cog in a ceaselessly moving mechanism" (1978:988; orig. 1921). Although formal organizations are intended to serve humanity, Weber worried that humanity would eventually serve formal organizations.

The ambivalence of many Americans toward bureaucracy, then, comes as no surprise. On the one hand, formal organizations advance many dominant American values, noted in Chapter 2 ("Culture"), including efficiency, practicality, and achievement. On the other hand, bureaucracies threaten the cherished ideals of democracy and individual freedom. Bureaucratic organizations affect our lives in countless ways, yet we have little sense of participation in their operation. In addition, the growth of formal organizations has prompted a decline in individual privacy (Long, 1967; Smith, 1979). The box provides details.

Bureaucratic waste and incompetence. *"Work expands to fill the time available for its completion."* Enough truth underlies C. Northcote Parkinson's (1957) tongue-in-cheek assertion that it is known today as Parkinson's Law.

To illustrate, assume that a bureaucrat processes fifty applications in an average day. If one day this worker had only twenty-five applications to examine, how much time will the task require? The logical answer is half a day; but Parkinson's Law suggests that if a full day is available to complete the work, a full day is how long it will take. Because they are rarely rewarded for efficiency, few members of formal organizations seek extra work to fill any spare time. Bureaucrats strive to *appear* busy, however, prompting organizations to take on more employees. The added time and expense required to hire, train, supervise, and evaluate a larger staff makes everyone busier still, setting in motion a vicious cycle that results in *bureaucratic bloat*. Ironically, the larger organization may accomplish no more real work than it did before.

Laurence J. Peter (Peter & Hull, 1969) devised the Peter Principle, which states that *bureaucrats are*

CRITICAL THINKING

Bureaucracy: A Threat to Personal Privacy?

A century ago, personal privacy in the United States consisted of building a fence around one's house and hanging a "Beware of Dog" sign on the gate. Today, however, fences and dogs do little to protect us from some kinds of intrusions. More people now have access to more information about each one of us than ever before.

Why? Because of the growth of formal organizations. Without a doubt, bureaucracy is essential to a vast and complex society, but the cost is ever-enlarging banks of personal information. Automobile drivers must be licensed, but doing so requires gathering information about everyone who legally operates a vehicle. The Internal Revenue Service, the Social Security Administration, and programs that benefit veterans, students, the poor, and unemployed people must each collect extensive information.

The explosive growth of credit in the American economy has also fueled the drive for information. In the past, local merchants offered credit to customers with no more paperwork than an I.O.U. Today, Americans carry almost 1 billion credit cards, enabling them to receive credit from total strangers.

This information revolution has spawned a new business: maintaining files about people's place of residence, marital status, employment, income, debts, and history of paying their bills on time. Further eroding personal privacy, computers now disseminate information more widely and more rapidly than ever before. Because addresses can easily be added to mailing lists, most Americans are now deluged by so-called junk mail. Of greater concern, that information circulates among organizations of all kinds, generally without the knowledge or consent of the people in question.

Many states have responded by giving citizens the right to examine records kept about them by employers, banks, and credit bureaus. The U.S. Privacy Act of 1974 also places limitations on government agencies seeking to exchange information about individuals. Additionally, citizens now can inspect the information contained in most government files, and they may offer corrections that become part of the record.

Such laws have limited, but are unlikely to reverse, the erosion of personal privacy. The price of relying on formal organizations may be the sacrifice of much personal privacy.

SOURCE: Based on Robert Ellis Smith, *Personal Privacy: How to Protect What's Left of It* (Garden City, NY: Anchor/Doubleday, 1979).

promoted to their level of incompetence. The logic here is simple: Employees competent at any level of the organizational hierarchy are likely to be promoted to higher positions. Eventually, however, when they reach a position where they are in over their heads and perform poorly, they no longer are eligible for promotion. They are thereby doomed to a future of inefficiency. Adding to the problem, by this time they have almost certainly acquired enough power to protect their interests, avoiding demotion or dismissal by hiding behind rules and regulations and taking credit for work actually performed by their more competent subordinates.

Bureaucratic ritualism. For many Americans, the term *bureaucracy* conjures up images of *red tape* (derived from the red tape used by eighteenth-century English officials to wrap parcels and records; Shipley, 1985). Red tape refers to a tedious concern with organizational procedures. In Robert Merton's view (1968), red tape is one type of group conformity. He coined the term **bureaucratic ritualism** to signify *a preoccupation with rules and regulations as ends in themselves rather than as the means to organizational goals.* Bureaucratic ritualism occurs when people become so intent on conforming to rules that they thwart the goals of the organization. Besides reducing individual and organizational performance, ritualism stifles creativity and imagination, robbing the organization of the talents, dynamic ideas, and innovative

approaches necessary to operate efficiently as circumstances change (Whyte, 1957; Merton, 1968). In bureaucratic ritualism, we see one form of the alienation that Max Weber feared would arise from bureaucratic rigidity.

Bureaucratic inertia. Weber noted that "once fully established, bureaucracy is among the social structures which are hardest to destroy" (1978:987; orig. 1921). Through **bureaucratic inertia,** *the tendency of bureaucratic organizations to persist over time,* formal organizations tend to take on a life of their own and to perpetuate themselves. Occasionally, a formal organization that meets its organizational goals will simply disband—as the anti-British Sons of Liberty did after the American Revolution. More commonly, however, an organization redefines its goals so it can continue to provide a livelihood for its members. The National Association for Infantile Paralysis, the sponsor of the well-known March of Dimes, was created to help find a cure for polio. After the development of the Salk vaccine in the early 1950s, the organization did not dissolve but simply redirected its efforts toward other medical problems such as birth defects (Sills, 1969). It still exists today.

Once created, then, formal organizations may remain in operation whether or not they have any meaningful purpose. "Sunset laws," widely enacted in the United States, require government agencies that cannot justify their existence to be terminated. In Illinois, for example,

George Tooker's painting *Government Bureau* is a powerful statement about the human costs of bureaucracy whereby human beings are reduced to "cases" and "officials" devoid of personal distinctiveness. Note the sameness of all the people seeking assistance, how no complete faces are shown, and the bland uniformity of the setting.

George Tooker, Government Bureau, 1956. *Egg tempera on gesso panel. 19⅝ × 29⅝ inches. The Metropolitan Museum of Art, George A. Hearn Fund, 1956. (56.78).*

officials with the responsibility to review the qualifications of people who shoe horses were finally relieved of their duties decades after their usefulness had ceased. Despite such examples, bureaucratic inertia usually leads formal organizations to devise justifications for themselves long after they have outlived their originally intended purpose.

Oligarchy

Early in this century, Robert Michels (1876–1936) pointed out that bureaucracy encourages **oligarchy**, *the rule of the many by the few* (1949; orig. 1911). The earliest human societies did not possess the organizational means for even the most power-hungry ruler to control everyone. The development of more complex formal organizations, however, enhanced the opportunities for a small elite to dominate society. According to what Michels called "the iron law of oligarchy," the pyramid-like structure of bureaucracy places a few leaders in charge of entire government organizations.

Weber credited bureaucracy's strict hierarchy of responsibility for increasing organizational efficiency. Applying Weber's thesis to the organization of government, Michels added that this hierarchical model also discourages democracy. While organization officials are expected to subordinate personal interests to organizational goals, people who occupy powerful positions in government can—and often do—use their access to information, opportunity to influence others, and numerous other advantages to promote their personal interests. Such abuse of power goes on largely hidden from the public, undermining society's control over its elected leaders.

Sociologists have documented the prevalence of oligarchy in formal organizations (Lipset, Trow, & Coleman, 1977). Political competition and governmental checks and balances in the American system of government prevent the flagrant practice of oligarchy found in less democratic societies. Even so, among national office-holders, for example, incumbents enjoy far greater access to the mass media and receive more financial support than challengers do. In 1990, all but one incumbent senator was returned to office by the voters. But even the most entrenched oligarchs are not immune to forces of political change. In recent years, anti-government drives succeeded in the overthrow of the Marcos regime in the Philippines and the Somoza oligarchy in Nicaragua, as well as the popular uprisings that toppled Communist regimes in Eastern Europe.

Gender and Race in Organizations

Rosabeth Moss Kanter (1977; Kanter & Stein, 1979) has analyzed how ascribed statuses such as gender and race figure in the power structures of bureaucratic hierarchies. To the extent that an organization has a dominant social composition, the gender- or race-based ingroup enjoys greater social acceptance, respect, credibility, and access to informal social networks. In American society, the most powerful positions are generally held by well-to-do white men. By contrast, women, nonwhites, and those from economically disadvantaged backgrounds sometimes feel like part of socially isolated outgroups. Often uncomfortably visible, they are taken less seriously and have lower chances of promotion than others. These people generally believe that they must work twice as hard as those in dominant categories to maintain their present position, let alone advance to a higher position.

Kanter finds that providing greater power and opportunity to some members of formal organizations has important consequences for everyone's on-the-job performance. Beyond the popular wisdom that employees who get ahead are smart and "hustle" while those who do not are less able and less motivated, Kanter's (1977) research indicates that the *organizational environment* greatly influences employee performance.

The opportunity to advance is a key dimension of the organizational environment. According to Kanter, organizations that offer everyone a chance for promotion typically turn employees into "fast-trackers," raising their aspirations, self-esteem, and commitment to the organization. By contrast, "dead-end" jobs produce only "zombies" with little aspiration, poor self-concept, and little loyalty to the organization.

Kanter claims that power and opportunity encourage people to be flexible leaders who build the morale of others, including subordinates. By contrast, those holding positions of little power often jealously guard what privileges they do have, rigidly supervising subordinates. Table 5–3 summarizes Kanter's findings. In Kanter's view, organizations must "humanize" their structure to bring out the best in their employees and improve the "bottom line."

"Humanizing" Bureaucracy

"Humanizing" bureaucracy means *fostering an organizational environment that develops human resources.* Re-

Table 5-3 KANTER'S RESEARCH: A SUMMARY

	Advantaged Employees	Disadvantaged Employees
Social composition	Being represented in high proportions helps employees to more easily fit in and to enjoy greater credibility; they experience less stress, and are usually candidates for promotion	Being represented in low proportions puts employees visibly "on display" and results in their not being taken seriously; they tend to fear making mistakes and losing ground rather than optimistically looking toward advancement
Power	In powerful positions, employees contribute to high morale and support subordinates; such employees tend to be more democratic leaders	In positions of low power, employees tend to foster low morale and restrict opportunities for subordinates to advance; they tend to be more authoritarian leaders
Opportunity	High opportunity encourages optimism and high aspirations, loyalty to organization, use of higher-ups as reference groups, and constructive responses to problems	Low opportunity encourages pessimism and low aspirations, weak attachment to the job, use of peers as reference groups, and ineffective griping in response to problems

SOURCE: Based on Rosabeth Moss Kanter, *Men and Women of the Corporation* (New York: Basic Books, 1977), pp. 246–249.

search by Kanter (1977, 1983, 1989; Kanter & Stein, 1980) and others (cf. Peters & Waterman, Jr., 1982) shows that "humanizing" bureaucracy produces both happier employees and healthier profits. Based on the discussion so far, we can identify three paths to a more humane organizational environment:

1. **Social inclusiveness.** The social composition of the organization should make no one feel "out of place" because of gender, race, or ethnicity. The performance of all employees will improve to the extent that no one is subject to social exclusion.

2. **Sharing of responsibilities.** "Humanizing" bureaucracy means reducing rigid, oligarchical structures by spreading power and responsibility more widely. Managers cannot benefit from the ideas of employees who have no channels for expressing their opinions. Knowing that superiors are open to suggestions encourages all employees to think creatively, increasing organizational effectiveness.

3. **Expanding opportunities for advancement.** Expanding opportunity reduces the number of employees stuck in routine, dead-end jobs with little motivation to perform well. Employees at all levels, therefore, should be encouraged to share ideas and to try new approaches, and no position should be ruled out as the start of an upward career path.

Critical evaluation.   Kanter's work provides a fresh look at the concept of bureaucracy and its application to business organizations. Rigid formality may have made sense in the past, when uneducated organizational employees were hired simply as a source of physical labor. But today, workers can contribute a wealth of ideas to bolster organizational efficiency if the organizational environment encourages and rewards innovation.

Although Kanter's suggested changes may not be popular with everyone, such efforts are likely to produce significant returns. Comparing forty-seven rigidly bureaucratic companies to competitors of similar size but with more flexible organizational structures, Kanter (1983) found that flexibility increased profits. She argues, therefore, that bureaucratic structure limits an organization's success to the extent that it treats employees as a group to be controlled rather than as a resource to be developed. Thus, while the basic bureaucratic model may still promote efficiency, organizational effectiveness is enhanced by flexible management styles, coupled with efforts to disseminate power and promote opportunity throughout the organization (Kanter, 1985).

Bureaucracy: The Japanese Case

We can gain a better understanding of bureaucracy in America by comparing American organizational struc-

Japan is a fascinating blend of the old and the new. Traditional loyalties and patterns of deference—of the young toward the old and women toward men—are now displayed in the workplace. The corporation's responsibilities toward employees are also modeled on traditional family life.

tures with organizational patterns in Japan. Americans have focused considerable attention on organizations in this small society, which has experienced remarkable economic success. Since the end of World War II, Japan's economic growth has surged five times faster than America's. Although geographically no larger than the state of Montana, Japan's gross national product in 1990 was more than one-third that of the United States.

Formal organizations in Japan reflect that culture's strong traditions of collective identity and social solidarity. This cohesiveness results in relatively low levels of social problems—such as alcoholism, violence, and drug abuse—compared to more rootless and competitive societies like the United States. Japanese cities also lack the abject poverty and crime found in much of urban America: Even late at night, a person can walk safely through downtown Tokyo (Ouchi, 1981).

This social solidarity makes Japanese organizations extremely large primary groups. In the United States, by comparison, although a few companies have tried to model themselves on Japanese organizational principles, even "humanized" bureaucracy has many more secondary relationships. Indeed, as the box suggests, American workers often oppose highly personal Japanese policies.

William Ouchi (1981) highlights five distinctions between formal organizations in Japan and their counterparts in industrial societies of the West. In each case, the Japanese organization reflects a more collective orientation.

1. **Hiring and advancement.** In American organizations, promotions and higher salaries are prizes won through individual competition. In Japanese

organizations, however, new school graduates are hired together as a group and receive comparable salaries and responsibilities. As one employee moves ahead, so do they all. Only after many years is anyone likely to be singled out for special advancement. This corporate or collective approach generates a common identity among employees of the same age.

2. **Lifetime security.** American employees rarely remain with one company for their entire careers; rather, we expect to move from one company to another in pursuit of personal goals. American companies are also quick to lay off workers when economic setbacks strike. By contrast, Japanese companies typically hire employees for life, so companies and their employees have strong, mutual loyalties. Then, too, Japanese workers who spend years learning one organization's system may be unattractive to other firms. Japanese companies, moreover, avoid layoffs by providing workers with other jobs in the organization, along with any necessary retraining.

3. **Holistic involvement.** In the United States, work and private lives are usually distinct. Japanese organizations differ by playing a broader role in their employees' lives. Companies often provide dormitory housing or mortgages for the purchase of homes, sponsor recreational activities, and schedule a wide range of social events in which workers participate. Employee interaction outside the workplace strengthens collective identity, while offering the respectful Japanese worker an opportunity to more readily voice suggestions and criticisms.

4. **Nonspecialized training.** Bureaucratic organization in the United States is based on specialization; a person's entire career often has a single focus. From the outset, a Japanese organization trains employees in all phases of its operation, with the expectation that employees will remain with the organization for life. Ideally, this nonspecialized training helps workers understand how each job relates to the organization's overall operation. As a result, Japanese workers generally have more technical knowledge than their American counterparts (Sengoku, 1985). Broad training also enables the company to move employees from job to job more easily as circumstances dictate.

5. **Collective decision making.** Most major decisions in American organizations are made by a handful

CROSS-CULTURAL COMPARISON

The Japanese Model: Will It Work in America?

What the company wants is for us to work like the Japanese. Everybody go out and do jumping jacks in the morning and kiss each other when they go home at night. You work as a team, rat on each other, and lose control of your destiny. That's not going to work in this country.

John Brodie
President, United Paperworkers
   Local 448
Chester, Pennsylvania

Who can quarrel with the economic success of the Japanese? Increasing economic competition from Asia and Europe has forced American companies to consider novel techniques for involving their workers in day-to-day decision making. Yet some voices in the American workplace—workers, union leaders, and managers—have been no happier about importing Japanese organizational techniques than about importing Japanese cars.

There is little doubt that the Japanese model *could* be applied to the American workplace. Japanese companies, including Honda, Nissan, and Toyota, operate manufacturing plants in the United States and use American workers to achieve the same degree of efficiency and quality that they do in Japan. However, American corporate culture, with its hierarchy, its heritage of individualism, and its history of labor-management conflict, makes proposals for greater worker participation highly controversial.

Many American workers dislike worker participation because they see it as increasing their personal workload. While still responsible for building cars, for instance, workers are now asked to worry about quality control, unit costs, and overall company efficiency—tasks traditionally shouldered by management. At the extreme, Japanese-style policies require workers to learn about the operation of the entire company. Moreover, some American employees do not want to move from job to job, acquiring new skills that they may or may not master. Union leaders, too, are suspicious of new plans formulated by management, even those purporting to share power. American labor unions themselves introduced the idea of worker participation more than fifty years ago. Today, though, union leaders are wary that any alliance of workers and managers may undermine union strength, which has been declining steadily in recent decades (see Chapter 11, "Economics and Politics"). Some managers, too, have been slow to adopt worker participation programs; sharing with lower-level employees the power to procure supplies, direct production, and even schedule their own vacations does not come easily in light of past practices. Finally, in an age of corporate takeovers and short-term profits, those who control businesses may not wish to invest the time and money in this kind of reorganization.

Nonetheless, worker-participation programs are changing the American workplace. A recent government survey found that, despite reservations and outright resistance, about 70 percent of large American businesses had initiated some program of this kind. The advantages go right to the bottom line: Productivity and profits are usually higher when workers have a say in decision making. And most employees in worker-participation programs—even those who balk at signing up for morning jumping jacks—seem significantly happier about their jobs. Workers who have long used only their bodies are now enjoying the chance to use their brains as well.

SOURCE: Based on John Hoerr, "The Payoff from Teamwork," *Business Week*, No. 3114 (July 10, 1989):56–62.

of executives. Exemplifying this cultural pattern was the well-known sign on the desk of President Harry Truman: "The buck stops here." Although leaders of Japanese organizations also take responsibility for their company's performance, they involve workers in every decision that affects them. A closer working relationship is also encouraged by comparatively greater economic equality between management and workers: The salary differential between Japanese executives and workers is about half that found in the United States. Additionally, Japanese companies typically encompass many semiautonomous working groups, called "quality circles." Instead of responding simply to the directives of superiors, all employees in Japan share managerial responsibilities.

These characteristics give the Japanese a strong sense of organizational loyalty. The cultural emphasis on *individual* achievement in American society finds its parallel in Japanese *groupism*. By tying their personal interests to those of the organization, workers realize ambitions through the organization.

FORMAL ORGANIZATIONS AND SOCIETY

In recent years, the study of formal organizations has expanded from the organizations themselves to include the *social environment* in which they operate. Surely cultural factors account for many of the differences between formal organizations in the United States and in Japan. In addition, formal organizations everywhere change along with their environments.

As Ouchi (1981:62–64) explains, Max Weber's analysis of bureaucracy was rooted in nineteenth-century Europe, where most businesses were still small family undertakings. Primary social relationships predominated, but many people agreed with Weber that such ties (often criticized as nepotism and personal favoritism) undermined organizational efficiency. Weber's model of bureaucracy, now well-entrenched in European and North American societies, therefore focused on impersonal, secondary relationships emphasizing technical specialization, impartiality, and behavior strictly guided by rules and regulations.

In Japan, formal organizations also developed within a socially cohesive society. But formal organizations in Japan did not undermine primary relationships as they did in the West; rather, as Japan has modernized, traditional loyalties to family and locality have been largely *transferred to corporations*. In this way, the Japanese remain at once traditional and modern, using personal social ties as an organizational resource to promote efficiency. In recent years, many Japanese workers have become more individualistic; some are leaving the big industrial corporations, lured by higher salaries to newer financial organizations. Yet the Japanese model still reveals that organizational life need not be impersonal.

The startling Japanese economic advancement prompted Americans to take a closer look at their way of doing things and to "humanize" bureaucracy in the United States. However, calls for greater worker participation in decision making do not always earn high marks from American workers.

Beyond the benefits for American business organizations, there is another reason to study the Japanese approach carefully. American society is now less socially cohesive than the more family-based society Weber knew. A rigidly bureaucratic form of organization encourages further atomization of society. Perhaps by following the lead of the Japanese, our own formal organizations can promote—rather than diminish—a sense of collective identity and responsibility. While bolstering productivity, then, organizational reform may also foster the integration of society.

SUMMARY

1. Social groups are important building blocks of societies that foster common identity and guide patterns of interaction.
2. Primary groups tend to be small and person-oriented; secondary groups are typically large and goal-oriented.
3. Instrumental leadership concentrates on a group's goals; expressive leadership focuses on the members' collective well-being.
4. The process of group conformity is well documented by researchers. Because members often seek consensus, groups do not necessarily generate

a wider range of ideas than individuals working alone.

5. Individuals use reference groups—both ingroups and outgroups—to make decisions and evaluations.

6. Georg Simmel argued that dyads have a distinctive intensity but lack stability because of the effort necessary to maintain them. A triad can easily dissolve into a dyad by excluding one member.

7. Social networks are grouplike relational webs whose members usually have little common identity and sporadic interaction.

8. Formal organizations are large, secondary groups that seek to perform complex tasks efficiently. Depending on their members' reasons for joining, formal organizations can be classified as normative, coercive, or utilitarian.

9. Bureaucratic organization expands in modern societies and allows the efficient performance of many complex tasks.

10. Bureaucracy is based on specialization, hierarchy, rules and regulations, technical competence, impersonal interaction, and formal, written communications.

11. The limitations of bureaucracy include the inability to deal efficiently with special cases, depersonalizing the workplace, and fostering ritualism among some employees. Max Weber also recognized that bureaucracy resists change.

12. Formal organizations are often oligarchies. Rosabeth Moss Kanter's research has shown that the concentration of power and opportunity in American corporations tends to diminish organizational effectiveness.

13. "Humanizing" bureaucracy means recognizing that people are an organization's greatest resource. To develop human resources, the organizational environment must reduce the significance of ascribed statuses such as gender and race, spread decision-making power more widely, and broaden opportunity.

14. Formal organizations in Japan differ from the Western, bureaucratic model because of the collective spirit of Japanese culture. Formal organizations in Japan are based on more personal ties than their counterparts in the United States.

KEY CONCEPTS

bureaucracy an organizational model rationally designed to perform complex tasks efficiently

bureaucratic inertia the tendency of bureaucratic organizations to persist over time

bureaucratic ritualism a preoccupation with organizational rules and regulations as ends in themselves rather than as the means to organizational goals

dyad a social group with two members

expressive leadership group leadership that emphasizes collective well-being

formal organization a large, secondary group that is organized to achieve its goals efficiently

"groupthink" a reduced capacity for critical thinking caused by group conformity

"humanizing" bureaucracy fostering an organizational environment that develops human resources

ingroup an esteemed social group commanding a member's loyalty

instrumental leadership group leadership that emphasizes the completion of tasks

network a web of social ties that links people, often with little common identity and social interaction

oligarchy the rule of the many by the few

outgroup a scorned social group toward which one feels competition or opposition

primary group typically a small social group in which relationships are both personal and enduring

rationality deliberate, matter-of-fact calculation of the most efficient means to accomplish any particular task

rationalization Max Weber's term for the change from tradition to rationality as the dominant mode of human thought

reference group a social group that serves as a point of reference for people making evaluations and decisions

secondary group typically a large and impersonal social group based on some special interest or activity

social group two or more people who identify with one another and have a distinctive pattern of interaction

tradition sentiments and beliefs about the world that are passed from generation to generation

triad a social group with three members

Deviance

6

Chapter Outline

In 1984, a twenty-seven-year-old member of the Revolutionary Communist Youth Brigade named Gregory L. Johnson traveled to Houston, Texas, and staged a political protest outside the hall where the Republican National Convention was being held. Assisted by other demonstrators, Johnson tore down a nearby American flag, soaked it in lighter fluid, set it on fire, and as it went up in flames chanted, "America—the red, white, and blue; we spit on you!" For his part in the episode, Johnson was convicted of violating a Texas law against defiling the flag, was fined $2,000, and was sentenced to one year in prison. He appealed his conviction. In 1989, in a 5–4 decision, the Supreme Court ruled that the First Amendment to the American Constitution, which guarantees the right to free speech, protects the burning of the flag as a form of political protest.

This decision sparked an even greater furor. Many Americans blasted the ruling, outraged that such contempt for Old Glory—a symbol of our nation—could be protected by the law. The Senate expressed its "profound disappointment" with the court's action, and President George Bush suggested that the Constitution be amended to negate the High Court's stand. Public opinion surveys ran three to one against the Court.

The Johnson case reached deep into the heart of the timeless tension between deviance and conformity. On the one hand, we voice a passionate desire to support American principles by denouncing such an attack on them. On the other hand, we honor the flag precisely by tolerating those who dishonor it. This latter view was expressed by Justice William J. Brennan, writing for the majority of the Court: "If there is a bedrock principle underlying the First Amendment, it is that the Government may not prohibit the expression of an idea simply because society finds the idea itself offensive or disagreeable" (Isaacson, 1989; Jacoby, 1989).

This chapter examines the ways in which societies specify what is "offensive or disagreeable." How and why does deviance arise? What happens when competing views of right and wrong collide? Are all people who violate norms defined as deviant? Why do legal standards sometimes clash with public opinion? We begin to answer these questions by defining several basic concepts.

WHAT IS DEVIANCE?

Deviance is *the recognized violation of cultural norms.* Norms shape a wide range of human activities, and so the concept of deviance covers a correspondingly broad

spectrum. One familiar type of deviance is **crime,** *the violation of norms formally enacted into criminal law.* Even criminal deviance varies widely, ranging from minor traffic violations to serious offenses such as rape and murder. **Juvenile delinquency,** *the violation of legal standards that apply to the young,* forms a special category of crime.

Deviance encompasses many other types of nonconformity as well, some of which are viewed as mild (left-handedness, boastfulness, and Mohawk hairstyles), while others are defined as more serious (mental illness and violent political protest). To some who are in the majority, those belonging to a racial or ethnic minority may seem deviant. In addition, the poor—who may find it difficult to conform to many conventional middle-class patterns—are also widely defined as deviant. Even some physical traits may be considered deviant. Men with many highly visible tattoos may court criticism; women with any tattoo at all may bear the brunt of society's disapproval as well. Being unusually tall or short, or grossly fat or exceedingly thin, may brand a person as deviant. Physical disabilities serve as yet another reason some people are defined as nonconforming.

Deviance exists in relation to any and all normative patterns. Because many societies have traditional conceptions of femininity involving softness and submissiveness, women who develop their physical strength—and especially women body-builders—may be viewed as deviant.

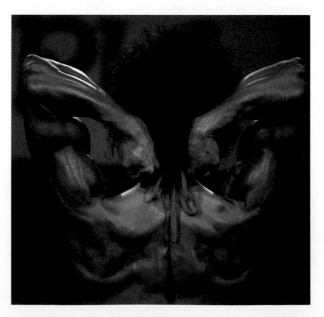

Most of the examples of nonconformity that come readily to mind involve *negative* definitions. However, the opposite may also be the case. Since we all have shortcomings, we might define especially righteous people as deviant, too, although we accord them a measure of respect (Huls, 1987). Deviance, then, centers on *difference*, both negative and positive, which causes us to react to others as "outsiders" (Becker, 1966).

Deviant people may be subject to **social control,** *attempts by society to regulate the behavior of individuals.* Like deviance itself, social control takes many forms. Socialization, the focus of Chapter 3, involves a complex process of social control in which family, peer groups, and the mass media influence people's attitudes and behavior. A more formal and multifaceted system of social control, the **criminal justice system,** *reacts to alleged violations of the law through the use of police, courts, and punishment.* A society exerts social control by giving individuals positive responses to conformity—praise from parents, high grades in school, and positive recognition from people in the community—and negative responses to deviance—including prison sentences. Both positive reinforcement for socially accepted actions and attitudes and fear of incurring society's wrath encourage conformity to conventional patterns of thought and behavior.

The Biological Context

But how do people come to be conformists or deviants in the first place? As noted in Chapter 3 ("Socialization: From Infancy to Aging"), human behavior was understood—or, more correctly, misunderstood—during the nineteenth century as an expression of biological instincts. Not surprisingly, then, the early investigation of criminality focused on biological causes.

In 1876, Caesare Lombroso (1835–1909), an Italian physician who worked in prisons, suggested that criminals had distinctive physical features—low foreheads, prominent jaws and cheekbones, protruding ears, extreme hairiness, and unusually long arms that made them resemble human beings' apelike ancestors. In essence, Lombroso viewed criminals as evolutionary throwbacks to lower forms of life. Toward the end of his career he did acknowledge the importance of social forces in criminality, but his early assertion that some people were literally born criminals gained great popularity, especially among powerful individuals who were not inclined to consider failings in social arrangements that

might account, in part, for criminal deviance (Jones, 1986).

Lombroso's research was flawed. He identified physical characteristics common among prisoners without realizing that the same traits also appeared in the population as a whole. Several decades later the British psychiatrist Charles Buckman Goring (1870–1919) probed the matter further—and more carefully—comparing thousands of convicts and noncriminals. He found great physical variation within both groups, but no overall physical differences, which distinguished criminals from noncriminals, of the kind suggested by Lombroso (1972; orig. 1913).

Although Lombroso's work had been discredited, others continued to search for alleged biological explanations for criminality. William Sheldon (1949) suggested that body structure played a significant role in criminality. He divided people into three general categories based on body structure: *ectomorphs,* who are tall, thin, and fragile; *endomorphs,* who are short and fat; and *mesomorphs,* who are muscular and athletic. After analyzing the body structure and criminal history of hundreds of young men, Sheldon reported a correlation between criminality and the mesomorphic body type. Criminality, according to Sheldon, was linked to a muscular, athletic build. Sheldon and Eleanor Glueck (1950) agreed. However, the Gluecks cautioned that mesomorphic body structure did not necessarily *cause* criminality. Mesomorphic males, they suggested, were somewhat more likely to be raised with little affection and understanding from family members; consequently, they showed less sensitivity toward others and tended to react aggressively to frustration. Young men with muscular builds also have the physical capacity to become the "bullies on the block" (Gibbons, 1981). If we expect muscular and athletic boys to display more physical aggression than others, we may treat them accordingly, thereby actually provoking aggressive behavior in a self-fulfilling prophecy.

More recently, increasing knowledge of genetics has rekindled interest in the biological causes of criminality. Some research has focused on unusual genetic flaws that may engender criminality in some people (Vold & Bernard, 1986). Yet no conclusive evidence substantiates the claim that such biological defects *cause* criminal activity (Hook, 1973; Suzuki & Knudtson, 1989). More promising research suggests that overall genetic composition, in combination with social influences, explains at least some variation in criminality (Rowe, 1983; Rowe & Osgood, 1984; Wilson & Herrnstein, 1985; Jencks, 1987). Sociobiologists (see Chapter 2, "Culture") are claiming already that biological factors partly answer some important questions, including why males engage in more violence than females and why disabled or foster children are more likely than healthy or natural children to be victimized by family violence (Daly & Wilson, 1988). Clearly, however, the biological forces at work in individual lives are enhanced or inhibited by the social environment.

Critical evaluation. Most biological theories have attempted to explain crime in terms of individual physical traits. Early biological research focused on rare and abnormal cases, which, under any circumstances, could explain only a small proportion of crimes. More recent sociobiological research suggests that common biological traits may be related to criminality but, as yet, too little is understood about the links between genetics and human behavior to warrant causal connections. In any case, an individualistic biological approach cannot address the issue of how some kinds of behaviors come to be defined as deviant in the first place. Therefore, although there is much to be learned about how human biology may affect behavior, research currently places far greater emphasis on social influences on human behavior (Gibbons & Krohn, 1986; Liska, 1987).

Personality Factors

Like biological theories, psychological explanations of deviance spotlight the individual, focusing on abnormalities in the personality. Though some abnormalities are hereditary, psychologists believe most result from socialization. Because personality is shaped by social experience throughout life, psychologists argue that deviance usually stems from "unsuccessful" socialization.

Walter Reckless and Simon Dinitz (1967) linked juvenile delinquency to the personality traits of young boys. They claimed that the drive to engage in delinquent activity can be curbed if boys develop strong moral values and a positive self-image. Reckless and Dinitz called their idea *containment theory.*

These researchers interviewed boys of about twelve years of age. Their teachers had identified which boys they believed were likely to engage in delinquent acts and which were not. The "good boys" seemed to have a strong conscience (or *superego*, in Sigmund Freud's terminology), generally coped well with frustration, and identified positively with cultural norms and values. The "bad boys" had a weaker conscience, had little tolerance for frustration, and identified less strongly with conven-

tional culture. Over a four-year period, the researchers found that the "good boys" did indeed have fewer contacts with the police than the "bad boys." Since all the boys studied lived in areas where delinquency was widespread, the researchers concluded that for the boys who managed to stay out of trouble the combination of a strong conscience and a positive self-concept served as "an internal buffer which protects people against (violation) of the social and legal norms" (Reckless, 1970:401).

Critical evaluation. Psychological research has linked personality patterns to delinquency and other types of deviance. Nevertheless, the vast majority of serious crimes are committed by people whose psychological profiles are normal; this finding limits the value of the psychological approach. Also, because this approach focuses on individuals, it ignores how definitions of what is "normal" and "abnormal" vary from society to society. Finally, psychological research sheds little light on why, among people who behave in the same manner, some are defined as deviant while others are not.

Both biological and psychological approaches view deviance as an individual attribute without exploring how conceptions of right and wrong initially arise and without investigating the deviant person's place in the larger society. We now address these issues by delving into the social foundations of deviant behavior.

The Social Foundations of Deviance

Although we tend to view deviance in terms of the free choice or personal failings of individuals, all behavior—deviance as well as conformity—is shaped by society. There are three *social* foundations of deviance.

1. **Deviance exists only in relation to cultural norms.** No thought or action is inherently deviant; it becomes deviant only in relation to particular norms. In the traditional village communities of Sicily, for example, norms demand the use of physical violence to avenge an insult to family honor (Wolfgang & Ferracuti, 1982). In that culture, peacefully ignoring an insult is defined as deviant. In most of American society, by contrast, norms forbid the use of violence in a comparable situation. What is viewed as honorable in one place, then, may result in arrest and prosecution in another.

    As norms change, so does deviance. A century ago, the lives of most American women centered on the home: Women seeking business ca-

On May 4, 1970, National Guard troops opened fire on students who had gathered for an antiwar demonstration at Kent State University in Ohio. Four students were killed and nine were wounded. Widespread opinion held that the shooting was justified, if regrettable, as a firm response to the many campus protests taking place at that time. None of the troops or their superiors was criminally prosecuted for taking part in the event.

reers were likely to be dismissed as deviant. Today most women pursue careers outside the home and receive widespread support for that choice.

2. **People become deviant as others define them that way.** Each of us violates cultural norms, perhaps even to the extent of breaking the law. For example, most of us have at some time walked around talking to ourselves or "borrowed" supplies, such as pens or papers, from the workplace. Such actions may or may not be sufficient to define us as mentally ill or criminal, depending on how others perceive, define, and respond to the situation.

3. **Both norms and the way people define situations involve social power.** As explained later in this chapter, Karl Marx considered norms, and especially laws, as devices to protect the interests of powerful people. For example, the owners of an unprofitable factory have a legal right to close their business, even if doing so puts thousands of people permanently out of work. If workers commit an act of vandalism that closes the same factory for a single day, however, they are likely to be defined as criminal. Also, poor people may be defined as deviant for exactly the same behavior that powerful people engage in with impunity. A homeless person who stands on a street corner denouncing the city government risks arrest for disturbing the peace; a mayoral candidate during an election campaign can do the same thing while receiving extensive police protection. In short, norms and their application are linked to social inequality.

THE FUNCTIONS OF DEVIANCE: THE STRUCTURAL-FUNCTIONAL APPROACH

Deviance is inherent in the operation of society. The structural-functional paradigm explains how deviance makes important contributions to a social system.

A pioneering study of the functions of deviance was carried out by Emile Durkheim (1964a, orig. 1895; 1964b, orig. 1893). He asserted that there is nothing abnormal about deviance; in fact, it forms an integral part of all societies. Durkheim cited four major functions of deviance.

1. **Deviance affirms cultural values and norms.** Culture is a matter of moral definition: Some attitudes and behaviors must be defined as preferable to others. Notions of what is morally right exist only in antithesis to notions of what is wrong. For example, patriotism grows stronger as a society condemns those who dishonor its flag. Deviance, therefore, is indispensable to the process of generating and sustaining cultural values.

2. **Responding to deviance clarifies moral boundaries.** Defining people as deviant also delineates the location of a society's moral boundaries. A college, for example, marks the line between academic honesty and dishonesty by using disciplinary procedures to declare some behavior—such as plagiarism—as wrong.

The arts allow members of society to explore alternatives to existing ideas and social arrangements. For this reason, artists historically have been celebrated but considered at the same time mildly deviant. Some provocative art has recently sparked controversy as to whether society should fund, or even permit, *any* type of artistic expression. This work provoked national attention because it required observers to walk on an American flag.

3. **Responding to deviance promotes social unity.** People typically react to serious deviance with collective outrage. In doing so, Durkheim explained, they reaffirm the moral ties that bind them. For example, Americans often respond with a surge of patriotism to terrorist actions against U.S. citizens.

4. **Deviance encourages social change.** By exploring a society's moral boundaries, deviants suggest alternatives to the status quo so that society does not remain static. Today's deviance, Durkheim noted, may well become tomorrow's morality (1964a:71).

The functions of deviance are illustrated by Kai Erikson's (1966) historical research about the early Puritans of Massachusetts Bay. This highly religious "society of saints," Erikson discovered, created deviance in order to clarify moral boundaries. The kind of deviance the Puritans encountered (challenging conventional religious beliefs) depended on the moral questions they needed to resolve (should the clergy control the community?). As they recognized "evil" in their midst, the early Puritans both enhanced their unity and affirmed common moral values.

Erikson's research also showed that a fixed proportion of people in Massachusetts Bay were defined as deviant over time. In his view, this shows that deviants, in relatively stable numbers, serve as moral markers, outlining the changing boundaries of conventional attitudes and behavior in a society. By consistently defining some of their members as deviant, the Puritans ensured that the social functions of deviance were carried out.

Merton's Strain Theory

Robert Merton (1938, 1968) has amplified Durkheim's structural-functional ideas by linking deviance to certain societal imbalances. Merton's theory begins with the observation that financial success constitutes a widespread American *goal*. People pursue financial success according to certain approved *means* such as education and hard work. Success gained through theft or other dishonest activities, however, violates cultural norms. Therefore, if people are socialized to seek success and to play by the rules, *conformity* should result.

But not everyone who desires success has the opportunity to achieve it. Moreover, even successful people may be motivated by the lure of further gain to violate cultural norms and perhaps the law. Corporate executives, for example, may embezzle company funds; certainly, many wealthy Americans misrepresent their income to the Internal Revenue Service. Merton called this type of deviance *innovation*—attempting to achieve culturally approved goals using unconventional means. Table 6–1 shows that innovation involves accepting the goal of success while rejecting conventional means to that goal.

Such innovation results from "strain" between the value of success and the limited opportunity to become successful in approved ways. The poor, especially, experience this strain to the extent that their aspirations are frustrated by a lack of educational and job opportunities. Responding to this strain, people may make their own rules, stealing, selling illegal drugs, or engaging in other kinds of street hustling and racketeering.

The inability to achieve wealth by normative means may also prompt a second response, called *ritualism* (see Table 6–1). This response to not achieving cultural

Table 6–1 MERTON'S STRAIN THEORY OF DEVIANCE

Individual Responses to Dominant Cultural Patterns	Cultural Goals	Cultural Means
Nondeviant Response		
Conformity	Accept	Accept
Deviant Responses		
Innovation	Accept	Reject
Ritualism	Reject	Accept
Retreatism	Reject	Reject
Rebellion	Reject current goals but promote new ones	Reject current means but promote new ones

SOURCE: Based on Robert K. Merton, *Social Theory and Social Structure* (New York: Free Press, 1968), pp. 230–246.

goals involves abandoning those goals while compulsively conforming to cultural norms as a means of seeking respectability. Ritualism, Merton suggests, predominates among people of modest social standing who have little opportunity to gain more in life but fear risking what they have through innovation. Consider the "bureaucratic ritualist," described in Chapter 5 ("Groups and Organizations"): the lower-level official who compulsively conforms to rules to the point of losing sight of their overall purpose. In Merton's view, such people are deviant because they have given up the pursuit of success; however, some may view them as "good citizens" because they rigidly adhere to the rules.

A third response to the inability to succeed is *retreatism*—the rejection of both the goals and the norms of one's culture. Retreatists are society's dropouts. They include some alcoholics and drug addicts, and some of the street people common to American cities. The deviance of retreatists comes out in their unconventional way of life and, perhaps more seriously, their acceptance of their situation.

The fourth response to failure is *rebellion*. Like retreatists, rebels reject both the cultural definition of success and the normative means of achieving it. Rebels, however, go further by advocating radical alternatives to the existing social order. They may promote unconventional values and norms through political revolution or through overzealous religious activity. Either way, rebels withdraw from established society, forming a counterculture subsequently viewed as deviant.

Merton's theory has gained much credibility, but it has also come under criticism because it explains some kinds of deviance (theft, for example) far better than others (such as crimes of passion or mental illness). In addition, Merton provides only a few clues as to why an individual would choose one response to strain over another. Finally, we must recognize that not everyone seeks success in conventional terms of wealth. As explained in Chapter 2 ("Culture"), Americans embrace many different cultural values and are motivated by various notions of personal success.

Deviant Subcultures

The societal imbalances cited in Merton's theory were also noted in a study of delinquent youth by Richard Cloward and Lloyd Ohlin (1966). They maintain that criminal deviance results not simply from limited legitimate opportunity but also from accessible illegitimate opportunity. In short, patterns of deviance and conformity reflect the *relative opportunity structure* various categories of young people face in their lives.

The life of Al Capone, a notorious American gangster of the prohibition era (which ran from 1920 to 1933), illustrates this concept. As a poor immigrant, Capone

Al Capone, perhaps the most notorious of America's gangsters, earned a fortune by selling liquor during the Prohibition era. He represents Merton's "innovator," pursuing a normative goal (wealth) through illegal means (bootlegging).

was denied legitimate paths to success, such as a college education. Yet his world did provide illegitimate opportunity for success as a bootlegger. Where relative opportunity favors what Merton might call "organized innovation," Cloward and Ohlin predict the development of *criminal subcultures*. These subcultures offer the knowledge, skills, and other resources needed to succeed in unconventional ways.

But in many poor and highly transient neighborhoods, organized innovation may be lacking. Here, delinquency is likely to surface in the form of *conflict subcultures* where violence explodes as an expression of frustration and a claim to prestige. Finally, among those who fail to achieve success, even using criminal means, *retreatist subcultures* may arise. Consistent with Merton's analysis, such subcultures comprise dropouts who may extensively use alcohol or other drugs.

Albert Cohen (1971) suggests that delinquency is most pronounced among lower-class youths because they are denied opportunity to attain success in a conventional way. Because conventional definitions of success call for achieving wealth and all its trappings, they find little basis for self-respect in their impoverished condition. In response, they may create a delinquent subculture that defines them in more favorable terms. These subcultures, Cohen says, "define as meritorious the characteristics [these youths] *do* possess, the kinds of conduct of which they *are* capable" (1971:66). For example, if the dominant culture values the calculated pursuit of wealth, a delinquent subculture may extol stealing "for the hell of it." In short, members of a delinquent subculture may publicly flout conventional norms while carefully conforming to their own standards.

Walter Miller (1970) agrees that delinquent subcultures are most likely to develop in the lower classes. In his view, however, the values and norms of delinquent gangs stem from the lack of legitimate opportunity in their world. He describes the following six focal concerns of delinquent subcultures. First is *trouble*, arising from frequent conflict with teachers and police. Second, especially among males, is *toughness*, value placed on physical size, strength, and athletic skills. Third is *smartness*, the ability to succeed on the streets, to outthink or "con" others, and to avoid being similarly taken advantage of. Fourth is *excitement*, the search for thrills, risk, or danger to gain needed release from a daily routine that is predictable and unsatisfying. Fifth is a concern with *fate*, derived from the lack of control these youths feel over their own lives. Sixth is *autonomy*, or the desire for freedom, often expressed as resentment toward authority figures.

Hirschi's Control Theory

A final argument that builds on Durkheim's analysis of deviance is Travis Hirschi's (1969) *control theory*. Hirschi assumes that individuals find deviance tempting; what requires explanation, then, is not deviance, but *conformity*. He suggests that conformity is a function of four types of social controls.

1. **Attachment.** Strong attachments to others enhance conformity; weak relationships in the family, peer group, and school leave people freer to engage in deviance.
2. **Commitment.** The higher one's commitment to legitimate opportunity, the greater the advantages of conformity. A young person bound for college, with good career prospects, has a high stake in conformity. In contrast, someone with little confidence in future success has a low investment in conformity and is more likely to follow a deviant path.
3. **Involvement.** Extensive involvement in legitimate activities, such as holding a job, going to school and completing homework, or pursuing hobbies, inhibits deviance. People with little legitimate involvement—who simply "hang out" waiting for something to happen—have time and energy for deviant activity.
4. **Belief.** Strong beliefs in conventional morality and respect for authority figures also restrain tendencies toward deviance; people with weak beliefs are more vulnerable to whatever temptation deviance presents.

Hirschi's analysis explains many kinds of deviant behavior, and it has gained support from subsequent research (Wiatrowski, Griswold, & Roberts, 1981). Here, again, a person's place in society is crucial in generating a stake in conformity or allowing everyday temptations to cross the line into actual deviance.

Critical evaluation. The various structural-functional theories derived from Durkheim's pioneering work reveal the functions of deviance for the larger society. Merton's strain theory links deviance to a lack of fit between society's goals and means. The general approach of Cloward and Ohlin, Cohen, Miller, and Hirschi—that deviance reflects the opportunity structure of society—has won a broad base of support (cf. Allan & Steffensmeier, 1989). Some of this research suggests that disadvantaged youths may try to expand the opportunities they do have by forming deviant subcultures.

However, these theories fall short in assuming that people use a single cultural standard for determining which attitudes and behavior are legitimate and illegitimate. American society upholds various, sometimes competing, ideas of what is and is not deviant. A second problem lies in defining deviance in terms that focus attention on poor people alone. If crime covers stock fraud as well as street theft, criminals are more likely to come from the ranks of affluent Americans. In addition, structural-functional theories imply that everyone who violates conventional cultural standards will be identified as deviant. Defining particular attitudes or actions as deviant, however, actually involves a highly complex process, as is explained in the next section.

THE LABELING APPROACH: SYMBOLIC INTERACTION AND DEVIANCE

The symbolic-interaction paradigm spotlights how people construct reality in countless situations. In the early 1950s, sociologists began to apply this theoretical paradigm to the study of deviance. Their work showed that surprising flexibility underscores definitions of deviance and conformity.

The central contribution of symbolic-interaction analysis, **labeling theory,** refers to *the assertion that deviance and conformity arise in the response of others.* Labeling theory stresses the relativity of deviance, meaning that the same behavior may be defined in any number of ways. Howard S. Becker therefore claims that deviance is nothing more than "behavior that people so label" (1966:9). Consider these situations: A woman takes an article of clothing from a roommate; a married man at a convention in a distant city sleeps with a prostitute; a member of Congress drives home intoxicated after a party. The first situation could be defined as borrowing or as theft. The consequences of the second situation depend largely on whether news of the man's action follows him back home. In the third situation, the official might be viewed as an active socialite or a dangerous drunk. In the social construction of reality, then, a highly variable process of detection, definition, and response comes into play.

People also may be labeled for involvement in situations completely beyond their control. For example, victims of violent rape are sometimes subjected to labeling as deviants because of the misguided assumption that they must have encouraged the offender. Similarly, people with serious diseases may come to be considered deviant by those who cannot cope with their illnesses. People with Acquired Immune Deficiency Syndrome (AIDS), for instance, are often shunned by employers, friends, and even family members.

The large proportion of homosexual men—people who have suffered from deviant labeling for their sexual orientation—among persons with acquired immune deficiency syndrome (AIDS) resulted in slow mobilization to fight this serious health problem. Public awareness that thousands of children are among the persons with AIDS has helped to change the way American society views this deadly disease.

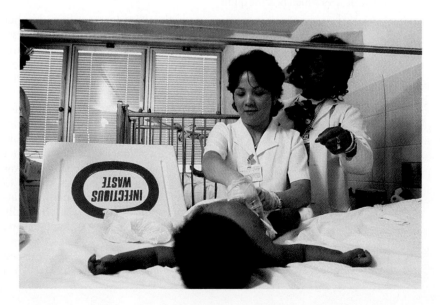

SOCIOLOGY OF EVERYDAY LIFE

Being Overweight: A Study in Deviant Labeling

"Joan," a sociologist, begins the story of her life by noting that she was born to two overweight parents. Probably through no fault of her own, she became heavy as a child. Yet she was unaware of being overweight—or of what it might mean to others—until she entered school.

> In the first grade, it was painfully pointed out to me—for the first time in my life—that I was different from other children. Other children's taunts of "fatty" and "pig" first brought shock, pain, tears, and later, guilt. I remember being afraid of the other children to the point of not wanting to walk home alone, and my mother frequently walked the one block from my home to the school to get me.
>
> The teasing, however, did not cause me to stop eating, for I still did not realize the connection between eating and being overweight. Instead, I started to develop . . . coping and protective devices which became quite elaborate later.

Ironically, Joan's "coping devices" deepened her deviant identity. She learned, for example, to avoid the embarrassment of engaging in sports (no one wanted her as a teammate) by pretending to be sick. Gradually, her "sick role" expanded:

> I also learned that by being "sick" I could avoid facing other people. . . . While in the third grade, I was in the school nurse's office almost every day with a wide range of ailments.

Another coping mechanism was lying. When her mother asked how much she weighed, Joan answered according to what she thought her mother would believe rather than revealing her actual weight. She knew her parents disliked lying, but she preferred to think of herself as a liar than as fat. Yet, this self-protection backfired:

> Like all good things, my deception came to an end when it was discovered during a visit to the doctor for a physical. Right up to the point of stepping on the scale . . . I had my mother convinced I weighed almost fifteen pounds less. The anxiety caused by the lying was terrible, but it was nothing compared with the way I felt when they found out. I cried hysterically. . . . The doctor suggested that my parents send me to a psychiatrist if I couldn't diet, which they did not do. This recommendation shocked me, and I entered high school with a much different picture of myself. At last I knew I was deviant; I accepted the fact, and I began to act accordingly.

In high school Joan continued in her deviant role, shunned and dateless. She was unable to lose weight, having accepted her self-image as a fat person. Her weight was no longer the problem; she saw herself simply as an outcast, someone with little for others to like. Entering college, Joan felt herself worthy of friendship only with others labeled as deviant—her roommate was a woman who was partly blind and who was known to have had extensive psychiatric treatment; another friend was physically disabled. These were unhappy years.

> I think my college depression can best be summarized by the way I felt when both my roommate and my paraplegic friend had dates on Friday night and I didn't. The only outlet I found that night for the anger I felt was the candy vending machine in the basement of the dormitory. How ironic that I should perpetuate the very thing that was helping to keep me home by eating candy.

There is no happy ending to Joan's story. She has now lost a great deal of weight and gained considerable understanding of her past. Yet she finds that her deviance has become so incorporated into her self-concept that her life simply hasn't changed:

> I now weigh 129 pounds and plan to lose at least another 10 pounds. The loss in weight, however, has not been accompanied by any increase in dates or change of mental attitude, and I fear that it is really my internal makeup that is deviant. I still feel fat, and no matter how many times my friends or parents tell me how nice I look, I don't believe them. . . . I do not know how to get dates, let alone what type of behavior is expected on a date.
>
> If I sound bitter, it's because I am tired of having to do all the changing. I don't like the fact that I have allowed my life to be regulated by the opinions and expectations of other people. . . . If nothing else, I hope I have shown to what extent being obese, and others' reactions to obesity, as well as the various rationalizations one entertains under these circumstances, can influence and even create a lifestyle.

SOURCE: Adapted from Anonymous, "Losing: An Attempt at Stigma Neutralization," in Jerry Jacobs, ed., *Deviance: Field Studies and Self-Disclosures* (Palo Alto, CA: National Press Books, 1974), pp. 69–72.

Edwin Lemert (1951, 1972) explains how deviant labeling affects a person's subsequent behavior. Lemert calls the activity that is initially labeled *primary deviance*. What Lemer terms *secondary deviance* may then follow if an individual incorporates the deviant label into his or her self-concept. Initial labeling, then, can encourage a person to fulfill, for better or worse, the expectations of others. The box shows how the primary deviance of being overweight in childhood led one woman to engage in secondary deviance.

Stigma

The development of secondary deviance marks the start of what Erving Goffman (1963) calls a *deviant career*. Typically, this occurs as a consequence of acquiring a **stigma,** *a powerfully negative label that radically changes a person's social identity and self-concept*. Stigma, then, operates as a master status (see Chapter 4, "Social Interaction in Everyday Life"), overpowering other dimensions of social identity so that a person is "reduced in our minds from a whole and usual person to a tainted, discounted one" (1963:3). The person who is stigmatized may become socially isolated, allegedly because of personal failings.

Children learn to devalue stigmatized categories of people as part of the socialization process. Those stigmatized may include not only lawbreakers but also people of certain races and social classes, as well as those who are physically disabled or unconventional in a host of other respects.

Sometimes condemnation rises to a level of formality that Harold Garfinkel (1956) calls a *degradation ceremony*. Consider a criminal prosecution, which resembles in many respects a high-school graduation, except that people stand before others to be formally labeled in a negative rather than positive way.

Acquiring a stigma can have serious long-term effects. As Joan's story indicates, even after losing weight a person may still view herself as unattractive. Yet Joan also expresses the determination to resist the negative judgments of others. Many people with physical disabilities, gay people, and members of racial minorities have countered stigma by recognizing and emphasizing their positive personal qualities. In the 1960s, for example, the expression "Black is beautiful" gained popularity as a boost to the self-image of African-Americans.

Once stigmatized, a person may be subject to **retrospective labeling**—*the interpretation of someone's past consistent with present deviance* (Scheff, 1984). For example, after discovering that a woman who has worked with the Girl Scouts for years has sexually molested a child, others rethink her past, perhaps musing, "She always did want to be around young children." Obviously, retrospective labeling involves a highly selective and prejudicial view of a person's past, guided more by the present stigma than by any attempt to be fair. But this process may nonetheless deepen a deviant identity.

Labeling and Mental Illness

Applying labeling theory to mental illness illustrates how society attaches a stigma to mental conditions that may be difficult to define. Generally speaking, psychiatrists believe that mental disorders have a concrete reality that parallels diseases of the body. Factors such as heredity, diet, stress, and chemical imbalances in the body do account, in part, for some mental disturbances. However, much of what we call "mental illness" is a matter of social definitions (Thoits, 1985). Sometimes defining and treating the "mentally ill" amounts to little more than an attempt to enforce conformity to conventional standards.

If a woman believes that Jesus rides the bus to work with her every day, is she seriously deluded or merely expressing her religious faith in a highly graphic way? If a man refuses to bathe or observe common etiquette, much to the dismay of his family, is he insane or simply choosing an unconventional way of life? Is a homeless woman loudly denouncing the city government on a street corner mentally ill or expressing justifiable anger?

According to psychiatrist Thomas Szasz, the label of insanity is widely applied to what is actually only "difference"; therefore, the notion of mental illness should be abandoned (1961, 1970; Vatz & Weinberg, 1983). Illness, Szasz argues, afflicts only the body. Mental illness, therefore, is a myth. Being "different" in thought or action may irritate others, but it does not justify defining someone as sick. To do so, Szasz claims, simply enforces conformity to the standards of people powerful enough to get their way. Thus, for example, political dissidents in the Soviet Union have reportedly been sent to psychiatric hospitals for "rehabilitation"; so have homeless people in New York City who refuse an offer of a bed in a city shelter.

Szasz's views have provoked controversy; many of

Because he chooses to express his religious convictions in an unconventional manner, should this man be labeled mentally ill?

his colleagues reject the notion that all mental illness is a fiction. Others have hailed his work, however, for pointing up the danger of abusing medical practice in the interest of conformity. Most of us, after all, experience periods of extreme stress or other mental disability at some time in our lives. Such episodes, although upsetting, are usually of passing importance. If, however, they form the basis of a social stigma, they may lead to a deviant career as a self-fulfilling prophecy (Scheff, 1984).

The Medicalization of Deviance

Labeling theory, and particularly the work of Thomas Szasz, has encouraged a historical shift in the way we understand deviance. Over the last fifty years, the growing influence of medicine—especially psychiatry—in American society has encouraged the **medicalization of deviance**, *the transformation of moral and legal issues into medical matters*. In essence, this amounts to changing labels. In moral terms, people and their behavior are defined as "bad" or "good." However, the scientific objectivity of medicine replaces moral judgments with clinical diagnoses of being "sick" or "well."

Changing views on alcoholism illustrate this process. Until the middle of this century, alcoholics were generally considered morally deficient, "drunks" too weak to act responsibly. Gradually, however, alcoholism was redefined as a medical problem. Now most people view alcoholism as an illness, affecting people who are "sick" rather than "bad." Similarly, obesity, drug addiction, child abuse, and other behaviors that used to come under the sway of morality are today widely defined as illnesses requiring help for sufferers rather than punishment.

How we define deviance—as a moral or medical issue—has a number of profound consequences. First, consider *who responds* to deviance. An offense against common morality typically provokes a response from members of the community or police. Applying medical labels, however, places the situation under the control of clinical specialists, including counselors, psychiatrists, and physicians. Second, we must address *how people respond* to the deviant. A moral approach defines the deviant as an "offender" subject to punishment; medically, however, "patients" cry out for treatment. Therefore, while punishment is designed to fit the crime, treatment programs are tailored to the patient and may involve virtually any therapy that might prevent future deviance (von Hirsh, 1986.) Third, and most important, we must look at *the personal competence of the person labeled as deviant*. Morally, people must take responsibility for their own behavior: They may do wrong, but they understand what they are doing and must face the consequences. Medically, sick people are not responsible for what they do. Defined as personally incompetent and unaware of what is in their own best interest, they become vulnerable to more intense, often involuntary, treatment. For this reason alone, attempts to define deviance in medical terms should be made with extreme caution.

Differential Association Theory

Related to the issue of how we define others' behavior is how we learn to define our own behavior. Edwin

Sutherland (1940) suggested that social patterns, including deviance, are learned through association with others, especially in primary groups. Because socialization is complex, people are exposed to forces encouraging criminality as well as those supporting conformity. The likelihood that a person will engage in criminal activity depends on the frequency of association with those who support norm violation compared with those who endorse conformity. This is Sutherland's theory of *differential association*.

Sutherland's theory is illustrated by a study of drug and alcohol use among young adults in the United States (Akers et al., 1979). In analyzing responses to a questionnaire by junior and senior high-school students, researchers discovered that the extent of alcohol and drug use among the respondents paralleled the degree to which the peer group they belonged to encouraged such activity. The researchers found that young people learn delinquent patterns as they receive praise and other rewards for deviance, and learn to define deviance rather than conformity in positive terms.

Critical evaluation. Labeling theory links deviance not to *action* but to the *reaction* of others. Thus some people are defined as deviant while others who think or behave in the same way are not. The concepts of stigma, secondary deviance, and the deviant career imply that the label of deviance can be incorporated into a lasting self-concept.

Yet labeling theory has several limitations. First, because this theory takes a highly relative view of deviance, it glosses over certain kinds of behavior, like murder, that are almost univerally condemned (Wellford, 1980). Labeling theory is thus most usefully applied to less serious deviance, such as certain kinds of sexual behavior and mental illness. Second, the consequences of deviant labeling are unclear. On the one hand, labeling may promote subsequent, long-term deviance. On the other hand, evidence suggests that labeling in the form of arrest, for example, discourages some people from further violations (Smith & Gartin, 1989). Thus questions remain as to when and how deviant labeling launches a deviant career. Third, labeling theory assumes that people resist the label of deviance. While most do, some people may seek to be defined as deviant (Vold & Bernard, 1986). For example, civil disobedience may lead to arrest but it may also call attention to social injustice. Fourth, we still have much to learn about how people respond to those who are labeled as deviant. One recent study found that the stigma of being a former mental patient typically resulted in social rejection but only in cases in which an individual was considered dangerous (Link et al., 1987).

Sutherland's differential association theory has had considerable influence in sociology, but it provides little insight into why society's norms and laws define certain kinds of activities as deviant in the first place. This important question is addressed by social-conflict analysis, described in the next section.

DEVIANCE AND SOCIAL CONFLICT

The social-conflict paradigm links deviance to social inequality. This approach suggests that *who* and *what* are labeled as deviant is based primarily on relative power.

Why, Alexander Liazos (1972) asks, do we tend to think of deviants as "nuts, sluts, and 'preverts'?" The answer, he suggests, is that such terms bring to mind powerless people. On the continuum of power, then, deviants inhabit the lowest reaches. Bag ladies (not tax evaders) and unemployed men on street corners (not those who profit from wars) carry the tag of deviance. Similarly, Americans tend to define the peer groups of poor youths as "street gangs," while those of affluent young people are simply called "cliques."

Social-conflict theory explains this pattern in three ways. First, the norms—including laws—of any society generally reflect the interests of the rich and powerful. People who threaten the wealthy, either by taking their property or by advocating a more egalitarian society, may find themselves defined as "thieves" or "political radicals." Karl Marx, one major architect of this approach, argued that social institutions by and large support the capitalist economic system and protect the interests of the rich, capitalist class. Richard Quinney makes the point succinctly: "Capitalist justice is by the capitalist class, for the capitalist class, and against the working class" (1977:3).

Second, even if their behavior is called into question, the powerful have the resources to resist deviant labels. Corporate executives who order or condone the dumping of hazardous wastes are rarely held personally accountable for these acts. While such mischief poses dangers for all of society, it is not necessarily viewed as criminal.

Third, the widespread belief that societal standards are natural and good obscures the political character of norms and laws. For this reason, we may condemn the

Hispanic artist Frank Romero painted *The Closing of Whittier Boulevard* based on a recollection of his youth in East Los Angeles. To many young Hispanics, portrayed here by their distinctive "low-rider" cars, police represent a hostile Anglo culture, likely to use heavy-handed tactics to discourage them from venturing out of their neighborhoods.

Frank Romero. The Closing of Whittier Boulevard, 1984. *Oil on canvas. 72 × 120 inches. Collection of Peter Schindler.*

unequal application of the law but give little thought to whether the *laws themselves* are inherently fair (Quinney, 1977).

Deviance and Capitalism

Steven Spitzer (1980) has explored how deviant labels come to be attached to people who impede the operation of capitalism. First, because capitalism is based on private control of property, people who threaten the property of others—especially the poor who steal from the rich— are prime candidates for labeling as deviants. Conversely, the rich who exploit the poor are unlikely to be defined as deviant. Landlords, for example, who charge poor tenants high rents and legally evict those who cannot pay are not considered a threat to society: They are simply "doing business."

Second, because capitalism depends on productive labor, those who cannot or will not work risk deviant labeling. Americans commonly think of people who are out of work—even if through no fault of their own—as deviant.

Third, capitalism depends on respect for figures of authority, so people who resist authority are generally labeled as deviant. These include children who skip school or talk back to parents and teachers, adults who do not cooperate with employers or police, and anyone who opposes "the system."

Fourth, capitalism, like all economic systems, rests on a widespread acceptance of the status quo. Those who undermine or challenge the capitalist system are subject to deviant labeling. In this category fall antiwar activists, environmentalists, labor organizers, and anyone who supports an alternative economic system.

By contrast, whatever enhances the operation of capitalism gains positive labels. Athletes, for example, are praised because sports expresses the values of individual achievement and competition vital to capitalism. Additionally, Spitzer notes, using drugs for escape (marijuana, psychedelics, heroin, and crack) is defined as deviant, while using drugs that promote adjustment to the status quo (such as caffeine) is widely endorsed.

Spitzer identifies two general types of "problem populations." The first constitutes what the system tends to define as *social junk*, that is, people who are a "costly yet relatively harmless burden" to capitalist society (1980:184). These people do not support the system by working, and they may depend on others or the government. Such nonproductive, but nonthreatening, members of society include Robert Merton's retreatists (for example, those addicted to alcohol or other drugs) and the elderly, physically disabled, mentally retarded, and mentally ill. Defined as moderately deviant, these people are typically subject to control by social welfare agencies.

The second type of problem population, that Spitzer terms *social dynamite*, encompasses people perceived as directly threatening to the capitalist system. These range from the inner-city "underclass" to alienated youths, radicals, and revolutionaries—in Merton's terms, society's innovators and rebels. To the extent that they become threatening, such people are subject to control by the criminal justice system and, in times of crisis, by military forces such as the National Guard.

Following Marx's ideas, Spitzer claims that capitalism itself produces both "social junk" and "social dynamite." The unemployment and poverty that overwhelm much of these populations stem from the workings of the capitalist system. Having created these categories of people, capitalism must also control them—through the

The popular "pro-democracy movement" in the People's Republic of China was brutally crushed on June 11, 1989, as 10,000 troops converged on Tiananmen Square at the center of Beijing. Thousands of Chinese people, who were demanding a greater voice in their government, were killed and wounded. The event demonstrated that "law and order," if not always moral rightness, is typically defined by the party with the greater power.

social welfare system and the criminal justice system. In the process, both systems apply labels that place responsibility for social problems on the people themselves. Those who receive welfare because they have no other source of income are considered unworthy; poor people who vent their rage at being deprived of a secure life are labeled as rioters; anyone who actively challenges the government is branded a radical or a communist; and those who attempt to gain illegally what they cannot otherwise acquire are called common thieves.

White-Collar Crime

Until 1989, few people other than Wall Street stockbrokers had ever heard of Michael Milken. Yet Milken had accomplished a stunning feat, becoming the highest-paid American in half a century. With salary and bonuses in 1987 totaling $550 million—*about $1.5 million a day*—Milken ranks behind only Al Capone, whose earnings in 1927 reached $600 million in current dollars (Swartz, 1989). Milken had something else in common with Capone: The government was after his fortune. Prosecutors accused him of one hundred violations of securities and exchange laws.

Such activities exemplify **white-collar crime**, defined by Edwin Sutherland in 1940 as *crimes committed by persons of high social position in the course of their occupations* (Sutherland & Cressey, 1978:44). As the Milken case suggests, white-collar crime rarely involves uniformed police converging on a scene with drawn guns. Thus it does not refer to crimes such as murder, assault, or rape that happen to be carried out by people of high social position. Instead, it includes crimes committed by powerful people making illegal use of their occupational positions to enrich themselves or others, often causing significant public harm in the process (Hagan & Parker, 1985; Vold & Bernard, 1986). In short, white-collar offenses that occur in government offices and corporate board rooms are commonly dubbed *crime in the suites* rather than *crime in the streets*.

The public harm wreaked by false advertising, marketing of unsafe products, embezzlement, and bribery of public officials extends far beyond what most people realize. Some researchers contend that white-collar crime causes greater public harm than the more visible "street crime" (Reiman, 1990). Estimates of the economic costs of business-related crimes range up to several hundred billion dollars a year—an amount far exceeding the economic costs of common theft (Reid, 1982; Reiman, 1984; U.S. Department of Justice, 1987). Although the responsibility for workplace safety rests primarily on employers, some 100,000 Americans die each year from occupational hazards—a figure five times greater than the total of all murders committed by street criminals (Simon & Eitzen, 1982:27; U.S. Federal Bureau of Investigation, 1987).

At the time Sutherland (1940) conducted his research, he claimed that all the largest American businesses had broken the law, causing considerable social harm. Yet only about one case in ten was officially treated as the criminal action of a specific person. Rather, he noted, violations by corporations or government agencies are far more likely to end up in a civil court than in a criminal court. *Civil law* refers to general regulations involving economic losses between private parties, while *criminal law* encompasses specific laws that define every individual's moral responsibility to society. In civil settlements, damage or injury is paid for but no one is branded as a criminal. Further, since corporations have the legal standing of persons, white-collar offenses commonly involve the organization as a whole rather than specific individuals. Today, as at the time of Sutherland's research, deviance by elites rarely results in criminal labeling of powerful people (Simon & Eitzen, 1986).

Ivan Boesky, another notorious Wall Street figure involved in an "insider-trading" scandal, was recently fined some $100 million and sentenced to three years in jail. But this outcome is rare: In 1988, of 9,008 people convicted of embezzlement in the U.S. District Court system, only 512 (5.7 percent) spent even a single day in prison; most were placed on probation (U.S. Bureau of Justice Statistics, 1990).

Sutherland also noted that the public voices less concern about white-collar crime than about street crime, partly because corporate crime victimizes everyone—and no one. White-collar criminals don't stick a gun in anyone's ribs, and the economic costs are usually spread throughout the population.

As the "backbone of capitalism," corporations have immense power, influencing both the mass media and the political process. High corporate officials frequently graduate from prestigious universities and professional schools, belong to exclusive social clubs, and have well-developed networks linking them to other powerful people in all walks of life. Many government officials, drawn from the ranks of corporate executives, regulate the very corporate enterprises in which they have spent most of their working lives. Not surprisingly, then, serious episodes of white-collar crime only make headlines from time to time.

Critical evaluation. According to social-conflict theory, the inequality in wealth and power that pervades capitalist systems also guides the creation and the application of laws and other norms. This theory also suggests that the criminal justice system and social welfare agencies act as political agents, controlling categories of people who threaten the capitalist system.

Like all approaches to deviance, however, social-conflict theory does have its critics. First, this approach tends to assume that laws and other cultural norms benefit only the rich and powerful. But laws also protect workers, consumers, and the environment, sometimes in opposition to the interests of capitalists. A second criticism holds that while social-conflict theory points up the social injury caused by the powerful, Americans remain more concerned about street crime. Third, this approach implies that criminality springs up only to the extent that a society treats its members unequally. However, according to Durkheim, all societies generate deviance, and in societies far more economically egalitarian than our own, extensive criminality still exists.

We have presented various sociological explanations for crime and other forms of deviance. Table 6–2 summarizes the contributions of each approach.

Deviance and Gender

Like much of sociological analysis, explanations of deviance tend to focus on the behavior of males. It is useful, then, to consider how gender figures in some of the theories we have already discussed.

Robert Merton's strain theory, for example, which falls within the structural-functional paradigm, defines cultural goals in terms of financial success. Traditionally, however, this preoccupation with material things has dominated the thinking of men while women have been socialized to define success in terms of relationships, that is, marriage and children (Leonard, 1982). Indeed, we have only recently begun to recognize the "strain" caused by American ideals of equality clashing with the reality of gender-based inequality.

Labeling theory, in symbolic-interaction analysis, offers some insights into the ways gender influences how we define deviance. Because the behavior of males and females is judged by somewhat different standards, the very process of labeling stems from sex-linked biases. Further, as Edwin Schur (1983) observes, in a society in which males have power over females, men often escape direct responsibility for actions that victimize women. Frequently, men who engage in sexual harassment, rape, or other assaults against women, for example, are tagged with only mildly deviant labels; sometimes, they suffer no adverse consequences and they may even win societal encouragement, depending on the surrounding culture. By contrast, women who are victimized may have to convince an unsympathetic audience that they are not to blame for what happened. Research confirms that whether or not people define any particular behavior as deviant depends, in part, on the sex of both the audience and the actors (King & Clayson, 1988).

Ironically, in light of its concern with social inequality, social-conflict analysis has neglected the importance of gender. If, as this approach asserts, oppression fostered by capitalism stands at the root of crime, why do women (whose economic position is much worse than their male counterparts') commit far *fewer* crimes than men do? In the next section we shall examine *both* male and female patterns of crime.

Table 6–2 SOCIOLOGICAL EXPLANATIONS OF DEVIANCE: A SUMMARY

Theoretical Paradigm	Major Contribution
Structural–functional analysis	While what is deviant may vary, deviance itself is found in all societies; deviance and the social response it provokes serve to maintain the moral foundation of society; deviance can also direct social change
Symbolic-interaction analysis	Nothing is inherently deviant but may become defined as such through the response of others; the reactions of others are highly variable; the label of deviance can lead to the emergence of secondary deviance and deviant careers
Social-conflict analysis	Laws and other norms reflect the interests of powerful members of society; those who threaten the status quo are likely to be defined as deviant; social injury caused by powerful people is less likely to be defined as criminal than social injury caused by people who have little social power

CRIME

Speak of crime and people immediately conjure up images of unsavory characters lurking in the shadows, waiting to prey on unsuspecting innocents. But crime covers a much wider range—including activities that in one time or place carry the stigma of deviance and in another hardly merit a raised eyebrow. In centuries past, for example, a commoner who simply looked at the Chinese emperor in public was charged as a serious criminal. Today a citizen of the People's Republic of China who expressed support for the nation's historic monarchy would likely face criminal sanctions. The American judicial system has also undergone sweeping changes, from first supporting slavery to eventually condemning racial discrimination.

All societies have a formal mechanism for dealing with perceived violations of law. Generally, then, crime amounts to a violation of the criminal law enacted by a local, state, or national government. Technically, a crime is constructed of two distinct elements: the *act* itself (or, in some cases, the failure to do what the law requires) and *criminal intent* (in legal terminology, *mens rea*, or "guilty mind"). Intent is a matter of degree ranging from a deliberate action to negligence, in which a person behaves in a manner that may reasonably be expected to cause harm. Juries weigh the degree of intent in determining whether, for example, someone who kills another is guilty of first-degree murder, second-degree murder, or negligent manslaughter (Reid, 1982).

Types of Crime

In the United States, the Federal Bureau of Investigation gathers information on criminal offenses. Two major types of offenses are used to generate the "crime index."

Crimes against the person constitute *crimes against people that involve violence or the threat of violence.* Such "violent crimes" include murder and nonnegligent manslaughter (legally defined as "the willful killing of one human being by another"), aggravated assault ("an unlawful attack by one person on another for the purpose of inflicting severe or aggravated bodily injury"), forcible rape ("the carnal knowledge of a female forcibly and against her will"), and robbery ("taking or attempting to take anything of value from the care, custody, or control of a person or persons by force or threat of force or violence and/or putting the victim in fear").

Crimes against property encompass *crimes that involve theft of property belonging to others.* "Property crimes" range from burglary ("the unlawful entry of a structure to commit a [serious crime] or a theft") to larceny-theft ("the unlawful taking, carrying, leading, or riding away of property from the possession of another"), auto theft ("the theft or attempted theft of a motor vehicle"), and arson ("any willful or malicious burning or attempt to burn the personal property of another").

A third category of offenses, not incorporated in major crime indexes, is **victimless crimes,** *violations of the law in which there are no readily apparent victims.* So-called "crimes without complaint" include illegal drug use, prostitution, and gambling. However, "victimless crime" is often a misnomer. How victimless is a crime when young people purchasing drugs may be embarking on a course that will force them into a life of deviant behavior to support a drug habit? How victimless is a crime when a young pregnant woman taking drugs can cause the death or permanent injury of her baby? How victimless is a crime when a young runaway is lured into prostitution and then brainwashed into thinking that's her only way to live? And how victimless is a crime when a gambler falls so deeply into debt that he cannot afford food for his family or mortgage payments? Indeed, those committing these crimes themselves can also be the victims.

Because public opinion about such activities varies considerably, the laws regulating victimless crimes differ from place to place. In the United States, gambling is legal in Nevada and part of New Jersey; prostitution is legal only in part of Nevada; homosexual (and some heterosexual) behavior is legally restricted in about half the states. Where such laws do exist, enforcement is generally uneven.

Criminal Statistics

Statistics gathered by the Federal Bureau of Investigation show that crime rates increased dramatically during the 1970s, declined during the early 1980s, and rose again after 1984. Figure 6–1 illustrates this trend, showing the relative frequency of various crimes.

Crime statistics should be read with considerable caution since they are based only on offenses known to the police. Police learn about almost all homicides, but assaults—especially among acquaintances—are far less likely to be reported. Police records include an even smaller proportion of all the property crimes that are committed, especially those involving items of little value. Some victims may not realize that a crime has occurred, or they may assume they have little chance of recovering their property even if they notify the police.

Rape statistics rarely reflect the actual incidence of sexual assault. Because of the traditional stigma attached to innocent victims of rape, many women have avoided reporting cases of rape to the police. However, in recent years public support for rape victims—including the establishment of rape crisis centers, and increased sensitivity to the trauma of rape by police officers and hospital personnel—has prompted more victims to come forward. As a result there has been a significant rise in the reporting of this crime (U.S. Federal Bureau of Investigation, 1989). Nevertheless, experts believe that only about half of all rapes are reported.

One way to evaluate official crime statistics is through a *victimization survey,* in which a representative sample of Americans is asked about being victimized. According to these surveys, the actual amount of crime in this country stands at almost three times what crime index reports indicate.

The "Street" Criminal: A Profile

Government statistics paint a broad-brush picture of people arrested for violent and property crimes. We now examine the breakdown of criminal behavior by age, sex, social class, and race.

Age. Official crime rates rise sharply during adolescence and the early 20s, declining thereafter (Hirschi & Gottfredson, 1983; Krisberg & Schwartz, 1983). Although representing only 15 percent of Americans, people between the ages of fifteen and twenty-four accounted for almost half the arrests for serious crimes in 1989: 41.7 percent for violent crimes and 46.1 percent for property crimes.

Sex. Official statistics suggest that crime is an overwhelmingly male activity. A disproportionately high percentage of arrests for serious crimes in 1989 involved males as opposed to females: 76.0 percent of property crime arrests were of males; 24.0 percent, females. For violent crimes, the disparity grows even greater: 88.6 percent males and only 11.4 percent females in 1989. Although some research suggests that the sex disparity

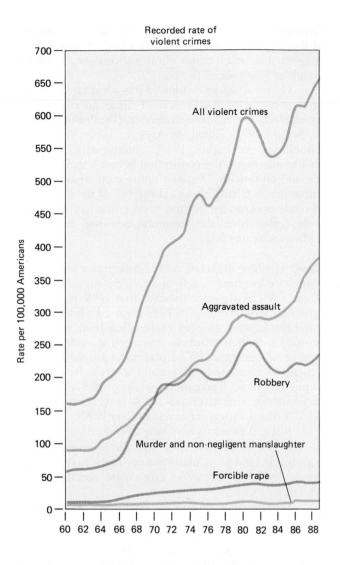

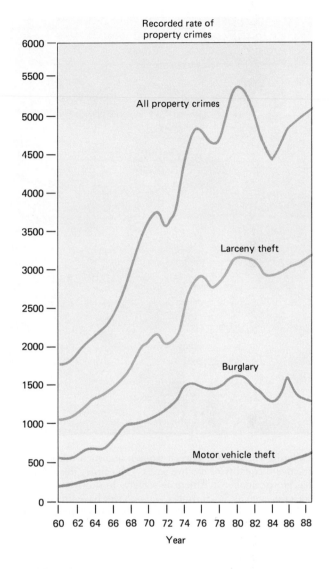

Figure 6–1 Crime Rates in the United States, 1960–1989
(U.S. Federal Bureau of Investigation, 1990)

among criminals diminishes in the lower social classes, this general pattern is striking (Hagan, Gillis, & Simpson, 1985).

In some measures, this difference stems from the reluctance of law enforcement officials to define women as criminals. Even so, the arrest rate for women has been moving closer to that of men, perhaps because of increasing sexual equality in American society. Between 1980 and 1989, the *increase* in arrests of women (47.9 percent) was twice that for men (23.9 percent) (U.S.

Federal Bureau of Investigation, 1990). In addition, girls and boys show similar patterns of delinquency in families where males and females share relative equality (Hagan, Simpson, & Gillis, 1987). Finally, research confirms that the greatest difference in crime rates between the two sexes appears in societies that most limit the social opportunities of women (Blum & Fisher, 1980).

Social class. Americans associate criminality with poverty. Sociological research suggests, however, that rich

Differing crime rates between women and men reflect the relative inequality of the two sexes. Over time, this disparity has grown smaller in American society. In strongly patriarchal societies such as Saudi Arabia, women still have little personal autonomy, and the crime rate among women is correspondingly low.

and poor alike commit crimes, albeit somewhat different *kinds* of offenses.

People arrested for violent and property crimes in the United States and elsewhere disproportionately have low social standing (Wolfgang, Figlio, & Sellin, 1972; Clinard & Abbott, 1973; Elliott & Ageton, 1980; Braithwaite, 1981; Thornberry & Farnsworth, 1982; Wolfgang, Thornberry, & Figlio, 1987). Here the disparity partly reflects the historical tendency to view poor people as less respectable than those whose wealth and power confer on them "respectability" (Tittle & Villemez, 1977; Tittle, Villemez, & Smith, 1978; Elias, 1986). Some contend that this bias in the criminal justice system has gradually

diminished, with criminality among various segments of the population becoming more equal. Evidence also suggests that street crime disproportionately *victimizes* people of lower social position.

Only a small proportion of less-advantaged people are ever convicted of crimes; most crimes are committed by relatively few hard-core offenders (Wolfgang, Figlio, & Sellin, 1972; Elliott & Ageton, 1980; Wolfgang, Thornberry, & Figlio, 1987). Additionally, as John Braithwaite notes, the connection between social standing and criminality "depends entirely on what form of crime one is talking about" (1981:47). If the definition of crime is expanded beyond street crime to encompass white-collar crime, the "common criminal" has much higher social standing.

Race. Probing the relationship between race and criminality, we confront a raft of complex issues. On the whole, official statistics indicate that 60.9 percent of arrests for serious crimes in 1989 involved whites. However, blacks were arrested more often than whites in proportion to their numbers, representing about 12 percent of Americans and 37.1 percent of arrests. African-Americans comprised 34.0 percent of arrests for property crimes (versus 63.9 percent for whites) and 47.7 percent of arrests for violent crimes (50.8 percent for whites) (U.S. Federal Bureau of Investigation, 1990).

Just as Americans have long considered criminality the province of the poor, they have also associated crime with blacks (and particularly young, black males). This despite evidence that most crimes are committed by whites.

We can draw no simple conclusions about crime and race for three reasons. First, arrest records do not qualify as statements of proven guilt. To the degree that *cultural prejudices* prompt police officers to arrest nonwhites more readily than whites, and lead white citizens more readily to report nonwhites to the police as suspected offenders, nonwhites are overly criminalized. The same prejudices work in the courtroom. In the long run, even small biases by law enforcement officials and the public substantially distort the official link between race and crime (Liska & Tausig, 1979; Unnever, Frazier, & Henretta, 1980; Smith & Visher, 1981).

Second, race in the United States is closely related to social standing, which, as we have already seen, affects the likelihood of engaging in street crimes. Research by Judith and Peter Blau (1982) helps to sort out the links among race, poverty, and criminality. Studying 125 large American cities, the Blaus concluded that high rates of criminality—especially violent crime—primarily stem from income disparity. Thus, deviant subcultures do not cause criminality; rather, crime results from poverty in the midst of affluence. Suffering the hardships of poverty in a rich society encourages people to view society and its laws as unjust. This perception, the Blaus maintain, provokes criminality. Because unemployment among African-American adults is two to three times higher than among whites, and because *almost half* of African-American children grow up in poverty (in contrast to about one in six white children), we should expect proportionately higher crime rates for African-Americans (Sampson, 1987). Research suggests that rigid systems of social inequality in other societies generate similar patterns of criminality (Messner, 1989).

Third, as noted earlier, white-collar crimes are excluded from the crime index. Clearly, this omission contributes to the view that the typical criminal is not simply poor but nonwhite. If our definition of crime is broadened to encompass insider business fraud, toxic-waste dumping, embezzlement, bribery, and cheating on income tax returns, the proportion of white criminals would certainly rise.

Crime in Global Perspective

By global standards, American society has a disproportionately high crime rate. Marshall Clinard (1978) observes that in Switzerland murders are relatively rare even in the largest cities. By contrast, New York City led all American cities, with 1,905 murders in 1989; rarely does a day pass with no murder in New York. Another forty-two cities had more than fifty murders each in 1989 (U.S. Federal Bureau of Investigation, 1990).

Although crime rates rose in Europe more than in the United States during the early 1980s, crime pervades American society to a much greater extent than it does in European countries. In a recent comparison, the American homicide rate stood five times higher than that of Europe; the rape rate, seven times higher; and property crime rates, twice as high. Truly global comparisons are difficult because nations define crimes differently and because data often are not accurately reported. Figure 6–2 on page 144 gives comparative data for rape and robbery. Although the patterns differ for each crime, we see that the United States contends with more crime than virtually any other country in the world (Kalish, 1988).

Elliot Currie (1985) suggests that crime is one product of our culture's emphasis on individual economic success, frequently at the expense of family and community cohesion. Currie also notes that, unlike European nations, the United States has neither a government-guaranteed minimum family income level nor publicly funded child-care programs. Such public policy decisions, he claims, erode the fabric of our society, give rise to increasing frustration among society's have-nots, and thus encourage criminal behavior. Furthermore, Currie asserts that the high level of unemployment and underemployment tolerated by Americans (and also by Europeans) helps create a large category of perpetually poor people whose opportunities to make money are often limited to crime. The key to reducing crime, then, lies in *social change*, Currie believes, not in hiring more police and building more prisons, politically expedient yet shortsighted responses.

Finally, Americans extol self-sufficiency and individualism, both embodied in the widespread private ownership of guns. This proliferation of guns encourages deadly crime. Recent controversy over "assault rifles" has focused renewed public attention on this issue, as the box on page 145 explains.

Available evidence indicates that crime rates in the nonindustrial societies of the world are also generally lower than in the United States. Some countries have high rates of violence (Colombia's recent drug war stands out), but the rate of property crime in this country dwarfs that of most Third-World nations. This lower crime rate in nonindustrial nations reflects the traditional nature of such societies; there, strong families and well-integrated residential areas informally control crime (Clinard & Abbott, 1973).

THE CRIMINAL JUSTICE SYSTEM

Through the criminal justice system, society formally responds to crime. We now examine key elements of this system: police, the courts, and the punishment of convicted offenders.

The Police

The police generally serve as the point of contact between the public and the criminal justice system. In principle, the police maintain public order by uniformly en-

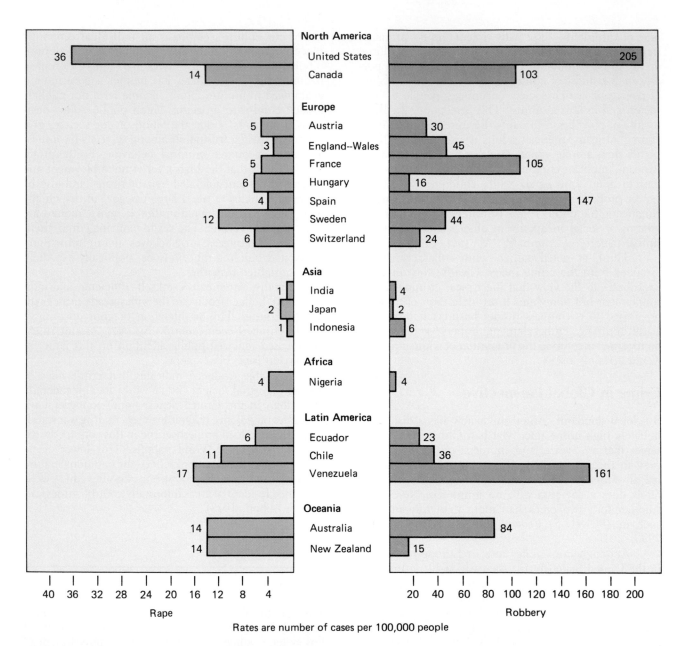

North America
- United States — Rape: 36, Robbery: 205
- Canada — Rape: 14, Robbery: 103

Europe
- Austria — Rape: 5, Robbery: 30
- England–Wales — Rape: 3, Robbery: 45
- France — Rape: 5, Robbery: 105
- Hungary — Rape: 6, Robbery: 16
- Spain — Rape: 4, Robbery: 147
- Sweden — Rape: 12, Robbery: 44
- Switzerland — Rape: 6, Robbery: 24

Asia
- India — Rape: 1, Robbery: 4
- Japan — Rape: 2, Robbery: 2
- Indonesia — Rape: 1, Robbery: 6

Africa
- Nigeria — Rape: 4, Robbery: 4

Latin America
- Ecuador — Rape: 6, Robbery: 23
- Chile — Rape: 11, Robbery: 36
- Venezuela — Rape: 17, Robbery: 161

Oceania
- Australia — Rape: 14, Robbery: 84
- New Zealand — Rape: 14, Robbery: 15

Rape

Robbery

Rates are number of cases per 100,000 people

Figure 6–2 Global Comparisons: Rates for Rape and Robbery
(Interpol data, as reported by Kalish, 1988)

"The Other Arms Race": Are Americans Really Safer?

On the afternoon of January 31, 1989, thirty-one-year-old Patrick Purdy paced nervously in a Stockton, California, schoolyard. After the final bell rang, as children were swarming from the building, Purdy opened fire with a high-powered, semiautomatic rifle, killing five and wounding thirty. We will never completely understand what provoked the shocking attack because Purdy ended the slaughter by taking his own life. But this event highlighted the latest chapter in the long controversy surrounding private ownership of firearms in the United States.

More than 21,500 Americans were murdered in 1989; about 62 percent were killed by guns. Currently, almost half of American households report owning at least one gun (N.O.R.C., 1989). In recent years, high-powered military-type weaponry, like the imitation AK-47 assault rifle Patrick Purdy used, are being added to the American arsenal. Capable of rapidly firing bullets through concrete walls, such assault rifles are readily available in stores in most states. They are especially popular among drug-dealing gangs that roam the streets of many cities, but increasing numbers are being purchased by "average Americans" convinced that their personal safety depends on owning a powerful firearm. Ironically, highly publicized cases such as the Purdy killings set in motion a vicious cycle: More violence increases the demand for firearms, which in turn generates further violence.

The raging controversy over privately owned firearms has sparked a number of ideas for reform. Some propose a waiting period of two weeks between the request for a firearm and the actual purchase to discourage impulse buying and to allow for a comprehensive background check. Another proposal would consolidate the current patchwork of state and local laws into uniform federal laws; in this way, no one could bypass a gun-control law merely by crossing a state border.

To date, most legislation on such proposals has been stalled by powerful opponents of gun control. Several months after the Purdy shooting, California managed to enact a ban on the manufacture and sale of assault rifles, but only by a narrow margin.

The federal government did not follow suit, instead restricting itself to blocking imports of such weapons.

Restricting gun ownership will never, in itself, resolve the American crime problem; the number of Californians killed each year by knives, for example, exceeds the number of Canadians killed by weapons of all kinds (Currie, 1985). Nevertheless, greater regulation of guns could reduce the extent and intensity of American violence. The issue of paramilitary firearms may well depend on the position taken by police officers, who face the sobering reality of being "out-gunned" by criminals. As Daryl Gates, the Los Angeles Chief of Police, recently pointed out, "There is no need for citizens to have highly sophisticated military assault rifles designed for the sole purpose of killing people on the battlefield."

SOURCES: Based on George J. Church, "The Other Arms Race," *Time*, Vol. 133, No. 6 (February 6, 1989):20–24, 25–26; Jacob V. Lamar, "Gunning for Assault Rifles," *Time*, Vol. 133, No. 13 (March 27, 1989):29; William R. Tonso, *Gun and Society: The Social and Existential Roots of the American Attachment to Firearms* (Lanham, MD: University Press of America, 1982).

---

forcing the law. In reality, the roughly 650,000 full-time police in the United States (in 1990) could never effectively monitor the activities of some 250 million Americans. As a result, the police exercise considerable discretion in deciding which situations warrant their attention and how to handle them.

In a study of police behavior in five cities, Douglas Smith and Christy Visher (1981; Smith, 1987) identified six factors that police take into account when confronted with apparent crime. Because they must often act quickly, police rely on external cues to guide their actions. First,

the more serious they perceive the situation to be, the more likely they are to make an arrest. Second, police assess the victim's preference in how the matter should be handled. In general, if a victim demands that an arrest be made, police are more likely to do so. Third, police more often arrest suspects who appear uncooperative. Fourth, they are more likely to arrest suspects with whom they have had prior contact, presumably because this suggests guilt. Fifth, the presence of bystanders increases the likelihood of arrest. According to Smith and Visher, a gathering of observers prompts police to act more assertively because they want to appear to be in control of the situation, and also because an arrest moves the interaction from the street (the suspect's turf) to the police department (where officers have the upper hand). Sixth, all else being equal, police are more likely to arrest nonwhite suspects than white ones. Smith and Visher concluded that police tend to consider nonwhite suspects as either more dangerous or more likely to be guilty. In their view, this perception contributes to the disproportionately high level of arrests of nonwhites.

Finally, the proportion of police relative to population is greatest in cities with high concentrations of nonwhites and with large income disparities between rich and poor (Jacobs, 1979). This finding accords with Judith and Peter Blau's (1982) conclusion that striking inequalities in income promote criminal violence. Thus police are concentrated where a volatile mix of social forces encourages disruption.

The Courts

After arrest, a suspect's guilt or innocence is determined by a court. In principle, our courts rely on an adversarial system of justice involving attorneys—who represent the defendant on one side and the state on the other—in the presence of a judge who upholds legal procedures. In practice, however, about 90 percent of criminal cases are resolved before they come to court through **plea bargaining,** *a legal negotiation in which the prosecution reduces a defendant's charge in exchange for a guilty plea.* For example, a defendant charged with burglary may agree to plead guilty to the lesser charge of possession of burglary tools; another charged with selling cocaine may go along with pleading guilty to mere possession.

Plea bargaining has gained widespread acceptance because it spares the system the time and expense of court trials. A trial is usually unnecessary if the prosecution and the defense agree on the basic facts of a case. By selectively trying only a small proportion of the cases, the courts can also channel their resources into those deemed most important (Reid, 1982).

But in the process, defendants (who are presumed innocent) are pressured to plead guilty. A person can exercise the right to a trial, but only at the risk of receiving a more severe sentence if found guilty. In essence, then, plea bargaining undercuts the rights of defendants as it circumvents the adversarial process. According to Abraham Blumberg (1970), defendants who have little understanding of the criminal justice system, as well as those

unable to afford a good lawyer, are likely to suffer from this system of "bargain-counter justice."

Punishment

In 1831 a nine-year-old English boy was hanged for the crime of setting fire to a house (Kittrie, 1971:103). American history reveals that 281 youths have been executed for crimes committed as juveniles, most recently a young man in Texas for a murder committed when he was seventeen. Twenty-seven other juveniles are currently on death row, awaiting Supreme Court rulings

Van Gogh's painting *Prisoner's Round* conveys the stark isolation and numbing depersonalization that characterized dungeon-like prisons of the late nineteenth century. One hundred years later, our prisons remain custodial institutions in which little rehabilitation occurs.

Vincent Van Gogh, 1853–1890. Prisoner's Round. *Dutch. Pushkin State Museum, Moscow.*

on whether their age should preclude their execution (Rosenbaum, 1989).

Such cases spark controversy because, in the United States, young people are widely regarded as having *diminished capacity* for crime. In addition, the issue of juvenile crime raises the question of why societies punish in the first place. Four justifications for punishment are commonly advanced.

Retribution. The most important justification for punishing is **retribution,** *subjecting an offender to suffering comparable to that caused by the offense.* As an act of social vengeance, retribution underlies a view of society as a system of moral balance. When criminality upsets this balance, punishment exacted in comparable measure restores the moral order, as suggested in the biblical dictum "an eye for an eye."

Retribution stands as the oldest justification for punishment. During the Middle Ages, crime was widely viewed as sin—an offense against God as well as society—therefore warranting harsh punishment. Although sometimes criticized today because it overlooks the issue of reforming the offender, retribution remains a strong justification for punishment.

Deterrence. A second justification for punishment, **deterrence,** amounts to *the attempt to discourage criminality through punishment.* Deterrence is based on the Enlightenment notion that humans are calculating and rational creatures. From this point of view, people engage in deviance for personal gain, but if they think that the drawbacks of punishment outweigh the benefits of crime, the incidence of criminal behavior will diminish.

Initially, deterrence was instituted to reform a system of excessive punishments based on retribution. Why put someone to death for a theft, for example, if the crime could be discouraged by a lesser penalty? As the concept of deterrence became better accepted, execution and physical mutilation of criminals were replaced by milder forms of punishment such as imprisonment.

Punishment may deter in two ways. *Specific deterrence* demonstrates to the offender individually that crime does not pay. *General deterrence* works as the punishment of one person serves as an example to others.

Rehabilitation. The third justification for punishment, **rehabilitation,** involves *reforming the offender to preclude subsequent offenses.* Rehabilitation paralleled the development of the social sciences in the nineteenth century. According to early social analysts, crime and other deviance sprang from an unfavorable social environment, one pervaded by poverty or lack of parental supervision,

for example. Many prisons, therefore, were called *reformatories* or *houses of correction,* and offered offenders a controlled environment (recall the description of total institutions in Chapter 3, "Socialization: From Infancy to Aging").

Rehabilitation resembles deterrence because it motivates the offender to conform to societal norms. But rehabilitation emphasizes constructive improvement while deterrence and retribution simply make the offender suffer. In addition, while retribution demands that the punishment fit the crime, rehabilitation focuses on the distinctive problems of each offender. Thus identical offenses might prompt similar acts of retribution, but different programs of rehabilitation.

Social protection. A final justification for punishment, **social protection,** refers to *rendering an offender incapable of further offenses either temporarily through incarceration or permanently by execution.* Like deterrence, social protection takes a rational approach to punishment and seeks to protect society from crime.

Table 6–3 summarizes these four justifications of punishment.

Table 6–3	FOUR JUSTIFICATIONS OF PUNISHMENT: A SUMMARY
Retribution	The oldest justification of punishment that remains important today. Punishment is atonement for a moral wrong by an individual; in principle, punishment should be comparable in severity to the deviance itself.
Deterrence	An early modern approach, deviance is viewed as social disruption, which society acts to control. People are viewed as rational and self-interested, so that deterrence requires that the pains of punishment outweigh the pleasures of deviance.
Rehabilitation	A modern approach linked to development of social sciences, deviance is viewed as the product of social problems (such as poverty) or of personal problems (such as mental illness). Social conditions are improved and offenders subjected to intervention appropriate to their condition.
Social protection	A modern approach easier to effect than rehabilitation. If society is unable or unwilling to improve offenders or reform social conditions, protection from further deviance is afforded by incarceration or execution.

Critical evaluation. We have described four purposes of punishment. Assessing the actual consequences of punishment, however, is no simple task.

The value of retribution relates to Durkheim's ideas about the functions of punishment. Recall that Durkheim believed that responding to deviance increases people's awareness of shared morality. Punishing a person for a moral offense, moreover, draws together disparate members of society by reinforcing a shared sense of justice. For this reason punishment was traditionally carried out in public. Public executions occurred in England until 1868; the last public execution in the United States took place in Kentucky in 1936. Today the mass media make sure that the public is aware of executions carried out in prisons (Kittrie, 1971). Nonetheless, it is difficult to prove scientifically that punishment upholds social morality. Often it advances one view of social morality at the expense of another, as when people who object to military service are imprisoned.

To some degree, punishment serves as a specific deterrent. Yet American society also has a high rate of **criminal recidivism,** *subsequent offenses committed by people previously convicted of crimes.* One recent study of people released from prison found that within three years, 63 percent had been rearrested and 41 percent had been returned to prison (U.S. Bureau of Justice Statistics, 1989). Such a high rate of recidivism raises questions about how well punishment actually deters crime. In addition, only about one-third of all crimes come to the attention of police, and of these, only about one in five results in an arrest. The old adage that "crime doesn't pay" rings rather hollow when we consider that a small proportion of offenses ever result in punishment.

General deterrence is even more difficult to investigate scientifically, since we have no way of knowing how people might act if they were unaware of punishments meted out to others. In the debate over capital punishment, which is now permitted in thirty-seven states, critics of the practice point to research suggesting that the death penalty has limited value as a general deterrent in the United States and elsewhere (Sellin, 1980; van den Haag & Conrad; 1983; Lester, 1987; Archer & Gartner, 1987; Bailey & Peterson, 1989).

Efforts at rehabilitation have also provoked controversy. Prisons do accomplish social protection simply by keeping offenders off the streets, but they offer little in the way of socially constructive learning. Penologists now concede that prisons rarely rehabilitate inmates (Carlson, 1976). Perhaps this is to be expected, since, according to Sutherland's theory of differential association, placing a person among criminals for a long period of time should simply strengthen criminal attitudes and skills. The prison environment also has a destructive level of physical and sexual violence. Once released, prison inmates also retain the stigma of being ex-convicts, an obstacle to successful integration into the larger society. One study of young offenders in Philadelphia found that boys who were sentenced to long prison terms, and were therefore more likely to acquire a criminal stigma, later committed both more crimes and more serious ones (Wolfgang, Figlio, & Sellin, 1972).

Finally, we must recognize that police, courts, and prisons can never effectively end crime. The reason, echoed throughout this chapter, is simple: Crime—in fact, all kinds of deviance—is more than simply the acts of "bad people;" it is inextricably bound up in the operation of society itself.

SUMMARY

1. Deviance refers to violations of all kinds of norms, from mild breaches of etiquette to serious violence.
2. Biological explanations of crime, from Lombroso's research in the nineteenth century to developing research in human genetics, has yet to produce much insight into the causes of crime.
3. Psychological explanations of deviance focus on abnormalities in the individual personality, which arise from either biological causes or the social environment. Psychological theories help to explain some kinds of deviance.
4. Social forces produce deviance because deviance (a) exists in relation to cultural norms, (b) involves a process of social definition, and (c) is shaped by the distribution of social power.
5. Sociology links deviance to the operation of society rather than the deficiencies of individuals. Using the structural-functional paradigm, Durkheim identified several functions of deviance for society as a whole.
6. The symbolic-interaction paradigm is the basis of labeling theory, which holds that deviance arises

from the reaction of some audience to a particular behavior. Labeling theory focuses on secondary deviance and deviant careers, which result from acquiring the stigma of deviance.

7. Social-conflict theory directs attention to the relationship between deviance and patterns of social inequality. Following the approach of Karl Marx, this paradigm notes that laws and other norms reflect the interests of the most powerful people in society. Social-conflict theory also spotlights white-collar crimes that cause extensive social harm, although the offenders are rarely defined as criminals.

8. Official statistics indicate that arrest rates peak in adolescence, then drop steadily with advancing age. Males are arrested about four times as often as females for serious street crimes. Three-fourths of property crime arrests are of males, as are almost nine out of ten arrests for personal crimes.

9. People of lower social position tend to commit more street crime than Americans with greater social privilege. When white-collar crimes are included in the overall category of criminal offenses, however, this disparity diminishes.

10. More whites than nonwhites are arrested for street crimes; however, African-Americans are arrested proportionately more often. Eliminating racial bias from the criminal justice system would lessen this disparity.

11. The police exercise considerable discretion in their work. Research suggests that factors such as the seriousness of the offense, the presence of bystanders, and the accused being male and nonwhite increase the likelihood of arrest.

12. Although ideally an adversarial system, American courts predominantly resolve cases through plea bargaining. An efficient method of handling cases where the facts are not in dispute, plea bargaining nevertheless places less powerful people at a disadvantage.

13. Punishment has been justified in terms of retribution, deterrence, rehabilitation, and social protection. Because its consequences are difficult to evaluate scientifically, punishment—like deviance itself—sparks considerable controversy among sociologists and the public as a whole.

KEY CONCEPTS

crime the violation of norms formally enacted into criminal law

crimes against property (property crimes) crimes that involve theft of property belonging to others

crimes against the person (violent crimes) crimes against people that involve violence or the threat of violence

criminal justice system a multifaceted system of social control that responds to alleged violations of the law through the use of police, courts, and punishment

criminal recidivism subsequent offenses committed by people previously convicted of crimes

deterrence the attempt to discourage criminality through punishment

deviance the recognized violation of cultural norms

juvenile delinquency the violation of legal standards that apply to the young

labeling theory the assertion that deviance and conformity arise in the response of others

medicalization of deviance the transformation of moral and legal issues into medical matters

plea bargaining a legal negotiation in which the prosecution reduces a defendant's charge in exchange for a guilty plea

rehabilitation reforming the offender to preclude subsequent offenses

retribution subjecting an offender to suffering comparable to that caused by the offense

retrospective labeling the interpretation of someone's past consistent with present deviance

social control attempts by society to regulate the behavior of individuals

social protection rendering an offender incapable of further offenses either temporarily through incarceration or permanently by execution

stigma a powerfully negative label that radically changes a person's social identity and self-concept

victimless crimes violations of law in which there are no readily apparent victims

white-collar crime crimes committed by people of high social position in the course of their occupations

Social Stratification

7

Chapter Outline

On April 10, 1912, the ocean liner *Titanic* left the docks of Southampton, England, on its maiden voyage across the North Atlantic to New York. A proud symbol of the new industrial age, the towering ship carried 2,300 passengers, some enjoying more luxury than most travelers today could imagine. The lower decks, however, were crowded with poor immigrants, journeying to what they hoped would be a better life in the United States.

On April 14, the crew received reports of icebergs in the area but paid little notice. Then, near midnight, as the ship steamed swiftly and silently westward, a lookout was stunned to see a massive shape rising out of the dark ocean directly ahead. Moments later, the ship collided with a huge iceberg, which ripped open the seams in the starboard hull. Sea water exploded into the ship's lower levels, and within twenty-five minutes people were cramming into the lifeboats. By 2 A.M. the bow of the *Titanic* was submerged and the stern was rising high above the water. There, silently observed by those in the lifeboats, hundreds of helpless passengers solemnly passed their final moments before the ship disappeared into the frigid water (Lord, 1976).

The tragic loss of more than 1,600 lives shocked the world. Looking back at this terrible event from a sociological perspective, however, we see that some categories of passengers had much better odds of survival than others. Of those holding first-class tickets, more than 60 percent survived, primarily because they were on the upper decks, where warnings were sounded first and lifeboats were accessible. Only 36 percent of the second-class passengers survived, and of the third-class passengers on the lower decks, only 24 percent escaped drowning. On board the *Titanic*, class turned out to mean more than the degree of luxury of accommodations: It was truly a matter of life or death.

This story dramatically illustrates the consequences of social inequality and the enormous difference it can make in the way people live, or sometimes whether they live at all. The chapter introduces a number of concepts and sociological ideas concerning social stratification and examines social inequality in American society. Chapter 8 explores how American society fits into a system of global inequality.

WHAT IS SOCIAL STRATIFICATION?

In every society, some people have more valued resources—money, housing, education, health, and power—than others. Such patterns are commonly called *social inequality*. Some social inequality reflects differences in people themselves—their varying abilities and efforts, for example. However, it also relates to the *society* in which they live. Sociologists use the term **social stratification** to refer to *a system by which categories of people in a society are ranked in a hierarchy*. Four key principles help explain social stratification.

1. **Social stratification is a characteristic of society, not simply a function of individual differences.** Social stratification involves how a society distributes what it produces. In the most technologically simple societies—the hunting and gathering societies described in Chapter 2 ("Culture")—so little was produced that people were more or less equal in social standing. More complex technology, however, allows bountiful production, although resources may be distributed quite unequally to people regardless of their individual abilities.

   Did a higher percentage of the first-class passengers on the *Titanic* survive because they were better swimmers than the second- and third-class passengers? Hardly. They fared better because of their privileged position on the ship. Similarly, American children born into wealthy families are more likely than those born into poverty to enjoy health and to live well into old age. Neither rich nor poor children are responsible for creating social stratification, yet this system shapes the lives of them all.

2. **Although variable in form, social stratification is universal.** No society is devoid of social stratification. Yet social stratification is also highly variable. As we shall explain, social stratification tends to be more rigid in agrarian societies of the world than in industrial societies. Less pronounced differences in systems of social inequality distinguish today's industrial societies from one another.

3. **Social stratification persists over generations.** Because social stratification is linked to the family, children assume the social positions of their parents. Especially in industrial societies, social position reflects some element of achievement, based on individual talent and effort. The concept of **social mobility** refers to such *changes in people's positions in a system of social stratification*. Even in industrial societies, however, social position is initially ascribed so that systems of social stratification tend to retain considerable stability.

4. **Social stratification is supported by patterns of**

The social position of Americans tends to remain fairly stable over generations. This is most true at the extremes, that is, among the very rich and the very poor. The most privileged Americans—those born to great wealth—employ rituals such as debutante balls to encourage their sons and daughters to marry one another, thus extending their privileges into another generation.

belief. Any system of social stratification is more likely to persist to the extent that it is thought to be fair. And just as systems of social stratification differ, so do the beliefs that legitimate them. Typically, people with the greatest social privileges express the strongest support for their society's system of social stratification, while those with fewer social resources are more likely to challenge the system.

SYSTEMS OF CASTE AND CLASS

In describing social stratification in particular societies, sociologists often use two opposing standards: systems that are relatively "closed"—allowing little social mobility—and those that are comparatively "open"—offering considerable change in social position (Tumin, 1985).

The Caste System

A **caste system** amounts to *social stratification based on ascription*. In a pure form, a caste system would allow individuals no social mobility at all; birth alone would determine one's destiny. Not surprisingly, then, people living in caste-like systems are very conscious of which social category they belong to.

Illustrations: India and South Africa. The nation of India—especially its traditional Hindu villages—illustrates caste-like social stratification. In the Indian caste system, people are born into one of several thousand caste groups, which place people in relation to one another in the local community.

In a caste system, birth determines the fundamental shape of people's lives in three crucial respects. First, traditional caste groups are linked to occupation; families in each caste group perform one type of work from generation to generation. Although some occupations (such as farming) are open to anyone, castes are socially identified with the work their members do (as priests, barbers, leather workers, and so on).

Second, a rigid system of social stratification mandates that each person marry someone of the same social standing. Sociologists call this pattern *endogamous* marriage (*endo* stems from the Greek, meaning "within"). The Indian tradition directs parents to select their children's marriage partners, often when the children are quite young. Only occasionally does a child of one caste (usually a female) marry a person of a higher position (Srinivas, 1971).

Third, powerful cultural beliefs underlie caste systems. In India, Hindu traditions define acceptance of one's fate as a moral duty; therefore, people must carry out their life's work, whatever it may be. Caste systems are commonly found in agrarian societies, and such beliefs foster the habits of diligence and discipline that agriculture demands. Cultural norms also specify appropriate social relationships. Traditional Indian Hinduism defines higher caste groups as relatively "pure," while lower caste groups are considered symbolically "polluted." The ingrained belief that a member of a higher caste is polluted by contact with a member of a lower caste creates a social distance between the two, virtually eliminating intermarriage. In the same way, many white South Africans justify apartheid by claiming they are morally superior to the black majority and, consequently, justified in dominating them.

Since the Industrial Revolution, beliefs that rank entire categories of people in this way have gradually diminished. As later chapters explain, such attitudes represent various "isms"—racism, sexism, ageism—that are increasingly denounced as unjust. Even in India, the caste system has been outlawed, although it still remains

South Africa: Race as Caste

At the southern tip of the African continent lies South Africa, a territory about the size of Alaska, with a population of almost 40 million. Social stratification in South Africa is based on race. About one South African in seven is of European ancestry (approximately the same proportion as that of Americans of African descent), yet South Africa's white minority holds the dominant share of wealth and power. Representing three-fourths of South Africans, blacks have far fewer rights and privileges. Another 4 million South Africans, known as "coloreds," are of mixed race, and about 1 million are Asians.

Apartheid, meaning the separation of the races, is the historical product of colonization by Europeans. The first Europeans to settle in southern Africa were Dutch traders who arrived in the mid-seventeenth century. Early in the nineteenth century, British colonization began, and the descendants of the Dutch settlers were pushed inland. By the beginning of the twentieth century, the British had

Recent reforms in South Africa have yet to fundamentally alter the caste barriers that divide the races in this industrial society. Whites dominate the economy and live in desirable urban areas, while blacks are constrained to live in shantytowns as poor as any in the world.

consolidated control of the region, calling it the Union of South Africa. In 1961 the Republic of South Africa won independence from Britain and became a sovereign nation.

The minority population of whites devised the rigid system of apartheid, and enforced racial separation with a pattern of brutality. An informal practice for many years, apartheid be-

---

deeply embedded in rural social life. In South Africa, a racially based caste system known as *apartheid* is still legally in force. Here, as the box explains, the white minority continues to dominate the black majority.

The Class System

A caste system bolsters stable, agrarian life; industrial societies, in contrast, depend on individual initiative, extensive education, and specialized skills. Social inequality in industrialized societies thus takes the form of a **class system,** *social stratification based on individual achievement.*

Social "classes" are not as rigidly defined as castes. As people develop their individual talents, they are likely to experience social mobility, blurring class distinctions. At the same time, clear social categories break down as more people migrate from rural areas to industrial cities and others immigrate from abroad. Paralleling these educational, demographic, and economic developments, governments in industrialized societies typically adopt democratic political systems, extending political rights to people of all social backgrounds, and giving them equal standing before the law.

Class systems are supported by the belief that individual talents and abilities should determine social position. Careers become more a matter of individual came law in 1948 and was used to deny the black majority South African citizenship, ownership of land, and any formal voice in the government. As a racial caste, blacks hold low-paying, menial jobs, and perform most of the hard labor; on average, they earn only one-fourth what whites do. In the past twenty-five years, some 3 million blacks have been forcibly relocated to homelands—dirt-poor districts set aside to confine and control them. In short, in a land with extensive natural resources, including diamonds and precious minerals, the majority of people live in abject poverty.

To maintain racial castes, South African laws have forbidden sexual relationships and marriage between the races. Such regulations have been gradually eased since 1985, but interracial marriage occurs infrequently because, for the most part, blacks and whites are still required to live in separate areas.

How is such an unequal system maintained? The prosperous white minority has traditionally defended it as an effort to protect their cultural traditions from influence by blacks, who are viewed as social inferiors. Increasingly, however, whites have relied on a powerful system of military repression to maintain their power. Lacking formal rights, blacks suspected of opposing white rule were for decades subject to arbitrary arrest and indefinite detention.

Despite its severity, this repression has not kept blacks—and a growing number of sympathetic whites—from challenging apartheid. Violent confrontations have become more frequent in recent years, especially among younger blacks impatient for political and economic opportunity. By the end of the 1980s, some 200 American corporations had severed direct economic ties with South Africa. This economic pressure has prompted reforms. In 1984, South Africans of mixed race and Asians were granted a limited voice in government. Additionally, a number of "petty apartheid" regulations, separating blacks and whites in public places, have been rescinded. Blacks have also won the right to form labor unions, resulting in economic gains for some workers. In 1990, the release from prison of Nelson Mandela and the legalization of the anti-apartheid African National Congress has raised the hope of more basic change.

In defending the slow pace of reform, South African officials urge Americans to remember that the United States, too, had a racial caste system in the past, and that the races are still far from equal today. Many whites also fear—perhaps with good reason—that granting full legal rights to the black majority will undermine their privileged position. However, the black majority, supported by world opinion, appears unlikely to settle for anything less.

SOURCES: George M. Fredrickson, *White Supremacy: A Comparative Study in American and South African History* (New York: Oxford University Press, 1981); also recent news reports.

achievement and choice, rather than being passed from generation to generation, as in caste systems. Greater individuality also translates into more freedom in marriage, with parents and cultural traditions playing a lesser role in children's selections of their mates.

Class systems also differ from caste systems in their degree of **status consistency**, *consistency of ranking across various dimensions of social standing*. Linking social ranking to birth (as in caste systems) generates high status consistency, meaning that across a lifetime an individual has roughly the same degree of privilege or deprivation when it comes to wealth, prestige, and power. Class systems, with their greater social mobility, offer less status consistency. In American society, some people with prestigious occupations (such as priests or professors) accumulate little wealth and only moderate social power. Such inconsistencies make the boundaries between classes less clear than those separating castes.

An illustration: Great Britain. The class system that has emerged in Great Britain since the Industrial Revolution reflects that society's long agrarian history. In the Middle Ages, social stratification took the form of a caste-like system of three *estates*. A hereditary nobility, or first estate, accounted for only 5 percent of the population. These nobles maintained wealth and power through the ownership of land (Laslett, 1984). Typically, nobles had no occupation at all; to be "engaged in trade" or any type of work for income was deemed "beneath" them. Well tended by servants, nobles used their extensive leisure time to cultivate refined tastes in art, music, and literature.

The law of *primogeniture* (from Latin meaning "first born") mandated that only the eldest son inherit property. This system protected large landholdings from division among children, so that many vast estates survived for centuries. In the process, younger sons of nobility had to find other ways to support themselves. Some entered the clergy—the second estate—where spiritual power was supplemented by the church's extensive landholdings. Others became military officers or lawyers, or took up other occupations that have come down to us today as "honorable" callings for "gentlemen." In an age when few women could expect to earn a living on their own, a daughter of nobility typically depended for her security on marrying well.

Below the nobility and the clergy, the vast majority of men and women formed the third estate, or commoners. Owning little or no land, most commoners or serfs were poor. They toiled for a lifetime on land owned by others, receiving little in return. Unlike the nobility and the clergy, commoners had little access to schooling, so most remained illiterate.

As the Industrial Revolution gradually transformed England's economy, some commoners, especially those in cities, gained wealth and power rivaling—and sometimes surpassing—that of the nobility. This economic transformation, along with the extension of education and legal rights to more people, soon blurred traditional social rankings as a class system emerged. Yet the legacy of Britain's feudal past remains in today's social stratification.

Many members of Great Britain's small upper class today enjoy wealth largely achieved through their own efforts. Others, descendants of traditional nobility, still maintain inherited wealth, savor the highest prestige, attend expensive, elite universities, and wield considerable power to shape British society. Note, too, that a traditional monarch stands as Britain's head of state, and Parliament's House of Lords is composed of "peers" of noble birth. Actual control of government, however, resides in the House of Commons, composed of commoners who are more likely to have achieved their position through individual effort than through ascription.

Below the upper class, perhaps one-fourth of the British population falls into the "middle class." Some are moderately wealthy, with high incomes from professions and business. These richer commoners, along with members of the upper class, make up the roughly 10 percent of Britons with investments in the form of stocks and bonds (Sherrid, 1986). Most members of today's British middle class, however, do not earn enough to accumulate substantial wealth.

Below the middle class, across a boundary that cannot be precisely defined, lie the half of all Britons known as the "working class." As in the United States, members of the working class earn modest incomes, commonly from manual labor. Although the British economy expanded during the 1980s, traditional industries such as coal mining and steel production declined, subjecting many working-class families to unemployment. Some slipped into poverty, joining the remaining one-fourth of Britons who are socially and economically deprived. Lower-class people—or, more simply, "the poor"—are heavily concentrated in northern and western regions plagued by economic decay.

Today Great Britain displays typical class-system traits: unequally distributed wealth, power, and prestige, but with some opportunity for significant movement up and down in the overall system. One legacy of the estate system, however, is that movement between social classes occurs less frequently than in the United States (Kerckhoff, Campbell, & Winfield-Laird, 1985). Compared with Americans, therefore, Britons are more resigned to remaining in the social position to which they were born (Snowman, 1977). The greater rigidity of British stratification is exemplified in the importance of accent as a mark of social position. Distinctive patterns of speech develop within any society as categories of people are socially segregated from one another over long periods. In Great Britain, families of long-standing affluence and those living in poverty speak with such different linguistic patterns that it hardly sounds as if they are speaking the same language.

Beyond Class? The Soviet Union

We have seen how industrialization has moved traditional caste systems toward class systems. Some industrial societies with socialist economies, such as the Union of Soviet Socialist Republics (U.S.S.R.), however, have long claimed to be classless. The Soviet Union was created through a revolution in 1917 that ended the feudal state system ruled by a hereditary nobility. This revolution transferred control of most farms, factories, and other productive property from private ownership to control

By American standards, leaders in the Soviet Union are not wealthy; their elite position is based on the enormous power that falls to those who control the governmental bureaucracy.

by the state. Karl Marx asserted that private ownership of productive property is the basis of social classes; the Soviet Union has traditionally based its claim as a classless society on the elimination of such private ownership.

Despite its claim of being classless, the Soviet Union has been undeniably socially stratified (Lane, 1984). Most occupations fall into one of four major categories, listed here in descending order of income, prestige, and power: (1) high government officials; (2) the Soviet intelligentsia, including lower government officials and professional workers—engineers, scientists, college professors, and physicians; (3) manual workers in state-controlled industries; and (4) the rural peasantry. According to Soviet doctrine, however, because factories, farms, colleges, and hospitals are owned and operated in the interest of everyone, socialist societies have less social inequality than capitalist societies.

Sweeping transformations of the socialist societies of Eastern Europe and the Soviet Union itself during 1989 and 1990 seriously undermined the claim of classlessness. It is now widely acknowledged that a powerful ruling class of party officials—served by military leaders and scientists—has for decades managed socialist societies. In the Soviet Union, where the communist party had retained a monopoly of power since 1917, roughly 18 million party members (about 6 percent of the population) have enjoyed privileges unavailable to others, such as vacation homes, chauffeured automobiles, and access to many consumer goods (Zaslavsky, 1982; Theen, 1984). The children of this elite have also gained special educational advantages and occupational opportunities.

Although Soviet society is not truly classless, the extremes of wealth and poverty in Great Britain and the United States are not found in the Soviet Union. Since Soviet elites have extensive *power* rather than *wealth*, very few people have the means to live without working. Even Mikhail Gorbachev, the Soviet leader who has encouraged drastic restructuring (*perestroika*) in the socialist world, has an income only slightly greater than that of the average American and far less than the American president. Though not wealthy, Gorbachev is certainly one of the most powerful people on earth.

And what about social mobility in so-called classless societies? Evidence suggests that during this century there has been somewhat more upward social mobility in the Soviet Union than in Great Britain, Japan, or even the United States. This is so partially because Soviet society lacks the concentrated wealth passed from generation to generation in other societies. Even more important, rapid industrialization and bureaucratization during this century have pushed a large proportion of the Soviet working class and rural peasantry upward to occupations in industry and government.

This exemplifies what sociologists call **structural social mobility,** *social mobility of large numbers of people that is due primarily to changes in society and the economy rather than to the efforts of individuals.* In Soviet society, industrialization created a vast number of new jobs that drew people to cities from rural farming villages. Similarly, the growth of bureaucracy propelled countless Soviet citizens from the fields into the offices. The effects of the recent introduction of private property into the Soviet economy are not yet clear. It seems likely that greater social stratification and economic inequality will result; the Soviets are hoping that even if this occurs, at least everyone will enjoy a higher standard of living.

Institutions, Ideology, and Social Stratification

Because of the extent of social inequality, we might wonder how a society can persist without distributing its resources more equally. The caste system of Great Britain lasted for centuries, placing most wealth and power in the hands of several hundred families. Even more striking, for two thousand years people in India apparently accepted the idea that they should be privileged or poor due to the accident of birth.

The ancient Greek philosopher Plato claimed that justice was primarily a matter of agreement about who should have what. To make that agreement work, most people in a society are socialized to view their system of social stratification as basically "fair."

Karl Marx believed that social institutions unjustly generate—and then seek to justify—the concentration of wealth and power in the hands of a few. Linked by marriage, well-to-do families can funnel wealth from generation to generation. According to Marx, society

Those who gathered at Plato's fabled academy were no cross-section of Greek society. They were wealthy males—the only people thought to be capable of intellectual pursuits. Like many Americans today, they accepted these privileges as a matter of personal merit.

then justifies such inherited wealth through the concept of private ownership of property, supported, as necessary, by the power of the state. With both resources and ideas under the institutional control of a society's elite, Marx concluded, most efforts to establish a more equitable social order have little chance for success.

Though Plato and Marx differed radically in their conclusions, both cited an essential truth about how societies work: Social stratification, they argued, is embedded in culture through **ideology**, *ideas that reflect and support the interests of some portion of a society.* Any cultural pattern—ideas as well as action—is ideological if it has consequences that favor some people over others. Ideology rarely consists of self-serving ideas deliberately generated by a privileged group in a conspiratorial fashion. Typically, it takes the form of established cultural patterns that support and justify specific social arrangements, thereby entitling certain categories of people to privileges denied to others. As the result of socialization, most people learn to accept social hierarchy; those who do challenge it commonly question their own position in the hierarchy rather than the system itself.

As a society's economy and technology change, so do the ideas used to justify social stratification. Caste systems, which depend on the routine labor of most people, come to define each person's work as a moral responsibility, ruling out the possibility of change based on individual desires. Both the European peasant during the Middle Ages and the farmer in a traditional Indian village were thus likely to see their respective caste systems as products of a "natural" order. With the Industrial Revolution, a new economic elite promoted the idea that valued resources come to those who show individual merit, rather than being conferred on the basis of birth. The poor, who had been the objects of charity under feudalism, were saddled with a double burden under industrial capitalism—their poverty *and* society's assumption that because of their lowly condition they were personally undeserving of better.

The history of human societies reveals that social stratification receives powerful institutional support. However, challenges to the status quo continue to arise as traditions weaken. People begin to question cultural "truths" when the political consequences of these assertions are unmasked. For example, American women have long been deprived of opportunity by traditional notions of "a woman's place." Even today, women are subjected to a caste-like system in which they are expected to perform traditional tasks out of altruism and duty, while men are financially rewarded for their efforts. (Consider the differences in power, prestige, and financial rewards, for instance, between a family cook, usually a woman, and a chef, typically a man.) Yet, while sexual equality is still not a reality in American society, there is little doubt that the sexes are steadily becoming more equal. The continuing struggle for racial equality in South Africa also signals widespread rejection of apartheid, which was never widely accepted by blacks, and is now losing support as a "natural" system among whites who condemn ideological racism (Friedrich, 1987).

THE FUNCTIONS OF SOCIAL STRATIFICATION

Why are societies stratified at all? One answer, consistent with the structural-functional paradigm, is that social stratification contributes to the operation of society. This argument was developed almost fifty years ago by Kingsley Davis and Wilbert Moore.

The Davis–Moore Thesis

In 1945 Davis and Moore proposed a theory of social stratification that remains influential—and controversial—to this day. According to the *Davis–Moore thesis*, all known societies exhibit some form of social inequality. Such universality, they suggest, indicates that inequality has vital functions for a social system.

To begin, Davis and Moore assert that every society encompasses many occupational positions of varying importance. Some jobs are performed easily by virtually anyone, while the most important positions can be carried out only by people with scarce talents who have received long and expensive education and training. Such functionally important positions also subject individuals to considerable pressure and day-to-day responsibility.

By conferring income, prestige, power, and leisure time on those who perform important tasks, a society encourages the discovery and development of human resources. Further, such stratification motivates individuals to engage in the most significant activities possible. Consider this: If a society values the work of a Supreme Court justice more than that of a government clerk, it accords greater benefits to the Supreme Court justice. Similarly, if more skills and training are required to be a physician than a hospital orderly, a society bestows greater rewards on the physician. Unequal rewards obviously give rise to a system of social stratification. According to the Davis–Moore thesis, a society could be egalitarian, but only to the extent that its members are prepared to have *any* person perform *any* job. Equality would also demand that someone who carries out a job well be rewarded no more than another who performs poorly. A system of equal rewards presumably would fail to motivate people toward their best efforts and would thereby reduce a society's productivity.

The Davis–Moore thesis seeks to explain why some kind of stratification exists everywhere; it is not a defense of any particular system of inequality. Davis and Moore do not, therefore, suggest precisely what reward should be attached to any occupational position. Their claim is merely that positions deemed more valuable by a society must yield sufficient rewards to draw talent away from less important positions.

Davis and Moore maintain that societies become more productive as they approach **meritocracy,** *a system linking rewards to personal merit.* Societies at different levels of technological development tend to define "merit" (from Latin, meaning "worthy of praise") differently. In agrarian caste systems, in which most people work in low-skill agriculture, the "merit" that is rewarded is dutiful persistence. Caste systems praise those who remain "in their place," conferring honor on people who perform their duties whatever their rank.

Davis and Moore assert that highly specialized industrial societies endeavor to develop the abilities and talents of each individual. The "merit" rewarded by class systems, then, is striving to "be all that you can be," as the Army recruiters say. Ideally, this means that class systems seek to provide equality of opportunity to everyone, although equality of condition is not expected, given individual differences. This overarching need to draw on people's individual talents and skills also explains the fluidity of classes in industrial societies.

No class system, however, distributes rewards solely based on individual talent and achievement. If that were the case, individual ambition and achievement might undermine the social fabric of family and community, while overriding standards of fairness. For example, we favor members of our families whether they are especially capable or not. In short, industrial class systems retain some elements of caste because of the needs for social cohesion and stability.

Critical evaluation.   Although the Davis–Moore thesis has made a lasting contribution to sociological analysis,

Melvin Tumin (1953) argues that it is flawed in several respects. First, Tumin points to the difficulty of quantifying the functional importance of any occupation. For example, the popular belief that society places great value on physicians partly results from a policy of limiting the number of people entering the medical profession (through medical school admission practices) to ensure that physicians remain greatly in demand.

Social rewards also may have little to do with an individual's functional importance to society. Thomas "Tip" O'Neill retired in 1988 as Speaker of the House of Representatives. He soon appeared on television commercials plugging such products as motel chains, credit cards, and beer. For a single day's work he received $100,000—about as much money as he used to earn in a year. Yet would anyone argue that a day spent as a TV pitchman was as valuable to society as a year's work as a Congressional leader?

Critics wonder, too, if what the market rewards

most is necessarily in the public interest. Market systems allow powerful people to manipulate the system for their own benefit. Thus American corporate executives pay themselves salaries and bonuses much higher than those of Japanese executives, even though many of Japan's corporations outperform their American counterparts. Michael Milken, described in Chapter 6 ("Deviance"), earned $550 million in 1987 selling so-called "junk bonds," which benefited only himself and a small number of investors while, according to Wall Street analysts, weakening the nation's overall economy. In contrast, Rachel Stuart spent 1987 counseling about thirty-five pregnant, mostly poor, women in rural Louisiana. Her work helped them to deliver healthy babies. Although the cost of neonatal care for a single premature baby may be $200,000, Stuart is paid only $4,000 a year for her work (Werman, 1989).

A second issue raised by Tumin is that Davis and Moore exaggerate the consequences of social stratification for the development of individual talents. American society does reward individual achievement, but families also transfer wealth and power from generation to generation regardless of talent. Additionally, for women or other minorities with limited opportunities, social stratification takes the form of barriers that ensure that much talent and ability will *never* be developed.

Third, by suggesting that social stratification benefits all of society, the Davis–Moore thesis ignores how social inequality may promote conflict and even revolution. This assertion leads us to the social-conflict paradigm, which provides a very different explanation for the persistence of social stratification.

According to the Davis–Moore thesis, the importance of any social role is measured by the rewards it generates. Entertainers, who were generally viewed as disreputable during the Middle Ages, now enjoy income and prestige that exceeds that of even the leaders of American government. What does this suggest about our society?

STRATIFICATION AND CONFLICT

Social-conflict analysis argues that, rather than benefiting society as a whole, social stratification advantages some categories of people at the expense of others. This analysis draws heavily on the ideas of Karl Marx; additional contributions were made by Max Weber.

Karl Marx: Class and Conflict

The striking social inequality of the nineteenth century, early in the Industrial Revolution, both saddened and angered Karl Marx. Through the technological miracle of industrialization, humanity could finally envision a society free from want. Yet, industrial capitalism had done little to improve the lives of most people. Marx's life was devoted to explaining this glaring contradiction: How could a society that was so rich have a majority that was so poor?

In Marx's view, social stratification is rooted in people's relationships to the means of production: either they are *owners* of productive property or they *provide labor* as part of the productive enterprises controlled by others. In feudal Europe, the nobility and clergy owned the productive land, and the peasantry supplied continual labor. The rise of industrial capitalism changed only the character of the contending classes. Class systems are dominated by **capitalists,** *people who own factories and other productive enterprises.* Capitalists (sometimes termed the *bourgeoisie,* a French word meaning "of the town") use their property in pursuit of profits. To do this, they must employ the **proletariat,** *people who provide productive labor.* Members of the industrial proletariat work to obtain the wages needed to live. Faced with irreconcilable interests and separated by great disparities in wealth and power, Marx maintained that the two classes would inevitably clash in a thunderous confrontation. At the center of Marx's analysis of capitalism, then, is **social conflict,** *struggle among segments of society over valued resources.*

Marx's analysis drew heavily on his observations of capitalism in the nineteenth century, when powerful new productive forces had elevated some to great wealth while subjecting many more to monotonous toil in early factories for low wages. During this period, wealthy American capitalists like Andrew Carnegie, J. P. Morgan, and John Jacob Astor (one of the few very rich passengers to perish on the *Titanic*) lived in fabulous mansions filled with priceless art objects and staffed by dozens of servants. Even by today's standards, their incomes were staggering. Carnegie, for example, made more than $20 million in 1900, at a time when the average worker earned perhaps $500 a year in wages (Baltzell, 1964).

In time, Marx believed, the working majority would organize to overthrow the capitalists and capitalism once and for all. Capitalism would bring about its own demise, Marx reasoned, because it steadily reduced the living standards of the working majority. Just as important, under a system of capitalism, workers had little control over the process and products of their labor. Thus, Marx asserted, work becomes a form of **alienation,** *the experience of powerlessness in social life,* rather than an expression of personal creativity. In place of capital-

This cartoon, entitled "Capital and Labour," appeared in the English press in 1843, the time at which the ideas of Karl Marx were gaining attention. It links the plight of England's coal miners to the privileges of the owners of coal-fired factories.

ism, Marx envisioned a *socialist system* that embraced the social needs of all—rather than promoting and protecting the profits of the few. Thus Marx, the relentless critic of the present, looked to the future with hope, claiming (1972:362; orig. 1848): "The proletarians have nothing to lose but their chains. They have a world to win."

Critical evaluation. By exploring how social inequality, and especially the capitalist economic system, generates conflict between classes, Marx's analysis of social classes has had an enormous influence on sociological thinking in recent decades. Because it is revolutionary, at least in a capitalist society, Marxism is also highly controversial. One of the strongest criticisms of Marx's approach is that it denies the central element of the Davis–Moore thesis: that motivating people to perform various social roles well requires some system of unequal rewards. Marx separated reward from performance, endorsing an egalitarian system based on the principle "from each according to ability, to each according to need" (1972:388). Critics note that this approach accounts for the generally low productivity of socialist economies around the world. That poor economic performance contributed to the upheavals in Eastern Europe and the Soviet Union.

Further, the revolutionary change Marx considered inevitable failed to materialize. Here lies perhaps the most important critique of his ideas. The next section explores why the socialist revolution Marx predicted and promoted has not occurred, at least in advanced capitalist societies.

Why No Marxist Revolution?

Obviously, capitalism is still thriving, in spite of Marx's prediction to the contrary. Even so, as we shall see, Western capitalism has evolved in at least some of the ways Marx anticipated.

Americans have not overthrown capitalism for several reasons (Dahrendorf, 1959). First, in the century since Marx's death, the American capitalist class has grown fragmented. Nineteenth-century companies were typically owned by *families*; today they are owned by numerous *stockholders*. Further, a large managerial class, whose members may or may not own a significant share of the companies they manage, has also emerged.

Second, Marx's industrial proletariat has also been transformed by the so-called white-collar revolution. As Chapter 11 ("Economics and Politics") explains, a century ago the vast majority of Americans filled the ranks of **blue-collar occupations,** *lower-prestige work involving mostly manual labor,* in factories or on farms. Today, most of the labor force is engaged in various **white-collar occupations,** *higher-prestige work involving mostly mental activity.* These jobs include positions in sales, management, and other service work, frequently in large, bureaucratic organizations. While these white-collar workers have much in common with the industrial working class described by Marx, evidence suggests that most do not think of themselves in those terms. For much of this century, then, the white-collar revolution has prompted many Americans to perceive their social positions as higher than those held by their parents and grandparents. As a result, American society seems less sharply divided between the rich and poor than it did during Marx's lifetime (Edwards, 1979; Gagliani, 1981; Wright & Martin, 1987).

Third, the plight of workers is not as desperate today as it was a century ago. Despite setbacks for many workers during the 1980s, living standards have greatly improved since the time of Marx. Moreover, workers have won the right to organize into labor unions that make demands of management backed by threats of work slowdowns and strikes. Although union membership has declined in recent decades, research suggests that well-established unions have substantially enhanced the economic standing of many workers (Rubin, 1986). Further, labor and management now regularly engage in contract negotiations. If not always peaceful, worker-management disputes are now institutionalized.

Fourth, legal protection has been widely extended during the last century. Laws now protect workers' rights, and provide greater access to the courts for redressing grievances. Government programs such as unemployment insurance, disability protection, and social security also provide workers with substantially greater financial security than the capitalists of the last century were willing to grant them.

Taken together, these developments suggest that despite persistent and marked stratification, many of capitalism's rough edges have been smoothed out. Consequently, social conflict today is less intense than it was a century ago. Even so, many sociologists continue to find value in Marx's analysis, often in modified form (Miliband 1969; Edwards, 1979; Giddens, 1982; Domhoff, 1983; Stephens, 1986).

Advocates of social-conflict analysis respond with four key points. First, wealth remains highly concentrated as Marx contended: About half of all privately controlled corporate stock is owned by just 1 percent of Americans. Second, the jobs produced by the white-collar revolution typically offer little more income and security than factory jobs did a century ago. Much white-collar work is as monotonous and routine as factory work, especially the low-level clerical jobs commonly held by women. Third, although labor organizations certainly have advanced the interests of workers over the last half century, regular negotiation between workers and management does not signal the end of social conflict. Many of the concessions workers have won came about precisely through the class conflict Marx described. Moreover, workers still struggle to gain concessions from capitalists and, in the 1990s, to hold on to the advances they already made. Even today, for instance, half of working Americans have no pension program. Fourth, workers have gained some legal protections, but the law has not changed the overall distribution of wealth in America, nor can "average" Americans use the legal system to the same advantage as the rich do.

Therefore, social-conflict theorists conclude, the fact that no socialist revolution has taken place in the United States hardly invalidates Marx's analysis of capitalism. American cultural values, emphasizing individualism and competition, may have curbed revolutionary

Table 7–1 TWO EXPLANATIONS OF SOCIAL STRATIFICATION: A SUMMARY

Structural-Functional Paradigm	Social-Conflict Paradigm
1. Social stratification keeps society operating. The linkage of greater rewards to more important social positions benefits society as a whole.	Social stratification is the result of social conflict. Differences in social resources serve the interests of some and harm the interests of others.
2. Social stratification encourages a matching of talents and abilities to appropriate positions.	Social stratification ensures that much talent and ability within the society will not be utilized at all.
3. Social stratification is both useful and inevitable.	Social stratification is useful to only some people; it is not inevitable.
4. The values and beliefs that legitimate social inequality are widely shared throughout society.	Values and beliefs tend to be ideological; they reflect the interests of the more powerful members of society.
5. Because systems of social stratification are useful to society and are supported by cultural values and beliefs, they are usually stable over time.	Because systems of social stratification reflect the interests of only part of the society, they are unlikely to remain stable over time.

SOURCE: Adapted in part from Arthur L. Stinchcombe, "Some Empirical Consequences of the Davis–Moore Theory of Stratification," *American Sociological Review*, Vol. 28, No. 5 (October 1963): 808.

aspirations in this country, but, as we shall see shortly, pronounced social inequality persists in American society, as does social conflict—albeit less overtly and violently than in the nineteenth century.

Table 7–1 summarizes the two contrasting approaches to social stratification.

Max Weber: Class, Status, and Power

Max Weber agreed with Karl Marx that social stratification sparks social conflict, but he differed with Marx in several important respects.

Weber considered Marx's two-class model simplistic. Instead, he viewed social stratification in terms of three distinct dimensions. First is economic inequality—the issue so vital to Marx—which Weber termed *class* position. Weber's use of "class" refers not to crude categories, but to a continuum on which anyone could be ranked from high to low. Second is *status*, meaning amount of social prestige. Third, Weber noted the importance of *power*, which he also placed on a continuum from high to low.

Marx believed that social prestige and power generally derived from economic position; thus he saw no reason to treat them as distinct dimensions of social inequality. But Weber asserted that status consistency in class systems is sometimes quite low, as we have already noted. For example, bureaucratic officials might wield considerable power yet have little wealth or social prestige. Weber's important contribution, then, is show-

ing that social stratification in industrial societies is not a matter of clearly defined categories but of rankings on a multidimensional hierarchy. Sociologists often use the term **socioeconomic status** to refer to *a composite social ranking based on various dimensions of social inequality*.

A population that varies widely in class, status, and power—Weber's dimensions of social inequality—creates a virtually infinite array of social groupings, all of which pursue their own interests. Thus, unlike Marx, who saw a clear conflict between two classes, Weber viewed social conflict as a highly variable and complex process.

Weber also suggested that each of his three dimensions of social inequality stands out at different points in the history of human societies. Agrarian societies, he maintained, emphasize social prestige or *status*, typically in the form of honor or symbolic purity. Members of these societies gain honor by conforming to cultural norms corresponding to their rank. Industrialization and the development of capitalism generate striking economic differences in the population, increasing the importance of the economic dimension of *class*. Mature industrial societies (especially socialist societies) witness a surging growth of the bureaucratic state and accord tremendous *power* to high-ranking officials.

Weber's concern with the growth of bureaucracy (detailed in Chapter 5, "Groups and Organizations") led him to disagree with Marx about the future of industrial-capitalist societies. Marx, who focused on economics, believed that social stratification could largely be eliminated by abolishing private ownership of productive property. Weber doubted that overthrowing capitalism would significantly diminish social stratification in modern societies, because of the growing importance of power in formal organizations. In fact, Weber thought that a socialist revolution might increase social inequality by expanding government and concentrating power in the hands of a political elite. Recent popular uprisings against entrenched socialist bureaucracies in Eastern Europe lend support to Weber's analysis.

Critical evaluation. American sociologists have embraced Weber's multidimensional analysis of social inequality. Some analysts (particularly those influenced by Marx) concede that social class boundaries have become less pronounced, but maintain that striking patterns of social inequality persist in American society as they do in other industrial societies. As we shall see presently, the enormous wealth of the most privileged Americans contrasts sharply with the grinding poverty of millions of people who are barely able to meet their day-to-day needs. During the last decade, the extent of economic inequality in the United States has actually increased; such economic polarization would seem to favor a model of "classes" rather than a "multidimensional hierarchy."

STRATIFICATION AND TECHNOLOGY

We can weave together a number of observations made in this chapter by considering the relationship between a society's technology and the type of social stratification it exhibits. Gerhard and Jean Lenski's model of sociocultural evolution, detailed in Chapter 2 ("Culture"), also draws on insights from both the structural-functional and social-conflict approaches (Lenski, 1966; Lenski & Lenski, 1987).

Simple technology limited the production of hunters and gatherers to daily necessities. No doubt, some individuals were more productive than others, but the group's survival depended on everyone sharing the fruits of the group's labor. With little or no surplus, therefore, no categories of people emerged as better off than others.

Technological advances historically generated a productive surplus but also promoted social inequality. In horticultural and pastoral societies, a small elite controls most of the surplus. Agrarian technology based on large-scale farming generates even greater abundance,

enabling various categories of people to lead strikingly different lives. The most favored strata—typically hereditary nobility—frequently wield godlike power over the society as a whole.

In industrial societies, however, social inequality tends to diminish. A drive for democratic thinking, prompted by the need to develop individual talents, erodes the power of elites. The greater productivity of industrial technology gradually raises the living standards of the historically poor majority. Specialized, technical work also encourages the expansion of schooling, sharply reducing illiteracy. And, as already noted, technological advances transform much blue-collar labor (offering low prestige and power) into white-collar work (carrying greater prestige). All these transformations help to explain why Marxist revolutions have occurred in agrarian societies—such as the Soviet Union (1917), Cuba (1959), and Nicaragua (1979)—where social inequality is historically most pronounced, rather than in industrial societies, as Marx predicted more than a century ago.

Figure 7–1 Social Stratification and Technological Development: The Kuznets Curve

The Kuznets Curve suggests that greater technological sophistication is generally accompanied by greater intensity of social stratification. The trend reverses itself, however, as industrial societies gradually become more egalitarian. Rigid caste-like distinctions are relaxed in favor of greater opportunity and equality before the law. Political rights are more widely extended, and there is even some leveling of economic differences. The Kuznets Curve may also be applied to the relative social standing of the two sexes.

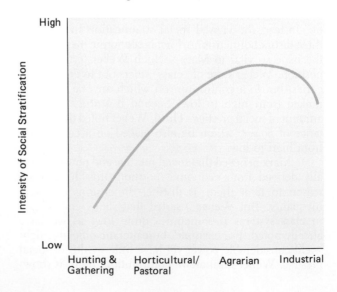

Additionally, the domination of women by men, generally strongest in agrarian societies, gradually diminishes with industrialization. The drive for gender equality derives from the demand for individual talent in the industrial economy and also from the growing belief in basic human equality.

In short, reducing the intensity of social stratification is actually functional for industrial societies. This historical pattern, recognized by Nobel-Prize–winning economist Simon Kuznets (1955, 1966), is illustrated by the "Kuznets Curve" (Figure 7–1).[1]

The trend suggested by Kuznets does not necessarily mean that industrial societies gradually become less and less stratified. The idea of equal opportunity for all is now widely endorsed by Americans, although this goal is unlikely to ever become a reality. In fact, Americans tend to understate the extent of social inequality in the United States, as we shall now see.

THE FOUNDATIONS OF CLASS

Americans have long considered theirs to be a society responsive to individual initiative. Unlike Japan or most European nations, the United States has never had a feudal aristocracy. With the significant exception of our racial history, Americans have never known a caste system that rigidly separated categories of people. In addition, as Chapter 8 ("Global Inequality") explains, in relation to a majority of the world's people, most Americans enjoy a high standard of living.

Even so, American society is highly stratified. The rich enjoy not only great wealth, but also more schooling, better health, and a greater share of almost all social resources that contribute to well-being. Such privilege contrasts sharply with the poverty of millions of poor Americans who struggle to meet their basic needs. The notion of "middle-class America" doesn't square with some important facts.

Income, Wealth, and Power

One important dimension of economic inequality involves **income**, *occupational wages or salaries and earnings from investments*. The government reports that the median American family income in 1989 was $34,210.

[1] The ideas of Simon Kuznets are discussed by Peter Berger (1986:43–46), whose interpretations are reflected in this material.

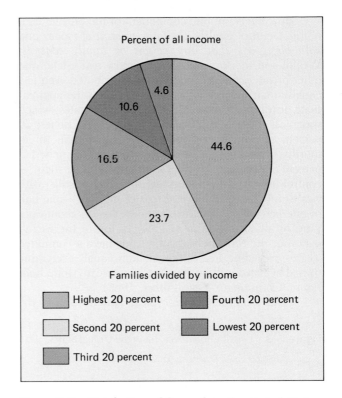

Figure 7–2 Distribution of Income in the United States, 1989

(U.S. Bureau of the Census, 1990)

Figure 7–2 shows the distribution of income among all American families. Note that the 20 percent of families with the highest earnings receive 44.6 percent of all income, while the bottom 20 percent make only about 4.6 percent. At the very top, the highest-paid 5 percent of American families receive 17.9 percent of all income, more than the income of the lowest-paid 40 percent.

Although generally stable since World War II, this income disparity increased during the 1980s as a result of the Reagan administration's budgetary priorities (Levy, 1987; Reich, 1989). Between 1979 and 1989, the income of the top fifth of American families rose 16.7 percent in constant 1989 dollars (a real gain of $15,200 for the average wealthy family). During the same period, the income share of the middle fifth remained about the same, while that of the lowest fifth actually fell 5.6 percent (an average family loss of $559). By the end of the 1980s, the income gap between rich and poor was greater than at any time since the end of World War II (Jaeger & Greenstein, 1989).

Income is but one component of the broader economic factor of **wealth,** *the total amount of money and valuable goods that any person or family controls.* Wealth—in the form of stocks, bonds, real estate, and other privately owned property—is distributed even less equally than income is. Figure 7–3 shows the approximate distribution of wealth in the United States, which was most recently calculated for 1983. The richest 20 percent of American families own more than three-fourths of the country's entire wealth. The richest 5 percent of American families—America's "super-rich"—control over half the nation's wealth. Richer still—with wealth into the millions and tens of millions—one half of one percent of American families possess about one-third of all wealth. And at the very top of the wealth pyramid, the *three* richest Americans have a combined wealth exceeding $12 billion, which equals everything owned by half a million "average" Americans (Joint Economic Committee, 1986; *Forbes*, 1989).

The wealth of more typical Americans—in the second and third fifths of Figure 7–3—lies in the range of the median annual income for families, or about $35,000. Lesser wealth also differs in *kind:* The richest Americans hold their wealth in the form of stocks and other income-producing investments. Other Americans' wealth resides primarily in nonincome-producing property such as a home. When financial liabilities are balanced against assets for the least wealthy 40 percent of American families, wealth simply does not exist. As the negative figure in Figure 7–3 shows, the bottom 20 percent are actually in debt.

In American society, wealth stands as an important source of power; therefore, the small proportion of families who control most of the wealth also have the ability to set the agenda for all of American society. As explained in Chapter 11 ("Economics and Politics"), some sociologists argue that such concentrated wealth undermines political democracy by distorting the political system so it serves the interests of the small proportion of "super-rich" families.

Figure 7–3 Distribution of Wealth in the United States, 1983

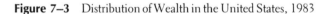

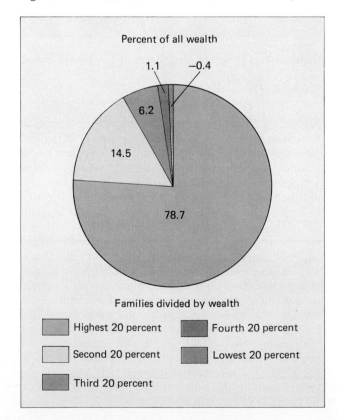

Occupational Prestige

Beyond generating income, occupation also is an important source of social prestige. Americans commonly evaluate each other according to the kind of work they do, envying and respecting some, shunning and looking down on others.

For more than sixty years, sociologists have measured the relative social prestige of various occupations (Counts, 1925; Hodge, Treiman, & Rossi, 1966; N.O.R.C., 1989). Based on a survey of Americans adults, Table 7–2 shows that high-prestige occupations are generally those that provide high income as well, such as physicians, lawyers, bankers, engineers. Prestige reflects more than high pay, however, since these occupations typically require considerable ability, education, and training. By contrast, less prestigious work—as a salesperson or janitor, for example—not only pays less, but usually requires less ability and education. Occupational prestige rankings follow similar patterns in all industrial societies.[2]

Although women are now represented in every occupation, their numbers are greatest in *pink-collar jobs* (Bernard, 1981). Primarily service occupations, pink-collar jobs—such as secretary, waitress, and beautician—tend to fall near the bottom of the prestige hierarchy.

---

[2] I am grateful to Dr. Li-Chen Ma of Lamar University for providing cross-cultural comparisons.

Table 7–2 THE RELATIVE SOCIAL PRESTIGE OF ONE HUNDRED OCCUPATIONS IN THE UNITED STATES

White-collar Occupations	Prestige Score	Blue-collar Occupations	White-collar Occupations	Prestige Score	Blue-collar Occupations
Physician	82		Bookkeeper	48	
College/university professor	78		Insurance agent	47	
Lawyer	76		Musician/composer	46	
Dentist	74			46	Secretary
Physicist/astronomer	74			44	Fireman
Bank officer	72		Air traffic controller	43	
Architect	71			42	Mail carrier
Aeronautical/astronautical engineer	71			41	Farmer
Psychologist	71		Buyer/shipper, farm products	41	
Airplane pilot	70			41	Tailor
Clergy	69		Photographer	41	
Chemist	69			40	Carpenter
Electrical engineer	69			40	Telephone operator
Geologist	67			40	Welder
Sociologist	66		Restaurant manager	39	
Secondary school teacher	63		Building superintendent	38	
Registered nurse	62			37	Auto body repairperson
Dental hygienist	61		Airline stewardess	36	
Pharmacist	61			36	Brick/stone mason
Radiologic technician	61			35	TV repairperson
Chiropractor	60			34	Baker
Elementary school teacher	60			33	Hairdresser
Veterinarian	60			33	Bulldozer operator
Postmaster	58		Auctioneer	32	
Union official	58			32	Bus driver
Accountant	57			32	Truck driver
Economist	57		Cashier	31	
Painter/sculptor	56		File clerk	30	
Actor	55			30	Upholsterer
Librarian	55			29	Drill-press operator
Industrial engineer	54			29	Furniture finisher
Forester and conservationist	54		Retail salesperson	29	
Surveyor	53			23	Midwife
Dietician	52			22	Gas station attendant
Funeral director	52			22	Security guard
Social worker	52			22	Taxi driver
Athlete	51			21	Elevator operator
Computer specialist	51			20	Bartender
Editor/reporter	51			20	Waiter/waitress
	51	Locomotive engineer		18	Clothing presser
Radio/TV announcer	51			18	Farm laborer
Bank teller	50			18	Household servant
	49	Electrician		17	Car washer
	48	Aircraft mechanic		17	Freight handler
	48	Machinist		17	Garbage collector
	48	Police officer		16	Janitor
				14	Bellhop
				09	Shoe shiner

SOURCE: Adapted from *General Social Surveys, 1972–1989: Cumulative Codebook* (Chicago: National Opinion Research Center, 1989), pp. 685–698.

Formal Education

Schooling is another dimension of social inequality in the United States. Table 7–3 indicates the formal education of Americans aged twenty-five and over in 1988. More than three-fourths had completed high school, although only about 20 percent were college graduates.

Formal education promotes more than personal development: It also affects a person's occupation and income. Most (but not all) of the white-collar occupations, shown in Table 7–2, that yield high income and greater social prestige require a college degree or other advanced education. Similarly, most of the blue-collar occupations that offer less income and lower social prestige are held by people with less schooling.

Ancestry, Race, and Gender

To some degree, the American class system rewards individual talent and initiative. But ascription is also important: Who we are at birth influences greatly what we become later in life.

Ancestry—or social background—determines our point of entry into the system of social inequality. The family into which we are born has a strong bearing on our future education, occupation, and income. Studies of the richest Americans—those with hundreds of millions of dollars in wealth—suggest that about half derived their fortunes primarily from inheritance (Thurow, 1987; Queenan, 1989). By the same token, the "inheritance" of poverty and the lack of opportunity that goes with it just as surely shapes the future for those in need.

Race is strongly related to social position in American society. Whites have a higher overall occupational standing than blacks, and greater educational achievement. As a result, the median income of black families in 1989—$20,260—was only 57 percent of that earned by white families, $35,549 (U.S. Bureau of the Census, 1990). Over time, this income differential creates a considerable "wealth gap," with average black wealth (about $4,000 in the mid-1980s) only about 10 percent of that found among whites (O'Hare, 1989). Even among affluent families, race makes a difference. The box takes a closer look.

Ethnic background also relates to social stratification in America (Hirschman & Wong, 1984). Traditionally, people of English ancestry have acquired the greatest wealth and the most power of all Americans. A detailed examination of how race and ethnicity affect social standing is presented in Chapter 9 ("Race and Ethnicity").

Societies also place men and women in different social positions. Of course, people of both sexes are born to families at every social level. Yet women gain less income, wealth, and occupational prestige, and place slightly lower in educational achievement than men do (Bernard, 1981; Lengermann & Wallace, 1985). Furthermore, as we shall see later in this chapter, households headed by women are ten times more likely to be poor than those headed by men. Chapter 10 ("Sex and Gender") further examines the link between gender and social stratification.

SOCIAL CLASSES IN THE UNITED STATES

As we have seen, rankings in a rigid caste system are usually obvious to all. Defining the social categories in a more fluid class system, however, poses a number of challenges. Using Karl Marx's analysis, we might identify only two major social classes; however, other sociologists have suggested that there are as many as six (Warner & Lunt, 1941) or seven (Coleman & Rainwater, 1978). Yet another approach, following Max Weber's lead, might be to reject the idea of clearly defined classes in favor of a multidimensional social hierarchy.

The difficulty in delineating classes arises from the relatively low status consistency among Americans. Especially toward the middle of the hierarchy, a person's social position on one dimension of social inequality

Table 7–3	EDUCATIONAL INEQUALITY IN THE UNITED STATES, 1988 (PERSONS AGED 25 AND OVER)	
Not a High-School Graduate		23.8%
0–7 years	6.8	
8 years	5.2	
9–11 years	11.7	
High-School Graduate		76.2
High school only	38.9	
Some college (1–3 years)	17.0	
College graduate or more	20.3	

SOURCE: U.S. Census Bureau, 1989.

Two Colors of Affluence: Do Blacks and Whites Differ?

The typical African-American family has only 57 percent of the income of the average white family. This creates a strong link between race and poverty. But there is another side to black America—an affluent side—that expanded dramatically during the 1980s.

The number of affluent black families—with annual incomes over $50,000—is increasing rapidly. In 1989, some 1,037,000 black families were affluent, a five-fold increase over two decades before in constant dollars. Today, 13.8 percent of African-American families are affluent—over 2 million adults and their children. Among Hispanic families, 14.7 percent are affluent, but this is well below the 30.9 percent of white families who have this much income.

But black and white affluence is not the same. First, rich blacks are not *as rich* as rich whites. Almost 40 percent of affluent white families earn over $75,000 a year; only 26.2

percent of affluent black families reach this income level. Second, blacks more than whites achieve affluence through multiple incomes—from two employed spouses, or employed parents and children. Third, affluent blacks are more likely to *earn* their income than whites are. Three-

fourths of affluent white families had unearned investment income, compared to only one-half of affluent African-American households.

Beyond differences in income, affluent blacks still contend with social barriers based on color. Even with the money to purchase a home, blacks may find they are unwelcome as neighbors. For this reason, affluent blacks are more likely to live in central-city areas (56 percent) than in the suburbs (40 percent). Affluent whites are much more likely to live in suburbs (61 percent).

Affluent Americans come in all colors. Yet, the social significance of race affects the lives of affluent people, as it does the lives of all Americans.

SOURCE: Based on William O'Hare, "In the Black," *American Demographics*, Vol. 11, no. 11 (November 1989):25–29. Data also drawn from U.S. Census Bureau, *Money Income and Poverty Status in the United States: 1989*, Washington, D.C.: U.S. Government Printing Office, 1990.

---

may contradict that same individual's position on another (Gilbert & Kahl, 1987). A government official, for example, may wield great power yet earn a relatively modest income and have accumulated no wealth. Similarly, a member of the clergy may enjoy high prestige while possessing only moderate power and little wealth. Finally, a lucky professional gambler may accumulate considerable wealth yet have little power, prestige, or education. Additionally, the social mobility typical of class systems—again, most pronounced near the middle—can allow a person to change social position during a lifetime, further complicating the task of defining social classes. Nonetheless, in the United States four general social classes emerge: the upper class, the middle class, the working class, and the lower class.

The Upper Class

The upper class contains no more than 3 or 4 percent of all Americans. The yearly income of upper-class families is at least $100,000 and can be ten times that amount or more. Much of this income may be in the form of investment earnings derived from inherited wealth. In 1990, *Forbes* magazine profiled the richest four hundred people in America, estimating their combined wealth at $273 billion (Seneker, 1990). These richest Americans had a minimum net worth of $260 million and included sixty-six billionaires. The upper class thus encompasses what Karl Marx called "capitalists" who own most of the nation's productive property. Besides their productive wealth, many members of the upper class work as top executives in large corporations and as senior government officials, further enhancing their power to shape events in the nation and, increasingly, the entire world. The upper class also gains the most education, typically in expensive and highly regarded schools and colleges. Historically, the upper class has been composed of white Anglo-Saxon Protestants (WASPs), although this is less true today (Baltzell, 1964, 1976, 1988).

A further distinction is sometimes made between the "upper-upper class" and the "lower-upper class." The *upper-upper class*, often described as "society" or "bluebloods," includes about 1 percent of the American population (Warner & Lunt, 1941; Coleman & Neugarten, 1971; Rossides, 1990). Membership is almost always the result of birth, as suggested by the old quip that the easiest way to become an "upper-upper" is to be born one. These families possess enormous wealth, primarily inherited rather than earned. For this reason, members of the upper-upper class are said to have *old money*. Noting the favor accorded to this segment of American society, C. Wright Mills commented that "prestige is the shadow of money and power" (1956:83).

Set apart by their wealth, members of the upper-upper class live in exclusive neighborhoods, such as Beacon Hill in Boston, the Rittenhouse Square area in Philadelphia, the Gold Coast of Chicago, and Nob Hill in San Francisco. Their children typically attend private secondary schools with others of similar background, completing their formal education at high-prestige colleges and universities. In the historical pattern of European aristocrats, they study liberal arts rather than vocationally directed subjects. Women of the upper-upper class often engage in volunteer work for charitable organizations. While helping the larger community, these activities also help forge networks that enhance this elite's social power (Ostrander, 1980, 1984).

The remaining 2 or 3 percent of the upper class may be termed the *lower-upper class*. For the lower-upper class, earnings rather than inheritance is the primary source of wealth. Few are bequeathed a vast fortune by their parents, although the majority inherit some wealth. While so-called "new rich" Americans generally live in expensive houses or condominiums, they may still be excluded from the highest-prestige clubs and associations of "old-money" families.

The Middle Class

The middle class includes 40 to 45 percent of all Americans. Because it is so large and embodies the aspirations of many more people, "middle-class America" has long been a powerful cultural image. Television and other mass media usually show middle-class Americans, and most commercial advertising is directed to this category. The middle class encompasses far more ethnic and racial diversity than the upper class. While many upper-class people (especially "upper-uppers") are likely to know each other personally, such exclusiveness and familiarity do not characterize the middle class.

The top third of this category is often termed the *upper*-middle class based on above-average income, from about $50,000 to $100,000 a year. This allows upper-middle-class families to gradually accumulate considerable property—an elegant house in a fairly expensive area, automobiles, and some investments. Virtually all upper-middle-class people receive college educations, and postgraduate degrees are common. Many work in white-collar fields such as medicine, engineering, and law, or as business executives. Lacking the power to influence national or international events, these Americans often play an important role in local political affairs.

The rest of the middle class typically works in less prestigious white-collar occupations (as bank tellers, lower-level managers, and sales clerks) or in highly skilled blue-collar jobs (including electrical work and carpentry). Commonly, family income is between $30,000 and $50,000 a year, depending on how many family members are working. This roughly equals the median family income for Americans (about $34,210 in 1989) and provides a secure, if modest, standard of living. Middle-class people generally accumulate a small amount of wealth over the course of their working lives, and most eventually own a house. Middle-class Americans are likely to be high-school graduates, but not all will be able to send their children to college. Limited income means that those who do go to college generally attend state-supported schools.

The Working Class

Including about one-third of all Americans, the working class refers to people who have lower incomes than those in the middle class and virtually no accumulated wealth. In Marxist terms, the working class forms the core of the industrial proletariat. The blue-collar occupations of the working class generally yield a family income of between $15,000 and $30,000 a year, somewhat below the national average. Working-class Americans thus find themselves especially vulnerable to financial problems brought on by unemployment or illness.

Television programming has generally portrayed a narrow range of Americans, from the middle class to the lower-upper class. In the last decade, however, an increasing number of shows has featured working-class people. Roseanne Barr, herself from a working-class family, is the star of one of the most popular shows in recent years.

Working-class jobs typically provide less personal satisfaction, and workers are usually subject to continual supervision by superiors (Edwards, 1979). Such jobs also provide fewer benefits such as medical insurance and pension programs. About half of working-class families own their homes, usually in lower-cost neighborhoods. College is an expense only a few can afford.

The Lower Class

The remaining 20 percent of Americans make up the lower class. A lack of income renders their lives unstable and insecure. Some 32 million Americans (roughly 13 percent of the population) are officially classified as poor. Millions more—the so-called "working poor"—are only marginally better off. The American poor typically work in low-prestige jobs that provide little intrinsic satisfaction. Only some manage to complete high school; a college degree is usually out of reach. Many lower-class Americans are functionally illiterate.

The lower class experiences considerable social segregation, especially when the poor belong to racial or ethnic minorities. Such segregation appears most starkly in urban areas where large numbers of poor people live in deteriorating neighborhoods or rental housing shunned by the other social classes.

Lower-class children learn early on the harsh reality that many people consider them only marginal members of society. Observing their parents and other lower-class adults, they may have little hope of breaking the cycle of poverty. Lower-class life, then, can generate self-defeating resignation to being cut off from the resources of an affluent society (Jacob, 1986).

Some may simply give up. Most poor people, however, work desperately—often at two or three jobs—to make ends meet. In a study conducted in a northern city, Carol Stack (1975) discovered that, far from lacking initiative and responsibility, many poor people devise ingenious means of survival. They do so, she concluded, because they simply have no choice.

THE DIFFERENCE CLASS MAKES

Social stratification affects nearly every dimension of social life. Health is one of the most important correlates of social standing. Children born into poor families are about 50 percent more likely to die during their first year of life than children born into more privileged families (Gortmaker, 1979). Among adults, affluent Americans are twice as likely to describe their health as excellent as are poor people. Moreover, affluence supports longer life expectancy by providing more nutritious foods, a safer and less stressful environment, and more extensive medical care.

Cultural values also vary somewhat from class to class. Americans with the highest social standing have an unusually strong sense of family history since their social position is based on wealth and social prestige passed down from generation to generation (Baltzell, 1979). Because their social standing is guaranteed as a birthright, the "old rich" also tend to be understated in their manners and tastes, as if to say, "I know who I am and I don't have to prove anything to anyone else." Below the upper class, patterns of consumption take on greater importance as class boundaries start to blur. Houses, clothes, and cars are often viewed as *status symbols* that "make a statement" about their owners.

Because of their greater personal and financial security, middle-class people display more tolerance than their working-class counterparts toward controversial behavior such as premarital sexual activity and homosexuality (Humphries, 1984). Working-class people grow up in an atmosphere of greater supervision and discipline, which they continue to experience on the job as adults. In socializing their children, too, they encourage greater conformity to conventional beliefs and practices (Kohn, 1977).

Even the meaning of time varies somewhat according to social class. Generations of wealth give upper-class families a strong sense of pride in the past. Middle-class people, especially those who are upwardly mobile, look optimistically to the future for a better life. By contrast, the drive for daily survival focuses the attention of lower-class people on the present. A pessimistic present-time orientation often reflects a pessimistic sense that there are limited opportunities for improving one's social position (Liebow, 1967; Lamar, Jr., 1985; Jacob, 1986).

Political attitudes also are class-linked. Generally, more privileged Americans support the Republican Party while less advantaged people favor the Democrats (Wolfinger, Shapiro, & Greenstein, 1980). A desire to protect their wealth prompts people who are well off to take a more conservative approach to economic issues. Thus, members of the higher social classes tend to favor a free-market economy unregulated by government. On social issues, such as support for the Equal Rights Amendment, abortion, and other feminist concerns, however, affluent people tend to be more liberal. People of lower social standing show the opposing pattern, favoring liberal economic policies and conservative social goals (Nunn, Crockett, & Williams, 1978; Erikson, Luttberg, & Tedin, 1980; Syzmanski, 1983; Humphries, 1984).

Finally, family life is also shaped by social class. Generally, lower-class families are somewhat larger than middle-class families, due to earlier marriage and less frequent use of birth control. Upper-class families, too, have more children, partly because they can afford added child-rearing expenses. Divorce is more common among disadvantaged Americans, due to stresses resulting from low income and unemployment (Kitson & Raschke, 1981; Fergusson, Horwood, & Shannon, 1984). Working-class marriages also reveal a more rigid division of tasks between husband and wife, while middle-class marriages involve spouses in more common activities (Bott, 1971). Finally, the number of households with children headed by women increased rapidly during the 1980s. This pattern appears most frequently among the poor—especially poor blacks—although more Americans of all classes are grappling with the economic challenges of single parenthood.

SOCIAL MOBILITY IN AMERICA

Ours is a dynamic society marked by a significant measure of social mobility. Earning a college degree, securing a higher-paying job, or succeeding in a business endeavor all contribute to *upward social mobility*, while dropping out of school, losing a job, or having a business enterprise fail may signal *downward social mobility*. *Horizontal social mobility*—as people change their occupation, for example, without changing their overall social standing—appears quite frequently in class systems.

Changes in society as a whole also affect social mobility. During the first half of this century, for example, industrialization expanded the economy, raising the standard of living for millions of Americans. Even without being very good swimmers, so to speak, people were able to "ride a rising tide of prosperity." As explained presently, *structural social mobility* in a downward direction has more recently forced many Americans to endure severe economic setbacks.

In studying social mobility, sociologists distinguish between one-generation and multigenerational transitions. **Intragenerational social mobility** refers to a *change in social position occurring during a person's lifetime*. Of even greater concern to sociologists is **intergenerational social mobility**, *the upward or downward social mobility of children in relation to their parents*. Social mobility across generations takes on special significance because it often reflects changes in society that affect virtually everyone.

Social Mobility: Myth and Reality

In few societies do people dwell on social mobility as much as in the United States: Historically, moving ahead has been central to the American Dream. The belief that people have the opportunity to realize their individual potential is a foundation of American social stratification (Kleugel & Smith, 1986).

Using the broad categories of blue-collar and white-collar jobs, studies of intergenerational mobility (that, unfortunately, have focused almost exclusively on men) show that almost 40 percent of the sons of blue-collar workers attain white-collar jobs and almost 30 percent of sons born into white-collar families accept blue-collar jobs. Comparisons of specific occupational categories show that about 80 percent of sons show some social mobility in relation to their fathers (Blau & Duncan, 1967; Featherman & Hauser, 1978). Research has shown that the extent of social mobility in the United States is comparable to that in other industrial societies (Lipset & Bendix, 1967; McRoberts and Selbee, 1981; Kaelble, 1986).

Among Americans, several patterns of social mobility emerge clearly. First, men have considerable social mobility, as we would expect in a class system. Second, until recently, the trend in social mobility had more commonly been upward than downward. Structural social mobility accounted for most of this upward movement as better-paying white-collar jobs steadily replaced the blue-collar and farming work more common several generations ago. Third, although significant changes appear over many generations, social mobility within a single generation has usually been incremental rather than dramatic. This means that Americans rarely move "from rags to riches," or the other way around. Social mobility typically involves subtle changes *within* a social class rather than dramatic changes *between* classes.

No patterns apply equally to *all* Americans, however. African-Americans have traditionally experienced less upward social mobility than whites, especially in recent years (Featherman & Hauser, 1978; Pomer, 1986). During the economic recovery of the 1980s, African-Americans actually lost ground in terms of income through much of the decade (Jacob, 1986). Hispanic families, too, were downwardly mobile throughout the 1980s, due to declining wage levels and their low overall age. Women also have less opportunity for upward mobility than men do since most American women in the labor force hold clerical positions (such as secretaries) and low-paying service jobs (such as waitresses).

The "Middle-Class Slide"

The expectation of upward social mobility is deeply rooted in American history and the American national consciousness. For much of our history, economic expansion has fulfilled the promise of prosperity by raising the overall standard of living. Since the 1960s, however, our traditional confidence in upward social mobility has diminished, with some sociologists claiming that American society has entered an "age of decline" (Blumberg, 1981). More and more Americans now seem to be simply trying to hold on to what they have.

This shift in attitude stems from changes in the economy. Figure 7–4 on page 174 shows median family income for Americans between 1950 and 1989 in constant 1989 dollars. Between 1950 and 1973, median family income for Americans grew by almost 65 percent, but it has remained roughly stable since then (U.S. Bureau of the Census, 1990).

Earlier in this century, economic growth fueled the notion that America was becoming an affluent, middle-class society (Kerckhoff, Campbell, & Winfield-Laird, 1985). But upward structural social mobility diminished after the early 1970s (Pampel, Land, & Felson, 1977; Levy, 1987). Since then, new jobs have offered less pay, causing more and more social mobility in the *downward* direction. Between 1963 and 1973, almost half of new jobs that were created provided relatively high income (over $30,000 annually in 1990 dollars). Through the remainder of the 1970s, income from more than 60 percent of new jobs was in the middle-income range (between about $15,000 and $30,000). During the first half of the 1980s, far fewer high- and middle-income jobs were created, and the proportion of low-income jobs (paying less than $15,000 annually) jumped sharply to more than 40 percent. Put simply, this loss of economic security for many "average" Americans is termed the *"middle-class slide."*

Underlying the "middle-class slide" is a global economic transformation: Much of the industrial production that offered Americans high-paying jobs a generation ago has been transferred overseas, while a growing proportion of new jobs in the United States require little skill and provide minimal income (Blumberg, 1981; Rosen, 1987; Thurow, 1987). Major industrial goods such as cars, and popular items such as electronic equipment, are now routinely imported from Japan, Korea, and other countries; at home, McDonald's now has more employees than USX (formerly United States Steel). While the expansion of global corporations has sparked upward mobility for some Americans—notably those who manage and invest in expanding global corporations—this transformation has hurt moderate-income Americans whose factory jobs have been "exported" overseas (Reich, 1989). Despite the fact that about half of today's families have two or more members in the labor force, double the proportion in 1950, many Americans are working harder just to hold on to the social standing they have. During the 1980s, some families were propelled into the ranks of the rich, but nearly twice as many suffered economic setbacks. As the rich became richer and the poor became poorer, the shine dimmed on the American Dream.

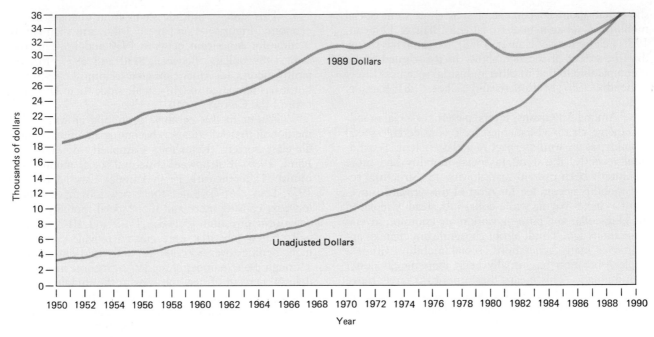

Figure 7–4 Median Family Income, 1950–1989

(*U.S. Bureau of the Census*)

Not surprisingly, the problem of poverty is receiving growing attention.

AMERICAN POVERTY

If more resources are enjoyed by some, others are inevitably deprived. Poverty is therefore a trait of all systems of social inequality. This concept, however, is used in two different ways. **Relative poverty,** the universal social trait, refers to *the deprivation of some people in relation to others.* Much more serious is **absolute poverty,** or *a deprivation of resources that is life-threatening.* Defined in this way, poverty is a pressing, if solvable, human problem.

As the next chapter ("Global Inequality") explains, the global dimensions of absolute poverty place the lives of perhaps 1 billion people—one in five of the earth's entire population—at risk. Even in affluent America, however, the wrenching reality of poverty results in hunger, inadequate housing, and poor health.

The Extent of American Poverty

Poverty in America has historically declined, although it rose during much of the 1980s. In 1989, 31.5 million people—12.8 percent of all Americans—were officially labeled as poor. The government defined a family of four living in an urban area as "poor" if the family had a total income below $12,675. Although this standard is somewhat arbitrary, it approximates three times the estimated minimum expense for food. Not all of the American poor are even this "well off": one recent study noted that 40 percent of poor people in the United States live in households with income that is less than half the official poverty level (Littman, 1989). Another 11 million Americans are not officially poor, but fall within 25 percent of the poverty line; they are known as the *marginally poor.*

Poverty means hunger. Estimates suggest that some 20 million Americans experience daily hunger (Schwartz-Nobel, 1981; Physicians' Task Force on Hunger, 1987). According to the Children's Defense Fund (1985), some ten thousand American children die each year for various reasons stemming from poverty, making this the leading cause of death among the youngest Americans. The richest society in the world, then, confronts the reality of widespread poverty, which many argue forms a barrier to becoming a "kinder and gentler nation."

Who Are the American Poor?

Although no single description covers all poor people, poverty is pronounced among certain categories of Americans.

Age. The burden of poverty falls most heavily on children. In 1989, 19.6 percent of Americans under eighteen were poor. From another perspective, 40 percent of the poor are under the age of eighteen.

A generation ago, the elderly were more likely to be poor than children were. In 1989, however, the poverty rate for Americans over the age of sixty-five stood at 11.4 percent, slightly below the overall poverty rate

People usually associate poverty with nonwhites in inner cities. But most poor people are white, and many struggle to survive in rural areas, unnoticed by the vast majority of Americans.

of 12.8 percent. In all, 10.7 percent of the poor are elderly people.

Race and ethnicity. Of all poor Americans, 65.9 percent are white, while 29.5 percent are black. But in relation to their overall numbers, African-Americans are about three times as likely as whites to be poor. In 1989, 30.7 percent of African-Americans lived in poverty, compared to 26.2 percent of Hispanics, 14.1 percent of Asians and Pacific Islanders, and 10 percent of whites. During the 1980s, this "poverty gap" between the races increased (U.S. Bureau of the Census, 1989). In 1989, 35.5 percent of Hispanic children, 43.2 percent of African-American children, and 18.9 percent of Asian-American children were poor.

Sex. Of all poor Americans over the age of eighteen, 63.2 percent are women and 36.8 percent are men. Women who head households bear the brunt of poverty. On their shoulders falls the financial burden of raising children, which makes working for income difficult. For those able to work, low-paying jobs are the norm. Of all poor families, 51.7 percent are headed by women with no husband present. In marked contrast, only 5.4 percent of poor families are households headed by single men. The **feminization of poverty** refers to *a trend by which females represent an increasing proportion of the poor.*

Area of residence. Poverty is more common in rural areas than in cities. In 1989, 15.7 percent of Americans living outside large urban areas were poor, in contrast to 12.2 percent of people living in cities (U.S. Bureau of the Census, 1990). Urban living tends to raise living standards because wealth, job opportunities, and social services are concentrated in cities. Yet, the largest pockets of poverty are concentrated in inner-city areas. Almost one in five residents of American inner cities is poor.

Explaining Poverty

The presence of tens of millions of poor people in one of the world's most affluent societies raises serious social and moral concerns. Theorists have developed two general approaches to the problem of poverty, which we now examine.

The poor are primarily responsible for their own poverty. Throughout our history, Americans have embraced the notion that people are largely responsible for their own social standing. This approach assumes that American society has considerable opportunity for

A common notion soon after the Industrial Revolution was that the poor were morally deficient people who, like other offenders, deserved to be punished. Debtors' prisons were the result, as depicted in this period engraving by an unknown artist. The poor are no longer physically imprisoned, but the idea that they are morally flawed and responsible for their own poverty remains strong.

anyone able and willing to take advantage of it. The poor, then, are those with fewer skills, less education, lower motivation, or, perhaps, a debilitating drug addiction—in sum, people who are somehow undeserving.

Anthropologist Oscar Lewis (1961) contributed to this approach through his research on Latin American poverty. Lewis claims that the poor become entrapped in a *culture of poverty* that fosters resignation to one's plight as a matter of fate. Socialized in this environment, children come to believe that there is little point in aspiring to a better life. The result is a self-perpetuating cycle of poverty. Edward Banfield (1974) adds that as poor people gather in inner cities, they forge a distinctive lower-class subculture that inhibits personal achievement. One element of this subculture is a present-time orientation, which encourages living for the moment rather than looking toward the future by engaging in hard work, saving, and other behavior likely to promote upward social mobility. In sum, Banfield portrays the poor as irresponsible, reaping more or less what they deserve.

Society is primarily responsible for poverty. An alter-native position, argued by William Ryan (1976), holds that society—not the poor—is primarily responsible for poverty. In his view, wealth and poverty stem from the ways a society distributes its resources. Poverty is therefore neither inevitable nor the fault of the poor themselves. From Ryan's point of view, any absence of ambition on the part of poor people is a *consequence* rather than a *cause* of their lack of opportunity. He argues that Banfield's analysis amounts to little more than "blaming the victims" for their own suffering. Ryan maintains that poverty should be addressed by offering greater economic opportunity for poor Americans and engineering more equality in our social arrangements.

Critical evaluation. Both these explanations of poverty have won their share of public support. About one-quarter of Americans believe that poor people should take care of themselves; about one-third think that assisting the poor is the government's job. The remainder express sympathy for both views (N.O.R.C., 1989).

As Banfield sees it, society should strive to encourage equality of opportunity, but should otherwise adopt a *laissez-faire* approach toward the poor. In Ryan's view, society should take an active role in reducing poverty by redistributing income in a more equal manner. This could be accomplished through programs such as a comprehensive child-care package to help poor mothers gain necessary skills or maintain jobs or a guaranteed minimum income level for every American family.

Little hard evidence conclusively substantiates either approach. But data reflecting patterns of work among the poor are suggestive. Banfield's position gains support from government data showing that more than half (50.8 percent) of the heads of poor families did not work at all during 1989. In fact, only about one in five of the heads of families in poverty worked steadily during 1989 (U.S. Bureau of the Census, 1990). So, from this point of view, the major cause of poverty is *not holding a job.*

But the *reasons* that people do not work seem more consistent with Ryan's position. Most women who are poor do not work because they need to care for children. In the United States, few employers provide child-care programs for workers, and few low-paid workers can afford to obtain child care on their own. Most poor men claim that there are no jobs to be found, that illness or disability has sidelined them, or, in the case of the elderly, that they have retired. Then, too, not all poor people are jobless. In 1989, 21.2 percent of the poor (1.4 million people) made up the *working poor,* heads of families who labored for at least fifty weeks of the year yet could not escape poverty. Another 23.6 percent (1.6 million people) worked 27 to 49 weeks, and 4.4 percent (300,000 people) worked fewer than 26 weeks. Such "working poverty" places a double burden on the poor: low wages and difficulty in seeking training or education to better themselves because they must struggle to make ends meet (Levitan & Shapiro, 1987). For most of the 1980s, the minimum wage remained at $3.35, rising to only $4.25 in 1991. Even at this level, an adult working full time could not support a family above the official poverty line.

Obviously, individual ability and initiative play a part in shaping everyone's social position. On balance, though, evidence points toward society—not individual character traits—as the primary source of poverty. Surely, some poor people lack ambition. Overall, however, the poor are *categories* of people—women who are heads of families, minorities, people isolated from the larger society in inner-city areas—without the same opportunities as others.

Homelessness

Many poor Americans lack the resources to support even basic housing. In light of the enormous wealth of the United States and its commitment to providing opportunity for everyone, homelessness may be fairly described as a national scandal demanding an effective response (Schutt, 1989).

There is no precise count of homeless Americans. Estimates suggest that some 500,000 people are homeless *on any given night*. Roughly 1.5 million Americans are homeless *at some time during the course of a year* (Kozol, 1988; Wright, 1989). The government also claims that 6 million people are at risk of homelessness. These people live below the poverty line and spend at least one-third of their income on housing (U.S. Commission on Security and Cooperation in Europe, 1990).

The traditional stereotypes of homeless people—men sleeping in doorways and women carrying everything they own in a shopping bag—have recently been undermined by the reality of the "new homeless." These are Americans thrown out of work because of plant closings, people forced out of apartments by rising rents or condominium conversions, and others unable to meet mortgage or rent payments because they must work for lower wages. Today, no stereotype of the homeless paints a complete picture because such people are now a highly varied category of Americans.

But virtually all homeless people have one thing in common: *poverty*. For that reason, the approaches already used to explain poverty also apply to homelessness. One side of the debate places responsibility on *personal* traits of the homeless themselves. Perhaps one-third of homeless people are mentally ill; others are addicted to alcohol or other drugs. Some, for whatever reason, seem unable to cope in a complex and highly competitive society (Bassuk, 1984; Whitman, 1989). On the other side of the debate, advocates assert that homelessness results from *societal* factors, including a lack of low-income housing in the United States and the economic transition toward low-paying jobs described earlier (Kozol, 1988; Schutt, 1989). One-third of all homeless people are now entire families, and children are the fastest growing category of the homeless. No one disputes that a large proportion of homeless people are personally impaired to some degree, although how much is cause and how much is effect is often difficult to untangle. But structural changes in the American economy, coupled with government policies reducing support for lower-income people, contribute substantially to homelessness.

Class and Welfare in America: Politics and Values

This chapter has explored the character of social stratification and presented many facts about social class in America. In the end, however, our understanding of what it means to be wealthy and privileged or poor and perhaps homeless also turns on politics and values. Not surprisingly, support for the notion that social standing reflects personal merit is strongest among well-off Americans. The idea that society should distribute wealth and other resources more equally finds greatest favor among those with relatively few advantages (Rytina, Form, & Pease, 1970; N.O.R.C., 1989).

The perceptions of *all* Americans are shaped by cultural values that hold people responsible for their own life circumstances. When a random sample of American adults was asked, "How important is hard work for getting ahead in life?" almost 90 percent responded that it was "essential" or "very important" (N.O.R.C., 1989:491). Such cultural values encourage us to see successful people as personally meritorious and the poor as personally deficient. Richard Sennett and Jonathan Cobb (1973) termed this judgment, applied to the poor, the *hidden injury of class*. In other words, poverty significantly lowers the self-image of disadvantaged people, while others display their affluence as a personal "badge of ability." Values supporting individual responsibility also contribute to the historically negative view of social welfare programs and those who receive such support in American society (Waxman, 1983). While advocates for the poor defend welfare programs as necessary for millions of Americans who are denied opportunities and advantages, American cultural values promote the view that social welfare programs undermine initiative. Accepting assistance of this kind thus becomes personally demeaning, which helps explain why half the Americans eligible for various forms of needed assistance do not apply for it (U.S. Bureau of the Census, 1989a).

Curiously, this same value system paints a more positive picture of government benefits provided to allegedly "deserving" wealthy Americans. Even as the Reagan administration cut government benefits to the poor in the early 1980s, for example, dozens of major corporations, including Boeing, General Electric, DuPont, Texaco, and Mobil, paid virtually no taxes on billions of dollars in earnings (Children's Defense Fund, 1985). A more recent case of government "wealth-fare" is the Bush Administration proposal to cut the capital gains tax, which no one denies would primarily enrich the wealthiest Americans. Clearly, government policy can aggravate or minimize social inequality, just as government policy itself is shaped by cultural and ideological definitions of rich and poor.

The drama of social stratification extends far beyond America's borders. The most striking social disparities are found not in the United States but in other parts of the world. Chapter 8 continues our investigation of social stratification, focusing on global inequality.

SUMMARY

1. Social stratification involves ranking categories of people in a hierarchy. Caste systems, common in agrarian societies, are based on ascription and permit little or no social mobility. Class systems, typical of industrial societies, allow more social mobility based on individual achievement.

2. Socialist societies claim to be classless because they are based on public ownership of productive property. Such societies, however, are unquestionably stratified.

3. The Davis–Moore thesis states that some degree of social stratification is universal because it helps society function. In class systems, unequal rewards encourage the most able people to assume the most important occupational positions. Criticism of the Davis–Moore thesis notes that (1) it is difficult to determine objectively the functional importance of any occupational position; (2) stratification prevents many people from developing their abilities; and (3) social stratification often generates social conflict.

4. Karl Marx recognized two major social classes in industrial societies: the capitalists, or *bourgeoisie*, which owns the means of production and seeks profits; and the proletariat, which provides labor in exchange for wages. The socialist revolution that Marx predicted has not occurred in industrial

societies such as the United States. While some sociologists see this fact as evidence that Marx's analysis was flawed, others point out that American society is still marked by pronounced social inequality and substantial class conflict.

5. Max Weber described social stratification in terms of three dimensions of social inequality: economic class, social status or prestige, and power. Taken together, these three dimensions form a complex hierarchy of socioeconomic standing.

6. Gerhard and Jean Lenski observe that, historically, technological advances have been associated with more pronounced social stratification. A limited reversal of this trend occurs in advanced industrial societies, as represented by the "Kuznets Curve."

7. Social inequality in American society involves disparity in a host of variables, including income, wealth, occupational prestige, and formal education.

8. The upper class, which is small (about 4 percent), includes the richest and most powerful Americans. The upper-upper class is the old rich, whose wealth has been transmitted over several generations; the lower-upper class, or the new rich, depends on earned income as their primary source of wealth.

9. The middle class includes 40 to 45 percent of Americans. The upper-middle class may be distin-

guished on the basis of higher income, higher-prestige occupations, and more schooling.

10. The working class includes about one-third of Americans. With below-average income, working-class families have less financial security than those in the middle class. Few working-class Americans have more than a high-school education, and they commonly work in blue-collar or lower white-collar jobs.

11. About one-fifth of Americans fall into the lower class. Most live near or below the official poverty line. African-Americans, Hispanic Americans, and women are disproportionately represented in the lower class.

12. Social mobility is common in the United States as in other industrial societies; typically, only small changes occur from one generation to the next.

13. Structural social mobility since the early 1970s has reduced the standard of living for many moderate-income Americans. This is the result of a decline in manufacturing industries in the United States, paralleling growth in low-paying service-sector jobs.

14. Some 32 million Americans are officially classified as poor. About 40 percent of the poor are children under the age of eighteen. Most poor Americans are white, but African-Americans, Hispanic Americans, and Asian Americans are disproportionately represented among the poor. A growing proportion of poor families is headed by women.

15. Oscar Lewis and Edward Banfield advanced the "culture of poverty" thesis, suggesting that much poverty is perpetuated by the personal characteristics of the poor themselves. Opposing this view, William Ryan argues that poverty is caused by the unequal distribution of wealth in society.

KEY CONCEPTS

absolute poverty a deprivation of resources that is life-threatening

alienation the experience of powerlessness in social life

blue-collar occupations lower-prestige work that involves mostly manual labor

capitalists people who own factories and other productive enterprises

caste system social stratification based on ascription

class system social stratification based on individual achievement

feminization of poverty a trend by which females represent an increasing proportion of the poor

ideology ideas that reflect and support the interests of some portion of a society

income occupational wages or salaries and earnings from investments

intergenerational social mobility a change in the social position of children in relation to that of their parents

intragenerational social mobility a change in social position occurring during a person's lifetime

meritocracy a system linking rewards to personal merit

proletariat people who provide productive labor

relative poverty being deprived of social resources in relation to those who have more

social conflict struggle among segments of society over valued resources

social mobility changes in people's positions in a system of social stratification

social stratification a system by which categories of people in a society are ranked in a hierarchy

socioeconomic status a composite social ranking based on various dimensions of social inequality

status consistency consistency of ranking across various dimensions of social standing

structural social mobility social mobility of large numbers of people that is due primarily to changes in society and the economy rather than to the efforts of individuals

wealth the total amount of money and valuable goods that any person or family controls

white-collar occupations higher-prestige work that involves mostly mental activity

Global Inequality

8

Chapter Outline

Half an hour from the center of Cairo, Egypt's capital city, the bus turned onto a dirt road and jerked to a stop. It was not quite dawn, and the Mo'edhdhins would soon climb the minarets of Cairo's many mosques to call the Islamic faithful to morning prayers. The driver turned to the busload of American students and their instructor, genuinely bewildered. "Why," he said, mixing English with some Arabic, "do you want to be here? And in the middle of the night?"

Why, indeed? No sooner had we stepped down from the bus than smoke and stench, the likes of which we had never before encountered, overcame us. Eyes squinting, handkerchiefs pressed against noses and mouths, we climbed the path ascending mountains of trash and garbage that extended for miles. We were entering the Cairo Dump, where the fifteen million people of one of the world's largest cities deposit their refuse.[1] We walked stiffly and with great care, since the only light came from small fires smoldering all around us. Suddenly, from the shadows, spectral shapes appeared. After a moment, we identified them as dogs peering curiously through the curtain of haze. As startled as we were, they quickly turned and vanished into the thick air. Ahead of us, large fires became visible with people clustered all around.

Human beings actually inhabit this inhuman place, creating a surreal scene, like the aftermath of the next war. As we approached, the fires cast an eerie light on their faces. We stopped some distance from them, separated by a vast chasm of culture and circumstances. But smiles eased the tension, and soon we were sharing the warmth of their flames. At that moment, the melodious call to prayer sounded across the city.

The people of the Cairo Dump, called the Zebaleen, belong to a religious minority—Coptic Christians—in a predominantly Muslim society. Barred by religious discrimination from many jobs, the Zebaleen use donkey carts and small trucks to pick up refuse throughout the city and bring it here. The night-long routine reaches a climax at dawn when the hundreds of Zebaleen gather at the dump, swarming over the new piles in search of anything valuable. That morning, we watched men, women, and children accumulate pieces of screen and bits of ribbon, examine scraps of discarded food, and slowly fill their baskets with what would get them through

[1] This portrayal of the Cairo Dump is based on the author's experiences in Cairo. It also draws on the discussion found in Spates & Macionis, 1987, and conversations with James L. Spates, who has also visited the Cairo Dump.

another day. Watching in silence, we became keenly aware of our sturdy shoes and warm clothing, and self-conscious that our watches and cameras represented more money than most of the Zebaleen might earn in a year.

Although unfamiliar to most Americans, the Zebaleen of the Cairo Dump are hardly unique. Their counterparts live in every nation on earth. Such destitute people are especially numerous in the Third World, where poverty is not only more common than in North America, but also far more acute.

THE IMPORTANCE OF GLOBAL PERSPECTIVE

Why should we study unfamiliar parts of the world, especially in a course primarily concerned with North America? Chapter 1 ("Sociology: Perspective, Theory, and Method") explained how American society shapes behavior, attitudes, and even our sense of ourselves. Taken one step further, the same logic applies to Ameri-

Even more than is the case in the United States, the burden of Third-World poverty falls most heavily on children.

can society's relationship to the world. To understand our own society we must explore how our part of the world fits into the larger global order. Extending the sociological perspective in this way is especially important today, as political changes sweep through Latin America, Eastern Europe, the Soviet Union, the Middle East, and South Africa, and rapid economic development reshapes many countries in Eastern Asia. All these global realignments affect the United States and the lives of every American.

This chapter also highlights how our world has grown increasingly interdependent. St. Augustine, an early leader of the Christian Church, once described the world as a book, noting that those who concentrate only on their own society read only a single page. With much of the contemporary world seized by political and economic change, looking beyond our own borders takes on greater importance than ever before.

THE THREE WORLDS

To gain a broader understanding of social inequality, then, we must look beyond the United States. While we recognize that pronounced social differences divide Americans (see Chapter 7, "Social Stratification"), the average American is quite well off by world standards. Even most Americans below our government's poverty line enjoy a much higher standard of living than the majority of people in the poorest nations on earth. We begin our study of global inequality by separating the world's societies into three broad categories or "worlds."

First, however, a word of caution. To place the roughly 175 nations on earth into three sweeping categories ignores striking differences in their ways of life. The societies in each category have rich and varied histories, speak dozens of languages, and encompass diverse peoples whose cultural distinctiveness serves as a source of pride. However, the three broad categories employed in this chapter are widely used to organize world nations based on (1) their level of technological development and (2) their political and economic system.

The First World

The term **First World** refers to *industrial societies that have predominantly capitalist economies*. They are not called "first" because they are "better" or "more impor-

tant" than other nations, but rather because the Industrial Revolution came first to these nations, beginning two centuries ago, vastly increasing their productive capacity. In historical context, the economic activity surrounding the care of household pets alone in the United States exceeds the economic enterprise in all of medieval Europe. This is reflected in a relatively high standard of living for the average American.

Figure 8–1 on pages 184–85 identifies countries of the First World. Shown in blue, this region includes the nations of Western Europe such as the United Kingdom (made up of England, Scotland, Wales, and Northern Ireland). It was in southwestern England that early industrialization appeared by 1775. Also part of the First World are the United States and Canada in North America, where the Industrial Revolution was under way around 1850. On the African continent, the advanced economic development of South Africa places this country (at least its *white minority*) in the First World. Also ranking in the First World is Japan, the most economically powerful nation in Asia. And, in the geographic region known as Oceania, Australia and New Zealand also belong to the First World.

Collectively, the First World covers roughly 25 percent of the earth's land area, includes parts of five continents, and mostly lies in the northern hemisphere. In 1990, the population of the First World was about 700 million, just over 15 percent of the earth's people. By global standards, the First World is not densely populated.

Despite historic and cultural differences among First-World nations, they now share an industrial capacity that generates, on average, a high standard of living for their people. Most of the world's income is enjoyed by the minority of humanity living in the First World. The economies of First-World nations are predominantly capitalist, so that a market system (or "private enterprise"), rather than government, controls production. Since World War I, the United States has been the dominant nation (often termed a "superpower") of the First World. Because the United States and its Western European allies are linked by political and economic alliances, the First World is sometimes referred to by the shorthand term "the West."

The Second World

The **Second World** is composed of *industrial societies that have predominantly socialist economies*. Industrial-

Figure 8–1 The Three Worlds

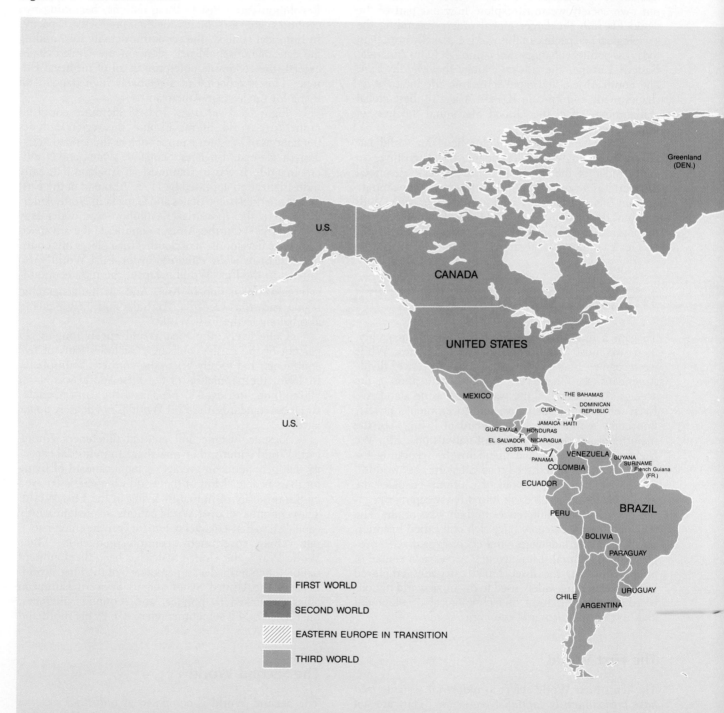

FIRST WORLD

SECOND WORLD

EASTERN EUROPE IN TRANSITION

THIRD WORLD

C.A.R. — CENTRAL AFRICAN REPUBLIC
U.A.E. — UNITED ARAB EMIRATES

ization took hold in much of this broad region of the world only in the twentieth century. This accounts, in part, for the lesser economic strength of the Second World in relation to the First World. Second-World nations have less powerful industrial capacities, and proportionately more of their people live in rural areas and remain in agricultural production. (Chapter 11, "Economics and Politics," provides a comparative look at the performance of capitalist and socialist economies.)

In Figure 8–1, the Second World appears in red. Dominating the Second World is the Union of Soviet Socialist Republics (U.S.S.R.), whose military strength gives it "superpower" status. Since World War II, the Second World has included the Eastern European nations of Poland, the German Democratic Republic (East Germany), Czechoslovakia, Hungary, Romania, and Bulgaria. During 1989, most of Eastern Europe was transformed by the popular overthrow of established socialist governments, the opening of borders to the West, and the call for Western-style market systems. In 1990, the "two Germanys" were rejoined, and the United Germany is now shown as part of the First World. Because the future course of other Eastern European countries is still unclear, these nations are shown with a striped pattern in Figure 8–1.

The Second World spans roughly 15 percent of the world's land area. Most of it lies in the Soviet Union, geographically the largest nation on earth, stretching from Europe to Asia. Roughly 500 million people or 10 percent of humanity live in the Second World. Like the First World, this region is not densely populated by global standards.

Second-World nations differ from one another in many respects. The Soviet Union itself comprises dozens of cultural groups, many of whom are fiercely nationalistic. Yet a historic reliance on predominantly socialist economies has joined the nations of the Second World together. Instead of the market systems of First-World nations, the economies of these Second-World countries have been largely directed by governments. Most of the societies of the Second World have been politically unified—at least until recent developments—under the leadership of the Soviet Union, and are sometimes described as the "Eastern Bloc."

The Third World

The **Third World** encompasses *primarily agrarian societies in which most people are poor*. In these societies, a

When natural disasters strike rich nations, property loss is great but loss of life is low; in poor societies, the converse is true. In 1985, a flood and mudslide wiped out the village of Armero in Colombia, killing more than 10,000 people.

majority of people live in rural areas, engage in farming, and follow the traditions of their ancestors. Industrial technology has had only a limited impact here, mostly in the Third-World cities. Therefore these societies are less productive by world standards. This pattern holds true even though some Third-World countries—notably the oil-rich nations of the Middle East—have an extremely high average standard of living due to the great wealth of *some* of their people.

Figure 8–1 indicates that the Third World, shown in green, encompasses *most* of the globe. On the southern border of the United States lies the Third-World nation of Mexico, beyond which is all of Central America. The nations of South America also belong to the Third World. Moving across the Atlantic Ocean, the continent of Africa (except for South Africa) falls into the Third World. Included, too, is the Middle East except Israel and all of Asia except Japan.

The Third World represents about 60 percent of the earth's area including most of the nations near and below the equator. More significantly, 77 percent of the world's 5.3 billion people live in the Third World. Because of its large and rapidly increasing population, low economic productivity, and unfavorable economic relations with rich societies, the Third World faces poverty on a massive scale. Hunger, unsafe housing, and high rates of disease all plague the Third World.

Despite the poverty they share, Third-World societies do not have an economic system in common. Some poor countries, such as the People's Republic of China (with 1.1 billion people, the world's most populous nation), have predominantly socialist economic systems. Other nations, like India and Egypt, blend elements of socialism and capitalism. Still others, including Brazil and much of Latin America, are primarily capitalist in nature.

This identification of "three worlds" is the foundation for understanding the problem of global inequality. For people living in an affluent nation such as the United States, the scope of the problem may be difficult to grasp. The televised scenes of famine in Ethiopia during the mid-1980s gave many Americans a shocking look at the absolute poverty that makes daily living a life-and-death struggle in much of the world today. Behind these images lie cultural, historical, and economic forces that will be the focus of the remainder of this chapter.

THIRD-WORLD POVERTY

Poverty always means struggle. Third-World poverty, however, typically involves more severe hardship than poverty in American society (see Chapter 7, "Social Stratification"). This does not mean that deprivation in the United States is a minor issue. Especially in a rich society, the lack of food, housing, and health care for tens of millions of people—many of them children—amounts to a national tragedy. Yet, in global perspective, poverty in the Third World is *more severe* and *more extensive* than in the United States.

The Severity of Poverty

Poverty in the Third World is more severe than it is in rich societies such as the United States. The data in Table 8–1 on page 188 suggest why. The first column of figures shows, for selected countries, the gross national product (abbreviated "GNP," and referring to the total value of all goods and services produced in a given year by everyone in that country). Industrial societies typically have a high GNP simply because industrial technology makes them extremely productive. A large, First-World nation like the United States had a 1990 GNP of over $4 trillion; the GNP of the Soviet Union, a large Second-World country, stood at about $2 trillion. The rest of the table shows that Third-World countries around the

Poverty in the Third World falls hardest upon children, a truth that is strikingly portrayed by David Alfaro Siqueiros in his painting *Echo of a Scream*.

David Alfaro Siqueiros, Echo of a Scream, 1937. Duco on wood, 48 × 36". Collection, The Museum of Modern Art, New York. Gift of M. M. Warburg.

Table 8–1 INCOME AND WEALTH IN WORLD PERSPECTIVE

Country	Gross National Product ($ billion)	Per-Person Income ($)
First World		
United States	4,200	15,400
Canada	367	13,100
United Kingdom	453	8,300
West Germany	898	11,000
Japan	1,900	10,400
Second World		
Soviet Union	2,000	7,300
Poland	240	6,100
Hungary	80	7,300
East Germany	93	9,800
Czechoslovakia	136	8,300
Third World		
Latin America		
Mexico	126	2,100
Argentina	65	2,300
El Salvador	4	700
Bolivia	4	550
Colombia	31	1,100
Nicaragua	3	850
Africa/Middle East		
Cameroon	8	800
Egypt	30	700
Nigeria	53	800
Burkina Faso	1	150
Zaire	5	150
Saudi Arabia	98	11,500
Lebanon	3	1,150
Iran	75	1,700
Asia		
P.R. of China	270	250
Taiwan	73	3,000
South Korea	90	2,200
Thailand	40	800
India	194	150
Pakistan	32	350
Bangladesh	15	100

Note: This table shows gross national product (GNP) and yearly per-person income in U.S. dollars for various nations. Available data are not always precisely comparable, but provide a generally accurate pattern. Most data are for the mid-1980s.

SOURCE: U.S. Arms Control and Disarmament Agency, *World Military Expenditures and Arms Transfers 1986* (Washington, DC: U.S. Government Printing Office, 1987); also *World Almanac and Book of Facts 1989* (New York: Pharos Books, 1988).

globe, with little industrial technology, have far lower GNPs.

The second column of figures in Table 8–1 indicates "per-person income" for these countries, calculated by dividing the country's total income by the total population. The figures for First-World nations are relatively high—more than $15,000 for the United States, for example. Income levels in Second-World societies are significantly lower than those in the First World. But the most dramatic difference involves the Third World. Here, per-person income levels are generally less than $2,000 (in many cases, below $1,000) a year. At approximately $150, the per-capita income in India amounts to only about 1 percent of that found in the United States. In simple terms, this means that the typical person in India labors all year to make what the average American earns in several days. [2]

Figure 8–2 shows the relative share of world income earned in each of the three "worlds." Clearly, the people of the First World are most advantaged: Representing just 15 percent of the world's population, they enjoy about two-thirds of the world's income. The people of the Second World are less well off, but they, too, claim a disproportionately large share of global income. In the Third World, three-fourths of humanity receive only about 20 percent of all income. For every dollar earned by a Third-World worker, five dollars go to a worker in the Second World. Even more privileged is a worker in the First World, who makes about sixteen dollars.

Beyond these global patterns, every society also has significant *internal* social stratification. This means that social differences between the most affluent Americans and the most disadvantaged Third-World people, such as the Zebaleen described in the chapter opening, are especially striking.

Relative versus absolute poverty. A distinction made in the last chapter has an important application to global inequality. In rich societies, most discussions of poverty focus on *relative poverty*, the lack of resources of some in comparison to others who have more. By definition, relative poverty exists in every society, even in the First World. But just as important—especially in a global context—is the concept of *absolute poverty*, a lack of

---

[2] The per-person income figures for the poorest of the world's societies are understated because a significant amount of income in the form of bartered products is not included in formal accountings. But even if the figures are doubled to overcome this bias, per capita income of Third-World societies would remain well below that of rich nations.

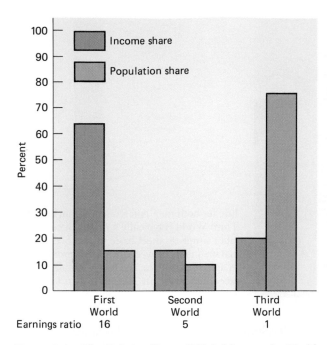

Figure 8–2 The Relative Share of Global Income by World Region

resources that is life-threatening. Most commonly, absolute poverty means lacking the minimum level of nutrition necessary for health.

In a rich society like the United States, poverty is often viewed in relative terms. Some degree of absolute poverty does exist, however; inadequate nutrition and even starvation are unfortunate realities in America. Yet such immediately life-threatening poverty strikes only a small proportion of the population. By contrast, societies of the Third World face a severe problem of absolute poverty, involving one-quarter of the population—1 billion people—who lack nutrition adequate for a safe and productive life.

The Extent of Poverty

Poverty in the Third World is more extensive than it is in the United States. Chapter 7 ("Social Stratification") indicated that about 13 percent of Americans are officially classified as poor. In the societies of the Third World, however, *most* people live no better than the American poor, and at any given time, perhaps 20 percent of the people are near absolute poverty. In some parts of the world (such as East Asia), the extent of absolute poverty

is not so great; in other regions (rural areas in Central America and Africa, for example), half the population may be ill-nourished. In the world as a whole, 100 million people have no shelter and approximately 1 billion people do not eat enough to allow them to work regularly. Of these, 800 million are at risk for their lives (Sivard, 1987; Helmuth, 1989).

Simply stated, people are dying, every minute of every day, from lack of basic nutrition. In the ten minutes it takes to read through this section of the chapter, about three hundred people in the world will die of starvation. This amounts to more than 40,000 people a day, or 15 million people each year. Even more than in the United States, the burden of poverty in the Third World falls on children. In the entire Third World, about one child in four dies before reaching the age of five.

Two further comparisons may make these statistics more meaningful. First, at the end of World War II, the United States obliterated the Japanese city of Hiroshima with an atomic bomb. The global loss of life from starvation *every three days* equals the Hiroshima death toll. Second, the number of people who have died in all the wars, revolutions, and murders during the last 150 years roughly equals the number of people who died from hunger in the last *five* years (Burch, 1983). World hunger must be considered one of the most serious problems facing humanity today.

Third-World Women: Work and Poverty

Even more than in rich societies, in the Third World women are disproportionately the poorest of the poor. In these societies, women have the primary responsibility for childbearing and maintaining the household.

In rural areas throughout the Third World, women have historically worked long hours—typically twelve hours a day for women compared to about eight hours for men (House of Representatives, 1988:43). Much of women's work—cleaning and repairing the home, gathering firewood, traveling to and from the market, tending to the needs of children, and preparing meals for the family—remains "invisible" to those who monitor the labor force. In comparison to rich societies, more of women's work in the Third World is not paid, making the economic position of women correspondingly weaker.

Paid work also places Third-World women at a greater disadvantage than their counterparts in rich societies. As Chapter 10 ("Sex and Gender") details, in the

Life for both men and women throughout the Third World is typically a matter of continual labor simply to meet basic needs. Because social inequality between the sexes is pronounced in agrarian societies, the relative disadvantages faced by women are greater than in industrial societies.

United States and the rest of the industrialized world, women receive less income for their labor than men do. In the largely agrarian societies of the Third World, where traditional subordination of women to men is more pronounced, the differential in salary between the two sexes is even greater. Third-World women have less access to education than men have, a pattern that is disappearing in many industrial societies (United Nations, 1988). Lacking education, women have far fewer choices about their lives.

Finally, the United Nations estimates that roughly 90 percent of land in the Third World is formally owned by males (in rich societies, the proportion is somewhat lower). In reality, as wives and mothers, women exert considerable control over property that formally belongs to males. Nevertheless, the strong traditions of family and the support of law give men ultimate control of the land, which is the most valuable resource in agrarian societies.

Overall, then, Third-World poverty is both severe and extensive. The burden of poverty is not shared equally, however; women are usually among the most disadvantaged.

Correlates of Third-World Poverty

What accounts for Third-World poverty? The rest of this chapter weaves various facts related to poverty into explanations.

1. **Technology.** The Third World is largely agrarian, lacking the productive capacity of industrial technology. Energy is supplied by the muscles of humans and other animals rather than by steam, oil, or nuclear energy, with corresponding limitations on machinery. The focus in agrarian societies on farming, rather than on specialized activities, also limits the development of human skills and abilities.

2. **Population growth.** As Chapter 14 ("Population and Urbanization") explains in detail, Third-World societies have the highest birth rates in the world. Despite high death rates from poverty, the populations of many poor societies of Africa, for example, are doubling every twenty-five years. In such societies, more than half the people are not yet beyond their teens, and are entering their childbearing years. Population growth in the future, therefore, is inevitable. Even a developing economy would not be able to absorb the likely surges in population. Economic growth, then, produces no real increase in standard of living for most of the population.

3. **Cultural patterns.** Societies that have yet to industrialize usually value tradition. Families and neighborhood groups pass down folkways and mores from generation to generation. Adhering to their traditions, such people tend to resist innovations—even those that promise a richer, more comfortable material life.

India: A Different Kind of Poverty

Most Americans know that India is one of the poorest societies of the world: Table 8–1 showed per-person income in India to be only $150 a year. One in three of the world's hungry lives in this vast society.

Few Americans can comprehend the reality of poverty in this Asian nation. There are rich people in India, just as everywhere else, but most of the country's 750 million people live in conditions far worse than Americans who are labeled "poor." An American's first experience of Indian life is sobering and sometimes shocking; in time, the outsider also sees that, in India, people experience poverty differently as well.

Arriving in Madras, one of India's largest cities, a visitor immediately recoils from the smell of human sewage, which fills the air in many areas and makes much of the region's water unsafe to drink. The sights and sounds, too, are strange and intense—the streets are choked by motorbikes, trucks, carts pulled by oxen, and waves of people. Along the roads, vendors sit on burlap cloth and hawk fruits, vegetables, and prepared foods. Seemingly oblivious to the urban chaos, people work, talk, defecate, and sleep in the streets. The cities of India contain literally millions of homeless people.

Madras is also dotted by more than a thousand shanty settlements, where

Third-World societies may be poor, but their traditions strengthen families. Thus poverty is endured amidst the support of kinship, which contrasts to the often isolating poverty of the United States.

about half a million people live in huts constructed of branches, leaves, and discarded material. These shanties offer little privacy and lack refrigeration, running water, and bathrooms. The American visitor may feel uneasy entering such a community, since the poorest sections of inner cities in the United States abound with frustration and, oftentimes, outright violence. But here, too, India offers a sharp contrast. No angry

young people hang out at the corner, no drugs pervade the area, and there is surprisingly little danger. Instead, the social units of shantytowns are strong families—children, parents, and sometimes elderly grandparents—who extend a smile and a welcome. In traditional societies like India, ways of life change little, even over many generations. Moreover, the lives of traditional Indians are shaped by *dharma*—the Hindu concept of duty and destiny—that encourages people to accept their fate, whatever it may be. Mother Teresa, who has won praise for her work among the poorest of India's people, goes to the heart of the cultural differences: "Americans have angry poverty; in India, there is worse poverty, but it is a happy poverty."

No one who lives on the edge of survival can be called truly "happy." The deadly horror of poverty in India, however, is eased by the strength of families and traditional communities, a sense of purpose to life, and a world view that encourages each person to accept whatever society offers. As a result, the American visitor comes away from the first encounter with Indian poverty in confusion: "How can people be so poor, and yet apparently content, vibrant, and so *alive*?"

SOURCE: Based on the author's research in Madras, India, November, 1988.

Traditionalism in poor societies often means accepting one's lot in life, although it may be poor, in order to maintain family vitality and cultural heritage. Although such attitudes may discourage

development, they also support strong social bonds. The box explains why traditional people in India respond to their poverty differently than poor people in the United States commonly do.

4. **Social stratification.** What little Third-World societies have is distributed very unequally *within* the population. Chapter 7 ("Social Stratification") explained that social inequality is generally more pronounced in agrarian societies, where land is a vital resource, than in industrial societies. In the farming regions of Bangladesh in Central Asia, for example, just 10 percent of all landowners own more than half the land, while almost half of all farming families have almost no land of their own (Hartmann & Boyce, 1982). According to another estimate, the richest 10 percent of landowners in Central America control more than three-fourths of the land in those poor societies (Barry, 1987). Such concentration of land and wealth has prompted widespread demands for land reform in many agrarian societies.

5. **Global power relationships.** A final cause of global poverty lies in the relationships among the nations of the world. Much of the wealth of the Third World has enriched the First World. Historically, this is due to **colonialism,** *the process by which some nations enrich themselves through political and economic control of other nations.* The nations of Western Europe colonized and maintained control over much of Latin America for more than 300 years; much of Africa endured a century of colonization; parts of Asia were also colonized for long periods. Some analysts claim that this global exploitation allowed some nations to *develop* economically while others were *underdeveloped.*

   During the nineteenth and twentieth centuries, most colonies gained their political independence; only a small number of formal colonies remain today. As we shall see, however, a continuing pattern of **neocolonialism** (*neo* comes from Greek, meaning "new") is emerging. This amounts to *a new form of economic exploitation that does not involve formal political control.* Charges of neocolonialism center on the business of **multinational corporations,** *large corporations that operate in many different countries.* As Chapter 11 ("Economics and Politics") explains, multinational corporations historically developed through rapid corporate growth and mergers. These corporations now wield such tremendous economic power that corporate decision makers can—and often do—influence the political systems in countries where they do business.

GLOBAL INEQUALITY: THEORETICAL ANALYSIS

There are two major explanations for the unequal distribution of the world's wealth and power—modernization theory and dependency theory. Each suggests not only why so many of the world's people are poor, but why we as North Americans enjoy such comparative advantages.

The two explanations overlap to some extent. Both acknowledge enormous inequality on our planet, and suggest that changes are needed to guarantee the future security of humanity, rich and poor alike. Yet, by emphasizing different factors, they reach differing conclusions about where responsibility lies for global poverty.

Modernization Theory

Modernization theory maintains that *global inequality reflects differing levels of technological development among societies.* Modernization theory developed in the 1950s, when the United States feared hostility to American interests in much of the Third World. At that time, socialist nations of the Second World were arguing that Third-World countries could not make economic progress under the influence of the capitalist First World. The American response was a broad defense of the First World that has shaped official foreign policy toward poor nations ever since.[3]

Historical perspective. According to modernization theory, the *entire world* was poor as recently as several centuries ago. Because poverty is the norm throughout human history, then, *affluence*—not deprivation—demands an explanation.

Affluence came within reach of a small part of humanity in the late Middle Ages as economic activity expanded in Western Europe. Initially, this economic growth involved trade within cities. By the beginning of the sixteenth century, exploration of other parts of the world revealed vast commercial potential. Then, the Industrial Revolution in the eighteenth and nineteenth centuries transformed Western Europe and, soon after, North America. Industrial technology and the innovations of countless entrepreneurs created new wealth

---

[3] The following discussion of modernization theory draws primarily on Rostow (1978), Bauer (1981), and Berger (1986).

In 1844, when an unknown artist produced this painting, hard and dangerous work was a fact of childhood in England. Initially, the Industrial Revolution did little to improve the lives of children, who had historically labored as adults did. Gradually, however, as machinery reduced the need for labor, the role of children was transformed so that they left mines and factories for schools.

on a grand scale. At the outset, this new wealth benefited only a few. Yet industrial technology was so productive that gradually the standard of living of even the poorest people began to rise. The specter of absolute poverty, which had cast a menacing shadow over humanity for its entire history, was finally being routed.

Since then, the standard of living in the region where the Industrial Revolution first began has continued to improve. Today, the benefits of industrialization are enjoyed primarily in the First World and, to a lesser extent, in the Second World. But without industrial technology, the Third World maintains the same low productivity it has had throughout history.

The importance of culture. Why didn't people the world over share in the Industrial Revolution so that they, too, could enjoy material plenty? Modernization theory holds that people are likely to exploit new technology only in a *cultural environment* that emphasizes the benefits of innovation and greater productivity.

The greatest barrier to economic development is, therefore, *traditionalism*. In traditional societies based on strong family systems, ancient ways of life provide powerful guides to understanding the present and shaping the future. Predictably, this creates a form of "cultural

inertia" that keeps societies from adopting technological advances that would improve their material standard of living. For example, Western innovations and technological advances have encountered fierce resistance in Iran because they threaten traditional Islamic family relationships, customs, and religious beliefs.

Max Weber (1958; orig. 1904–1905) argued that, toward the end of the Middle Ages, Western Europe developed a distinctive cultural environment that favored change. As explained in Chapter 12 ("Family and Religion"), this progress-oriented culture characterized societies where the Protestant Reformation had transformed traditional Catholicism. Material affluence, which the Catholic Church had regarded with suspicion, became a personal virtue, and individualism steadily eroded the traditional emphasis on kinship and community. Taken together, these changing cultural patterns nurtured the Industrial Revolution, which allowed one segment of humanity to prosper.

Rostow's stages of modernization. Modernization theory does not condemn the poor regions of the globe to a future as poor as their past. Due to technological advances, all societies are gradually converging on one general form: the industrial model. According to

W. W. Rostow (1978), the process of modernization follows four general stages.

1. **Traditional stage.** In this stage, poor societies rely on strong traditions, and their cultures resist technological innovation. People in traditional societies cannot easily conceive of how life could be different. Such societies place great significance on family and community, granting little exercise of individual freedom of the sort that initiates change. Life may be spiritually rich, therefore, but lacking in material abundance.

    A century ago, much of the world was in this initial stage of economic development. Today, according to modernization theory, the extreme poverty of societies like Bangladesh in Central Asia and Burkina Faso in Central Africa stems from their still being at the traditional, or first, stage of development.

2. **Take-off stage.** As traditions begin to weaken, the economy slowly grows. A limited market emerges as people produce not just for their own consumption but to engage in profitable trade with others. Paralleling these developments is a greater achievement orientation, which often comes at the expense of family ties and longstanding norms and values.

    Great Britain reached this stage by about 1800; the United States did soon afterward. Many of the nations of the Third World have made economic gains in recent decades, and are now at this stage. Thailand in Eastern Asia is a prime example.

    Rostow argues that economic "take-off" in Third-World societies depends on progressive influences—including foreign aid, introduction of advanced technology and investment capital, and schooling abroad—that only rich nations can provide.

3. **Drive to technological maturity.** At this stage, a society has embraced the pursuit of a higher standard of living. An active, diversified economy is driven by a population eager to enjoy the benefits of industrial technology. At the same time, however, people begin to recognize (and sometimes lament) that industrialization is eroding traditional life in families and local communities. Great Britain reached this point by about 1840, the United States by about 1860. Today, Mexico and the People's Republic of China are among the nations driving to technological maturity.

    At this stage of economic development, absolute poverty is greatly reduced. Cities swell to great size, occupational specialization makes relationships less personal, and heightened individualism often sparks movements pressing for greater political rights. Societies at this level of development also recognize the need to educate all their people, and to provide advanced training for some. As adherence to tradition declines, women tend to assume a social position more equal to that of men. Initially, however, the process of development subjects women to new and unanticipated stresses, as the box explains.

4. **High mass consumption.** Economic development through industrial technology eventually raises living standards. This occurs, Rostow argues, as mass production stimulates mass consumption. The United States reached this stage of development by the beginning of the twentieth century. Other First-World societies were not far behind. For example, Japan became a military power early in this century. After recovering from the destruction of World War II, the Japanese enjoyed high mass consumption, and Japan now rivals the United States as an economic power. The Soviet Union claimed to be approaching this stage by about 1950, but its sluggish economy since then still limits the availability of many goods and services. Fast nearing this level of economic development are some of the most prosperous East Asian societies of the Third World: South Korea, Taiwan, Hong Kong, and Singapore.

The role of rich nations. Modernization theory claims that the First World plays an important role in global economic development. Rather than being the *cause* of the abject poverty that afflicts much of humanity, rich societies form part of the *solution* to global inequality in the following ways:

1. **Assisting in population control.** As we have already noted, population growth is greatest in the poorest societies of the world and can easily overtake economic advances. First-World nations can help curb global population by exporting birth control technology and promoting its use. Once economic development is under way, birth rates should decline as they have in industrialized societies.

2. **Increasing food production.** Modernization theory suggests that "high-tech" farming methods, ex-

ported from rich societies to poor nations, can significantly raise agricultural yields. Such techniques—collectively referred to as the "*Green Revolution*"—involve the use of new hybrid seeds, modern irrigation methods, chemical fertilizers, and pesticides for insect control.

3. **Introducing industrial technology.** Rich nations can accelerate the economic growth of poor societies by introducing industrial technology. This form of cultural diffusion helps to transform the labor force of poor countries from lower-skill agricultural work to higher-skill industrial work, improving productivity.

4. **Instituting programs of foreign aid.** Investment capital from rich nations allows poor societies to reach the "take-off" stage. Developing countries

CRITICAL THINKING

Modernization and Women: What are the Drawbacks?

In global perspective, gender inequality is most pronounced in the poorest societies. Economic development advances the interests of women by weakening traditional patterns of male domination and giving women more opportunities to work outside the home. Women also benefit from more formal education and from access to birth control.

Yet economic development also has drawbacks for women, even as their standard of living rises. Investigating a poor, rural district of Bangladesh, Sultana Alam (1985) identified several problems women face as a result of modernization.

First, economic opportunity often draws men from rural areas to cities in search of work, leaving women and children to fend for themselves. Men sometimes sell their land and simply abandon women, who are left with nothing but their children.

Second, the eroding strength of the family and neighborhood leaves women who are deserted in this way with few sources of assistance. The same holds true for women who become single through divorce or the death of a spouse. In the past, Alam reports, family or neighbors readily took in a Bangladeshi woman who found herself alone. Today, as Ban-

One consequence of modernization in Third-World societies might be termed "the sexualization of women." Rather than being defined in terms of traditional kinship roles, women are increasingly valued for their sexual attractiveness. Perhaps significantly, many of the growing number of prostitutes in large Third-World cities have discarded traditional dress for Western styles of clothing.

gladesh struggles to advance economically, the number of female-headed poor households is increasing. Rather than enhancing women's autonomy, Alam argues, this spirit of individualism has reduced the social standing of women.

Third, economic development undermines traditional roles as wives, sisters, and mothers, while redefining women as objects of sexual attention. Today, especially under the influence of the Western mass media, a "modern" emphasis on sexuality has encouraged men to desert aging spouses for younger, more physically attractive women.

Modernization, then, does not affect men and women in the same ways. In the long run, the evidence suggests that modernization does make the sexes more equal. In the short run, however, the economic position of many women declines, and women are also forced to contend with new problems that were virtually unknown in traditional societies.

SOURCE: Based on Sultana Alam, "Women and Poverty in Bangladesh," *Women's Studies International Forum*, Vol. 8, No. 4 (1985), pp. 361–371; also Barbara Mink, "How Modernization Affects Women," *Cornell Alumni News*, Vol. III, No. 3 (April 1989):10–11.

can use foreign aid to purchase high technology—in the form of fertilizers and irrigation projects—to raise agricultural productivity. Similarly, building power-generating plants and factories greatly improves industrial output.

Critical evaluation.   Modernization theory has influential supporters among social scientists (Parsons, 1966; W. Moore, 1977, 1979; Bauer, 1981; Berger, 1986). In identifying how industrialization affects other dimensions of social life, this approach has helped to explain how and why industrialization changes a society. Modernization theory has also shaped the foreign policy of the United States and other First-World nations. Proponents cite a number of poor societies that have made impressive strides with the assistance of rich countries. For instance, the Asian nations of South Korea, Taiwan, the former British colony of Singapore, and the current British colony of Hong Kong each receive extensive First-World assistance, and each has shown significant economic development. Similarly, concerted efforts to modernize by nations like Turkey have greatly improved national living standards.

From the outset, however, modernization theory has come under fire from nations of the Second World as a thinly veiled defense of capitalism. By the 1960s, a growing number of critics in First-World societies also detected major flaws in this approach. Perhaps the most serious failing, according to critics, is that modernization theory has fallen short of its own standards of success. Instead of making the industrial model widely accessible, only limited modernization has occurred. Critics argue that global inequality is as striking as ever.

A second criticism is that modernization theory tends to ignore historical forces that thwart development in the Third World today. Modernization theory holds that the opportunities for growth available to rich nations several centuries ago are still available to the Third World. (Indeed, according to this theory, opportunities today are even *greater* since rich nations can offer assistance to the Third World.) However, critics claim that political and economic barriers to development have emerged in the two centuries since Europe's Industrial Revolution that almost ensure the perpetuation of global poverty. In essence, they argue, the First World industrialized from a position of global *strength*; the Third World cannot be expected to modernize from a position of global *weakness*.

Third, by minimizing the connections between rich and poor societies, modernization theory offers little insight into how global development continues to affect *rich* societies. For example, many traditional American industries, such as steel and auto production, have declined in large measure because of the growth of these industries abroad, notably in Japan and South Korea. As a result, low-paid service work is replacing high-paid factory work in the United States, as explained in Chapter 7 ("Social Stratification").

Fourth, critics contend that by holding up the First World as the standard by which the rest of humanity should be judged, modernization theory betrays an ethnocentric bias. As Chapter 15 ("Social Change and Modernity") explains, "progress" is reducing the cultural diversity of our world, promoting a materialistic, Western way of life around the globe.

Fifth, and finally, modernization theory draws criticism for suggesting that the causes of global poverty lie almost entirely in the poor societies themselves. This amounts to "blaming the victims" for their own plight. Instead, critics argue, an analysis of global inequality should focus as much attention on the behavior of *rich* nations as that of poor nations (Wiarda, 1987).

From all these concerns has emerged a second major approach to understanding global inequality: dependency theory.

Dependency Theory

Dependency theory maintains that *global poverty historically stems from the exploitation of poor societies by rich societies.* This analysis places primary responsibility for global poverty on rich nations. Dependency theory holds that rich societies have impoverished the Third World by making poor nations *dependent* on richer ones. The roots of this destructive process, which continues today, extend back several centuries.

Historical perspective.   Before the Industrial Revolution, there was little of the affluence present in some of the world today. Dependency theory asserts, however, that most of the people living in what we now call the Third World were actually better off economically in the past. André Gunder Frank (1975), a noted proponent of this approach, argues that the development of rich societies paralleled the *underdevelopment* of poor societies.

Dependency theory directly links the economic positions of the rich and poor nations of the globe. Modernization theory, its critics argue, errs by suggesting

According to dependency theory, the poverty of much of the world was created through centuries of unfavorable economic relations. During the so-called "Age of Exploration" beginning in the late fifteenth century, European societies dispatched expeditions that systematically plundered other societies, often killing many people in the process. As the conquerors reduced these societies to European colonies, an enduring global pattern was established: The First World began to prosper, while the Third World fell into a state of economic decline and dependency.

that poor societies are lagging behind rich ones on a single "path of progress." According to dependency theory, the increasing prosperity of the First World has come largely at the expense of the Third World. In short, some nations have become rich *only because others have become poor*. This complex process, which began centuries ago with the onset of global commerce, continues in much of the world today.

The importance of colonialism. Some five hundred years ago, Europeans set out to explore the "New World" of North America to the west, the massive continent of Africa to the south, and Asia to the east. As vast new wealth was discovered, the economic fortunes of the First World began to rise. By the late fifteenth century, the Third World began to fall under the domination of European governments. Spain and Portugal colonized nearly all of Latin America. By the beginning of the twentieth century, Great Britain had colonies around the world and boasted that "The sun never sets on the British Empire." The United States, itself originally a British colony, colonized the Virgin Islands, Haiti, Puerto Rico, and part of Cuba in the western hemisphere, and Guam and the Philippines in Asia.

Overt colonialism has largely disappeared from the world. Most Latin American nations achieved political independence during the first half of the nineteenth century, and most African and Asian colonies gained their freedom during this century. However, according to dependency theory, political liberation has not meant economic autonomy. Far from it: Poor societies of the Third World maintain economic relationships with rich nations that carry on the colonial pattern. This neocolonialism is fueled by a capitalist world economy.

Wallerstein's capitalist world economy. Immanuel Wallerstein (1974, 1979, 1983, 1984) developed a model of the "capitalist world economy" to explain the origins of contemporary global inequality.[4] Wallerstein's term *world economy* suggests that interacting national economies comprise a global economic system. He argues that this global economic system has expanded over the last five hundred years beyond the control of the traditional political units we call nations. The dominant character of this global system is capitalist.

The nations of the First World stand at the *core* of the world economy. Colonialism established this core

---

[4] While based largely on Wallerstein's ideas, this section also is informed by the work of Frank (1980, 1981), Delacroix & Ragin (1981), and Bergesen (1983).

as raw materials, funneled to Western Europe from the rest of the world, fueled the Industrial Revolution. Today, multinational corporations that operate profitably around the globe are headquartered in the core nations of North America, Western Europe, and Japan. By contrast, the Third World encompasses countries at the *periphery* of the world economy. Drawn into the world economy by colonial exploitation, these poor countries continue to support industrial societies by providing inexpensive labor and an enormous market for First-World products.

According to this approach, the world economy benefits the First World (in terms of profits) and harms the Third World (by perpetuating poverty). The world economy thus fosters a state of dependency in which poor nations remain under the control of rich ones. This dependency is caused primarily by the following three factors:

1. **Narrow, export-oriented economies.** Unlike the economies of core nations, those of Third-World countries are not diversified. Historically, colonial powers have forced local farmers to stop growing a variety of traditional crops for local consumption in favor of producing a small number of products for export. Most colonial economies export only a few products—mostly raw materials. Coffee and fruits from Latin American countries, oil from Nigeria, hardwoods from the Philippines, and palm oil from Malaysia are some of the key products central to the economies of poor nations. Multinational corporations maintain this pattern today as they purchase raw materials cheaply in poor societies and process them profitably in core societies. Corporations have also increased their landholdings, transforming traditional farmers into low-paid laborers in foreign-owned industries. The result is that Third-World societies cannot develop industries of their own.

2. **Lack of industrial capacity.** Without an industrial base, poor societies face a double bind: They rely on rich nations to buy their inexpensive raw materials, and to sell them whatever expensive manufactured goods they can afford. In a classic example of this double-dependency, British colonialists allowed the people of India to raise cotton, but prohibited them from manufacturing their own cloth. Instead, Indian cotton was shipped to the textile mills of Birmingham and Manchester in England, woven into cloth, and shipped back for profitable sale in India.

    Underdevelopment theorists also blast the "Green Revolution," widely praised by modernization theory, for fostering dependency. To promote agricultural productivity, poor countries must purchase expensive fertilizers, pesticides, and mechanical equipment from core nations. Typically, rich countries profit more than poor societies do.

3. **Foreign debt.** Such unequal trade patterns have

Struggling under massive foreign debt, the economy of Argentina has been devastated by inflation. As a result, tens of thousands of Argentinos took to the streets in 1990 to press for change. Their demands were simple, as suggested by the banner that reads "Argentinos Are Hungry."

forced Third-World countries into deeper and deeper debt to industrialized nations. Collectively, the Third World owes First-World countries roughly $1 trillion, including hundreds of billions of dollars owed to the United States. This staggering debt is a financial burden few poor societies can bear. Excessive debt can destabilize a country's economy, and many poor nations are already reeling from high unemployment and rampant inflation. Besides further impoverishing peripheral societies, massive foreign debt makes poor countries all the more dependent on rich nations. According to dependency theorists, this results in a vicious circle that makes rich nations richer and poor nations poorer.

Seeing no way out of the "debt trap," some Third-World countries have simply stopped making payments. Cuba, for example, refused to make further payments on its $7 billion foreign debt in 1986. Because this threatens the economic growth of rich nations, countries such as the United States strongly oppose such actions.

The role of rich nations. Nowhere is the difference between modernization theory and dependency theory sharper than in the role they assign to rich nations.

Modernization theory maintains that rich societies create new wealth through technological innovation. According to this view, the economic success of the First World does not cause world poverty. Rather, as Third-World nations modernize, absolute poverty will decrease. In contrast, dependency theory argues that rich societies have unjustly seized the wealth of the world for their own purposes. That is, the *over*development of some of the globe is directly tied to the *under*development of the rest of it.

Dependency theorists deny that First-World programs of population control, agricultural and industrial technology, and foreign aid help poor societies. Instead, they contend that rich nations act simply in pursuit of profit. Selling technology makes money, and foreign aid typically goes to ruling elites (rather than the poor majority) who will maintain a favorable "business climate" for multinational corporations (Lappé, Collins, & Kinley, 1981).

Additionally, dependency theory maintains, the capitalist culture of the United States encourages people to think of poverty as natural or inevitable. Following this line of reasoning, poverty results from "natural" processes including having (too many) children, and disasters such as droughts. World hunger activists Frances Moore Lappé and Joseph Collins (1986) argue that global poverty is far from inevitable because it stems from deliberate policies. They point out that the world already produces enough food to allow every person on the planet to grow quite fat. Moreover, India and most of Africa *export* food in spite of the fact that most of their people are poor. Agricultural production—and, more important, distribution—must simply be guided by the needs of the many rather than the profits of the few.

Critical evaluation. Dependency theory makes the important observation that no society develops (or fails to develop) in isolation, and this approach highlights how global inequality shapes the destiny of all nations. Dependency theorists point to Latin America and elsewhere, claiming that development simply cannot proceed under present international conditions. To address global poverty, they conclude, more than change within poor societies is needed; instead, the world economy must be reformed so it operates in the interests of the majority of people.

Critics of the dependency approach identify some important weaknesses in the theory. First, the theory assumes that the wealth of the First World is based solely on appropriating resources from poor societies. Not so, critics contend: Farmers, small-business owners, and industrialists can and do create new wealth through their imagination and drive. Wealth is not a zero-sum resource; the entire world's wealth has grown during this century, largely due to technological advances and other innovations.

Second, if dependency theory were correct in condemning the First World for creating global poverty, those nations with the strongest ties to rich societies would be among the poorest. However, the most impoverished nations of the world (such as Ethiopia and other countries in Central Africa) have had little contact with rich societies. Similarly, critics suggest, a long history of trade with rich countries has dramatically improved the economies of nations including Singapore, South Korea, Japan, and Hong Kong (which became a British colony in 1841 and will remain so until 1997). Then, too, many of the nations most active as colonizers in the past (Portugal and Spain, for example) are far from "superpowers" today.

Third, critics contend that dependency theory simplistically assumes that a single factor—world capitalism—has produced global inequality. Directing attention to forces *outside* of poor societies, dependency theory views poor societies as victims, ignoring factors *within* these countries that may contribute to their economic plight. Sociologists have long recognized that culture shapes human behavior. World cultural patterns vary greatly, with some societies embracing change readily and others staunchly resisting economic development. As we noted earlier, for example, Iran's fundamentalist Islamic society deliberately avoids bolstering its economic ties with other countries. Capitalist societies can hardly be blamed for Iran's resulting economic stagnation. Nor can rich societies be saddled with responsibility for the behavior of every foreign leader. Governments of poor societies must assume some responsibility for widespread poverty insofar as leaders engage in far-reaching corruption and militaristic campaigns to enhance their own power (examples include the regimes of Marcos in the Philippines, Duvalier in Haiti, Noriega in Panama, and Saddam Hussein in Iraq). Some governments also use food supplies as a weapon in internal political struggles (this occurred in Ethiopia and the Sudan in Africa). Other regimes (including many nations of Latin America and Africa) fail to support programs to improve the status of women or control population growth.

Fourth, dependency theory tends to downplay economic dependency fostered by the Soviet Union, the leading power of the Second World. While the Soviet Union never colonized the Third World, it seized control of most of Eastern Europe during World War II and subsequently dominated these nations politically and economically. The popular uprisings against Soviet-installed governments, beginning in 1989, suggest a widespread belief that this domination was a form of exploitation that prevented economic development. Eastern European nations were forced to buy Soviet-manufactured goods and Soviet-produced energy, and they were prevented from trading more profitably on the world market. In the Third World, Cuba and Angola are among the nations that remain highly dependent on the Soviet Union.

Fifth, the policy implications of dependency theory are vague. This approach suggests that poor societies should end all contact with the First World, and perhaps nationalize foreign-owned industries. On a broader scale, however, dependency theory implies that global poverty could be eliminated by a world overthrow of international capitalism. What form emerging economies would take, and whether they would be capable of meeting the economic needs of a growing world population (in light of the economic weaknesses of current socialist societies) remains unclear.

THE FUTURE OF GLOBAL INEQUALITY

Faced with such differing analyses, we might wonder which is the "right" explanation of global inequality. As with many controversies in sociology, each view has some validity as well as limitations. Table 8–2 summarizes important arguments made by advocates of each approach.

We must also consider empirical evidence. In some regions of the world, such as the "Pacific Rim" of Eastern Asia, the market forces endorsed by modernization theory are raising living standards rapidly. At the same time, other societies of the Third World, especially in Latin America, are experiencing economic turmoil that frustrates hopes for market-based development.

The Third-World societies that have surged ahead economically have two factors in common. First, they are relatively small.[5] Combined, the Asian societies of South Korea, Taiwan, Hong Kong, Singapore, and Japan equal only about one-fifth of the land area and population of India. The economic problems smaller countries face are more manageable; consequently, small societies more effectively administer programs of development. Second, these "best case" societies have cultural traits in common, especially traditions emphasizing individual achievement and economic success. In other areas of the world, where powerful group forces inhibit individual achievement, smaller nations have a record of lesser development.

The picture now emerging tends to call into question arguments put forward by both approaches. The major "paths to development" advanced by modernization and dependency theories are both currently undergoing significant transformation. On the one hand, few societies seeking economic growth now adopt a capitalist economy completely free of government control. This view challenges modernization theory, which has favored a free-market approach over government-directed development. Also, as recent upheavals in the Soviet Union and Eastern Europe demonstrate, a global reevaluation of socialism is currently under way. These events, following decades of poor economic performance and political repression, make many Third-World societies reluctant to consider this path to development. Because depen-

---

[5] This argument was suggested by Professor Alan Frishman of Hobart College.

Table 8–2 MODERNIZATION THEORY AND DEPENDENCY THEORY: A SUMMARY

	Modernization Theory	Dependency Theory
Historical Pattern	The entire world was poor just two centuries ago; the Industrial Revolution brought affluence to the First World; as industrialization gradually transforms the Third World, all societies are likely to become more equal and alike.	Global parity was disrupted by colonialism, which developed the First World and simultaneously underdeveloped the Third World; barring change in the world capitalist system, rich nations will grow richer and poor nations will become poorer.
Primary Causes of Global Poverty	Characteristics of Third-World societies cause poverty, including lack of industrial technology, traditional cultural patterns that discourage innovation, and rapid population growth.	Global economic relations—historical colonialism and the operation of multinational corporations—have enriched the First World while placing the Third World in a state of economic dependency.
Role of Rich Nations	First-World countries can and do assist Third-World nations through programs of population control, technology transfers that increase food production and stimulate industrial development, and by providing investment capital in the form of foreign aid.	First-World countries have concentrated global resources, advantaging themselves while producing massive foreign debt in the Third World; rich nations represent a barrier to economic development in the Third World.

Hong Kong, an economic marketplace that operates as freely as any in the world, is a monument to the power of capitalism to generate wealth. Land values in Hong Kong are among the highest in the world, and many of the British colony's people are extremely wealthy. At the same time, however, there is a striking contrast between the rich and the poor. In Aberdeen, shown here, thousands of Chinese people live in a floating neighborhood where the chances of getting ahead are quite small.

dency theory has historically supported socialist economic systems, changes in world socialism will surely generate new thinking here as well.

In the immediate future, no plan for development is likely to effectively reduce the pressing problems of world hunger and rapid population growth. Looking to the next century, however, there are reasons for hope. The approaches described in this chapter identify the two keys to combating global inequality. One, revealed by modernization theory, is that world hunger is at least partly a *problem of technology*, because a higher standard of living for a rapidly increasing world population will require greater agricultural and industrial productivity.

The second, derived from dependency theory, is that global inequality is also a *political issue*. Even with higher productivity, crucial questions concerning how resources are distributed—both within societies and around the globe—remain.

As debate over global inequality continues, people are coming to recognize that the security of everyone in the world depends on reducing the destabilizing extremes of contemporary global poverty. We can only hope that, as the Cold War between the superpowers winds down, energy and resources be redirected to the needs of the vast majority of humanity trapped in a desperate struggle for life itself.

SUMMARY

1. A global perspective reveals the full extent of the social stratification that characterizes humanity. The "three worlds" are broad categories based on patterns of economic development. The First World encompasses industrialized, capitalist societies including the United States; the Second World is composed largely of industrialized, socialist societies including the Soviet Union; the Third World represents the remaining poor societies that have yet to industrialize.

2. In addition to relative poverty, the Third World contends with widespread absolute poverty. The typical member of a Third-World society struggles to survive on an income far below that of the typical American.

3. Poverty places about 20 percent of the Third-World population—at least 800 million people—at risk. Some 15 million people, many of them children, die of starvation every year.

4. Women are more likely than men to be poor nearly everywhere in the world. In poor societies, women's relative and absolute disadvantages are greater than in the United States.

5. The poverty of Third-World societies is a complex problem rooted in a lack of industrial technology, rapid population growth, traditional cultural patterns, internal social stratification, and global power relationships.

6. Modernization theory maintains that acquiring advanced productive technology is crucial to economic development. Traditional cultural patterns are viewed as a barrier to modernization.

7. Modernization theorist W. W. Rostow identifies four stages of development: traditional, take-off, drive to technological maturity, and high mass consumption.

8. Arguing that rich societies create their own wealth, modernization theory cites four ways rich nations can assist poor nations: through population control, food-producing technologies, industrial development, and investment and other foreign aid.

9. Policies based on modernization theory are criticized for producing only limited economic development in the world, and for assuming ethnocentrically that poor societies can follow the path to development taken by rich nations centuries ago.

10. Dependency theory claims global wealth and poverty are directly linked to the historical operation of the capitalist world economy.

11. The dependency of Third-World countries is rooted in colonialism. In this century, neocolonialism represents the continued exploitation of politically independent societies of the Third World by multinational corporations.

12. Immanuel Wallerstein views the First World as the advantaged "core" of the capitalist world economy; poor societies of the Third World form the global "periphery."

13. Three key factors—export-oriented economies, a lack of industrial capacity, and foreign debt—perpetuate Third-World dependency on rich nations.

14. Dependency theory is criticized for overlooking how some nations have created new wealth. Further, contrary to the implications of this approach, the poorest societies are not those with the strongest ties to the First World.

15. Both modernization and dependency approaches offer useful insights into the development of global inequality. Some evidence supports each view. Less controversial is the urgent need to address the various problems caused by worldwide poverty.

KEY CONCEPTS

colonialism the process by which some nations enrich themselves through political and economic control of other nations

dependency theory an approach maintaining that global inequality stems from the exploitation of poor societies by rich ones

First World a category of industrial societies with predominantly capitalist economies

modernization theory an approach maintaining that global inequality reflects differing levels of technological development among world societies

multinational corporation a large corporation that operates in many different countries

neocolonialism a new form of economic exploitation involving not formal political control but the operation of multinational corporations

Second World a category of industrial societies with predominantly socialist economies

Third World a category of primarily agrarian societies in which most people are poor

Race and Ethnicity

9

Chapter Outline

Almost forty years ago, in the city of Topeka, Kansas, a minister walked hand in hand with his seven-year-old daughter to a public elementary school four blocks from their home. Linda Brown wanted to enroll in the second grade, but school officials refused to admit her. Instead, they required her to attend another school two miles away. Because of their decision, the little girl had to walk six blocks every day to a bus stop, where she sometimes waited half an hour for the bus. In bad weather, she would be soaking wet by the time the bus came; one day she became so cold at the bus stop that she walked back home. Why, she asked her parents, couldn't she attend the school that was nearby?

With the answer—one difficult for loving parents to give their child—came Linda Brown's realization that her skin color made her a second-class citizen in American society. Her parents began to speak to other blacks in the city about the injustice of separate schools for black and white children. Ultimately, a suit was filed on behalf of Linda Brown and several other children, and in 1954 their case came before the Supreme Court of the United States. In *Brown v. the Board of Education*

of Topeka, the Supreme Court unanimously rejected the idea that schools for the two races were "separate but equal." Instead, they concluded, racially segregated schools inevitably provide African-Americans with an inferior education. A generation later, Linda Brown looked back on this decision as a "turning point for black America" (U.S. Commission on Civil Rights, 1974:17).

Throughout the world, skin color and cultural background provoke struggles that are frequently more intense than those linked to social class. In South Africa, blacks continue to press a white minority government for equal political rights. In the United Kingdom, an uneasy tension exists between whites and darker-skinned immigrants from former European colonies such as India. Canada, too, has been wrenched by conflict between people of French and English backgrounds. And the Soviet Union is confronting ongoing demands for independence from many of its ethnically distinct republics.

In American society, as throughout the world, race and ethnicity are used to define members of society, trumpeting personal identity and group pride, but often

The range of biological variation in human beings is far greater than any system of racial classification allows. This is made obvious by trying to place all of the people pictured here into simple racial categories.

creating tension and even sparking violence. This chapter examines the meaning and consequences of race and ethnicity.

THE SOCIAL SIGNIFICANCE OF RACE AND ETHNICITY

Americans frequently use the terms "race" and "ethnicity" imprecisely and interchangeably. For this reason, we begin with important definitions.

Race

A **race** is *a category composed of men and women who share biologically transmitted traits that are defined as socially significant*. Races are commonly distinguished by physical characteristics such as skin color, hair texture, shape of facial features, and body type. All humans are members of a single biological species, but the biological variations we describe as "racial characteristics" are the result of living for thousands of generations in different geographical regions of the world (Molnar, 1983). In regions of intense heat, for example, humans developed darker skin that offers protection from the sun; in regions with moderate climates, humans have lighter skin.

Over the course of history, migration encouraged intermarriage, so that many genetic characteristics once common to a single region have spread through much of the world. In regions that historically have been "crossroads" of human migration, like the Middle East, people display striking racial variation. More isolated people, such as the Japanese, display greater uniformity of racial characteristics. No society, however, lacks genetic mixture, and increasing contact among the world's people will enhance racial mixing in the future.

Attempting to make sense of what can be bewildering human variety, nineteenth-century biologists developed a three-part scheme of racial classifications: People with relatively light skin and fine hair were called *Caucasian*; the term *Negroid* was applied to those with darker skin and coarser, curlier hair; people with yellow or brown skin and distinctive folds on the eyelids were labeled as *Mongoloid*. As we know now, however, there are no biologically pure races. In fact, the traveler moving from region to region notices gradual and subtle racial variations the world over. The people commonly called "Caucasians" or "whites" actually display skin color that ranges from very light to very dark, and the same variation occurs among so-called "Negroids" and "Mongoloids." Some "whites" (such as the Caucasians of southern India) actually have darker skin and hair than some "blacks" (including the blond Negroid aborigines of Australia).

Although Americans distinguish "white" and "black" people, research confirms that many Americans are genetically mixed. Over many generations, the genetic traits of Negroid Africans, Caucasian Europeans, and Mongoloid Native Americans have spread widely through the American population. Many "black" people, therefore, have a large proportion of Caucasian genes, and many "white" people have at least some Negroid genes. In short, race is not a black-and-white issue.

Biological facts notwithstanding, most societies of the world use race to rank people in systems of social inequality. Racial hierarchy has often been defended by assertions that physical traits are linked to innate intelligence and other mental abilities, although there is no scientific foundation for such beliefs. With so much at stake, societies commonly strive to make social rankings clear and enforceable. Earlier in this century, for example, many states in the South labeled as "colored" anyone who had at least one thirty-second black ancestry. That is, having at least one African-American great-great grandparent (or any closer ancestor) was grounds for being legally considered "black." Because race has become less of a caste distinction in American society, by law parents may now declare the race of a child.

Ethnicity

Ethnicity is *a cultural heritage shared by a category of people*. Members of an *ethnic category* may have a common place of ancestral origin, language, and religion which, together, confer a distinctive social identity. The forebears of Polish, Hispanic, and Chinese Americans, for example, live in particular nations of the world. As Chapter 2 ("Culture") explained, millions of Americans speak Spanish, Italian, German, French, or other languages in their homes. The United States and Canada are predominantly Protestant societies, but most Americans and Canadians of Spanish, Italian, and Polish ancestry are Roman Catholic, while many others of Greek, Ukrainian, and Russian ancestry are members of the Eastern Orthodox Church. More than 6 million Jewish-Americans (with ancestral ties to various nations) share a common religious history. Similarly, several million Americans have a Muslim religious heritage.

Race and ethnicity, then, are quite different: The first is biological and the second, cultural. But the two sometimes go hand in hand. Japanese Americans, for example, have distinctive physical traits and—for those who maintain a traditional way of life—cultural traits as well. But ethnic attributes should not be viewed as racial. For example, Jews are sometimes described as a race although they are distinctive only in their religious beliefs as well as their history of persecution (Goldsby, 1977). Finally, people can change their ethnicity by adopting a different way of life. Polish immigrants who discard their cultural background over time may cease to have a particular ethnicity. Assuming people mate with others like themselves, however, the physical traits of race persist for generations.

Minorities

A racial or ethnic **minority**[1] is *a category of people, defined by physical or cultural traits, who are socially disadvantaged*. Minorities are of many kinds, including people with physical disabilities and (as Chapter 10, "Sex and Gender," suggests) women.

Table 9–1 presents the broad categories of racial and ethnic variation in the United States. The table shows that almost three-quarters of the population are whites of non-Hispanic background. These include primarily people of European ancestry (from the countries

---

[1] The commonly used term "minority group" is incorrect. Chapter 5 ("Groups and Organizations") differentiates categories from groups.

Table 9–1 THE RACIAL AND ETHNIC COMPOSITION OF THE UNITED STATES, 1989

Category	Number	Percent
Whites (non-Hispanic)	179,434,000	72.9%
African-Americans	30,332,000	12.3
Hispanic Americans	20,746,000	8.4
Asian Americans and Pacific Islanders	6,673,000	2.7
Other races (including Native Americans)	8,807,000	3.6
Total		99.9

SOURCE: U.S. Bureau of the Census.

of England, Germany, and Ireland especially). However, the African-American, Hispanic, and Asian-American populations are rapidly increasing and projections are that these minorities, taken collectively, may well become a majority in the next century.

Minorities have two major characteristics. First, they share a *distinctive identity*. Because race is highly visible (and virtually impossible for a person to change), blacks in the United States or Chinese in South Africa are often keenly aware of their race. The significance of ethnicity (which can be changed) is more variable. Throughout American history, some people (many Reform Jews among them) have downplayed their ethnicity, while others (including many Orthodox Jews) have maintained distinctive cultural traditions and lived in ethnic neighborhoods.

A second characteristic of minorities is *subordination*. Chapter 7 ("Social Stratification") explained that American minorities typically have lower incomes and less occupational prestige and education. But not all members of a minority are equally disadvantaged. Some Hispanic Americans have accumulated considerable wealth, certain Chinese Americans are celebrated business leaders, and African-Americans are included among our nation's leading scholars. But even successful individuals may be viewed negatively on the basis of their social category. Race or ethnicity often serves as a master status (as described in Chapter 4, "Social Interaction in Everyday Life") that overpowers other personal traits.

Minorities usually constitute a small proportion of a society's population, but there are exceptions. For example, blacks in South Africa are a numerical majority that is grossly deprived of economic and political power by whites. In the United States, women represent slightly more than half the population but are still denied opportunities and privileges enjoyed by men.

Social conflict involving minorities and the majority is common around the world, as one category of people—African-Americans in the United States, Christians in Egypt, Sikhs in India, Azerbaijanis in the Soviet Union—struggles for rights formally guaranteed by law. Malaysia represents an unusual and interesting case: a society in which ethnic minorities are *unequal* under the law. The box provides details.

Prejudice

Prejudice amounts to *a rigid and irrational generalization about an entire category of people*. The word preju-

Unequal Under the Law: Race and Ethnicity in Malaysia

The 17 million people of Malaysia live in a nation roughly the size of New Mexico. This small society, on the southeast tip of Asia, also includes the northern part of the island of Borneo. As a Third-World nation, Malaysia is still poor in comparison to America, but its standard of living is rising.

Race and ethnicity are fundamental to Malaysian society. The earliest inhabitants of the region, called Malays, make up just over half the population. People of Chinese ancestry account for one-third, while an additional 10 percent are Indians whose ancestors came to work on agricultural plantations. The languages of this nation are various combinations of Malay, Chinese, English, and Indian tongues, although most Malaysians manage to communicate with one another.

Social differences among Malaysians generate controversy and conflict. The Chinese are wealthy and concentrated in large cities; they control the most prosperous businesses and live in expensive neighborhoods. Indians, too, live in urban areas, but the majority own small businesses or work for wages. The typical Indian Malaysian earns only about two-thirds of what the Chinese Malaysian does. The Malays, despite being the region's first inhabitants, are the poorest. Most are rural farm laborers earning about half what the Chinese Malaysians do.

These disparities erupted into violence in 1969, leading to years of martial law. In an effort to help the Malay majority advance socially, the government adopted policies granting them special privileges. The growing government bureaucracy now gives hiring preference to Malays. A quota system requires state-supported universities to admit applicants according to their proportion in the population as a whole; thus, half the places in the universities are reserved for Malays, regardless of academic performance. Similarly, most government licenses to operate small businesses, such as taxi services, are given to Malays. The government also supports the prominence of traditional Malay culture.

Malaysia defends such unequal and categorical treatment of its people as necessary to help the Malays catch up to the wealthy Chinese. But many Malays—and Indians—still feel disadvantaged and resentful. For their part, the Chinese community has become embittered by what it sees as an official policy of favoritism for the Malays. For instance, many Chinese complain that the quota system forces them to send their children abroad for a college education.

Most world societies are composed of distinctive races and ethnicities, which usually have different social standing. Malaysia is one of the few societies in which special treatment for racial and ethnic categories is enshrined in the constitution. Unlike the apartheid system under attack in South Africa, however, this policy is intended not to create but to eliminate social disparities. Whether it will do so—and at what cost—remains to be seen.

SOURCE: Based on information provided by Professor Steven Chee, University of Malaysia, and travel by the author in Malaysia.

---

dice is closely related to the word *prejudgment*. Prejudice is therefore irrational insofar as people hold strong, inflexible attitudes supported by little or no direct evidence. Prejudice can be directed toward people of a particular social class, sex, sexual orientation, age, political affiliation, race, or ethnicity. Prejudices can be positive or negative, and most people hold some of each type. Positive prejudices tend to exaggerate the virtues of people like ourselves, while negative prejudices condemn people who are different from us. Negative prejudice also runs along a continuum, ranging from mild aversion to outright hostility. Because attitudes are rooted in our culture, everyone has at least some measure of prejudice.

Stereotypes. A common form of prejudice is the **stereotype** (*stereo* is derived from Greek meaning "hard" or "solid"), *a set of prejudices concerning some category of people.* Because stereotypes often involve emotions of love (generally toward members of ingroups) and hate or fear (toward outgroups), they are hard to change even in the face of contradictory evidence. For example, some people have a stereotypical understanding of the poor as lazy and irresponsible freeloaders who would rather rely on welfare than support themselves (Waxman, 1983; N.O.R.C., 1989). As was explained in Chapter 7 ("Social Stratification"), this stereotype distorts reality: More than half of poor Americans are children and working adults.

Stereotypes have been devised for virtually every racial and ethnic minority, and they often form part of a society's culture. In the United States, many white people stereotype nonwhites in much the same way that wealthy people stereotype the poor, as lacking motivation to improve their own lives (N.O.R.C., 1989:287). Such attitudes assume poverty is mostly a matter of personal deficiency and, more to the point, they ignore the fact that most poor people in America are white and that most blacks work as hard as anyone else and are *not* poor. In this case the bit of truth in the stereotype is that blacks are more likely than whites to be poor. But by building a rigid attitude out of a few selected facts, stereotypes grossly distort reality.

Racism. A powerful and destructive form of prejudice, **racism** refers to *the belief that one racial category is innately superior or inferior to another.* Racism has pervaded world history. The ancient Greeks, various peoples of India, and many Asian societies viewed anyone unlike themselves as inferior. Racism has historically been widespread in American society; today overt racism has been weakened by a more egalitarian culture, yet it surfaces periodically, as we can see in news accounts.

By asserting that certain categories of people exhibit allegedly *innate* inferiority, dominant groups have historically subjected people to *social* inferiority. By the end of the nineteenth century, Great Britain, France, Spain, and the United States had forged colonial empires throughout the Third World. Exploiting colonies often involved ruthless oppression defended by the argument that the subjugated people were inferior beings.

In this century, racism was central to the Nazi regime in Germany. Nazi racial doctrine proclaimed a so-called "Aryan race" of blond-haired, blue-eyed Caucasians that was allegedly superior to all others and destined to rule the world. Such racism supported the murder of any "inferior beings," including some 6 million European Jews and millions of Poles, gypsies, homosexuals, and people with physical and mental disabilities.

More recently, racial conflict has intensified in European societies as whites confront millions of immigrants from former colonies (Glenn & Kennedy-Keel, 1986). Similarly, in the United States the last decade has been marked by increasing racial tensions in cities and on college campuses across the country.

Theories of Prejudice

If prejudice has little basis in a rational assessment of facts, what are its origins? Social scientists have provided various answers to this vexing question.

Scapegoat theory of prejudice. One explanation, commonly termed *scapegoat theory*, claims that prejudice is the product of frustration among people who are themselves disadvantaged (Dollard, 1939). A white woman working in a textile factory for low wages, for example, may direct hostility not at the powerful people who operate the factory but at powerless minority co-workers. Prejudice of this kind is not likely to improve the woman's situation in the factory, but it is a relatively safe way to vent anger and it may give her the feeling that at least she is superior to someone.

A **scapegoat** is thus *a person or category of people unfairly blamed for the troubles of others.* Because they typically have little social power, minorities are easily used as scapegoats. For example, the Nazis used Jews as scapegoats, blaming them for Germany's ills.

Authoritarian personality theory. T. W. Adorno (1950) and others claim that extreme prejudice may develop as a personality trait. Adorno's research indicated that people who display strong prejudice toward one minority are usually prejudiced against all minorities. Such people—described as having *authoritarian personalities*—rigidly conform to conventional cultural values, believe most moral issues to be clear matters of right and wrong, and are strongly ethnocentric. Such people also view society as naturally competitive and hierarchical, with "better" people (such as themselves) inevitably dominating those who are weaker. In contrast, Adorno found that people who are tolerant toward any minority are likely to be accepting of all. They tend to be more flexible in their moral judgments and believe that, ideally, society should be relatively egalitarian. They feel uncomfortable in any situation in which some people are able to exercise power over others.

The researchers claimed that authoritarian personalities tend to develop in people with little education and those raised by harsh and demanding parents. Faced with cold and insistent authority figures, they theorized, children may become angry and anxious, and ultimately hostile and aggressive toward scapegoats—others they define as their social inferiors.

Cultural theory of prejudice. A third approach suggests that some prejudice is embedded in cultural values. As noted in Chapter 2 ("Culture"), the social superiority of some categories of people is a core American value (Williams, 1970).

Emory Bogardus (1968) studied this issue for more than forty years using the concept of *social distance*, or how closely people are willing to interact with members of various racial and ethnic categories. His research shows that Americans generally offer similar evaluations of various racial and ethnic categories, presumably because such attitudes have become normative in our culture. Americans view others of English, Canadian, and Scottish background most positively, and welcome close relationships with them. Less favorable attitudes are expressed toward the French, Germans, Swedes, and Dutch. According to Bogardus, Americans are most negative toward blacks, Chinese, and Koreans and avoid close social ties with them. The fact that such evaluations were found to be widespread suggests that prejudice is not simply a trait of abnormal people, as Adorno's research implies, but surfaces in people well adjusted to a "culture of prejudice."

Conflict theory of prejudice. A fourth approach views prejudice as the product of social conflict. According to this theory, an ideology of prejudice is used to justify the oppression of minorities. To the extent that illegal immigrants in the Southwest are devalued, for example, they deserve little more than hard work at low wages.

In Marxist terms, prejudice also divides workers to the advantage of elites. There is ample evidence in American history that whites have used minority co-workers as scapegoats, in the process decreasing the chances that *all* workers will join together to advance their common interests (Geschwender, 1978; Olzak, 1989).

Discrimination

Closely related to prejudice is **discrimination**, *treating various categories of people unequally*. While prejudice refers to attitudes, discrimination is a matter of action. Like prejudice, discrimination can be either positive (providing special advantages) or negative (subjecting categories of people to disadvantages). Discrimination also varies along a continuum, ranging from subtle to blatant.

Prejudice and discrimination may occur together. A personnel manager prejudiced against members of a particular minority may refuse to hire them. Robert Merton (1976) describes such a person as an *active bigot* (see Figure 9–1). Fearing legal action, however, the prejudiced personnel manager may not discriminate, thereby becoming a *timid bigot*. What Merton calls *fair-weather*

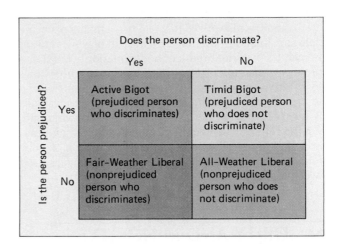

Figure 9–1 Patterns of Prejudice and Discrimination
(Merton, 1976)

liberals may discriminate without being prejudiced, as in the case of our manager discriminating only because a superior demands it. Finally, Merton's *all-weather liberal* is free of both prejudice and discrimination.

Institutional discrimination. Like prejudice, discrimination can involve the operation of society as well as individuals. **Institutional discrimination** refers to *patterns of discrimination that are woven into the fabric of a society*. As the story of Linda Brown at the beginning of this chapter illustrates, traditional ideas of people's "place," sometimes enforced by law, historically have stood between minorities and quality education, good jobs and housing, and even the right to own land and to vote.

Despite legal changes that advance equality for all categories of Americans, discrimination in many forms persists. Almost forty years after the 1954 Supreme Court ruling that outlawed segregated schools, for example, many young Americans still attend racially imbalanced schools.

Prejudice and Discrimination: The Vicious Cycle

Prejudice and discrimination persist because they tend to reinforce each other. W. I. Thomas offered a simple explanation for this fact, noted in Chapter 4 ("Social Interaction in Everyday Life") as the Thomas theorem: *If situations are defined as real, they are real in their consequences* (1966:301; orig. 1931).

Thomas recognized that reality is a matter of people defining situations. Prejudice on the part of whites toward nonwhites does not produce *innate* inferiority but it can produce *social* inferiority, consigning many nonwhites to poverty, low-prestige occupations, and poor housing in racially segregated neighborhoods. If this disadvantage is interpreted by whites as evidence that nonwhites are not their equal, a new round of prejudice and discrimination may result. Prejudice and discrimination thereby form a *vicious cycle*—a situation that perpetuates itself over time, even from generation to generation.

MAJORITY AND MINORITY: PATTERNS OF INTERACTION

Patterns of interaction between minorities and more privileged members of a society can be described in terms of four models: pluralism, assimilation, segregation, and genocide.

Pluralism

Pluralism is *a state in which racial and ethnic minorities are distinct but have social parity*. Many Americans take pride in the racial and ethnic diversity of our society. Large cities contain countless "ethnic villages" where people display the cultural traditions of their immigrant ancestors (Greeley, 1971; Gans, 1982). In New York these include Spanish Harlem, Little Italy, and Chinatown; in Philadelphia, Polish Kensington and Italian "South Philly"; in Chicago, Vietnamese "Little Saigon"; and in Los Angeles, Hispanic East Los Angeles.

Nevertheless, American society is not entirely pluralistic. First, while many Americans appreciate their cultural heritage, only a small proportion want their race or ethnicity to set them clearly apart from others

This piece of "neon art," entitled *Nation of Nations*, suggests the ethnic complexity of the United States. Various combinations of cultures provide a kaleidoscope of new social patterns that add vitality to American life.

and to live only with their "own kind" (N.O.R.C., 1989). Second, American tolerance for social diversity is limited. Chapter 2 ("Culture") described the social movement to make English the official language of the United States; this drive hardly encourages pluralism. Third, some racial and ethnic identity is forced on people by others. For example, many communities in the Appalachian Mountains of the eastern United States remain culturally distinctive because their members are snubbed as "hill-billies" and subjected to discrimination that perpetuates their poverty (Sacks, 1986).

Assimilation

Assimilation is *the process by which minorities gradually adopt patterns of the dominant culture.* Assimilation involves changing modes of dress, values, religion, language, or friends.

Americans have traditionally viewed the United States as a "melting pot" in which various nationalities were fused into an entirely new way of life. This melting-pot characterization of American society is misleading, however. Rather than everyone "melting" into some new cultural pattern, minorities have typically adopted the traits of the dominant culture established by the earliest settlers. They did so to improve their social position and to escape the prejudice and discrimination directed against foreigners (Newman, 1973). This is not to deny the rich contributions to American culture made by various minorities; cultural contact, however, generally involves more change on the part of less powerful minorities.

While assimilation has certainly occurred in American history (witness the disappearance of many European immigrant neighborhoods over the course of this century), many ethnic enclaves remain—and others are now forming—suggesting that race and ethnicity are still the building blocks of American society (Glazer & Moynihan, 1970; Alba, 1985).

As a cultural process, assimilation involves changes in ethnicity but not in race. For example, many descendants of Japanese immigrants have discarded a traditionally Japanese way of life but still have their racial identity. However, distinguishing racial traits may diminish over generations as the result of **miscegenation,** *the biological process of interbreeding among racial categories.* Although resistance to such biological mixing remains strong, miscegenation (often outside of marriage) has occurred throughout American history.

Segregation

Segregation refers to *the physical and social separation of categories of people.* Sometimes minorities, especially religious groups, voluntarily segregate themselves. Usually, however, minorities are involuntarily segregated by others who exclude them. Various degrees of segregation characterize residential neighborhoods, schools, occupations, hospitals, and even cemeteries. While pluralism fosters distinctiveness without disadvantage, segregation enforces separation to the detriment of a minority.

Racial segregation also has a long history in the United States, involving centuries of slavery, and racially linked lodging and transportation. Decisions such as the 1954 *Brown* case have reduced overt and *de jure* (Latin meaning "by law") discrimination in the United States. However, *de facto* ("in fact") segregation continues. In the 1960s, Karl and Alma Taeuber (1965) measured the residential segregation of blacks and whites in more than two hundred American cities. On a numerical scale ranging from zero (a mixing of races in all neighborhoods) to 100 (total racial segregation), they calculated an *average* segregation score of 86.2. In the decades since, segregation has decreased little, even among African-Americans with substantial economic standing, despite their desire to live in racially integrated neighborhoods (Van Valey, Roof, & Wilcox, 1977; Hwang et al., 1985; Calmore, 1986; N.O.R.C., 1989:187).

Recent research by Douglas Massey and Nancy Denton (1989a) suggests that segregation involves more than neighborhood composition. These researchers discovered a pattern of racial segregation in which black neighborhoods cluster together into a larger ghetto in the inner city that allows residents little social contact with the outside world. Such *hypersegregation* is common among African-Americans, they conclude, far more than among any other minority in the United States.

Segregation and the principle of second-class citizenship that supports it are understandably opposed by minorities. Sometimes the action of even a single individual can have lasting consequences. On December 1, 1955, Rosa Parks was riding a bus in Montgomery, Alabama, sitting in a section designated by law for blacks. When a crowd of white passengers boarded the bus, the driver asked four blacks to give up their seats to whites. Three did so, but Rosa Parks refused. The driver left the bus and returned with police, who arrested her for violating the racial segregation laws. She was later convicted in court and fined $14 for an action that sparked the black community of Montgomery to boycott city buses, ultimately ending this form of segregation (King, 1969).

Genocide

Genocide is *the systematic killing of one category of people by another.* This brutal form of racism and ethnocentrism

Political regimes sometimes engage in the inhuman madness of mass murder. These shoes are silent testimony to the methodical death wrought by the Nazis during World War II against Jews, Gypsies, homosexuals, and a host of other people deemed "undesirable." More recently, the Pol Pot government turned Cambodia into "killing fields," murdering some two million people.

violates nearly every recognized moral standard; nonetheless, it has recurred time and again in human history.

Genocide has figured prominently in centuries of contact between Europeans and the original inhabitants of the Americas. From the sixteenth century on, the Spanish, Portuguese, English, French, and Dutch forcefully established vast colonial empires. The native populations of North and South America were systematically killed so that Europeans could gain control of their wealth. Beyond the intentional killing, diseases introduced by Europeans eventually resulted in the death of most of this hemisphere's indigenous population (Hardoy, 1975; Cottrell, 1979; Butterworth & Chance, 1981; Matthiessen, 1984).

Genocide has also occurred in the twentieth century. Unimaginable horror befell European Jews in the 1930s and 1940s, as the Nazi regime seized control of much of Europe. During Adolf Hitler's reign of terror, known as the Holocaust, the Nazis exterminated more than 6 million Jews. Between 1976 and 1980 the Communist regime of Pol Pot in Cambodia slaughtered anyone thought to represent capitalist cultural influences. Condemned to death were people who knew any Western language and even those who wore eyeglasses, viewed as a symbol of capitalist culture. In the "killing fields" of Cambodia, 2 million people (one-fourth of the population) perished (Shawcross, 1979).

These four patterns of minority-majority contact can coexist in a society. For example, Americans proudly point to patterns of pluralism and assimilation but only reluctantly acknowledge the degree to which our society has been built on segregation (of African-Americans, for example) and annihilation (of Native Americans).

The remainder of this chapter suggests how these four types of majority-minority contact have shaped the history and present social standing of major racial and ethnic categories in American society.

RACE AND ETHNICITY IN THE UNITED STATES

Give me your tired, your poor,
Your huddled masses yearning to breathe free,
The wretched refuse of your teeming shore,
Send these, the homeless, tempest-tossed to me:
I lift my lamp beside the golden door.

These words by Emma Lazarus, inscribed on the Statue of Liberty, express the American ideals of human dignity, personal freedom, and opportunity. But America's golden door has opened more widely for some than for others. Social inequality, entrenched in American society since its beginnings, is readily evident in the history of America's racial and ethnic minorities.

White Anglo-Saxon Protestants

White Anglo-Saxon Protestants (WASPs) historically have dominated American society. Most WASPs are of English ancestry, but Scots and Welsh are also included. WASPs predominated among America's early European settlers; not until the nineteenth century did substantial immigration of non-WASPs begin. With more than 50 million Americans of English ancestry, roughly one in four Americans can claim some WASP background.

Historically, WASP immigrants were highly skilled and motivated toward achievement by what came to be called the Protestant work ethic. Also, as the majority, WASPs were not subject to the prejudice and discrimination experienced by other categories of Americans. The historical dominance of WASPs has been so great that, as noted earlier, assimilation into American society has meant becoming more like the WASPs (Gordon, 1964).

Many WASPs responded to growing social diversity in the nineteenth century with prejudice and discrimination toward new arrivals they saw as undesirable foreigners. Nativist political movements sought legal limits on the rapidly growing immigration. Some, who could afford to, pursued a personal solution to the "problem" by isolating themselves, in exclusive suburbs and social clubs, from those they deemed their social inferiors. Thus the 1880s—the decade in which the Statue of Liberty first welcomed immigrants to America—also saw the founding of the first American country club (with all WASP members). Soon afterward, WASPs began publishing the *Social Register* (1887), a listing of members of "society," and established various genealogical societies such as the Daughters of the American Revolution (1890) and the Society of Mayflower Descendants (1894). These efforts served to socially distance wealthy WASPs from newly arrived immigrants (Baltzell, 1964).

By about 1930, pushed by the growing wealth of other categories of Americans and more egalitarian values, WASPs began to share their privileges (Baltzell, 1964, 1976, 1988). This changing trend was symbolized in 1960 by the election of John Fitzgerald Kennedy as the first non-WASP (Irish-Catholic) president of the United States. Even so, WASPs continue to have great influence in American society; with extensive education, they work in high-prestige occupations, and enjoy above-average incomes (Neidert & Farley, 1985). The majority of people in the upper-upper class are still WASPs (Greeley, 1974; Baltzell, 1979; Roof, 1981). The WASP cultural legacy also continues: English remains the dominant language of the United States, and Protestantism is the majority religion. Our legal system, too, reflects its English origins. Perhaps the historical dominance of WASPs is most evident in the widespread use of the terms "race" and "ethnicity" to describe everyone but them.

Native Americans

The term *Native Americans* refers to the hundreds of distinct societies—including Aleuts, Cherokee, Zuni, Sioux, Mohawk, Aztec, and Inca—who were the original inhabitants of the Americas. Thousands of years ago, migrating peoples crossed a land bridge from Asia to North America where the Bering Strait (off the coast of Alaska) is today, and over the centuries they spread throughout the Western hemisphere. When the first Europeans arrived late in the fifteenth century, Native Americans numbered in the millions and had a thirty-thousand-year history on this continent (Dobyns, 1966).

From the start, contact with Europeans was disastrous for Native Americans. What some Europeans ethnocentrically called "taming the wilderness" actually amounted to the destruction of many ancient civilizations. Exposure to European diseases took a terrible toll among Native Americans, and tens of thousands more were the victims of genocide at the hands of Europeans seeking wealth and land. By the beginning of the twentieth century, the "vanishing Americans" numbered a mere 250,000 (Tyler, 1973).

Native Americans were first referred to as *Indians* by Christopher Columbus (1446–1506), who is said to have mistaken the Antilles in the Caribbean for India. Columbus found indigenous Americans to be passive and peaceful (Matthiessen, 1984). Such values clashed with those of Europeans, whose way of life was more competitive and aggressive. Even as Europeans seized the land of Native Americans, sometimes violently, the invaders demeaned their victims as thieves and murderers, in an effort to justify their actions (Unruh, 1979; Josephy, 1982).

Trail of Tears was painted by Robert Lindneux (1942) to commemorate the suffering caused by the policy of forced migration—often at gunpoint—of native Americans living east of the Mississippi after 1830. Uprooted from traditional homelands, the Shawnee, Cherokee, and other peoples were marched for hundreds of miles westward to supposedly "reserved" territories on the plains. Often they arrived only to confront still more hostile whites who had already settled on what the government had promised were to be Indian lands.

Robert Lindneux, The Trail of Tears, 1942. Woolaroc Museum, Bartlesville, OK.

After the Revolutionary War, the new United States government adopted a pluralist approach to Native-American societies and sought to gain more land through treaties. Payment for land was far from fair, however, and when Native Americans resisted surrender of their homelands, superior military power was used to evict them. Thousands of Cherokees, for example, died on a forced march—the Trail of Tears—from their homes in the southeastern United States to segregated reservations in the Midwest. By the early 1800s, few Native Americans remained east of the Mississippi River.

After 1871, the United States made Native Americans wards of the government and tried to resolve "the Indian problem" through forced assimilation. Native Americans continued to lose their land, and they were losing their culture as well. Reservation life fostered dependency, replacing ancestral languages with English and eroding traditional religion in favor of Christianity. Many children were taken from their parents and placed in boarding schools, operated by the Bureau of Indian Affairs, to be resocialized as "Americans." Local control of reservations was given to the few Native Americans who supported government policies, and reservation land—traditionally held collectively—was distributed as the private property of individual families (Tyler, 1973). In the process, some whites managed to grab still more land for themselves.

Not until 1924 were Native Americans entitled to citizenship. Since then, the government has encouraged their migration from reservations. Some have adopted mainstream cultural patterns and married non-

Native Americans. Many large cities now have sizable Native-American populations. As is shown in Table 9–2, however, median family income for Native Americans was far below the American average when last calculated in 1980, and Native Americans were much less likely to earn a college degree (7.7 percent) than Americans as a whole (17.1 percent).

From in-depth interviews with Native Americans in a western city, Joan Albon (1971) concluded that many were disadvantaged by little education, few marketable skills, less than perfect English, and dark skin that

Table 9–2 THE SOCIAL STANDING OF NATIVE AMERICANS, 1980*

	Native Americans	Entire United States
Median Family Income	$16,672	$19,917
Proportion in Poverty	27.5%	12.4%
Median Education (age 25 and over)	12.2 years	12.5 years
Completion of Four or More Years of College (age 25 and over)	7.7%	17.1%

* The data used in this chapter are the most recent available at the time of publication. Comparisons of all racial and ethnic categories are possible only through using data from the 1980 census, but more recent statistics are also included wherever possible.

SOURCE: U.S. Bureau of the Census.

provokes prejudice and discrimination. Additionally, she noted, Native Americans often lacked the individualism and competitiveness that contribute to success in America. These traits stemmed from both traditional values and long dependence on government assistance.

Like other racial and ethnic minorities in the United States, Native Americans have recently reasserted pride in their cultural heritage and sought greater rights and opportunity for themselves. They have sued the national government for return of lands forcibly taken in the past, and organizations such as the Pan-Indian American Indian Movement seek democratic control of reservation lands by Native Americans themselves. In some instances, violent confrontations with federal officials have erupted. Few Native Americans support this means of addressing grievances, but the vast majority share a profound sense of the injustice endured at the hands of whites (Josephy, 1982; Matthiessen, 1983).

African-Americans

Although African-Americans accompanied Spanish explorers to the New World in the fifteenth century, the beginning of black history in the United States is usually set at 1619, when a Dutch trading ship brought twenty Africans to Jamestown, Virginia (Holt, 1980). It is unclear whether these people arrived as slaves or as indentured servants, people obligated to perform labor for a specified period in return for passage across the Atlantic Ocean. Nevertheless, being black in America soon became virtually synonymous with being a slave. In 1661 the first law recognizing slavery was passed in Virginia (Sowell, 1981).

Slavery became the foundation of the plantation system in the colonies' agrarian economy. Whites prospered as plantation owners, and also as slave traders—a legal occupation until 1808. Some 10 million Africans were forcibly brought to various countries of the Western hemisphere; about 400,000 entered the United States (Sowell, 1981). Hundreds of slaves were chained on board small sailing ships as human cargo during a voyage of several weeks across the Atlantic Ocean. Filth and disease killed many; others were driven to suicide. Overall, perhaps half died en route (Tannenbaum, 1946; Franklin, 1967).

Surviving the journey was a mixed blessing, bringing a life of servitude as the property of white owners. Most slaves engaged in farming, although some worked in cities at a variety of trades (Franklin, 1967). Work usually lasted from daybreak to sunset, and for up to

The official record reveals some five thousand lynchings in the United States between 1880 and 1930. Lynch mobs were formed by whites as a terrorist measure aimed at maintaining their dominance over African-Americans and other minorities.

Beginning in the mid-1950s, a renewed Civil Rights movement struggled for racial equality in the United States. Resistance by whites was often fierce, as suggested by the common tactic of turning fire hoses on protesters.

twenty hours a day during the harvest. The law allowed slave owners to impose whatever disciplinary measures they deemed necessary to ensure that slaves labored continuously. Even the killing of a slave by an owner rarely prompted legal action. Owners also divided slave families at public auctions where human beings were bought and sold like pieces of property. This system further controlled slaves by eliminating any opportunity for schooling and by ensuring that slaves remained dependent on their owners for their basic needs (Sowell, 1981).

There were, however, free persons of color in both the North and the South, small-scale farmers, skilled workers, and small-business owners (Murray, 1978). But the lives of most African-Americans stood in glaring contradiction to the principles of equality and freedom on which the United States was founded. The Declaration of Independence states:

> We hold these Truths to be self-evident, that all Men are created equal, that they are endowed by their Creator with certain inalienable Rights, that among these are Life, Liberty, and the Pursuit of Happiness. . . .

Most white Americans did not apply these ideals to blacks. In the Dred Scott case in 1857, the U.S. Supreme Court addressed the question, "Are blacks citizens?" and answered, "We think they are not, and that they are not included, and were not intended to be included, under the word 'citizens' in the Constitution, and can therefore claim none of the rights and privileges which that instrument provides for and secures for citizens of the United States" (Blaustein & Zangrando, 1968:160). Thus arose what Swedish sociologist Gunnar Myrdal (1944) termed the *American dilemma*: the denial of basic rights and freedoms to an entire category of Americans. To resolve this dilemma, many whites simply defined blacks as innately inferior.

In 1865 the Thirteenth Amendment to the Constitution outlawed slavery. Three years later the Fourteenth Amendment reversed the Dred Scott ruling, giving citizenship to all people born in the United States. The Fifteenth Amendment, ratified in 1870, stated that neither race nor previous condition of servitude should deprive anyone of the right to vote. However, so-called Jim Crow laws still divided American society into two racial castes (Woodward, 1974). Especially in the South, whites beat and lynched blacks (and some whites) who challenged the racial hierarchy.

The twentieth century has brought dramatic changes to African-Americans. In the decades after World War I, tens of thousands left the rural South for jobs in northern factories. While they did find more economic opportunity up North, they did not escape racial prejudice and discrimination, which set them apart from white immigrants arriving from Europe at the same time (Lieberson, 1980). In the 1950s and 1960s, blacks and sympathetic whites launched a wide-ranging attack on racism in America that grew into a national civil rights movement. During this period, landmark judicial decisions outlawed racially segregated schools and overt racial discrimination in employment and public accommodations. In addition, the "black power movement" gave African-Americans a renewed sense of purpose and pride, making many less willing to be defined in terms of the white culture.

Gains notwithstanding, blacks continue to occupy a subordinate position in American society, as shown in Table 9–3. The median income of black families in 1989 ($20,209) was substantially below that of Americans as a whole ($34,213). Black families are also three times as likely as white families to be poor. In general, black Americans made significant economic gains from the 1940s through the 1960s; the 1970s brought economic stagnation, and much of the 1980s saw a decline in economic position (Jacob, 1986; Jaynes & Williams, 1989; Littman, 1989; Welniak & Littman, 1989).

This recent downturn reflects changes in the American economy, described in Chapter 7 ("Social Stratification"). In the 1980s, millions of factory jobs—a vital resource for those in America's inner cities—were lost to other countries, where labor costs are substantially lower. Thus black unemployment stands at more than

Table 9–3 THE SOCIAL STANDING OF BLACK AMERICANS, 1980 AND 1989

	Black Americans	Entire United States
Median Family Income	$12,598 ($20,209) in 1989	$19,917 ($34,213 in 1989)
Proportion in Poverty	29.9% (30.7% in 1989)	12.4% (12.8% in 1989)
Median Education (age 25 and over)	12.0 yrs (12.5 yrs in 1988)	12.5 yrs (12.8 yrs in 1988)
Completion of Four or More Years of College (age 25 and over)	8.4% (11.3% in 1988)	17.1% (22.7% in 1988)

SOURCE: U.S. Bureau of the Census.

twice the level among whites; among African-American teenagers in many cities, the figure exceeds 40 percent (Wilson, 1984; Jacob, 1986; Lichter, 1989).

The median schooling for blacks over the age of 25 in 1960 was 8.2 years compared to 10.9 years for whites. By 1988 this gap had mostly closed: The respective figures were 12.5 years and 12.8 years. Even so, as Table 9–3 shows, African-Americans are still only about half as likely as whites to complete four years of college. In recent years the number of African-Americans enrolling in college and graduate schools has actually fallen. In the mid-1980s, only about one-fourth of black high-school graduates entered college, compared with about one-third a decade earlier (American Council on Education, 1987; *Black Issues in Higher Education*, 1987).

No less distressing is evidence that education provides less upward mobility for blacks than it does for whites (Blau & Duncan, 1967; Tienda & Lii, 1987). About one in four black families in the United States is now securely anchored in the middle class, and one in ten has an annual income exceeding $50,000 a year. But these gains stand out against the persistent poverty of millions of African-Americans—especially women and children—who represent an economically desperate underclass (Wilson, 1984; O'Hare, 1989).

The political clout of African-Americans has increased along with the number of registered voters and elected officials. Black migration to cities, together with white movement to the suburbs, has resulted in black majorities in many large cities; by 1990 half of America's

The election of Douglas Wilder in 1989 was a symbolic victory for all African-Americans. Not only was this descendant of slaves elected to the highest political office in Virginia—a state of the old Confederacy—but his achievement marked the first time in American history that an African-American was elected as governor of any state.

ten largest cities had elected black mayors. In 1989, Virginia elected the first black governor (Douglas Wilder, a grandson of slaves) in American history. At the national level, however, only 1 percent of elected officials are people of color. After the 1990 elections, 26 blacks (of 435) sat in the House of Representatives and no black person (of 100) was in the Senate.

In sum, for more than 350 years, people of African ancestry have struggled for social equality in the United States. Americans can certainly take pride in how far we have come in pursuit of racial equality. A century ago slavery was outlawed and, during this century, many forms of overt discrimination were legally banned. According to some research, our society is moving along a path of long-term decline in antiblack prejudice, suggesting that Americans are coming to see racial justice as a matter of basic fairness (Firebaugh & Davis, 1988). For example, during the 1970s about 60 percent of Americans supported the rights of whites to sell their homes only to other whites; by 1989 that proportion had dropped below 40 percent (N.O.R.C., 1989:180).

Still, such figures reveal that racial bigotry remains strong in America. One response has been the government policy of affirmative action, or preferential treatment for categories of people historically subject to prejudice and discrimination. The box provides details.

Asian Americans

Although Asian Americans share some racial traits, enormous cultural diversity marks this category of people. The 1980 census placed their number at about 3 million—approaching 2 percent of the population. In 1990, the largest category was estimated to be Filipinos, with 1.4 million people, followed by those of Chinese ancestry (1.2 million) and Japanese ancestry (700,000). Most Asian Americans live in the West.

Migration from China and Japan to the United States began over a century ago. More recent immigrants from Asia include Filipinos, Koreans, and Vietnamese. Overall, Asian Americans account for 40 percent of all immigrants to the United States and constitute our society's fastest-growing minority.

Asian immigrants—especially young people—have commanded both attention and respect in recent years as high achievers. Young Asian Americans are disproportionately represented among students at the best colleges and universities in the country (Brand, 1987). Many of their elders have also made significant economic and

Affirmative Action: Problem or Solution?

The phrase "Equal Justice Under Law" over the entrance to the Supreme Court building in Washington, D.C., certainly has not applied to many American minorities. One reaction to this historical pattern is affirmative action, which entails special efforts to increase opportunity for minorities. Affirmative action means, for example, that employers encourage applications from all racial and ethnic categories and carefully monitor hiring and promotion policies to eliminate discrimination, even unintentional discrimination, against minorities. The goal is the representation of all categories of people in various occupations and educational programs in proportion to their numbers in the overall population.

The most controversial element of affirmative action involves establishing quotas to ensure the hiring and promotion of minorities. Under a quota system, a fixed number of minority members are guaranteed favorable treatment regardless of how they

stack up against other applicants. In most cases, rigid quota systems have been rejected by American courts, but the *principle* of affirmative action has been upheld; in other words, race and ethnicity can be used as the basis of preference in hiring and promotions.

Advocates see affirmative action as a fair and necessary corrective for historical discrimination. Everybody alive today, they argue, has been affected by privileges accorded or denied to their parents and grandparents. "Special treatment," then, is nothing new and is necessary for those denied opportunity through no fault of their own. Only in this way, advocates claim, can we break the vicious cycle of prejudice and discrimination.

Opponents of affirmative action agree that minorities have historically suffered from discrimination, but they see affirmative action as *reverse discrimination*. Why should whites today—many of whom are far from privileged—be penalized for past dis-

crimination for which they were in no way responsible? Opponents also claim that minorities have largely overcome historical barriers to opportunity and that those who have made the greatest efforts have had the most success—which is as it should be. Giving minorities special treatment inevitably compromises standards, fosters race-awareness, and undermines public perceptions of the real accomplishments of minorities.

As applied to blacks, Americans tend to oppose such policies, as the following survey item suggests:

> Some people think that blacks have been discriminated against for so long that the government has a special obligation to help improve their living standards. Others believe that the government should not be giving special treatment to blacks. (N.O.R.C., 1989:331)

The numbers 1 through 5 show the range of opinion in relation to the three responses.

1		3		5
I strongly agree that the government is obligated to help blacks.		I agree with both answers.		I strongly agree that the government shouldn't give blacks special treatment.
1	2	3	4	5
8.7%	9.4%	26.9%	18.4%	33.0%
	No Response = 3.7%		Total = 1,035 respondents	

SOURCE: Survey data from N.O.R.C., *General Social Surveys* (Chicago: National Opinion Research Center, 1989), p. 331.

social gains in recent years. Yet in the past, Americans have expressed attitudes ranging from aloofness to outright hostility in their relations with Asian Americans. Moreover, as we shall see, the "model minority" image that Asian Americans have cultivated obscures the poverty of some among their ranks.

Chinese Americans. Chinese immigration to America began when the California Gold Rush of 1849 sparked an economic boom in the West. As new towns and businesses sprang up virtually overnight, American entrepreneurs met the pressing need for cheap labor by bringing to this country about 100,000 Chinese immigrants

The success of many Asians is testimony to their cultural emphasis on achievement. But such success is common only in a few fields. Immigrant minorities tend to excel in mathematics, science, or music because these pursuits do not depend on extensive knowledge of a new language or culture. Instead, they utilize systems of thought (especially numbers) that are familiar to people of all societies. Asian immigrants have won several Nobel prizes in physics, for instance, but none for literature.

in the decades that followed. Most were young, hard-working males willing to take lower-status jobs shunned by whites (Ling, 1971). When the economy soured in the 1870s, desperate whites began competing with the Chinese for jobs. Suddenly the industriousness of the Chinese and their willingness to work for low wages posed a threat. Repeating a well-known pattern, economic hard times led to mounting prejudice and discrimination (Boswell, 1986).

Soon, laws barred the Chinese from many occupations. Courts also withdrew legal protections, encouraging whites to initiate vicious campaigns against the so-called "Yellow Peril" (Sowell, 1981). American society seemed to line up against the Chinese, and the saying that a person didn't have "a Chinaman's chance" gained popular use (Sung, 1967:56).

In 1882, the U.S. government passed the first of several laws curtailing Chinese immigration. This action created great domestic hardship because, of the Chinese already in the United States, males outnumbered females by almost twenty to one (Hsu, 1971; Lai, 1980). This sex imbalance caused the Chinese population to fall to about 60,000 by 1920. Chinese women already in the United States benefited from the situation, however: In high demand, they soon became far less submissive to men (Sowell, 1981).

Responding to their plight, some Chinese moved eastward; many more sought the relative safety of urban Chinatowns (Wong, 1971). There Chinese traditions flourished, and kinship networks, called *clans*, gave fi-

nancial assistance to individuals and served as political organizations representing the interests of all. With the help of the clans, Chinese immigrants obtained loans to start businesses and find jobs. At the same time, however, those living in a Chinatown had little incentive to learn the English language or pursue other forms of cultural assimilation.

With the onset of World War II, a renewed need for labor increased the opportunities of the Chinese (Lai, 1980). In 1943 President Roosevelt ended the ban on Chinese immigration and extended the rights of citizenship to Chinese Americans born abroad. Many responded by moving out of Chinatowns and seeking cultural assimilation. In turn-of-the-century Honolulu, for example, 70 percent of the Chinese people lived in Chinatown; by 1980, only 20 percent did (Lai, 1980).

By 1950, many Chinese Americans were enjoying considerable upward social mobility. Today, Americans of Chinese ancestry are no longer restricted to self-employment in laundries and restaurants; many now work in high-prestige occupations. Their achievement has been outstanding in science and technology, fields in which many Chinese Americans—including several Nobel Prize winners—have excelled (Sowell, 1981). As shown in Table 9–4, the median household income of Chinese Americans in 1980 ($22,259) was above the national average ($19,917), and Chinese Americans have twice the proportion of college graduates as Americans taken as a whole. A more recent income figure available for all categories of Asian Americans shows a median

Table 9–4 THE SOCIAL STANDING OF CHINESE AND JAPANESE AMERICANS, 1980

	Chinese Americans	Japanese Americans	Entire United States
Median Family Income	$22,259	$27,354	$19,917
Proportion in Poverty	13.5%	6.5%	12.4%
Median Education (age 25 and over)	13.4 yrs.	12.9 yrs.	12.5 yrs.
Completion of Four or More Years of College (age 25 and over)	36.6%	26.4%	17.1%

SOURCE: U.S. Bureau of the Census.

household income of $36,100 in 1989. Although this is several thousand dollars above the comparable income for whites, Asian-American homes also had more people in the labor force (U.S. Bureau of the Census, 1990).

Nevertheless, many Chinese Americans still grapple with serious problems. Overt prejudice and discrimination have diminished, but racial hostility persists. Poverty among Chinese Americans stands above the national average, especially among those who remain in the protective circle of Chinatowns. At the beginning of the 1980s, the poverty level of New York's Chinatown was twice as high as that of the city as a whole, with half of all Chinese males working in restaurants and three-fourths of Chinese females stuck in low-paying jobs in the garment industry (Sowell, 1981). This economic picture has sparked a debate over whether racial and ethnic enclaves exploit or economically assist their residents (Portes & Jensen, 1989; Zhou & Logan, 1989).

Japanese Americans. Japanese immigration to the United States began slowly in the 1860s, reaching only 3,000 by 1890. Japanese immigrants were welcomed to the Hawaiian Islands (a state since 1959) as a source of cheap labor on sugar plantations. Early in this century, however, Japanese immigration rose along with demands for better pay, and whites sought to curb their immigration (Daniels, 1971). In 1908 the United States signed an agreement with Japan limiting male immigration, which was viewed as the major economic threat, while allowing Japanese women to immigrate to ease the sex-

ratio imbalance. But by the early 1920s, in California and elsewhere, new laws mandated segregation and prohibited interracial marriage, virtually ending Japanese immigration. The United States denied foreign-born Japanese citizenship until 1952.

Japanese immigrants differed from the Chinese in two ways. First, the Japanese knew more about the United States before migrating than the Chinese did; this encouraged assimilation (Sowell, 1981). Second, fewer Japanese immigrants clustered in cities; instead, many became farmers in rural areas.

Whites reacted swiftly to Japanese purchases of farmland in California. In 1913, no noncitizen was permitted to own farmland. Such laws were principally motivated by economic considerations, but they also reflected a measure of racial hostility as suggested by this comment from the state's attorney general:

The fundamental basis of all legislation has been, and is, race undesirability. It seeks to limit [Japanese] presence by curtailing the privileges which they may enjoy here, for they will not come here in large numbers and abide with us if they may not acquire land. (Kitano, 1980:563)

Foreign-born Japanese (called the *Issei*) responded by placing farmland in the names of their American-born children (*Nisei*), who were automatically U.S. citizens under the Constitution. Others leased farmland with great success.

The Japanese faced their greatest struggle after December 7, 1941, when the nation of Japan destroyed much of the U.S. naval fleet at Hawaii's Pearl Harbor. Rage toward Japan was directed at the Japanese living in America. Some feared the Japanese here would commit acts of espionage and sabotage on behalf of Japan. Within a year, President Roosevelt had signed Executive Order 9066, an unprecedented act intended to protect the national security of the United States. Areas of the West Coast were designated as military zones from which anyone considered likely to be disloyal would be relocated inland to remote military reservations. Ninety percent of Americans of Japanese ancestry—110,000 in all—were interned in security camps.

While concern about national security always rises in times of war, this policy was criticized, first, because it targeted an entire category of people, not one of whom was ever convicted of any disloyal act. Second, roughly two-thirds of those imprisoned were Nisei American, citizens by birth; their individual rights were undermined by fear and racism (Kitano, 1985:244). Third, the United States was also at war with Germany and Italy, yet no such action was taken against whites of German or Italian ancestry.

Relocation meant selling homes, furnishings, and businesses on short notice for whatever price could be obtained. As a result, almost the entire Japanese-American population was devastated economically. In the military prison camps—surrounded by barbed wire and armed soldiers—families suffered greatly as they were crowded into single rooms, often in buildings that had previously been used for livestock (Fujimoto, 1971; Bloom, 1980). The internment ended in 1944, when it was declared unconstitutional by the Supreme Court. In 1988 Congress awarded $20,000 as compensation to each victim of this policy—token recognition of the economic loss and personal suffering endured by Japanese Americans.

After World War II, Japanese Americans staged a dramatic recovery. Having lost their traditional businesses, they entered a wide range of new occupations. Because their culture places a high value on education and hard work, Japanese Americans have enjoyed remarkable success. As shown in Table 9–4, the 1980 median income of a Japanese-American household was more than 30 percent above the national average. And the rate of poverty among Japanese Americans was only half that for the United States as a whole.

Upward social mobility has encouraged cultural assimilation. The third and fourth generations of Japanese Americans (the *Sansei* and *Yonsei*) rarely live in residential enclaves, as many Chinese Americans still do, and a significant number have married non-Japanese Americans. In the process, many have abandoned their traditions, including the ability to speak Japanese. But a high proportion of Japanese Americans participate in ethnic associations as a way of maintaining some ethnic identity (Fugita & O'Brien, 1985). Still, some appear to be caught between two worlds, belonging to neither. As one Japanese-American man claims, "I never considered myself 100 percent American because of obvious physical differences. Nor did I think of myself as Japanese" (Okimoto, 1971:14).

Hispanic Americans

In 1990, there were at least 20 million Hispanic Americans, representing one in twelve people in the United States. Although some are of purely Spanish descent, most have some combination of Spanish, African, and Native-American ancestry. Hispanic Americans also represent a variety of cultures. More than half (at least 13

million) are Mexican Americans, commonly called *Chicanos*. Puerto Ricans are next in population size (3 million), followed by Cuban Americans (1 million). Many other societies of Latin America are represented in smaller numbers. Because of a high birth rate, the Hispanic-American population is currently increasing by almost a million a year. If this trend continues, Hispanics may outnumber African-Americans in the United States early in the next century (Moore & Pachon, 1985).

The social standing of Hispanics improved in some respects during the 1980s. Between 1984 and 1988, for instance, the number of Hispanic men in managerial and professional occupations jumped 42 percent; among Hispanic women, the increase was a remarkable 61 percent (Schwartz, 1989). Nevertheless family income for Hispanics remained steady during the 1980s. Furthermore, as the following sections reveal, some categories of Hispanics have fared better than others.

Mexican Americans. Some Mexican Americans are descendants of people who were living in a part of Mexico that was annexed by the United States after the Mexican-American War (1846–1848). Most Mexican Americans, however, are recent immigrants. During the 1970s and 1980s, more immigrants came to the United States from Mexico than from any other nation. By the end of the 1980s, almost 13 million Mexican Americans were officially recorded as living in the United States, most in the West and Southwest. The actual figure could be far higher because large numbers of Mexican Americans enter the United States illegally (Weintraub & Ross, 1982).

Attitudes toward Mexican Americans vary along with the need for the inexpensive labor many of them provide, especially as farm workers. As was true of Japanese and Chinese immigrants in the West a century ago, many Mexican Americans hold low-paying jobs. Table 9–5 shows that in 1989 the median family income for Mexican Americans was $21,025, about 65 percent of the comparable national figure of $32,191, a drop from 74 percent at the beginning of the decade. In 1989, one-fourth of Chicano families were classified as poor—more than twice the national average but less than the proportion of blacks living in poverty. Finally, despite improvement since 1980, Mexican Americans have significantly less education than Americans as a whole.

Puerto Ricans. Puerto Rico has been a possession of the United States since the end of the Spanish-American War in 1898. In 1917, these islanders became American citizens, and Puerto Ricans now move freely to and from the mainland (Fitzpatrick, 1980).

Table 9–5 THE SOCIAL STANDING OF HISPANIC AMERICANS, 1980 AND 1989

	All Hispanics		Mexican Americans		Puerto Ricans		Cuban Americans		Entire United States	
	1980	1989	1980	1989	1980	1989	1980	1989	1980	1989
Median Family Income	$14,712	$21,769	$14,765	$21,025	$10,734	$18,932	$18,245	$28,858	$19,917	$32,191
Proportion in Poverty	23.5%	23.7%	23.3%	24.9%	36.3%	30.8%	13.2%	16.9%	12.4%	10.4%
Median Education (years) (age 25 and over)	10.8	12.0	9.6	10.8	10.5	12.0	12.2	12.4	12.5	12.7
Completion of Four or More Years of College (age 25 and over)	7.6%	9.9%	4.9%	6.1%	5.6%	9.8%	16.2%	19.8%	17.1%	21.1%

SOURCE: U.S. Bureau of the Census.

New York City is the center of Puerto Rican life in the continental United States. In 1910 about 500 Puerto Ricans lived in New York; by 1940, about 70,000. After World War II, however, regular airline service between New York City and San Juan, the capital of Puerto Rico, sparked even greater migration; by 1950, New York's Puerto Rican population had reached 187,000 (Glazer & Moynihan, 1970).

However, life in New York has not met the expectations of many Puerto Ricans. By the mid-1960s, half of the Puerto Ricans in New York were living in poverty (Moore & Pachon, 1985). Today, half of the more than 2 million Puerto Ricans in the continental United States live in New York's Spanish Harlem, and many continue to be severely disadvantaged. Adjusting to cultural patterns on the mainland—including, for many, learning English—is a major challenge; Puerto Ricans with darker skin encounter especially strong prejudice and discrimination. As a result, each year about as many Puerto Ricans return to Puerto Rico as arrive from the island.

This "revolving door" pattern has hampered cultural assimilation. About three-fourths of Puerto Rican families in the United States continue to speak Spanish at home, compared with about half of Mexican-American families (Sowell, 1981; Stevens & Swicegood, 1987). Speaking only Spanish helps maintain a strong ethnic identity but may also limit economic opportunity. Puerto Ricans also have a higher incidence of female-headed households than do other Hispanics, a pattern linked to poverty (Reimers, 1984). Table 9–5 shows that in

1989 the median household income for Puerto Ricans was $18,932—59 percent of the national average. Throughout the 1980s, therefore, Puerto Ricans were the most socially disadvantaged Hispanic minority.

Cuban Americans. Large numbers of Cubans came to the United States after the 1959 Marxist revolution led by Fidel Castro. By 1972, aided by special legislation, 400,000 Cubans had immigrated (Perez, 1980). Most settled in Miami, although the Cuban community in New York now numbers over 50,000. Those who fled Castro's Cuba were generally not the "huddled masses" described on the Statue of Liberty, but highly educated business and professional people. They wasted little time building much the same success in the United States that they had enjoyed in their homeland (Fallows, 1983). Table 9–5 shows that the median household income for Cuban Americans in 1989 was $26,858—well above that of other Hispanics although still well below the national average. Poverty among Cuban Americans is substantially higher than for all Americans.

Cuban Americans have managed a delicate balancing act—achieving success in the larger society while retaining much of their traditional culture. Of the categories of Hispanics we have considered, they are the most likely to speak Spanish in their homes; eight out of ten families do (Sowell, 1981). However, cultural distinctiveness and living in highly visible communities, like Miami's Little Havana district, provoke hostility from some whites. While some whites in Miami applaud the eco-

Hispanic Americans represent a majority of the residents of Miami, Florida. In the Little Havana district of the city, Cuban immigrants have blended their traditional way of life with the surrounding cultures.

nomic and social strengths of the city's Cuban community, others angrily denounce the Cubans as outsiders who are taking over their domain. As a bumper sticker states bluntly, "Will the last American to leave Miami remember to bring the flag?"

In 1989 the total number of Cuban Americans was estimated to stand at more than a million (U.S. Bureau of the Census, 1990). Substantial population growth during the 1980s followed the so-called Mariel boat lift, the influx of 125,000 refugees from Mariel Harbor in Cuba. Several thousand of these "boat people" had been released from Cuban prisons and mental hospitals, and they became the focus of mass-media accounts fueling prejudice toward Cuban Americans (Clark, Lasaga, & Regue, 1981; Portes, 1984).

About 90,000 of this second wave of Cuban immigrants settled in the Miami area while others—especially those with darker skin—entered cities in the Northeast (Perez, 1980). Typically poorer and less educated than those who arrived a generation earlier, these recent immigrants clashed with the more established Cuban community in Miami (Fallows, 1983). But they too are quickly becoming established. Soon after their arrival, most applied for resident status so that their relatives abroad could also be admitted to the United States.

White Ethnic Americans

In the 1960s, the term *white ethnics* was coined in recognition of the visible ethnic heritage of many white Americans. White ethnics are non-WASP people of European ancestry, including people of German, Irish, and French background. Overall, more than half of all Americans fall into some white ethnic category.

Unprecedented immigration from Europe during the nineteenth century greatly increased American social diversity. Initially, the Germans and Irish predominated. Italians, and Jews from many European countries, followed. Despite cultural differences, all shared the hope that America would offer greater political freedom and economic opportunity than they had known in their homelands. The belief that the streets of America were paved with gold was, of course, a far cry from the reality experienced by the vast majority of immigrants. Jobs were not always easy to find, and most demanded hard labor for low wages.

Economic problems were aggravated by prejudice and discrimination, which rose with the increasing tide of immigration. Nativist organizations opposed the entry of non-WASP Europeans to America and denounced those already here. Newspaper ads seeking workers in the mid-nineteenth century often carried a warning to new arrivals: "None need apply but Americans" (Handlin, 1941:67).

Some of the prejudice and discrimination actually involved class, since immigrants were typically poor and often had little command of English. But even distinguished achievers faced hostility. Fiorello La Guardia, the son of immigrants, half Italian and half Jewish, who served as mayor of New York between 1933 and 1945, was once rebuked by President Herbert Hoover in words that reveal unambiguous ethnic hatred:

You should go back where you belong and advise Mussolini

how to make good honest citizens in Italy. The Italians are preponderantly our murderers and bootleggers. . . . Like a lot of other foreign spawn, you do not appreciate the country that supports and tolerates you. (Mann, 1959, cited in Baltzell, 1964:30)

Nativists were finally victorious. Between 1921 and 1968, immigration quotas were applied to each foreign country. The greatest restrictions were placed on southern and eastern Europeans—people likely to have darker skin and to differ culturally from the dominant WASPs (Fallows, 1983).

In response to widespread bigotry, white ethnics followed the pattern of forming supportive residential enclaves. Some also gained footholds in specialized trades: Italian Americans entered the construction industry; Irish Americans worked in various building trades and civil service jobs; Jews predominated in the garment industry; many Greeks (like the Chinese) worked in the retail food business (Newman, 1973).

White ethnics who prospered were typically assimilated into the larger society. Many working-class people, however, still live in traditional neighborhoods. Despite continuing problems, white ethnics have achieved considerable success over the course of this century. Many descendants of immigrants who labored in sweatshops and lived in overcrowded tenements now hold respectable positions—both socially and economically. As a result, ethnic heritage now serves as a source of pride to many white Americans.

AMERICAN MINORITIES: A HUNDRED-YEAR PERSPECTIVE

The United States has been, and is likely to remain, a land of immigrants. Its striking cultural diversity stems from immigration, which peaked at the beginning of this century and subsided with World War I (1914–1918) and restrictive legislation enacted during the 1920s (Easterlin, 1980).

For most of those who came to America, the first half of this century brought gradual economic gains and at least some cultural assimilation. American society slowly granted basic freedoms where they had earlier been denied: Citizenship was extended to Native Americans (1924) and to foreign-born Chinese Americans (1943) and Japanese Americans (1952). In the 1950s, black Americans organized the civil rights movement in response to centuries of oppression.

Immigration to this country has been rising again since the 1930s, reaching about 400,000 people during the 1980s—the same as during the "Great Immigration" a century ago (although newcomers now enter a country with five times as many people). But today the names, faces, and cultural patterns of these immigrants are different. Now most immigrants come from Latin America and Asia, not Europe. During the 1980s, Mexicans, Filipinos, and Koreans arrived in the largest numbers. Rather than entering the large cities on the "European" side of the United States, most new immigrants are bringing profound cultural changes to cities in the South and West.

New arrivals face many of the same problems of prejudice and discrimination experienced by those who came before them. Also, like European immigrants of the past, many now struggle to enter the "golden door" of American society without entirely losing their traditional culture. Some have also built racial and ethnic enclaves: The Little Havana and Little Saigon of today stand alongside the Little Italy and Germantown of the past. New Americans also share the hope that racial and ethnic diversity will be viewed as a matter of difference rather than inferiority.

SUMMARY

1. Race involves a cluster of biological traits that form three broad overarching categories: Caucasians, Negroids, and Mongoloids. There are, however, no pure races. Ethnicity is based on shared cultural heritage. Minorities are people—including those of certain races and ethnicities—who are socially distinctive and have a subordinate social position.

2. A prejudice is an inflexible and distorted generalization about a category of people. Racism is a powerful type of prejudice, asserting that one race is innately superior or inferior to another.

3. Discrimination involves action—treating various categories of people differently.

4. Pluralism exists to the extent that distinct racial

and ethnic categories have equal social standing. Assimilation is a process by which minorities gradually adopt the patterns of the dominant culture. Segregation is the physical and social separation of categories of people. The segregation of minorities is typically involuntary. Genocide is the extermination of a category of people.

5. WASPs predominated among the original European settlers of America, and they continue to enjoy a high social position today.

6. Native Americans—the original inhabitants of the Americas—have endured genocide, segregation, and forced assimilation. Today the social standing of Native Americans is well below the national average.

7. Black Americans lived for two centuries as slaves. Emancipation in 1865 led to rigid segregation by law. Despite formal equality under the law, blacks are still relatively disadvantaged today.

8. Chinese and Japanese Americans suffered due to both racial and ethnic differences. Today, however, both categories have above-average income and education.

9. Hispanic Americans represent many ethnicities sharing a Spanish heritage. Mexican Americans are the largest Hispanic minority, heavily concentrated in the Southwest. Puerto Ricans, most of whom live in New York, are poorer. Cubans, concentrated in Miami, are the most affluent category of Hispanics.

10. White ethnic Americans include non-WASPs of European ancestry. While making gains during the last century, many white ethnics are still struggling for economic security.

11. Immigration has increased in recent years. No longer primarily from Europe, immigrants now come mostly from Latin America and Asia.

KEY CONCEPTS

assimilation the process by which minorities gradually adopt patterns of the dominant culture

discrimination treating various categories of people unequally

ethnicity a cultural heritage shared by a category of people

genocide the systematic killing of one category of people by another

institutional discrimination patterns of discrimination that are woven into the fabric of a society

minority a category of people, defined by physical or cultural traits, who are socially disadvantaged

miscegenation the biological process of interbreeding among racial categories

pluralism a state in which racial and ethnic minorities are distinct but have social parity

prejudice a rigid and irrational generalization about a category of people

race a category composed of men and women who share biologically transmitted traits that are defined as socially significant

racism the belief that one racial category is innately superior or inferior to another

scapegoat a person or category of people unfairly blamed for the troubles of others

segregation the physical and social separation of categories of people

stereotype a set of prejudices concerning some category of people

Sex and Gender

10

Chapter Outline

In 1840 an American couple traveled to London to attend the World Anti-Slavery Convention. Henry Brewster Stanton, an eloquent speaker, was welcomed as a delegate. His wife, Elizabeth Cady Stanton, was barred at the door, by people allegedly opposed to social inequality, because she was a woman.

Elizabeth Cady Stanton soon encountered Lucretia Mott, who had also been excluded from the meeting. The two women shared their dismay at how even abolitionists discriminated against women of all races. Stanton and Mott discussed organizing a meeting of their own, and eight years later in Seneca Falls, New York, the first women's rights gathering was held. Delegates to this convention described how women and blacks suffered from similar prejudice and discrimination. Like black slaves, they observed, most women could not own property, keep their earnings, enter into business, testify in court against their husbands, or legally vote.

In 1865, the Thirteenth Amendment to the Constitution outlawed slavery in the United States. Congress soon extended citizenship to all African-Americans (the Fourteenth Amendment), but the right to vote was granted only to black *men* (the Fifteenth Amendment). Women of all races were still denied suffrage. Elizabeth Cady Stanton and other feminists responded by forming the National Woman Suffrage Association. In 1920 their long-sought goal was finally achieved with the adoption of the Nineteenth Amendment to the Constitution, granting women the right to vote (McGlen & O'Connor, 1983; Friedrich, 1984).

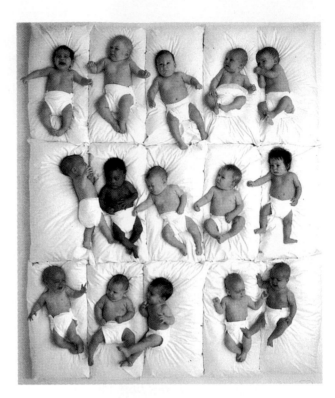

Sex is a biological distinction that develops prior to birth. Gender is the meaning that a society attaches to being female or male—that is, feelings, thoughts, and behavior that are defined as feminine or masculine. Gender differences are not evident among infants, although over a lifetime the social worlds of males and females are distinguished in countless ways.

SEX AND GENDER

Now, more than seventy years later, women have made other important gains but remain socially disadvantaged in relation to men. This inequality is often thought to reflect innate differences between the sexes but, as this chapter will explain, it is more a creation of society itself. To begin, we shall explore the key concepts of sex and gender.

Sex: A Biological Distinction

Sex refers to *the division of humanity into biological categories of male and female.* Sex is determined at the moment a child is conceived through sexual intercourse. The female ovum and the male sperm, which join to form a fertilized embryo, each contain twenty-three pairs of chromosomes—biological codes that guide physical development. One of these pairs of chromosomes determines the child's sex: The mother contributes an X chromosome; the father contributes either an X or a Y. If the father contributes an X chromosome, a female embryo (XX) develops, whereas a Y results in a male embryo (XY).

Within six weeks, sex differentiation in the embryo begins. If the embryo is male, testicular tissue produces testosterone, a hormone that stimulates the development of the male genitals. Without testosterone, the embryo develops female genitals. At birth, males and females are distinguished by **primary sex characteristics**, *the genitals, used to reproduce the human species.* When they reach puberty, in the early teens, people become capable of reproduction. At this point, humans experience further biological differentiation, developing **secondary sex characteristics,** *physical traits, other than the genitals, that distinguish physiologically mature males and females.* To accommodate pregnancy, giving birth, and nurturing infants, adolescent females develop wider hips, breasts, and soft fatty tissue, thereby providing a reserve supply of nutrition for pregnancy and breast-feeding (Brownmiller, 1984). Usually slightly taller and heavier than females from birth, males, in adolescence, typically develop more muscles in the upper body, more extensive body hair, and voices deeper in tone. These are only general differences, however. Many males are smaller and lighter than many females; some males have less body hair than some females; and some males speak in a higher tone than some females do.

In rare cases, a hormone imbalance before birth produces a **hermaphrodite** (a word derived from Hermaphroditus, the offspring of the mythological Greek gods Hermes and Aphrodite, who embodied both sexes), *a human being with some combination of male and female internal and external genitalia.* Because our culture tends to frown on sexual ambiguity, we often regard hermaphrodites with confusion and even disgust. In contrast, the Pokot of Eastern Africa are indifferent to what they define as a simple biological error, and the Navajo look on hermaphrodites with awe, viewing them as the embodiment of the full potential of both the male and the female (Geertz, 1975).

There are cases of people who choose to change their sex. Hermaphrodites may have their genitals surgically altered to gain the appearance (and occasionally the function) of a sexually normal man or woman. Surgery may also be considered by **transsexuals,** *people who feel they are one sex though biologically they are the other.* Some 20,000 transsexuals in the United States have medically altered their genitals to escape the sense of being "trapped in the wrong body" (Restak, 1979, cited in Offir, 1982:146).

Sexual Orientation

Sexual orientation is *the manner in which people experience sexual arousal and achieve sexual pleasure.* For most living things, sexuality is biologically programmed. In humans, however, sexual orientation is bound up in the complex web of culture. The norm in all industrial societies is *heterosexuality* (*hetero* is a Greek word meaning "the other of two"), by which a person is sexually attracted to the opposite sex. However, *homosexuality* (*homo* is the Greek word for "the same"), by which a person is sexually attracted to people of the same sex, is not uncommon.

More broadly, all cultures endorse heterosexuality, although many tolerate—and some even encourage—homosexuality. Among the ancient Greeks, for instance, elite male intellectuals celebrated homosexuality as the highest form of relationship, while devaluing relations with women, whom they considered to be incapable of philosophical discussion. Heterosexuality was thus seen as little more than a reproductive necessity and men who did not engage in homosexuality were defined as deviant. But because homosexual relations do not permit reproduction, no society has been known to favor homosexuality over heterosexuality (Kluckhohn, 1948; Ford & Beach, 1951; Greenberg, 1988).

Tolerance of gay people (a label homosexuals adopted in the 1960s) has increased during this century. In 1974 the American Psychiatric Association removed homosexuality from its listing of mental disorders. Gays were subject to increasing prejudice and discrimination during the 1980s, however, when the deadly disease AIDS became publicly identified with homosexual men. Today, although three-fourths of American adults continue to define homosexuality as morally wrong, the same proportion think American society should provide equal workplace opportunities for gays and straights (N.O.R.C., 1989:258; Salholz, 1990). For their part, many organizations of gay people are struggling to overcome the stereotypes of gay men and gay women (commonly called *lesbians*). Supporters of gay rights now use the term *homophobia* (with Greek roots meaning "fear of sameness") to indicate an irrational fear of gay people (Weinberg, 1973). This label implies that people intolerant of gays, rather than those who engage in homosexuality, are misguided.

Pioneering research by Alfred Kinsey (1948, 1953) suggested that about 4 percent of males and roughly 2 percent of females have an exclusively same-sex orientation. Nevertheless, perhaps 25 percent of Americans have had at least one sexual experience with someone of the same sex. In many cases, sexual orientations are not mutually exclusive; some people have a *bisexual* (combining homosexual and heterosexual) orientation.

How does a person develop a particular sexual orientation? There is growing evidence that sexual orientation is rooted in biological factors present at birth and is further reinforced by the hormone balance in the body as we grow (Gladue, Green & Hellman, 1984; Weinrich, 1987; Isay, 1989). Still other research points to the importance of the social environment in encouraging sexual attitudes and behaviors (Troiden, 1988). According to these researchers, humans are born with the capacity and desire to be sexual, but *how* we express our sexuality is learned as our personality develops in society. Most likely, both nature and nurture play a part. To complicate matters further, sexual orientation is not established in precisely the same way for everyone. One influential study concluded that a complete explanation for sexual orientation simply does not exist at present (Bell, Weinberg, & Kiefer-Hammersmith, 1981).

Gender: A Cultural Distinction

Gender refers to *human traits linked by culture to each sex.* Gender guides how males and females think about

The stereotypical view of females as "the weaker sex" is challenged by the everyday lives of women throughout the world. Especially in poor societies that depend on human labor, women perform work that would be physically challenging to most American men.

themselves, how they interact with others, and what positions they occupy in society as a whole.

Gender involves how a society defines the humanity of its people and confers power on each of the sexes. Gender is thus also a matter of inequality. Societies base the patterns of gender on certain biological differences between males and females, although these are complex and inconsistent. Beyond the primary and secondary sex characteristics already noted, males have more muscle in the arms and shoulders, so the average man can lift more weight than the average woman can. Furthermore, males have greater strength over short periods of time. Yet, females can outperform males in some tests of long-term endurance because they can draw on the energy derived from greater body fat. Females also outperform males in life itself. According to the National Center for Health Statistics (1990), the average life expectancy for males born in 1989 is 71.8 years, while females born that same year can expect to live 78.6 years.

Research indicates no difference in overall intelligence between males and females. Adolescent males exhibit greater mathematical ability, while adolescent females outperform males in verbal skills (Maccoby & Jacklin, 1974; Baker et al., 1980; Lengermann & Wallace, 1985).

Biologically, then, only limited differences characterize males and females, with neither sex naturally superior. Nevertheless, the deep-rooted *cultural* notion of male superiority may seem so natural that we assume it is the inevitable consequence of sex itself. But society, much more than biology, is at work here, as the global variability of gender attests.

Cultural variability in gender. Fascinating gender research has focused on collective settlements in Israel called *kibbutzim.* The kibbutz (the singular form) compels our interest because its members have historically embraced social equality, sharing in necessary work and decision making.

Members of kibbutzim typically endorse conceptions of gender that give females and males comparable social standing. Both sexes perform all types of work including child care, building repair, cooking, and cleaning. Boys and girls are raised in the same way and, from the first weeks of life, live in dormitories under the care of specially trained personnel. To members of kibbutzim, then, sex is defined as irrelevant to much of everyday life.

Some observers suggest that women in the kibbutzim have been returning to more traditional social roles.

Sociobiologists (see Chapter 2, "Culture") wonder if subtle but persistent biological predispositions may undermine efforts at gender equality (Tiger & Shepher, 1975). Even if this were so, the kibbutzim demonstrate wide cultural latitude in defining what is masculine and feminine. They also exemplify how, through conscious efforts, a society can encourage sexual equality.

Comparative research on gender was also carried out earlier in this century by anthropologist Margaret Mead. To the extent that gender reflects the biological facts of sex, she reasoned, the human traits defined as masculine and feminine should be everywhere the same; if gender is cultural, these conceptions should vary.

Mead's best-known research of this kind involved three societies of New Guinea (1963; orig. 1935). In the mountains of New Guinea, Mead observed that both the men and women of Arapesh had remarkably similar attitudes and behavior. Both sexes, she reported, were cooperative and sensitive to others: in short, what American culture would term "feminine." Among the Mundugumor, who lived to the south, Mead also found females and males to be alike; yet, the Mundugumor culture of head-hunting and cannibalism stood in striking contrast to the gentle ways of the Arapesh. Both sexes were typically selfish and aggressive, traits defined as more "masculine" by American culture. Finally, traveling west to observe the Tchambuli, Mead discovered a culture that, like our own, defined males and females differently. Yet the Tchambuli *reversed* many of our notions of gender: Females were dominant and rational, while males were submissive, emotional, and nurturing toward children.

Mead concluded that cultures can exaggerate or minimize social distinctions based on sex. Additionally, where differences are pronounced, what one culture defines as masculine may be considered feminine by another. Mead's research therefore strongly supports the conclusion that gender is a variable creation of society.

A broader study of more than two hundred preindustrial societies by George Murdock (1937) revealed some general agreement about which tasks are feminine or masculine. Hunting and warfare, Murdock found, generally fall to males, while home-centered tasks such as cooking and child care tend to be defined as female tasks. With only simple technology, preindustrial societies apparently adopted this strategy to benefit from males' typically greater size and short-term strength; because females bear children, their activities were likely to be more domestic.

But within these general patterns, Murdock found significant variation. Just as many societies considered agriculture—the core of preindustrial production—to be feminine as masculine. For most, in fact, farming responsibilities were shouldered by both males and females. When it came to many other tasks—from building shelters to tattooing the body—Murdock observed considerable variation from culture to culture.

Overall, the record suggests that only a few specific activities have been universally defined as masculine or feminine. And as societies industrialize, with a resulting decrease in the significance of muscle power, these distinctions are lessened (Lenski & Lenski, 1987). Gender, therefore, varies too much across cultures to be considered a simple expression of the biological categories of sex. Instead, as with many other elements of culture, what it means to be male and female is mostly a creation of society.

Patriarchy and Sexism

Although conceptions of gender do vary, one universal pattern characterizes all societies to some degree: **patriarchy** (literally, "the rule of fathers"), *a form of social organization in which males dominate females.* Despite mythical tales of societies dominated by female "Amazons," the pattern of **matriarchy,** *a form of social organization in which females dominate males,* is not at present part of the human record (Gough, 1971; Harris, 1977; Kipp, 1980; Lengermann & Wallace, 1985). While a tendency toward patriarchy may be universal, however, world societies reveal significant variation in the relative power and privilege of males and females.

An important ideological underpinning of patriarchy is **sexism,** *the belief that one sex is innately superior to the other.* Patriarchy historically has been supported by a belief in the innate superiority of males who, therefore, legitimately dominate females. As Table 10–1 on page 234 shows, sexism has much in common with racism, which was covered in Chapter 9 ("Race and Ethnicity"). Just as racism constitutes an ideology supporting white domination of nonwhites, so sexism is an ideology supporting (allegedly superior) males dominating (allegedly inferior) females.

In addition to the obvious costs to females, sexism burdens society by stunting the talents and abilities of females—half the population. Men too suffer from sexism because, as Marilyn French (1985) argues, patriarchy compels males to relentlessly seek control—not only of women, but of themselves and the entire world. Such

Table 10–1 WAYS IN WHICH SEXISM AND RACISM ARE ALIKE

	Women	Blacks
Link to highly visible personal traits	Secondary sex characteristics.	Skin color.
Assertion of innate inferiority	Women are mentally inferior. Women are irresponsible, unreliable, and emotional.	Blacks are mentally inferior. Blacks are irresponsible, unreliable, and pleasure-seeking.
Assertion that those who are disadvantaged are content with their "proper place" in society	"A woman's place is in the home." All women really enjoy being treated "like a woman."	"Blacks should remain in their place." Blacks are content living just as they do.
Assertion that victims are under the protection of their oppressors	"Men put women on a pedestal."	Whites "take care of" blacks.
Coping strategies on the part of victims	Behavior flattering to men; letting men think they are better even when they are not. Hiding one's real feelings. Attempting to outwit men.	Deferential behavior toward whites; letting whites think they are better even when they are not. Hiding one's real feelings. Attempting to outwit whites.
Barriers to opportunity	Women don't need an education. Confined to "women's work." Women should stay out of politics.	Blacks don't need an education. Confined to "black occupations." Blacks should stay out of politics.
Criticism of those who do not "stay in their place"	Assertive women are "pushy." Ambitious women are trying to be like men. Women as traditional targets of violence by men.	Assertive blacks are "uppity." Ambitious blacks are trying to be like whites. Blacks as traditional targets of violence by whites.

SOURCE: Adapted from Helen Mayer Hacker, "Women as a Minority Group," *Social Forces*, Vol. 30 (October 1951): 60–69; and "Women as a Minority Group: Twenty Years Later," in Florence Denmark, ed., *Who Discriminates Against Women?* (Beverly Hills, CA: Sage, 1974), pp. 124–134.

impossible goals extract a high price in terms of accidents, stress, heart attacks, and other diseases that result in a higher death rate among males of all ages. The so-called Type A personality—characterized by impatience, driving ambition, and competitiveness, and known to be linked to heart disease—behaviorally describes what our culture defines as masculine (Ehrenreich, 1983). Furthermore, insofar as males seek control over others, they lose the ability to experience intimacy and trust (French, 1985). One recent study concluded that although developing masculinity is supposed to separate "the men from the boys," in practice it separates men from men (Raphael, 1988:184).

Overall, when human feelings, thoughts, and actions are rigidly scripted according to a culture's conceptions of gender, people cannot develop and freely express the full range of their humanity. In Western culture, males are strongly pressured to be assertive, competitive, and in control, a weighty burden for many to bear. Females are constrained to be submissive, dependent, and self-effacing, regardless of their individual talents and personalities.

Is patriarchy inevitable? Patriarchy in technologically simple societies largely stems from individuals having little control over the natural differences of sex. Pregnancy and childbirth limit the scope of women's lives, while men's greater height and short-term strength typically allow them to overpower females. Technological advances, however, give members of industrial societies greater choice in defining the relation of the two sexes. Birth control has given women greater control over pregnancy, just as industrial machinery has diminished the primacy of muscle power in everyday life. Today, then, biological differences provide little justification for patriarchy.

Categorical social inequality—whether based on race, ethnicity, or sex—also comes under attack in the more egalitarian culture of industrial societies. In many industrial nations, laws mandate that women and men have equal opportunity in at least most occupations and receive equal pay for equal work. Nonetheless, in all industrial societies, the two sexes tend to hold different jobs; moreover, women still have primary responsibility for maintaining the household, while men wield the lion's share of economic and political power.

Does the persistence of patriarchy mean that it is inevitable? Some researchers claim that biological factors encourage different behaviors and motivations in the two sexes, making the complete eradication of patriarchy difficult, if not impossible (Goldberg, 1974, 1987). Many sociologists acknowledge that biological differences between the sexes have *some* effect on human behavior (Rossi, 1985), but overwhelmingly, they believe that gender is primarily a social construction. As such, it is subject to change. Simply because no society has yet eliminated patriarchy, then, does not mean that patriarchy as it has existed in the past must inevitably shape the human future.

To understand the persistence of patriarchy, we now examine how gender is deeply rooted in society, from the way children learn to think of themselves, to how sexual inequality affects men and women as adults.

GENDER AND SOCIALIZATION

From birth until death, human feelings, thoughts, and actions reflect social definitions of the sexes. As children interact with others, they quickly learn that males and females are considered different kinds of human beings; by about the age of three or four, they apply gender standards to themselves (Kohlberg, 1966, cited in Lengermann & Wallace, 1985:37; Bem, 1981). Table 10–2 lists traits that traditionally have been used to define American males and females in different and opposing terms. Dividing human qualities according to sex is still widespread in American society, although research suggests that most young people do not develop consistently "masculine" or "feminine" personalities (L. Bernard, 1980).

Table 10–2 TRADITIONAL GENDER IDENTITY

Masculine Traits	Feminine Traits
Dominant	Submissive
Independent	Dependent
Intelligent and competent	Unintelligent and incapable
Rational	Emotional
Assertive	Receptive
Analytical	Intuitive
Strong	Weak
Brave	Timid
Ambitious	Content
Active	Passive
Competitive	Cooperative
Insensitive	Sensitive
Sexually aggressive	Sex object
Attractive because of achievement	Attractive because of physical appearance

Just as socialization incorporates gender into personal identity, so it teaches us to *act* according to cultural conceptions of what is masculine and feminine. **Gender roles** (or sex roles) are *attitudes and activities that a culture links to each sex.* Through gender roles, people express their gender identity. In other words, insofar as our culture defines males as ambitious and competitive, we expect them to engage in team sports and seek out positions of leadership. To the extent that females are defined as deferential and emotional, we expect them to be good listeners and supportive of others.

Gender and the Family

The first question usually asked about a newborn child is, "Is it a boy or a girl?" The question is important because the answer involves more than sex; it carries a great deal of significance for the child's entire life.

Sociologist Jessie Bernard suggests that, soon after birth, family members introduce infants to the "pink world" of girls or the "blue world" of boys (1981). In fact, gender is at work even before the birth of a child, since parents generally hope to have a boy rather than a girl (cited in Lengermann & Wallace, 1985:61). In China and other strongly patriarchal societies, female embryos are sometimes aborted and female infants killed so that parents can raise male children, whose social value is greater.

The lifetime contribution of Jessie Bernard to sociology has been concerned largely with gender. She points out that many sociologists have ignored the lives of women in their work; this is true even of those (like Karl Marx) who were otherwise outspoken critics of society.

Research on parental attitudes suggests that both fathers and mothers encourage sons to be strong, aggressive achievers while expecting daughters to be weaker, delicate, and less assertive (Witkin-Lanoil, 1984). Parents may even convey these expectations unconsciously in the way they handle their children. A researcher at an English university presented an infant dressed as either a boy or a girl to a number of women. Videotapes revealed that the women handled the "female" child tenderly, with frequent hugs and caresses, while treating the "male" child more aggressively, often lifting him up high in the air or bouncing him on the knee (Bonner, 1984). Other research shows that mothers have more overall physical contact with infant boys than with infant girls (Major, 1981). The message is clear: The female world revolves around passivity and emotion, while the male world involves substantial independence and action.

Gender and the Peer Group

As children reach school age, they interact more outside the family, especially with others their own age. Peer groups further distinguish the pink and blue worlds of girls and boys. The box explains how play groups shaped one young boy's sense of himself as masculine.

Observing fifth graders at play for a year, Janet Lever (1978) concluded that male and female peer groups provide boys and girls with distinctive socialization. Boys, Lever reported, engage more in team sports—such as baseball and football—that involve many roles, complex rules, and clear objectives such as scoring a run or a touchdown. These games are nearly always competitive, separating winners from losers. Male peer activities reinforce masculine traits of aggression and remaining in control.

By contrast, the peer groups of girls play hopscotch or jumprope, or simply talk, sing, or dance together. Spontaneous activities with fewer formal rules, such games rarely have "victory" as their ultimate goal, and girls rarely oppose one another. Instead of teaching girls to be competitive, female peer groups promote interpersonal skills of communication and cooperation—presumably the basis for family life.

Carol Gilligan (1982) reports similar results in research concerning how children engage in moral reasoning. Boys learn to reason according to rules and principles: For them, "rightness" consists largely of "playing by the rules." In the female world, morality is more a matter of responsibility to other people; "rightness" lies in maintaining close relationships with others. Such distinctive patterns of moral reasoning, too, are reinforced by the different peer-group activities of boys and girls.

Gender and Schooling

Even before children enter school, their reading tends to promote distinctions of gender. In one study, conducted some twenty years ago, a group of researchers examined books read by parents to pre-elementary school children (Weitzman et al., 1972). Males rather than females were the focus of attention in most of these books. For example, the ratio of males to females in illustrations was ten to one. Three times as many book titles mentioned males as females. These researchers concluded that children "are bound to receive the impression that girls are not very important because no one has bothered to write books about them" (1972:1129).

Play may appear to be simply a matter of having fun, but it is also a serious way to teach children how their culture defines the roles of each sex.

The books also presented the lives of males and females in stereotypical ways: Males engaged in diverse and interesting activities, while females usually stayed home. The females depicted in these books were usually concerned with pleasing males: Girls courted the favor of their father and brothers, and women endeavored to please their husbands. More like dolls than living beings, the girls in these books were mostly attractive and compliant objects, sources of support and pleasure to males.

In the last decade, the growing awareness among authors, teachers, and readers that childhood learning shapes people's lives as adults has led to changes. Today's books for children portray males and females in a more balanced way.

In addition to the formal lessons of school, what Raphaela Best (1983) calls "the second curriculum"— the informal messages and experiences of school life— encourages children to embrace appropriate gender patterns. By the time children reach high school, topics of study reflect the different roles males and females are expected to assume as adults. Instruction in typing and such home-centered skills as nutrition, cooking,

SOCIOLOGY OF EVERYDAY LIFE

Masculinity as Contest

By the time I was ten, the central fact in my life was the demand that I become a man. By then, the most important relationships by which I was taught to define myself were those I had with other boys. I already knew that I must see every encounter with another boy as a contest in which I must win or at least hold my own. . . . The same lesson continued (in school), after school, even in Sunday School. My parents, relatives,

teachers, the books I read, movies I saw, all taught me that my self-worth depended on my manliness, my willingness to stand up to the other boys. This usually didn't mean a physical fight, though the willingness to stand up and "fight like a man" always remained a final test. But the relationships between us usually had the character of an armed truce. Girls weren't part of this social world at all yet, just because they weren't part of this con-

test. They didn't have to be bluffed, no credit was gained by cowing them, so they were more or less ignored. Sometimes when there were no grownups around we would let each other know that we liked each other, but most of the time we did as we were taught.

SOURCE: Michael Silverstein, in Jon Snodgrass, ed., *A Book of Readings for Men Against Sexism* (Albion, CA: Times Change Press, 1977), pp. 178–179.

and sewing has long been provided to classes composed almost entirely of females. Classes in woodworking and auto mechanics, conversely, are still mostly all-male.

In college, males and females follow this same pattern, tending toward different majors. Traditionally, the natural sciences—including physics, chemistry, biology, and mathematics—have been defined as part of the male province. Women have been expected to major in the humanities (such as English), the fine arts (painting, music, dance, and drama), or the social sciences (including anthropology and sociology). New areas of study are also likely to be sex linked. Computer science, for example, with its grounding in engineering, logic, and abstract mathematics, has predominantly attracted male students (Klein, 1984); courses in gender studies, by contrast, tend to enroll females.

Extracurricular activities also segregate the two sexes. Athletics and other activities for men benefit from more attention and more funding. Mass media coverage of men's athletics also far outstrips that devoted to female sports. This male dominance encourages females to assume supportive roles as observers or cheerleaders.

Gender and the Mass Media

Chapter 3 ("Socialization: From Infancy to Aging") explained that the mass media have a powerful influence on the socialization process. Films, magazines, and television significantly affect our thoughts and actions.

Since it first captured the public imagination in the 1950s, television has placed the dominant category of Americans—white males—at center stage. Racial and ethnic minorities were all but absent from television until the early 1970s, and only in the last decade have a number of programs featured female characters in major roles.

Even when both sexes appear on camera, men generally play the brilliant detectives, fearless explorers, and skilled surgeons. Men take charge, give orders, and exude competence. Women, by contrast, generally rely on men, are less capable, and are more often the targets of comedy (Busby, 1975). Women have also been traditionally portrayed as objects valued for their sexual attractiveness. Such stereotypes persisted during the 1980s, although more programming now involves interesting and responsible roles for women.

Change has come most slowly to advertising. Advertising, after all, sells products by conforming to widely established cultural patterns. Historically, television and magazine advertising has presented women in the home, rather than in the workplace, to sell household items such as cleaning products, foods, clothing, and appliances. Men, on the other hand, predominate in ads for cars, travel, banking services, industrial companies, and alcoholic beverages. The authoritative "voiceover" in television and radio advertising is almost always male (Busby, 1975; Courtney & Whipple, 1983).

Erving Goffman (1979) studied magazine and newspaper ads, concluding that men were photographed to appear taller than women, implying male superiority. Women were more frequently presented lying down (on sofas and beds) or, like children, seated on the floor. The expressions and gestures of men conveyed competence and authority, whereas women were more likely to appear in childlike poses. While men tend to focus on the products being advertised, the attention of women is generally directed toward men, conveying their supportive and submissive role.

Advertising tries to persuade us that embracing traditional notions of masculinity and femininity contributes enormously to our personal and professional success. With that groundwork in place, advertising then dictates what we should consume. For example, the masculine man drives the "right" car and vacations in the "right" place. The truly feminine woman buys clothing and cosmetics that make her look younger and more attractive to men.

Gender and Adult Socialization

Our gender identity and gender roles typically come to feel natural well before we become adults. Thus the attitudes and behavior of adults commonly follow feminine and masculine patterns (Spender, 1980; Kramarae, 1981).

In a simple but revealing bit of research, Pamela Fishman (1977, 1978) tape-recorded two weeks of conversations by three young, white, middle-class married couples in their homes. Even casual exchanges, she discovered, reinforce male dominance. For example, when the men began a conversation, the women usually kept it going; yet when the women initiated a conversation, the men frequently allowed it to collapse. This suggests that what males have to say is considered more important. Women, but rarely men, opened conversations with remarks like "This is interesting" or "Do you know what?" Fishman interpreted this pattern—also common to the speech of children—as women's way of finding out if men really want to hear what they had to say. Starting a conversation with "This is interesting," for example, is a request to the male to pay attention to what follows. Opening with "Do you know what?" amounts to stating, "I have something to say; are you willing to listen?"

The women also asked many more questions than the men did, a further indication of deference. Both the men and women used various "minimal responses" (such as "yeah," "umm," and "huh"), but in different ways. For the men, such responses expressed minimal interest, as if to say, "I guess I'll continue to listen if you insist on speaking." For the women, however, minimal responses were a form of "support work," inserted continually to show their interest in the conversation.

Years of gender-based socialization set the foundation for marriages between adults who inhabit different social worlds. Not surprisingly, husbands and wives may have considerable difficulty simply communicating with each other. Studies of verbal interaction in marriage confirm that this is a common problem among spouses (Komarovsky, 1967; Rubin, 1976, 1983).

GENDER AND SOCIAL STRATIFICATION

Gender implies more than how people think and act. The concept of **gender stratification** refers to *the unequal distribution of wealth, power, and privilege between the two sexes.* Specifically, females have less of a society's valued resources than males do.

Working Men and Women

In 1989, 66.5 percent of Americans over the age of fifteen were working for income; the American labor force includes 76.4 percent of men and 57.4 percent of women (U.S. Bureau of Labor Statistics, 1990). In 1900, only about one-fifth of women were in the labor force; as is shown in Figure 10–1, that proportion has increased steadily in recent decades. Furthermore, 74.5 percent of women in the labor force in 1989 were working full time. The traditional view that earning an income is a "man's job" thus no longer holds true.

Among the key factors contributing to these changes in the American labor force are the increasing number of service jobs in the American economy, the

Some recent advertising reverses traditional gender roles by portraying men as the sex objects of successful women. Although the role reversal is new, the use of gender stereotypes to sell consumer products is very old indeed.

growth of cities, declining family size, and more flexible norms regarding appropriate roles for women. In addition, because economic decline reduced the income of many Americans during the last fifteen years (see Chapter 7, "Social Stratification"), an increasing proportion of families require more than one income to maintain a comfortable standard of living. In 1989, 59.4 percent of married couples had two incomes.

A common misconception holds that women in the labor force are single or, if married, without children. In 1989, 57 percent of all married women were working, and the proportion stays the same for married women with children under six. Among married women with children between six and seventeen years of age, 73 percent were employed. For divorced women with chil-

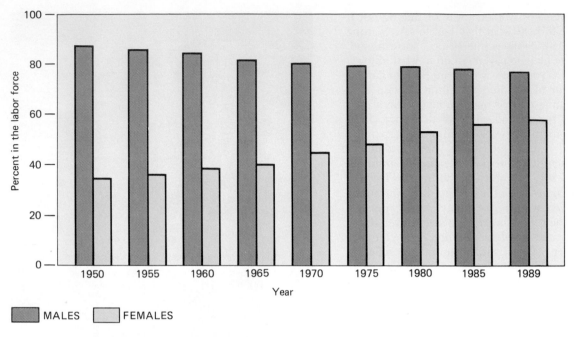

Figure 10–1 Men and Women in the American Labor Force
(U.S. Bureau of Labor Statistics)

dren, the comparable figures were higher still: 70.1 percent of women with younger children and 83.9 percent of women with older children (U.S. Bureau of the Census, 1989). A gradual increase in employer-sponsored child-care programs is giving more women and men the opportunity to combine the responsibilities of being workers and parents, a trend that is especially important for divorced mothers.

Gender and occupations. While the proportions of men and women in the labor force are converging (Jacobs, 1989), the work done by the two sexes remains quite different. According to the U.S. Bureau of Labor Statistics (1990), women have a relatively small range of occupations, with almost half of working women holding two types of jobs. First, 28 percent of working women perform clerical work as secretaries, typists, or stenographers; within this category, women represent 80 percent of all "pink-collar" clerical workers. Second, 18 percent of working women engage in service jobs, including waitressing and other food service employment as well as nursing and other health care work. Both categories of jobs lie at the low end of the pay scale and offer limited opportunities for advancement.

Table 10–3 shows the ten occupations with the highest concentrations of women in 1989. Although increasing numbers of women, both married and single, are working, women remain highly segregated in the labor force in a society that continues to link work to gender (Roos, 1983; Kemp & Coverman, 1989; U.S. Bureau of Labor Statistics, 1990).

Men predominate in most job categories beyond the ten occupations noted in the table. The highest proportion of men work in the trades: 99.5 percent of brickmasons, stonemasons, structural metal workers, and heavy-equipment mechanics are male. Males also predominate in jobs that provide a great deal of income, prestige, and power. For example, more than 90 percent of engineers, 80 percent of physicians and lawyers, and more than 60 percent of managers, administrators, and computer specialists are men. Only a few women appear as the top executives of America's largest corporations. Even where men and women do much the same work, titles (and consequently pay) benefit men. A "special assistant to the president," for example, is likely to be a man, while an "executive secretary" is nearly always a woman.

One exception to this pattern is the growing number

Table 10–3 JOBS WITH THE HIGHEST CONCENTRATIONS OF WOMEN, 1989

	Occupation	Number of Women Employed	Percent in Occupation Who Are Women
1.	Dental hygienist	79,360	99.2%
2.	Secretary	3,973,910	99.1%
3.	Dental assistant	184,943	98.7%
4.	Prekindergarten and kindergarten teachers	421,518	98.2%
5.	Receptionist	792,180	97.2%
6.	Private household child-care worker	347,618	97.1%
7.	Child-care worker	829,143	96.3%
8.	Licensed practical nurse	397,854	96.0%
9.	Teacher's aide	418,440	95.1%
10.	Typist	694,450	95.0%

SOURCE: U.S. Bureau of Labor Statistics.

of women who own and operate small businesses. Women now own 30 percent of all American firms, and the number of women-owned firms jumped 50 percent between 1982 and 1987. Most of these businesses are small; 90 percent are sole proprietorships with a single employee (U.S. Bureau of the Census, 1990). Even so, the success of these talented entrepreneurs suggests that women can create opportunities for themselves, sometimes more than those provided by male-dominated companies.

Overall, then, gender stratification permeates the workplace, where men tend to hold occupational positions that confer more wealth and power than those typically held by women. This hierarchy along gender lines is often easy to spot in the job setting: Male physicians are assisted by female nurses, male executives have female secretaries, and male airline pilots work with female flight attendants. In any occupation, the greater a job's income and prestige, the more likely it is that the position will be held by a man. Among teachers, for example, women make up 98 percent at the kindergarten level; 85 percent in the elementary grades; and 53 percent at the secondary school level. But only 39 percent of professors in colleges and universities are women (U.S. Bureau of Labor Statistics, 1990). At the top of the pyramid, just 12 percent of college and university presidents are women, and these usually preside over smaller institu-

tions, many with an all-female student body (American Council on Education, 1984).

Housework: Women's "Second Shift"

Just as men traditionally have been required to work outside the home, so housework—maintaining the home and caring for children—has been the province of women. Housework has always embodied a cultural contradiction: touted as essential to American life on the one hand, carrying little reward or social prestige on the other (J. Bernard, 1981).

Women's rapid entry into the labor force has prompted little change in the pattern of responsibility for housework. One estimate indicates that the hours of housework performed by women declined only slightly in recent decades and the proportion of housework shared by men remained the same (Fuchs, 1986). Typically, American couples share the disciplining of children and managing finances, but little else. Men routinely perform home repairs and mow the lawn; women see to the daily shopping, cooking, and cleaning. Thus women commonly return from the workplace to face a "second shift" of unpaid work on the homefront (Schooler et al., 1984; Benokraitis & Feagin, 1986; Hochschild, 1989).

Most men support the idea of women entering

Women in the American labor force historically have been concentrated in a few occupations such as garment making. Much of women's work also has been under the supervision of men.

the labor force, yet refuse to modify their own behavior to help their partners do so (Komarovsky, 1973). Only in rare cases, such as the Israeli kibbutzim, is housework shared to any great extent. Even in Sweden—a society with a strong belief in the social equality of the sexes—only one in five couples shares housework equitably (Haas, 1981).

Gender, Income, and Wealth

Because women predominate in clerical and service jobs while men hold most business and professional positions, women earn less than men do. Thus, income—a major measure of self-worth—reinforces women's disadvantaged position in the occupational hierarchy.

In 1989, the median earnings for women working full time were $19,643, while men working full time earned $28,605. Thus men earned in about seven days what women earned in ten days; more simply, for every dollar earned by men, women earned about 69 cents. This income disparity between males and females has declined gradually over the last two decades.

Put in different terms, one in five women working full time earned less than $10,000 in 1989, whereas only one in ten men did. One in four women earned more than $25,000, compared to one in two men. Men were also almost eight times more likely than women (4.3 percent versus 0.6 percent) to earn more than $75,000 (U.S. Bureau of the Census, 1990).

This earning disparity primarily stems from the different jobs held by men and women. Taking a closer look, we discover that jobs and gender interact: Jobs

CRITICAL THINKING

Corporate Women: The "Mommy-Track" Controversy

The facts of corporate life are changing. Once the preserve of male executives and female support workers, management positions are now being occupied by women in record numbers. This is good news for corporations, because women are among the top college and business school graduates in America. The end of the post–World War II baby boom has reduced the supply of corporate workers, while the rapid growth in administrative positions in the new "information economy" has increased the demand for talented people. Overall, there are no longer enough men (and far fewer *good* men) to fill all the positions. Speaking purely in terms of the bottom line, corporate America needs women.

Even so, the corporate world is decidedly unfriendly to women. Felice N. Schwartz—founder and president of Catalyst, an organization that seeks to develop the careers of

women—explains the problem this way: By trying to make women equal to men in the workplace, we have chosen to all but ignore *maternity*, the most crucial difference between the two sexes. Many young adults want to divide their time and energy between a career and young children. Currently, Schwartz claims, doing this is much more difficult for women than for men. As evidence, she points out that, by age forty, 90 percent of male executives have children, but only 35 percent of female executives do. Men, after all, do not face a conflict between family and career, as long as their wives take responsibility for child care.

However, businesses have long been uneasy about women employees having children because, under current policies, motherhood takes women away from their jobs. Professional women usually consider having children in their early thirties,

with less clout are considered "women's work," and jobs are devalued to the extent that they are performed by women (Parcel, Mueller, & Cuvelier, 1986). During the 1980s, this disparity was challenged by the "comparable worth" movement, which claims that women's work has been historically undervalued, and that women and men should receive equal pay for work that has equal, or comparable, worth.

A second cause of this gender-based income disparity has to do with the family. Both men and women have children, of course, but parenthood disadvantages mothers in the workplace much more than working fathers. Pregnancy, childbirth, and raising small children keep some younger women out of the labor force altogether at a time when men of the same age commonly make significant occupational gains. As a result, women workers have less job seniority than their male counter-

parts (Fuchs, 1986). Moreover, women who choose to have children may be reluctant or unable to maintain fast-paced jobs that demand evening and weekend work. Career mothers therefore may seek less demanding jobs that offer advantages such as a shorter commuting distance, flexible hours, and child-care services (Schwartz, 1989). The box examines a recent, controversial proposal intended to benefit corporate women.

The two factors noted so far—type of work and family responsibilities—account for roughly two-thirds of the earnings disparity between women and men. A third factor, then, which we can assume accounts for the remainder of the income gap, is simple discrimination against women (Pear, 1987). Because discrimination is illegal, it is often subtle, but it remains a major cause of economic disadvantage for working women (Benokraitis & Feagin, 1986). Corporate women, for example,

after corporations have invested almost a decade in training them. Paradoxically, when a corporate woman becomes a mother, her company typically pressures her to decide between the company and her family. But the choice is unfair because women usually want both career and family. Currently, however, many mothers end up leaving their careers; when that occurs, both the corporations and the women themselves lose out.

The solution to this problem, Schwartz suggests, is for corporations to develop two tracks for women executives, a "career track" and a "career and family track." Women who wish to put their careers first (even if they have children) should be identified early and given as much opportunity and encouragement as the best and most ambitious men.

"Career and family women"—the majority of women, in Schwartz's view—value their careers, but are

willing to forgo some professional advancement to care for their children. These women can make a significant contribution to a company, especially in the middle-management positions currently staffed with less successful men. Positions of moderate responsibility, with part-time, flex-time, or job-sharing options, allow women to combine career and childrearing. Women often bring much-needed creativity and enthusiasm to jobs traditionally held by male colleagues who have stalled in their careers. A "career and family" option would also allow mothers to return to the "career track" at a later time. In any case, such a program allows corporations to recover their investment from past training and gain future benefits from loyal workers whose personal needs are being met.

Schwartz's proposal generated much controversy. Some critics feared that creating a "mommy track"

would strengthen stereotypes holding that women have less attachment to careers, thereby undermining women's gains in the workplace. Because such a plan is unlikely to be applied to men, critics charge, it may reinforce the traditional notion that women are unsuitable for management. Thus, Schwartz's proposal may hurt rather than help corporate women.

Schwartz disagrees. Women, she claims, have demonstrated that they are the equal of men in any kind of work. About 40 percent of management positions are now held by women, so that corporations must give women more choice in the workplace. By doing so, careers and children will no longer be in conflict, and corporations will enjoy more productive and satisfied employees.

SOURCE: Felice N. Schwartz, "Management, Women, and the New Facts of Life," *Harvard Business Review*, Vol. 89, no. 1 (January–February 1989):65–76.

often encounter a "glass ceiling," a barrier that is not formally acknowledged in the company, but that nonetheless prevents women from rising beyond middle-management positions.

For several reasons, then, women earn less than men even within a single occupational category. As shown in Table 10–4, this disparity varies according to type of work, but in only one job classification do women earn more than 80 percent as much as men do.

Finally, perhaps because women typically outlive men, many Americans think that women own most of the country's wealth. Government statistics (calculated for 1982) reveal a different story: 53 percent of all Americans with $500,000 or more in assets were men, although widows were highly represented. Among people with more modest wealth ($100,000 or more in assets), 58 percent were men (U.S. Department of Labor, 1983; U.S. Bureau of the Census, 1985). More recently, *Forbes* magazine found only fifty-four women (13.5 percent) among the four hundred richest Americans in 1989 (Queenan, 1989).

Gender and Education

Women have traditionally been discouraged, and sometimes formally excluded, from higher education because advanced schooling was thought to be unnecessary for homemakers. In 1989, however, 54.2 percent of all college students were women, and women received 52.6 percent of all higher-education degrees awarded that year (Cohen & Croe, 1988; Kroc, 1989).

As noted earlier, men and women still tend to pursue different courses of study in college although less so than in the past. In 1970, for example, only 17 percent of the bachelor's degrees in natural sciences, computer science, and engineering were awarded to women; by 1987 the proportion had risen to 28 percent (U.S. Center for Education Statistics, 1989).

Women now enjoy more opportunities for postgraduate education, often a springboard to high-prestige jobs. Today, when all areas of study are counted, women earn as many master's degrees as men do. Furthermore, a growing number of women are pursuing programs that were until recently virtually all male. For example, in 1970 only a few hundred women received master's of business administration (M.B.A.) degrees; in 1980 the number reached 12,000 (25 percent of such degrees); by 1987, the number exceeded 22,000 (33 percent of M.B.A.s) (Kaufman, 1982; U.S. Center for Education Statistics, 1989).

However, men still outnumber women in many professional fields. In 1987, males received 64.8 percent of doctorates (although, in 1990, women earned 52 percent of all Ph.D.s in sociology). Men also received 59.8 percent of law degrees (LL.B. and J.D.), 69.2 percent of medical degrees (M.D.), and 76.0 percent of dental degrees (D.D.S. and D.M.D.) (U.S. Center for Education Statistics, 1989). In a culture that still defines high-paying professions (and the drive and competitiveness needed to succeed in them) as masculine, women may be discouraged from completing professional education after having enrolled (Fiorentine, 1987). Nonetheless, the proportion of women in professional schools and the professions is rising steadily.

Table 10–4 EARNINGS OF FULL-TIME AMERICAN WORKERS, BY SEX, 1989*

Selected Occupational Categories	Median Income (dollars)		Women's Income as a Percentage of Men's
	Men	Women	
Executives, administrators, and managers	$40,103	$24,589	61.3%
Professional specialties	$39,449	$27,933	70.8%
Technical workers	$31,371	$21,768	69.4%
Sales	$29,676	$16,057	54.1%
Precision production, craft, and repair workers	$26,499	$17,457	65.9%
Clerical and other administrative support workers	$25,138	$17,517	69.7%
Transportation workers	$23,612	$16,288	69.0%
Machine operators and tenders	$22,343	$14,463	64.7%
Service workers	$18,903	$11,669	61.7%
Farming, forestry, and fishing workers	$13,885	$11,305	81.4%
All occupations listed above	$27,430	$18,778	68.5%

* Workers aged 15 and over.

SOURCE: U.S. Bureau of the Census. *Money Income and Poverty Status in the United States 1989.* Washington, DC: U.S. Government Printing Office, 1990.

Gender and Politics

A century ago, virtually no women held elected office. Women were legally barred from voting in national elections in Canada until 1917, and in the United States until 1920. A few women were candidates for political office, however, even before they could vote. The Equal Rights Party supported Victoria Woodhull for the American presidency in 1872; perhaps it was a sign of the times that she spent election day in a New York City jail. Table 10–5 cites milestones in women's gradual movement into American politics.

Today, several thousand women serve as mayors of cities and towns across the United States, and tens of thousands more hold responsible administrative posts in the federal government (Mashek & Avery, 1983;

Table 10–5 SIGNIFICANT "FIRSTS" FOR WOMEN IN AMERICAN POLITICS

1872	First woman to run for the presidency (Victoria Woodhull) represents the Equal Rights Party.
1917	First woman elected to the House of Representatives (Jeannette Rankin of Montana).
1924	First women elected state governors (Nellie Tyloe Ross of Wyoming and Miriam Ferguson of Texas); both followed their husbands into office. First woman to have her name placed in nomination for the vice presidency at the convention of a major political party (Lena Jones Spring).
1931	First woman to serve in the Senate (Hattie Caraway of Arkansas); completed the term of her husband upon his death and was reelected in 1932.
1932	First woman appointed to a presidential cabinet (Frances Perkins, Secretary of Labor); as of 1990, only eight women have been so appointed.
1964	First woman to have her name placed in nomination for the presidency at the convention of a major political party (Margaret Chase Smith).
1972	First black woman to have her name placed in nomination for the presidency at the convention of a major political party (Shirley Chisholm).
1981	First woman appointed to the U.S. Supreme Court (Sandra Day O'Connor).
1984	First woman to be successfully nominated for the vice presidency (Geraldine Ferraro).
1988	First woman chief executive to be elected to consecutive third term (Madeleine Kunin, governor of Vermont).

SOURCE: Adapted from Sandra Salmans, "Women Ran for Office Before They Could Vote," *New York Times*, July 13, 1984, p. A 11.

Schreiner, 1984). Less change has occurred at the highest levels of politics, although a majority of Americans claim that they would support a woman for any office, including the presidency. In 1991, 3 of the 50 state governors were women (6 percent); in Congress, 29 of 435 members of the House of Representatives (6 percent) and 2 of 100 senators (2 percent) were women.

Minority Women

If minorities (see Chapter 9, "Race and Ethnicity") are socially disadvantaged, are minority women doubly so? Generally, yes. First, there is the disadvantage associated with race and ethnicity. For example, in 1989, black women working full time earned 90.1 percent as much as white women; for Hispanic women, the figure was 80.5 percent. Second, there is the obstacle associated with sex. Thus, black women earned 86.5 percent as much as black men, while Hispanic women earned about 86.2 percent as much as Hispanic men. When these disadvantages are combined, black women earned 62.6 percent as much as white men and Hispanic women earned 56.0 percent as much (U.S. Bureau of the Census, 1990).

The reduced income of minority women reflects their lower position on the occupational ladder in comparison to white women. Whenever the economy sags, as it has in the early 1990s, minority women are especially likely to experience declining income and unemployment.

Chapter 7 ("Social Stratification") explained that women are becoming a larger proportion of the American poor. In 1988, 51.7 percent of poor households were headed by women, in contrast to 5.1 percent headed by men. Poverty is especially dramatic among minority women. In 1989, about 25.4 percent of households headed by white women (with no husband present) were poor, compared to 46.5 percent of comparable black households and 47.5 percent among Hispanics.

Are Women a Minority?

In Chapter 9 ("Race and Ethnicity") a minority was defined as a category of people whose social disadvantage is linked to physical or cultural traits. In a patriarchal society, women must be considered to be a minority, since physical traits of sex result in various social barriers, as we have explained.

Even so, most white women do *not* think of themselves as a minority (Hacker, 1951; Lengermann & Wallace, 1985). This is partly because, more than racial and ethnic minorities, white women are part of families at the highest social levels. Yet, within every social class, women typically have less income, wealth, education, and power than men do. In fact, patriarchy makes women dependent for much of their social standing on men—first their fathers and later their husbands (Bernard, 1981).

Another reason many white women do not consider themselves as members of a minority is that they have been socialized to accept their situation as natural. A woman taught conventional ideas about gender believes that she should be deferential to men.

In sum, some women—especially the relatively privileged—may not think of themselves as part of a minority. Yet as a category of Americans, women have a distinctive identity that forces them to contend with numerous social barriers just as other minorities do.

THEORETICAL ANALYSIS OF GENDER

Each of sociology's major theoretical paradigms points to some of the significance of gender in American society.

Structural-Functional Analysis

The structural-functional paradigm views society as a complex system of many separate but integrated parts. In this approach, every social structure contributes to the overall operation of society.

As explained in Chapter 2 ("Culture"), the earliest hunting and gathering societies had limited ability to challenge biological facts and forces. Lacking effective birth control, women contended with frequent pregnancies and the related responsibilities of child care (Lengermann & Wallace, 1985). As a result, social norms encouraged women to center their lives around home and children. Likewise, based on their greater short-term strength, norms guided men to engage in capturing game and other tasks away from the home. The overall result was a sexual division of labor into feminine and masculine worlds.

As long as technology remains simple, the biological facts of sex and the cultural facts of gender are closely linked. This is not a matter of biological necessity but a cultural strategy that most preindustrial societies adopt to survive. Over many generations, the sex-based division of labor becomes institutionalized, built into the structure of society and taken for granted.

Industrial technology opens up a vastly greater range of cultural possibilities. The muscles of humans and other animals no longer serve as the primary sources of energy, so the physical strength of males loses much of its earlier significance. At the same time, the ability to control reproduction gives females greater choice in shaping their lives. Such societies can release considerable amounts of talent by eroding traditional conceptions of gender. Yet change comes slowly, especially if gender-based behavior is deeply embedded in social mores.

In addition, as Talcott Parsons (1951, 1954) has explained, gender differences make up a social fabric that integrates society—at least in its traditional form. Gender, Parsons claimed, defines a *complementary* set of roles that links males and females into family units that, in turn, support the operation of society. Women are charged with maintaining the internal cohesion of the family, managing the household, and taking primary responsibility for raising children; males connect the family to the larger world, primarily by participating in the labor force.

Parsons further argued that distinctive patterns of socialization prepare males and females to assume their respective adult roles. Both sexes learn their appropriate gender identity and acquire necessary skills and attitudes. Destined for the labor force, boys are taught to be rational, self-assured, and competitive—a complex of traits that Parsons described as *instrumental*. To prepare females for childrearing, their socialization stresses what Parsons called *expressive* qualities, such as emotional responsiveness and sensitivity to others.

Finally, according to Parsons, society encourages gender-linked behavior through various means of social control. This social guidance is partly internal: As people incorporate cultural definitions into their own identities, violations of gender norms give rise to guilt. It is also partly external, since the failure to display the personal traits appropriate to one's sex can lead to criticism from others. Further, society militates against gender deviance by conveying subtle and not-so-subtle messages that straying too far from accepted gender roles courts rejection by members of the opposite sex. In simple terms, women are likely to view nonmasculine men as sexually unattractive, while unfeminine women risk rejection by men.

Critical evaluation. Structural-functionalism highlights the traditional complementarity of gender roles. From this point of view, gender integrates society both structurally (in terms of what people do) and morally (in terms of what people believe).

However, this approach assumes a singular vision of society that is simply not shared by everyone. For example, many women have traditionally worked outside the home because of economic necessity. Also, critics charge, Parsons's analysis ignores personal strains and social costs produced by rigid, traditional gender roles (Giele, 1988). Finally, this analysis serves to legitimate the unequal status quo. Increasingly, as traditional norms and values have weakened, what Parsons saw as gender "complementarity" is seen as male "domination."

Social-Conflict Analysis

Focusing on the issue of power, social-conflict analysis suggests that gender has historically benefited men while subjecting women to prejudice and discrimination comparable to that experienced by racial and ethnic minorities (Hacker, 1951, 1974; Collins, 1971; Lengermann & Wallace, 1985). From this point of view, gender promotes not cohesion but tension and conflict as men seek to protect their privileges while women challenge the status quo. Traditional gender beliefs are viewed as sexist ideology that justifies "keeping women in their place." Patriarchy can persist only to the extent that men are believed to be innately superior and women are defined as less capable as workers or political leaders. In the home, patriarchy inhibits marital communication and contributes to violence against women (F. Klein, 1982).

As was noted in earlier chapters, the social-conflict paradigm draws heavily on the ideas of Karl Marx. Yet Marx was a product of his time insofar as his writings focused almost exclusively on men. His friend and collaborator Friedrich Engels, however, did explore the link between gender and social classes (1902; orig. 1884).

Engels suggested that the different activities of women and men in hunting and gathering societies had comparable importance. A successful hunt may have brought men great prestige but women were responsible for gathering most of the society's food in the form of vegetation (Leacock, 1978). As technological advances led to a productive surplus, however, social equality and communal sharing gave way to social classes based on the idea of private property. At this point, male power over females became pronounced. Surplus wealth fostered concern for heirs, to whom men would transmit

"Hire him. He's got great legs."

SEX DISCRIMINATION ISN'T FUNNY.
SUPPORT THE NATIONAL ORGANIZATION FOR WOMEN.
28 EAST 56 STREET N.Y.C. 10022

For generations, the evaluation of women in terms of physical appearance instead of job performance contributed to unequal occupational opportunities. By turning the tables, this educational poster helps people to see how grossly unfair this practice really is.

their property. This encouraged the creation of monogamous marriage and the family, so that men could identify their offspring, especially sons, and ensure that their wealth would be passed on to them. Within families, the lives of women became centered on bearing and rearing children.

Engels claimed that capitalism intensified male domination. First, capitalism created more wealth, which further empowered men as the owners of property, the heirs of property, and the primary wage earners. Second, an expanding capitalist economy depended on defining people—especially women—as consumers and encouraging them to seek personal fulfillment through purchasing products. Third, to support males working in factories, females were assigned the task of maintaining the home. The double exploitation of capitalism, then, lies in paying low wages for male labor and *no* wages for female work (Eisenstein, 1979; Barry, 1983; Jagger, 1983; Vogel, 1983).

Social-conflict analysis holds that disadvantaged people will try to establish a more egalitarian social order. Thus, efforts to transform gender roles will materialize as political acts against an oppressive system. But as William Goode (1983) points out, men may be slow to recognize gender as a source of social conflict, resisting change simply because they see no inherent inequality between the sexes. Goode suggests that women, in their subordinate role, are well aware of the prejudice and discrimination linked to gender while men, as the dominant category, tend to view success or failure simply as a result of personal merit. Even men who acknowledge the plight of women may think that they themselves are not personally responsible for patriarchy. And because men are emotionally tied to women—as lovers, husbands, fathers, and sons—many view male dominance merely as protecting and providing; at worst, they consider themselves benevolent despots. For these reasons, Goode concludes, men may be hurt and confused by women's claims of being victimized.

Critical evaluation. Social-conflict analysis stresses the domination of society by males. This approach explains the growing criticism of conventional gender roles as a consequence of the inequality of the sexes.

Yet social-conflict analysis minimizes the extent to which males and females live together cooperatively in families. People who endorse traditional notions of gender may resist redefining as "political ideology" what they view as morality. Another problem with this approach is its assertion that capitalism stands at the root of gender stratification. As we shall see, even societies with socialist economic systems are strongly patriarchal.

FEMINISM

Feminism, *the advocacy of social equality for the sexes, in opposition to patriarchy and sexism,* is not new to America. As described at the beginning of this chapter, women opposed to slavery, including Elizabeth Cady Stanton and Lucretia Mott, began the "first wave" of feminism in the 1840s when they drew parallels between the oppression of African-Americans and the oppression of women (Randall, 1982). The primary objective of the women's movement at that time was securing the right to vote, but after suffrage for women was achieved in 1920, other disadvantages persisted. Thus, the "second wave" of feminism arose in the 1960s, and continues today.

Basic Feminist Ideas

Feminism links the personal experiences of women and men to the significance of gender. In feminist terms, how we think of ourselves (gender identity), how we act (gender roles), and our degree of privilege or deprivation relative to that of the opposite sex (gender stratification) are derived from the operation of our society.

Feminism is decidedly political and critical, challenging traditional ideas about the two sexes, insofar as they contribute to patriarchy. For example, our culture traditionally defines masculinity largely in terms of power over others. By contrast, femininity in our culture revolves around altruism—selflessly responding to the needs of other people, especially males. Feminism holds that examining, and ultimately rejecting, such values can lead to equal power and dignity for both sexes.

Feminists (both women and men) also pursue a "reintegration of humanity" (French, 1985:443). They argue that cultural conceptions of gender divide the full range of human qualities into two distinct and limited spheres: the male world of rationality and competition, and the female world of emotions and cooperation. Feminism disputes the assertion that masculine traits are inherently superior to feminine traits. Instead, feminists contend that every human being is capable of developing *all* these traits. Through a process of feminist resocialization, then, all people are promised the possibility of expressing the full range of their human potential.

Also critical of gender stratification, feminism seeks to end laws and cultural norms that limit the income, education, and occupational opportunities of women. Supporters of women's rights oppose the historical pattern by which the female half of the population has been subject to decisions made by the male half—whether in the privacy of the home or in the public world of national politics. For this reason, feminists support the Equal Rights Amendment (ERA) to the U.S. Constitution, which states simply:

More than a century after the women's movement in the United States began, a "second wave" of feminism sought to reduce gender-based inequality. Women's control of their own sexuality is widely viewed as crucial to these efforts. This accounts for the centrality of the abortion controversy to the women's movement in recent years. After declaring abortion to be a woman's choice in 1973, the Supreme Court stepped back in the 1989 Webster decision, supporting the ability of states to regulate that right.

Equality of rights under the law shall not be denied or abridged by the United States or any State on account of sex.

The ERA, first proposed in Congress in 1923, has the support of almost three-fourths of American adults although it has yet to become law (N.O.R.C., 1989:280).

Finally, feminists focus on human sexuality. In a patriarchal society, sexual relationships between men and women often mirror the male power structure in the larger society (Millet, 1970; J. Bernard, 1973; Dworkin, 1987). One reflection of women's inequality is the widespread pattern of sexual harassment. On college campuses, for example, as many as one-third of female students report unwanted sexual advances from their male teachers (Dziech & Weiner, 1984). Another survey found that about one-fourth of college women had been victims of rape—often what is commonly called *date rape*, in which a date is transformed into a violent crime, with the man forcing himself sexually on the woman (Sweet, 1985). Surveys of men and women in the workplace also indicate that a majority of both sexes believe sexual harassment constitutes a serious problem (Loy & Stewart, 1984).

More generally, feminism supports the right of females to control their own sexuality and reproduction. For this reason, feminists advocate the right of women to obtain birth control information—something that was illegal in some states as recently as the 1960s. In addition, most feminists support a woman's right to choose whether to bear children or to terminate a pregnancy. Feminism as an ideology does not favor abortion, but it holds that the decision to bear children should be made by women themselves rather than by men—such as husbands, physicians, or legislators. Many feminists also support gay peoples' drive to overcome prejudice and discrimination in a culture dominated by heterosexuality. Such social disadvantages are even greater for lesbians than for gay men because lesbians violate not only the cultural norm of heterosexuality, but also the norm that men should control the sexuality of women (Deckard, 1979; Barry, 1983; Jagger, 1983).

Variations within Feminism

Because the goal of sexual equality can be pursued in various ways, more than one kind of feminism exists today. Although the distinctions among them are not clear-cut, three general types of feminist thinking can be identified (Barry, 1983; Jagger, 1983; Stacey, 1983; Vogel, 1983).

Liberal feminism accepts the basic organization of American society but seeks to ensure that females have the same rights as males. Liberal feminism endorses the Equal Rights Amendment and stresses the need to eliminate the prejudice and discrimination that have historically limited women's opportunities. Those endorsing this approach support reproductive freedom for all women. While accepting the family as a central social institution, liberal feminism advocates the availability of maternity leave and child care for women who wish to work. It is striking that more than one hundred nations guarantee maternity leaves for all working women, but the United States has no such public policy (Hewlett, 1986).

Socialist feminism, based on the ideas of Karl Marx and Friedrich Engels, links patriarchy to the capitalist economic system. Thus, socialist feminists view the reforms sought by liberal feminism as necessary but insufficient. Only through a socialist revolution, these feminists claim, can women win equality with men. (Further discussion of socialism is found in Chapter 11, "Economics and Politics.")

Radical feminism endorses liberal feminist reforms but, like socialist feminism, considers them inadequate. According to radical feminists, even a socialist revolution would not end patriarchy. Instead, this variant of feminism claims gender equality can be realized only through the elimination of the cultural notion of gender itself. This does not mean, of course, that males and females will cease to differ biologically in terms of sex, but rather that culture should not define sex in terms that divide human capacities into masculine and feminine worlds. Radical feminists, then, seek a gender-free society.

Resistance to Feminism

Feminism has encountered resistance from both men and women who embrace the dominant cultural ideas about gender. Some men oppose feminism for the same reasons that many whites have historically opposed social equality for nonwhites: They do not want to lose privileges linked to their social position. Other men, including those who are neither rich nor powerful, distrust a social movement that challenges the traditional family and rejects time-honored male-female relationships. Further, for some men, feminism threatens an important basis of their status and self-respect: their masculinity. Men who have been socialized to value strength and dominance understandably feel threatened by the feminist notion that they can also be gentle and warm (Doyle, 1983).

Some women, as well, shy away from feminism. For example, women who center their lives around their husbands and children may consider feminism as a threat to their most cherished values. From this point of view, feminism amounts to an effort to revise the law, to change the workplace, to restructure marriage and childbearing—in short, to remake all of society—according to the radical political agenda of a few, tearing down the traditional values that have guided American life for centuries. Additionally, some women believe that demands for sexual equality threaten the conventional "feminine" spheres of life, including the home and the family, that have traditionally conferred power and personal identity on women (Marshall, 1985).

A final area of resistance to feminism involves *how* women's social standing should be improved. Although

Since the emergence of feminism in the United States, some people have feared sexual equality. As this 1869 Currier and Ives drawing suggests, males may fear the loss of privileges central to their masculine identity.

a large majority of Americans believe women should have equal rights, most also believe that women should advance individually, according to their abilities. In a national survey, 70 percent of American adults claimed that women should expect to get ahead on the basis of their own training and qualifications; only 10 percent thought women's rights groups represented the best approach (N.O.R.C., 1989:391).

GENDER IN THE TWENTY-FIRST CENTURY

Predictions about the future are, at best, informed speculation. Just as economists disagree about the likely inflation rate a year from now, sociologists differ in their views of the future state of our society. Yet we can venture some general observations about the future of gender in American society.

Recall, first, the position of American women more than a century ago. Husbands controlled property in marriage, women were barred from most areas of the labor force, and no woman could vote. Although women remain socially disadvantaged, the movement toward greater equality has been remarkable.

Many factors have contributed to this change. Perhaps most important, industrialization has both broadened the range of human activity and shifted the nature of work from physically demanding tasks that favored male strength to jobs that require human thought and imagination, placing the talents of men and women on an even footing. Additionally, medical technology has given us control over reproduction, so women's lives are less circumscribed by unwanted pregnancies.

Many women and men have also made deliberate efforts to lessen the power of patriarchy. Feminism seeks to end constraints imposed on people by a society that assigns activities and forms of self-expression simply on the basis of sex. As these efforts continue, the social changes in the twenty-first century may be even greater than those we have already witnessed.

In the midst of change, strong opposition to feminism persists. Gender still forms an important foundation of personal identity and of family life, and it is deeply woven into the moral fabric of America. We should expect, therefore, that attempts to change cultural ideas about the two sexes will continue to provoke considerable opposition.

On balance, while dramatic and radical change in American society's view of gender may not occur in the short run, the movement toward a society in which males and females enjoy equal rights and opportunities seems certain to gain strength.

SUMMARY

1. Sex is a biological concept; human beings are male or female from the moment of conception. People with the rare condition of hermaphroditism combine the biological traits of both sexes. Transsexuals are people who deliberately have their sex altered surgically.

2. Heterosexuality is the dominant sexual orientation in virtually every society in the world. Homosexuals make up a small proportion of the American population. Sexual orientation is not always clear-cut, however; some people are bisexual.

3. Gender involves human traits that a culture attaches to each sex. Gender varies historically and across cultures.

4. Some degree of patriarchy exists in every society. Male dominance has been defended by sexism, just as racial dominance has been defended by racism.

5. The socialization process links gender to personal identity (gender identity) and distinctive activities (gender roles). The major agents of socialization—family, peer groups, schools, and the mass media—reinforce cultural definitions of what is masculine and feminine.

6. Gender stratification entails numerous social disadvantages for women. Although most women are now in the paid labor force, a majority of working women hold clerical or service jobs. Unpaid housework also remains predominantly a feminine activity.

7. On the average, women earn about 69 percent as much as men do, for a number of reasons, including discrimination. This discrepancy has led to the demand for equal pay for work of equal worth.

8. Historically excluded from higher education, women now form a slight majority of all college students and receive half of all master's degrees. Most doctorates and professional degrees are still earned by men.

9. The number of women in politics has increased sharply in recent decades. Still, the vast majority of national elected officials are men.

10. Minority women have greater social disadvantages than white women. Overall, minority women earn only half as much as white men, and almost half the households headed by minority women are poor.

11. On the basis of their distinctive identity and social disadvantages, all women can be considered members of a social minority.

12. Structural-functional analysis suggests that distinctive roles for males and females constitute a survival strategy in preindustrial societies. In industrial societies, extensive gender inequality becomes dysfunctional, although long-established cultural norms related to gender change slowly. According to Talcott Parsons, complementary gender roles increase the social integration of the family.

13. Social-conflict analysis views gender as a dimension of social inequality and conflict. Friedrich Engels linked gender stratification to the development of private property. Engels claimed that capitalism increased male dominance by devaluing females as homemakers working for no pay.

14. Feminism supports the social equality of the sexes and actively opposes patriarchy and sexism. It challenges the cultural pattern of dividing human capabilities into masculine and feminine traits, and it seeks to eliminate the historical social disadvantages faced by females. Three types of feminism include liberal feminism, socialist feminism, and radical feminism.

15. Because gender distinctions stand at the core of American society, feminism has encountered strong resistance. Although two-thirds of Americans express support for the Equal Rights Amendment, this legislation—first proposed in Congress in 1923—has yet to become part of the U.S. Constitution.

KEY CONCEPTS

feminism the advocacy of social equality for the sexes, in opposition to patriarchy and sexism

gender human traits that are linked by culture to each sex

gender roles (sex roles) attitudes and activities that a culture links to each sex

gender stratification the unequal distribution of wealth, power, and privilege between the two sexes

hermaphrodite a human being with some combination of male and female internal and external genitalia

matriarchy a form of social organization in which females dominate males

patriarchy a form of social organization in which males dominate females

primary sex characteristics the genitals, used to reproduce the human species

secondary sex characteristics physical traits, other than the genitals, that distinguish physiologically mature males and females

sex the division of humanity into biological categories of male and female

sexism the belief that one sex is innately superior to the other

sexual orientation the manner in which people experience sexual arousal and achieve sexual pleasure

transsexuals people who feel they are one sex though biologically they are the other

Economics and Politics

Chapter Outline

In a joke making the rounds in the Soviet Union, Lenin (1870–1924)—the architect of Soviet socialism—returns to life, but in New York. Thinking he is in Moscow, he wanders around the streets of Manhattan eagerly seeking evidence of the fate of socialism. Seeing merchandise lavishly displayed in store windows, he exclaims with joy: "Wonderful! It's exactly the way I imagined it!" (cited in Watson, 1989).

This joke provides small comfort to residents of Moscow, where, in recent years, life has been difficult. Coal for heating homes is scarce in the wake of a miners' strike. Steam locomotives without fuel stand idle, delaying deliveries of food and other consumer goods. Many store shelves are empty, while some overflow with poorly made goods no one wants to buy.

The Soviet Union's deepening crisis has prompted Soviet President Mikhail Gorbachev to initiate a program of *perestroika*, or "restructuring" of his country's economic and political life. Although Gorbachev's ambitious plans may not succeed, Americans have warmly praised his approach, citing that it seems to mirror Western ways of doing things. Yet, Americans have their own woes in the 1990s: deepening economic recession, loss of competitiveness in world markets, and a population that seems indifferent to the political rights we have enjoyed for centuries.

This chapter, and the two that follow, explore **social institutions,** *major structural parts of society that address one or more basic activities.* This chapter examines the economy and the polity. Sociologists recognize that economics and politics lie at the core of social organization; some sociologists, especially Marxists, argue that these are the dominant institutions (Mills, 1956). First, we shall explore the character of the economy, with special attention to the Industrial Revolution and the growth of global corporations. Second, politics will command our attention, as we investigate the expansion and changing character of government. Both discussions provide insights into how and why socialist societies such as the Soviet Union are changing, and how their way of life differs from that of the United States.

THE ECONOMY: HISTORICAL OVERVIEW

The **economy** is *the institutionalized system for production, distribution, and consumption of goods and services.* The term *goods* refers to commodities ranging from necessities (such as food, clothing, and shelter) to luxury items (including automobiles and swimming pools). *Services* encompasses any activity that benefits others (consider the work of religious leaders, physicians, police officers, and telephone operators).

The complex economies of modern industrial societies grew out of centuries of technological innovation and social change. As Chapter 2 ("Culture") explained, early hunting and gathering societies were small nomadic groups that lived off the land—hunting game, gathering vegetation, and fashioning rudimentary clothing, tools, and shelters. Production, distribution, and consumption all took place within the bounds of kinship.

The Agricultural Revolution

Agriculture emerged as human inventiveness brought together plows and animal power. Ten to twenty times more productive than hunting and gathering societies, agrarian societies generate a significant surplus. Because producing food no longer consumes the time and energy of all, individuals assume specialized economic roles in permanent settlements, producing crafts, designing tools, and constructing dwellings. Trading networks increasingly link towns, exchanging food, animals, and other goods (Jacobs, 1970). These four factors—agricultural technology, productive specialization, permanent settlements, and trade—were the keys to a revolutionary expansion of the economy.

In agrarian societies, the economy becomes a social institution distinct from family life, although production usually occurs close to home. In medieval Europe, for instance, most people farmed the fields near their homes. People living in cities often worked at home, too—a pattern called *cottage industry*—producing goods sold in outdoor markets.

The Industrial Revolution

Beginning in mid-eighteenth-century England, industrialization introduced five revolutionary changes to the economies of Western societies.

1. **New forms of energy.** Since the earliest hunting and gathering societies, energy had been produced by the muscles of human beings and animals. At the dawn of industrialization in 1765, James Watt applied a steam engine to the production of material

The Industrial Revolution unleashed unprecedented productive power, leading to optimistic predictions that technology would greatly improve people's everyday lives. This 1897 lithograph, *The Triumph of Steam and Electricity*, celebrates the changes brought to English society by new sources of energy.

goods. Steam power surpassed muscle power one hundredfold, allowing the operation of many large machines.

2. **The spread of factories.** Steam-powered machinery soon made cottage industries obsolete. Factories—centralized workplaces separate from the home—sprang up rapidly. Although more productive, factory work was also impersonal compared to the close ties that had characterized family-based cottage industries.

3. **Manufacturing and mass production.** Before the Industrial Revolution, most work involved producing raw materials, such as wool and wood. The industrial economy shifted that focus to manufacturing raw materials into a wide range of salable products. For example, factories mass produced clothing from wool and furniture from lumber.

4. **Specialization.** A worker in a cottage industry fashioned a product from beginning to end based on skill acquired from years of apprenticeship. Factory work, however, was highly specialized; laborers repeated a single task, making a small contribution to the product. Factories raised productivity, but also lowered the skill level of the average worker (Warner & Low, 1947).

5. **Wage labor.** Instead of working for themselves or under the supervision of a member of the household, factory workers became wage laborers. This meant they sold their labor to strangers to whom they often mattered less than the machines they operated. Supervision became routine and intense.

The impact of the Industrial Revolution gradually rippled outward from the factories to transform society as a whole. Greater productivity steadily raised the standard of living as countless new products filled an expanding economy. Especially at the outset, these benefits were very unequally shared. Some factory owners made vast fortunes, while the majority of workers remained perilously close to poverty. Children worked in factories or deep in coal mines for pennies a day. Women factory workers were also among the lowest paid, as the box on page 258 explains.

The Postindustrial Society

Industrialization is an ongoing process. In Europe and North America, workers gradually organized into labor unions in opposition to factory owners. Governments also outlawed child labor, improved working conditions, and extended political rights to more of the population.

By the mid-twentieth century, America was becoming a **postindustrial economy,** in which *economic activity centers on service work and high technology.* Computerized machinery has reduced the role of human labor in production. Simultaneously, bureaucracy has expanded the ranks of clerical workers and managers. Service industries—such as public relations, advertising, banking, and sales—now employ most of the American labor force. The postindustrial era, then, is marked by workers moving from industrial production to service jobs.

Women in the Factories of Lowell, Massachusetts

The American textile industry began in 1822 in the Massachusetts town of Lowell—named for Francis Cabot Lowell, a descendant of two prominent Boston families, the Cabots and the Lowells—who brought plans for a textile factory from England.

About 75 percent of Lowell workers were women. The factory owners preferred women because, at $2 to $3 a week, they earned half the wages men did. In addition, prejudiced factory owners favored native New England women over male immigrants, who were also willing to work for low wages.

Factory recruiters drove wagons through the region, encouraging parents to send their daughters to learn skills and receive moral training in the factories. The offer appealed to many families that could not provide for their children; after all, the few occupations open to women at that time, such as teaching and household service, paid even less than factory work.

The Lowell factory provided dormitory-type housing and meals, at a

cost of one-third of a worker's wages. Women were subject to a curfew and, as a condition of employment, attended church regularly. Any morally questionable conduct (such as bringing men to their rooms) brought firm disciplinary action against offenders. These strict policies were imposed for more than moral reasons; closely supervised women had no opportunity to organize among themselves. Working almost thirteen hours a day,

six days a week, the Lowell employees had good reason to seek improvements in their working conditions. Yet any open criticism of the factory, or even the possession of "radical" literature, could cost a worker her job.

SOURCE: Based on Benita Eisler, *The Lowell Offering: Writings by New England Mill Women 1840–1845* (Philadelphia and New York: J. B. Lippincott Company, 1977).

The crucial postindustrial technology involves information. Computer technology stands at the center of an *information revolution*, generating a host of new, specialized occupations. Just as gaining technical skills was the key to success in the past, opportunity now depends on literacy skills.

The postindustrial society also changes the location of work. Industrialization initially centralized the workforce in factories; today, however, computers, facsimile (fax) machines, mobile cellular telephones, and other new forms of information technology allow workers to perform many jobs at home or even while driving in their cars. More educated and skilled workers also no

longer require—and often do not tolerate—close supervision.

Sectors of the Modern Economy

In the broad historical changes just described, we can see a shifting balance among three sectors of a society's economy. The **primary sector** refers to *the segment of the economy generating raw materials directly from the natural environment*. The primary sector, which includes agriculture, animal husbandry, fishing, forestry, and mining, predominates in preindustrial societies.

The **secondary sector** is *the segment of the economy that transforms raw materials into manufactured goods.* This sector gains prominence as societies industrialize. Such economic activity ranges from the refining of petroleum to the manufacture of metals into tools, building materials, and automobiles.

The **tertiary sector** makes up *the segment of the economy generating services rather than goods.* Accounting for only a tiny share of work in preindustrial economies, the tertiary sector grows with industrialization and becomes the dominant economic sector in postindustrial societies. Almost 65 percent of the American labor force is now employed in service occupations, including secretarial and clerical work and positions in food service, sales, law, advertising, and teaching.

COMPARATIVE ECONOMIC SYSTEMS

Two overarching economic models—capitalism and socialism—represent the two ends of a theoretical spectrum. Every real-world economy falls somewhere between the two.

Capitalism

Capitalism represents *an economic system in which natural resources and the means of producing goods and services are privately owned.* Ideally, a capitalist economy has three distinctive features.

1. **Private ownership of property.** A capitalist economy legally and morally supports the right of individuals to own almost anything. The more purely capitalist an economy is, the more widespread private ownership is, allowing private holdings of wealth-producing property such as factories, real estate, and natural resources.
2. **Pursuit of personal profit.** A capitalist society encourages the accumulation of private property and defines a self-centered, profit-minded orientation as a natural matter of "doing business." In practical terms, according to Scottish economist Adam Smith (1723–1790), when individuals adopt a selfish orientation, the entire society benefits from greater "wealth and prosperity" (1937:508; orig. 1776).

3. **Free competition and consumer sovereignty.** A purely capitalist economy would operate with no interference from government. The state thereby assumes a *laissez-faire* (a French expression meaning "to leave alone") approach to the marketplace. Adam Smith claimed that a freely competitive economy would regulate itself by the "invisible hand" of the laws of supply and demand.

   According to Smith, whose *Enquiry into the Nature and Causes of the Wealth of Nations* (1776) became the bible of the free-trade movement, the market system is dominated by consumers who select goods and services providing the greatest value. Producers compete with one another by offering the highest-quality goods and services at the lowest possible price. Thus, although motivated by personal gain, everyone benefits from more efficient production and ever-increasing value. Smith's time-honored assertion was that from narrow self-interest comes the greatest good for the greatest number of people. Government control of an economy would distort market forces, reducing producer motivation, diminishing the quality of goods produced, and short-changing consumers.

The United States is the leading capitalist society, yet even here the guiding hand of government plays an extensive role in economic affairs. Through various regulatory agencies, government policies affect what is produced, the quality and cost of products, what is imported and exported, and how the country develops or conserves natural resources. The federal government also owns and operates a host of productive organizations, which includes the Department of Housing and Urban Development (HUD) and the Nuclear Regulatory Commission (which conducts atomic research and produces nuclear materials). The entire American military apparatus is operated by the federal government as well. Federal officials may prevent the collapse of businesses, as in the "bailout" of Amtrak, the Chrysler Corporation, and the American savings and loan industry. In addition, the government sets minimum wage levels and safety standards for the workplace; antitrust regulations affect mergers of large corporations; price supports bolster particular agricultural crops; and payments in the form of Social Security, welfare, student loans, and veterans' benefits regularly benefit millions of Americans. Finally, federal, state, and local governments directly employ about 15 percent of the American labor force (U.S. Bureau of the Census, 1990).

Socialism

Socialism describes *an economic system in which natural resources and the means of producing goods and services are collectively owned*. In its ideal form, a socialist economy is antithetical to each of the three characteristics of capitalism just outlined. Here are the key elements of socialist economies.

1. **Collective ownership of property.** An economy is socialist to the extent that it limits the ownership of private property, especially that used in producing goods and services. The goal is to ensure that products such as housing go not just to those with the most money but to everyone.

   Karl Marx asserted that private ownership of productive property creates social classes and invariably generates an economic elite. Because socialist doctrine views the antagonism among social classes as a destructive force in society, socialism prevents class formation by forbidding the private ownership of property.

2. **Pursuit of collective goals.** The individualistic pursuit of profit is also at odds with the collective orientation of socialism. Cultural values and norms in socialist societies define what capitalists call the entrepreneurial spirit as antisocial.

3. **Government control of the economy.** Socialism rejects the idea that a free-market economy regulates itself. Instead of a laissez-faire approach, socialist societies place the economy under government control. Thus, socialism creates a *centrally controlled* economy.

   Socialism also rejects the notion that consumers drive capitalist production. Marx contended that consumers lack the information necessary to evaluate products and are manipulated by advertising to buy what is profitable to others rather than what they genuinely need. Commercial advertising thus plays little role in a socialist economy.

The People's Republic of China and some societies in Asia, Africa, and Latin America pattern their economies on the socialist ideal, placing almost all wealth-generating property under state control (Gregory & Stuart, 1985). Recently, the Soviet Union, the most powerful socialist society in the world, has begun to reshape its economy along free-market lines. Eastern European societies, under the political control of the Soviet Union since the end of World War II, were dra-

matically transformed during 1989. Breaking free of Soviet domination, these nations—including Poland, the German Democratic Republic (now part of a united Germany), Czechoslovakia, Hungary, Romania, and Bulgaria—have rapidly introduced capitalist elements into what had for decades been centrally controlled economies.

Socialism and Communism

Americans often mistakenly equate *socialism* with *communism*. An abstract goal of socialism, **communism** is *a hypothetical economic and political system in which all people have social equality*. In many socialist societies today, the dominant political party describes itself as communist, but nowhere has the communist goal been realized.

Why? For one thing, social stratification involves differences of power as well as wealth. Socialist societies have generally succeeded in reducing the disparity in material plenty only through expanding government bureaucracies, giving officials extensive power over the people. In the process, government has not "withered away" as Marx imagined. On the contrary, during this century political and bureaucratic elites have gained enormous power and privilege in socialist societies.

Marx would have been the first to agree that communism is a *utopia* (from Greek words meaning "not a place"). Yet Marx considered communism a worthy goal, and would probably have disparaged existing "Marxist" societies like the Soviet Union for falling far short of his communist ideal.

Democratic Socialism

Some Western European nations—including Great Britain, Sweden, and Italy—have merged socialist policies with capitalist economies through elections rather than revolution. The hybrid that emerged is called **democratic socialism,** *a political and economic system in which free elections coexist with a market system modified by government policies to minimize social inequality*. Under democratic socialism, the government owns some of the largest industries and services, such as transportation, public utilities, education, and health care. Private industry also exists, but it is subject to extensive regulation. High taxation (aimed especially at the rich) transfers wealth, in the form of welfare programs, to less advantaged members of society.

Relative Advantages of Capitalism and Socialism

Recent economic changes in the world have heightened debate over the relative advantages of capitalism and socialism. Assessing these economic models is difficult because nowhere do they exist in their pure states. Societies mix capitalism and socialism to varying degrees, and each has distinctive cultural attitudes toward work, unequal natural resources, different levels of technological development, and disparate patterns of trade (Gregory & Stuart, 1985). Despite these complicating factors, we can make some crude comparisons.

Table 11–1 on page 262 compares economic performance for a number of societies with predominantly capitalist or predominantly socialist economies. "Gross National Product" (GNP) is the total value of all goods and services produced annually by a nation's economy; by calculating "per capita" (or per person) GNP (dividing the total GNP by the total number of people), we can compare societies with unequal populations. Among societies with predominantly capitalist economies, Japan had the highest per capita GNP ($19,410), closely followed by the United States ($18,570) and the Federal German Republic (West Germany before unification in 1990) ($18,450). Greece had the lowest per capita GNP ($4,677). Taken together, the per capita GNP of these nine predominantly capitalist societies yields an unweighted average of $14,821 ("unweighted" means that the varying size of the countries is ignored). This figure roughly measures the value of goods and services produced per person in predominantly capitalist societies.

The productivity of capitalist societies is suggested by the consumer culture of central cities; the Ginza district of Tokyo is awash in commercial neon signs. Since social equality is a primary concern of socialist societies, "downtown" generally means government buildings rather than a central business district. In Moscow, the central location of Red Square and the Kremlin convey the unmistakable importance of government.

Table 11–1 ECONOMIC PERFORMANCE OF CAPITALIST AND SOCIALIST ECONOMIES, 1987

	Per Capita GNP (U.S. Dollars)
Predominantly Capitalist Economies	
Austria	15,440
Belgium	13,940
Canada	15,550
Federal Republic of Germany (West Germany)	18,450
France	15,620
Great Britain	11,730
Greece	4,677
Hong Kong	8,260
Japan	19,410
Sweden	15,630
United States	18,570
Unweighted average	14,821
Predominantly Socialist Economies	
Czechoslovakia	9,709
German Democratic Republic (East Germany)	11,860
Hungary	8,260
Poland	6,879
Soviet Union	8,662
Yugoslavia	2,580
Unweighted average	7,992

SOURCE: U.S. Arms Control and Disarmament Agency, *World Military Expenditures and Arms Transfers 1988* (Washington, DC: U.S. Government Printing Office, 1989).

Looking at primarily socialist nations, the German Democratic Republic (East Germany prior to unification) had the highest economic output per person ($11,860), while Yugoslavia had the lowest ($2,580). Overall, these socialist economies produced considerably less than their capitalist counterparts. The unweighted average is $7,992 or 56 percent of the figure for capitalist societies.

How wealth is distributed is also important in comparing capitalist and socialist economies. Table 11–2 shows income inequality in selected capitalist and socialist societies. The income ratios indicate how many times more income is received by highly paid people than is earned by poorly paid people.[1]

Of the five primarily capitalist societies listed in

[1] Specifically, income ratio is derived from dividing the 95th percentile income by the 5th percentile income.

Table 11–2, the United States had the greatest income inequality, with a rich person earning almost thirteen times more than a poor person. The income ratios of Canada (12.0) and Italy (11.2) are only slightly less. Both Sweden (5.5) and Great Britain (5.0) have much less income inequality because they incorporate socialist principles into traditionally capitalist economies. The unweighted average shows that a rich person earns more than nine times as much as a poor person in predominantly capitalist societies.

With an unweighted average of 4.5, primarily socialist societies have about half as much income inequality. This comparison of economic performance reveals that capitalist economies are more productive but generate greater social inequality; socialist economies, by contrast, produce greater social equality, but a lower overall standard of living.

As explained later in this chapter, economics and politics are closely linked. Capitalism depends on the freedom of producers and consumers to interact in a market setting without extensive interference from the state. Thus economic capitalism flourishes in a political environment that confers broad civil liberties and political freedom. Socialist governments strive to maximize economic and social equality. This requires considerable state intervention in the economy, limiting the personal liberty of citizens. Humanity has yet to resolve the time-

Table 11–2 DISTRIBUTION OF INCOME IN CAPITALIST AND SOCIALIST ECONOMIES

	Income Ratio
Predominantly Capitalist Economies	
United States (1968)	12.7
Canada (1971)	12.0
Italy (1969)	11.2
Sweden (1971)	5.5
Great Britain (1969)	5.0
Unweighted average	9.3
Predominantly Socialist Economies	
Soviet Union (1966)	5.7
Czechoslovakia (1965)	4.3
Hungary (1964)	4.0
Bulgaria (1963–1965)	3.8
Unweighted average	4.5

SOURCE: Adapted from P. J. D. Wiles, *Economic Institutions Compared* (New York: Halsted Press, 1977), as cited in Paul R. Gregory and Robert C. Stuart, *Comparative Economic Systems*, 2nd ed. (Boston: Houghton Mifflin, 1985), p. 503.

less tension between the goals of personal liberty and economic equality. With this in mind, we might well expect that Soviet and Eastern European efforts to expand market forces in the interest of greater liberty and productivity will produce greater inequality.

Perestroika

Economic reform throughout the socialist world accelerated after 1985 when Mikhail Gorbachev assumed leadership of the Soviet Union. His approach, popularly known as *perestroika* ("restructuring"), is a response to the poor performance of the Soviet economy. Decades of rigid centralized control and expanding bureaucracy have left the Soviet economy almost paralyzed with a standard of living substantially below that of nearly every Western society (Berger, 1986; Brzezinski, 1989; U.S. Bureau of the Census, 1989).

More than mere reform, *perestroika* actually constitutes a second socialist revolution. The Russian Revolution in 1917 deposed the aristocratic ruling class; Gorbachev has initiated the overthrow of the entrenched bureaucracy that has ruled the Soviet Union ever since. Supporters of *perestroika* criticize the rigid central administration of the Soviet economy for producing *plans* rather than *products*. Economic success has been defined as meeting the goals of bureaucrats, often ignoring the actual needs of the people. For this reason, Soviet goods have little value on world markets, while Soviet shoppers can find few desirable items on which to spend their earnings.

Economic restructuring has swept even more rapidly through Eastern Europe, where productivity has also been low. Restricted since the end of World War II to trading with the Soviet Union and among themselves, Eastern European nations now seek to broaden economic ties to attract foreign investment. Because of the stunning rate of change, the future of Eastern European *perestroika* cannot be predicted. Nevertheless, Eastern Europe is unlikely to ever return to the economic situation it faced at the beginning of the 1980s.

WORK IN THE POSTINDUSTRIAL ECONOMY

The economy of the United States has also changed dramatically during the last century. In 1989, 124 million

Table 11–3 PARTICIPATION IN THE LABOR FORCE BY SEX AND RACE, 1989

Category of the Population	In the Labor Force	
	Number (millions)	Percent
Males (aged 16 and over)	67.8	76.4
White	59.0	77.1
Black	6.7	71.0
Females (aged 16 and over)	56.0	57.4
White	47.4	57.2
Black	6.8	58.7

SOURCE: U.S. Bureau of Labor Statistics, *Employment and Earnings*, Vol. 37, No. 1 (January 1990), pp. 162–164.

people belonged to the labor force, representing two-thirds of Americans over the age of sixteen. As shown in Table 11–3, a larger proportion of American men (76.4 percent) than women (57.4 percent) held income-producing jobs. As noted in Chapter 10 ("Sex and Gender"), this gap has been narrowing. Among males, the proportion of blacks in the labor force (71.0 percent) is somewhat lower than the proportion of whites (77.1 percent); among women, a slightly greater share of blacks (58.7 percent) than whites (57.2 percent) are employed.

The Changing Workplace

In 1900, 40 percent of the American labor force engaged in farming. By 1991, this proportion had fallen to less than 3 percent. Figure 11–1 on page 264 illustrates this rapid decline, which reflects the diminished role of the primary sector in the American economy.

Industrialization swelled the ranks of blue-collar workers early in this century. By mid-century, however, a white-collar revolution carried a majority of Americans into service occupations. In 1990, more than two-thirds of employed Americans held white-collar jobs.

The growth of white-collar positions accounts for the widespread—if misleading—assessment of the United States as a middle-class society. As explained in Chapter 7 ("Social Stratification"), many so-called "white-collar" jobs actually fall into the category of low-paying "service work," including sales positions, clerical jobs, and health-care occupations. Such work yields little of the income and prestige of traditional white-collar occupations, and often provides fewer rewards than factory work. There-

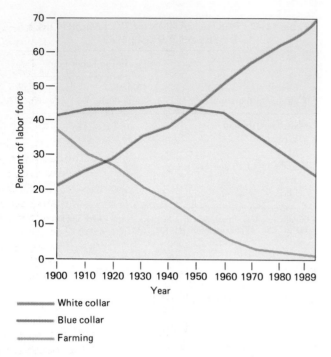

y-axis: Percent of labor force

x-axis: Year — 1900 1910 1920 1930 1940 1950 1960 1970 1980 1989

━━━━━ White collar

━━━━━ Blue collar

━━━━━ Farming

Figure 11–1 The Changing Pattern of Work in the United States, 1900–1989

(U.S. Bureau of the Census)

fore, an increasing proportion of work in postindustrial America generates only a modest standard of living.

Labor Unions

The changing American economy has been accompanied by a decline in **labor unions,** *organizations of workers that attempt to improve wages and working conditions through various strategies, including negotiations and strikes.* Membership in labor unions increased rapidly after 1935, encompassing more than one-third of non-farm workers after World War II. Union membership peaked during the 1970s at almost 25 million. Since then, it has steadily declined to about 14 percent of the non-farm labor force, or about 17 million men and women.

Proportionately fewer workers in the United States belong to unions than in other industrial societies. More than 90 percent of workers in Denmark and Sweden join unions, as do half in Great Britain and about one-third in Canada, Switzerland, and Japan.

This pattern stems from a decrease in the highly unionized industrial sector of the American economy. In addition, newly created service jobs are far less likely to be unionized. Unions still exert a great deal of power in the American workplace and in national politics. Yet, the erosion of union strength seems likely to continue (Goldfield, 1987).

Professions

Many kinds of work are commonly called *professional*; consider the professional exterminator or the professional tennis player. As distinct from the *amateur* (from Latin for "lover," meaning activity simply for the love of it), professionals pursue their task for a living.

More precisely, a **profession** is *a prestigious, white-collar occupation that requires extensive formal education.* Originally, some "professed vows" to become priests; other professionals entered medicine, the law, or academia. Today, several characteristics mark occupations deemed professional (Ritzer, 1972). One is theoretical knowledge of their field rather than mere technical training. Anyone can learn first aid, for example, but physicians claim a theoretical knowledge of human health. Second, the typical professional is self-employed, "in practice" rather than working for a business. Third, based on their extensive training, professionals claim authority over clients, and expect "lay people" to follow their direction. Fourth, professionals frequently assert that they serve clients and the community rather than merely seeking personal enrichment. Some professionals, including physicians, are even barred by professional codes from advertising.

Self-Employment

Self-employment, earning a living without working for a large organization, is an American tradition that has waned in recent years. From about 80 percent of the American labor force in 1800, self-employment now accounts for 8.2 percent of the labor force (9.9 percent of men and 6.2 percent of women) (U.S. Bureau of Labor Statistics, 1990).

Professionals have always been strongly represented among the self-employed because they possess valued education and skills. But most self-employed workers are small business owners, plumbers, carpenters, freelance writers, editors, artists, and long-distance truck drivers. Overall, the self-employed are more likely to hold blue-collar than white-collar jobs.

Unemployment

Some unemployment is found in every society. Few young people entering the labor force find a job immediately; some workers temporarily leave the labor force to seek a new job or because of a labor strike; others suffer from long-term illnesses; and still others who are illiterate or without skills cannot perform useful work. Unemployment is also caused by the economy itself. Jobs disappear due to recession, because occupations become obsolete, or because businesses close in the face of foreign competition. During the 1980s, for example, the decline of some American industries increased unemployment among blue-collar workers (Kasarda, 1983).

In 1989, 6.5 million Americans over the age of sixteen were unemployed—about 5 percent of the civilian labor force. In some regions of the United States, such as parts of West Virginia and New Mexico, unemployment may be twice the national average. Unemployment has generally declined since 1982, the year of the highest annual unemployment rate (9.7 percent) since the Great Depression ended in the early 1940s.

During the Great Depression, a time of catastrophic unemployment in the United States, Isaac Soyer painted *Employment Agency* to reveal the personal collapse and despair that can afflict men and women who are out of work.

Figure 11–2 shows the official unemployment rate for various categories of American workers in 1989 (U.S. Bureau of Labor Statistics, 1990). Black unemployment stood more than twice as high (11.4 percent) as white

Figure 11–2 Official Unemployment Rate among Various Categories of Americans, 1989
(*U.S. Bureau of Labor Statistics, 1990*)

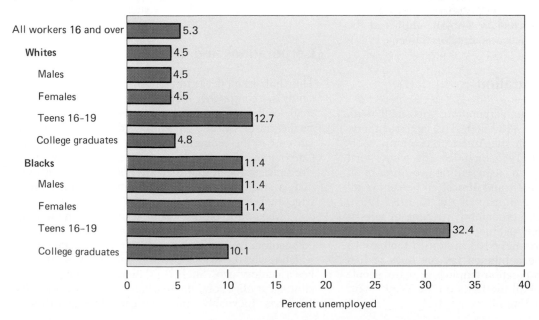

unemployment (4.5 percent), due to the historical concentration of blacks in jobs with less security (DiPrete, 1981). For both races, women's level of unemployment remained the same as men's during the 1980s; before that, women consistently faced higher unemployment than men. The economic recession of the early 1980s, which hit male-dominated blue-collar industrial jobs especially hard, explains why men now suffer from joblessness as much as women do.

CORPORATIONS

At the core of today's capitalist economy we find the **corporation,** *an organization with a legal existence including rights and liabilities apart from those of its members*. By incorporating, an organization becomes a legal entity with the power to enter into contracts and own property. Of perhaps 18 million businesses in the United States in the mid-1980s, 3.4 million were incorporated (*Statistics of Income Bulletin*, 1989).

The largest corporations are owned by millions of stockholders (including other corporations) rather than by single families. This dispersion of corporate ownership has spread wealth to some extent, making more Americans small-scale capitalists. Ralf Dahrendorf (1959) points out that the day-to-day operation of a corporation falls to white-collar executives who may or may not be major stockholders. In practice, however, a great deal of corporate stock is owned by a small number of the corporation's top executives and directors (Useem, 1980).

Economic Concentration

About half of American corporations are small, with assets totaling less than $100,000. The largest corporations, however, dominate the American economy. Corporations of record in 1985 included 281 whose total assets exceeded $1 billion, representing two-thirds of all American corporate assets and almost 70 percent of all corporate profits (U.S. Bureau of the Census, 1987). The largest American corporation in terms of sales is General Motors, which had income exceeding $120 billion in 1988; GM also has $163 billion in total assets. GM's sales equal the combined tax revenues of half the states, and the corporation employs as many people as the governments of all the states on the West Coast, including Alaska and Hawaii.

Conglomerates and Corporate Linkages

Economic concentration has created *conglomerates*, giant corporations composed of many smaller corporations. Conglomerates result when corporations enter new markets. That is, as corporations grow, they spawn new companies. More recently, corporate executives have favored "takeovers" of existing firms as a means of building companies. Beatrice Foods, for example, is a corporate "umbrella" encompassing more than fifty smaller companies that manufacture well-known products such as Redi-Whip, Wesson cooking oils, Peter Pan peanut butter, Hunt's foods, Tropicana fruit juices, La Choy Chinese foods, Orville Redenbacher popcorn, Max Factor cosmetics, Playtex clothing, and Samsonite luggage (Beatrice, 1985).

Another type of corporate linkage, the *interlocking directorate*, constitutes a social network of people who simultaneously serve on the boards of directors of many corporations (Marlios, 1975; Herman, 1981; Scott & Griff, 1985). These connections give corporations access to insider information that can be extremely valuable. Beth Mintz and Michael Schwartz (1981) found that General Motors is linked through board-of-director memberships to twenty-nine other major corporations. The members of these boards, in turn, serve on the boards of almost seven hundred other corporations. Although corporate linkages do not necessarily run contrary to the public interest, they certainly concentrate power and may encourage illegal activity such as price-fixing.

Corporations and Competition

The capitalist model assumes businesses operate independently in a competitive market. However, the *competitive sector* of the American economy is actually limited to smaller businesses and self-employed people. The corporate core of the economy forms a *noncompetitive sector*. Corporations do not truly compete because, first, extensive linkages mean that they are not independent. Second, a small number of corporations dominate many large markets.

Maximum profits would result from **monopoly,** *domination of a market by a single producer*. With no competitors, a company could simply dictate prices, which is why the federal government outlawed monopolies a century ago. Such legislation, however, has not eliminated **oligopoly,** *domination of a market by a few producers*. Inevitably, industrial capitalism gives rise to oligopoly. For example, to enter today's automobile market against the existing giants, a new manufacturer would have to invest billions of dollars. True competition means risk, which big business tries to avoid.

Ideally, capitalism supports minimal government intervention in the economy. But corporate power is now so great—and competition among corporations so limited—that government regulation is often the only means to protect the public interest. Yet paradoxes abound in the relationship between government and big business. The government is the single biggest customer of large corporations (Madsen, 1980). Washington also frequently intervenes to support struggling corporations, as in the savings and loan bailout of the late 1980s. Corporations and government typically work together to make the entire economy more stable and more profitable.

Corporations and the Global Economy

Corporations will soon account for most of the world's economic activity. The largest corporations—centered in the United States, Japan, and Western Europe—have spilled across national borders and now view the world as one vast marketplace.

As Chapter 8 ("Global Inequality") explained, multinationals are large corporations that produce and market products in many different nations. Beatrice Foods, for example, operates factories in thirty countries and sells products in more than one hundred. Corporations become multinational in order to make more money. Three-fourths of the world's people and most of the planet's resources are found in Third-World societies. Worldwide operations, then, offer raw materials, inexpensive labor, and vast markets. Developing a "global reach" also permits corporations to lower their tax liabilities and to move money from country to country, profiting from fluctuating currency values.

The effects of multinationals on poor societies of the Third World are controversial, as Chapter 8 explained in detail. Modernization theorists claim that multinationals unleash the great productivity of the capitalist economic system in the service of world economic development (Rostow, 1978; Madsen, 1980; Berger, 1986). Supporters of this approach argue that corporations offer poor societies needed employment in the secondary (manufacturing) and tertiary (service) sectors, as well as

The expansion of Western multinational corporations has changed patterns of consumption throughout the world, creating a "corporate culture" that is—for better or worse—undermining countless traditional ways of life.

capital and new technology that accelerates economic growth. Host countries gain short-term advantages, in the form of wages and taxes, and multinationals also stimulate long-term development by expanding the local economy with new products and services.

But many disagree. Critics claim that multinationals have intensified global inequality (Vaughan, 1978; Wallerstein, 1979; Delacroix & Ragin, 1981; Bergesen, 1983). Multinational investment, they argue, is mostly capital-intensive, actually creating few jobs. In fact, critics maintain, the tremendously powerful multinationals may actually inhibit the development of labor-intensive local industries, the real source of employment. Another charge leveled against multinationals is that they generally produce expensive consumer goods for export rather than food and other necessities that would bolster local communities. Critics conclude that multinationals make poor societies poorer and increasingly dependent on the rich societies of the capitalist First World. From this perspective, the growth of multinationals simply amounts to a new form of colonialism.

The emerging global economy also means that more of America is foreign-owned. In 1990, foreign corporations owned more property in the United States than American corporations owned abroad ("Buy America," 1989). Foreign investors now own half of commercial property in downtown Los Angeles, 40 percent in Houston, 35 percent in Minneapolis, and 25 percent in Manhattan (Selimuddin, 1989). This, together with growing industrial production overseas, is likely to further transform the American economy in the coming decade.

On the horizon, the economic forecast worldwide is emerging from trends in place today, as the national economies of the past increasingly are overshadowed by a global economic system.

POLITICS: HISTORICAL OVERVIEW

Closely related to economics is **politics,** *the institutionalized system by which a society distributes power and makes decisions.* Early in this century, Max Weber (1978; orig. 1921) defined **power** as *the ability to achieve desired ends despite resistance from others.*

History shows sheer force—physical or psychological coercion—to be the most basic form of power. No society can long exist, however, if power *only* derives from force, because people will break the rules at the first opportunity. Social organization, therefore, depends on building significant consensus about proper goals (cultural values) and the suitable means of attaining them (cultural norms). The key to social stability and justice, Weber argued, lies in **authority,** *power widely perceived as legitimate rather than coercive.* Authority is legitimated by the explicit or implicit acceptance of everyone to whom it applies.

According to Weber, preindustrial societies rely on **traditional authority,** *power legitimated by respect for long-established cultural patterns.* After it becomes woven into a society's collective memory, power may seem almost sacred. The power of Chinese emperors

All governments desire the stability that comes from the widespread perception of legitimacy. Even in Haiti, one of the most politically volatile countries in the world, leaders seek to convey a sense of security and confidence. Nonetheless, in many countries, governmental authority is often hard to distinguish from military power.

in antiquity was legitimated by tradition, as was the rule of nobility in medieval Europe. In both cases, hereditary family rule supported by tradition renders leaders almost godlike.

Traditional authority declines with industrialization. Royal families still exist in several European countries, but democratic forces have shifted power to commoners who are elected to office. Yet, Weber continued, the expansion of rational bureaucracy provides a distinctly modern means to legitimate power. Weber defined **rational-legal authority** (sometimes called *bureaucratic authority*) as *power legitimated by legally enacted rules and regulations*.

Rationally enacted rules underlie most authority in the United States today. The authority of political leaders now stems from offices in vast governmental organizations. In contrast to traditional authority, bureaucratic authority stresses not ascription but achievement. An officeholder presumably exercises rational-legal authority on the basis of talent and special training, not birth. A king's brother, for example, is a prince; but sisters and brothers of American presidents rarely attract much public notice, and exercise no authority unless they, too, hold office.

Weber described a final form of authority, one that has surfaced throughout human history. Chapter 12 ("Family and Religion") explores *charisma*, exceptional personal qualities that play an important role in many religious movements. Weber recognized **charismatic authority** as *power legitimated through extraordinary personal abilities that inspire devotion and obedience*. Unlike its traditional and rational-legal counterparts, charismatic authority depends little on a person's ancestry or office; it derives from the force of individual personality. Charisma sometimes enhances the power of traditional or rational-legal rulers. More commonly, however, charismatics lead people away from traditional customs and established organizations. The personal magnetism that draws people to charismatic leaders makes followers feel the charismatic gains strength from some higher power. This extraordinary trait characterized leaders from Jesus of Nazareth to Hitler to the Ayatollah Khomeini. As different as these three were, all preached an alternative to the status quo and inspired followers to transform the existing social order.

Because charismatic authority emanates from a single individual, Weber warned, charismatic movements are threatened by the eventual loss of their leader. Their survival depends on the **routinization of charisma,** *the transformation of charismatic authority into some combination of traditional and bureaucratic authority.* Christianity, for example, emerged from the personal charisma of Jesus of Nazareth. After the death of Jesus, the Roman Catholic Church gradually became established on a foundation of tradition and bureaucracy. Such a routinization of charisma is by no means certain, however. Most charismatic movements disintegrate when the inspirational leader dies or moves on. The nineteenth-century Christian sect in the Oneida region of upstate New York, founded by the charismatic clergyman John Humphrey Noyes, declined soon after its aging leader left the community.

GOVERNMENT AND POLITICAL SYSTEMS

Government refers to *formal organization that directs a society's political life.* The governments of the world's 175 different nations differ in countless ways. Yet virtually all bear a close resemblance to one of four political systems.

Monarchy

Monarchy is *a type of political system in which power is passed from generation to generation within a single family.* Monarchy has a long history: The Bible, for example, tells of great kings such as David and Solomon; British monarchs trace their ancestry through centuries of nobility. In terms of Weber's analysis, monarchy is legitimated by tradition.

During the medieval era, *absolute monarchy*, in which hereditary rulers claimed a virtual monopoly of power based on divine right, flourished from England to China. Monarchs in some nations—including Saudi Arabia—still exercise virtually absolute power over their people. During this century, however, elected officials have gradually replaced hereditary nobility. In those European societies where royal families still exist—including Great Britain, Spain, Norway, Sweden, Belgium, Denmark, and the Netherlands—they now preside over *constitutional monarchies*, in which monarchs are merely symbolic heads of state. Actual governing is now the responsibility of elected officials, led by a prime minister, and guided by a constitution. In these nations, then, the nobility may reign, but elected officials rule (Roskin, 1982).

Democracy

Increasingly common in the modern world is **democracy,** *a political system in which power is exercised by the people as a whole.* In large and complex societies, individuals rarely participate directly in decision making. Instead, a system of *representative democracy* places authority in the hands of elected leaders who are accountable to the people.

Democratic political systems flourish in affluent, industrial societies (Hannan & Carroll, 1981). The highly specialized economies of these societies demand a literate populace, and a highly educated people generally reject traditional rulers in favor of the broader citizen participation that marks representative democracy. Additionally, in every industrial society, a wide range of formal organizations strive to advance their interests in the political arena. Thus, in contrast to the high concentration of power found in the absolute monarchies common to preindustrial societies, industrial societies have a more complex and diffuse political system.

The traditional legitimation of power in a monarchy gives way in democratic political systems to rational-legal patterns of authority. A rational election process places leaders in offices that provide authority only as defined by law. Thus democracy and rational-legal authority are linked just as monarchy and traditional authority are. In addition, democratic societies are extensively bureaucratic. Most of the almost 19 million Americans who operate federal, state, and local governments are not elected. Thus much decision making in nominally democratic societies is actually performed in an undemocratic way (Scaff, 1981; Edwards, 1985; Etzioni-Halevy, 1985).

Although their political systems differ, during most of this century both socialist and capitalist societies have claimed to provide democracy and freedom. The dramatic changes sweeping Eastern Europe and the Soviet Union, which began in 1989, lessened traditional differences between the two political camps and, as the box explains, highlighted two competing approaches to defining freedom.

Authoritarianism and Totalitarianism

Authoritarianism refers to *denying the majority participation in government.* No society involves all its citizens in the daily activities of government, and thus each is, to some degree, authoritarian. Truly authoritarian political systems take no interest in people's lives, and offer no legal means to remove leaders from office. The absolute monarchies that remain today are highly authoritarian, as are the more common military juntas (like the one in Chile) or the dictatorships that have ruled the Philippines, Haiti, and Panama.

More intense political control characterizes **totalitarianism,** *denying the majority participation in a government that extensively regulates people's lives.* Totalitarian governments have emerged only within the last century, as societies have developed the technological means to rigidly regulate the lives of citizens. The Nazi regime in Germany, finally crushed at the end of World War II, maintained control over its citizens through an extensive system of surveillance and terror. More recently, advanced electronic technology—especially computers for storing vast amounts of information—has increased the potential for government control and manipulation of a large population.

Although totalitarian governments may claim to represent the will of the people, the reverse is more accurate: They seek to bend people to the will of the government. Such governments exert *total* control, allowing no organized political opposition. Denying the populace the right to assemble for political purposes, totalitarian regimes thrive in an environment of social atomization. Beyond widespread repression of any opposition, these governments limit the access of citizens to information: In the Soviet Union, for example, the mass media have only recently begun to act independently of the government. Further, totalitarianism weakens the public by restricting access to items such as telephone directories, accurate city maps, and copying and facsimile machines. Totalitarian governments also encourage citizens to report the unpatriotic activities of others. After the government of the People's Republic of China overwhelmed the pro-democracy movement with a bloody show of force in Beijing's Tiananmen Square in 1989, leaders demanded that citizens report anyone—even family members—who had been involved in the movement.

Socialization in totalitarian societies is intensely political, seeking not just outward obedience but inward commitment to the system. In North Korea, one of the most totalitarian states in the modern world, political banners, pictures of leaders, and political messages over loudspeakers appear nearly everywhere to remind citizens that they owe total support to the state. In the aftermath of the pro-democracy movement, Chinese officials subjected students at the sixty-seven Beijing universities to mandatory political "refresher" courses. The mass media

The Meaning of Freedom: Changes in Eastern Europe

Underlying the changes in Eastern Europe are pivotal political and economic debates. As explained earlier in this chapter, the free-market principles of Western societies support a vision of political freedom as *personal liberty*. This means *freedom to* vote or otherwise act in one's own interest with minimal interference from the government. At the same time, capitalism fosters considerable inequality of wealth, which had prompted Eastern European societies to criticize their Western counterparts as neither free nor truly democratic because the rich impose their interests on others. Popular elections are unlikely to undermine the rule of the rich, according to this view, and thus such political rituals have little practical significance.

In contrast to the Western emphasis on personal liberty, Eastern European societies have traditionally pursued *freedom from* basic want, by seeking to provide every citizen with jobs, housing, education, and health care. This version of freedom requires establishing rough *economic equality* among all people. Eastern European societies with socialist economic systems were, until recently, undemocratic in that their people had no elec-

These lines, written on the Berlin Wall shortly after its opening at the end of 1989, reveal powerful causes of change in Eastern Europe: extensive political control by socialist governments coupled with a low standard of living. Yet the market-based conception of freedom embraced by Western nations may also come under fire from those who believe that political liberty depends on controlling the amount of economic inequality.

toral voice and no right to form opposition parties. But the benefits of equality were offered as justification for the extensive government involvement in the lives of all citizens.

Mikhail Gorbachev's restructuring of the Soviet Union opened the way for the people of Eastern Europe to

express widespread dissatisfaction with their political systems. Accompanying the introduction of market principles has been increased political pluralism—a number of parties competing for popular support—breaking the monopoly of power held by national communist parties since World War II. Some Westerners view this sweeping transformation as evidence of the collapse of socialism (Brzezinski, 1989). Others interpret these events as an evolution toward a political system that may meet human needs better than either the traditional Eastern or Western models.

The changes in Eastern Europe reveal the underlying incompatibility of political liberty and economic equality. Should these nations move toward Western-style political liberty and greater personal freedom, they will soon contend with greater economic inequality (as some, through individual initiative and drive, accumulate greater wealth than others). Should their governments continue to enforce economic equality, they will have to limit personal liberty. The debate over this dilemma rages among leaders in Poland, Romania, Czechoslovakia, and other Eastern European nations.

---

offer further support for totalitarian regimes by presenting only official versions of events (Arendt, 1958; Kornhauser, 1959; Friedrich & Brzezinski, 1965; Nisbet, 1966; Goldfarb, 1989). The bloody crackdown at Tiananmen Square, according to Chinese government reports, was merely a skirmish, sparked by attacks of "hooligan" and "counter-revolutionary" students on soldiers.

Totalitarian governments span the political spec-

trum from the far right (including Nazi Germany) to the far left (such as the People's Republic of China and Albania). Bear in mind that socialism (an economic system) is not synonymous with totalitarianism (a political system). Formal socialism does demand pervasive government involvement in everyday life. But democratic socialism—as it exists in Sweden or the United Kingdom—has operated successfully for decades. By contrast, some capitalist societies, such as Chile and South Africa, exercise sufficient control over the lives of most of their citizens to be considered totalitarian.

THE AMERICAN POLITICAL SYSTEM

The founding of the United States was a bold political experiment. Originally part of a colonial empire, Americans fought a war against Great Britain to gain political independence.

Early American leaders sought to replace the British monarchy with a democratic political system. The commitment of Americans to democratic principles has persisted, although our political system is now vastly larger and more complex. The American version of democracy is also distinctive, shaped by our particular history, economy, and cultural traditions.

Culture, Economics, and Politics

Americans have historically prized hardy individualists who seek success commensurate with their abilities and effort. The Bill of Rights, which guarantees freedom to act without undue government interference, politically embodies this American brand of individualism. Many Americans, no doubt, share the sentiment of nineteenth-century philosopher and poet Ralph Waldo Emerson: "The government that governs best is the government that governs least."

Yet few Americans would actually want to do away with government entirely because almost everyone thinks it is necessary for specific purposes, including national defense, education, and public law and order. As the United States has grown larger and more complex, our government has expanded dramatically, regardless of which political party was in power.

In 1789, the federal budget amounted to a mere $4.5 million; by 1988 the federal budget had passed the $1 trillion mark. Government has become so expensive that even our leaders have trouble grasping its scope. The late senator Everett Dirksen once quipped that members of Congress spend "a billion here and a billion there, pretty soon you're talking about a lot of money." The government workforce has also expanded greatly. During the early 1800s, the federal government employed only a few thousand people compared to more than 3 million today.

Growth of government has outstripped America's expansion in geographical size and population. Early in the nineteenth century, one federal civilian employee served every eighteen hundred Americans; today, the corresponding ratio is one government official for every seventy-nine people (U.S. Bureau of the Census, 1990). Even a century ago, the federal government's presence in most communities was limited to a post office. Now, universal education; civil rights legislation; safety standards that protect consumers and workers; expanded support for students, veterans, and the elderly; and a larger and more complex system of national defense mean that government—at the federal, state, and local levels—touches almost everyone's life (Devine, 1985). A majority of Americans also depend on government for at least part of their income (Caplow et al., 1982).

The Political Spectrum in America

Political labels—including "conservative," "liberal," and "middle-of-the-roader"—reflect an individual's attitudes on what is commonly called the *political spectrum*, ranging from extreme liberalism on the left to extreme conservatism on the right.

One cluster of political attitudes, called *economic issues*, deals with economic inequality. Economic liberals support an extensive role for government in the economy in the interest of limiting disparities of income and wealth. Economic conservatives seek to limit the role of government in the economy, allowing market forces freer reign.

Social issues comprise a second set of political attitudes, ranging from moral questions regarding abortion and the death penalty to the legal standing of minorities. Social liberals support equal rights and opportunities for all categories of Americans, view abortion as a matter of individual choice, and oppose the death penalty because it has been unfairly applied to minorities. Social conservatives support traditional social distinctions between the sexes, and oppose affirmative action and other "special programs" for minority groups. Social conservatives tend to condemn abortion as morally wrong and support the death penalty as a response to very serious crimes.

With regard to both kinds of issues, the Republican Party takes a more conservative stance while the Democratic Party follows a more liberal line. Yet each party has conservative and liberal wings, so that a liberal Republican and a conservative Democrat may share nearly identical views. Further, Republicans as well as Democrats favor extensive government—when it advances their aims. Liberal Democrats, for instance, support government guarantees of equal treatment for women through an Equal Rights Amendment (ERA) to the Constitution. Conservative Republicans, however, have long favored legislation prohibiting abortion.

With wealth to protect, well-to-do Americans tend to adopt a conservative approach to economic issues. Yet because of their extensive education and secure social standing, privileged Americans tend to take a liberal stand on social concerns. Americans of low social position with less education show the opposite pattern; they tend to express more liberal views on economic issues while supporting a socially conservative agenda. They seek more economic opportunity, but take pride in conforming to conventional cultural patterns (Nunn, Crocket, & Williams, 1978; Erikson, Luttbeg, & Tedin, 1980; Syzmanski, 1983; Humphries, 1984).

Blacks of any social standing are likely to be both economically and socially liberal and, for half a century, have been strongly Democratic. Hispanic Americans and Jews historically have also supported the Democratic Party. Since about 1950, however, ethnicity—although not race—appears to have declined as a force in American politics (Knoke & Felson, 1974).

Because many voice neither liberal nor conservative positions consistently, party identification is understandably weak among Americans. In this respect, the United States differs from European democracies where people generally adhere strongly to one political party (Wolfinger, Shapiro, & Greenstein, 1980). Table 11–4 shows the results of a national survey of party identification among American adults (N.O.R.C., 1989). About 45 percent identified themselves—to some degree—as Democrats and about 40 percent as Republicans. Twelve percent claimed to be independents, expressing no preference for either major party. Although more than eight in ten do have a preference, most are not strongly committed to their party. In any election, then, Americans may swing from one party to the other.

Why this political vacillation? For one thing, the two major parties have much in common. Both support the capitalist economic system, a strong national defense, and the basic principles of the United States Constitution. Republicans as well as Democrats also favor some government intervention in the American economy.

Political parties in most other democracies represent a wider range of positions. In Great Britain, the Labour party (on the left) and the Conservative Party

Table 11–4 POLITICAL PARTY IDENTIFICATION IN THE UNITED STATES, 1989

Party Identification	Proportion of Respondents
Democrat	45.7%
Strong Democrat	15.2
Not very strong Democrat	21.8
Independent, close to Democrat	8.7
Republican	40.6
Strong Republican	11.4
Not very strong Republican	21.5
Independent, close to Republican	7.7
Independent	12.5
Other Party, No Response	1.2

SOURCE: N.O.R.C., *General Social Surveys, 1972–1989* (Chicago: National Opinion Research Center, 1989), p. 95.

(on the right) are further apart politically than are the two major parties in the United States. Sweden, the Netherlands, Switzerland, Belgium, and Israel each have more than two parties representing sizeable proportions of voters across a wide political spectrum (Roskin, 1982).

Special-Interest Groups

In 1989, President Bush proposed a tax-cut on capital gains—profits from the sale of investments—that he claimed would encourage economic growth. Wealthy Americans and people in the financial industry applauded this proposal, while organizations representing less affluent people denounced it as a giveaway for rich Americans that would increase the federal debt.

American political life encompasses many **special-interest groups,** *political alliances of people with an interest in a particular economic or social issue.* Special-interest groups flourish in nations like the United States where political parties are relatively weak (Burnham, 1983). Here we find a vast array of special-interest groups, representing businesses and professions, religions, recreational and leisure activities, as well as Americans of particular races and ethnicities. Special-interest groups employ thousands of *lobbyists* to present their concerns to political officials (Sheler, 1985).

The most powerful special-interest groups focus their lobbying efforts on economic issues. Tremendous wealth gives corporations vast power in the American political system. Although declining in influence, labor

During the 1980s Vietnam veterans organized into a special-interest group seeking belated recognition for their sacrifices in fighting an unpopular war.

unions retain the clout of 17 million American workers. Other special-interest groups offer opinions on social issues. Examples include the National Organization of Women (NOW), numerous consumer-protection organizations such as those headed by Ralph Nader, environmentalist groups like the Sierra Club, and the American Civil Liberties Union (ACLU).

Political action committees (PACs) are *organizations formed by special-interest groups, independent of political parties, to pursue political aims by raising and spending money.* Usually, political action committees raise money, which is then channeled directly to candidates likely to support their interests. There are now more than five thousand PACs in the United States (Federal Election Commission, 1989a).

As the cost of political campaigns skyrockets, political candidates increasingly court the financial support of political action committees. Between 1972 and 1987, fifty-one U.S. senators each received more than $1 million in PAC contributions. During the 1988 Congressional campaigns, PACs contributed $150 million—one-third of all money raised during that campaign (U.S. Federal Election Commission, 1989b). Because of the huge sums of money PACs inject into the American political process, controversy has swirled around them. Supporters maintain that PACs represent the interests of many Americans—whose businesses, unions, or churches provide financial support—thereby increasing political participation. Critics charge that organizations supplying cash to politicians expect to be treated favorably in return; PACs, in short, engage in buying political influence (Sabato, 1984).

Voter Apathy

Even as people around the world strive to gain a greater voice in government—sometimes at the cost of their lives—many Americans show a surprising indifference to their own political rights. Americans are less likely to vote today than they were a century ago. *Voter apathy* was recently found to be worse in the United States than in twenty-three other industrialized democracies (Harvard/ABC News Symposium, cited in Piven & Cloward, 1988). In the 1988 presidential election, only 57 percent of eligible voters went to the polls.

Who is and is not likely to vote? Historically, sex is significant. Women gained the right to vote only in 1920, and for decades afterward they voted in lower proportions than men. In 1988, however, women were slightly more likely to vote (58.3 percent of those eligible voted) than men (56.5 percent). The likelihood of voting also increases dramatically with age. Of eligible Americans between eighteen and twenty-four years of age in 1988, only 36.2 percent voted. By contrast, among Americans over sixty-five, 68.8 percent went to the polls. Voting was also higher among whites (59.1 percent) than among African-Americans (51.5 percent); Hispanic Americans (28.8 percent) were even less likely to vote. Some of this variation along racial and ethnic lines stems from greater voter apathy among people with lower incomes, less prestigious jobs, and less schooling (Wolfinger & Rosenstone, 1980; U.S. Bureau of the Census, 1989).

What accounts for apparent voter apathy? First, at any given time, millions of people are sick or otherwise disabled; millions more, who are out of town, make no arrangements to submit an absentee ballot. Second, many people forget to re-register after moving from one election district to another. Third, registration and voting require the ability to read and write, which may discourage tens of millions of functionally illiterate Americans.

Generally, conservatives see voter apathy as evidence of *indifference* to politics, suggesting that Americans are by and large content with their lives. Radicals counter that many Americans are deeply dissatisfied with society but doubt elections will significantly change anything for the better. From this perspective, voter apathy signifies *alienation* from politics. A third explanation holds that many people are apathetic because our two major parties have so much in common. If the parties represented a wider spectrum of political opinion, some suggest, Americans would have more incentive to vote (Zipp & Smith, 1982; Zipp, 1985).

THEORETICAL ANALYSIS OF POLITICS

Sociologists and political scientists have long debated the basic questions of politics: How is power distributed? Who makes decisions? In whose interest are they made?

Political power is one of the most difficult topics of scientific inquiry. Decision making is complex, and often occurs informally behind closed doors. Rarely do decision makers welcome the scrutiny of social scientists. Moreover, as Plato recognized more than two thousand years ago, theories about power are difficult to separate from the beliefs and interests of social thinkers themselves. This dynamic mix of research and political debate has produced two competing models of power in the United States.

The Pluralist Model: A Structural-Functional View

The first approach, related to the structural-functional paradigm, sees politics as a system responding to various constituencies in a complex society. The **pluralist model,** then, is *an analysis of politics that views power as dispersed among many competing interest groups.*

Pluralists claim, first, that politics mediates an array of competing organizational interests. With limited resources, no group is likely to achieve all its goals. Organi-

zations, therefore, operate as *veto groups*, gaining some of their objectives while keeping their competitors from achieving all their goals. The political process, then, relies heavily on negotiating alliances and compromises that bridge differences among various interest groups so societal conflict is minimized and the public policies that emerge from the crucible of politics have wide support (Dahl, 1961, 1982).

In the pluralists' view, power is dispersed widely through American society. Studying the power structure of New Haven, Connecticut, Nelson Polsby (1959) found that key decisions involving urban renewal, nominations of political candidates, and the educational system were made by different groups. Polsby also noted that few members of the New Haven upper class—people listed in that city's *Social Register*—held major positions of economic leadership. Thus, Polsby concluded that no one segment of society has a monopoly on power.

The pluralist model implies that American society is reasonably democratic, granting at least some power to everyone. Pluralists assert that not even the most influential Americans always get their way, and even the disadvantaged are able to band together to ensure that at least some of their political interests are addressed.

The Power-Elite Model: A Social-Conflict Analysis

A second approach, allied with the social-conflict paradigm in sociology, is the **power-elite model,** *an analysis of politics that views power as concentrated among the rich.*

C. Wright Mills (1956) introduced the term *power elite* into America's vocabulary, arguing that the upper class (described in Chapter 7, "Social Stratification") holds most of society's wealth, prestige, and power. The power elite are America's "super-rich"—a handful of families who forge alliances in corporate boardrooms and at the altar to perpetuate their privileges by dominating national politics.

The power elite has historically overseen the three major sectors of American society—the economy, the government, and the military. According to Mills, elites circulate from one sector to another, consolidating their power. Alexander Haig, for example, has held top positions in private business, was secretary of state under Ronald Reagan as well as a 1988 presidential candidate, and is a retired army general. A large majority of national political leaders enter public life from powerful and

Table 11–5 THE PLURALIST AND POWER-ELITE MODELS: A COMPARISON

	Pluralist Model	Power-Elite Model
How is power distributed in the United States?	Highly dispersed.	High concentrated.
How many centers of power exist?	Many, each with a limited scope.	Few, with power that extends to many areas.
How do centers of power relate to one another?	They represent different political interests and thus provide checks on one another.	They represent the same political interests and face little opposition.
What is the relation between power and the system of social stratification?	Some people have more power than others, but even minority groups can organize to gain power. Wealth, social prestige, and political office are rarely combined.	Most people have little power and the upper class dominates society. Wealth, social prestige, and political office are commonly combined.
What is the importance of voting?	Voting provides the public as a whole with a political voice.	Voting cannot create significant political change.
What, then, is the most accurate description of the American political system?	A pluralist democracy.	An oligarchy—rule by the wealthy few.

highly paid positions in private business—and return there later (Brownstein & Easton, 1983).

According to the power-elite model, the concentration of wealth and power in the hands of a few undermines claims of American democracy. Rejecting pluralist assertions that various centers of power serve as checks and balances on one another, the power-elite model suggests that those at the top encounter no real opposition.

Supporting the power-elite model, Robert and Helen Lynd (1937) studied Muncie, Indiana (which they called Middletown, to suggest that it was a typical American city). They concluded that members of a single family who had amassed a fortune from the manufacture of glass canning jars—the Balls—dominated most dimensions of city life. Thus the family name appeared on almost all the local institutions, including the bank, the college, the hospital, and the department store. The Balls financially involved themselves in dozens of other businesses and charities. At the local level, then, the power elite can constitute a single family.

Critical evaluation. The debate between pluralists and "elitists," summarized in Table 11–5, is unlikely to be resolved anytime soon, primarily because some evidence supports each analysis. Just as important, issues of this kind reach into deeply held political values.

The balance of research lends greater support to the power-elite model. Even Robert Dahl (1982)—one of the stalwart supporters of the pluralist model—has recently conceded that the marked disparity in American wealth, as well as the barriers to equal opportunity faced by minorities, are basic flaws in America's quest for a truly pluralist democracy. This does not mean that American politics lacks pluralism. But it does suggest that our political system falls short of the democratic ideal many Americans endorse. The right to vote is a pluralist achievement; yet major candidates usually support only those positions acceptable to the most powerful segments of American society (Bachrach & Baratz, 1970).

POWER BEYOND THE RULES

Politics always concerns disagreement about goals and the means to achieve them. Yet those engaging in political struggles generally play by the rules. The basic doctrine of the American political system is the Constitution and its twenty-six amendments. Other regulations guide each political official from the president to the county tax assessor. Sometimes, however, political activity spills beyond established standards.

Revolution

Revolution is *the overthrow of one political system to establish another.* In contrast to reform, which refers to change *within* a system, revolution implies change *of the system itself.* Reform may also involve conflict, but rarely violence. Even when one leader overthrows another—in a *coup d'état* (in French, literally "stroke of state")—violence is usually limited. Not so in the case of revolution. Although revolutionary change in Eastern Europe during 1989 occurred largely without bloodshed, the weeklong uprising against Romanian dictator Nicolae Ceausescu resulted in the deaths of thousands of citizens as soldiers fired on unarmed crowds.

No political system is immune to revolution; nor does revolution invariably produce any one kind of government. The American Revolution transformed colonial rule by the British monarchy into democratic government. French revolutionaries in 1789 also overthrew a monarch, only to set the stage for the return of monarchy in the person of Napoleon. In 1917, the Russian Revolution replaced monarchy with a socialist government guided by the ideas of Karl Marx. As recent events have shown, socialist societies too are vulnerable to demands for democratic reforms.

Despite these differences, revolutions have several common traits (Tocqueville, 1955, orig. 1856; Davies, 1962; Brinton, 1965; Skocpol, 1979; Lewis, 1984).

1. **Rising expectations.** Although common sense suggests that revolution is more likely under conditions of extreme deprivation, history shows that revolutions occur most often when people's lives are improving. Rising expectations, rather than resignation, fuel revolutionary fervor.

2. **Unresponsive government.** Revolutionary zeal rises to the extent that a government is unable or unwilling to reform, especially when demands for change are made by powerful segments of society (Tilly, 1986). The Ceausescu regime in Romania, for example, defied popular demands for reforms in the weeks before it was toppled.

3. **Radical leadership by intellectuals.** The English philosopher Thomas Hobbes (1588–1679) pointed out that universities play a pivotal role in political rebellion. Students often lead political insurgencies, as they did in China's recent pro-democracy movement. By articulating principles in support of revolution, intellectuals define the ideology underlying calls for change.

4. **Establishing a new legitimacy.** The overthrow of an old political system does not ensure a revolution's long-term success. Some successful revolutionary movements, unified by hatred of the past regime, fall victim to division. A new government, formed in the wake of a revolution, must also guard against counterrevolution led by ousted leaders. For this reason, victorious forces in Romania, following a common pattern, quickly executed the deposed dictator.

Revolution, in and of itself, cannot be defined as good or bad; the full consequences of any such upheaval become evident only after many years pass. Revolutions have created many nations—including the United States and the Soviet Union—which went on to achieve world prominence. Following the revolutions in 1989, the nations of Eastern Europe remained unsettled as the 1990s began, their long-term development uncertain.

Terrorism

Terrorism constitutes *the use of violence or the threat of violence by an individual or group as a political strategy.* Like revolution, terrorism falls outside the rules of established political systems. Paul Johnson (1981) offers three insights about terrorism.

First, terrorism favors violence over legitimate political tactics. Terrorists reject standards of morality and human dignity recognized by nearly every culture. They also ignore (or are excluded from) established channels of political negotiation. Thus terrorism is often used by weaker groups as a way of paralyzing a stronger foe. For example, with a massive army on its border in 1990, the Iraqi leadership detained thousands of foreign nationals as a "human shield" to discourage an invasion.

Second, although terrorism can be used by any political system, it dovetails especially well with totalitarianism. Totalitarian regimes have the means and desire to sustain widespread fear and intimidation.

Charges of "terrorism" are often traded by nations in conflict in the absence of a declared war. To many Americans, the aggressive seizure of the American embassy in 1979 and the subsequent holding of its staff as hostages, were clear acts of terrorism by Iran. A different version of truth is vividly shown by these Iranian stamps—printed in English to be circulated around the world.

Third, extensive civil liberties make democratic societies vulnerable to terrorism. For this reason, the threat of terrorism has sometimes resulted in the suspension of civil liberties for some Americans. After the Japanese attack on Pearl Harbor at the outset of World War II, fears that Japanese Americans might engage in terrorism provoked a government decision to imprison more than one hundred thousand Japanese-American citizens for the duration of the war.

For all but nine months of the 1980s, somewhere in the world Americans were held hostage by terrorists. The immediate difficulty in responding to terrorism is identifying those responsible. Because terrorist groups often operate in the shadows, with no formal connection to any established state, targeting reprisals is frequently impossible. Yet, terrorism expert Brian Jenkins warns, the failure to respond "encourages other terrorist groups, who begin to realize that this can be a pretty cheap way to wage war on the United States" (cited in Whitaker, 1985:29). Then, too, a military reaction to terrorism may trigger more violence, and may also increase the risk of confrontation with other governments.

Terrorism is not limited to small organizations. Some nations engage in *state terrorism*, using violence against individuals or groups with or without support of law. In an act of state terrorism, French revolutionaries executed an estimated seventeen thousand people during

the "reign of terror" in 1789 (Stohl & Lopez, 1984). In Iraq, Saddam Hussein demonstrated how state power can be used to crush any political opposition. A further instance of state terrorism is the "death squads" used by various Latin American governments to intimidate their populations and eliminate political opponents.

WAR AND PEACE

The most critical issue political leaders face is **war,** *armed conflict among the people of various societies,* *formally initiated by their governments.* War is as old as humanity, but recent technological advances, which give us the capacity to destroy ourselves, make war a danger to the entire planet. **Peace** implies *the absence of war,* but not necessarily of all conflict.

Although Americans often think of war as extraordinary, it is global peace that has been rare during this century. Our own history includes nine major wars, which, as shown in Figure 11–3, resulted in the deaths of more than 1.3 million Americans and injury to many times that number (Vinovskis, 1989). Thousands of other Americans have died in undeclared wars and other military actions, in countries including the Dominican Republic, Lebanon, Grenada, and Panama.

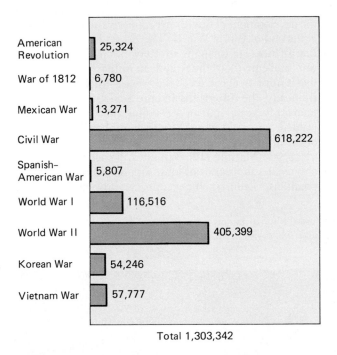

American Revolution	25,324
War of 1812	6,780
Mexican War	13,271
Civil War	618,222
Spanish-American War	5,807
World War I	116,516
World War II	405,399
Korean War	54,246
Vietnam War	57,777

Total 1,303,342

Figure 11–3 Deaths of Americans in Nine Major Wars
(*Compiled from various sources by Maris A. Vinovskis, 1989:37*)

Causes of War

Is war a "natural" part of the human condition? While some animals are naturally aggressive (Lorenz, 1966), research does not support the conclusion that human beings inevitably go to war under any particular circumstances. As Ashley Montagu (1976) observes, governments around the world must resort to considerable coercion to enlist the support of their people for wars.

Like other forms of social behavior, warfare is a product of society that varies in purpose and intensity from culture to culture. The Tasaday in the Philippines, among the most peace-loving of all societies, rarely resort to violence. In contrast, the Yanomämo, described in Chapter 2 ("Culture"), readily take up arms.

Under what circumstances *do* humans engage in war? Quincy Wright (1987) cites several factors that promote war.

1. **Perceived threats.** Societies mobilize in response to a perceived threat to their people, territory, or culture. The likelihood of war is increased to the extent that Americans, for example, define the Soviet Union as seeking to subvert our way of life.

2. **Social problems.** Internal problems may prompt a society to engage in aggressive action against its neighbors. Enemies, therefore, can be created as a form of scapegoating. In the People's Republic of China, for example, the lack of economic development has fueled hostility toward Vietnam, Tibet, and the Soviet Union.

3. **Political objectives.** War may be viewed as a desirable political strategy. Poor societies, such as Vietnam, have fought wars to end foreign domination. For powerful societies like the United States, a periodic "show of force" (such as the invasion of Panama or the Iraqi conflict) may win concessions from an opponent (Patchen, 1987).

4. **Moral objectives.** Rarely do nations claim to wage war simply for tangible rewards, such as territory or wealth. They infuse military campaigns with moral urgency, so that people fight to defend (or extend) compelling symbols, such as "freedom" of the "fatherland." Although few doubted that the 1990 American military deployment in Saudi Arabia was primarily about *oil*, President Bush portrayed the mission as halting a Hitler-like Saddam Hussein.

5. **The absence of alternatives.** Beyond Wright's list, a fifth factor promoting war is the lack of other means to resolve conflict. Mediation by the United Nations offers one alternative to war; Article 1 of its charter defines the UN's goal as "maintaining international peace." Despite some notable successes, however, the UN's ability to resolve tensions among self-interested nations has been limited.

Militarism and the Arms Race

Militarism costs more than human lives lost in warfare. Together, the world's nations spend more than $5 billion annually on military buildups. Although such expenditures, at least in part, may be justified, they divert resources from the desperate struggle for survival by millions of poor people throughout the world (see Chapter 8, "Global Inequality"). Assuming the will to do so, the resources currently spent on militarism are sufficient to eradicate global poverty. A large proportion of the world's scientists also engage in military research; this resource, too, is thus siphoned away from other activity that might benefit humanity.

Defense is the largest single category of American government expenditures, representing about 30 percent of all spending or about $300 billion in fiscal year 1990. Officials defend this sum—roughly $1200 for every man, woman, and child—as a reasonable cost for ensuring national security.

Much of the expenditure on munitions worldwide goes to the **arms race,** *a mutually reinforcing escalation of military power.* The modern arms race began with the development of nuclear weapons by the United States at the end of World War II. The Soviet Union's production of nuclear weapons in 1949 intensified the "cold war" and convinced the American military establishment that it must meet or exceed the Soviets' nuclear potential. Ironically, the Americans and the Soviets have, for more than forty years, pursued a policy that neither nation wanted nor could afford. The box probes the dynamics of the arms race.

Sam Marullo (1987) points out that the arms race also creates thousands of jobs, supports hundreds of corporations, stabilizes the economy, and stimulates re-

Although the coalition forces led by the United States fought the recent Gulf War largely for economic reasons, they justified the war primarily on moral grounds, portraying Iraqi leader Saddam Hussein as a modern-day Hitler.

The Arms Race: Is Security Enhanced?

Dwight D. Eisenhower, the retired general who became our nation's thirty-fourth president, reportedly asked Soviet leader Nikita Khrushchev why they each routinely approved higher and higher military expenditures. Eisenhower began:

Perhaps first I should tell you how it is with us. It's like this. My military leaders say, "Mr. President, we need such and such a sum for such and such a program." I say, "Sorry, we don't have the funds." They say, "We have reliable information that the Soviet Union has already allocated funds

for their own such program." So I give in. That's how they wring money out of me. Now tell me, how is it with you?

Khrushchev replied:

It's just the same. They say, "Comrade Khrushchev, look at this! The Americans are developing such and such a system." I tell them there's no money. So we discuss it some more, and I end up giving them the money they asked for.

Both governments assume that mili-

tary parity—at levels well beyond what is needed to destroy the other—enhances national security. Yet evidence suggests that the arms race, in which increasingly sophisticated missile systems are computer-driven and less subject to human control, may actually increase the possibility of war (Frei, 1988; Dedrick, 1990).

SOURCE: Quotation from Clayton Fritchey, syndicated column, June 16, 1973, cited in James MacGregor Burns, J. W. Peltason, and Thomas E. Cronin, *Government by the People*, 13th ed. (Englewood Cliffs, NJ: Prentice Hall, 1987), p. 473.

---

search that frequently leads to new civilian products. Yet, he wonders if the enormous resources devoted to the arms race would be more beneficial to Americans if invested in conventional industries.

C. Wright Mills (1956, 1958) claims that the arms race benefits the power elite. Drawing on the ideas of Karl Marx, Mills suggests that expanding the military-industrial complex produces vast profits for the small number of capitalists who control the economy. A related charge against militarism points up its propensity to undermine democracy. In his final speech as president in 1961, Dwight Eisenhower warned of the increasing power of the **military-industrial complex,** *the close association between the government, the military, and defense industries.* Echoing the sentiments of C. Wright Mills, Eisenhower claimed that a corporate and military establishment had acquired enormous power and was less and less responsive to the American people.

Nuclear Weapons and War

Humanity has produced an estimated fifty thousand nuclear weapons, representing a destructive power equivalent to five tons of TNT for every person on the planet.

Should even a significant fraction of this arsenal be consumed in war, life as we know it will cease on much of the earth. Nuclear weapons are also becoming more deadly: Figure 11–4 on page 282 shows that the relatively small warhead of an MX missile can destroy sixty times the area leveled by the primitive atomic bomb used by the United States against the Japanese city of Hiroshima in 1945. Albert Einstein, whose genius contributed to the development of nuclear weapons, reflected, "The unleashed power of the atom has changed everything save our modes of thinking, and we thus drift toward unparalleled catastrophe."

At present, most nuclear weapons are held by the United States and the Soviet Union; three other nations—Great Britain, France, and the People's Republic of China—also have a substantial nuclear capability. The danger of catastrophic war is increasing with *nuclear proliferation*, acquisition of nuclear weapons by more societies. Israel, India, Pakistan, and South Africa are believed to possess some nuclear weapons. Other nations (such as Argentina, Brazil, Iraq, and Libya) are in the process of developing them. By the end of this century, fifty nations may have the capacity to engage in nuclear war. Because many of these nations have histories of conflict with neighboring states, nuclear proliferation places the entire world at risk (Spector, 1988).

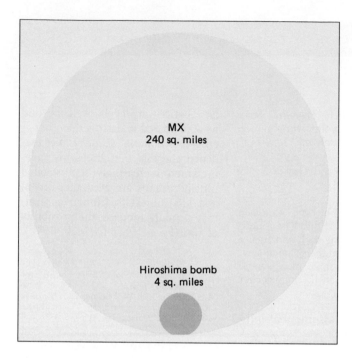

MX
240 sq. miles

Hiroshima bomb
4 sq. miles

Figure 11–4 Area of Destruction: MX Missile Compared with Hiroshima Bomb

The Pursuit of Peace

How can the world reduce the dangers of nuclear war? Several approaches have been advanced.

1. **Maintaining the status quo.** The logic of the present arms race holds that security derives from a balance of terror between the superpowers. Thus a principle of *mutually assured destruction* (MAD) demands that either superpower launching a first strike against the other sustain massive retaliation. This policy of deterrence has kept the peace for forty years; yet it has two major flaws. First, by encouraging the arms race, deterrence burdens the economies of the United States and the Soviet Union. Second, deterrence cannot control nuclear proliferation, which poses a growing threat to peace.

2. **High-technology defense.** If technology created the threat of war, perhaps it can also save us. This is the idea behind the *strategic defense initiative*

(SDI), proposed by the Reagan administration. The complex SDI plan calls for satellites and ground installations that would create a protective shield against enemy attack. Missiles would be detected soon after launch and destroyed by lasers and particle beams before reentering the atmosphere. If perfected, advocates argue, the "star wars" defense would render nuclear weapons obsolete.

This proposal has provoked tremendous controversy. Some claim that such a program, even after years and trillions of dollars, would produce at best a leaky umbrella. Just as serious, the Soviets argue that SDI constitutes an offensive system that could assist an American first strike. Thus its development would almost certainly prompt the Soviets to devise countermeasures, launching another costly round in the arms race (Kurtz, 1988).

3. **Diplomacy and disarmament.** This approach views the problem of achieving peace as diplomatic rather than technological (Dedrick & Yinger, 1990). Diplomacy has the appeal of achieving security through reducing rather than increasing weapons stockpiles. But disarmament has its own dangers. No nation wishes to become vulnerable by reducing its defenses. Successful diplomacy, then, depends not on "soft" concession-making or "hard" demands, but on all parties sharing responsibility for a common problem (Fisher & Ury, 1988). The rising costs of the arms race, the pressing domestic social problems of the two superpowers, and their warming relations in recent years offer hope for some disarmament during the 1990s.

4. **Resolving underlying conflict.** In the end, reducing the dangers of war may depend on resolving the issues that have fueled the arms race. Even in the "post–cold war" era, heralded by superpower leaders, basic political differences between the United States and the Soviet Union will remain. Tensions also erupt in regions like Latin America, Africa, Asia, and especially, the Middle East; these may embroil other nations in a larger conflict. Why, then, does the world spend 3,000 times as much money on militarism as it does on peacekeeping (Sivard, 1988)?

The danger of war remains great: We face vast stockpiles of weapons, proliferating nuclear technology, and powerful military establishments at home. The forces working for peace and stability are also great, however, from organizations such as the United Nations, to expanding international trade (multinationals have a vested interest in maintaining international stability), and improving superpower relations. Perhaps most crucial is the growing realization that human technological progress demands nonviolent solutions to the age-old problem of war.

SUMMARY

Economics

1. The economy is the institutional means by which goods and services are produced, distributed, and consumed.

2. Industrialization sparks economic expansion with new sources of energy, specialization, and mass production. Postindustrial economies shift production from goods to services.

3. The primary sector of the economy, generating raw materials, dominates preindustrial societies. The secondary, manufacturing sector prevails in industrial societies. The tertiary service sector has the greatest importance in postindustrial societies.

4. Capitalism is based on private ownership of productive property and the pursuit of personal profit in a competitive marketplace. Socialism is based on collective ownership of productive property and the pursuit of collective well-being through government control of the economy.

5. Capitalism is highly productive, creating a high overall standard of living. Socialist economies are less productive but generate more economic equality.

6. Agricultural work has sharply declined in the United States during this century. Today, only one-fourth of the labor force remains in blue-collar jobs. About two-thirds of American workers hold white-collar service jobs.

7. A profession is a special category of white-collar work based on theoretical knowledge, occupational autonomy, authority over clients, and an orientation toward community service.

8. Today, 8 percent of Americans are self-employed. Most self-employed workers have blue-collar occupations.

9. Corporations stand at the core of the American economy. The largest corporations, which are conglomerates, account for most corporate assets and profits.

10. Multinational corporations have grown in number and size during this century. The consequences for global economic development are a matter of continuing controversy.

Politics

1. Politics is the institutional organization of power in society. Political leaders seek legitimacy, transforming power into authority through tradition, rationally enacted rules and regulations, and personal charisma.

2. Monarchy based on traditional authority has been common in preindustrial societies. Although constitutional monarchies persist in some industrial nations, industrialization tends to increase democracy.

3. Authoritarian political systems deny popular participation in government. Totalitarian political systems do so as well, but seek additionally to control people's everyday lives.

4. The United States has two major political parties: the more conservative Republican Party and the more liberal Democratic Party. The political spectrum—from extreme liberalism on the left to extreme conservatism on the right—spans both economic and social issues. Economic issues deal with the degree of government regulation of the economy; social issues focus on the rights and opportunities of all segments of the population.

5. Special-interest groups advance the political aims of specific segments of the population. They make use of lobbyists and political action committees to raise money to fund campaigns.

6. Most Americans are weakly affiliated with one political party. Only about half of those eligible actually vote.

7. The pluralist model views political power as widely dispersed; the power-elite model claims that politi-

cal power is concentrated in the hands of a small, wealthy segment of American society.

8. Political revolution radically transforms a political system. Political revolutions have created diverse political systems.

9. Terrorism employs violence in pursuit of political aims. Although attention has long focused on group

terrorism, state terrorism is potentially more powerful.

10. War is armed conflict between governments. The development of nuclear weapons, and their proliferation, has increased the danger of global catastrophe.

KEY CONCEPTS

Economics

capitalism an economic system in which natural resources and the means of producing goods and services are privately owned

communism a hypothetical economic and political system in which all people have social equality

corporation an organization with a legal existence including rights and liabilities apart from those of its members

democratic socialism a political and economic system in which free elections coexist with a market system modified by government policies to minimize social inequality

economy the institutionalized system for production, distribution, and consumption of goods and services

labor unions organizations of workers that attempt to improve wages and working conditions through various strategies, including negotiations and strikes

monopoly domination of a market by a single producer

oligopoly domination of a market by a few producers

postindustrial economy economic activity centered on service work and high technology

primary sector the segment of the economy that generates raw materials directly from the natural environment

profession a prestigious, white-collar occupation that requires extensive formal education

secondary sector the segment of the economy that transforms raw materials into manufactured goods

social institution a major structural part of society, such as the family or the economy, that addresses one or more basic activities

socialism an economic system in which natural resources and the means of producing goods and services are collectively owned

tertiary sector the segment of the economy that generates services rather than goods

Politics

arms race a mutually reinforcing escalation of military power

authoritarianism denying the majority participation in government

authority power that is widely perceived as legitimate rather than coercive

charismatic authority power legitimated through extraordinary personal abilities that inspire devotion and obedience

democracy a type of political system in which power is exercised by the people as a whole

government formal organization that directs a society's political life

military-industrial complex the close association between the government, the military, and defense industries

monarchy a type of political system in which power is passed from generation to generation within a single family

peace the absence of war

pluralist model an analysis of politics that views power as dispersed among many competing interest groups

political action committee (PAC) an organization formed by a special-interest group, independent of political parties, to pursue specific aims by raising and spending money

politics the institutionalized system by which a society distributes power and makes decisions

power the ability to achieve desired ends despite resistance from others

power-elite model an analysis of politics that views power as concentrated among the rich

rational-legal authority (bureaucratic authority) power legitimated by legally enacted rules and regulations

revolution the overthrow of one political system to establish another

routinization of charisma the transformation of charis-matic authority into some combination of traditional and bureaucratic authority

special-interest group a political alliance of people with an interest in a particular economic or social issue

terrorism the use of violence or the threat of violence by an individual or group as a political strategy

totalitarianism denying the majority participation in a government that extensively regulates people's lives

traditional authority power that is legitimated through respect for long-established cultural patterns

war armed conflict among the people of various societies, formally initiated by their governments

Faith Ringgold, *The Wedding: Lover's Quilt #1*, 1986. Oil on canvas, tie-dyed, printed, pieced fabric. 77½ x 58″. Collection of Marilyn Lanfear, Texas; Photographs courtesy Bernice Steinbaum Gallery, New York City.

Family and Religion

Chapter Outline

Marriage and the family, in the words of Johann Wolfgang von Goethe, the German novelist, are "the beginning and the end of all culture." From the historian's point of view, Goethe's notable assertion would seem quite true, since human societies have always been organized around some type of family. Similarly, the family is a basic social unit in every society in the world today.

Another thoughtful observer of the social world, English historian Arnold J. Toynbee, declared that "All civilizations are based on religion." Like the family, some form of religion appears to be a universal element of human society, from our earliest nomadic ancestors clustering in remote sacred places to the religious appeals broadcast by satellite technology now heard the world over.

The family and religion have special significance to human societies as the prominent *symbolic institutions*. This means that both the family and religion are central to establishing morality, maintaining traditions, and binding people together into meaningful and durable social units.

Controversy also surrounds the family and religion today, with both prompting spirited debate and experiencing rapid change. Not long ago, Americans spoke of a traditional family—a working father, homemaker mother, with one or more children; today, only about one in ten American families fits this description. Although Americans still vow to remain married "till death do us part," divorce ends more marriages than death. Because of the prevalence of divorce, and the growing trend of women choosing to have children outside of marriage, half of all young Americans spend some time before their eighteenth birthday living with a single parent.

Similar changes have shaken the foundations of American religion. Membership in most traditional churches is falling, while controversial sects and cults flourish. In some respects, television has forever changed the face of religion, making many Americans wonder if preachers are more concerned with raising moral standards or raising cash.

In examining these two fundamental social institutions—the family and religion—we shall see how both are faring in the United States today, and make numerous comparisons to those institutions in other world societies.

THE FAMILY: BASIC CONCEPTS

Kinship refers to *social relationships based on blood, marriage, or adoption*. We designate kin with the shorthand term "relative," which means that much of our

In modern industrial societies, members of extended families usually do not live together. In fact, kinship is somewhat a matter of personal choice as people decide what relationship, if any, they wish to have with more distant family members. Commonly, however, extended families assemble for rituals such as weddings, funerals, and annual reunions.

social identity and many of our social roles are performed *relative* to these others. In small preindustrial societies, people depend on kin to meet most of their everyday needs. Kinship has somewhat less functional importance in industrial societies, as secondary groups play a wider role in everyday life.

The **family** is typically defined as *a relatively permanent social group of two or more people, who are related by blood, marriage, or adoption and who usually live together.* Families are commonly formed by **marriage,** *a socially approved relationship that is expected to be enduring, involving economic cooperation and allowing sexual activity leading to childbearing.* The expectation that marriage precedes procreation explains the traditional attachment of the label of *illegitimacy* to children born out of wedlock. This expectation is also evident in the word *matrimony,* with Latin roots meaning "the condition of motherhood." The norm linking childbearing to marriage is weakening, however, and the proportion of children born to unmarried women is increasing.

Few generalizations apply to every American family today. Some Americans object to limiting the use of the term "family" to married couples and children. For example, an unmarried couple and their children may think of themselves as a family, even if some Americans disapprove of this arrangement. Many gay male and lesbian couples, perhaps living with children of one or both partners, also consider themselves to be families. Some people, however, argue that because the family is central to American society, social approval should not be extended to any relationship simply because those involved wish to be defined as a family (Dedrick, 1990). Precisely what constitutes a family, then, is a matter of political debate. Courts have a part in this controversy, too: They have recognized the right of partners—married or not—to make claims on each other's property. Such rulings suggest that the concept of family—legally as well as socially—is taking on a broader meaning.

THE FAMILY: CULTURAL VARIATIONS

Although all societies recognize families, kinship varies significantly from culture to culture (Murdock, 1945). Preindustrial societies attach great importance to the **extended family,** *a social unit including parents, children, and other kin.* This is also called the *consanguine family,* meaning that it is based on blood ties. The onset of industrialization, described in Chapter 11 ("Economics and Politics"), encourages the **nuclear family,** *a social unit composed of one or, more commonly, two parents and children.* Typically based on marriage, the nuclear family is also known as the *conjugal family.*

Although many Americans live in extended families, the nuclear family predominates in the United States (Laslett, 1978; Degler, 1980). Industrialization promotes nuclear families; as productive work moves away from the home, children grow up to pursue their careers and form new families of their own. Both the geographical and social mobility that accompany industrialization tend to weaken extended families.

Marriage Patterns

Cultural norms, often in the form of law, regulate whom a person may marry. Marriage norms of one type, found in every society, promote **endogamy,** *marriage between people within a social group or category.* Such norms define as suitable marriage partners people of the same age, tribe, race, religion, or social class. A second type of marriage norms encourages **exogamy,** *marriage between people of different social groups or categories.* People are subject to both kinds of norms. The young person in a traditional Indian village, for example, must marry someone from the same caste category but from a different village. In most societies, people are expected to marry someone of their own social background, yet outside their own extended family.

In every industrial society, both law and cultural norms prescribe a form of marriage called **monogamy** (from the Greek meaning "one union"), *marriage involving one relationship between two partners.* In preindustrial societies, a more common marital pattern is **polygamy** ("many unions"), defined as *marriage that unites three or more people.* In polygamous marriage two or more nuclear families are combined to form an extended family.

Polygamy takes two forms. By far the more common is *polygyny* (Greek meaning "many women" or "many wives"), a form of marriage that joins one male with more than one female. Islamic societies in the Middle East and Africa, for example, allow men to have up to four wives. However, in societies that endorse this marital pattern, most families are nonetheless monogamous because great wealth is required to support several wives and even more children. *Polyandry* (from the Greek, meaning "many men" or "many husbands") unites one female with more than one male. Quite rare in our world, this pattern appears in only a few societies, including Tibetan Buddhists. Polyandry discourages the division of land into parcels too small to support a family and divides the burdensome costs of supporting a wife among many men. Polyandry has also been found in societies that engage in female infanticide, which reduces the female population so that men must share women.

Three-fourths of world societies endorse some form of marriage in addition to monogamy. Most marriages in the world are monogamous, however, partly because of the financial burden of multiple spouses and partly because the numerical parity of the sexes limits the possibility of polygamy (Murdock, 1965).

Residential Patterns

Families also differ with regard to residence. In preindustrial societies, newlyweds commonly reside with one set of parents, gaining economic security and protection in the process. *Patrilocality* (Greek for "place of the father") means that a married couple lives with or near the husband's family. Worldwide, this is the most common pattern (Murdock, 1965). *Matrilocality* (meaning "place of the mother") places a married couple with or near the wife's family. This pattern is rare, occurring where families define daughters as more valuable economic assets than sons (Ember & Ember, 1971, 1985). Industrial societies typically favor *neolocality* (Greek meaning "new place"), by which a married couple lives apart from the parents of both spouses.

Patterns of Descent

Descent refers to *the system by which kinship is traced over generations.* Preindustrial societies usually trace kinship only through one parent, meaning that just the father's or just the mother's ancestors are defined as relatives. The more common pattern is *patrilineal descent*, meaning kinship traced through males. In this pattern, property as well as social identity is passed across the generations from fathers to sons. Less common is *matrilineal descent*, kinship traced through women. Here, only the mother's side of the family is defined as kin, with property passing from mothers to daughters. Patrilineal descent is common among pastoral and agrarian societies, in which men produce the most valued resources. Matrilineal descent predominates in horticul-

tural societies, where women are often the primary breadwinners (Haviland, 1985).

Industrial societies recognize a pattern of *bilateral descent* ("two-sided descent"), kinship traced through both men and women. In this pattern, children count as relatives members of both parents' families.

Patterns of Authority

The predominance of polygyny, patrilocality, and patrilineal descent in the world reflects the universal presence of some degree of patriarchy, examined in Chapter 10 ("Sex and Gender"). Wives and mothers have considerable power in every society, but no record exists of a truly matriarchal society. In industrial societies such as the United States, men usually head households, just as they dominate most areas of social life. More egalitarian family patterns are gradually evolving, especially as increasing numbers of women enter the labor force. However, the social status of wives is still typically lower than that of husbands. Americans still prefer males as first children, and most children are given their father's last name.

THEORETICAL ANALYSIS OF THE FAMILY

The theoretical analyses used in earlier chapters can offer some keen insights when applied to the family.

Functions of the Family: Structural-Functional Analysis

The structural-functional paradigm suggests that the family has important social functions. Together, these consequences support the notion of the family as the backbone of society.

1. **Socialization.** As explained in Chapter 3 ("Socialization: From Infancy to Aging"), the family is the first and most influential agent of socialization. Ideally, families guide their children toward becoming well-integrated and contributing members of society (Parsons & Bales, 1955). Of course, family socialization continues throughout the life cy-

cle. Adults change within marriage, and, as any parent knows, mothers and fathers learn as much from their children as children learn from them.

2. **Regulation of sexual activity.** Because sex is the basis of human reproduction and economic inheritance, every culture restricts sexual behavior. One cultural universal is the **incest taboo,** *a cultural norm forbidding sexual relations or marriage between certain kin.* Precisely which kin are subject to the incest taboo varies from culture to culture. The Navajo, for example, forbid marrying any relative of one's mother. Americans apply the incest taboo to both sides of the family but limit it to close relatives, including parents, grandparents, siblings, aunts, and uncles. However, brother-sister marriages, condemned by Americans, were common among the ancient Egyptian, Incan, and Hawaiian nobility (Murdock, 1965).

Widespread sexual activity between close relatives may adversely affect the mental and physical well-being of offspring. But this does not explain why the incest taboo is observed by only one species of life: human beings. As Robert Murphy (1979) suggests, the incest taboo functions to maintain family life. First, it minimizes sexual competition within families by restricting legitimate sexuality to spouses. Second, it forces people to marry outside of their immediate families, forging links throughout the society. Third, since kinship defines people's rights and obligations toward one another, reproduction among close relatives would transform kinship into relational chaos.

3. **Social placement.** Although not biologically necessary for people to have children, families provide for the social placement of children. Social identity based on race, ethnicity, religion, and social class is ascribed at birth through the family. This fact explains the long-standing concern that children be born within socially sanctioned marriages. Legitimate birth, especially when parents are of similar social position, clarifies inheritance rights and allows for the stable transmission of social standing from parents to children.

4. **Material and emotional security.** The family has long been considered a "haven in a heartless world" because kin are presumed to provide physical protection, emotional support, and financial assistance to "their own." Research bears out this popular wisdom: People living in families tend to be healthier than those living alone.

"Family resemblance" means more than sharing physical features. Children's range of interests and opportunities depends on the social position of their parents. Thus each new generation in many ways "follows in the footsteps" of the preceding generation, as illustrated by the careers of Kirk and Michael Douglas.

Critical evaluation. Structural-functional analysis identifies a number of the major functions of the family. From this point of view, it is easy to see that society as we know it could not exist without families.

However, critics charge that this approach implies support for the narrow conception of a "traditional" family and overlooks the great diversity of American family life. It also focuses little attention on the problems of family life. Established family forms support patriarchy, and also evince a surprising measure of violence that undermines individual self-confidence, health, and well-being.

Inequality and the Family: Social-Conflict Analysis

The social-conflict paradigm also considers the family as central to the operation of society, but as a mirror of the social inequality found in the larger society. As noted in Chapter 10 ("Sex and Gender"), Friedrich Engels (1902; orig. 1884) traced the origin of the family to the transmission of private property from generation to generation. Families are thus crucial to concentrating wealth in the hands of an economic elite. Recall from Chapter 7 ("Social Stratification") that about half of the four hundred richest Americans received great wealth through inheritance (Forbes, 1989). The family thus supports social stratification, limits social mobility, and perpetuates racial and ethnic differences.

The family, Engels continued, also promotes patriarchy. During his own lifetime, wives were widely viewed (and often legally defined) as the property of men. The earnings of nineteenth-century American women typically belonged to their husbands as heads of households. Even today, women continue to be responsible for housework and childrearing, although most women are now in the workforce (Haas, 1981; Schooler et al., 1984; Fuchs, 1986).

Critical evaluation. Social-conflict analysis reveals another side of family life: its role in maintaining social inequality. During his era, Engels condemned the family as part and parcel of capitalism. Yet the societies that have rejected the capitalist economy have families all the same. Criticisms notwithstanding, therefore, the family carries out essential social functions not easily accomplished by other means.

Micro-Level Analysis

As a micro-level paradigm, symbolic-interaction analysis views family life as socially constructed and variable. Women and men, for example, are likely to view their marriages very differently (Bernard, 1982). Similarly, children usually perceive their parents only in terms of parental roles, with little understanding of marital sexual relationships. Furthermore, a couple's expectations as they exchange their wedding vows are usually transformed considerably by the daily realities of married life. A change in the role of one spouse, such as a wife entering law school, may also alter the roles of other family members. Thus the symbolic-interaction approach suggests the inadequacy of describing marriage and the family in terms of rigid patterns.

Social-exchange analysis, another micro-level approach, views courtship and marriage as a negotiation in which people offer each other various resources (Blau, 1964). In courtship, each person assesses the likely advantages and disadvantages of taking the other as a spouse. Physical attractiveness is one critical dimension of ex-

change. In patriarchal societies around the world, beauty has long been a commodity offered by women on the marriage market. The social value assigned to beauty explains females' traditional concern with physical appearance and their sensitivity about revealing their age. By contrast, a man's considerable financial resources may prompt an attractive woman to take an interest in him regardless of his looks (Melville, 1983). The terms of exchange are converging for men and women now that both are in the labor force and women are less dependent on men to support them and their children.

STAGES OF FAMILY LIFE

The family is dynamic, changing through the life course. Sociologists have identified several stages of family life common to American society.

Courtship and Romantic Love

Members of preindustrial societies generally consider courtship too important to be left to the young (Stone, 1977; Haviland, 1985). *Arranged marriages* represent an alliance between two extended families that affects the wealth, power, and prestige of them both. Parents often make such arrangements when their children are very young. In nineteenth-century India, for example, half of all girls were married before reaching the age of fifteen (Mayo, 1927; Mace & Mace, 1969).

Industrialization erodes the importance of extended families, weakens traditions, and enhances personal choice in courtship. Young people are expected to marry only after having gained the experience needed to select a compatible marriage partner. Dating is also a period of sexual experimentation, and today many couples even live together before deciding to marry.

American culture views *romantic love*—the feeling of deep affection and sexual passion toward another person—as the basis for marriage. For us, marriage without love is difficult to imagine, and the mass media—from traditional fairy tales like "Cinderella" to contemporary paperback romance novels—present romantic love as the keystone of successful marriage. Not surprisingly, then, Americans view romantic love as the most important element in courtship (Roper, 1974). Romantic love also encourages individuals to leave the original family of orientation to form a new family of procreation. Romantic love is usually most intense when people first marry, and it may therefore carry a newly married couple through the difficult period of adjusting to the realities of married life (Goode, 1959). Yet, based on feelings that may change, romantic love forms a less stable foundation for marriage than social and economic considerations.

Sociologists have long recognized that Cupid's arrow is aimed by society more carefully than individualistic Americans like to believe. Even today, people fall in love with others of the same race and of comparable age and social class. The forces of society guide courtship toward **homogamy** (literally, "like marrying like"), *marriage between people with the same social characteristics*.

Settling In: Ideal and Real Marriage

Socialization often instills unrealistic expectations of marriage. For those who idealize family life, marriage may be disappointing, especially for women—who, more than men, are taught to view marriage as the key to future happiness. Research also suggests that a good deal of fantasy infuses romantic love: People fall in love with others, not necessarily as they are, but as they want them to be (Berscheid & Hatfield, 1983). Only after marriage do spouses confront each other regularly, for better or for worse, as they face the day-to-day challenges of maintaining a household.

Sexuality may also fall short of romantic expectations. In the romantic haze of falling in love, people may glamorize marriage, envisioning an extended sexual honeymoon only to face the sobering realization that marital sex has become less than an all-consuming passion. Although 70 percent of married people claim to be satisfied with the sexual dimension of their marriage, marital sexual activity declines over time, as Table 12–1 illustrates (Blumstein & Schwartz, 1983).

Research indicates that couples with the most fulfilling sexual relationships have the greatest overall satisfaction with their marriages. This does not mean sex is the key to marital bliss, but rather that good sex and good relationships go together (Hunt, 1974; Tavris & Sadd, 1977; Blumstein & Schwartz, 1983).

Childrearing

Almost all Americans think that a family should include at least one child, as shown by survey results in Table 12–2. Few Americans want more than four children,

Table 12–1 FREQUENCY OF SEXUAL ACTIVITY AMONG MARRIED COUPLES

Years Together	Sexual Frequency (times per month)			
	1 or less	1–4	4–12	12 or more
0–2	6%	11%	38%	45%
2–10	6	21	46	27
10 or more	16	22	45	18

SOURCE: Adapted from Philip Blumstein and Pepper Schwartz, *American Couples* (New York: William Morrow, 1983), p. 196.

however—a change from two centuries ago, when *eight* children was the American average (Newman & Matzke, 1984). Before the Industrial Revolution (and still in preindustrial societies), production was based on human labor, so children were essential. This meant that having children was regarded as a wife's duty, and unreliable birth control technology made childbearing a regular event. Even so, family size was limited by high infant mortality; as late as 1900, about one-third of American children died before adolescence (Wall, 1980).

Industrialization transforms children, economically speaking, from an asset to a liability. Children today rarely reach financial independence until after the age of eighteen (and often not until the mid-twenties), and the expense of raising them can be staggering. One estimate placed the cost of rearing a typical child to age eighteen at more than $100,000, adding another $50,000 to $150,000 if the child goes to college (*Family*

Table 12–2 THE IDEAL NUMBER OF CHILDREN FOR AMERICANS, 1989

Number of Children	Proportion of Respondents
0	1.1
1	2.7
2	53.3
3	21.2
4	8.8
5	2.6
6 or more	1.4
As many as you want	5.3
No response	3.7

SOURCE: N.O.R.C., *General Social Surveys, 1972–1989* (Chicago: National Opinion Research Center, 1989), p. 253.

Economics Review, 1989). Not surprisingly, then, family size has dropped steadily during this century to about two children per American woman today. The median number of children among Japanese women is 1.5, a decline from 4.5 fifty years ago.

As explained in Chapter 10 ("Sex and Gender"), the recent entry of American women into the labor force has been dramatic. In 1989, 57.4 percent of women over the age of fifteen were in the workforce; two-thirds of women with children under eighteen were working outside the home (U.S. Bureau of Labor Statistics, 1990). Women working outside the home continue to bear the traditional responsibility for raising children and doing housework. Although some American men are enlarging their roles as parents, most resist sharing responsibility for household tasks that our culture has historically defined as feminine (Radin, 1982).

Because parenting competes with other personal interests and needs, more and more Americans are choosing to delay childbirth or to remain childless. In 1960, 12.6 percent of women between 25 and 29 who had ever been married had no children; by 1988 this proportion had risen to 29.1 percent (U.S. Bureau of the Census, 1990). Why this shift? Many working women have low-paying jobs and cannot support children, others wish to use their income to gain more education, while still others want to become established in a career before assuming the responsibilities of parenthood (Blumstein & Schwartz, 1983).

Aging and Family Life

The increasing life expectancy of Americans means that, barring divorce, couples typically remain married for a long time. By about age fifty, most have completed the major task of raising children. For the remaining years of marriage, couples commonly face an "empty nest" because, just as at the beginning of marriage, there are no children living at home.

While the departure of children requires adjustments, the marital relationship often becomes closer and more satisfying (Kalish, 1982). Perhaps the best characterization of a healthy marriage at this stage of life is companionship. Years of living together may have diminished a couple's sexual passion for each other, but mutual understanding and commitment, plus a common history, are likely to deepen and enrich their relationship.

Personal contact with children usually continues, since most older adults live within a short distance of

at least one of their children (Shanas, 1979). People's incomes peak in late middle age, as the expenses of childrearing diminish. Thus at this stage in family life, parenting may involve helping children make large purchases (a car or a house) and, of course, periodically babysitting the grandchildren.

Retirement brings further change to family life. If the wife has been a homemaker, the husband's retirement means the two spouses will be spending much more time together. Although the husband's presence is often a source of pleasure to both, it may dramatically change wives' established routines. Some wives find the presence of retired husbands an intrusion, as suggested by one woman's blunt reaction: "I may have married him for better or worse, but not for lunch" (Kalish, 1982:96). Because retirement from the labor force is becoming common among women as well as men, this final stage of family life may hold new and shared delights.

The most difficult transition in married life comes with the death of a spouse. Wives typically outlive husbands because women have a longer life expectancy than men, and also because women usually marry men who are several years older to begin with. Wives can thus expect to spend a significant period of time as widows. The bereavement and loneliness accompanying the death of a spouse pose serious challenges. This experience may be even more difficult for husbands, who usually have fewer friends than their wives and must suddenly adjust to the unfamiliar responsibility of housework (Berardo, 1970).

AMERICAN FAMILIES: CLASS, RACE, AND GENDER

Dimensions of inequality, including social class, ethnicity and race, and gender, generate considerable variation in marriage and family life.

Social class shapes a family's range of opportunities and financial security. Working-class wives interviewed by Lillian Rubin (1976) deemed a man a good husband to the extent that he refrained from violence and excessive drinking and held a steady job. Rubin's middle-class respondents, by contrast, never mentioned such things. Assuming a husband would provide a safe and secure home, they described their ideal spouse as a man with whom they could share thoughts and feelings and be more intimate. Overall, research indicates that spouses of higher social class are more open and expressive with each other (Komarovsky, 1967; Bott, 1971; Rubin, 1976).

Ethnicity, too, shapes family life. Many Hispanic Americans maintain extended families based on strong loyalties and mutual support. Hispanic-American parents traditionally exercise considerable control over their children's courtship, defining marriage as an alliance of families rather than a union of individuals. Adherence to conventional gender roles also characterizes Hispanic families. *Machismo*—masculine strength, daring, and sexual prowess—is pronounced, while women are closely supervised. Assimilation into the larger American culture is gradually altering these traditional patterns, however. Puerto Ricans who migrate to New York rarely maintain the strong extended families found in Puerto Rico. Affluence also seems to weaken traditional male authority among Hispanic families (Fitzpatrick, 1971; Moore & Pachon, 1985).

Family life among African Americans is strained by a poverty rate three times that of whites. Overall household income among blacks in 1989 was about 60 percent that of whites (U.S. Bureau of the Census, 1990). One consequence of this economic uncertainty is a tendency to remain single: 25 percent of black women born in the early 1950s have never married, compared with about 10 percent of their white counterparts (Bennett, Bloom, & Craig, 1989). Another consequence of economic disadvantage is the pronounced pattern of women heading households. Women headed 43.8 percent of

black families in 1989, compared with 23.1 percent of Hispanic families and 12.9 percent of white families (U.S. Bureau of the Census, 1990). Figure 12–1 on page 296 shows that, among Americans, households headed by women are likely to be poor; this is especially true of women who are black and Hispanic. Just as striking is that roughly two-thirds of black children are born to women who are unmarried and, in many cases, poor (Hogan & Kitagawa, 1985).

The decline of traditional industries during the 1980s hit African-American families especially hard. During a decade of prosperity for some Americans, poor black families became poorer, and some families' hold on middle-class standing became tenuous (Updegrave, 1989). A black underclass now exists in urban America, increasingly cut off from opportunity and hope. Amid despair and violence, the use of crack-cocaine and other dangerous drugs reached epidemic proportions by the beginning of the 1990s. More than half of African-American children now grow up in poverty. This fact, coupled with the rise in motherhood among poor teenagers, has led some researchers to conclude that an expanding cycle of poverty now entraps many black women and their children (Ladner, 1986; Furstenberg, Brooks-Gunn, & Morgan, 1987).

For all social classes, ethnicities, and races, gender shapes marriage and family life. Jessie Bernard (1982) asserts that every marriage is actually *two* different marriages: a woman's marriage and a man's marriage.

Hispanic cultures have traditionally maintained strong kinship ties. Carmen Lomas Garza's painting, *Sandia*, *Watermelon*, portrays the three-generation family pattern common to Hispanic Americans.

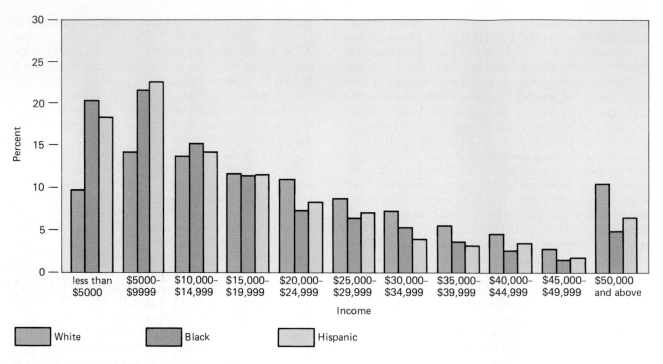

Figure 12–1 Families Headed by Women, by Income, 1989
(*U.S. Bureau of the Census*)

During the last century, the extent of male domination of the family has diminished, but still few marriages are composed of two equal partners. Mirra Komarovsky (1973, 1976) found that men were the stronger partner in the ideal marriage envisioned by most college seniors of both sexes. Perhaps this is not surprising, since Americans expect husbands to be older and taller than wives, and have long defined the husband's career as more important (McRae, 1986).

In light of these patterns, it is hard to fathom the basis for the traditional idea that marriage is more beneficial for women than for men (Bernard, 1982). The positive stereotype of the carefree bachelor contrasts sharply with the negative stereotype of the lonely spinster. The notion that marriage favors women is probably rooted in women's historical exclusion from the labor force: A woman's financial security depended on having a husband to provide for her. But in most respects, Jessie Bernard claims, marriage favors men. In comparison to single women, she notes, married women have poorer mental health and more passive attitudes toward life, and they report greater personal unhappiness. Married men, by contrast, live longer than single men, have

better mental health, and report greater personal happiness. After divorce many more women than men report happier lives, and women are less likely than men to remarry. Bernard asserts that there is no better guarantor of long life, health, and happiness for a man than a woman well socialized to perform the "duties of a wife," willing to devote her life to taking care of him and providing the security of a well-ordered home. She adds that marriage *could* be healthful for women if American society would only end the "anachronistic way in which marriage is structured," meaning husbands dominating wives and consigning them to tedious work in the home.

TRANSITIONS AND PROBLEMS IN FAMILY LIFE

Ann Landers, one of the best-known observers of the American scene, once remarked, "One marriage out of twenty is wonderful, four are good, ten are tolerable, and five are pure hell" (Landers, 1984). Families can be a source of joy, but the reality of family life often falls short of the ideal.

Divorce

Americans strongly favor marriage, and about nine of ten Americans eventually marry. But today's marriages often do not endure. Figure 12–2 shows that the divorce rate—the number of divorces for every one thousand people over the age of fifteen—has risen about tenfold during this century. By the 1970s, half of American marriages were expected to end in divorce (for blacks, about two-thirds). In world context, the American divorce rate is second to none, and marriages are now more likely to be ended by divorce than by death (Cherlin, 1981; Kitson & Raschke, 1981; Weitzman, 1985).

The rising divorce rate has a number of causes (Huber & Spitze, 1980; Kitson & Raschke, 1981). First, Americans now spend less time in family activities than in the past. Americans have become more individualistic, seemingly more concerned with personal happiness and success than committed to the well-being of families. Second, participation in the labor force has reduced women's financial dependence on their husbands so that,

as a practical matter, marriages are easier to end. Third, divorce no longer carries the powerful negative stigma common a century ago (Thornton, 1985; Gerstel, 1987). Fourth, because the United States has a high remarriage rate, people may initiate divorce with confidence that they can find another, more suitable, partner.

Most likely to divorce are young spouses, especially teenagers, who often have a brief courtship, little financial stability, and limited emotional maturity. Divorce also occurs more often when a couple marries in response to an unexpected pregnancy, and when one or both have alcohol or other drug problems. Divorce also is more common among women who have successful careers, partly because of the strains of a two-career marriage and partly because such women are less constrained to stay in an unhappy marriage. Moving, which weakens ties with family and friends, also increases the chances of divorce (Booth & White, 1980; Yoder & Nichols, 1980; Glenn & Shelton, 1985). Finally, people who divorce once tend to divorce again, presumably because personal problems follow them from one marriage to another.

Remarriage

As the divorce rate has increased, so has the rate of remarriage. Four out of five people who divorce remarry, most within five years. Men, especially those who are older, are more likely to remarry than women. Because women are expected to "marry up," the more education a woman has, and the better her job, the less likely she is to find a suitable husband (Leslie & Korman, 1989).

Remarriage often creates *blended families*, composed of biological parents and stepparents; children in one household may have two, one, or no common parents. With one biological parent typically living elsewhere, blended families must define precisely who makes up the child's nuclear family (Furstenberg, 1984). Blended families also subject children to new relationships: An only child, for example, may suddenly find she has two older brothers. Remarriages involving children are often stressful and, probably for that reason, show higher rates of divorce (Kalmuss & Seltzer, 1984).

Family Violence

Ideally, families offer their members pleasure and support. Yet the disturbing reality of many families centers

Figure 12–2 The Divorce Rate for the United States, 1890–1990

(U.S. Bureau of the Census)

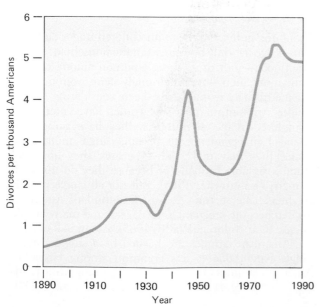

American society has reluctantly come to the conclusion that the home can be a dangerous place. This is especially true for women: At least 1 million women are the victims of family violence each year.

on *family violence*, emotional, physical, or sexual abuse of one family member by another. Richard J. Gelles calls the family "the most violent group in society with the exception of the police and the military" (cited in Roesch, 1984:75).

Family brutality often goes unreported to police, but researchers estimate that about 9 million couples—or one in six—experience some violence each year. For 1 to 2 million of these couples the violence is serious, including kicking, biting, and punching; sometimes such assaults escalate to murder. Although violence commonly involves both partners, women suffer the most serious injuries (Straus & Gelles, 1986; Schwartz, 1987).

Physically abused women have traditionally had few options. In the past, the law regarded domestic violence as a private concern of families. Now, even without separation or divorce, a woman can seek court protection in the hope that an abusive spouse will be punished. In addition, communities across North America are establishing shelters for victims of domestic abuse that provide counseling as well as temporary housing for women driven from their homes by violence.

Family violence also victimizes children. Child abuse entails more than physical injury: Adults undermine their children's emotional health by misusing power and trust. Perhaps 2.2 million children each year are abused, including several thousand who die as a result (U.S. House of Representatives, 1989). Child abuse is most common among young children who are most vulnerable (Straus & Gelles, 1986).

Most child abusers are men, but they conform to no simple stereotype. As one man who entered a therapy group reported, "I kept waiting for all the guys with raincoats and greasy hair to show up. But everyone looked like regular middle-class people" (Lubenow, 1984). However, these men are likely to have one thing in common: Most abusers suffered abuse themselves as children. Researchers have found that violent behavior in close personal relationships is learned; in the family, then, violence begets violence (Gwartney-Gibbs, Stockard, & Bohmer, 1987).

ALTERNATIVE FAMILY FORMS

In recent decades, American society has embraced a great variety of models in family living. While more traditional forms are still preferred by most, marriage and the family now encompass a range of lifestyles.

One-Parent Families

About one in five families with children under eighteen years of age has only one parent in the household. Single parenthood—four times more common among women than among men—overwhelmingly stems from divorce, but increasingly women have been considering having children without marriage. As women have entered the labor force in record numbers, they have gained the financial independence to become single mothers, a choice they may make either because they have not found a suitable husband or because they do not wish to marry (Kantrowitz, 1985). But not all single parents are financially secure. At least one-third of American women become pregnant as teenagers, and many decide to raise their children (Wallis, 1985). About half of African-American families are headed by a single parent. Single parenthood is less common among Hispanic-American families (30.0 percent) and among white families (17.0 percent) (U.S. Bureau of the Census, 1990).

Most research supports the conclusion that growing up in a one-parent family does not, in itself, disadvantage children. Divorce is certainly stressful, sometimes leaving emotional scars that remain for decades (Wallerstein & Blakeslee, 1989). But a more common problem among families with one parent—especially if that parent is female—is poverty. Pervasive poverty, rather than the absence of a parent, disadvantages such children, increasing their likelihood of remaining poor as adults, divorcing, and having children outside of marriage themselves (McLanahan, 1985; Weisner & Eiduson, 1986).

Cohabitation

Cohabitation is *the sharing of a household by an unmarried couple*. The number of cohabiting couples in the United States increased from about 500,000 in 1970 to over 2.5 million by the end of the 1980s. This practice is common on college and university campuses, where perhaps one-fourth of students cohabit at some time. Although most cohabitation does not lead to marriage, this living arrangement is gaining popularity as a way to test a serious relationship while saving the expense of a second residence.

Gay Male and Lesbian Couples

In 1989, Denmark became the first country to recognize homosexual marriages, thereby extending to gay and lesbian couples legal advantages in inheritance, taxation, and joint property ownership. Danish law, however, does not allow homosexual couples to adopt children. In the United States, laws enacted in San Francisco, New York, and elsewhere confer some of the legal benefits of marriage on gay male and lesbian couples.

Despite scorn rooted in the heterosexuality of American culture and barriers to legal marriage, many gay men and lesbians form long-term, committed partnerships they themselves honor as marriages and view as the basis of families (Bell, Weinberg, & Kiefer-Hammersmith, 1981). Like heterosexual couples, gays and lesbians enter relationships with romantic ideals and then adjust to day-to-day realities, and they share the strains of financial and household responsibilities. Some homosexual couples also raise children, usually from previous heterosexual relationships. Artificial insemination, however, has given women the option of having children without a male partner.

On October 1, 1989, Denmark became the first society to permit gay people to marry. Here, the first Danish couple to formalize their relationship celebrates at Copenhagen's city hall.

Singlehood

Because nine out of ten Americans eventually marry, singlehood is often seen simply as a premarital stage of life. In recent decades, however, more Americans have deliberately chosen the freedom and independence of living alone, remaining both single and childless. In 1950 only one household in ten included a single adult. By 1990, this proportion was about one in four: a total of 23 million single adults.

The greatest change in singlehood is among young women. In 1960 only 28 percent of women aged twenty to twenty-four were single; by 1988 the proportion had soared to 61 percent. Underlying this trend is greater female participation in the labor force, since women who are economically secure view marriage as a matter of choice rather than a financial necessity.

By midlife, however, women confront a lack of available men. Because our culture discourages women (but not men) from marrying partners much younger than they are, middle-aged women who wish to marry find the odds against them rising. In 1988, there were 133 unmarried women between forty and forty-four for every 100 unmarried men of that age (U.S. Bureau of the Census, 1990).

New Reproductive Technology and the Family

Recent medical advances, generally called *new reproductive technology*, are changing families. In the fifteen years since England's Louise Brown became the world's first "test-tube" baby, thousands of people have been conceived in this way. Early in the next century, 2 or 3 percent of the population of industrial societies may be the result of "new birth technologies" (Vines, 1986; Ostling, 1987).

Test-tube babies are created through *in vitro fertilization*: uniting the male sperm and the female ovum "in glass" rather than in a woman's body. In this complex medical procedure, drugs are often used to stimulate the production of more than one egg in each ovary during a woman's reproductive cycle. Then these eggs are surgically "harvested" from the ovaries and combined with sperm in a laboratory dish. The successful fusion of eggs and sperm produces embryos, which are placed in the womb of the woman who is to bear the child. The embryos may be implanted immediately or may be frozen for use at a later time.

In vitro fertilization helps some couples who cannot conceive children normally to become parents. In the longer term, many medical experts believe that new birth technologies will reduce the incidence of birth defects. By genetically screening sperm and eggs, medical specialists will be able to reasonably predict that the baby will be born healthy and normal (Vines, 1986).

By allowing people to exert control over life itself, new reproductive technology has sparked heated debate. One concern focuses on its high cost (exceeding $5,000), placing this procedure out of reach of many people. Also problematic, such technology allows medical experts to define what constitutes a proper "family." In most cases, *in vitro* fertilization has been made available only to women who are under forty years of age and are part of a heterosexual marriage. Single women, older women, and lesbian couples have so far been denied access to this technology.

A third ethical problem concerns *surrogate motherhood*, by which one woman bears a child for another. One type of surrogate motherhood involves joining one couple's ovum and sperm to produce an embryo that is implanted into the body of another woman—the surrogate—who gives birth to the child. In other cases, a surrogate agrees to bear a child for a couple by having her own ovum artificially fertilized by the man's sperm. Both types of surrogate motherhood raise difficult ethical issues and blur the traditional definition of parenthood. The Catholic Church opposes new reproductive technologies, charging that this approach to human reproduction reduces human life to an object for manipulation, as the box explains.

THE FAMILY IN THE TWENTY-FIRST CENTURY

American family life has changed dramatically in recent decades, and new reproductive technology may cause even greater change in the future. Yet advocates of traditional family values challenge proponents of new family forms and greater personal choice, fueling a raging public debate (Berger & Berger, 1983).

Our discussion suggests four likely directions of change as we approach the next century. First, marriage will almost certainly be less durable than it was in the 1950s. Divorce rates are likely to remain high. Because increasing numbers of women are able to support themselves, a traditional marriage appeals to fewer of them. Men, too, are beginning to embrace change. Still, most divorces lead to remarriage, suggesting that we are witnessing the transformation of marriage rather than its demise. As women's and men's lives change, new forms of family life will emerge that may prove more stable and more satisfying.

Second, family life is becoming more varied. More and more Americans are choosing cohabitation, or living in one-parent families and blended families. People are also embracing additional alternatives, such as lifelong singlehood and childless marriage. Taken together, these alternatives represent a growing conception of family life as a matter of choice.

Third, the importance of men in childrearing is waning. Certainly many fathers today are deeply involved in raising their children. But the number of women rearing children outside of marriage—because of either divorce or single motherhood—is increasing. As a result, more American children are growing up with weak ties to their fathers. Most research suggests that the absence of fathers does not significantly hurt children, but there is little doubt that this pattern contributes to the feminization of poverty in American society.

Fourth, and finally, new reproductive technology will continue to expand the range of options open to couples. While opposition will surely slow these develop-

Are New Reproductive Technologies Immoral? The Catholic Church's View

Americans generally assume technological advances are beneficial. New reproductive technologies, including *in vitro* fertilization and genetic research, are celebrated because they allow more women who want children to conceive and reduce birth defects.

Yet the Catholic Church condemns any childbirth that is "the product of an intervention of medical or biological techniques." Such efforts, the Church claims, reduce human life simply to an object of research. Not long ago, church officials remind us, similar research led Nazis to envision creating a new race of "superhumans."

Despite some useful results, the Church concludes, manipulation of an embryo in a laboratory is never justified. In support of the Church's position, half the states in the United States currently restrict genetic research, as do many European countries.

There is less support, however, for the Church's opposition to new reproductive technologies that assist infertile couples wishing to have children.

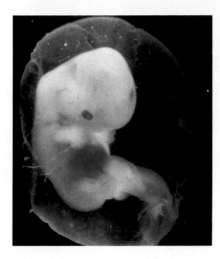

In vitro fertilization, the Church maintains, separates the act of procreation from the loving union of two parents. Catholics will recognize this argument as an extension of the Church's long-time prohibition against artificial contraception. Once separated from human sexuality, the argument goes, reproduction is in danger of becoming a business rather than a family concern.

Many people, including some Catholics, question whether sexual intercourse between husband and wife is the only moral way to conceive children. Since certain loving couples cannot conceive in this way, they argue, artificial insemination or *in vitro* fertilization provides hope for having a child. Moreover, critics complain that this prohibition strikes hardest at Catholics who accept the Church's view that Catholic families are incomplete without children.

Some Catholics will ignore the Church's recent pronouncements, just as many have overlooked prohibitions against artificial birth control in the past. But few people—whether Catholic or not—can easily dismiss the Church's concern that what is technologically possible may not always be morally desirable.

SOURCE: Based on Congregation for the Doctrine of the Faith, *Instruction on Respect for Human Life in Its Origin and on the Dignity of Procreation: Replies to Certain Questions of the Day* (Vatican City, 1987); also Richard N. Ostling, "Technology and the Womb," *Time*, Vol. 129, No. 12 (March 23, 1987):58–59; and Kenneth L. Woodward, "Rules for Making Love and Babies," *Newsweek*, Vol. 109, No. 12 (March 23, 1987):42–43.

ments, new forms of reproduction are likely to alter traditional meanings of parenthood.

Despite social changes that have buffeted the American family, most Americans still report being happy as partners and as parents (Cherlin & Furstenberg, 1983). Marriage and family life may now be taking on new forms, but they are likely to remain the foundation of our society well into the future.

RELIGION: BASIC CONCEPTS

Like the family, religion plays a central part in human history. Members of the earliest societies attributed birth, death, and success or failure in human endeavors to supernatural forces. French sociologist Emile Durkheim claimed that religion the world over deals with "all sorts

Every religion distinguishes the sacred from the secular. Japanese Buddhists reverently remove their shoes—which touch the profane ground—before entering this sacred temple in Kyoto.

of things that surpass the limits of our knowledge" (1965:62; orig. 1915). Humanity, Durkheim explained, divides ideas, objects, events, and experiences into one of two categories. Most are considered **profane** (from the Latin for "outside the temple"), meaning that they comprise *ordinary elements of everyday life*. Some, however, are set apart as **sacred,** as *extraordinary, inspiring a sense of awe, reverence, and even fear*. Distinguishing the sacred from the profane is the key to all religious belief. **Religion,** therefore, constitutes *a system of beliefs and practices based on recognizing the sacred.*

Because religion deals with ideas that transcend everyday experience, neither common sense nor science can establish religious truth. Religion is a matter of **faith:** *belief that is not based on scientific evidence*. In the New Testament of the Bible, Christians are said to "walk by faith, not by sight" (II Corinthians 5:7), and faith is described as "the conviction of things not seen" (Hebrews 11:1).

Matters of faith vary greatly throughout the world. Nothing is sacred to everyone on earth; something becomes sacred or profane as a community of people agree to define it as such. Although most books are profane, the Torah (the first five books of the Hebrew Bible or Old Testament) is sacred to Jews, as is the entire Bible to Christians and the Qur'an (Koran) to Muslims.

Durkheim (1965:62) claimed that profane things are understood in terms of their usefulness as, for instance, we use a computer or a car in everyday routines. That which is sacred, however, is separated from daily life—"set apart and forbidden"—evoking a reverent and submissive response. To maintain the boundary between the sacred and the profane, Muslims remove their shoes before entering a mosque; in this way they avoid defiling a sacred place with shoes that have touched the profane ground outside.

The sacred is the focus of *ritual*, or formal, ceremonial behavior. Holy communion forms the central ritual of Christianity; the wafer and wine consumed during communion are never defined as food but, rather, symbolize the body and blood of Jesus Christ.

Sociological analysis of religion may make some people uneasy. Yet looking at religion from a sociological standpoint implies no offense or threat to anyone's religious faith. Just as sociologists study the family, passing no judgments on various family structures, we seek to understand the religious beliefs and practices of human societies. Here, through scientific inquiry, sociological analysis delves into the social consequences of religious activity, making no assessments about the *validity* of any religious doctrine. That is a matter of faith rather than empirical evidence.

THEORETICAL ANALYSIS OF RELIGION

Sociologists have applied various theoretical paradigms to the study of religion. Each offers distinctive insights into religious life.

Functions of Religion: Structural-Functional Analysis

Emile Durkheim asserted that society has an existence and power of its own beyond the lives of the people who collectively create it. Thus, he concluded, society itself is "godlike," surviving the ultimate deaths of the members whose lives it shapes. According to Durkheim (1965; orig. 1915), society has the sacred qualities of immortality and power over us. Religion, then, celebrates society's awesome potency.

People transform everyday objects into sacred symbols that represent elements of their collective life. Technologically simple societies do this with the **totem,** *an object in the natural world imbued with sacred qualities.* As the focus of ritual activity, the totem stands as a sacred representation of the entire society. For today's Americans, the flag has taken on the aura of a quasi-religious totem that should never be used in a profane manner or allowed to touch the ground.

Durkheim identified the following three major functions of religion for the operation of society:

1. **Social cohesion.** Religion unites members of a society through shared symbolism, values, and norms. Religious thought and ritual underlie the morality and rules of "fair play" that make organized social life possible.
2. **Social control.** Each society promotes conformity and obedience by invoking a religious justification for its way of life. In medieval Europe, monarchs claimed to rule by divine right. Few of today's political leaders use religion so explicitly, but many publicly ask for God's blessing, implying to audiences that their efforts are both right and just.
3. **Providing meaning and purpose.** Religious beliefs hold out the comforting notion that the vulnerable human condition serves some greater purpose. Strengthened by such beliefs, people are less likely to collapse with despair when confronted by life's uncertainties and calamities. For this reason, major life transitions—including birth, marriage, and death—are usually marked by religious observances.

Critical evaluation. Durkheim's structural-functional analysis of religion highlights the importance of symbolism in collective life. However, to its detriment, this approach downplays the dysfunctional consequences of religion—especially the capacity of beliefs to generate destructive conflict. Nations have long marched to war under the banner of their god (from the European Crusades a thousand years ago to today's unrest in the Middle East) and religions divide humanity in ways that may encourage such turmoil. Historically, more conflict probably has been caused by differences in religious beliefs than by social inequality.

Constructing the Sacred: Symbolic-Interaction Analysis

"Society," asserts Peter Berger (1967:3), "is a human product and nothing but a human product, that yet continuously acts back upon its producer." Religion, from a symbolic-interactionist standpoint, is socially constructed (perhaps with divine inspiration). We construct the sacred, Berger explains, because society is subject to so much disruption. Placing life within a "cosmic frame of reference" confers on the fallible, transitory creations of human beings (and on human beings themselves) "the semblance of ultimate security and permanence" (1967:35–36).

For instance, if marriage were defined as just an agreement between two people, its violation would be a simple matter of changing one's mind. Defined as holy matrimony, however, marriage makes moral claims on us and infuses our lives with sacred meaning. Especially when humans face uncertainty and life-threatening situations—such as illness, war, and natural disaster—sacred symbols come to the fore. By socially creating the sacred, humanity rises above the ultimate reality of death, so that society—if not its individual members—becomes immortal.

Critical evaluation. The symbolic-interaction approach views religion as the construction of a "sacred canopy" of meaning over everyday life (Berger, 1967). But, Berger cautions, the ability of sacred notions and symbols to legitimate and stabilize society depends on a form of subterfuge: The constructed character of the sacred must go unrecognized so people attribute the process to supernatural forces. After all, we could derive little strength from sacred beliefs we recognized as mere devices for coping with tragedy. One reason many people are uncomfortable with the sociological study of religion is that it brings them face to face with the assertion that we construct the sacred in the same manner as we create the rest of society.

Religion and Inequality: Social-Conflict Analysis

The social-conflict paradigm links religion to social inequality. According to Karl Marx, religion amounts to ideology that serves elites by legitimating the status quo and diverting people's attention from social inequities.

The British monarch, for example, has traditionally been crowned by the head of the Church of England, illustrating the close alliance between religious and political hierarchy. Thus, to oppose existing social arrangements means challenging the church—and, by implication, God. Religion also encourages people to look hopefully to a "better world to come" while ignoring social problems of *this* world. One of Marx's best-known statements is a stinging criticism of religion as "the sigh of the oppressed creature, the sentiment of a heartless world, and the soul of soulless conditions. It is the opium of the people" (1964:27; orig. 1848).

An additional link between religion and social inequality involves gender. Virtually all the world's major religions are historically patriarchal. For example, the Qur'an (Koran), the sacred text of Islam, asserts that men have social dominance over women:

> Men are in charge of women. . . . Hence good women are obedient. . . . As for those whose rebelliousness you fear, admonish them, banish them from your bed, and scourge them. (cited in Kaufman, 1976:163)

Christianity—the dominant religion of the Western world—has also supported patriarchy. Although Christians revere Mary, the mother of Jesus, the New Testament instructs us:

> A man . . . is the image and glory of God; but woman is the glory of man. For man was not made from woman, but woman from man. Neither was man created for woman, but woman for man. (I Corinthians 11:7–9)

> As in all the churches of the saints, the women should keep silence in the churches. For they are not permitted to speak, but should be subordinate, as even the law says. If there is anything they desire to know, let them ask their husbands at home. For it is shameful for a woman to speak in church. (I Corinthians 14:33–35)

> Wives, be subject to your husbands, as to the Lord. For the husband is the head of the wife as Christ is the head of the church. . . . As the church is subject to Christ, so let wives also be subject in everything to their husbands. (Ephesians 5:22–24)

Judaism, too, has traditionally supported patriarchy. Male Orthodox Jews include the following words in daily prayer:

> Blessed art thou, O Lord our God, King of the Universe, that I was not born a gentile. Blessed art thou, O Lord our God, King of the Universe, that I was not born a slave. Blessed art thou, O Lord our God, King of the Universe, that I was not born a woman.

Despite patriarchal traditions, many religious organizations are gradually placing women in leadership roles. Such developments, coupled with linguistic revi-

One way that religions support social inequality is by designating only some categories of people as eligible for leadership. Historically, this has meant the dominance of white males, but this pattern has eroded in recent years. In 1989, for example, Barbara Harris became the first black woman to be ordained as a bishop in the Episcopal Church.

sions in hymnals and prayers, have delighted progressives while outraging traditionalists. The consequences of such changes involve not just organizational patterns but conceptions of God. Theologian Mary Daly puts the matter bluntly: "If God is male, then male is God" (cited in Woodward, 1989:58).

Critical evaluation. Social-conflict analysis points up how religion reinforces social inequality. Yet critics of religion's conservative face, including Karl Marx, minimize the ways in which religion has promoted change and, sometimes, social equality. Nineteenth-century American religious groups played a key role in the abolition of slavery. During the 1950s and 1960s, religious organizations were at the core of the civil rights movement. The black church has been especially active in the struggle for racial equality in the United States; perhaps the most outstanding leader in this movement was Martin Luther King, Jr., a minister. During the 1960s and 1970s, clergy members actively opposed the Vietnam War and, as we shall explain presently, some have supported revolutionary change in Latin America and elsewhere.

RELIGION AND SOCIAL CHANGE

Religion is not only the conservative force portrayed by Karl Marx. Historically, as Max Weber (1958; orig. 1904–1905) explained, religion can promote dramatic social change.

Max Weber: Protestantism and Capitalism

Weber pointed out that the development of industrial capitalism in Europe paralleled the rise of Calvinism—a Christian religious movement emerging from the Protestant Reformation. Central to the religious thought of John Calvin (1509–1564) is the doctrine of *predestination.* This means that God, with complete control over the universe, selects some people for salvation and others for eternal damnation. Each individual's fate—known only to God—is thus predestined before birth, with heavenly glory or hellfire for all eternity awaiting everyone at the end of life.

With their lives framed by anxious visions of salvation or damnation, Calvinists began to seek signs of God's favor in this world. For Calvinists, worldly prosper-

ity constituted one important indication that God was singling out particular individuals. Thus Calvinists became absorbed in a quest for material success. However, gaining riches could never be used for self-indulgent spending; nor did Calvinists share wealth with the poor, since poverty signaled rejection by God, in the Calvinist view. Their ever-present purpose was to carry out God's will as a life-long "calling."

Calvinists established the roots of capitalism by reinvesting their profits, leading to ever-greater success. Beyond practicing personal thrift, they readily embraced the technological advances that accompanied the Industrial Revolution.

For Weber, the success-oriented Calvinist creed provided striking evidence of the power of religious ideas to promote social change. While the religious fervor that motivated early Calvinists weakened in later generations, he noted, their success-seeking personal discipline remained. Calvinists thus transformed a religious ethic into a profane "work ethic," with profit pursued for its own sake, rather than for the glory of God. From this point of view, Weber concluded, industrial capitalism can be thought of as a "disenchanted" religion. In a revealing bit of linguistic history, the term *accounting,* which early Calvinists called their written record of daily moral deeds, has come down to us today solely with a monetary meaning. Here we see how the "Protestant ethic" reemerged as the "spirit of capitalism."

Liberation Theology

The power of religion to effect social change also takes shape in the contemporary Christian movement known as "liberation theology." Christianity has long addressed the suffering of poor and oppressed people. Historically, this has meant strengthening the faith of the believer in a better life to come. In recent decades, however, some church leaders and theologians have embraced **liberation theology,** *a fusion of Christian principles with political activism, often Marxist in character.*

Liberation theology developed in the late 1960s in Latin America's Roman Catholic Church. In addition to the Church's efforts to liberate humanity from sin, Christian activists are helping people to liberate themselves from the abysmal poverty of the Third World, described in Chapter 8 ("Global Inequality"). Their message is that human suffering is not just pervasive, it is inconsistent with Christian morality. Further, global poverty is preventable. Therefore, as a matter of faith and conscience, Christians must act to reduce this suffering.

Religion has always held a special promise to the poor, reaffirming the dignity of people flogged by famine and offering hope of a better life to come. Christian churches are currently thriving in the poorest regions of southern Africa, where Christian ideals are passionately expressed in some of the world's most inspiring religious art.

The radicalization of the church has, in some instances, strengthened support for Catholicism among Latin American people (Neuhouser, 1989). Yet Pope John Paul II has condemned liberation theology for mixing politics with traditional church doctrine. In response, the Vatican has forbidden church officials to take sides in any political conflicts, contending that liberation theology endangers the Catholic faith by diverting attention from the otherworldly concerns of Christianity and embroiling the church in political controversy. Despite this opposition, the liberation theology movement continues apace in Latin America, fueled by the belief that Christian faith and a sense of human justice require clerics to press for immediate improvements in the condition of the world's poor (Boff, 1984).

CHURCH, SECT, AND CULT

Religious organization can be described in terms of three general types: church, sect, and cult. Ernst Troeltsch (1931), a student of Max Weber, defined a **church** as *a formal religious organization that is well integrated into the larger society*. Churches typically persist for centuries, usually encompassing members of a family over many generations. Bureaucratic organization further enhances a church's stability: Officials are formally ordained and work within a hierarchy of offices according to specific policies and regulations.

Although concerned with the sacred, churches ac-

cept the profane world. They advance morality in abstract terms, often turning a blind eye to specific social arrangements that violate their principles. For example, many churches have historically celebrated the unity of all people even though their congregations are composed of only whites. Such duality minimizes conflict between the church and the political state (Troeltsch, 1931; Johnstone, 1983; O'Dea & Aviad, 1983).

A church generally takes one of two forms. An **ecclesia** is *a church that is formally allied with the state*. Ecclesias have been common in human history: The Catholic Church was for centuries bound to the Holy Roman Empire; the Anglican Church has been the official Church of England since the sixteenth century; Confucianism was the state religion in China until early in this century; and Islam remains the official religion of Pakistan and Iran. In societies where everyone is legally defined as a member of an ecclesia, there is no tolerance of religious diversity.

A second type of church is called a **denomination,** *a church that recognizes religious pluralism*. Denominations usually exist in societies that formally separate church and state. The United States has dozens of Christian denominations, including Catholics, Baptists, Methodists, and Lutherans. Each denomination holds certain religious beliefs but recognizes the right of others to disagree.

Distinct from all churches are **sects,** *informal religious organizations that stand apart from the larger society*. Sects often lack the rigid hierarchy of established churches, exalting personal experience and emotion over

The formality of traditional churches is evident in the relatively subdued and passive behavior of members during worship services. In contrast, the charismatic leaders of sects encourage their followers to experience personally a divine presence, often generating strong emotion.

the more formal ritual and established doctrine embraced by churches. Sects often view established churches as having lost the true path as they seek to restore "authentic" religious beliefs and practices (Stark & Bainbridge, 1979).

Churches have formal officials, such as priests, rabbis, and ministers. By contrast, leaders of sects can be anyone who displays **charisma,** *extraordinary personal qualities that can turn an audience into followers.* Sect members respond to the emotional appeal of charismatics, viewing their leaders as divinely inspired.

Unlike churches, sects tend to withdraw from society to practice their religion without interference. To members of sects, the outside world has grown misguided—sometimes even evil—so members are urged to cluster together apart from nonmembers. The Amish, found in large numbers in Pennsylvania and the American midwest, form a religious sect that remains isolated from the larger society (Hostetler, 1980). Insofar as sects view their own beliefs as the only true religion, members are intolerant of other religious beliefs.

To sustain their membership, many sects rely on active recruitment, or *proselytizing,* of new members. Proselytizing leads to *conversion,* or personal religious transformation. Members of Jehovah's Witnesses, for example, share their faith with others in the hope of attracting new members.

Finally, churches and sects differ in their social composition. Well-established churches tend to include people of high social standing; sects often attract those who are disadvantaged or living at the fringes of society. A sect's openness to new members and promise of salvation and personal fulfillment may be especially appealing to people who perceive themselves as social outsiders.

Sects generally form as breakaway groups from established churches or other religious organizations (Stark & Bainbridge, 1979). Less stable than churches because of their psychic intensity and lack of formal structure, many sects emerge only to disappear soon after. The sects that do endure become more like churches, losing fervor as they become more bureaucratic, established, and respectable.

A **cult** is *a religious movement that is highly unconventional in terms of the surrounding society.* Whereas a sect breaks away from an established religious organization, a cult represents something else entirely. Cults typically form around a highly charismatic leader who offers a compelling message. An example of cult formation is the founding of the Church of Jesus Christ of Latter-Day Saints (the Mormons) by Joseph Smith in New York State in 1830. Although Smith accepted many established Christian principles, he distinguished Mormonism with some unconventional religious ideas, including polygynous marriage. Over their history, however, Mormons have abandoned such practices and become an established church.

Cults can also arise from the diffusion of religious ideas from one society (where they are conventional) to another society (where they are not). Transcendental Meditation (TM) attracted many devotees in the United States when Maharishi Mahesh Yogi introduced Hindu ideas to American society in the late 1950s. During the 1970s, TM had perhaps 500,000 followers, although its popularity has declined considerably since then (Bainbridge & Jackson, 1981).

Cults tend to be even more at odds with established society than sects. Many cults demand that members not only accept their doctrine but embrace an entire *lifestyle* involving a radical change in self-identity. For this reason, cults are sometimes accused of brainwashing new members. Research suggests, however, that most people who join cults suffer no psychological harm (Barker, 1981; Kilbourne, 1983).

Cults tend to form and disperse rather quickly, with little public notice. Some endure, gradually becoming bureaucratic and conventional, and seeking peace with the surrounding society.

RELIGION IN HISTORY

Religion exists in every society of the world. But like the family and other institutions, religion shows significant historical variation.

Religion in Preindustrial Societies

Religion predates written history. Archaeological evidence suggests that, at least forty thousand years ago, our human ancestors routinely engaged in religious rituals.

Hunting and gathering peoples embraced **animism** (from the Latin meaning "the breath of life"): *the belief that natural objects are conscious forms of life that can affect humanity*. Animistic people view forests, oceans, mountains, and the wind as spiritual forces. Many early Native American societies were animistic, which accounts for their historical reverence for the natural environment.

In pastoral and horticultural societies, whose members focus their energies on growing crops and raising

livestock, a belief arose in a divine power who created the world. Pastoral peoples typically recognize a Creator God directly involved in the well-being of the universe. This view of God is widespread among Americans because Christianity, Judaism, and Islam all emerged from pastoral societies. Agrarian societies, too, have powerful religious organizations, as evidenced by the centrality of the church in medieval Europe. In England, for example, the church was a major landowner and its leaders were closely allied (often through kinship) with the ruling nobility.

Religion in Industrial Societies

The Industrial Revolution heralded the primacy of the scientific approach, diminishing the scope of religious thinking. Even so, science has hardly banished religion from our world. On the contrary, religious thought persists because science cannot address issues of ultimate meaning in human life. Scientific investigation can reveal *how* this world works; but science has no answers as to *why* we and the rest of the universe exist at all. Whatever the benefits of science, then, religion has a unique capacity to probe essential dimensions of human existence.

Still, science and religion have often been placed in opposition to each other. A notable case involves the controversy over human origins, which pits scientific facts about human evolution against the religious beliefs commonly called *creationism*. The box provides details.

RELIGION IN THE UNITED STATES

Is religion becoming a weaker force in American society? Research reveals some transformations but confirms the continuing role of religion in social life (Collins, 1982; Greeley, 1989).

Religious Commitment

National surveys show that 90 percent of Americans identify with a particular religion (Gallup, 1984; N.O.R.C., 1989). Two-thirds formally affiliate with a religious organization for at least some period of their lives; this pattern has not declined in the past fifty years (N.O.R.C., 1989; U.S. Bureau of the Census, 1989).

Does Science Threaten Religion? The Creation Debate

"In the beginning God created the heavens and the earth." So states Genesis in the Bible, a sacred text for millions of Christians and Jews. A literal reading of Genesis puts the origin of life on earth at the third day when God created vegetation; on the fifth and sixth days, God created animal life including human beings, fashioned in God's own image.

In 1859, the English scientist Charles Darwin published the scientific treatise *On the Origin of Species*, a biological account of human origins. Darwin's theory of evolution states that, far from being present at the earth's creation, humans evolved from lower forms of life over the course of a billion years.

Darwin's theory immediately generated controversy. What some celebrated as a great contribution to science, others saw as an attack on centuries-old sacred beliefs. On the surface, Darwin's scientific assertions do seem to contradict the biblical text, setting in motion the *creation debate*.

This simmering controversy erupted in 1925 in the little town of Dayton, Tennessee. At that time, a new state law outlawed teaching "any theory that denies the story of the Divine Creation of man as taught in the Bible," and especially forbade the claim that "man descended from a lower order of animals." One afternoon in Doc Robinson's drugstore, John Thomas Scopes, a science teacher in the local high school, conceded that he had, on occasion, taught the theory of evolution in his classroom. To test the law, Scopes agreed to stand charged with defying it.

The "Scopes Monkey Trial" (so designated because of evolution's contention that humans evolved from lower primates) drew national attention when William Jennings Bryan, a three-time presidential candidate and a fundamentalist Christian opposed to evolutionary science, enthusiastically agreed to prosecute the case. Clarence Darrow, a renowned criminal lawyer, defended Scopes.

Darrow turned in one of his finest performances at the trial, while Bryan, aging, ill, and only days from death, did little to advance the creationist cause. Yet the community applauded when Scopes was found guilty and fined $100. His conviction was reversed on appeal (perhaps to prevent the case from reaching the U.S. Supreme Court), and Tennessee law banned teaching evolution until 1967. However, in 1968, the U.S. Supreme Court struck down all such laws as a violation of the constitutional prohibition against government-supported religion.

But creationists persisted, adopting a new strategy: If teaching the theory of evolution was permitted in schools, creationism should also be taught to balance this view. Creationism, stripped of its obvious religious overtones, became *creation science*. Some state legislatures, responding to the politically powerful creationist movement, soon required that creation science be included in school curricula. Such legislation, however, was rejected by the courts in 1985 as a violation of the constitutionally mandated separation of church and state.

Creation science suffered a further blow with charges that it was scientifically invalid. To qualify as science, judges asserted, a body of knowledge must have a provisional character, changing as new empirical evidence surfaces. The theory of evolution has been transformed by research, but creation science has not; thus, the court concluded, creationism is religion, not science.

Despite court rulings, 44 percent of Americans endorse the creation science belief that God created human beings in their present form within the last ten thousand years. Only 9 percent claim a nonreligious evolutionary view that human life evolved from lower forms of life over millions of years, with God having no part in the process. Evolution—directed by God—is favored by 38 percent. The remaining 9 percent profess no knowledge of how humans came into being (Severo, 1982).

Americans clearly remain divided over the creationism question. But many, including church leaders, insist that the conflict itself is based on faulty thinking. John S. Spong, the Episcopal bishop of Newark, New Jersey, states that scientists and biblical scholars alike must accept the "enormous amount of evidence" that humanity did evolve over a billion years. But, he adds, science merely investigates *how* the natural world operates; only religion can address *why* we exist in terms of God's role in this process. In considering human creation, then, we must look to both scientific fact and faith.

SOURCE: Based on Harry Nelson and Robert Jermain, *Introduction to Physical Anthropology*, 3rd ed. (St. Paul, MN: West, 1985), pp. 22–24; Stephen J. Gould, "Evolution as Fact and Theory," *Discover*, May 1981, pp. 35–37; Ronald L. Numbers, "Creationism in 20th-Century America," *Science*, Vol. 218, No. 5 (November 1982): 538–544; Richard Severo, "Poll Finds Americans Split on Creation Idea," *New York Times*, August 29, 1982, p. 22. Professor J. Kenneth Smail of Kenyon College also contributed ideas to this section.

Religious affiliation is somewhat less common in western states, apparently the result of more frequent geographical movement (Welch, 1983; Gallup, 1984). Table 12–3 indicates the religious identification of Americans.

Religiosity is *the importance of religion in a person's life*. By world standards, Americans and Canadians are a religious people, more so, for example, than Europeans or the Japanese. But precisely how religious Americans are depends on how we assess religiosity. Almost everyone in the United States (95 percent) professes belief in a divine power, although only about 65 percent claim to "know that God exists and have no doubts about it" (N.O.R.C., 1989:405). As already noted, 90 percent of Americans identify with a specific religion. And 84 percent claim to "feel closeness to God" (N.O.R.C., 1987:140).

Yet just 70 percent of Americans assert their belief in a life after death, half claim to pray at least once a day, and only one-third attend religious services on a weekly or almost-weekly basis (N.O.R.C., 1989).

Determining the degree of American religiosity, therefore, is no simple matter. Because belief in God is normative in American culture, many people may make such a claim simply as a matter of conformity. Similarly, people may attend religious services not out of piety but rather in search of identity and belonging and perhaps even social prestige. Most Americans, then, are marginally religious, although a large minority are deeply religious. This assessment is supported by a recent survey of American adults, illustrated in Figure 12–3.

Religiosity also varies among religious organizations. Rodney Stark and Charles Glock (1968) found Catholics to be more religious than Protestants, with sect members the most religious of all.

Class, Ethnicity, and Race

Religious affiliation is related to a number of other factors. Wade Roof (1979) found that Episcopalians, Presbyterians, and Jews had the highest overall social standing in American society. In a middle position were Congregationalists and Methodists; somewhat lower social standing characterized Catholics, Lutherans, Baptists, and members of sects.

Figure 12–3 The Strength of American Religious Beliefs, 1989

(National Opinion Research Center, 1989:144)

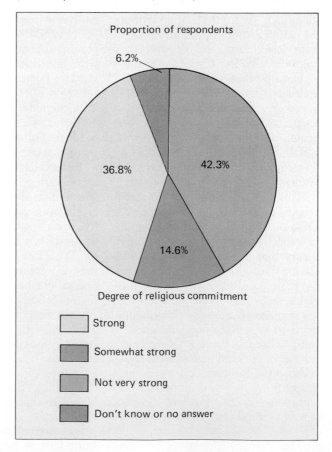

Table 12–3 RELIGIOUS IDENTIFICATION AMONG AMERICANS, 1989*

Religion	Proportion Indicating Preference
Protestant denominations	63.1%
Baptist	19.8
Methodist	9.6
Lutheran	7.3
Presbyterian	4.6
Episcopalian	2.8
All others, or no denomination	19.3
Catholic	25.1
Jewish	1.5
Other or no answer	2.5
No religious preference	7.8

* Based on a national sample of persons aged 18 or over.

SOURCE: N.O.R.C., *General Social Surveys, 1972–1989* (Chicago: National Opinion Research Center, 1989), pp. 140–41.

Throughout the world, religion is also linked to ethnicity. Many religions predominate in a single region or society. Islam pervades the Arab cultures of the Middle East, for example, as Hinduism is woven into the culture of India. By contrast, Christianity, like Judaism, thrives in numerous cultures.

In American society we find *Anglo-Saxon* Protestants, *Irish* Catholics, *Russian* Jews, and *Greek* Orthodox. This fusion of nationality and religion stems from an influx of immigrants to the United States from societies with a single major religion. Still, nearly every American ethnic group contains at least some religious diversity. Americans of English ancestry, for instance, include members of many Protestant denominations, Roman Catholics, Jews, and adherents of other religions.

The church has historically been central to the lives of African-Americans. After arrival in the Western hemisphere, most African-Americans became Christians—the dominant religion in the Americas—but fused Christian belief and practice with elements of African religions. This history, and the harsh discipline of slavery, generated among black Christians a series of rituals that was—by white standards—highly emotional and spontaneous. These rituals persist in some black churches today (Frazier, 1965; Roberts, 1980). As blacks migrated from the rural South to the industrial cities of the North, the church addressed problems of dislocation, prejudice, and poverty. For a category of Americans sometimes cut off from the larger society, black churches also provide opportunity for talented men and women to distinguish themselves. Black ministers, such as Ralph Abernathy, Martin Luther King, Jr., and Jesse Jackson, gained international recognition as leaders of black America.

RELIGION IN A CHANGING SOCIETY

Every society changes over time. Along with patterns of family life, religion continues to change in the United States. We now consider some of the ways religion is changing in contemporary America.

Secularization

Among the most important and controversial patterns of social change is **secularization,** *the historic decline in the influence of religion.* Secularization (derived from the Latin, meaning "the present age") is commonly associated with modern, technologically advanced societies (Cox, 1971; O'Dea & Aviad, 1983). Thus secularization involves a shift from a *religious* view of the world (based on faith) to a *scientific* understanding (based on empirical evidence).

Today few Americans see in birth, illness, or death the workings of a divine power. As a result, these transitions are now more likely to occur in the presence of physicians (whose knowledge is based on science) than church leaders (whose knowledge is based on faith). In practice, then, secularization has diminished religion's sphere of influence. Theologian Harvey Cox elaborates:

> The world looks less and less to religious rules and rituals for its morality or its meanings. For some, religion provides a hobby, for others a mark of national or ethnic identification, for still others an esthetic delight. For fewer and fewer does it provide an inclusive and commanding system of personal and cosmic values and explanations. (1971:3)

If Cox is correct, should we expect that religion will some day disappear entirely? Not according to many sociologists (Hammond, 1985; McGuire, 1987). Recall that the vast majority of Americans continue to profess a belief in God. Two-thirds of Americans affiliate with a religious organization, a proportion that is actually twice as high as it was in 1900 and four times as high as in 1850. There is also little evidence of a decline in church attendance (Hout & Greeley, 1987).

American society, then, is *not* undergoing a progressive elimination of religion; instead, a decline in some dimensions of religion is paralleling an increase in others. Moreover, Americans do not agree about the meaning of the secularization that has occurred: Some see religious decline as a lamentable loss of traditional American values; for others, secularization liberates society from the all-encompassing beliefs of the past, so that people now take greater responsibility for what they choose to believe. Secularization has also brought the practices of many religious organizations more in line with widespread social attitudes. The Catholic Church, for example, has abandoned Latin in religious services in favor of the vernacular (commonly spoken languages the world over), and other religions have recently sanctioned the ordination of women.

Overall, the extent of secularization can easily be exaggerated. As we saw earlier when we considered the family, the fears of some that religion may disappear are almost certainly unfounded.

Civil Religion

Robert Bellah (1975) uses the term **civil religion** to refer to *a quasi-religious loyalty binding individuals in a basically secular society*. The term *civil* refers to the ordinary life of citizens of a political state. In a secular society, then, patriotism itself assumes many religious qualities.

A vast majority of American citizens consider the American way of life to be morally good, and believe that American involvement in the world benefits other nations. By contrast, most Americans perceive communism as evil (N.O.R.C., 1983, 1989). Civil religion among Americans is bolstered by rituals such as rising to sing the national anthem before sporting events. Much like the Christian cross and the Jewish Star of David, the flag serves as a sacred symbol that Americans treat with reverence and respect.

Finally, participants in a patriotic celebration often feel the same sense of reverence and awe shared by people at religious services. The explanation lies in Emile Durkheim's insight that all rituals reinforce our collective identity and focus our attention on the power of society.

Religious Revival in America

The steady level of church attendance in the United States in recent decades masks an underlying shift in the popularity of various religious organizations. During the last twenty-five years, membership in established, "mainstream" churches (including Episcopalian, Presbyterian, and Lutheran denominations) has decreased by about 20 percent, while membership in other religious organizations (including the Mormons, Seventh-Day Adventists, and many Christian sects) has risen dramatically (Jacquet, 1988). The drive for secularization goes only so far: As secularization takes root in a society, prompting the decline of established religions, the timeless human quest for meaning and security gives rise to new forms of religious activity (Stark & Bainbridge, 1981).

Underlying this trend is the growth of **religious fundamentalism,** *conservative religious organizations that seek to restore what are viewed as fundamental elements of religion*. Fundamentalism came to the attention of many Americans when conservative Christian organizations rallied behind President Ronald Reagan in the 1980s. In fact, fundamentalism has been gaining support throughout this century (Bromley & Shupe, 1984).

In response to the growing influence of science, expanding cities, and erosion of the conventional family, religious fundamentalists have launched a campaign on behalf of the so-called traditional values of rural, God-fearing America. From a fundamentalist point of view, some churches have even succumbed to the temptations of secularization by modifying their doctrines with a liberal tolerance for diversity and openness to change. One way fundamentalists challenge secularization and divergent viewpoints is by insisting on a literal interpreta-

Arts of the South, by American painter Thomas Hart Benton (1889–1975), suggests that religious fundamentalism is strongly integrated into the community life of rural people in the southern United States.

Thomas Hart Benton, Arts of the South. Tempera with oil glaze, 8 × 13 feet, 1953.20. From the collection of the New Britain Museum of American Art, Connecticut. Harriet Russell Stanley Fund.

tion of the Gospels (the first four books of the New Testament) as the basis of "true" religion (Johnstone, 1983). Thus, fundamentalism appeals to those seeking certainty in an uncertain world. What some—including many faithful Christians—consider dogmatic, then, others find distinctly reassuring.

Fundamentalism also places a sectlike emphasis on the personal experience of religion. In contrast to the reserve and self-control common to more established religious organizations, Christian fundamentalism promotes spiritual revival through the process of being "born again"—establishing a personal relationship with Jesus that imbues daily life with meaning. In addition, fundamentalist churches reveal a sectlike detachment, shunning the modern world to some extent because of its embrace of "secular humanism," a doctrine that undermines religious conviction in the eyes of fundamentalists. Even so, some fundamentalist leaders have joined the political fray to oppose the so-called "liberal agenda" of social issues—the proposed Equal Rights Amendment; abortion as a matter of choice; and civil rights for homosexuals. They have also pressed for the return of prayer to American public schools—a forum for moral permissiveness in their view—while scolding the mass media for coloring news and entertainment with liberal sentiments (Hunter, 1983).

Some religious organizations are more "fundamentalist" than others. The most fundamentalist Christians belong to conservative organizations in the larger evangelical tradition, including Pentecostals, Southern Baptists, Seventh-Day Adventists, and the Assembly of God. The precise number of Americans who can accurately be described as religious fundamentalists can only be approximated, but about 20 percent of American adults claim to interpret the Bible literally (N.O.R.C., 1989:168).

Christian fundamentalism in the United States has expanded its educational efforts beyond the doors of the church. There are now thousands of Christian elementary and secondary schools, along with several hundred fundamentalist Bible colleges. Fundamentalist organizations also spread their message through hundreds of periodicals (Hunter, 1985). Additionally, during the 1980s, fundamentalist Christianity made increasing use of the most powerful medium of communication: television.

The Electronic Church

The mass media now play a major role in religious life, especially among fundamentalists. The *electronic church*, with its congregation in the form of radio and television audiences around the world, is dominated by a number of highly visible prime-time preachers (Hadden & Swain, 1981). Some members of more established churches charge that the electronic church undermines religion with emotional simplicity. In any case, about 5 percent of the national television audience (about 15 million Americans) regularly tune in to religious television, while perhaps 20 percent (about 60 million) watch at least some religious programming every month (Martin, 1981; Gallup, 1982; N.O.R.C., 1989).

Using the mass media to regularly solicit contributions brought a financial windfall—in some cases totaling hundreds of millions of dollars a year—to mass-media religious organizations. The power of money, however, compromised some church leaders. In 1989, Jim Bakker began a jail term following a conviction for defrauding contributors. From a modest beginning hosting a children's puppet show in 1965, Jim and Tammy Bakker rose to national attention during the 1980s as founders of the PTL (Praise the Lord) Club and developers of the twenty-three hundred acre Heritage, USA, Christian theme park in South Carolina. As the money poured in, the couple's income soared to more than $1 million a year, prompting a federal investigation.

In the wake of this scandal, support for television preachers has waned. Many believe televangelism empires have grown too rich, and, for the single charismatic leaders and their families who control an embarrassment of riches, temptation may be overwhelming.

The power of media ministries, the growth of cults and sects, and the adherence of millions of Americans to traditional churches—all substantiate the stronghold religion has over modern society (Stark & Brainbridge, 1981; Bateson & Ventis, 1982; Hunter, 1985). Few would argue that our complex and rapidly changing world creates in many people a longing for a more secure individual identity and sense of larger purpose.

Despite impressive scientific advances in our understanding of the natural world, science is simply unable to provide answers to essential questions concerning the *meaning* of life. And some scientific technology—nuclear armaments, for example—has only increased anxiety about the future of the human species. Because religion has the power to imbue life with meaning, purpose, and a sense of belonging, many people rely on their faith for a sense of security and hope in a puzzling and uncertain world (Cox, 1977; Barker, 1981; Johnstone, 1983).

SUMMARY

Family

1. All societies are built on kinship, although family forms vary considerably across cultures and over time.

2. In industrial societies such as the United States, conventional marriage is monogamous. Many preindustrial societies, however, recognize polygamy, of which there are two types: polygyny and polyandry.

3. Cross-culturally, families differ in residential patterns. Industrial societies favor neolocality; patrilocality is more common throughout the world; and a few cultures have matrilocal households. Industrial societies utilize bilateral descent, while preindustrial societies tend to be either patrilineal or matrilineal.

4. Structural-functional analysis identifies the major functions of the family: socializing the young, regulating sexual activity, social placement, and providing emotional support. Social-conflict theory points up how the family perpetuates social inequality by strengthening distinctions in class and gender, and ethnic and racial divisions. Symbolic-interaction analysis highlights the dynamic and changeable nature of family life.

Religion

1. Religion is a major social institution based on distinguishing the sacred from the profane.

2. Religion is a matter of faith, not scientific evidence. Therefore, sociological study of religion's role in society can make no claim as to the ultimate truth or falsity of any religious belief.

3. Emile Durkheim argued that religion expresses the power of society over individuals. His structural-functional analysis suggests that religion promotes social cohesion, social control, and infuses life with meaning and purpose.

4. Using the symbolic-interaction paradigm, Peter Berger explains that religious beliefs are socially constructed. Religion is especially important as a response to life's disruptions.

5. Using the social-conflict paradigm, Karl Marx claimed religion supported social inequality. Reli-

5. Families begin with the process of courtship, which, for Americans, is centered on romantic love. The vast majority of married couples have children, although family size has decreased over time. In later life, families change as children leave home. In the final stage of marriage, a spouse dies, usually the husband.

6. The divorce rate today is ten times higher than it was a century ago; half of current marriages will end in divorce. Most people who divorce—especially men—remarry.

7. Family violence, involving both spouse abuse and child abuse, is now an important public concern.

8. American family life has become increasingly varied. Cohabitation and single-parent families have proliferated in recent years. Although gay men and lesbians cannot legally marry, many form long-lasting relationships. The practice of adults remaining single is also increasingly common.

9. New reproductive technology may alter patterns of parenting and challenge traditional definitions of parenthood. Critics of reproductive technology argue that what is technically possible may not be morally desirable.

gious ideals, however, have also motivated some people to seek greater social equality.

6. Churches, formal religious organizations that are well integrated into the larger society, fall into two types—ecclesias and denominations. Sects, often the result of religious division, are characterized by less integration into the larger society and charismatic leadership. Cults are religious organizations that embrace new and unconventional beliefs and practices.

7. Almost all American adults identify with a religion; about 60 percent have a formal religious affiliation, with the largest number belonging to various Protestant denominations. Almost all American adults claim to believe in God; about half engage in daily prayer; about one-third regularly attend religious services.

8. Secularization, an important dimension of social change, reflects the diminishing importance of reli-

gion. To some secularization signals a breakdown of traditional morality; others consider it a form of liberation and a source of greater tolerance.

9. Although membership in many "mainstream" churches has declined, other religious organizations (notably Christian sects) have gained in popularity. This suggests that secularization is unlikely to result in the demise of religion.

10. Fundamentalist Christianity stresses a literal interpretation of the Bible, intolerance of religious diversity, and the personal experience of religious faith. Fundamentalist Christian organizations in the United States typically support conservative political goals.

KEY CONCEPTS

Family

cohabitation the sharing of a household by an unmarried couple

descent the system by which kinship is traced over generations

endogamy marriage between people within a social group or category

exogamy marriage between people of different social groups or categories

extended family (consanguine family) a social unit including parents, children, and other kin

family a relatively permanent social group of two or more people, who are related by blood, marriage, or adoption and who usually live together

homogamy marriage between people with the same social characteristics

incest taboo a cultural norm forbidding sexual relations or marriage between certain kin

kinship social relationships based on blood, marriage, or adoption

marriage a socially approved relationship that is expected to be enduring, involving economic cooperation and allowing sexual activity leading to childbearing

monogamy a form of marriage with one relationship between two partners

nuclear family (conjugal family) a social unit composed of one or, more commonly, two parents and children

polygamy a form of marriage that unites three or more people

Religion

animism the belief that natural objects are conscious forms of life that can affect humanity

charisma extraordinary personal qualities that can turn an audience into followers

church a formal religious organization that is well integrated into the larger society

civil religion a quasi-religious loyalty binding individuals in a basically secular society

cult a religious movement that is highly unconventional in terms of the surrounding society

denomination a church that recognizes religious pluralism

ecclesia a church that is formally allied with the state

faith belief that is not based on scientific evidence

liberation theology a fusion of Christian principles with political activism, often Marxist in character

profane that which is defined as an ordinary element of everyday life

religion a system of beliefs and practices based on recognizing the sacred

religiosity the importance of religion in a person's life

religious fundamentalism conservative religious organizations that seek to restore what are viewed as fundamental elements of religion

sacred that which is defined as extraordinary, inspiring a sense of awe, reverence, and even fear

sect an informal religious organization that stands apart from the larger society

secularization the historic decline in the influence of religion

totem an object in the natural world imbued with sacred qualities

Education
and Medicine

Chapter Outline

Thirteen-year-old Naoko Masuo has just returned from school to her home in suburban Yokohama, Japan. Instead of dropping off her books and beginning an afternoon of play, she settles into her homework. Several hours later, her mother reminds her that it is time to leave for the *juku* or "cram school" that she attends three evenings a week. After a short subway trip downtown, Naoko joins dozens of other girls and boys for intensive training in Japanese, English, math, and science.

The Masuo family spends several hundred dollars a month so that their daughter can attend *juku*. They know, however, that the realities of Japanese schooling make such an investment necessary. Naoko will soon take a national examination, which will determine her school placement. In three years, she will repeat the process with the high-school competition. Then will come the final test: the college entrance examination. Only by working hard to become one of the best and the brightest can Naoko hope to be included in the one-third of Japanese students who enter an exclusive national university (Simons, 1989).

Why do the Japanese pay such attention to schooling? Because in this modern, industrial society, admission to an elite university virtually ensures a high-paying, prestigious career. This chapter begins by exploring *education*, a vital institution in societies like Japan and the United States. We shall see how *who* is schooled, for *how long*, and *in what* course of study is linked to various historical and cultural factors. The second half of the chapter examines *medicine*, another social institution that has gained great importance in the modern world. Like formal education, health is distributed quite unequally throughout any nation's population. And like schooling, medicine reveals distinctive variation from society to society.

EDUCATION IN CROSS-CULTURAL PERSPECTIVE

Education refers to *the various ways in which knowledge—including facts, skills, and values—is transmitted to members of society.* In industrial societies, a vital kind of education is **schooling**, *formal instruction under the direction of specially trained teachers.*

In preindustrial societies, families and local communities teach their members specialized productive skills, but schooling—especially instruction not linked to the world of work—is generally available only to the

Early in the twentieth century, mandatory education laws had been passed by every state. For the half of Americans who lived in rural areas, formal education meant the one-room schoolhouse, where children received a basic education from one teacher.

wealthy. The English word *school*, in fact, is derived from a Greek word for "leisure." In ancient Greece, renowned teachers such as Plato, Socrates, and Aristotle presided over a fabled academy for aristocratic males. In ancient China, the famous philosopher Confucius also taught a privileged few (Rohlen, 1983).

Industrial societies, by contrast, embrace the principle of mass education. Industrialization demands a labor force with a grasp of at least the basic skills of reading, writing, and arithmetic. During the last century, Americans also viewed schooling as a means to forge a literate citizenry able to participate actively and intelligently in political life. More recently, the steady growth of bureaucracy and a postindustrial economy based on written communication have made schooling even more important.

In 1850, only half of Americans between the ages of five and nineteen were enrolled in school. By 1918, however, every state had *mandatory education laws*, typically requiring schooling to age sixteen or completion of the eighth grade. These laws drew America's children from farms and factories to classrooms. Table 13–1 shows that by the mid-1960s, a majority of American adults had completed high school. Today more than 75 percent of American adults have a high-school education and 20 percent have completed four years of college.

Table 13–1 EDUCATIONAL ACHIEVEMENT
IN THE UNITED STATES, 1910–1988*

Year	High-School Graduates	College Graduates	Median Years of Schooling
1910	13.5%	2.7%	8.1
1920	16.4	3.3	8.2
1930	19.1	3.9	8.4
1940	24.1	4.6	8.6
1950	33.4	6.0	9.3
1960	41.1	7.7	10.5
1970	55.2	11.0	12.2
1980	68.7	17.0	12.5
1988	76.2	20.3	12.7

* For persons twenty-five years of age and over.

SOURCE: National Center for Education Statistics, 1989.

Japan. Until the enactment of mandatory education laws in 1872, schooling in Japan was limited to the privileged few. Today, however, Japan's educational system is widely praised for generating some of the world's highest achievers.

Schooling in the early grades instills Japanese traditions, including obligation to family (Benedict, 1974). By their early teens, students encounter Japan's system of rigorous and competitive examinations. These written tests, which all but determine their future, resemble the Scholastic Aptitude Tests (SATs) used for college admissions in the United States.

More Japanese graduate from high school (90 percent) than do Americans (76 percent). But the system of competitive examinations sharply restricts college matriculation, so that only about 30 percent of high-school graduates—half the proportion of Americans—continue their schooling (Simons, 1989). Understandably, Japanese students approach these entrance examinations with the utmost seriousness and about half attend *juku* "cram schools." In a society in which women have yet to enter the labor force in large numbers, Japanese mothers often devote themselves to their children's success at school (Brinton, 1988; Simons, 1989).

Despite—or perhaps because of—the pressure it places on students, the Japanese educational system produces impressive results. In a number of fields, notably mathematics and science, young Japanese outperform students in every other industrial society, including the United States (Hayneman & Loxley, 1983; Rohlen, 1983).

Great Britain. As explained in Chapter 7 ("Social Stratification"), the legacy of a feudal past still influences today's British society. During the Middle Ages, schooling was a privilege reserved for the nobility, who studied classical subjects since they had little need for skills related to earning a living.

As the Industrial Revolution generated a demand for educated workers, an increasing proportion of people went to school. Demands by the working class that the educational system be opened to their children had the same effect. As a result, every British child is now required to attend school until age sixteen.

Yet, traditional social distinctions persist in British education. Many wealthy families send their children to what the British call *public schools*, the equivalent of American private boarding schools. But because public schools are beyond the financial reach of most British parents, the majority send their children to state-supported schools, just as most American families do. Elite public schools in Britain do more than teach academic subjects; they also socialize children from wealthy (especially *new rich*) families into a distinctive way of life. Students learn patterns of speech, mannerisms, and social graces that distinguish members of the upper class from other Britons.

The 1960s and 1970s saw a marked expansion in the British university system (Sampson, 1982). Today British students compete for university admission by taking examinations during their high-school years. But unlike the educational arrangement in the United States, in Britain the government pays most of the tuition and living expenses for those who gain admission. Compared with Japan, examinations are less significant in Britain, and social background plays a greater role. Thus a disproportionate number of well-to-do children attend Oxford and Cambridge, the British universities with the highest social prestige (roughly comparable to Yale, Harvard, and Princeton in the United States).

The Soviet Union. At the time of the socialist revolution of 1917, Russia was an agrarian society with schooling reserved primarily for nobles. By the 1930s, however, the Soviet Union had enacted mandatory education laws. While the social disruption of World War II slowed educational programs, by 1950 half of all young people were in school. In forging a national educational system, the Soviets have long contended with striking cultural diversity in the largest country, geographically, in the world. By 1975 the Soviets finally claimed nearly universal schooling (Ballantine, 1983; Matthews, 1983).

Under Soviet policy, educational opportunity is

Schooling is a means of teaching the values and attitudes that a society deems important. Groups such as the "Young Pioneers" in the People's Republic of China meet after school to advance the political goals of socialism; the Boy Scouts and Girl Scouts represent comparable groups in the United States that teach their members our political beliefs.

open to all. The sexes are represented in fairly equal numbers in college, although women make up a greater percentage of students in lower-prestige fields (such as education and medicine), while men predominate in higher-prestige studies (agriculture and engineering, for example). The Soviets are also facing mounting demands from ethnic minorities for the same privileges (including the right to learn their traditional language in school) as the Russian majority.

As in all countries, schooling in the Soviet Union reinforces important cultural values. Although changing with *perestroika* (see Chapter 11, "Economics and Politics"), the Soviet educational system remains under the rigid control of the government, and schools teach the norms and values of socialist living (Matthews, 1983; Tomiak, 1983). Through competitive examinations, the Soviets channel the most academically talented students to higher education. However, the support of Communist party officials (especially if they are family members) has long played an important part in educational opportunity (Ballantine, 1983).

The United States. American schooling has also been shaped by distinct cultural patterns. Compared to the British, Americans have a stronger tradition of political participation. Thomas Jefferson argued that an educated populace is vital to the practice of democracy so the people can "read and understand what is going on in the world" (cited in Honeywell, 1931:13). The United States now has a larger proportion of its people attending

colleges and universities than any other industrial society (Rubinson, 1986).

Schooling in the United States also is informed by the value of *equal opportunity*. National surveys show that the vast majority of Americans think schooling is crucial to personal success (Gallup, 1982). Americans also assume that our society offers broad educational opportunity: 70 percent endorse the notion that people have a chance to get an education consistent with their abilities and talents (N.O.R.C., 1989:120). But this view better mirrors our aspirations than our achievement. Until this century, women were all but excluded from higher education, and only among the wealthy do a majority of young people attend college even today.

The cultural value of *practicality* means that, in many areas, American schools teach what has a direct bearing on people's lives, and especially their work. The educational philosopher John Dewey (1859–1952) advocated schooling with practical consequences. Rejecting the traditionalist emphasis on conveying a fixed body of knowledge to each generation, Dewey (1968; orig. 1938) endorsed *progressive education* that reflected people's changing concerns and needs. George Herbert Mead, the architect of the symbolic-interaction paradigm in sociology and a friend of Dewey's, echoed these sentiments, claiming that "any education that is worthy of the name [provides] the solution to problems that we all carry with us" (1938:52).

True to this tradition, today's college students select major areas of study with an eye toward future jobs. Figure 13–1 shows recent trends; note especially the rapid growth during the 1980s in the study of computer science, a consequence of America's high-tech revolution.

THE FUNCTIONS OF SCHOOLING

Structural-functional analysis has identified several ways in which formal education enhances the integration and stability of society.

1. **Socialization.** In technologically simple societies, the family transmits a way of life from one generation to another. As societies acquire complex technology, a formal system of education emerges that makes use of specially trained personnel to convey a wide range of specialized knowledge.

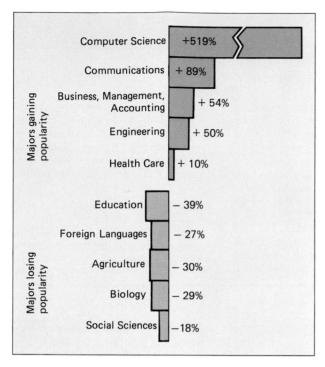

Figure 13–1 Changes in Bachelor's Degrees Conferred, 1986–1987 Compared with 1976–1977

(National Center for Education Statistics, 1979, 1989)

2. **Social integration.** By teaching approved norms and values, schooling fosters social unity. This function is especially important in societies, such as the United States, that encompass many diverse cultures. The enactment of mandatory education laws corresponded to the arrival of millions of immigrants a century ago. In many of today's cities, a majority of students belong to racial and ethnic minorities; schools help them blend their traditions with existing American culture.

3. **Social placement.** Through screening and selection, schools develop people's various abilities. Schools begin this process by evaluating students' performance primarily in terms of achievement rather than social background. Ideally, the "best and the brightest" are encouraged to pursue the most challenging and advanced studies, while students of modest abilities are guided into educational programs and occupations suited to their talents. Historically, this meritocracy function has been a key to upward social mobility in American society (Hurn, 1978).

4. **Cultural innovation.** Educational systems create as well as transmit culture. Schools are centers of critical inquiry and research that lead to discovery and innovation.

5. **Latent functions of schooling.** Formal education has additional functions that are less widely recognized. Schools serve the rising number of one-parent families and two-career marriages by providing parents with child care. Among teens, schooling consumes much time and considerable energy, inhibiting social disruption at a time of life when the likelihood of unlawful behavior is high. Schooling also occupies thousands of young people in their twenties for whom few jobs may be available. Finally, high schools, colleges, and universities bring together people of marriageable age, many of whom meet their future spouse in classes or other school-related settings. School networks provide not only friendship but valuable career opportunities and resources as well.

Critical evaluation. The structural-functional analysis of formal education stresses the various ways in which schools support the operation of an industrialized society. However, this approach overlooks the extent to which quality schooling is a privilege enjoyed by some people and far less by others. In the next section, social-conflict analysis focuses on that issue.

SCHOOLING AND SOCIAL INEQUALITY

Social-conflict analysis links formal education to social inequality. From this point of view, schooling perpetuates social inequality and acceptance of the status quo.

1. **Social control.** Schooling promotes acceptance of the status quo with its inherent inequities. Samuel Bowles and Herbert Gintis (1976) claim that the expansion of public education in the late nineteenth century provided American capitalists with a docile and disciplined work force. Mandatory education laws ensured that immigrants learned the English language as well as cultural values supporting capitalism. Compliance, punctuality, and discipline were—and still are—part of what is sometimes called the *hidden curriculum* of American schools.

American Schools: Is Disadvantage Labeled "Deficiency"?

Disadvantaged students labeled as "dumb" in school are likely, over time, to accept the idea that they are personally deficient. The process sets into motion a self-fulfilling prophecy by which students become as deficient as they are told they are. Eleven-year-old Ollie Taylor describes his own situation in these words:

The only thing that matters in my life is school and there they think I'm dumb and always will be. I'm starting to think they're right. Hell, I know they put all the black kids together in one group if they can, but that doesn't make any difference either. I'm still dumb. Even if I look around and know that I'm the smartest in my group, all that means is that I'm the smartest of the dumbest, so I haven't got anywhere at all, have I? I'm right where I always was. Every word those teachers tell me, even the ones I like most, I can hear in their voice that what they're really saying is "All right you dumb kids. I'll make it as easy as I can, and if you don't get it then, you'll never get it. Ever." That's what I hear every day, man. From every one of them. Even the other kids talk that way to me too.

SOURCE: Thomas J. Cottle, "What Tracking Did to Ollie Taylor," *Social Policy*, Vol. 5, No. 2 (July–August 1974), 22–24.

2. **Testing and social inequality.** Standardized testing recasts privilege as personal merit. Intelligence and aptitude tests were developed early in this century to evaluate innate ability, not social background. But such tests have questionable validity insofar as scores also reflect a test taker's cultural environment. In the United States, tests designed by affluent, white educators generally contain some elements of bias in favor of affluent, white students (Crouse & Trusheim, 1988; Owen, 1985).

3. **Tracking and social inequality.** Despite their shortcomings, many schools in most industrial societies use standardized tests as the basis for **tracking,** *assigning students to different educational programs.* Defenders of the tracking system argue that tracking gives students an education appropriate to their individual aptitude and interests, in classes with others of comparable abilities. Thus some enroll in college preparatory classes while others receive a general education, and still others gain vocational and technical training. But critics charge that tracking undermines the goal of meritocracy because social background plays a major role in how students are evaluated (Bowles & Gintis, 1976; Persell, 1977; Davis & Haller, 1981; Oakes, 1982). In practice, students from privileged backgrounds are typically placed in higher tracks with the best teachers and the greatest opportunities for creative learning. Those from disadvantaged backgrounds, by contrast, are likely to end up in lower tracks, with the least inspiring teachers, in which rote memorization and classroom drill make up the daily routine. Because the classroom also shapes friendships, tracking enhances the segregation of privileged and disadvantaged students (Persell, 1977; Oakes, 1982, 1985; Hallinan & Williams, 1989). The box explores one boy's experience with tracking.

Public and Private Education

Just as students are treated differently in school, so schools themselves vary. In 1990 almost 90 percent of America's 65 million primary- and secondary-school children attended state-funded public schools. The remainder were educated in private schools.

Most private-school students attend Christian church schools. Most of these are *parochial* (from the Latin meaning "of the parish") schools developed by the Catholic Church a century ago as millions of Catholics entered the predominantly Protestant United States. More recently, fundamentalist Protestants have established religious schools to provide religious instruction—and sometimes a more rigorous academic environment. Some so-called Christian schools, however, are also established to maintain racial segregation (James, 1989).

A small number of American private schools enroll

young people mostly from the upper classes. These prestigious and expensive preparatory schools send many of their graduates to equally prestigious and expensive universities. Prep schools not only provide a strong academic program, but inculcate the mannerisms, attitudes, and social graces of the socially prominent. Many "preppies" maintain lifelong social networks with other graduates of their school that provide numerous social advantages.

Two influential reports (Coleman, Hoffer, & Kilgore, 1981; Coleman & Hoffer, 1987) indicate that, holding social background constant, students in private schools perform better academically than public-school students. This appears to be due to the private schools' smaller classes, more rigorous curricula, and better discipline. Graduates of private schools are more likely than public-school alumni to complete college and subsequently enter high-paying occupations.

The public schools attended by the majority of Americans also show striking inequalities from one to another. The 1988 per-student expenditures of the fifty states ranged from a high of $8,748 in Alaska to about $2,693 in Utah (U.S. Office of Educational Research and Improvement, 1990). Much but not all of this variation reflects cost-of-living differences. Some states provide better schooling than others, and schools in wealthy, largely white suburbs have greater financial resources (because of a higher property-tax base) than schools in central cities, where financially disadvantaged minority students predominate.

Such differences prompted a policy of *busing*—transporting students to achieve greater racial balance in schools. Although this policy affects only 5 percent of American school children, it has generated enormous controversy. Advocates of busing claim governments are likely to provide adequate funding to schools in poor neighborhoods only if children from across the city attend them. Critics respond that busing is expensive and undermines the concept of neighborhood schools. But both sides acknowledge that inner cities contain too few white students to generate racial parity, whatever schools they attend. To be effective, busing would have to join cities (where blacks are concentrated) and suburbs (which are overwhelmingly white). Rarely has this been politically feasible.

A report by a research team headed by James Coleman (1966) confirmed that predominantly black schools stand at a distinct disadvantage in terms of funding, and documented further disadvantages including larger class size, insufficient libraries, and fewer science classes. But the Coleman report concluded that funding was not the key to academic quality. More important are educational attitudes on the part of teachers, children's families, and children themselves. Supporting this conclusion, Christopher Jencks (1972) claimed that even if schools were exactly the same for all, some students would perform better than others because of broader social advantages.

The point is that schools alone cannot overcome marked social inequality in American society. Yet our society can no longer afford to ignore the educational needs of poor minority children, who represent a steadily increasing proportion of the American workforce (Cohen, 1989).

Access to Higher Education

Higher education is a path to occupational achievement; for this reason most American parents want their children to attend college (Gallup, 1982). Government support for higher education has raised the proportion of Americans entering college during this century. Today about 60 percent of high-school graduates enroll in college the following fall, although college graduates make up only one-fifth of Americans over twenty-five.

Not all high-school students, of course, want to continue their academic schooling, and the intellectual demands of college may discourage others. But a crucial factor affecting access to higher education is money, since a college education must be purchased and the cost is high. Even at state-supported colleges and universities, tuition is at least several thousand dollars a year, and the annual cost of attending the most expensive private schools exceeds $20,000. Thus, as Figure 13–2 on page 324 shows, family income has a significant effect on the college attendance of young Americans.

Because of the financial burden of higher education, minorities, typically with below-average incomes, have difficulty managing to attend college. Figure 13–3 shows that whites are overly represented at every stage in American education from high school to graduate school. During the 1980s, the number of Hispanic-American students in college rose by about 50 percent, while African-American enrollments stayed fairly steady (U.S. Bureau of the Census, 1988).

The advantages of a college education seem well worth the cost. Beyond intellectual and personal growth, more schooling translates into more income. As Table 13–2 shows, males who do not complete high school typically earn $600,000 by age sixty-four, roughly half

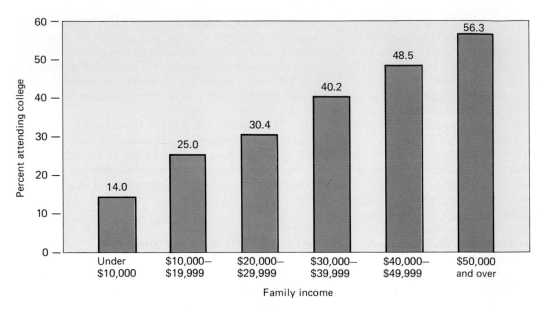

Figure 13–2   College Attendance and Family Income, 1986
Americans between 18 and 24 Years of Age
(U.S. Bureau of the Census, 1988)

the earnings of a college graduate. Among women, the financial gains of education are even greater. At each level of educational achievement, however, women earn considerably less than men. Based on differences in job types, fewer years in the labor force, and lesser pay for the same work, the lifetime earnings of a woman college graduate are less than those of a man who does not complete high school.

The high earnings of college graduates have to do with more than education. Americans who attend college are likely to come from relatively well-to-do fami-

lies and to enjoy social and economic advantages which make college possible in the first place.

Credentialism

Sociologist Randall Collins (1979) calls the United States a *credential society*, where people view diplomas and degrees as evidence of ability to perform specialized occupational roles. As modern societies have become more technologically advanced, culturally diverse, and socially mobile, credentials have assumed much of the significance once attached to family background.

Credentialism, then, amounts to *evaluating people for employment on the basis of educational degrees*. Functionally speaking, credentialism involves placing well-trained people into occupational roles for which they have the necessary aptitude. But social-conflict analysis contends that credentials often bear little relation to the skills and responsibilities a specific job demands. Collins (1979) argues that advanced degrees signal to employers, in a shorthand way, people with the manners and attitudes that speak of privilege. Credentialism thus serves a gate-keeping function, restricting powerful and lucrative positions to a small segment of the population.

Table 13–2   EDUCATION AND LIFETIME EARNINGS

Education	Lifetime Earnings*	
	Males	Females
College graduate (4 years)	$1,190,000	$523,000
Some college	957,000	460,000
High-school graduate	861,000	381,000
Less than 12 years	601,000	211,000

* Figures reflect earnings up to age sixty-four, in constant 1981 dollars.
SOURCE: U.S. Bureau of the Census, 1984.

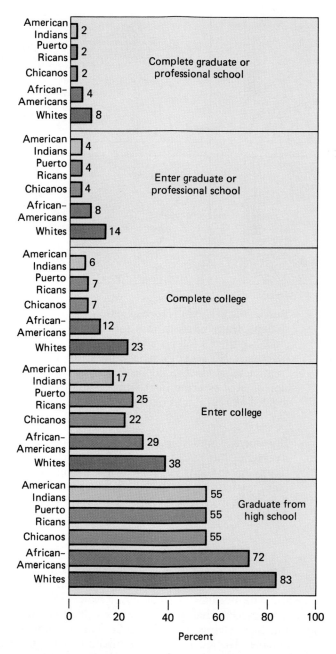

Figure 13–3 Educational Achievement of Whites
and Minorities

(Higher Education Research Institute, 1982)

Critical evaluation.   Social-conflict analysis links formal education to social inequality by contending that schooling is unequal for different categories of people. In this view, schooling transforms privilege into personal ability and social disadvantage into personal deficiency.

Social-conflict analysis can be criticized for minimizing the value of schooling for individuals and for society as a whole. Moreover, significant meritocracy in the educational system has permitted upward social mobility for many talented Americans.

PROBLEMS IN AMERICAN EDUCATION

During the 1980s, intense debate centered on American schooling. Surveys indicate that only half of Americans think our schools do a satisfactory job (Gallup, 1984).

Discipline and Violence

The government estimates that several hundred thousand students and at least one thousand teachers are physically assaulted on school grounds every year. Disorder spills into schools from the surrounding society. Nevertheless, schools do have the power to effect change for the better. Research indicates that school violence can be curbed by imposing firm disciplinary policies, supported by parents and, when necessary, law enforcement officials (Burns, 1985). Schools are unlikely to solve problems of violence that have roots deep in American society (Reed, 1983), but they can control violence within their walls by forging alliances with parents and community leaders.

Bureaucracy and Student Passivity

Another dilemma today's educators are facing is pervasive *student passivity.* This problem confronts both public and private schools at all grade levels (Coleman, Hoffer, & Kilgore, 1981).

Too many students perceive the opportunities provided by schooling not as a privilege but as a series of hurdles to be cleared in pursuit of credentials. In short, students are bored. Some of the blame must be placed on students themselves, who lack the initiative to become partners in education. Television, which now consumes

more of young people's time than school does, may also be a culprit. Even so, much of the passivity of American students stems from the educational system itself.

The small, highly personal schools of countless local communities have disappeared, replaced by impersonal educational factories. In a study of high schools across the United States, Theodore Sizer (1984) identified five ways in which large, bureaucratic schools undermine education (1984:207–209).

1. **Bureaucracy means uniformity.** Schooling has become insensitive to the cultural variation in local communities. Schools now fall under the control of outside "specialists" who may have little understanding of the everyday lives of students.

2. **Bureaucracy means numerical ratings.** School officials focus on attendance rates, dropout rates, and achievement test scores. In doing so, they overlook dimensions of schooling that are difficult to quantify, such as the creativity of students and the energy and enthusiasm of teachers.

3. **Bureaucracy fosters rigid expectations.** Fifteen-year-olds are expected to be in the tenth grade, and eleventh-grade students are expected to score at a certain level on a standardized verbal achievement test. Rarely are exceptionally bright and motivated students permitted to graduate early. Likewise, the system demands that students who have learned little graduate with their class.

4. **Bureaucracy demands specialization.** High-school students learn English from one teacher, receive guidance from another, and are coached in sports by others. No school official comes to know the "complete" student. Students experience this division of labor as a continual shuffling among rigidly divided fifty-minute periods throughout the school day.

5. **Bureaucracy undermines individual responsibility.** Highly bureaucratic schools place little responsibility on students for their own learning. Similarly, teachers have little latitude in what and how they teach their classes; they dare not accelerate learning for fear of disrupting "the system."

To some degree, bureaucracy in schools is inevitably given the immense task of educating millions of students. The number of students in New York City alone now exceeds that of the entire country a century ago. But, Sizer claims, schools can be more responsive and humane. He recommends eliminating rigid class schedules, reducing class size, and training teachers more broadly so they can become involved more fully in the lives of their students. His most radical departure from the status quo calls for making graduation from high school dependent on what a student has learned rather than simply on the length of time spent in school.

College: The Silent Classroom[1]

Student passivity is also common in colleges and universities. Curiously, sociologists have done little research on the college classroom considering how much time most spend there.

In one study, David Karp and William Yoels (1976) systematically observed classes and surveyed students at a coeducational university. Even in small classes, they found, only a few students were active participants. On the contrary, the classroom norm was passive silence. Sometimes, they observed, students themselves became irritated when one of their peers was especially talkative.

Even so, students express dismay at the silent classroom, and most blame themselves for being so passive. But, Karp and Yoels suggest, the educational system promotes passivity by instructing students to view teachers as "experts" who convey the "truth." Students come to see their proper role as quietly listening and taking notes. As a result, the researchers estimate, only 10 percent of college class time is devoted to discussion. Generally speaking, instructors enter a classroom ready to deliver a lecture, and students learn that teachers often dislike being sidetracked by student questions or comments (Boyer, 1987). Early in a course, a handful of students emerge as those who will provide the limited responses that instructors desire.

Academic Standards and Quality

While little public attention has been paid to student passivity (perhaps because bureaucratic organization and its sometimes-numbing effect on individual initiative are an accepted part of American social life), the glare of public scrutiny has been focused on the declining academic performance of American students.

A *Nation at Risk*, a 1983 study of the quality of American schools prepared by the National Commission on Excellence in Education, began with an alarming statement:

> If an unfriendly foreign power had attempted to impose on America the mediocre educational performance that

exists today, we might well have viewed it as an act of war. As it stands, we have allowed this to happen to ourselves. (1983:5)

In support of this conclusion, the report pointed out that "nearly 40 percent of 17-year-olds cannot draw inferences from written material; only one-fifth can write a persuasive essay; and only one-third can solve mathematical problems requiring several steps" (1983:9). Furthermore, scores on the Scholastic Aptitude Test (SAT) have declined since the early 1960s. Then, median scores for American students were 500 on the mathematical test and 480 on the verbal test; by 1990, the averages had slipped to 476 and 424. Some of this decline may be due to a growing pool of students taking these tests (Owen, 1985). But few doubt that American education has suffered a setback.

A *Nation at Risk* also noted with alarm the preponderance of **functional illiteracy**, *reading and writing skills inadequate for everyday needs.* Roughly one in eight children—one in three minorities—completes secondary school without learning to read or write very well. As a result, 25 million American adults (15 percent) read and write at no more than a fourth-grade level. Functional illiteracy costs our society an estimated $100 billion a year in decreased productivity, accidents, and unnecessary welfare or prison costs (Kozol, 1980, 1985).

A *Nation at Risk* recommends drastic educational change. First, it calls for rigorous academic standards: All students should be required to complete several years of English, mathematics, social studies, general science, and computer science. Second, students should remain in school as long as necessary to learn basic skills. Third, teachers' salaries should be raised to attract talent into the profession, and teacher training must be improved. A *Nation at Risk* concludes that educators must ensure that schools meet public expectations, and the American people must be prepared to bear the costs of good schools.

RECENT ISSUES IN AMERICAN EDUCATION

America's schools must respond to new challenges and technological innovation. We now turn to several contemporary educational issues.

---

[1] The phrase "silent classroom" is taken from Martha E. Gimenez (1989).

Magnet Schools

During the 1970s, school districts in many American cities established **magnet schools,** *schools that attract students through special facilities and programs promoting educational excellence.* The 1,000 magnet schools in American cities offer unusual classroom and athletic facilities and provide intensive instruction in subjects such as computer science, foreign languages, or science and mathematics.

Magnet schools are designed, first, to improve academic quality. By demanding higher achievement, magnet schools generally enhance student performance. Even schools with a history of high dropout rates now find students eagerly learning and regularly completing homework assignments.

In addition, magnet schools make inner-city schools more attractive to more affluent people—especially whites—who are likely to educate their children privately. Magnet schools can thus promote voluntary integration, reducing controversial court-ordered busing. But, in this respect, their performance has been mixed. In some cities, magnet schools have lessened racial segregation. However, in most cities there are simply not enough white students left to make for racial balance in schools. To meet a court-mandated plan for racial balance in its schools, Kansas City, in a strange twist, had to limit the enrollment of blacks in magnet schools to the available number of whites (King, 1989). While magnet schools do hold promise, then, they seem unlikely to solve the deeply entrenched problem of racial segregation in America's schools.

Schooling for the Disabled

Mandatory education laws not only require children to attend school, they also embody the American ideal of providing a basic education to everyone. Nevertheless, millions of people with mental or physical disabilities receive little or no schooling. A highly bureaucratized system of mass education does not readily meet the needs of such children, who are sometimes simply defined as unteachable.

Educating children with disabilities poses a great challenge. Many children with physical limitations have difficulty getting to and from school and, once there, stairs in school buildings form insurmountable barriers to those using crutches or wheelchairs. Children with developmental disabilities (including mental retardation)

or those with emotional problems require extensive personal attention from specially trained teachers. As a result, many children with mental and physical disabilities receive a public education only after parents and other concerned citizens persistently demand that schools meet their obligation to educate all citizens.

A recent trend called *mainstreaming,* or integrating students with disabilities into the overall educational program, is an alternative to segregated "special education" classes. Mainstreaming works well for physically impaired students who have no difficulty keeping up with the rest of the class. As an added plus, children with disabilities learn to interact with other children just as other children learn to interact with them. Mainstreaming is typically less successful among students with mental or emotional disabilities for two reasons. They may have difficulty matching the performance of other students, while simultaneously being deprived of appropriate special education. Mainstreaming is also expensive, requiring changes in physical facilities and the hiring of teachers capable of meeting the special needs of children with disabilities.

Adult Education

Most schooling is directed toward children and adolescents. However, an increasing proportion of students are adults, many of whom return to the classroom after a considerable length of time.

By the mid-1980s, 25 million American adults were enrolled in school. They range in age from the mid-twenties to well past sixty-five. Adult students generally come from a fairly privileged segment of the population: Most are white and have above-average incomes.

Why do adults return to school? There are many reasons, but usually the motivation is work-related. Most adults pursue study linked to their careers, including courses in business, health, and engineering. Others return to school simply for the challenge of intellectual stimulation.

Schooling, Computers, and the Future

Computers are now used in virtually every occupation. Not surprisingly, then, more than 95 percent of public schools have instructional computers (U.S. Bureau of the Census, 1989). Other industrial societies share America's enthusiasm for computers in schools: The Soviet

The number of foreign students in the United States—exceeding 350,000—has increased dramatically in recent years. Most of these students are from Third-World societies, 60 percent from Asian nations. The majority will return to their countries with the goal of speeding economic development.

Union began requiring computer education in its high schools in 1985 (Alexander, 1985).

The advantages of educational computing are not limited to learning job-related skills. Computers can also improve the quality of schooling itself. In a new field called computer-aided instruction (CAI), computers can be programmed to interact with students by reacting to students' input. Computers also allow students to progress at their own pace. For students with disabilities, who are unable to write with pencil and paper, computers may permit easier self-expression. The introduction of computers into schools—in some cases, as early as kindergarten—has also sparked a new passion for learning among many students. Research suggests that computer-assisted instruction significantly increases learning speed and retention of information (Fantini, 1986).

But some educators have strong reservations about the use of computers in school. After all, no matter how cleverly it is programmed, a machine will never prompt a series of keen personal insights the way a motivated human teacher can. And while computers are ideally suited for quantitative pursuits, their capacity is limited when it comes to inspiring a love of poetry or drawing students into complex ethical controversies.

Introducing computers into American education will not solve many of the problems that plague our schools. Yet there is little doubt that they will continue to shape classroom learning in the twenty-first century.

MEDICINE

Another social institution concerned with human well-being is **medicine,** *the institutionalized means of combating disease and promoting health.* As in the case of educating the young, health has been a major concern of human societies throughout history. The World Health Organization describes the ideal of **health** as *a state of complete physical, mental, and social well-being* (1946:3).

Health and Society

As we shall see in the remainder of this chapter, health is as much a social as a biological issue. To begin, society affects health in three basic ways.

1. **Cultural patterns affect health.** Standards of health vary from culture to culture. René Dubos (1980; orig. 1965) points out that early in this century, yaws, a contagious skin disease, was so common in tropical Africa that people there considered it normal.

    Lifestyles a society views as healthy are also closely linked to what it defines as morally good; by contrast, behavior considered unhealthy is often perceived as morally bad. Americans who believe homosexuality is morally wrong may view this sexual orientation as "sick," although it is quite natural from a medical point of view. Americans, especially men, tend to define a competitive, stressful way of life as normal, despite strong evidence that such behavior lies at the root of two-thirds of physician visits and most heart disease—the leading cause of death in the United States (Wallis, 1983). Ideas about health, therefore, translate into a form of social control, encouraging conformity to cultural standards.

2. **Technology and resources affect health.** Many of the technologies to combat disease were developed in this century. By current standards, in fact, America has a history of malnutrition, poor sanitation, and infectious disease. Similarly, what today's relatively affluent Americans consider poor health, people in Third-World countries take as the norm.

3. **Health relates to social inequality.** Throughout the world, the resources that promote personal well-being are distributed unequally. The physical, mental, and emotional health of wealthier people is far better than that of poor people. Affluence is also linked to longevity. Because of their relative affluence, whites in the United States live an average of six years longer than blacks.

Health in Cross-Cultural Perspective

The marked variations in health from nation to nation provide strong evidence of the link between health and society. Historical patterns, too, confirm this connection.

Preindustrial societies. Their simple technology limited the ability of hunting and gathering societies to generate a healthful environment. As Gerhard and Jean Lenski (1987) suggest, a food shortage sometimes meant a nursing mother had to abandon a child. Those surviving infancy were still vulnerable: Perhaps half the members of such societies died before age twenty, and few lived past forty.

The agricultural revolution expanded the supply of food and other resources. Yet, due to increasing social inequality, elites enjoyed better health than peasants and slaves. Hunger, hard work, and crowded, unsanitary shelters took their toll on the majority. Especially in the growing cities of medieval Europe, human waste and other refuse triggered infectious diseases, including plague that periodically wiped out entire towns (Mumford, 1961).

Industrial societies. The Industrial Revolution in Europe and North America, beginning in the mid-eighteenth century, initially did little to improve public health. On the contrary, factories attracted to the cities thousands of people from the countryside, further aggravating sanitation problems. Even the most well-paid industrial work-

ers lived in crowded, contaminated tenements. Factories continuously fouled the air with smoke, a health threat unrecognized until well into the twentieth century. Workplace accidents were common.

Then, during the nineteenth century, health in Western Europe and North America began to improve. A rising standard of living meant better nutrition and safer housing. After 1850, scientific advances in medicine improved health further, especially in the cities plagued with infectious diseases. In 1854, John Snow examined the street addresses of cholera victims in London and succeeded in tracing the source of this disease to contaminated drinking water (Mechanic, 1978). Within several decades, scientists had linked cholera to specific bacteria and developed a protective vaccine. Increasing medical knowledge brought an end to age-old unsanitary practices such as discharging raw sewage into rivers used for drinking water. By the early twentieth century, death rates from infectious diseases had declined sharply.

Dramatic improvement in the health of industrialized societies has continued. The leading killers in 1900—influenza and pneumonia—accounted for 25 percent of all deaths. Today, because of antibiotics and other medical breakthroughs, these diseases cause fewer than 3 percent of deaths in the United States. Table 13–3 lists other infectious diseases—the cause of significant numbers of deaths in 1900—which no longer pose a major threat to public health.

Today heart disease, cancer, and cerebrovascular diseases such as stroke account for almost 60 percent of deaths in the United States. The preponderance of these diseases partly stems from increased use of work-saving devices that reduce the need for healthful exercise, and partly from consumption of cigarettes and high-cholesterol foods. In short, fewer Americans die of acute infectious diseases (such as influenza and pneumonia) and more die of chronic illnesses (including heart disease and cancer) associated with advancing age.

Third-World health today. The striking poverty of the Third World (see Chapter 8, "Global Inequality") limits life expectancy there to roughly sixty years, ten years below the average in industrial societies. People in the poorest societies in the world, such as Cambodia and Ethiopia, generally live only to about forty. Paul Harrison (1984) estimates that 10 percent of Third-World children die during their first year of life; in the poorest nations of the world, half the children do not survive into adulthood. These startling statistics roughly mirror the situation in Europe in 1750 (George, 1977).

Table 13–3 THE CHANGING CAUSES OF DEATH
                IN THE UNITED STATES

The Ten Leading Causes of Death in 1900
 1. Influenza and pneumonia
 2. Tuberculosis
 3. Stomach and intestinal diseases
 4. Heart disease
 5. Cerebral hemorrhage
 6. Kidney disease
 7. Accidents
 8. Cancer
 9. Diseases of early infancy
10. Diphtheria

The Ten Leading Causes of Death in 1987
 1. Heart disease
 2. Cancer
 3. Cerebrovascular diseases
 4. Accidents
 5. Lung disease (noncancerous)
 6. Influenza and pneumonia
 7. Diabetes
 8. Suicide
 9. Cirrhosis and related liver disease
10. Artery disease

SOURCE: Information for 1900 is from William C. Cockerham, *Medical Sociology*, 2nd ed. (Englewood Cliffs, NJ: Prentice-Hall, 1986), p. 24; information for 1987 is from U.S. National Center for Health Statistics, *Monthly Vital Statistics Report*, Vol. 36, No. 3 (June 22, 1987): Table 6.

According to the World Health Organization, one billion people around the world suffer from poor health. Poverty translates into hunger and poor sanitation, resulting in widespread infectious disease. Diseases that killed most Americans in 1900 thus are still the leading causes of death in poor nations. In sum, a majority of Americans die in old age from heart disease and cancer; most people in the Third World die throughout the life cycle from infectious and parasitic diseases.

Improving Third-World health poses a monumental challenge. First, poverty and poor health form a vicious cycle: Poverty breeds disease, which in turn undermines economic productivity (Harrison, 1984). Second, as medical technology is brought in to combat infectious disease, the populations of poor countries increase. Lacking the resources to ensure the well-being of the people they have now, poor nations can ill-afford population growth. Thus, reducing death rates carries the moral obligation to reduce birth rates as well.

HEALTH IN THE UNITED STATES

In global perspective, Americans enjoy very favorable patterns of health. Some categories of Americans, however, are far healthier than others.

Social Epidemiology: Who Is Healthy?

Social epidemiology is *the study of the distribution of health and disease in a society's population.* Just as early social epidemiologists examined the origin and spread of epidemic diseases, researchers today link health to the physical and social environment (Cockerham, 1986). At the root of such analysis, researchers compare the health of different categories of Americans.

Age and sex. Although death is now rare among young people, accidental death among Americans under age twenty-five has become more likely. Such cases are usually automobile-related.

Across the life course, women have better health than men. Biological factors cause slightly more deaths of males at or soon after birth. The subsequent socialization of children into gender roles also favors females. Males, encouraged to be aggressive and individualistic, are the primary victims of accidents, violence, and suicide. As adults, men are more competitive, repress their emotions, and consume more cigarettes and alcohol.

Social class and race. Infant mortality—the death rate among newborns—is twice as high for socially disadvantaged Americans as for their more privileged counterparts. While the richest American children fare best of all, the poorest are as vulnerable as children in Third-World nations such as Libya and Lebanon.

Table 13–4 shows that almost 80 percent of Americans with family incomes over $35,000 assess their health as excellent or very good, in contrast to about half of those in families earning less than $10,000. Conversely, while only about 4 percent of higher-income people described their own health as fair or poor, more than 22 percent of poor Americans made this claim. This difference shows up in school and the workplace. On average, Americans with family income under $10,000 miss twenty-five days of school or work a year due to illness, while those earning over $35,000 take off only ten days for medical reasons (U.S. National Center for Health Statistics, 1990).

Table 13–4 ASSESSMENT OF PERSONAL HEALTH BY INCOME, 1989

Family Income	Excellent	Very Good	Good	Fair	Poor
Under $10,000	24.3%	23.4%	29.2%	14.8%	7.8%
$10,000–$19,999	30.9	26.7	28.0	10.5	3.8
$20,000–$34,999	40.7	30.2	21.7	5.7	1.6
$35,000 and over	50.5	29.0	16.8	3.0	0.8

SOURCE: U.S. National Center for Health Statistics, *Current Estimates from the National Health Survey*, 1989, Series 10, No. 176 (Washington, DC: Government Printing Office, 1990), Table 70, p. 114.

Because African Americans are three times as likely as whites to be poor, they are more likely to die in infancy and to suffer illness as adults. Table 13–5 shows the average life expectancy for American children born in 1988. Whites can expect to live more than seventy-five years; nonwhites, about seventy-one years. Sex is a stronger predictor of health than race, since nonwhite females born in 1988 can expect to outlive males of either race. Table 13–5 also indicates that 75 percent of white males—but only about 58 percent of nonwhite males—will live to sixty-five. The comparable chances for women are about 86 percent for whites and 75 percent for nonwhites.

Poor Americans often live in crowded, unsanitary dwellings that breed infectious diseases. Poor people also suffer from nutritional deficiencies. Perhaps 20 percent of Americans—some 45 million people—can afford neither a healthful diet nor adequate medical care. As a result, while wealthy Americans are likely to die of long-term chronic illnesses, such as heart disease and cancer, poor Americans tend to die at a younger age from infectious diseases and illnesses resulting from poor nutrition.

Poverty also breeds stress and violence. The leading cause of death for African-American males aged fifteen to twenty-four—who are heavily represented in the urban underclass—is homicide. In 1988 about 4,500 African-Americans were killed by other blacks—more than half the number of black soldiers killed in the entire Vietnam War. Increased drug use, especially crack cocaine, during the 1980s escalated inner-city violence.

Environmental Pollution

Industrial technology has generated a number of environmental hazards to health. Air pollution from automobiles and industry poses a growing health threat. For example, the air in Los Angeles is considered unhealthful about half the days of the year. Across the country, industries have polluted the soil and groundwater with poisonous chemicals.

Some 30,000 waste sites in the United States threaten drinking-water supplies. The Environmental Protection Agency has targeted 1,200 of these for urgent action, but to date fewer than fifty have been cleaned up. Bureaucratic delays, mismanagement of public funds, and disagreement as to who should pay the costs have all contributed to the slow pace of this process.

Nuclear power has the potential to provide inexpensive energy without depleting the finite resources of coal and oil. In 1990, 110 nuclear reactors produced about 20 percent of the electricity consumed by Americans. However, nuclear power has its own inherent environmental hazards: One major malfunction could release massive clouds of radiation into the atmosphere for hundreds of miles, as deadly as fallout from an atomic bomb. Nuclear accidents have occurred in Canada, Great Britain, the United States, and—most seriously—at the Chernobyl plant near Kiev in the Soviet Union in 1986. Radiation from this accident spread throughout much of the world. The immediate death toll was thirty, but long-term casualties from radiation exposure might number into the tens of thousands.

Table 13–5 LIFE EXPECTANCY FOR AMERICAN CHILDREN BORN IN 1988

	Males	Females	Both Sexes
Whites	72.1	78.9	75.5
	(75%)	(86%)	(81%)
Nonwhites	67.4	75.5	71.5
	(58%)	(75%)	(66%)
All races	71.4	78.3	74.9
	(73%)	(85%)	(79%)

Figures in parentheses indicate the chances of living to age 65.
SOURCE: U.S. Bureau of the Census, 1990.

Nuclear power plants also produce waste materials that remain highly radioactive for hundreds of thousands of years. Currently, there is no way to safely dispose of such wastes; the danger of future radioactive contamination looms over every disposal plan.

Cigarette Smoking

Cigarette smoking became popular among Americans during this century. Evidence of its dangers appeared early, but smoking was still socially acceptable as recently as a generation ago. Today smoking is recognized as the leading, preventable cause of illness and death among Americans and is becoming defined as a mild form of social deviance.

Consumption of cigarettes has fallen since 1970, when 37 percent of American adults smoked. In 1989, about 29 percent of Americans were smokers, consuming some 550 billion cigarettes. Further declines are expected during the 1990s (U.S. Department of Commerce, 1989).

Cigarette smoke contains nicotine, which is physically addictive. When used as a means of coping with stress, cigarettes also foster psychological dependence. People who are divorced or separated are likely smokers, as are the unemployed and people in the armed forces. Blue-collar workers are more likely to smoke than white-collar workers, and people with less education smoke more than those with more schooling. Among adults, blacks (40 percent) are more likely to smoke than whites (30 percent), and males of all races (32 percent) smoke

more than females (27 percent). Cigarettes are the only form of tobacco to gain popularity among women; the number of women smokers has risen since World War II, and in 1987 lung cancer surpassed breast cancer as the cause of death among young American women.

Nearly 400,000 Americans die each year as a direct result of cigarette smoking—about seven times the number killed during the Vietnam War. Smoking has been linked to heart disease; cancer of the mouth, throat, and lungs; and emphysema. Smokers also contract more minor illnesses, such as flu, than nonsmokers, and pregnant women who smoke increase the likelihood of spontaneous abortion, low-birth-weight babies, and prenatal death. Research indicates that even passive exposure to smoke (so-called secondhand smoke) increases the risk of disease (Shephard, 1982).

Tobacco, in all its forms, constituted a $21 billion industry in the United States in 1987. The tobacco industry maintains that the precise link between cigarettes and disease has not been specified, so the health effects of smoking remain "an open question" (Rudolph, 1985). But the American tobacco industry is not breathing as easily today as it once did. Laws mandating a smoke-free environment are spreading rapidly. Furthermore, courts have increased the liability of cigarette manufacturers in lawsuits brought by victims of smoking-related illnesses, or their survivors.

In response to these developments, the tobacco industry is rapidly diversifying into non-tobacco products. In addition, it has launched intensive sales campaigns in the Third World, where regulation of tobacco sales and advertising are lenient.

Critics claim that the American tobacco industry has targeted minorities, partly accounting for higher rates of cigarettte smoking among African-Americans. Several communities, including this neighborhood in Washington, D.C., have organized to demand removal of such billboards.

Sexually Transmitted Diseases

Sexual activity may be pleasurable, but people can transmit more than fifty diseases in this way. What are commonly called *venereal diseases* (from Venus, the Roman goddess of love) date back to humanity's origins; they are even mentioned in the Bible. Because Americans have traditionally linked sex to sin, many people regard venereal disease not only as illness, but also as punishment for immorality.

Sexually transmitted diseases (STDs) attracted national attention during the so-called "sexual revolution" of the 1960s. Thus STDs stand out as an exception to the general decline of infectious ailments during this century.

Gonorrhea and syphilis. Gonorrhea and syphilis have plagued humanity for centuries. Caused by a microscopic organism, they are almost always transmitted by sexual contact. Untreated, gonorrhea can cause sterility, while syphilis can damage major organs and result in blindness, mental illness, and death.

More than a million cases of gonorrhea are reported annually, although the actual number is probably several times greater (Masters, Johnson, & Kolodny, 1988). Gonorrhea is more common among minorities than whites. Of the total number of reported cases in 1988, 78 percent involved blacks, 16 percent whites, and 5 percent Hispanics. African-Americans also had the highest rate of syphilis, accounting for 76 percent of cases; whites and Hispanics each accounted for about 12 percent (Moran et al., 1989).

Gonorrhea and syphilis are now easily cured with penicillin, an antibiotic drug developed in the 1940s. Therefore neither disease currently represents a serious health problem in the United States.

Genital herpes. An estimated one in eight American adults carries the genital herpes virus. The infection rate among African-Americans, however, is estimated to be about three times higher than the overall average (Moran et al., 1989).

Although far less serious than gonorrhea and syphilis, herpes is incurable. It can be asymptomatic or it can cause periodic, painful blisters on the genitals, accompanied by fever and headache. Although not fatal to adults, women with active genital herpes can transmit the disease, during a vaginal delivery, to infants, for whom it may be deadly. Such women, therefore, often give birth by cesarean section.

AIDS. The most serious sexually transmitted disease is acquired immune deficiency syndrome, or AIDS. Identified in 1981, this fatal disease has no cure. About forty thousand new cases were reported in the United States during 1990, bringing the total through 1990 to 155,000. More than 94,000 of these people have already died.

AIDS is caused by a human immunodeficiency virus (HIV). This virus attacks white blood cells, the core of the immune system, rendering a person vulnerable to a wide range of infectious diseases that eventually lead to death.

According to 1990 estimates, about 1.5 million Americans were infected with HIV. The majority of those with the virus show no symptoms and are probably unaware of their infection. The presence of HIV does not necessarily mean that a person will develop AIDS; in any case, symptoms do not usually appear for at least a year. Within about five years, 25 percent of infected people will come down with AIDS; most but perhaps not all will eventually develop the disease. Estimates place the number of Americans actively battling the disease in 1992 at 365,000. AIDS thus represents a catastrophic development—potentially the most serious epidemic of modern times.

Transmission of HIV almost always occurs through blood, semen, or breast milk. This means that AIDS is not spread through casual contact with an infected person, including shaking hands or hugging. There is no known case of the virus being transmitted through coughing and sneezing, through the sharing of towels, dishes, or telephones, or through water in a bath, pool, or hot tub. The risk of transmitting AIDS through saliva (as in kissing) appears to be extremely low. Oral, genital, and especially anal sex carry risk, which can be greatly reduced by use of condoms. There is no danger of becoming infected by donating blood, and receiving a blood transfusion is now virtually safe, thanks to extensive screening of the nation's blood supply. In short, AIDS is deadly but it is also hard to get.

Specific behaviors place people at high risk for AIDS. The first, anal sex, can cause rectal bleeding, allowing easy transmission of HIV. This practice is extremely dangerous, and the greater the number of sexual partners, the greater the risk. Anal sex is commonly practiced by gay males, in some cases with many sexual partners. For this reason, about two-thirds of people with AIDS are homosexual and bisexual males. During the 1980s, however, promiscuity among gays (and nongays) declined greatly as a result of concern about this

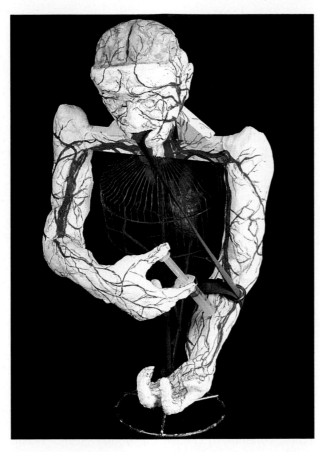

The sculpture *The Junkie,* by Paul Marcus, graphically depicts the loss of humanity that often accompanies intravenous drug use. The age of AIDS has added yet another deadly consequence to such behavior, the transmission of HIV through the sharing of needles. Many cities have proposed programs for giving clean needles to addicts, but almost all of them have been defeated by those concerned that this encourages illegal drug use.

disease (McKusick et al., 1985; Kain, 1987; Kain & Hart, 1987).

Sharing needles used for intravenous drugs constitutes a second high-risk behavior. At present, such drug users account for 22 percent of those with AIDS. Sex with a drug user also poses high risks. Because intravenous drug use is more common among poor Americans, AIDS is becoming a disease of the socially disadvantaged. Overall, 55 percent of AIDS victims are white, yet blacks (12 percent of Americans) account for 28 percent of people with AIDS, and Hispanics (7 percent of Ameri-

cans) represent 16 percent of AIDS cases (U.S. Center for Disease Control, 1990). Among children, the linkage between AIDS and minorities is even more pronounced: Almost 80 percent of AIDS victims under thirteen are minorities (U.S. Department of Health and Human Services, 1989).

In 1990, only 5 percent of AIDS cases in the United States were thought to have been caused by heterosexual contact (although heterosexuals, infected in various ways, account for about 30 percent of AIDS cases). The likelihood of a runaway "breakout" of AIDS into the heterosexual population seems less likely than it did several years ago (Fumento, 1989). But heterosexual activity can and does transmit AIDS, and the risk rises with the number of sexual partners, especially those in high-risk categories.

Strictly from an economic standpoint, AIDS is already reaching catastrophic proportions. The cost of treatment today exceeds $150,000 per person and may rise further as new therapies are developed. The national medical bill for AIDS now stands at some $10 billion; tens of billions more in lost earnings and productivity can be added to that as well. Government health programs, private insurance, and personal savings will cover only a small fraction of this total. There is little doubt, then, that AIDS represents both a medical and a social problem of monumental dimensions.

The government responded slowly to the AIDS crisis, largely because gays and intravenous drug users are widely viewed as deviant. More recently, funding for AIDS research has risen rapidly, and progress is being made. For example, researchers have found that the drug AZT slows the progress of the disease. Nevertheless, educational programs remain the most effective weapon against AIDS, since prevention is the only way to stop a deadly disease that currently has no cure.

Ethical Issues Surrounding Death

Technological advances have given human beings greater control over life itself. Ethical issues arise as we struggle to decide how to use these new powers, or whether to use them at all.

When is a person dead? Common sense suggests that life ceases when breathing and heartbeat stop. But a heart can be revived or replaced, and respiration can be artificially sustained. In short, the line between life and death has become clouded by new medical technologies. Medical and legal experts in the United States now define death as an irreversible state involving no response to stimulation, no movement or breathing, no reflexes, and no indication of brain activity (Ladd, 1979; Wall, 1980).

Do people have a right to die? With increasing frequency, the deaths of terminally ill people depend on a human decision. Who should assume this responsibility? In 1990, twenty-six-year-old Nancy Cruzan fell into an irreversible coma after an automobile accident. Physicians assured Cruzan's parents that their daughter would never recover. Certain that their daughter would not wish to live in a permanent vegetative state, the Cruzans sought to let Nancy die, taking their case all the way to the U.S. Supreme Court. In 1990, the court supported a patient's right to die by declaring that any person judged competent could choose to refuse medical treatment or nutrition. Because the Cruzans were able to present "clear and convincing evidence" of their daughter's wishes, the feeding tube keeping her alive was removed. Nancy Cruzan died twelve days later (Mauro, 1990).

Ten thousand Americans are in the same kind of permanent vegetative state as Nancy Cruzan was (Howlett, 1990). Thousands more, faced with a terminal illness that may cause suffering, consider ending their own life. American courts and government commissions continue to wrestle with the ethical dilemma pitting patients' rights against the need to afford all appropriate care to those in need. A 1983 presidential commission noted that the first obligation of physicians and hospitals is to protect the patient's life. Doctors must explain every medical option available to patients or, when patients are incapacitated, to family members. Even so, terminally ill patients can refuse heroic treatment that may extend their lives but not offer hope of recovery. According to the commission, however, a family decision such as that faced by the Cruzans must be made in the interest of the patient, not others.

What about mercy killing? *Mercy killing* is the common term for **euthanasia,** *assisting in the death of a person suffering from an incurable disease.* Euthanasia (from the Greek, meaning "a good death") thus amounts to causing the death of another person out of kindness. Although the patient's right to die has gained widespread support in the United States, assisting in the death of another person is more controversial. *Passive* euthanasia—withholding heroic treatment by, say, not reviving a heart attack victim—allows a patient to die; *active* euthanasia—such as turning off a respirator, removing

a feeding tube, or administering a lethal injection—entails a more serious responsibility.

Those who categorically view life—even with suffering—as better than death reject all forms of euthanasia. Those who recognize circumstances under which death is preferable may support euthanasia, but face the practical problem of determining just when life is no longer worth living.

Such a decision can place an enormous burden on family members. Surely in most cases they try to imagine what the terminally ill person would desire. Yet, medical expenses may be difficult to ignore. A single attempt to revive a patient whose heart has stopped may cost $1,500. Two weeks of heroic lifesaving efforts may cost tens of thousands of dollars in medical expenses. Opponents of euthanasia express concern that such costs may enter into a family's decision regarding heroic treatment. Financial concerns obviously only further complicate an already perplexing ethical issue.

THE MEDICAL ESTABLISHMENT

Through most of human history, health care was a responsibility of individuals and their families. In preindustrial societies, medical practitioners range from herbalists to acupuncturists; in much of the Third World, such people continue to combat the world's greatest health problems (Ayensu, 1981).

As a society industrializes, healing becomes the responsibility of specially trained and legally licensed healers. A scientific approach to health has come to dominate the American medical establishment.

The Rise of Scientific Medicine

Scientific medicine applies the logic of science to the treatment of disease and injury. The herbalists, druggists, midwives, and ministers who engaged in some form of healing arts in colonial America rarely agreed about how this work should be done (Stevens, 1971). Unsanitary instruments, lack of anesthesia, and widespread ignorance made surgery a terrible ordeal; doctors probably killed as many patients as they saved.

Medical specialists gradually learned about human anatomy, physiology, and biochemistry. By about 1850, with the establishment of medical schools, doctors assumed their place as self-regulating professionals. The American Medical Association (AMA), founded in 1847, heralded broad acceptance of a scientific model of medicine and laid the groundwork for today's medical establishment. The AMA widely publicized the medical successes of its members in tracing the cause of life-threatening diseases to bacteria and viruses, and developing vaccines to combat disease.

Although other approaches to health care, such as regulating nutrition, were also popular, the AMA boldly—some thought arrogantly—asserted the superiority of its approach. It won a victory in the early 1900s as state licensing boards agreed to certify only physicians competent in the scientific programs approved by the AMA (Starr, 1982). With control of the certification process, the AMA effectively closed down schools teaching other healing skills, limiting the practice of medicine to those with an M.D. degree. In the process, both the prestige and income of physicians rose dramatically. They are now among the highest-paid Americans, earning an average of $125,000 in 1988.

Osteopathic physicians, who originally promoted health by manipulating the skeleton and muscles, concluded that they had no choice but to accept scientific medicine. Thus osteopaths (with D.O. degrees) today treat illness in the same fashion as medical doctors (with M.D. degrees). Other practitioners—such as chiropractors, herbal healers, and midwives—have held to traditional practices at the cost of being relegated to the fringes of the medical profession. With far less social prestige and income than physicians, these professionals now have a small, if devoted, following among Americans (Gordon, 1980).

The rise of scientific medicine, taught in expensive, urban medical schools, also changed the social profile of doctors. More and more, physicians came from privileged backgrounds and practiced in cities. Furthermore, women had long played a role in the traditional forms of health care denigrated by the AMA. Some medical schools did train mostly women and African-Americans but, with little public support or financial resources, few of these schools survived. Thus only in recent decades has the number of blacks and women in medicine begun to increase (Stevens, 1971; Starr, 1982; Huet-Cox, 1984).

Holistic Medicine

The scientific medical establishment still has its critics. A traditional view of health that has gained growing

Medieval medical practice was heavily influenced by astrology, and diseases were often thought to arise from astral influence; this is the root of our word "influenza." Thus, as midwives attend a childbirth in this woodcut by Swiss artist Jost Amman (1580), an astrologer casts a horoscope for the newborn.

support among Americans is called **holistic medicine,** *an approach to health care that emphasizes prevention of illness and takes account of the whole person within a physical and social environment.*

Holistic practitioners claim that drugs, surgery, artificial organs, and high technology have transformed medical doctors into narrow specialists concerned with symptoms rather than people, and with disease rather than health. The following are the foundations of holistic health care (Gordon, 1980):

1. **Patients are people.** Holistic practitioners are concerned not only with symptoms, but with how an overall social environment affects each person's health. For example, the likelihood of illness increases under stress caused by poverty or intense competition at work (Duhl, 1980). Holistic practitioners work to actively combat environmental pollution and other dangers to public health.

2. **Responsibility, not dependency.** Scientific medicine views health as a complex issue only physicians can understand, fostering patients' dependency on medical doctors. Holistic medicine acknowledges the role of experts in a crisis, but generally seeks to help people enhance their own ability to engage in health-promoting behavior (Ferguson, 1980). Holistic medicine is an *active* approach to *health*, whereas scientific medicine is a *reactive* approach to *disease*.

3. **Personal treatment environment.** Conventional medicine has shifted health care from the home to impersonal offices and hospitals, which are disease-centered rather than health-oriented, and which reinforce reliance on medical experts. As much as possible, holistic medicine places health care in personal, relaxed settings.

4. **Optimum health for all.** The goal of holistic medicine is the highest possible level of well-being for everyone. Beyond treating illness, the holistic approach helps people who are "well" to realize "a state of extraordinary vigor, joy, and creativity" (Gordon, 1980:17).

Perhaps most important, holistic medicine seeks to reestablish the personal social ties that united healers and patients before the era of specialists. The AMA currently recognizes more than fifty specialized areas of medical practice, and a growing proportion of M.D.s are entering these high-paying specialties rather than family practice. Thus there is a need for practitioners who are concerned with the patient in holistic perspective.

Medicine and Economics

As medical technology has become more complex, the costs of health care have skyrocketed. Nations around the world have various ways to meet this expense.

The Soviet Union. In socialist societies, such as the Soviet Union, the government controls medical care. Because basic health care is defined as a right, the government uses public funds to pay medical costs. It owns and operates medical facilities and it pays the salaries of practitioners, who are government employees (Fuchs, 1974; Knaus, 1981). Soviet people cannot choose their own physician, as many Americans do, but report to a government health facility near their home.

The transformation of Eastern Europe has revealed that some socialist societies have not placed a high value on the health of their people. Romania is perhaps the worst offender, for decades subjecting its people to industrial pollutants. In the town of Copsa Mica, death rates have been extremely high, raising doubts about the long-term health of children such as these.

Soviet physicians receive about the same salary as skilled industrial workers, a reflection of socialist attempts at economic equality. The relatively low income of Soviet physicians is also a gender issue. About 70 percent of Soviet physicians are women, compared with about 18 percent in the United States, and, as in the United States, occupations dominated by women are financially less rewarding (Knaus, 1981).

Although the Soviet system does provide basic care to a large population, its rigid bureaucracy makes for highly standardized and impersonal treatment. This institutionalized lack of flexibility limits the Soviet system's ability to embrace holistic health concerns.

The People's Republic of China. The People's Republic of China is a poor, agrarian society only beginning to industrialize. Attending to the health of more than a billion people is a truly monumental task. The Chinese make use of traditional acupuncture, medicinal herbs, as well as scientific techniques, and retain a strong holistic concern for the interplay of mind and body (Sidel & Sidel, 1982b; Kaptchuk, 1985).

China recently experimented with private medical care, but in 1989 reestablished tight government controls over every area of life. China's so-called barefoot doctors, roughly comparable to American paramedics, continue to bring at least some modern medical care to millions of peasants in remote rural villages.

Sweden. In nations with predominantly capitalist economies, health is largely a commodity to be purchased privately. Many free-market countries, however, provide considerable government support for medical care.

In 1891 Sweden instituted a program of compulsory, comprehensive medical care funded through taxes. Most physicians receive salaries from the government rather than fees from patients, and most hospitals are government-managed. Because this medical system resembles that of socialist societies, it is often described as **socialized medicine**, *a health-care system in which most medical facilities are owned and operated by the government, and most physicians are salaried government employees.*

Great Britain. In 1948 Great Britain instituted socialized medicine as an outgrowth of a medical insurance program launched in 1911. Even so, some physicians and hospitals operate privately. Thus all British citizens can use the National Health Service, but those who can afford it purchase more extensive care from private practitioners. This "dual system" results in better care for some but basic care for all.

Canada. The Canadian government reimburses its people for hospitalization and physician services. Because physicians operate privately, Canada does not offer true socialized medicine. Moreover, some physicians work entirely outside the government-funded system, charging whatever fees they wish. The schedule of reimbursable fees is set annually by the federal government and the governments of the ten Canadian provinces in consultation with professional medical associations (Grant, 1984; Vayda & Deber, 1984).

Japan. Physicians in Japan operate privately, and a combination of insurance and government programs pays most costs. Many large businesses provide comprehensive health coverage as an employee benefit. For those without such programs, government medical insurance covers 70 percent of all costs, and the elderly receive free care (Vogel, 1979).

Medicine in the United States

The United States is unique among industrialized nations in having no government-sponsored medical program for every citizen. On average, European governments pay about 75 percent of medical costs; the U.S. government pays 40 percent. The state pays most medical expenses but only for some categories of people, so that American medicine is primarily a private, profit-making industry. This **direct-fee system** is *a medical-care system in which patients pay directly for the services of physicians and hospitals.*

Affluent Americans can purchase outstanding medical care; yet poorer Americans fare worse than their counterparts in Europe. Witness the relatively high death rates among both infants and adults in the United States compared to many European countries (Fuchs, 1974; United Nations, 1983).

Why does the United States have no national health-care program? First, Americans have historically favored limited government. Second, support for a national medical program has not been strong, even among members of labor unions, which have concentrated on winning health-care benefits from employers. Third, the AMA and the insurance industry have strongly and consistently lobbied against any such program (Starr, 1982).

Figure 13–4 shows that medical expenditures in the United States increased dramatically between 1950 and 1988. Americans spent about 5 percent of the gross national product on medical care in 1950; by 1988, medical care was absorbing 11 percent of GNP. How do Americans pay for medical care?

Private insurance programs. In 1987, 147 million Americans (61 percent) received medical-care benefits from a family member's employer or labor union. Another 35 million Americans (14 percent) purchased private coverage on their own. Although these programs rarely pay all medical costs, three-fourths of the American population has some private medical insurance (Health Insurance Association of America, 1989).

Public insurance programs. In 1965, Congress created Medicare and Medicaid. Medicare pays some of the medical costs of Americans over sixty-five; in 1988, it covered almost 33 million Americans, about 16 percent of the population. Medicaid, a medical insurance program for the poor, provided benefits to almost 23 million Americans, or about 10 percent of the population. An additional 10 million veterans (4 percent of the popula-

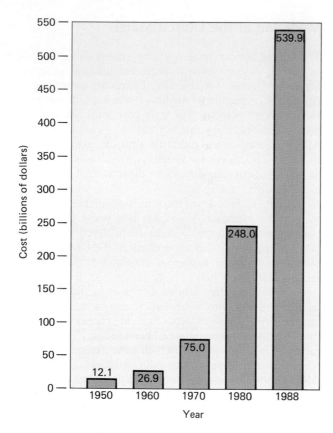

Figure 13–4 The Rising Cost of Medical Care in the United States

(U.S. Bureau of the Census)

tion) can obtain free care in government-operated hospitals. In all, about 30 percent of Americans enjoy some medical benefits from the government, although most are also covered by private insurance programs.

Health maintenance organizations. An increasing number of Americans belong to a **health maintenance organization** (HMO), *an association that provides comprehensive medical care for a fixed fee.* In 1988, 653 HMOs had some 27 million members, or almost 13 percent of the population. HMOs vary in their costs and benefits, and none provides full coverage. But fixed costs give these organizations a financial interest in keeping their subscribers healthy; therefore many HMOs have embraced the preventive principles of holistic medicine (Ginsburg, 1983).

In all, 85 percent of Americans rely on some medical insurance coverage, either private or public. Yet this coverage may fall short, first, because the health-insurance plans of perhaps 50 million Americans pay only part of the cost of a catastrophic illness, threatening even middle-class people with financial ruin. Second, most programs exclude many medical services, such as dental care (Eve, 1984). Third, and most serious, 35 million Americans (about 15 percent) lack any medical insurance (Altman et al., 1989; *Sourcebook of Health Insurance Data*, 1989). Caught in a terrible bind, most of those with no insurance are poor or moderate-income people who simply cannot afford to become ill or to purchase the medical care they need to remain healthy.

THEORETICAL ANALYSIS OF MEDICINE

Each theoretical paradigm in sociology highlights some of the social dimensions of medicine.

Structural-Functional Analysis

Talcott Parsons (1951) argued that maintaining the good health of its members is a basic task of any social system. Illness is thus dysfunctional, undermining the performance of social roles.

The sick role. Parsons claimed that one social response to poor health is the **sick role,** *patterns of behavior socially defined as appropriate for those who are ill.* Insofar as people suffer from poor health, in other words, they are exempted from everyday responsibilities. However, Parsons added, people cannot simply declare themselves as ill; they must seek the assessment of a recognized medical expert. He notes further that assuming the sick role carries the expectations that a person wishes to regain good health and will cooperate with health professionals to that end.

The physician's role. The function of physicians is to assess claims of sickness, and to provide the medical care needed to restore those who are ill to health and their normal routines. Parsons claimed that specialized knowledge gives the physician both power and responsibility in relation to the patient. Physicians expect patients to follow "doctor's orders," and to provide whatever personal information may reasonably assist their efforts.

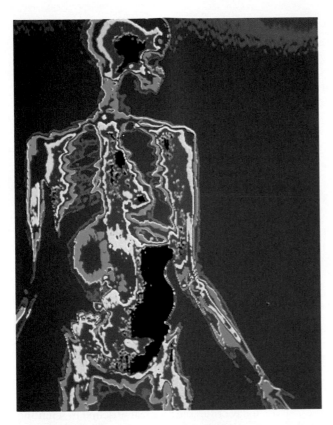

Advances in medicine utilizing computers and other new technology offer significant benefits to many Americans. But they have also contributed to the soaring cost of medical care. This has sparked charges that the United States has two standards of health: one for those who can afford the best care and another for everyone else.

Critical evaluation. Parsons's work links illness and medicine to the broader organization of society. The concept of the sick role is especially useful, and has been extended to some non-illness situations such as pregnancy (Myers & Grasmick, 1989). Bear in mind, however, that the sick person's ability to regain health depends on available resources. Many impoverished Americans cannot afford either effective health care or time off from work.

Parsons's view of the physician's role has also come under fire for positively embracing conventional, scientific medicine. Treatment-oriented physicians typically claim more authority over patients, in contrast to holistic practitioners, who seek an egalitarian partnership in which people assume responsibility for their own health.

Symbolic-Interaction Analysis

According to the symbolic-interaction paradigm, life is the ongoing construction of reality. The reality of health, then, hinges on subjective perceptions. British sociologist Ann Holohan recounts a visit to her physician for what she assumed was a breast infection only to be informed that she might have cancer. She left the physician's office in a state of shock:

> It seemed incredible that nothing had changed—the sun was still shining, the road sweeper gathering the leaves. I sat in my car [and] immense waves of panic engulfed me. I drove blindly home and recall very little of the actual journey. . . . Yet I was no "sicker" than before my consultation. All that had changed was the possibility of a medical label for my symptom. (1977, cited in Cockerham, 1982:95)

When a hospital report indicated that Holohan did not have cancer, her world changed again—this time for the better. Some medical professionals have noted that perceptions are real enough to affect human health. They have long pointed to the *psychosomatic* character of health, that sickness or healing is affected by a person's emotional state (Hamrick, Anspaugh, & Ezell, 1986). Here, again, we see that situations defined as real may become real in their consequences (Thomas, 1931).

More broadly, people the world over socially define matters of health and illness in a variety of ways. In poor societies, where malnutrition predominates, an underfed child may be viewed as normal. In much the same way, affluent societies have long consumed rich foods, tobacco, and alcohol with little regard for the consequences to individual health. In every society, how people respond to those thought to be ill is yet another matter of social definitions. For instance, people with AIDS contend with fear and sometimes outright bigotry that has no basis in medical fact.

Even "expert opinions" are influenced by nonmedical factors. David Mechanic (1978) explains, for example, that military physicians may define flu symptoms as illness during peacetime but not in desperate times of war. And college students have been known to dismiss signs of illness on the eve of a vacation, yet readily report to the infirmary the night before a difficult examination. In other words, we often use medical experts to socially construct a claim to health or illness for a host of reasons. Defining sickness and health, then, has as much to do with social negotiation as with scientific assessment.

Critical evaluation. To its credit, the symbolic-interaction paradigm reveals the subjective relativity of health. However, some physical conditions do cause measurable changes in human capacities, no matter how we define them. In short, even if people in poor societies view themselves as relatively healthy, they still do not live as long as people in richer societies.

Social-Conflict Analysis

Social-conflict analysis links health to social inequality and, especially, to capitalism. Researchers have focused on three key issues.

1. **Unequal access.** Health is the foundation of social life. Yet by turning health into a commodity, capitalist societies make wealth a precondition for health. As already noted, the problem of access to medical care is more serious in the United States than in most other industrial societies.

   In the view of radical critics, capitalist health problems are rooted in the class system. They claim that inequality of wealth makes equal medical care impossible, even if a comprehensive government program were enacted. Only a redistribution of economic resources would make medical care uniformly available (Bodenheimer, 1977; Navarro, 1977).

2. **The profit motive.** Some critics argue that the key issue is not *access* to medical care but the *character* of capitalist medicine itself. Driven by the profit motive, physicians, hospitals, and the drug industry become multibillion-dollar corporate conglomerates (Ehrenreich, 1978). The quest for ever-increasing profits underlies the push for unnecessary tests and surgery as well as an overreliance on prescription drugs (Kaplan et al., 1985). The antianxiety drug valium, for example, is prescribed more than 25 million times each year to reduce stress, although it can also lead to psychological (and physical) addiction (Myers, 1986). Moreover, some 1 million Americans enter hospitals each year because of an adverse reaction to a prescription drug (Illich, 1976).

   Of the 26 million surgical operations performed in the United States in 1987, three-fourths were "elective," meaning that they were not prompted by a medical emergency. Growing evidence suggests that the decision to perform surgery reflects both the financial interests of surgeons and hospitals as well as the medical needs of patients (Illich, 1976). Perhaps 10 percent of this elective surgery could safely be refused or deferred, saving patients more than $1 billion each year. More important, since about one in two hundred patients dies from elective surgery (because surgery itself is dangerous), 13,000 lives a year are needlessly lost (Sidel & Sidel, 1982a). From this point of view, improving the American health-care system requires moving toward socialized medicine so that public health, not individual profit, is of primary importance.

3. **Medicine as politics.** While scientific medicine claims to be politically neutral, evidence shows that the medical establishment takes sides on significant social issues. For example, the medical establishment (embodied by the AMA) strongly opposes government health-care programs. The history of medicine, critics charge, is replete with racial and sexual discrimination based on "scientific" facts about women and other minorities (Zola, 1978; Brown, 1979; Leavitt, 1984). The box suggests that science has been tainted by sexism when it comes to women's health.

Even today critics see political mischief in scientific medicine. Scientific medicine explains illness in terms of bacteria and viruses rather than showing the health effects of social inequality. In this way, scientific medicine transforms potentially explosive issues involving the health of Americans into matters of simple biology.

Critical evaluation. Social-conflict analysis provides still another view of the relationships among health, medicine, and society. While many people celebrate American medicine for developing artificial hearts and CAT scans, social-conflict theorists point out that millions of people still lack basic medical care.

However, the social-conflict approach minimizes the dramatic achievements of American scientific medicine. Though there is plenty of room for improvement, health indicators for Americans have risen steadily during this century.

Together, sociology's three theoretical paradigms demonstrate the many ways in which health and medicine emerge as social issues. The illustrious French scientist Louis Pasteur (1822–1895) spent much of his life studying how bacteria cause disease. Yet, just before his death,

Medicine and Victorian Women: Science or Sexism?

A century ago medical science re-acted strongly to the changing roles of women. With men firmly in control, American medicine strongly opposed greater sexual equality.

Medical opinion held that conventional gender distinctions were both natural and inevitable. Beyond differences in size and strength, physicians pronounced men naturally rational while claiming that women are dominated by their emotions and hypersensitive nervous systems. Thus women's natural work was childbearing and childrearing. Writing in 1890, one physician remarked that "the Almighty, in creating the female sex, had taken the uterus and built up a woman around it" (cited in Smith-Rosenberg & Rosenberg, 1984:13). Thus medical opinion equated motherhood and health, arguing that childless women risked physical and mental illness and a shortened life.

The Victorian medical establishment also obstructed women's demands for schooling. Physicians warned that too much thinking rendered a woman weak and sickly and decreased her capacity to bear healthy children. Describing the educated woman in 1901, one gynecologist complacently predicted, "She may become highly cultured and accomplished and shine in society, but her future husband will discover too late that he has married a large outfit of headaches, backaches, and spine aches, instead of a woman fitted to take up the duties of life" (cited in Smith-Rosenberg & Rosenberg, 1984:16). Another member of the

Leon-Augustin Lhermitte's painting, *Claude Bernard Operates for his Students*, shows Victorian medicine to be the domain of men who commonly mixed their science with politics and patriarchal values.

Harvard medical faculty warned that "If she puts as much force into her brain education as a boy, the brain or the special apparatus [reproductive system] will suffer" (cited in Bollough & Voght, 1984:30).

Victorian physicians also opposed women's efforts to control their own sexuality. Women, they argued, had no interest in sexual activity beyond having children, and had neither the desire nor the ability to achieve orgasm. Men, by contrast, required orgasms to prevent the dangerous buildup of nervous energy. Male orgasms, unimpeded by contraceptive devices such as condoms, also enhanced a woman's health by "bathing the female reproductive organs" (cited

in Smith-Rosenberg & Rosenberg, 1984:19). Well into this century, in fact, the American Medical Association opposed contraception and abortion allegedly on medical grounds.

Some Victorians challenged conventional medical opinions. Martha Carey Thomas, president of Bryn Mawr College, denounced the scientific wisdom of her day. She won much support for her conclusion that men holding such ungenerous attitudes toward women were themselves "pathological, blinded by neurotic mists of sex, unable to see that women form one-half of the kindly race of normal, healthy human creatures in the world" (cited in Bollough & Voght, 1984:34).

he concluded that health depends less on bacteria than on the social environment in which bacteria operate (Gordon, 1980:7). Explaining Pasteur's insight is sociology's contribution to human health.

SUMMARY

Education

1. Education is a major social institution for transmitting knowledge and skills as well as cultural norms and values. In preindustrial societies, education occurs informally within the family; industrial societies, by contrast, develop formal systems of schooling.

2. The United States was among the first nations to develop compulsory mass education, reflecting both democratic political ideals and the needs of the industrial-capitalist economy.

3. The functions of schooling include socialization, social placement, and promoting both social integration and innovation. Additional latent functions involve child care and forging social networks.

4. Social-conflict analysis points up the unequal opportunity for schooling among Americans. Formal education also acts as an agent of social control, instilling conformity to produce compliant adult workers.

5. Based on standardized testing, tracking provides students with schooling corresponding to their ability. Critics charge that tracking has more to do with students' social background than their individual abilities. Thus, tracking justifies allocating more educational resources for privileged students.

6. The great majority of young Americans attend state-funded public schools. Most privately funded schools are affiliated with religious organizations. A very small proportion of young people—generally of privileged social background—attend private preparatory schools.

7. One-fifth of Americans over the age of twenty-five are college graduates. Most attended state-funded institutions, with expensive, private education generally accessible only to members of wealthy families.

8. American public schools have come under criticism in recent years. School violence is a highly visible problem, especially in poor neighborhoods. The bureaucratic character of American schools has also fostered widespread student passivity.

9. Declining academic standards, a major problem in America, are reflected in lower average scores today on academic achievement tests and functional illiteracy among a significant proportion of high-school graduates.

10. Magnet schools have improved urban education, although they have not significantly reduced racial segregation.

11. Children with mental or physical disabilities historically have been schooled in special classes or not at all. Mainstreaming, a recent innovation, provides handicapped students with broader opportunities for social interaction and academic achievement. Other educational trends include increasing numbers of adult students and more widespread use of computers for instruction.

Medicine

1. As a social issue, health depends on a society's technology and distribution of resources. Culture shapes both definitions of health and responses to illness.

2. Health improved dramatically in Western Europe and North America in the nineteenth century due to industrialization and medical advances.

3. Most Americans died from infectious diseases at the beginning of this century. Today most people die in old age of heart disease, cancer, or stroke.

4. Third-World health suffers from inadequate sanitation, hunger, and other problems linked to poverty. Average life expectancy is about twenty years less than that of the United States; in the poorest nations, half the children do not survive to adulthood.

5. Three-fourths of American children can expect to live to at least age sixty-five. Throughout the life course, females have relatively better health than males, and people of high social position enjoy better health than others.

6. Although industrialization has raised living standards in the United States, environmental pollution threatens the future health of Americans.

7. Cigarette smoking has increased during this century, becoming the greatest preventable cause of death among Americans. Health hazards and the decreasing social tolerance of smokers have combined to reduce cigarette consumption.

8. Unlike other kinds of infections, sexually transmitted diseases are on the rise. As a result, fewer people are engaging in casual sexual relations.

9. Advancing technology has transformed the point of death into a human decision; this has generated ethical dilemmas surrounding the rights of the dying.

10. Scientific medicine dominates the American medical establishment. Holistic medicine, an alternative approach, seeks to promote health as well as treat disease and to make people more responsible for their own health.

11. Socialist societies define medical care as a right that governments offer equally to everyone. Capitalist societies view medical care as a commodity to be purchased, although most capitalist governments support medical care through socialized medicine or national health insurance. The United States is the only industrialized society with no comprehensive government-sponsored medical-care program.

12. Structural-functional analysis spotlights the sick role, in which illness brings release from routine social responsibilities as long as patients seek to regain their health. The symbolic-interaction paradigm reveals that health is largely a matter of subjective perception and social definition. Social-conflict analysis focuses on unequal health patterns between rich and poor and criticizes American medicine for emphasizing the biological rather than the social causes of illness.

KEY CONCEPTS

Education

credentialism evaluating people for employment on the basis of educational degrees

education the various ways in which knowledge—including facts, skills, and values—is transmitted to members of society

functional illiteracy reading and writing skills inadequate for everyday needs

magnet schools schools that attract students through special facilities and programs promoting educational excellence

schooling formal instruction under the direction of specially trained teachers

tracking assigning students to different types of educational programs

Medicine

direct-fee system a medical-care system in which patients pay directly for the services of physicians and hospitals

euthanasia (mercy killing) assisting in the death of a person suffering from an incurable illness

health a state of complete physical, mental, and social well-being

health maintenance organization (HMO) an organization that provides comprehensive medical care for which subscribers pay a fixed fee

holistic medicine an approach to health care that emphasizes prevention of illness and takes account of the whole person within a physical and social environment

medicine the institutionalized system for combating disease and promoting health

sick role patterns of behavior that are socially defined as appropriate for those who are ill

social epidemiology the study of the distribution of health and disease in a society's population

socialized medicine a health-care system in which most medical facilities are owned and operated by the government, and most physicians are salaried government employees

Population and Urbanization

14

In 1519 a band of Spanish conquistadors led by Hernando Cortés reached Tenochtitlán, the capital of the Aztec empire. They were stunned by a lake-encircled city teeming with over 300,000 people, more people than were found in any European city at that time. As they gazed down broad streets, explored magnificent stone temples, and examined the golden treasures of the royal palace, Cortés and his soldiers often felt as if they were dreaming.

Tenochtitlán was more than Cortés could resist; he soon set his mind and his men to looting the city. Unable at first to overcome the superior forces of the Aztecs and their leader Montezuma, Cortés spent two years raising a vast army and finally destroyed Tenochtitlán. In its place, Cortes began construction of a new European center—*Ciudad Imperial de México*—Mexico City.

Today Mexico City is again fighting for its life. Its soaring population is expected to reach 30 million by the end of this decade—one hundred times the number that so impressed Cortés. Its people are struggling to survive in a Third-World nation burdened with poverty, foreign debt, and a rapidly deteriorating environment.

This pattern—rising population fueling urban growth amid stunning poverty—is found in much of today's world. This chapter examines population growth and urbanization—two powerful forces that are changing our planet. Increasing population will pose one of the most serious challenges facing the world in the coming century; more and more, this vital drama is being played out in cities of unprecedented size.

Each year about 4 million children are born in the United States. Fertility among Americans has been relatively low in recent decades partly because parents are waiting longer to have children.

DEMOGRAPHY: THE STUDY OF POPULATION

From the emergence of the human species some 200,000 years ago until recently, the population of the earth was small and vulnerable to disease and natural disaster. Ironically, perhaps, the world population is now so large (5.5 billion in 1990), and growing so rapidly, that the fate of humanity is again uncertain.

This growth is the focus of **demography,** *the study of human population.* Demography (from the Greek, meaning "description of people") is a close cousin of sociology that investigates the size, age, and sex composition of a society's people, as well as how they move from place to place. Although much demographic research is quantitative, demography is more than a num-

bers game. The discipline poses crucial questions about the causes and consequences of population growth.

The following sections focus on key demographic concepts.

Fertility

The study of human population looks first to how many people are born. **Fertility** is *the incidence of childbearing in a society's population.* Women in the childbearing years, from the onset of menstruation (typically in the early teens) to menopause (usually in the late forties), are capable of bearing perhaps twenty children. But *fecundity,* or potential childbearing, is greatly reduced by health, financial concerns, and cultural norms.

A basic measurement of fertility is the **crude birth rate**, *the number of live births in a given year for every thousand people in a population*. The crude birth rate is calculated by dividing the number of live births in a given year by a society's total population, and multiplying the result by 1,000. In 1988, there were 3.9 million live births among 246 million Americans (Hollman, 1990). According to this formula, then, there were 15.9 live births for every thousand people, or a crude birth rate of 15.9.

This birth rate is "crude" because the population encompasses males as well as females not in their childbearing years. A comparison of crude birth rates can be misleading, then, if one society has a higher proportion of women of childbearing age than another. A crude birth rate also provides no information about birth rates among different races, ethnicities, and religions. It has the advantage, however, of being easy to calculate, and it is a good measure of a society's overall fertility. Table 14–1 shows that the crude birth rates of the United States and other industrial societies are low in world context.

Mortality

Population size is also affected by **mortality**, *the incidence of death in a society's population*. Mortality is often measured in terms of the **crude death rate**, *the number of deaths in a given year for every thousand people in a population*. This time, we take the number of deaths in a given year, divide by the total population, and multiply the result by 1,000. In 1988 there were 2.2 million deaths in the U.S. population of 246 million, yielding a crude death rate of 8.9. As Table 14–1 shows, this rate is low by world standards.

Another common demographic measure is the **infant mortality rate**, *the number of infant deaths for each thousand live births in a given year*. We come up with this rate by dividing the number of deaths of children under one year of age by the number of live births during the same year and multiplying the result by 1,000. In 1988, there were 38,910 infant deaths and about 3.9 million live births in the United States. Dividing the first number by the second and multiplying the result by 1,000 produces an infant mortality rate of 10.0. Here again, bear in mind variation among different categories of Americans. For example, the infant mortality of poor Americans is twice as high as that among the well-to-do (Stockwell, Swanson, & Wicks, 1987).

Table 14–1 FERTILITY AND MORTALITY RATES AMONG WORLD SOCIETIES, 1989

	Crude Birth Rate	Crude Death Rate	Infant Mortality Rate
North America			
United States	16	9	10
Canada	14	7	7
Europe			
Belgium	12	11	8
Denmark	11	11	7
France	14	10	9
Spain	13	8	11
United Kingdom	13	12	9
U.S.S.R.	18	11	25
Latin America			
Chile	21	6	18
Cuba	17	6	14
Haiti	31	12	92
Mexico	30	6	42
Nicaragua	39	8	65
Puerto Rico	19	7	16
Africa			
Algeria	38	8	73
Cameroon	42	16	123
Egypt	35	10	93
Ethiopia	45	15	113
Nigeria	46	17	121
South Africa	35	8	53
Asia			
Afghanistan	44	21	173
Bangladesh	43	15	138
India	31	11	91
Israel	22	7	9
Japan	11	7	5
Vietnam	33	8	51

SOURCE: U.S. Bureau of the Census, *World Population Profile 1989* (Washington, DC: Government Printing Office, 1989).

Infant mortality offers a good general measure of overall quality of life. Table 14–1 shows that infant mortality in the United States, Canada, and other industrial societies is considerably lower than that in poor nations of the Third World.

Low infant mortality greatly raises **life expectancy**, *the average lifespan of a society's population*. American males born in 1988 can expect to live 71.5 years, while females, on average, reach the age of 78.3. In Third-World societies with high infant mortality, however, life expectancy is about twenty years less.

Migration

Population size also changes as people move from one place to another. Demographers define **migration** as *the movement of people into and out of a specific territory.* Some migration is involuntary, such as the forcible transport of 10 million Africans to the Western Hemisphere as slaves (Sowell, 1981). Voluntary migration is usually motivated by complex "push-pull" factors. "Push" factors often begin the process, as rural villagers, for example, become dissatisfied with their poverty. A common "pull" factor is the attraction of a big city, where people envision greater opportunity. As explained later in this chapter, this precise scenario is causing rapid urban growth in the Third World. In other cases, people simply seek a more agreeable climate, which explains some of the population growth in the American Sunbelt.

People's movement into a territory—commonly termed immigration—is measured in terms of the *in-migration rate*, the number of people entering an area for every thousand people in the total population. Movement out of a territory—or emigration—is measured in terms of the *out-migration rate*, the number leaving for every thousand people in the total population. Both types of migration usually occur simultaneously; demographers describe the difference between the two as the *net-migration rate*.

Population Growth

Migration, and especially fertility and mortality, affect the size of any society's population. Demographers calculate a population's *natural growth rate* by subtracting the crude death rate from the crude birth rate. In 1988, a crude birth rate of 15.9 minus a crude death rate of 8.9 yields a natural growth rate for Americans of 7.0, which is the same as about 0.7 percent annual growth. During the 1990s this growth rate is projected to remain far below the world average, as shown in Figure 14–1.

As Figure 14–1 shows, the population growth in the industrialized regions of the world—including Europe (0.2 percent), North America (0.7 percent), and Oceania (1.3 percent)—is well below the world average. By contrast, annual growth is far higher in the Third World—including Asia (1.7 percent), Latin America (1.8 percent), and Africa (3.1 percent). Annual growth of about 2 percent (as in Latin America) will double a population in thirty-five years, and a 3 percent growth rate (as in Africa) will double a population in twenty-

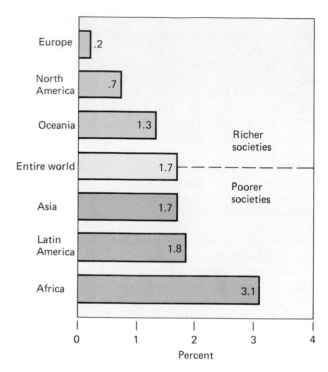

Figure 14–1 Projected Rate of Population Growth by World Region, 1990–2000

(U.S. Bureau of the Census, 1989)

four years. Rapid population growth in poor countries is deeply troubling because those nations can barely support the populations they have now.

Population Composition

Demographers also study the composition of a society's population at any point in time. One simple variable is the **sex ratio,** *the number of males for every hundred females in a given population.* In 1988 the sex ratio in the United States was 95.0, or 95.0 males for every 100 females. Sex ratios are usually lower than 100 because women typically outlive men.

A more complex measure is the **age-sex pyramid,** *a graphic representation of the age and sex of a population.* Figure 14–2 presents the age-sex pyramid for the United States in 1989. The left side represents the number of males of various ages, while the right side shows the corresponding number of females. The rough pyramid shape results from higher mortality as people age. After

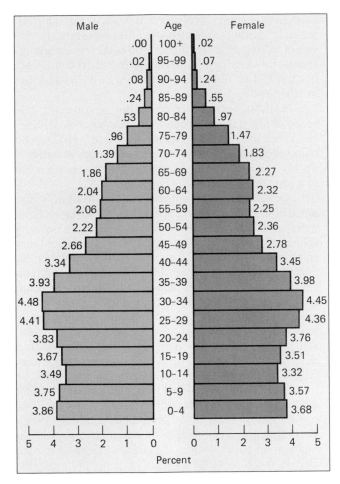

Male	Age	Female
.00	100+	.02
.02	95–99	.07
.08	90–94	.24
.24	85–89	.55
.53	80–84	.97
.96	75–79	1.47
1.39	70–74	1.83
1.86	65–69	2.27
2.04	60–64	2.32
2.06	55–59	2.25
2.22	50–54	2.36
2.66	45–49	2.78
3.34	40–44	3.45
3.93	35–39	3.98
4.48	30–34	4.45
4.41	25–29	4.36
3.83	20–24	3.76
3.67	15–19	3.51
3.49	10–14	3.32
3.75	5–9	3.57
3.86	0–4	3.68

Percent

Figure 14–2 Age–Sex Population Pyramid for the United States, 1989

(U.S. Bureau of the Census, 1989)

about thirty-five, females increasingly outnumber males in the American population. The bulge corresponding to ages fifteen through forty-four stems from high birth rates between the mid-1940s and the late 1960s, commonly called the *baby boom*. The contraction just below shows that the baby boom was followed by a *baby bust*. From a peak of 25.3 in 1957, the crude birth rate dropped to 15.3 in 1986.

Bulges and contractions in age-sex pyramids reveal a society's demographic history and likely future. The relatively box-like profile of the population of industrial societies derives from a relatively low and stable birth rate. The age-sex pyramids of Third-World societies,

however, are very narrow at the top and very wide at the bottom. This indicates high death rates after what we think of as middle age and very high birth rates. More ominous still, the birth rate in typical Third-World societies is continuing to rise, since the majority of females have yet to enter their childbearing years. When they do—unless measures are taken to effectively limit births—the exploding population will further strain limited social resources.

HISTORY AND THEORY OF POPULATION GROWTH

Through most of human history, societies favored high birth rates because human labor was vital to productivity. For that matter, controlling birth was uncertain until the invention of rubber condoms 150 years ago. But high death rates, the result of infectious diseases, kept population growth fairly low. At the dawn of civilization, about 6000 B.C.E., global population stood at approximately 20 million; gradual growth resulted in a tenfold increase by the beginning of the common era. In Europe, population grew slowly throughout the Middle Ages, as gains were periodically erased by outbreaks of deadly plague, such as the Black Death that swept across Western Europe in the mid-fourteenth century.

Then, about 1750, death rates began to fall with the onset of the Industrial Revolution so that the earth's population turned sharply upward, reaching 1 billion within a century. This achievement, some forty thousand years in the making, was repeated by 1930—only eighty years later—when a second billion had been added to the planet. In other words, not only did population increase, but the *rate* of growth accelerated. A third billion was added by 1962—after just thirty-two years—and a fourth billion by 1974, a scant twelve years later. The rate of world population increase has recently slowed, but we passed the 5 billion mark in mid-1987. In no previous century did the world's population even double; in the twentieth century, it has increased *fourfold*.

Currently, world population is predicted to exceed 6 billion early in the twenty-first century, probably reaching 8 billion by 2025. Little wonder, then, that global population has become a matter of urgent concern.

Malthusian Theory

Concern over population growth sparked the development of demography. Thomas Robert Malthus (1766–

1834), an English clergyman and economist, developed a demographic theory that warned of impending social chaos. Malthus (1926; orig. 1798) considered the human species driven to reproduction by timeless sexual passion. The resulting population increase, he predicted, would approximate what mathematicians call a geometric progression, as illustrated by the series of numbers 2, 4, 8, 16, 32, and so on. Malthus concluded that world population would soon soar out of control.

Food production would also increase, Malthus reasoned, but only in arithmetic progression (as in the series 2, 3, 4, 5, 6) because, even with technological innovations in agriculture, farmland is limited. Malthus envisioned a bleak future indeed, with people reproducing beyond what the planet could feed, leading ultimately to catastrophic starvation.

Malthus saw two limits to population growth: *positive checks* such as famine, disease, and war; and *preventive checks* including artificial birth control, sexual abstinence, and delayed marriages. His religious principles precluded birth control, and common sense told him people would not abstain from sex or marry later, unless facing imminent famine. His pessimistic forecast thus earned him the moniker the "dismal parson."

Critical evaluation. Fortunately, Malthus's predictions were flawed in several respects. First, by 1850 the birth rate in Europe began to slow, partly because children were more of an economic liability than an asset, and partly because artificial birth control was widely adopted. Second, Malthus underestimated human ingenuity: Advances in irrigation, fertilizers, and pesticides greatly increased the output of farmers, and industrial technology has resulted in unforeseen increases in the production of other goods.

Malthus was also criticized for ignoring the role of social inequality as a cause of abundance or famine. His views irritated Karl Marx (1967; orig. 1867), who objected to linking human suffering to a "law of nature." To Marx, such suffering was human mischief, the result of a capitalist economy.

Still, we cannot entirely dismiss Malthus's dire prediction. First, resources such as habitable land, clean water, and unpolluted air are certainly finite. In boosting economic productivity, technology has also created new and threatening problems, such as environmental pollution, described in Chapter 13 ("Education and Medicine"). Medical advances, which have lowered the death rate, have at the same time increased world population.

Second, although the population is rising slowly in North America, the poorest societies of Africa, Asia, and Latin America are facing the catastrophe Malthus envisioned. Throughout the Third World, perhaps one-fifth of the world's people are already in jeopardy.

Third, although global population growth has not approached the levels feared by Malthus, in the long run no rate of increase is acceptable (Ehrlich, 1978). Even if humanity manages to curtail the population explosion in poor societies, the entire world must remain alert to the long-range dangers of population growth.

Demographic Transition Theory

Malthus's rather crude analysis has been superseded by **demographic transition theory,** *the thesis that population patterns are linked to a society's level of technological development.*

This relationship can be illustrated by comparing three stages of technological change, as shown in Figure 14–3. Stage 1 is typical of preindustrial agrarian societies. Birth rates are high because of the economic value of children and the absence of effective birth control. Death rates are also high, the result of a low standard of living and the lack of medical technology. Because the high number of deaths neutralizes the high number of births, population increase was modest for thousands of years before the Industrial Revolution began in eighteenth-century Europe.

Among the poorest countries on earth, Bangladesh is struggling to meet the needs of approximately 115 million people in a land area smaller than the state of Wisconsin. With a high birth rate, the population problem is likely to become more serious in the future.

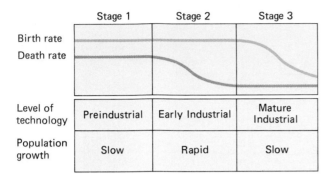

	Stage 1	Stage 2	Stage 3
Birth rate Death rate			
Level of technology	Preindustrial	Early Industrial	Mature Industrial
Population growth	Slow	Rapid	Slow

Figure 14–3 Demographic Transition Theory

Stage 2, the beginning of the demographic transition, accompanies the onset of industrialization. Technology expands food supplies and combats disease. Birth rates remain high, but death rates fall sharply, with the predictable result of rapid population growth. It was in this era that Malthus developed his ideas, so his pessimism is understandable. This high-growth stage characterizes most Third-World societies today.

In Stage 3, a fully industrial economy is established, and several factors combine to lower the birth rate. First, a high standard of living makes children expensive to raise, so large families become an economic liability rather than an asset. Women working outside the home also prefer smaller families. Furthermore, birth control becomes increasingly effective. As birth rates begin to fall into line with low death rates, fertility and mortality reach a balance and once again population growth slows. Western industrial societies have been in this stage for much of this century.

Critical evaluation. Demographic transition theory provides more grounds for optimism than does Malthusian theory. Instead of a runaway population increase, this analysis foresees both a lower rate of population growth and more material resources as a result of technological development.

Demographic transition theory dovetails with modernization theory, the approach to global development discussed in Chapter 8 ("Global Inequality"). This theory implies that Third-World countries will solve their population problem if and when they industrialize. Yet, as dependency theorists argue, current global economic arrangements are likely to ensure that poor societies remain poor. Unless there is a significant redistribution of world resources, they claim, our planet will become increasingly divided, with industrialized "haves" enjoying low

population growth while nonindustrialized "have-nots" struggle in vain to feed soaring populations.

WORLD POPULATION TODAY

What demographic patterns characterize today's world? Drawing on the theories discussed so far, we can discern a number of patterns and draw some conclusions.

Industrial societies. Soon after the Industrial Revolution began, population growth in Western Europe and North America peaked at about 3 percent annually. It subsequently declined and, since 1970, has remained below 1 percent. Having now reached Stage 3, the American birthrate is close to the replacement level of 2.1 children per woman, a point termed **zero population growth,** *the level of reproduction that maintains population at a steady state.* Several European societies have already experienced an absolute decline in population, prompting some analysts to anticipate a fourth demo-

The birthrate in Europe has dropped so low that some analysts foresee a decline in population. In France, the government has turned to advertising to encourage people to have children. The ad implies that children are becoming so rare that this baby can remark, "It appears that I am a sociocultural phenomenon." At the bottom right is added, "France needs children."

Il paraît que je suis un phénomène socio-culturel.

LA FRANCE
A BESOIN
D'ENFANTS.

graphic stage, characterized by a falling population (van de Kaa, 1987). Because the American population is still relatively young—with a median age of 32.7 in 1989—modest population growth is expected to continue during the next several decades. Yet the "graying of America" discussed in Chapter 3 ("Socialization: From Infancy to Aging") may eventually bring us to or below zero population growth.

Factors placing downward pressure on population include the high costs of raising children, the rising proportion of women in the labor force, and trends toward later marriages, singlehood, and childlessness (see Chapter 12, "Family and Religion"). Contraceptive use has increased as well: About two-thirds of women in the childbearing years regularly practice artificial birth control. Voluntary sterilization has increased dramatically, becoming the most common form of birth control in the United States. Even Catholics, whose religious doctrine prohibits artificial birth control, no longer differ from other Americans in their contraceptive practices (Westoff & Jones, 1977; Moore & Pachon, 1985). Abortion was criminalized across the United States during the nineteenth century, although it was declared legal again in 1973. In the wake of that decision, during the 1980s, about 1.3 million women annually aborted their pregnancies (Ellerbrock et al., 1987; *Morbidity and Mortality Weekly Report*, 1989). Poor Americans still have somewhat larger than average families and, as was noted in Chapter 7 ("Social Stratification"), the largest category of the American poor is children. Overall, however, population growth in industrial nations such as the United States does not present the pressing problem that it does in poor countries.

Nonindustrial societies. Today only a few societies, untouched by industrial technology, fall within demographic transition theory's Stage 1. Most societies in Latin America, Africa, and Asia have agrarian economies with limited industrialization, which places them at Stage 2. Advanced medical technology supplied by First-World societies has sharply reduced death rates, but birth rates remain high. Figure 14–4 shows the result. These societies now account for about two-thirds of the earth's people and demographers predict that the percentage will increase to about three-fourths as the earth's population reaches 6 billion (Piotrow, 1980).

Third-World birth rates are high now for many of the same reasons they were high in industrial societies in past centuries. There, children are still economic assets, frequently working eight- or ten-hour days to con-

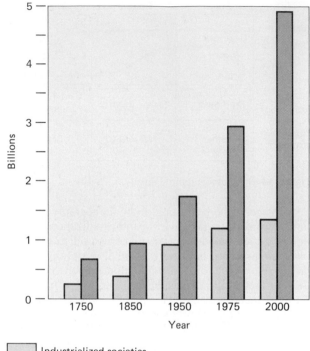

Industrialized societies

Nonindustrial societies

Figure 14–4 Population Distribution, Industrial and Nonindustrial Societies, 1750–2000

(Piotrow, 1980)

tribute to their families' income. Parents also look to children for economic support in old age. The economic value of children, coupled with high mortality among infants and children, encourages parents to have large families. Throughout the Third World, average family size is about four or five children; in rural areas the number is frequently higher (The World Bank, 1984).

The social position of women also remains a crucial factor in today's population picture. Agrarian societies tend to be strongly patriarchal, so women's primary responsibilities are to bear and raise children. Thus in Latin America, for example, a combination of economic need, traditional patriarchy, and Roman Catholic doctrine discourages women from using birth control devices. In much of Africa, village women have no opportunity even to learn about effective forms of birth control (Salas, 1985). Asia is a mixed case: While some women have little access to effective contraception, others in

CROSS-CULTURAL COMPARISON

Birth Control in China

Third-World governments have responded to rapid population growth with a variety of programs aimed at reducing fertility. Nowhere is population more of a concern than in the People's Republic of China, which contains one-fourth of the world's people (1.1 billion in 1990). Ominously, more than half the Chinese people are under thirty, raising the specter of a baby boom without parallel in human history.

In 1979, the government initiated a tough policy limiting couples to a single child. Local officials strongly encourage people to delay childbirth, and, once a child is born, to submit to sterilization or abort subsequent pregnancies. One-baby couples receive income bonuses, and single children are promised priority in school enrollment, health care, and, later, in employment and housing. Family planning is thus defined as everyone's social responsibility. The result was a significant drop in the birth rate from 2.0 percent annual growth in the 1960s to about 1.8 percent in the 1980s.

Controlling births in this way, however, has provoked controversy and created other problems in its wake. First, widespread sterilization during the early 1980s sparked inter-

Population policies often have unanticipated consequences. Now that government policies limit couples to a single child on which parents and grandparents lavish attention, some Chinese wonder if they may be raising a generation of "little empresses" and "little emperors."

national protest that China was forcing its people to undergo surgery. Second, the one-child policy has had the unintended effect of encouraging abortion of female fetuses and female infanticide. Chinese traditions give sons the responsibility of caring for elderly parents; daughters serve their husband's parents. Thus few Chinese couples wish to face old age without a son. In cities where ultrasound technology allows parents to know the sex of a fetus, selective abortion of females is common. In rural areas, couples may kill first-born girls in order to try again for a boy. In a related development, privileges accorded to only children are now disproportionately enjoyed by sons, increasing sexual inequality.

By 1990, social strains had caused the government to become more lenient. Yet even the present rate of growth will double the population of China by 2025, undermining the struggle of a vast society to raise its standard of living.

SOURCE: *World Development Report 1984* (New York: Oxford University Press, 1984); Gwenda Brophy, "China, Part I" and "China, Part II," *Population Today*, Vol. 17, no. 3 (March 1989):12 and no. 4 (April 1989):12; H. Yuan Tien, "Second Thoughts on the Second Child," *Population Today*, Vol. 17, no. 4 (April 1989):6–9.

India and China have been mobilized by government programs to control birth rates. The current situation in the People's Republic of China, the world's most populous society, is examined in the box.

There is also a connection between population growth and the social position of women. Women who are restricted to the traditional roles of childrearing and homemaking have many children. Similarly, men with-

out economic and educational opportunities are likely to define their masculinity in terms of virility. Thus schooling and rewarding work hold the key not only to economic development, but to population control. Research in the Sudan (Africa) and Colombia (South America) suggests that women with seven years of schooling had half as many children as those without any education (Ross, 1985; Salas, 1985).

Where efforts to control fertility in the Third World have been most intense, average family size fell by 20 percent between 1975 and 1985. This decline may continue through the end of this century, but at a slower pace (Salas, 1985). Birth rates will still remain high, however, and since death rates are falling at the same time, Third-World population is expected to continue increasing.

Actually, *most* population growth in the Third World stems from declining death rates. After about 1920, when Europe and North America began to export technology improving medicine, nutrition, and sanitation, Latin America, Africa, and Asia witnessed a sharp decline in death rates. Inoculations against infectious diseases, treatment with antibiotics, and the use of insecticides have combined to reduce death rates with stunning effectiveness. For example, in Sri Lanka, malaria caused half of all deaths in the mid-1930s; a decade later, insecticide used to kill malaria-carrying mosquitoes cut the malaria death toll in half (Ehrlich, 1978). Although there is reason to rejoice at such an achievement, the long-term effect was a dramatic increase in Sri Lanka's population. Similarly, India's infant mortality rate fell from 130 in 1975 to 95 in 1990, but its population now exceeds 850 million. In response, current birth control programs are attempting to limit the sharp increase in population growth brought on by the successful "death control" campaigns several generations ago (Piotrow, 1980).

The Importance of Demography

Demographic analysis is vital for understanding how and why the world population is reaching unprecedented levels. Only through such study can humanity address this pressing problem.

The technological advances that caused the populations of Europe and North America to swell during the past centuries simultaneously raised their standard of living. But this is not the case in the societies presently experiencing unprecedented population growth. Third-World countries lack the productive capacity to cope with their present populations, much less future ones. Because population is growing fastest in the poorest societies, demographic forces are central to understanding global inequality, as explained in Chapter 8.

The problems of feeding a hungry world seem overwhelming. Every year the world population grows by 90 million people, who need housing, education, and employment. The well-being of the entire planet may ultimately depend on resolving the economic and social problems of poor, overly-populated countries and bridging the widening gulf between "have" and "have-not" societies. Describing recent population growth as "a great wave," one official of the United States government concluded:

> I see the world population movement as the effort to construct a breakwater—a structure that will stop the wave and prevent it from engulfing and sweeping away centuries of human development and civilization. (cited in Gupte, 1984:323)

URBANIZATION: THE GROWTH OF CITIES

For most of human history, people lived in small nomadic groups, moving as vegetation was depleted or in pursuit of migratory game. As civilization emerged in the Middle East some eight thousand years ago, only a small fraction of the earth's population lived in widely scattered settlements. Today single cities contain as many people as the entire planet did then.

Urbanization is *the concentration of humanity into cities.* Not only does urbanization redistribute population within a society, it also transforms many patterns of social life. The remainder of this chapter will point out the consequences of three urban revolutions that have shaped today's world.

The Evolution of Cities

In the long course of human history, cities are a relative newcomer. Only after hundreds of thousands of years of evolutionary development did our ancestors grasp the idea of the city as a permanent settlement. Two factors set the stage for the *first urban revolution* about ten thousand years ago.

Preconditions of cities. The first precondition of urban development was *a favorable ecology:* As glaciers began to melt at the end of the last ice age, people were drawn to warm regions with fertile soil. The second was *changing technology:* At about the same time, humans learned how to raise animals and crops. Together, these factors produced a surplus of food. Whereas hunting and gathering had demanded continual movement, raising food required people to remain in one place (Lenski & Lenski,

Early urban settlements in Latin America often took the form of ceremonial centers. Shown here is the massive Pyramid of the Sun at Teotihuacán, near Mexico City.

1982). Thus settlements became permanent. Freed by the surplus from having to engage in food production, some people proceeded for the first time to build shelters, make tools and clothing, and become religious leaders. The founding of cities was truly revolutionary, then, and resulted in a higher standard of living based on productive specialization.

The first cities. Evidence suggests that the first city was Jericho, a settlement to the north of the Dead Sea in land currently occupied by Israel. In 8000 B.C.E., Jericho's population stood at about 600 people (Kenyon, 1957; Hamblin, 1973; Spates & Macionis, 1987). By 4000 B.C.E., numerous cities were flourishing in the Fertile Crescent between the Tigris and Euphrates rivers in present-day Iraq and, soon afterward, along the Nile River in Egypt. Some, with populations of 50,000, became centers of urban empires dominating large regions. Priest-kings with absolute power were served by lesser nobles, administrators, artisans, soldiers, and farmers. Slaves, captured in frequent military campaigns, provided labor to build monumental structures such as the Egyptian pyramids (Wenke, 1980; Stavrianos, 1983; Lenski & Lenski, 1987).

Cities originated independently in at least three other parts of the world. Several large, complex cities sprang up along the Indus River of present-day Pakistan

about 2500 B.C.E. Chinese cities are believed to date from 2000 B.C.E. In Central and South America, urban centers arose about 1500 B.C.E. In North America, however, significant urbanization did not begin until the arrival of European settlers in the sixteenth century (Lamberg-Karlovsky, 1973; Change, 1977; Coe & Diehl, 1980).

Preindustrial European cities. Urbanization in Europe began about 1800 B.C.E. on the Mediterranean island of Crete and spread throughout Greece. In all, Greece boasted more than one hundred city-states, of which Athens is the most famous. During its Golden Age (roughly 500–400 B.C.E.), some 300,000 people living within one square mile devised the elements of culture still central to the Western way of life, including philosophy, the arts, the principles of democracy, and a blending of physical and mental fitness exemplified by the Olympic games (Mumford, 1961; Carlton, 1977; Stavrianos, 1983). Despite such lofty achievements, Athenian society depended on the labor of slaves, perhaps one-third of the population. Democratic principles notwithstanding, Athenian men also denied the rights of citizenship to women and foreigners (Mumford, 1961; Gouldner, 1965).

As Greek civilization faded, the city of Rome grew to almost 1 million inhabitants, becoming the center of a vast empire. By the first century C.E., the militaristic Romans had subdued much of northern Africa, Europe, and the Middle East. In the process, Rome spread its language, arts, and technological innovations. By the fifth century C.E., the Roman Empire had fallen into disarray, a victim of its own gargantuan size, internal corruption, and militaristic appetite. Yet, between them, the Greeks and Romans had founded cities across Europe, including London, Paris, and Vienna.

With the fall of the Roman Empire, an era of urban decline and stagnation began. Cities shrank to about 25,000 people, living within defensive walls. Competing warlords battled for territory, inhibiting urban trade. Not until the eleventh century did a semblance of peace allow cities to develop into economic centers.

Medieval cities slowly tore down their walls to facilitate trade. As their economies expanded, the narrow and winding streets of London, Brussels, and Florence teemed with artisans, merchants, priests, peddlers, jugglers, nobles, and servants. Typically, occupational groups such as bakers, keymakers, and carpenters clustered together in distinct sections or "quarters." In the medieval cities of Europe, cathedrals towered above all

Table 14–2 POPULATION GROWTH IN SELECTED INDUSTRIAL CITIES OF EUROPE (IN THOUSANDS)

City	Year			
	1700	1800	1900	1988
Amsterdam	172	201	510	695
Berlin	100	172	2,424	3,353
Lisbon	188	237	363	818
London	550	861	6,480	6,735
Madrid	110	169	539	3,124
Paris	530	547	3,330	2,189*
Rome	149	153	487	2,816
Vienna	105	231	1,662	1,483

* 1982
SOURCE: Based on data from Tertius Chandler and Gerald Fox, *3000 Years of Urban History* (New York: Academic Press, 1974), pp. 17–19; and *The Statesman's Year-Book 1990–1991*, 127th ed. (New York: St. Martin's Press, 1990).

other buildings, symbolizing the preeminence of Christianity.

By today's standards, medieval cities were surprisingly personal (Sjoberg, 1965). Family ties were strong, and the people living and working in each city "quarter" shared a trade and often religious and ethnic traditions. In some cases, this clustering was involuntary; ethnic minorities were often legally restricted to certain districts. Jews were targets of widespread prejudice and discrimination in an era dominated by the Roman Catholic Church. Laws in Venice, and later in most of Europe, confined Jews to areas known as *ghettos*.

Industrial European cities. Throughout the Middle Ages, steadily increasing commerce created an affluent urban middle class or *bourgeoisie* (French for "of the town"). By the fifteenth century, this wealth conferred sufficient power for the bourgeoisie to rival the hereditary nobility. European colonization of much of the world played a major part in the political ascent of the new trading class.

By about 1750 the Industrial Revolution was under way, triggering a *second urban revolution*, first in Europe and then in North America. Factories unleashed productive power as never before, causing cities to grow to unprecedented size, as shown in Table 14–2. During the nineteenth century the population of Paris rose from 500,000 to over 3 million, and that of London from 800,000 to 6.5 million (A. Weber, 1963, orig. 1899; Chandler & Fox, 1974). Most of this increase was due

to migration from rural areas by people seeking jobs in the new factories.

Cities changed in other ways as well during this period. Commerce so dominated the industrial-capitalist city that a new urban form arose. Broad, straight boulevards replaced the old irregular streets to accommodate the flow of commercial traffic and eventually, motor vehicles. Steam and electric trolleys criss-crossed the expanding European cities. Lewis Mumford (1961) explains that the city was divided into regular-sized lots as land became a commodity, bought and sold in the capitalist economy. Finally, the cathedrals that had guided the life of medieval cities were dwarfed by a central business district of factories, banks, retail stores, and offices, as even-taller buildings proclaimed the power of the capitalist economy.

Urban social life also changed. Cities became impersonal and increasingly crowded. People routinely came into contact with vast numbers of strangers in the workplace and the neighborhood. Crime rates increased. A small number of industrialists lived in grand style, while for most men, women, and children, factory work proved exhausting and provided bare subsistence.

European cities continued to grow during the twentieth century, although at a declining rate. Worker organization and political struggle brought improvements, including legal regulation of the workplace, better housing, and the right to vote. Public utilities, such as water, sewage, and electricity, further changed urban living for the better. Today poverty remains the daily plight of many workers, but a rising standard of living has partly fulfilled the city's historical promise of a better life.

The Growth of American Cities

Although Native Americans have inhabited North America for tens of thousands of years, they established few permanent settlements. Cities emerged only after European colonization. The Spanish made an initial settlement at St. Augustine, Florida, in 1565, and the English founded Jamestown, Virginia, in 1607. New Amsterdam (later renamed New York) was established in 1624 by the Dutch, and soon overshadowed these smaller settlements.

Colonial settlement: 1624–1800. Dutch New Amsterdam at the tip of Manhattan Island (1624) and English Boston (1630) were originally tiny settlements in a vast, unknown wilderness. Both resembled medieval European towns, with narrow, winding streets that still exist in lower Manhattan and downtown Boston. New Amsterdam was walled on the north, the site of today's Wall Street. In 1700, Boston was the largest American settlement with a population of barely 7,000.

The expansion of capitalism soon transformed villages into thriving towns with gridlike streets. Figure 14–5 contrasts the traditional shape of New Amsterdam with the regular design of Philadelphia founded a half-century later in 1680.

Although growing steadily, colonial American cities remained small enough to permit residents to maintain a network of personal relationships. The lack of industrial technology prevented rapid movement, so pedestrians and horse-drawn wagons and carriages often clogged the cobblestone streets.

At this point, the United States was still an overwhelmingly rural society. In 1790 the government's first census counted roughly 4 million Americans. As Table 14–3 shows, only about 5 percent of them resided in cities. The vast majority lived on farms and in small villages scattered along the Eastern seaboard.

Urban expansion: 1800–1860. Early in the nineteenth century, dozens of new cities sprang up as transportation routes opened the American West. In 1818, the National Road (now Interstate 40) linked Baltimore to the Ohio

Table 14–3	THE URBAN POPULATION OF THE UNITED STATES, 1790–1988	
Year	Population (millions)	Percent Urban
1790	3.9	5.1
1800	5.3	6.1
1820	9.6	7.3
1840	17.1	10.5
1860	31.4	19.7
1880	50.2	28.1
1900	76.0	39.7
1920	105.7	51.3
1940	131.7	56.5
1960	179.3	69.9
1980	226.5	73.7
1988	245.8	77.1

SOURCE: U.S. Bureau of the Census.

Valley. A decade later the Baltimore and Ohio Railroad transported people and products far faster. The Erie Canal (1825) connected New York to the Great Lakes and sparked the development of cities such as Buffalo, Cleveland, and Detroit. Because of the importance of water transportation during this period, most cities took root on the shores of lakes and rivers.

Figure 14–5   The Street Plans of Colonial New Amsterdam and Philadelphia

The plan of colonial New Amsterdam (New York), shown on the left, reflects the preindustrial urban pattern of walls enclosing a city of narrow, irregular streets. Colonial Philadelphia, founded fifty years later, reflects the industrial urban pattern of accessible cities containing wide, regular streets to facilitate economic activity.

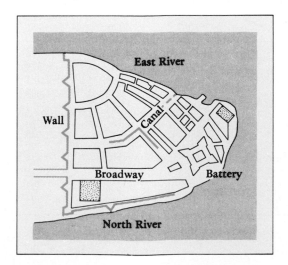

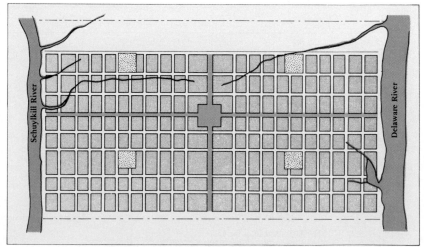

By 1860, about one-third of Americans were city dwellers. Some greeted this trend as progress; others mourned the passing of traditional agrarian life. Rural-urban tensions were inflamed by negative stereotypes: Urbanites sneered at "ignorant country cousins" while those living in rural areas condemned "untrustworthy city slickers" (Callow, 1969).

Driving this urban expansion was industrial capitalism, which was concentrated primarily in the northern states. In 1850, for example, New York City had a population ten times greater than that of Charleston. This division of American society into the industrial-urban North and the agrarian-rural South fueled many of the tensions leading to the Civil War (Schlesinger, 1969).

The metropolitan era: 1860–1950. Industrialization intensified after the Civil War. Now millions of Americans fled the countryside for cities, in hopes that factory jobs would offer greater economic opportunity. Cities also absorbed tens of millions of immigrants, most from Europe. Table 14–4 shows the rapid growth of American cities in the late nineteenth century.

By 1900, New York boasted 4 million residents, and Chicago, which had scarcely 100,000 people in 1860, was approaching 2 million. This growth marked the era of the **metropolis,** *a large city that dominates an urban area socially and economically.* Industrializa-

tion had transformed cities into vast commercial, manufacturing, and residential centers.

Industrial technology further changed the shape of urban America. Until 1850, few buildings exceeded three or four stories. By the 1880s, steel girders and mechanical elevators raised structures over ten stories high. In 1930, New York's Empire State Building became an urban wonder, a true "skyscraper" stretching 102 stories into the clouds. Railroads and highways enabled cities to expand outward, with unprecedented efficiency (Warner, 1962). Now most Americans were urbanites; America had become, and would remain, an urban society.

Urban decentralization: 1950–present. The industrial metropolis peaked about 1950. Since then, many people have moved away from the central cities in a process known as *urban decentralization* (Edmonston & Guterbock, 1984). As Table 14–4 shows, the largest central cities of the Northeast and Midwest have stopped growing; many have even lost population. New York, for example, has 600,000 fewer people today than in 1950.

Over the course of 350 years, American society has been transformed from a string of rural villages to a nation of vast urban regions. Today, three-fourths of Americans are city dwellers, living on a tiny fraction of this country's land area. As we approach the new

Table 14–4 POPULATION GROWTH IN SELECTED AMERICAN CITIES, 1870–1990

City	Population (in thousands)						
	1870	1890	1910	1930	1950	1970	1990
Baltimore	267	434	558	805	950	905	736
Boston	251	448	671	781	801	641	574
Chicago	299	1,100	2,185	3,376	3,621	3,369	2,784
Dallas	7	38	92	260	434	844	1,007
Detroit	80	206	466	1,569	1,850	1,514	1,027
Los Angeles	6	50	319	1,238	1,970	2,812	3,485
Milwaukee	71	204	374	578	637	717	628
New Orleans	191	242	339	459	570	593	497
New York*	942	2,507	4,767	6,930	7,892	7,896	7,323
Philadelphia	674	1,047	1,549	1,951	2,072	1,949	1,586
St. Louis	311	452	687	822	857	622	397
San Francisco	149	299	417	634	775	716	724

* Population figures for New York in 1870 and 1890 reflect that city as presently constituted.
SOURCE: U.S. Bureau of the Census.

century, urbanization is continuing although cities are assuming a new form. Instead of residing in densely populated central cities, Americans have spread out into large urban regions, a trend closely tied to the growth of suburbs.

Suburbs and Central Cities

Recent decades have seen the rapid expansion of **suburbs,** *the urban area beyond the political boundaries of a city.* Suburbs began to grow late in the nineteenth century, as railroad and trolley lines enabled people to live beyond the commotion of the city and to commute to work "downtown." The first commuters were the well-to-do, imitating the pattern of the European nobility who periodically traveled between country estates and town houses (Baltzell, 1979). The growth of suburbs was also fueled by racial and ethnic intolerance: Rising immigration was giving the central city a socially diverse makeup, prompting many to favor homogeneous, high-prestige suburbs. In time, less wealthy Americans also began to view a single-family house on its own piece of leafy suburban ground as a key element of the American Dream.

The economic boom of the late 1940s, government-backed mortgages for veterans, and increasingly affordable automobiles placed suburbia within the grasp of the average family. After World War II, Americans eagerly returned to family life, igniting the baby boom described earlier in this chapter. Since central cities contained little space for new housing construction, suburbs blossomed almost overnight.

Some of the most successful postwar suburbs were designed for moderate-income Americans. Levittown, built on the potato fields of New York's Long Island in the late 1940s, inaugurated a trend toward inexpensive suburban housing (Wattel, 1958). What some dismissed as prefabricated, look-alike homes were bought as fast as they were built. By 1970, more Americans lived in the suburbs than in the central cities.

Not surprisingly, business also began to look to the suburbs. By 1970, the suburban mall was well on its way to replacing the downtown stores of the metropolitan era (Rosenthal, 1974; Tobin, 1976; Geist, 1985). The interstate highway system, built during the postwar period, also brought industry to the suburbs. Old factory districts in the inner city had become expensive because of high taxes and increasing crime, and were also inconvenient for large trucks. Cities were soon surrounded by commercial parks encompassing both industry and offices.

This rapid shift from cities to suburbs created financial problems for the older cities of the Northeast and Midwest. Population decline reduced tax revenues. Cities

Urban renewal has transformed many decayed central-city districts into vital business centers. Baltimore's Inner Harbor, a commercial venture by developer James Rouse, is visually exciting and full of wonderful shops and restaurants. But renewal of this kind, critics claim, does little to address the basic housing needs of the American poor.

lost relatively affluent residents to the suburbs and were faced with financing ever more expensive social programs for the poor who remained (Gluck & Meister, 1979). The predictable result was the gradual decay of the inner city after about 1950 (Sternlieb & Hughes, 1983). Some major cities, including Cleveland, New York, and Philadelphia, have reached the brink of financial bankruptcy. To many white Americans, the deteriorating inner city became synonymous with low-quality housing, crime, drugs, unemployment, the poor, and the nonwhite. This perception fueled the ongoing "white flight," setting in motion a vicious cycle of decline (Clark, 1979; Logan & Schneider, 1984; Stahura 1986).

In response to the plight of the central cities, the federal government established a policy of **urban renewal,** *government programs intended to revitalize cities.* Many inner cities have been rebuilt, usually with substantial federal funding. Yet these programs have been criticized for benefiting the business community far more than low-income residents in need of housing (Jacobs, 1961; Greer, 1965; Gans, 1982).

The Sunbelt: Postindustrial Cities

Not only are urban Americans spreading beyond the boundaries of central cities, they are also migrating from the traditional industrial heartland of America. In 1940 the Snowbelt (the Northeast and Midwest) contained almost 60 percent of all Americans. By 1975, however, the Sunbelt (the South and the West) passed the Snowbelt in overall population, and by 1990 it was home to almost 60 percent of the population. This regional migration, linked to the emergence of a postindustrial economy (discussed in Chapter 11, "Economics and Politics"), has further eroded the population of older Snowbelt cities.

Sunbelt cities continue their rapid growth. This demographic shift is shown in Table 14–5, which compares the ten largest cities in the United States in 1950 and in 1990. In 1950, eight of the top ten were Snowbelt industrial cities, whereas in 1990, six of ten were in the Sunbelt. The office-tower service jobs that dominate in Sunbelt cities are likely to proliferate in the next decade. Thus, this century, which opened with tremendous urban growth in the North and Midwest, will close with rapid urban growth in the South and West.

Unlike industrial cities of the Snowbelt, the postindustrial cities of the Sunbelt grew *after* urban decentral-

Table 14–5   THE TEN LARGEST CITIES IN THE UNITED STATES, 1950 AND 1990

1950		
Rank	City	Population
1	New York	7,892,000
2	Chicago	3,621,000
3	Philadelphia	2,072,000
4	Los Angeles	1,970,000
5	Detroit	1,850,000
6	Baltimore	950,000
7	Cleveland	915,000
8	St. Louis	857,000
9	Boston	801,000
10	San Francisco	775,000

1990		
Rank	City	Population
1	New York	7,322,564
2	Los Angeles	3,485,398
3	Chicago	2,783,726
4	Houston	1,630,553
5	Philadelphia	1,585,577
6	San Diego	1,110,549
7	Detroit	1,027,974
8	Dallas	1,006,877
9	Phoenix	983,403
10	San Antonio	935,933

SOURCE: U.S. Bureau of the Census

ization began. Since Snowbelt cities have long been enclosed by a ring of politically independent suburbs, outward migration came at the expense of the central city. Suburbs have played a much smaller role in the life of Sunbelt cities, which have simply expanded as population has grown. Thus Chicago covers 228 square miles, whereas Houston sprawls over 565. This physical expansion has enhanced the financial strength of Sunbelt cities. But movement across town is difficult, especially for those unable to afford an automobile. Lower densities also mean that Sunbelt cities generate less social intensity than urban centers like New York or Chicago. For example, critics sometimes charge that Los Angeles is a vast cluster of suburbs in search of a center.

Megalopolis: Regional Cities

The decentralization of urban America has produced large urban areas that contain countless individual cities. In 1988, the Bureau of the Census (1990) reports, the United States contained 283 urban regions, or *metropolitan statistical areas* (MSAs). Each MSA contains a city with at least 50,000 people plus densely populated surrounding counties. Almost all of the fifty fastest-growing MSAs are located in the Sunbelt.

The twenty biggest MSAs, encompassing more than 1 million people, are called *consolidated metropolitan statistical areas* (CMSAs). The largest is New York and adjacent Long Island and northern New Jersey, with a total population of about 18 million. Next in size is the CMSA in Southern California that includes Los Angeles, Riverside, and Anaheim, with a population of some 14 million (U.S. Bureau of the Census, 1989).

Many of these urban regions have grown so large that they have collided with one another. The East Coast now comprises a 400-mile supercity extending from southern New England to northern Virginia. In the early 1960s, French geographer Jean Gottmann (1961) coined the term **megalopolis** to designate *a vast urban region containing a number of cities and their surrounding suburbs.* Although composed of hundreds of politically independent cities and suburbs, from an airplane at night, a megalopolis appears as one continuous city. Other such supercities include the eastern coast of Florida, much of Southern California, and the urban strip extending from Cleveland to Chicago. Future urban regions will undoubtedly emerge, especially in the fast-growing Sunbelt.

URBANISM AS A WAY OF LIFE

Rapid urban growth since the Industrial Revolution has transformed American society in various ways. Both European and American sociologists have explored differences between urban life and rural life.

Marc Chagall's painting *I and the Village* (1911) conveys the essential unity of rural life, by which people are linked by tradition and their common work on the land. In contrast, Edouard Manet's *The Bar at the Folies Bergeres* suggests the isolating character of urban life. Here a woman stands alone—despite being in the middle of a crowd—her contact with others limited to the impersonal role she performs. Note, too, that the people in the room are depicted only indirectly in a mirror.

Marc Chagall, I and the Village, *1911. Oil on canvas, 63⅝″ × 59⅝″. Collection, The Museum of Modern Art, New York. Mrs. Simon Guggenheim Fund.*

Ferdinand Toennies. In the late nineteenth century, the German sociologist Ferdinand Toennies (1963; orig. 1887) used the German word *Gemeinschaft* (meaning roughly "community") to refer to *a type of social organization based on tradition and enduring, personal relationships*. People who lived in rural villages, Toennies claimed, were bound together by kinship, neighborhood, and friendship. *Gemeinschaft*, then, characterizes any social setting in which people form what is more or less a single primary group.

By contrast, *Gesellschaft* (a German word meaning roughly "association") refers to *a type of social organization based on cultural pluralism and transitory, impersonal relationships*. In *Gesellschaft*, people are motivated by self-interest rather than the well-being of the entire community. With little common identity, Toennies suggested, city dwellers view other people as a means of achieving their own goals. Toennies believed the growth of cities heralded the erosion of traditional social relations in favor of the temporary and impersonal ties typical of business. The tension between rural and urban social patterns can sometimes cause conflict, as suggested in the box.

Émile Durkheim. The French sociologist Émile Durkheim understood the spread of urban life in much the same way as Toennies. Durkheim's concept of **mechanical solidarity** refers to *social bonds, typical of people in rural settings, based on conforming to tradition*. Durkheim's concept of mechanical solidarity and Toennies's *Gemeinschaft*, then, are virtually synonymous.

Industrial societies with an expanding urban life are joined by what Durkheim called **organic solidarity**, *social bonds, typical of people in industrial cities, based on specialization and interdependence*. This concept parallels Toennies's *Gesellschaft*. Although the two agreed that the expansion of industry and cities were undermining traditional social patterns, Durkheim was more optimistic about this historical transformation. For him, urban society offered far more individual choice, moral tolerance, and personal privacy than had ever been found in the rural village. In short, if something was lost in urbanization, much was gained.

Georg Simmel. Georg Simmel offered a micro-analysis of cities; that is, he analyzed how urban life shaped people's behavior and attitudes (1964; orig. 1905). Because the city presents a crush of people, objects, and events, Simmel argued, the urbanite is easily overwhelmed with stimulation. Consequently, city people typically develop a *blasé attitude*, learning to respond selectively by tuning out much of what goes on around them. City dwellers are not without sensitivity and compassion for others; they simply must be discriminating in their responses because of the social intensity of the city.

Robert Park. American sociologists soon joined the exploration of rapidly growing cities. Robert Park (1864–1944) was a leader of the first major American sociology program at the University of Chicago. Although Park was influenced by the Europeans noted above, he sought to give American urban studies a decidedly more empirical emphasis by advocating the detailed study of actual cities. One of Park's most memorable comments described his own life as a student of the city:

> I suspect that I have actually covered more ground, tramping about in cities in different parts of the world, than any other living man. (1950:viii)

Park concluded that the city comprised a highly ordered mosaic of distinctive ethnic communities, vice districts, and industrial sectors. These "natural areas," all part of a complex social organism, develop and change in relation to one another over time. To Park, the city formed an ever-changing human kaleidoscope.

Louis Wirth. Another major figure in the Chicago School of urban sociology was Louis Wirth (1897–1952). In 1938, Wirth published an influential essay that systematically integrated the ideas of Toennies, Simmel, Durkheim, and Park into a theory of urban life.

Wirth defined the city as a setting marked by large population, dense settlement, and social diversity. These characteristics, he argued, confer special qualities on urban life. Urbanism as a way of life is largely impersonal, superficial, and transitory. Living among millions of others, a city resident comes in contact with countless people, yet knows most only in terms of what they do: as bus driver, office manager, grocery store clerk. Urban social relationships are also founded on self-interest. For example, shoppers see merchants as suppliers of goods, while merchants see shoppers as the source of income. They may exchange greetings, but friendship is not the reason for their interaction. This self-centeredness and also greater diversity make city dwellers tolerant. Rural communities often vigorously enforce narrowly defined social mores, but the heterogeneous population of a city rarely shares precisely the same moral values (Wilson, 1985).

SOCIOLOGY OF EVERYDAY LIFE

When Worlds Collide: The Invasion of the City Slickers

Historically, population increase in the United States has gone hand in hand with the development of cities. Urbanization sometimes brings the most dramatic changes to people living in rural villages and small towns that are drawn into the orbit of expanding cities. While some small-town residents may applaud this change, others resist it.

When city people move to the country, Noel Perrin explains, they bring with them "a series of unconscious assumptions. It might be better for rural America if they brought a few sticks of dynamite. . . ."

Echoing the view of Toennies, Perrin also recognizes that the historical direction of change has favored the city.

Take a typical example. Mr. and Mrs. Nice are Bostonians. They live a couple of miles off Route 128 in a four-bedroom house. He's a partner in an ad agency; she has considerable talent as an artist. For some years they've had a second home in northern New Hampshire. The kids love it up there in Grafton County.

For some years, too, both Nices have been feeling they'd like to simplify their lives. They look with increasing envy on their New Hampshire neighbors, who never face a morning traffic jam, or an evening one, either; who don't have a long drive to the country on Friday night and a long drive back on Sunday; who aren't cramped into a suburban lot; who live in harmony with the natural rhythm of the year; who think the rat race is probably some minor event at a county fair.

One Thursday evening Don Nice says to Sue that he's been talking to the other partners, and they've agreed there's no reason he can't do some of his work at home. If he's in the office Wednesday and Thursday every week, why the rest of the time he can stay in touch by telephone. Sue, who has been trapped all year as a Brownie Scout leader and who has recently had the aerial snapped off her car in Boston, is delighted. She reflects happily that in their little mountain village you don't even need to lock your house, and there is no Brownie troop.

So the move occurs. In most ways Don and Sue are very happy. They raise practically all their own vegetables the first year; Sue takes up cross-country skiing. Don personally splits some of the wood they burn in their new woodstove.

But there are some problems. The first one Sue is conscious of is the school. It's just not very good. It's clear to Sue almost immediately that the town desperately needs a new school building—and also modern playground equipment, new school buses, more and better art instruction at the high school, a different principal. Don is as upset as Sue when they discover that only about 40 percent of the kids who graduate from that high school go on to any form of college. The rest do native things like becoming farmers, and mechanics, and joining the Air Force. An appalling number of the girls marry within twelve months after graduation. How are Jeanie and Don, Jr., going to get into good colleges from this school? . . . Pretty soon Sue and Don join an informal group of newcomers in town who are working to upgrade education. All they want for starters is the new building ($5.6 million) and a majority of their kind on the school board.

As for Don, though he really enjoys splitting the wood—in fact, next year he's planning to get a chainsaw and start cutting a few trees of his own—he also likes to play golf. There's no course within twenty miles. Some of the nice people he's met in the education lobby feel just as he does. They begin to discuss the possibility of a nine-hole course. The old farmer who owns the land they have in mind seems to be keeping only four or five cows on it, anyway. Besides, taxes are going up, and the old fellow is going to have to sell, sooner or later. (Which is too bad, of course. Don and Sue both admire the local farmers, and they're sincerely sorry whenever one has to quit.)

Over the next several years, Don and Sue get more and more adjusted to rural living—and they also gradually discover more things that need changing. For example, the area needs a good French restaurant. And it needs a much better airport. At present there are only two flights a day to Boston, and because of the lack of sophisticated equipment, even they are quite often canceled. If Don wants to be sure of getting down for an important meeting, he has to drive. Sue would be glad of more organized activities for the kids. There's even talk of starting a Brownie troop.

In short, if enough upper-middle-class people move to a rural town, they are naturally going to turn it into a suburb of the nearest city. For one generation it will be a nice and truly rustic suburb, with real farms dotted around it, and real natives speaking their minds at town meetings. Then as the local people are gradually taxed out of existence (or at least out of town), one more piece of rural America has died.

SOURCE: Noel Perrin, "Rural Area: Permit Required," *Country Journal*, April 1980, pp. 34–35.

Robert Ezra Park (1864–1944) had a passion for cities. Leaving a newspaper job, Park embarked upon a thirty-year career at the University of Chicago leading a group of sociologists in direct, systematic observations of urban life.

On balance, Wirth's evaluation of urbanism seems rather negative. The rapid urbanization of Europe and North America troubled him, as it did Toennies and others. There is little doubt that the personal ties and traditional morality of rural life fall to the wayside in the anonymous rush of the city. But, echoing Durkheim and Park, Wirth noted a positive side to these changes, including greater personal autonomy and a wider range of life choices.

Critical evaluation. In Europe and the United States, early sociologists concentrated much research on cities and their implications for human beings. Decades of additional research, however, have provided mixed support for their conclusions.

Urban settings do engender a weaker sense of community than rural areas, but it is easy to exaggerate the social cohesion in rural life. In reality, conflict and interpersonal antagonisms of various stripes undermine community life in the countryside as well as the city. Furthermore, while urbanites treat most others impersonally,

they do establish and maintain close personal relationships. The public anonymity of cities means that people "walk lonely in the crowd," but many welcome such privacy (Keller, 1968; Cox, 1971; Macionis, 1978; Wellman, 1979; Lee et al., 1984).

Although urbanism does foster a way of life more tolerant of diversity, the pioneering sociologists were wrong to imply that it neutralizes the effects of class, race, and sex. On the contrary, cities often intensify the social forces at work in class struggles, racism, and sexism (Spates & Macionis, 1987). Herbert Gans (1968) criticized Wirth's view of urbanism as a single way of life, suggesting that rich and poor, white and black, male and female lead distinctive lives in cities.

Urban Ecology

Sociologists have also explored **urban ecology,** *the link between the physical and social dimensions of cities.* Chapter 2 ("Culture") focused on cultural ecology, the study of how a way of life is related to the physical environment. Urban ecology reveals that urban life is closely linked to the physical form of the city.

Consider first the location of cities. The first cities emerged in fertile regions where the ecology favored settlement. Later in history, cities were sited according to cultural priorities. For example, early medieval societies concerned with defense used the natural environment for self-protection. Athens is situated on an outcropping of rock; Paris and Mexico City were established on islands. After the Industrial Revolution, the unparalleled importance of economics opened cities to the outside and fueled urban growth near rivers and natural harbors that facilitated trade.

A second issue studied by urban ecologists is the physical design of cities. In 1925, Ernest W. Burgess, a student and colleague of Robert Park, described land use in Chicago in terms of a series of concentric zones. City centers, Burgess observed, are business districts bordered by a ring of factories. Beyond this commercial hub lie residential rings that become more expensive with greater distance from the noise and pollution of the city's center.

Homer Hoyt (1939) refined these observations by noting that distinctive districts often form wedge-shaped sectors. For example, one fashionable area may be built next to another, or development may grow outward from a city's center along a train or trolley line.

Chauncey Harris and Edward Ullman (1945) added that decentralization results in multicentered cities. As growth occurs, zoning typically separates certain activities from one another. Few people wish to live close to industrial areas, for example, and owners of fashionable retail shops usually want to distance themselves from pornography and areas where vice thrives, such as Boston's Combat Zone. Thus the complexity and diversity of urban life give rise to a mosaic of distinctive districts.

Subsequent research has identified several factors—family patterns, social class, and race and ethnicity—that account for considerable variation in urban land use (Shevky & Bell, 1955; Johnston, 1976). Families with children gravitate to areas offering large apartments or single-family homes and good schools. The rich generally seek high-prestige neighborhoods away from low-income people—sometimes in exclusive central-city areas. People with a common cultural heritage tend to cluster together. The poor and some minorities, whose choices are limited, also live in distinct areas.

Brian Berry and Philip Rees (1969) argue that particular factors influence urban land use in specific ways. In accordance with Ernest Burgess's theory, distinctive family types tend to form concentric zones. Households with few children tend to live near the city's center, while those with more children live farther away. Differences in social class generate the sector-shaped districts described by Homer Hoyt as, for instance, the rich and the poor each occupy an opposing "side of the tracks." Racial and ethnic groups cluster together at various points throughout the city, consistent with Harris and Ullman's multiple-center model.

Critical evaluation.   Almost a century of research in urban ecology has linked the physical and social dimensions of urban life. But, as ecologists themselves concede, we have gained only an idealized picture of city life that may not apply well to particular settings. Some critics of this approach point out that urban ecology also suffers from a tendency to minimize the extent to which development is guided by power elites (Molotch, 1976; Feagin, 1983). Also, because urban ecologists have studied American cities during a brief historical period, their conclusions may lack universal application. Preindustrial towns differ from industrial cities in important ways, and postindustrial cities are introducing still more new forms. No single model is likely to take into account the full range of urban diversity.

THIRD-WORLD URBANIZATION

Twice in human history, the world has experienced a revolutionary expansion of cities. The first urban revolution began about 8000 B.C.E., when the first cities emerged, continuing for thousands of years as permanent settlements appeared on different continents. The second urban revolution lasted for two centuries after 1750 as the Industrial Revolution sparked the rapid growth of cities in Europe and North America.

A third urban revolution began about 1950, and is once again transforming the world. But this change is not taking place in the industrial societies of the world, where 75 percent of people already are city dwellers. Extraordinary urban growth is now occurring in the Third World. In 1950, about 25 percent of the Third-World population inhabited cities; in 1990, the proportion had risen to 40 percent. By 2000, half the people in the Third World will be urbanites. In 1950, there were only seven cities in the world with a population over 5 million, and only two of these were in the Third World. By 1985, twenty-six cities had more than 5 million residents, and eighteen were in the Third World (Fornos, 1986). By the end of this century, several Third-World cities will dwarf even the largest cities in industrialized societies.

Table 14–6 identifies the world's ten largest urban areas—cities and their densely populated surroundings—in 1981 and includes estimates of the ten biggest in 2000. In 1981, six of the ten were in industrialized societies. Within a decade, however, only three of the top ten will be situated in industrialized societies. Most will be in less economically developed societies of the Third World. These urban areas not only will be the world's largest, they will contain an unprecedented number of inhabitants. Relatively rich nations such as Japan may be able to meet the needs of 15 to 30 million people in emerging megacities, but it is doubtful that the same is true of Mexico, Brazil, or India.

Causes of Third-World Urban Growth

A primary cause of this third urban revolution is that many nonindustrial societies are now entering the high-growth stage of demographic transition. Declining death rates have resulted in a population explosion in Latin America, Africa, and Asia. For urban areas, the rate

Table 14–6 THE WORLD'S TEN LARGEST URBAN AREAS, 1981 and 2000

1981

Urban Area	Population (in millions)
New York, U.S.A.	16.5
Tokyo–Yokohama, Japan	14.4
Mexico City, Mexico	14.0
Los Angeles–Long Beach, U.S.A.	10.6
Shanghai, China	10.0
Buenos Aires, Argentina	9.7
Paris, France	8.5
Moscow, U.S.S.R.	8.0
Beijing, China	8.0
Chicago, U.S.A.	7.7

2000

Urban Area	Population (in millions)
Tokyo–Yokohama, Japan	30.0
Mexico City, Mexico	27.9
São Paulo, Brazil	25.4
Seoul, South Korea	22.0
Bombay, India	15.4
New York, U.S.A.	14.7
Osaka–Kobe–Kyoto, Japan	14.3
Tehran, Iran	14.3
Rio de Janeiro, Brazil	14.2
Calcutta, India	14.1

SOURCE: 1981 data from various reports of the United Nations; 2000 data from U.S. Bureau of the Census, *World Population Profile: 1989* (Washington, DC: Government Printing Office, 1989), Table 15, pp. 83–84.

of growth is *twice* as high because of urban migration in search of better jobs, health care, education, and conveniences like running water and electricity. Additionally, the seizure of land by elites sometimes forces peasants to migrate to cities (London, 1987).

Cities do offer more opportunities than rural areas, but they provide no panacea for the massive problems generated by an escalating population and oppressive poverty. Many Third-World cities are simply unable to meet the basic needs of their people. In Mexico City, described at the beginning of this chapter, thousands of people from rural areas come in search of work and housing every day, although more than 10 percent of

current residents have no running water in their homes; 15 percent lack sewage facilities; half the trash and garbage produced each day cannot be processed; and exhaust from factories and cars chokes everyone, rich and poor alike (Friedrich, 1984). Like other major cities throughout Latin America, Africa, and Asia, Mexico City is surrounded by wretched shantytowns—settlements of makeshift homes built from discarded materials. As was noted in Chapter 8 ("Global Inequality"), city dumps are home to thousands of poor, who pick through the waste hoping to find enough to ensure their survival for another day.

The Future of Third-World Cities

The problems now facing Third-World cities seem to defy solution, and the end to this remarkable urban growth is nowhere in sight. What hope is there of relieving the plight of people in these emerging megacities?

Earlier chapters have suggested two different answers to this question. One view, linked to modernization theory, holds that as the Third World undergoes industrialization (as Western Europe and North America did in past centuries), greater productivity will simultaneously raise living standards and reduce population growth. A second view, associated with dependency theory, argues that such progress is unlikely as long as Third-World societies remain economically dependent on rich societies.

Urbanist Jane Jacobs (1984), combining elements of each approach, concludes that expanding trade will meet the challenge of population growth, but only if Third-World nations focus trading ties not on rich countries but among themselves. Then their economies can move beyond providing raw materials and inexpensive labor to corporate interests in rich, First-World nations.

Jacob's argument remains controversial. Defenders of multinational corporations insist that contact with rich societies is necessary for obtaining much-needed technology. Critics of the capitalist world system maintain that nothing less than a revolutionary redistribution of global wealth will open the way for an end to grinding poverty in much of the world (Gilbert & Gugler, 1983).

Whatever the course of events, the drama of overpopulation in the Third World will be played out in the cities. Throughout history, and around the world, cities have held out the promise of a better life. But if cities have generated the best in human culture, they have also concentrated the greatest human ills—includ-

Many Third-World cities provide striking social contrasts: Rio de Janeiro is both a playground for the world's rich and home to millions who are desperately poor. Perhaps not surprisingly, in recent years this city has experienced a rapid rise in crime, much of it directed at affluent tourists.

ing poverty, crime, racial tension, and environmental pollution.

In short, the city weaves an intricate pattern of noble accomplishments and wretched shortcomings. As we approach the twenty-first century, the greatest test of the urban promise will occur in societies of the Third World.

SUMMARY

Population

1. Fertility and mortality are major components of population growth. In global terms, the fertility, mortality, and population growth in North America are relatively low.

2. Migration, another key demographic concept, has special importance to the historical growth of cities.

3. Age-sex pyramids allow demographers to describe the composition of a population and to project future population patterns.
4. Historically, world population grew slowly because high birth rates were offset by high death rates. About 1750, a demographic transition began as death rates declined, causing world population to rise sharply.
5. Malthus warned that population would outpace food production, leading to social calamity. Contrary to Malthus's ominous predictions, demographic transition theory holds that technological advance brings gradually declining birth rates. Although this has occurred in industrialized societies, the Third World has declining death rates coupled with continued high birth rates, prompting population to swell to unprecedented levels.

Urbanization

1. Closely related to population growth is urbanization. The first urban revolution began with the appearance of cities after 8000 B.C.E.; by the start of the common era, cities had emerged in every region of the world.
2. Preindustrial cities are characterized by small buildings, narrow, winding streets, personal and social ties, and rigid patterns of social inequality.
3. A second urban revolution began about 1750 as the Industrial Revolution caused rapid urban growth in Europe. Cities adopted wide, regular streets to facilitate trade. In the process, social anonymity increased.
4. Urbanism came to North America with European settlers. From a string of colonial towns dotting the Atlantic coastline, by 1920 a majority of Americans lived in urban places, and several metropolises contained millions of inhabitants. By 1950, as a result of the emergence of a postindustrial economy, American cities began to decentralize in vast urban regions.

5. Rapid urbanization in Europe during the nineteenth century led early sociologists to contrast rural and urban life. Ferdinand Toennies built an analysis on the concepts of *Gemeinschaft* and *Gesellschaft*, which correspond closely to Émile Durkheim's concepts of mechanical solidarity and organic solidarity. Georg Simmel claimed that overstimulation produced a blasé attitude in urbanites.
6. At the University of Chicago, Robert Park saw the city as an internally differentiated organism that permits its residents considerable social freedom. Louis Wirth suggested that the size, density, and heterogeneity of cities give rise to impersonality, self-interest, and tolerance. Other researchers have explored urban ecology, the interplay of social and physical dimensions of cities.
7. A third urban revolution is now occurring in the Third World, where most of the world's largest urban areas will soon be found. These megacities will be far larger than any in history.

KEY CONCEPTS

Population

age-sex pyramid a graphic representation of the age and sex of a population

crude birth rate the number of live births in a given year for every thousand people in a population

crude death rate the number of deaths in a given year for every thousand people in a population

demographic transition theory the thesis that population patterns are linked to a society's level of technological development

demography the study of human population

fertility the incidence of childbearing in a society's population

infant mortality rate the number of infant deaths for each thousand live births in a given year

life expectancy the average lifespan of a society's population

migration the movement of people into and out of a specific territory

mortality the incidence of death in a society's population

sex ratio the number of males for every hundred females in a given population

zero population growth the level of reproduction that maintains population at a steady state

Urbanization

Gemeinschaft a type of social organization based on tradition and enduring, personal relationships

Gesellschaft a type of social organization based on cultural pluralism and transitory, impersonal social relationships

mechanical solidarity social bonds, typical of people in rural settings, based on conforming to tradition

megalopolis a vast urban region containing a number of cities and their surrounding suburbs

metropolis a large city that dominates an urban area socially and economically

organic solidarity social bonds, typical of people in industrial cities, based on specialization and interdependence

suburbs the urban area beyond the political boundaries of a city

urban ecology study of the link between the physical and social dimensions of cities

urbanization the concentration of humanity into cities

urban renewal government programs intended to revitalize cities

Social Change and Modernity

Chapter Outline

The firelight flickers in the gathering darkness. Chief Kanhonk sits, as he has done every evening for many years, to begin an evening of animated talk and storytelling.[1] This is the hour when the Kaiapo, a small society of Brazil's Amazon rainforest, celebrate their culture. Because the Kaiapo are a traditional people with no written language, the elders use such occasions to instruct their grandchildren in their history and way of life. In the past, evenings like this have been filled with tales of brave Kaiapo warriors fighting off Portuguese traders in pursuit of slaves and gold.

But as the minutes pass, only a few villagers assemble for the evening ritual. "It is the Big Ghost," one grumbles. The presence of the "Big Ghost" is evident in the soft glow spilling from windows of homes. Most of the Kaiapo are watching television. Three years ago, their leaders installed a satellite dish in the village, and the consequences of this one act have been greater than anyone imagined. What outsiders failed to do to the Kaiapo with guns they may yet accomplish with prime-time programming. Those around the fire sit silently, knowing that their culture is again under attack. This time there may be no defense (Simons, 1989).

The Kaiapo, a small group among the 230,000 native people of Brazil, are easily identified by their striking body paint and ornate ceremonial dress. Recently, profits from gold-mining and cutting mahogany trees have made them rich. But the Kaiapo wonder whether their new-found fortune is a blessing or a curse. To some, affluence means the opportunity to learn about the outside world through television. Others, like Chief Kanhonk, express a different view. Sitting by the fire, he thinks aloud, "I have been saying that people must buy useful things like knives and fishing hooks. Television does not fill the stomach. It only shows our children and grandchildren white people's things." Bebtopup, the oldest priest, agrees: "The night is the time the old people teach the young people. Television has stolen the night" (Simons 1989:37).

The transformation of the Kaiapo raises important questions about what causes social change; their current plight also makes us wonder whether change—even toward a higher standard of living—is always for the better. Such questions affect not just the Kaiapo, of course, since around the globe traditional cultures are being drawn away from their past by the materialism and affluence of the First World.

---

[1] This opening is a selective adaptation of the account provided by Simons (1989).

A vexing dilemma is that economic development often is achieved only at the cost of a traditional society's culture. The resources of Brazil's Amazon region place a richer material life within reach of the Kaiapo. But many of their number fear that television and other modern "conveniences" will quickly destroy the Kaiapo's distinctive way of life.

This chapter, then, explores social change as a process with both positive and negative consequences. Of particular interest to Americans is what sociologists call *modernity*, the social world as it emerged from changes wrought by the Industrial Revolution. We shall also consider how powerful, industrial nations, including the United States, are involved in changes affecting the rest of the world.

WHAT IS SOCIAL CHANGE?

Earlier chapters have explored complex human societies in terms of both stability and change. On the one hand, we have examined social structure, the relatively *static* patterns involving status and role, social inequality, and various institutions. On the other hand, societies grapple with *dynamic* forces including conflict, technological innovation, the growth of bureaucracy, population increase and the expansion of cities, and social movements.

The result of these factors is **social change**, *the transformation of culture and social institutions over time*. This complex process has four general characteristics.

1. **Social change is universal although the rate of change varies.** "Nothing is certain except death

and taxes," so the saying goes. Actually, the odds of dying at an early age, the reasons people die, and even the definition of death have changed in recent centuries. The notion that taxes are certain is a distinctly modern notion; taxes were unknown for most of human history. In short, one would be hard pressed to identify anything that is not subject to the forces of social change.

Still, some societies change faster than others. As explained in Chapter 2 ("Culture"), hunters and gatherers remained much the same over thousands of years. By contrast, societies with complex technology change rapidly, so that people are keenly aware of change even within a single lifetime. Moreover, in modern societies some cultural elements change more quickly than others. William Ogburn's (1964) theory of *cultural lag* (see Chapter 2) asserts that material culture typically changes faster than nonmaterial culture. For example, medical devices that prolong the life of seriously ill people have developed more rapidly than ethical standards for deciding when and how to employ this technology.

2. **Social change is both intentional and unplanned.** Industrial societies actively encourage many kinds of change. For example, scientists seek more efficient forms of energy, advertisers try to convince consumers that some new gadget is a "necessity," and government officials seek ways to increase equality of opportunity in the workplace. Yet even the experts rarely envision all the consequences of the changes they propose. Early automobile manufacturers understood that cars would allow Americans to travel in a single day distances that had required weeks or months a century before. But no one foresaw that the mobility provided by automobiles would also dramatically affect American families, reshape cities and suburbs, alter our environment, and result in some 50,000 accidental deaths each year.

3. **Social change is often controversial.** As the history of the automobile demonstrates, all social change involves both good and bad consequences. Any transformation of society is likely to draw praise from some people and provoke opposition from others. Capitalists welcomed the Industrial Revolution because advancing technology increased productivity and profits. Many workers, however, fearing that machines would make their skills obsolete, strongly resisted "progress." Similarly, most blacks in South Africa have celebrated the weakening of apartheid in recent years, while these changes have been unsettling to many whites. In the United States, changing social patterns between blacks and whites, between women and men, and between gays and heterosexuals remain controversial public issues.

4. **Some changes matter more than others.** Some changes have only passing significance, while other transformations have far-reaching ramifications. At one extreme, fads, such as Teenage Mutant Ninja Turtles, arise and dissipate quickly, with little long-term effect. At the other, Americans are still adjusting to powerful technological advances such as television half a century after its introduction. And we can scarcely imagine how the computer revolution will transform the entire world during the next century. Like the automobile and television, computers will have both positive and negative effects, providing new kinds of jobs while eliminating old ones, and facilitating the processing of information while reducing personal privacy.

CAUSES OF SOCIAL CHANGE

There are many causes of social change. Some change emerges within a particular society. But in a world linked by sophisticated communication and transportation technology, change in one place often prompts change elsewhere.

Culture and Change

Culture is a dynamic system of symbols that continually acquires new elements and loses others. Chapter 2 ("Culture") identified three important sources of cultural change. First, *invention* produces mechanical objects, ideas, and social patterns that reshape society to some degree. Rocket propulsion research, beginning in the 1940s, has produced increasingly sophisticated vehicles for space flight. Today we take such technology for granted, and during the next century a significant number of Americans will probably travel in space.

A second process, *discovery*, occurs when people recognize existing elements of the world or learn to see them in a new way. For example, medical advances offer a growing understanding of how the human body operates. Beyond the direct effects for human health, medical discoveries have also increased average life expectancy, contributing to the "graying of America."

Third, *diffusion* creates change as cultural elements spread from one society to another through trade, migration, and mass communication. Ralph Linton (1937) recognized that many familiar elements of American life have come to us from other lands—for example, cloth (developed in Asia), clocks (invented in Europe), and coins (devised in Turkey). Generally, material things diffuse more readily than nonmaterial cultural traits. The Kaiapo, described at the beginning of this chapter, have been quick to adopt television but are reluctant to embrace the materialism and individualism that gradually seizes those who spend hours watching Western, commercial programming.

For its entire history, the United States has been transformed by cultural diffusion accompanying immigration. In recent decades, people from Latin America and Asia have introduced new cultural patterns, clearly evident in the sights, smells, and sounds of cities across the country (Fallows, 1983; Muller & Espenshade, 1985). The global dominance of the United States ensures that much American culture—from hamburgers to Harlem rap music to the skills of Harvard M.B.A.s—has diffused to other societies.

Bear in mind, too, that some cultures are more likely to embrace change than others. Recall from Chapter 12 ("Family and Religion") Max Weber's (1958; orig. 1904–05) claim that the deliberate rationality of early Calvinists was vital to the development of Western industrial-capitalism.

Conflict and Change

Tension and conflict within a society also causes change. This is a central idea in the work of Karl Marx, who claimed that conflict between social classes drives societies from one historical era to another. Under industrial-capitalism, he maintained, the struggle between capitalists and workers propels society toward a system of socialist production. In the century since Marx's death, this model has proven simplistic, yet he was correct in foreseeing that social conflict arising from patterns of inequality (involving race and gender as well as social class) would modify every society, including the United States.

The Physical Environment and Change

Because human societies are closely related to the natural environment, change in one tends to produce change in the other. Many Native American cultures viewed the natural world with reverence, living according to natural rhythms. European settlers who came to North America generally saw nature in a strikingly different way: as an adversary to be tamed and then molded to human purposes. Confronting a wilderness, these newcomers systematically cut down forests to clear space and amass materials for building, established towns, extended roads in every direction, and dammed rivers as a means of creating water and energy supplies. Consider that, early in the seventeenth century, Manhattan Island was covered with woods and streams; today the center

Americans have achieved a high standard of living partly through indifference to the long-term consequences of our way of life for the natural environment. Some resources are in danger of being depleted, clean air and water can no longer be taken for granted, and only a small fraction of waste materials is currently recycled in urban centers now awash in their own refuse.

of New York City is twenty-two square miles of almost unbroken concrete and buildings that soar thousands of feet into the sky. Such human construction reveals both the American determination to master the natural environment and the centrality of ideas like "growth" in America's capitalist culture.

Technological development renders societies increasingly capable of threatening the natural environment. Americans' high standard of living generates more than 300 billion pounds of refuse each year. Where is it to go? The operation of hundreds of millions of motor vehicles, tens of thousands of factories, and the routine use of dozens of household products all release hazardous chemicals into the environment. Only in the last few decades have we begun to realize the potential effects of our way of life on the environment; devising solutions to this problem will surely require decades more.

In addition to being acted on, the natural environment also affects human societies, sometimes with devastating effect. Throughout history, entire civilizations have succumbed to natural disasters in the form of floods, volcanic eruptions, and earthquakes. Today, life is still periodically disrupted by such natural calamities. In recent years, major earthquakes have killed tens of thousands in Armenia and Iran, just as droughts in central Africa have devastated the lives of millions. Routinely, of course, air and water pollution as well as climatic change will affect our lives in more ways than we can easily predict.

Population and Change

Demographic factors (described in Chapter 14, "Population and Urbanization") also cause social change. Increasing population places escalating demands on the environment and shapes social relationships. In some industrial societies, including the Netherlands and Japan, limited space already affects virtually every facet of life. For example, homes in Amsterdam are small and narrow by American standards, and staircases are extremely steep to make efficient use of space. In Tokyo, bus drivers routinely negotiate city streets that many American commuters would consider too narrow for even a car. Although the United States and Canada have enjoyed a bounty of physical space, urbanization and industrialization have also changed our way of life and will continue to do so. About three out of four North Americans live in cities, which cover only a small percentage of the land surface. The way of life that results barely resembles that found in the rural villages and small towns of the past.

Profound change also results from the shifting composition of a population. Americans, collectively speaking, are growing older. In 1990, almost 13 percent were over sixty-five, three times the proportion in 1900. By the year 2030, seniors will account for about one in four Americans (U.S. Bureau of the Census, 1989). Medical research and health-care services will increasingly focus on the elderly, and negative stereotypes about old people will be challenged as more Americans enter this stage of life (Barberis, 1981). American life may change in countless additional ways as homes and household products are redesigned to meet the needs of older consumers.

Migration within and among societies often promotes dramatic social change. Between 1870 and 1930, tens of millions of foreign immigrants swelled the industrial cities in the United States. Millions of rural Americans joined them. As a result, farm communities declined as metropolises expanded, and, for the first time, the United States became a predominantly urban society. In the process, cultural patterns from around the world diffused throughout American society. Similar changes are taking place today, as people move from Snowbelt to Sunbelt states, where they mingle increasingly with immigrants from Latin America and Asia.

Social Movements and Change

Social change also stems from the intentional efforts of people themselves. When people band together, these efforts take the form of **social movements**, *organized activity that encourages or opposes some dimension of change.* Sociologists study social movements as part of the field of **collective behavior**, defined as *relatively spontaneous activity involving large numbers of people that does not conform to established norms.* Collective behavior encompasses a broad array of human actions, from fashions and fads, to riots, and even lynch mobs. As we have already suggested, fads typically have little lasting effect on a society; riots, however, have played a central part in American history. Race relations, for example, have been shaped by both white riots directed against blacks and black rioting in protest of unjust treatment by whites.

Types of social movements. Social movements can be classified in terms of the kind of change they seek (Aberle, 1966; Cameron, 1966; Blumer, 1969). One variable is *breadth*: Some social movements seek to change only a specific category of people, while others try to change society as a whole. A second variable is *depth*: Some attempt only superficial change, while others pursue extensive transformation of people or institutions. Combining these variables produces four types of social movements, shown in Figure 15–1.

Alternative social movements pursue limited change in certain individuals, encouraging them to discard specific attitudes or behaviors in favor of alternatives. Planned Parenthood, for example, is part of the social movement concerned with population growth. This organization urges individuals to acknowledge the consequences of sexual activity by practicing birth control if they do not want children.

Redemptive social movements also target certain individuals, but attempt to radically change their lives. For example, fundamentalist Christian organizations that seek new members through conversion are redemptive social movements. The resulting transformation is sometimes so momentous that converts are described as being "born again."

Reformative social movements pursue social reform of the entire society. The holistic health-care movement, described in Chapter 13 ("Education and Medicine"), for example, supports revision of American health-care practices. Reformative social movements generally work within the existing institutional framework. They can be progressive (promoting a new social pattern) or reactionary (countermovements seeking to preserve the status quo or to reinstate past social patterns). In the ongoing

Figure 15–1 Four Types of Social Movements
(Aberle, 1966)

		BREADTH OF CHANGE	
		Specific individuals	Entire society
DEPTH OF CHANGE	Limited	1 Alternative social movement	3 Reformative social movement
	Radical	2 Redemptive social movement	4 Revolutionary social movement

debate about abortion in the United States, both the pro-life and pro-choice organizations are reformative social movements.

Revolutionary social movements advocate sweeping transformation. Sometimes mapping out specific plans, sometimes spinning utopian dreams, they reject existing social institutions in favor of radical change. Revolutionary social movements in eighteenth-century colonial America and in czarist Russia early in this century led to the overthrow of existing governments by new political regimes. Until recently, most Americans linked revolution to the establishment of leftist governments, but recent events in Eastern Europe have shown that socialism, too, is subject to popular overthrow. Revolutionary social movements also emerge on the far right. The John Birch Society and the organization headed by Lyndon LaRouche each claim that socialism is undermining the American way of life; in response, they seek radical alteration of our social institutions (Broyles, 1978).

Explaining social movements. Several approaches have dominated the study of social movements. *Deprivation theory* suggests that people advocate social change when they perceive themselves to be deprived of what they deserve. Research has not discovered any absolute level of deprivation that triggers activism. Rather, people tend to see their situation in terms of **relative deprivation,** *a perceived disadvantage based on some standard of comparison.* Therefore revolutionary movements have emerged in both better and worse times; what seems to matter more is how people subjectively evaluate their own situation (Tocqueville, 1955, orig. 1856; Davies, 1962; Merton, 1968).

A second approach, *mass-society theory,* claims that organized efforts toward social change predominate in industrial societies because movements offer rootless individuals a sense of membership and purpose. Thus social movements have a personal as well as a political purpose (Kornhauser, 1959; Melucci, 1989).

Resource-mobilization theory, a third analysis, highlights the importance of resources—money, human labor, access to the mass media, and moral strength—to the outcome of any social movement. From this point of view, logistics—or the extent to which an organization manages to mobilize resources successfully—underlies the success of deliberate movements for social change (McCarthy & Zald, 1977; Killian, 1984; Snow, Rochfoird, Jr., Worden, & Benford, 1986).

A fourth analysis, called *new social movements theory,* holds that contemporary social movements tend to reach beyond local boundaries, becoming national

Environmentalists are a prominent example of what are called "new social movements." Such efforts for change typically involve people in many countries, and are concerned with "quality of life" issues that participants believe are vital to the future of humanity. Here, throngs of people in Paris celebrate Earth Day, 1990.

or international in scope. In addition, they are likely to focus on quality-of-life issues—including global ecology, world peace, and animal rights—rather than economic issues. Social movements are expanding their scope in response to the growing global economy and the increasing linkages among governments (Melucci, 1980; McAdam, McCarthy & Zald, 1988; Kriesi, 1989).

Stages in social movements. Organized efforts for social change typically follow four stages. The *emergence* of a social movement generally stems from the widespread perception that a particular form of social change is necessary. In some cases (the women's movement), activism may emerge from the everyday experiences of countless people; in others (the AIDS crisis), the public may be mobilized by a small number of individuals.

The *coalescence* of a social movement depends on the availability of resources. After emerging, a movement must clearly define itself, recruit new members, and devise policies and tactics to achieve its goals. In addition, leaders must secure access to the mass media and forge alliances with other organizations to sustain the movement's momentum.

In time, a social movement tends to undergo *bureaucratization*. As it becomes more established, the movement depends less on the charisma and talents of a few leaders and more on a capable staff. As movements become more bureaucratic, members may lose some initial fervor, but the movement as a whole has a better chance of long-term survival.

Finally, social movements *decline* for a variety of reasons. They may succeed in their goals, lose resources, or meet overwhelming opposition. In some cases, movements become so well established that they persist even after reaching their objectives, setting their sights on new goals in the face of earlier successes (Piven & Cloward, 1977; Miller, 1983).

MODERNITY

Underlying the study of social change is **modernity,** *patterns of social life linked to industrialization.* In everyday usage, modernity refers to the present in relation to the past. Sociologists include in this catch-all concept all social patterns that arose in the wake of the Industrial Revolution that began in Western Europe in the late eighteenth century. **Modernization** thus refers to *the process of social change initiated by industrialization.* Peter Berger (1977) cites four general characteristics of modernization.

1. **The decline of small, traditional communities.** Modernization involves "the progressive weakening, if not destruction, of the concrete and relatively cohesive communities in which human beings have found solidarity and meaning throughout most of history" (Berger, 1977:72). For thousands

of years, in the camps of hunters and gatherers and in the rural villages of early North American settlers, people lived in small-scale communities of family and neighbors. Each person had a well-defined place in a traditional world based on sentiments and beliefs that were passed from generation to generation. Living in small primary groups certainly limited the range of personal experience, but conferred a strong sense of personal identity, belonging, and purpose.

Industrialization undermines small, isolated communities in several ways. Population growth and efficient communication and transportation expand the scale of social life. The family no longer forms the unrivaled center of everyday activities; as Talcott Parsons (1966) noted, modern life is carried out in distinct social institutions—schools, workplaces, hospitals, prisons, and places of worship.

2. **The expansion of personal choice.** People in traditional preindustrial societies recognize powerful forces beyond human control—gods, spirits, or simply fate. Jealously protecting their traditions, these societies grant members a narrow range of personal choices.

As the power of tradition diminishes, people come to see their lives as an unending series of options. Berger calls this process *individualization*.

Americans, for instance, adopt one "lifestyle" or another, since a way of life that one person finds suitable may hold little appeal to another. Recognizing alternatives in everyday life, of course, parallels a willingness to embrace change. Modern people, then, readily imagine that "things could be other than what they have been" (1977:77).

3. **Increasing diversity in beliefs.** In preindustrial societies, strong family ties and powerful religious convictions enforce conformity, discouraging diversity and change. Modernization promotes a more rational, scientific world view, in which traditional beliefs weaken and morality increasingly becomes a matter of individual attitude. The growth of cities, the expansion of impersonal, bureaucratic organizations, and the social interaction of immigrants from around the world combine to foster a diversity of beliefs and behavior as well as an openness to those who differ from ourselves.

Chapter 12 ("Family and Religion") spotlighted *secularization*, the historical decline of the importance of religion. This weakening of religious doctrine, and especially the official separation of religion and politics, supports expanding the range of personal beliefs in modern society.

4. **Future orientation and growing awareness of time.** People in modern societies have a distinctive understanding of time. First, we tend to think more

In response to the rapid change in the industrial world, Paul Gauguin left France for the South Seas, where he was captivated by a simpler and seemingly timeless way of life. He romanticized this environment in his 1894 painting *Mahana no Atud* (*Day of the Gods*).

Paul Gaugin, Day of the Gods (Mahana no Atua), *1894. Oil on canvas, 68.3 × 91.5 cm. The Art Institute of Chicago. Helen Birch Bartlett Memorial Collection.*

about the future than about the past. Preindustrial people are guided by traditions. Lacking these traditional roots, modern people look toward the future, imagining that inventions and discoveries will make life immeasurably better. Second, modern societies organize daily routines according to precise units of time. Preindustrial peoples think of time in terms of the days and seasons. With the introduction of clocks late in the Middle Ages, Europeans began thinking in terms of hours and minutes. Why? Because of the growing importance of economic activity. Industrial technology demands precise measurement of time; shortly after the Industrial Revolution, people began claiming "Time is money!" Berger suggests that the more people wear wristwatches, the more a traditional society is industrializing.

According to Berger, then, modernization emancipates people from the tyranny of tradition, but leaves them without the comforting security of heritage and roots. No longer do people live in tightly knit communities where traditional religious beliefs provide each person with a strong sense of belonging and little individual freedom. Modern societies offer far more autonomy but less sense of purpose and fewer enduring social ties.

Finally, recall that modernization underlies sociology itself. As was noted in Chapter 1 ("Sociology: Perspective, Theory, and Method"), the discipline originated in the wake of the Industrial Revolution in Western Europe, precisely where social change was most intense. Early European and American sociologists strove to describe and explain the rise of modern society and its consequences for human beings.

Ferdinand Toennies: The Loss of Community

The German sociologist Ferdinand Toennies produced a highly influential account of modernization, detailed in Chapter 14 ("Population and Urbanization"). Like Peter Berger, whose work he influenced, Toennies viewed modernization as the progressive loss of human community, or *Gemeinschaft*, based on personal ties fostering group membership and loyalty. As Toennies saw it, the Industrial Revolution undermined this strong social fabric by introducing a businesslike emphasis on facts and efficiency. European and North American societies gradually became rootless and impersonal and people came to associate mostly on the basis of self-interest—a state Toennies called *Gesellschaft* (1963; orig. 1887).

Ferdinand Toennies (1855–1936) was a pioneering sociologist in Germany during a time of rapid social change. His work cautions us about assuming that what may pass for "progress" is in every sense beneficial.

Early in this century, at least some of American society approximated Toennies's concept of *Gemeinschaft*. Families living in small villages and towns for many generations were deeply bound together in a hardworking, slow-moving way of life. This social world was limited in space as well as choice. Telephones (invented in 1876) were rare even after 1915, when the first coast-to-coast call was placed in the United States. Living without television (introduced in 1939, and uncommon until the 1950s), families entertained themselves, often gathering with friends in the evening—much like Brazil's Kaiapo—to share stories, sorrows, or song. Without rapid transportation (although Henry Ford's assembly line began in 1908, cars became commonplace only after World War II), many people thought of their own town as their entire world.

Inevitable tensions and conflicts—often based on race, ethnicity, and religion—characterized past communities. According to Toennies, however, the traditional ties of *Gemeinschaft* bound the people of a community together, "essentially united in spite of all separating factors" (1963:65).

Modern societies are closer to Toennies's concept of *Gesellschaft*, in which people are "essentially separated in spite of uniting factors" (1963:65). In large cities, for example, most people live among strangers and ignore people they pass on the street; many do not even expect others to treat them fairly. No wonder, as one recent news report indicated, 15 million Americans attend weekly support groups—also made up of strangers—in which they establish temporary emotional ties and find someone who is willing simply to *listen* (Leerhsen, 1990).

A major contributor to American society's rootlessness is geographic mobility. Table 15–1 shows that almost 20 percent of Americans change their residence each year because of a new job, divorce, or simply in search of something better.

Modern life is not completely devoid of *Gemeinschaft*. Even in a world of strangers, people form friendships where they live or where they work that are sometimes lasting and powerful. Traditions are especially strong in many ethnic neighborhoods where residents maintain strong local community. But in cosmopolitan districts of large cities, indifference to those outside of an immediate circle—the attitude that disturbed Toennies in the 1880s—continues to pose an ethical dilemma today, as the box explains.

Critical evaluation. Toennies's theory of *Gemeinschaft* and *Gesellschaft* is the most widely cited model for describing the rise of modern societies. The theory's strength lies in its synthesis of various dimensions of change—growing population, the rise of cities, greater impersonality. However, Toennies's approach falls short by failing to specify which factors are cause and which are effect. Critics also assert that Toennies favored—even romanticized—traditional societies.

Émile Durkheim: The Division of Labor

The French sociologist Émile Durkheim shared Toennies's interest in the profound social changes wrought by the Industrial Revolution. For Durkheim, the rise of modernity is marked by the increasing *division of labor*, or specialized economic activity (1964b; orig. 1893). Whereas traditional societies involve everyone in similar daily activities, modern societies function by having people perform countless, highly distinctive roles.

Durkheim claimed that members of preindustrial societies are held together by *mechanical solidarity*, social bonds resulting from shared moral sentiments and a sense that everyone is basically alike and belongs together. Mechanical solidarity depends on a minimal division of labor, so that every person's life is essentially the same. Durkheim's mechanical solidarity mirrors Toennies's *Gemeinschaft*.

As the division of labor becomes more pronounced, a society develops *organic solidarity*, bonds of mutual dependency based on specialization. In simple terms, modern societies are held together not by likeness but by difference. Since specialization characterizes such societies, individuals engage in only a single activity and are dependent on others to meet their various needs. Organic solidarity corresponds to Toennies's concept of *Gesellschaft*.

Despite obvious similarities, Durkheim and Toennies interpreted modernity somewhat differently. To Toennies, modern *Gesellschaft* lacks social solidarity, as "natural" and "organic" traditions of the rural past are eroded by the "artificial" and "mechanical" life of contemporary cities. Durkheim disagreed, maintaining that the city is no less natural than the village. He made this point by reversing Toennies's language: He labeled modern social life as "organic" and traditional societies as "mechanical" because they were so regimented. Thus Durkheim viewed modernization not so much as a loss of community as a *change* in the basis of community—from bonds of likeness (kinship and neighborhood) to

Table 15–1   MOVING ON IN MODERN AMERICA

	Residence in 1987				
Region	Same House as 1986	Different House than in 1986	Different House Same County	Different County Same State	Different State
Northeast	87.6%	11.9%	7.6%	2.7%	1.6%
Midwest	83.0	16.7	10.7	3.6	2.4
South	79.4	20.3	12.9	4.0	3.4
West	76.6	22.4	14.5	4.5	3.4
Total U.S.	81.4	18.1	11.6	3.7	2.8

SOURCE: U.S. Census Bureau, *Geographical Mobility: March 1986 to March 1987* (Washington, D.C.: Government Printing Office, 1989), pp. 16–17.

Modern Society: What Do We Owe One Another?

In today's society, how much should we bother with the lives of others? Few people would welcome a return to the "tyranny of the tribe" by which members of traditional societies suspiciously monitor one another's every activity. But does the modern notion of "individual freedom" mean that we should be indifferent to everyone around us, including those in need?

Modern society poses a dilemma that might be described as the principle of privacy versus the principle of human community. We don't expect others to interfere in our lives, yet we do expect others to display basic human concern for us. Striking the right balance between these two conflicting principles is no easy task.

Consider the 1964 murder of Kitty Genovese in New York City. On one level, the crime was all too common. Returning from work late at night, Genovese was stabbed to death in the parking lot near her apartment building. But investigators made a stunning discovery: The brutal attack had lasted more than thirty minutes and was observed by at least thirty-eight of her neighbors, not one of whom came to her assistance or even called the police. For months after the crime, Americans debated the issue of just what people in a modern, industrial society owe one another.

For some, the murder of Kitty Genovese brings to mind the New Testament book of Luke (10:30–47), in which Jesus is asked "Who is my neighbor?" He responds with the tale of the Good Samaritan. A man on the road to Jericho was robbed and left for dead; several travelers passed by without offering any help. Then a Samaritan stopped, attended to the man's wounds, took him to an inn, and even left money to pay for further care. The Samaritan made no effort to establish a personal relationship with the victim; he did not even try to learn his name. The victim, it seems, was just another stranger. But while the Samaritan behaved impersonally, he acted compassionately, doing what was necessary for a fellow human being in need.

This ancient biblical parable offers an important lesson for today's world. Perhaps it is possible for members of modern societies to express their common humanity simply and compassionately, but without unduly surrendering their privacy.

---

economic interdependence (the division of labor). Durkheim's view of modernity is both more complex and more positive than that of Toennies.

Critical evaluation. Durkheim's work stands alongside that of Toennies, which it closely resembles, as a highly influential analysis of modernity. Of the two, Durkheim is clearly the more optimistic; still, he feared that modern societies would become so internally diverse that they would collapse into **anomie**, *a condition in which society provides little moral guidance to individuals.* Modern people thus tend toward egocentrism, placing their own needs above those of others.

Evidence supports Durkheim's contention that anomie plagues modern societies. Suicide rates, which Durkheim considered a prime index of anomie, have risen during this century. But despite any rise of egocentrism, shared norms and values are still strong enough to give our lives meaning. Additionally, whatever the hazards of social atomization, most people seem to value the privacy and personal autonomy it affords.

One indication of modernization is that all people no longer engage in traditional activities such as farming. Instead, individuals assume increasingly specialized roles. Hoping to secure a day's work in Mexico City, these men offer their services as electricians, contractors, painters, and plumbers.

Max Weber: Rationalization

Max Weber argued that modernity involves replacing a traditional world view with a rational way of thinking. In preindustrial societies, tradition acts as a constant brake to change. To traditional people, "truth" is roughly synonymous with what has always been (1978:36; orig. 1921). In modern societies, however, people see truth as the product of deliberate calculation. Because efficiency is valued more than reverence of the past, individuals embrace whatever new social patterns allow them to readily achieve their goals. A rational view of the world, then, leads people to seek out and assess various options according to their specific consequences rather than according to any absolute standard of rightness. For Weber, this is the essential distinction between traditional families and modern bureaucracies.

Echoing the claim by Toennies and Durkheim that industrialization weakens tradition, Weber declared that modern society had become "disenchanted." What were once unquestioned truths have become subject to matter-of-fact evaluation. Embracing rational, scientific thought in a secular framework, modern society turns away from the gods, Weber noted. Weber's works explore various modern "types"—the capitalist, the scientist, and the bureaucrat—all of whom share the detached world view he believed was coming to dominate human interaction.

Critical evaluation. Compared with Toennies and, especially, Durkheim, Weber was a profound critic of modern society. He recognized that science could produce technological and organizational wonders, yet he worried that it was unable to answer the most basic questions about the meaning and purpose of human existence. Weber feared that rationalization, especially in bureaucracies, would erode the human spirit with endless rules and regulations. Some critics of Weber believe that the alienation he attributed to bureaucracy actually stemmed from economic and social inequality. This leads us to the work of Karl Marx.

Karl Marx: Capitalism

While other analysts of modernity examined shifting patterns of social order, Marx focused on social conflict. For Marx, modernity was synonymous with capitalism; he saw the Industrial Revolution primarily as a *capitalist revolution*. Marx asserted that the bourgeoisie emerged in medieval Europe as a social class intent on wresting

control of society from the feudal nobility. The bourgeoisie finally succeeded when the Industrial Revolution placed a powerful new productive system under their control.

Marx agreed that modernity weakened small-scale communities (as described by Toennies), increased the division of labor (as noted by Durkheim), and fostered a rational world view (as asserted by Weber). But he saw these factors simply as conditions necessary for capitalism to flourish: Capitalism draws people from farms and small towns into an ever-growing market system centered in the cities; specialization underlies efficient factories; and rationality is exemplified in the capitalists' relentless quest for profits.

Earlier chapters showed Marx to have been a spirited critic of capitalist society, but his vision of modernity also contains an element of optimism. Unlike Weber, who viewed modern society as an "iron cage" of bureaucracy, Marx believed that social conflict fueled by capitalism would produce revolutionary social change leading to an egalitarian socialism. Such a society, he claimed, would allow the wonders of industrial technology to enrich the lives of the many rather than the few—and thereby rid the world of social conflict and dehumanization. While Marx's evaluation of modern capitalist society was highly negative, he anticipated a future with greater human freedom and a renewed sense of human community.

Critical evaluation. To its credit, Marx's analysis links various dimensions of social change to the rise of capitalism. However, Marx underestimated the significance of bureaucracy in shaping modern societies. The stifling effects of bureaucracy on humanity may well be worse in the socialist societies he envisioned, with their expanded government apparatus. The recent political unrest in Eastern Europe and the Soviet Union reveals the depth of popular opposition to entrenched bureaucracies.

UNDERSTANDING MODERNITY: THE THEORY OF MASS SOCIETY

The rise of modernity is a complex process involving many dimensions of change, described in previous chapters and summarized in Table 15–2. One broad approach integrates various forms of change by equating modernity with *mass societies* (Dahrendorf, 1959; Kornhauser, 1959;

Table 15–2 TRADITIONAL AND MODERN SOCIETIES: DIMENSIONS OF DIFFERENCE

	Characteristics of Traditional Societies	Characteristics of Modern Societies
	Scale of Life	
	Small scale; population typically small and widely dispersed in rural villages and small towns	Large scale; population typically large and concentrated in cities
	Social Structure	
Status and role	Few statuses, most ascribed; few specialized roles	Many statuses, some ascribed and some achieved; many specialized roles
Relationships	Typically primary; little anonymity and privacy	Typically secondary; considerable anonymity and privacy
Communication	Face-to-face	Face-to-face communication supplemented by extensive mass media
Social control	Informal gossip	Formal police and legal system
Social stratification	Rigid patterns of social inequality; little mobility	Fluid patterns of social inequality; considerable social mobility
Gender patterns	Pronounced patriarchy; few women in the paid labor force	Declining patriarchy; increasing number of women in the paid labor force
Family	Extended family as the primary means of socialization and economic production	Nuclear family retains some socialization function but is a unit of consumption rather than production
Religion	Religion guides world view; little religious pluralism	Religion weakens with the rise of science; extensive religious pluralism
Education	Formal schooling limited to elites	Basic schooling becomes universal, with growing proportion receiving advanced education
State	Small-scale government; little state intervention into society	Large-scale government; considerable state intervention into society
Economy	Based on agriculture; some manufacturing within the home; little white-collar work	Based on industrial mass production; factories become centers of production; increasing white-collar work
Health	High birth and death rates; brief life expectancy because of low standard of living and simple medical technology	Low birth and death rates; longer life expectancy because of higher standard of living and complex medical technology
	Cultural Patterns	
Values	Homogeneous; sacred character; few subcultures and countercultures	Heterogeneous; secular character; many subcultures and countercultures
Norms	High moral significance; little tolerance of diversity	Variable moral significance; high tolerance of diversity
Orientation	Present linked to past	Present linked to future
Technology	Preindustrial; human and animal energy	Industrial; advanced energy sources
	Social Change	
	Slow; change evident over many generations	Rapid; change evident within a single generation

Nisbet, 1966, 1969; Baltzell, 1968; Stein, 1972; Berger, Berger, & Kellner, 1974).

A **mass society** is *a society in which industrialization and expanding bureaucracy have weakened traditional social bonds.* A mass society emerges with the erosion of traditional kinship and neighborhood so that people become socially isolated or atomized. Feelings of moral uncertainty and personal powerlessness are widespread. Mass-society theory draws on many ideas derived from Ferdinand Toennies, Emile Durkheim, and Max Weber.

Expanding scale of life. Mass-society theory argues, first, that the scale of modern life has expanded significantly. Before the Industrial Revolution, Europe and North America formed an intricate mosaic of countless rural villages and small towns. In these small communities, which inspired Toennies's concept of *Gemeinschaft*, people lived together their entire lives, bound by kinship and a shared heritage. Gossip was an informal, yet highly effective, means of maintaining rigid conformity to community standards. Limited population, social isolation, and a strong, traditional religion combined to generate cultural homogeneity—the mechanical solidarity described by Durkheim. For example, in England before 1690, law and local custom demanded that everyone regularly partake in the Christian ritual of Holy Communion (Laslett, 1984). Similarly, New England's colonies offered little support for religious dissent. Because social differences were repressed, subcultures and countercultures rarely flourished and the pace of social change was slow. Also characterized by rigid social stratification based on birth, these societies offered little social mobility.

A surge in population, the growth of cities, and the specialization of economic activity during the Industrial Revolution gradually changed all this. People came to be known by their function (for example, as the "doctor" or the "bank clerk") rather than by their kinship group or hometown. The majority of people were simply a mass of strangers to one another. The face-to-face communication of the village was eventually replaced by the mass media—newspapers, radio, and television— that furthered the process of social atomization. Large organizations steadily assumed more and more responsibility for daily needs that had once been fulfilled by family, friends, and neighbors; universal public education enlarged the scope of learning; police, lawyers, and formal courts supervised a criminal justice system. Even charity became the work of impersonal bureaucracies, such as the Red Cross and public welfare agencies, rather than extended families.

Geographical mobility, mass communications, and exposure to diverse ways of life eroded traditional values. Less certain about what was worth believing, people became more tolerant of social diversity and placed increasing value on individual rights and freedom of choice. Subcultures and countercultures multiplied. Making categorical distinctions among people fell out of favor; to treat someone according to race, sex, or religion has come to be defined as backwards and unjust. In the process, traditionally marginal minorities have gained broader participation in society. Yet, mass-society theorists fear, transforming people of various backgrounds into a generic mass may end up dehumanizing everyone.

The rise of the state. In the small-scale, preindustrial societies of Europe, government exerted only limited control over the population. A royal family formally reigned but, without efficient transportation and communication, the power of even absolute monarchs fell far short of that wielded by today's political leaders.

Technological innovation allowed government to expand, and the centralized state grew in size and importance. At the time of American independence, the federal government was a tiny organization whose function was little more than national defense. Since then, government has entered more and more areas of social life: regulating wages and working conditions, establishing standards for products of all kinds, educating the population, and providing financial assistance to the ill and the unemployed. Taxes have correspondingly increased, so that today's average American works four months a year to pay for various government services.

In a mass society, power resides in large bureaucracies, leaving people in local communities with limited control over their lives. For example, state officials require a local school to have a standardized educational program, just as local products must carry government-mandated labels, and every citizen must maintain extensive records for purposes of taxation. While such regulations may protect people and enhance uniformity of treatment, they depersonalize human decision making and limit the autonomy of neighborhoods, families, and individuals.

Critical evaluation. The theory of mass society acknowledges that the transformation of small-scale societies has positive aspects, but tends to see historical change as the loss of an irreplaceable heritage. Modern societies increase individual rights, magnify tolerance of social differences, and raise standards of living. But they seem prone to what Max Weber feared most—excessive bureaucracy—and to Emile Durkheim's anomie. Their size, complexity, and tolerance of diversity all but doom traditional values and family patterns, leaving individuals isolated, powerless, and prone to materialism. As we noted in Chapter 11 ("Economics and Politics"), only about half of Americans eligible to vote do so. But should we be surprised that people in vast, impersonal societies often conclude that no one person can make a difference?

One criticism of mass-society theory is that it tends to romanticize the past. Presumably, many people in the small towns of America's past were actually quite eager to set out for a better life in the cities. And who would actually wish to give up the improved standard of living that industrial technology has made possible? In addition, this approach offers little praise for deliberate efforts to lessen social inequality. Mass-society analysis, critics claim, attracts social and economic conservatives who defend conventional morality and often seem indifferent to the historical plight of women and other minorities.

UNDERSTANDING MODERNITY: THE THEORY OF CLASS SOCIETY

A second interpretation of modernity derives largely from the ideas of Karl Marx. From this point of view, modernity takes the form of a **class society**, *a capitalist society with pronounced social stratification*. Class-society theorists hold that social inequality, with the majority suffering feelings of powerlessness, stands at the core of modernity. Modern technology has failed to fulfill its promise of a good life for everyone since poverty still assails millions. The culprit, according to this theory, is the capitalist system itself, which continues to produce and distribute goods and services according to the logic of private property and profit; thus, a further social revolution, following the Industrial Revolution, is needed (Miliband, 1969; Habermas, 1970; Polenberg, 1980; Blumberg, 1981; Harrington, 1984).

Capitalism. Class-society theory holds that the increasing scale of social life stems from the insatiable appetite of capitalism. Because a capitalist economy pursues ever-increasing profits, both production and consumption expand. Marx considered the Industrial Revolution as a significant stage in the enlarging capitalist economic system.

According to Marx, capitalism emphasizes "naked self-interest" and individual greed (1972:337; orig. 1848).

In the process, it undermines the social ties that once cemented small-scale communities. Capitalism favors impersonality and anonymity by transforming people into commodities—laborers in factories and buyers for material goods produced by capitalist enterprises. The net result: Capitalism reduces human beings to cogs in the machinery of material production.

Science, the key to greater productivity, constitutes a modern ideology that justifies capitalism, in Marx's view. In preindustrial Europe, the nobility defended their rule with traditional notions of moral obligation and responsibility. In modern societies, science legitimates the capitalist status quo by encouraging people to view social well-being as a technical puzzle to be solved by engineers and other experts rather than a matter of social justice (Habermas, 1970). Poor health, for example, is attacked with scientific medicine rather than by eliminating the poverty that undermines health in the first place.

Businesses also employ scientific logic, claiming that efficiency demands continual growth. As Chapter 11 ("Economics and Politics") explained, capitalist corporations have reached enormous size and control almost unimaginable wealth. Nevertheless, to increase profits even more, they have transformed themselves into multinationals operating throughout the world. From the class-society point of view, then, the expanding scale of modern life is the inevitable and destructive consequence of capitalism.

Persistent inequality. Modernity has gradually eroded rigid categorical distinctions that divided preindustrial societies. Class-society theory maintains, however, that elites persist in the form of capitalist millionaires rather than family-based nobility. In the United States, the richest 5 percent control more than half of all property. As Paul Blumberg (1981) notes, despite a rising standard of living in America during this century, a small minority still enjoys unimaginable wealth while many continue to live in poverty.

What of the state, which mass-society theory suggests has an expanding role in combating social problems? The capitalist state, Marx argued, does little to encourage meaningful change; for the most part, government defends the wealth and privileges of capitalists. Working Americans and minorities do enjoy greater political rights and economic benefits today, but these are more the fruits of political struggle than expressions of government benevolence. And despite pretensions of democracy, power still rests primarily in the hands of those with the money. Throughout the 1980s, conservative political leaders, in the name of economic growth and free-market efficiency, attempted to curtail government funding for programs that benefited less-privileged Americans (Harrington, 1984; Jacob, 1986).

Critical evaluation. Key differences in the interpretations of modernity offered by class-society theory and mass-society theory are shown in Table 15–3. In place of mass-society theory's focus on the increasing scale of social life and the rise of large formal organizations, class-society theory stresses the expansion of capitalism and persistent inequality. Class-society theory also dismisses Durkheim's argument that people in modern societies suffer from moral collapse and anomie. Instead, the malaise of modern life comes from alienation and powerlessness. Not surprisingly, then, the class-society interpretation of modernity enjoys widespread support among social and economic liberals who favor greater equality and seek extensive regulation of the capitalist marketplace.

Critics of this theory argue, however, that it ignores the many ways in which modern societies have grown more egalitarian. After all, categorical distinctions of race, ethnicity, religion, and sex are still made, but they are now widely defined as social problems. As Chapter 7 ("Social Stratification") explained, considerable social inequality remains in the United States, but our society has become more equal since the early Industrial Revolution. In addition, critics blast the implication, inherent in this approach, that a centralized economy would cure the ills of modernity. Socialism, they contend, has not shown itself capable of generating a high standard of living. Furthermore, many social problems found in the United States—including unemployment, homelessness, industrial pollution, and unresponsive government—have also plagued the socialist nations of Eastern Europe and the Soviet Union.

Table 15–3 TWO INTERPRETATIONS OF MODERNITY: A SUMMARY

	Key Process of Modernization	Key Effects of Modernization
Mass-society theory	Industrialization; growth of bureaucracy	Increasing scale of life; rise of the state and other formal organizations
Class-society theory	Rise of capitalism	Expansion of capitalist economy; persistence of social inequality

MODERNITY AND THE INDIVIDUAL

Both mass- and class-society theories focus on broad patterns of change since the Industrial Revolution. Each "macro-level" approach also offers "micro-level" insights into how modernity shapes individual lives.

Mass society: Problems of identity. Modernity liberated individuals from small, tightly knit communities of the past. Modern Americans possess unprecedented privacy and freedom to express their individuality. Mass-society theory suggests, however, that extensive social diversity, atomization, and rapid social change make it difficult for many people to establish any identity at all (Wheelis, 1958; Reisman, 1970; Berger, Berger, & Kellner, 1974).

Chapter 3 ("Socialization: From Infancy to Aging") explained that people forge distinctive personalities based on their social experience. The small, homogeneous, and slowly changing societies of the past provided a firm foundation for building a meaningful personal identity. For example, the Amish communities that still flourish in the United States and Canada provide their members with strong historical and cultural roots. Young Amish men and women know the meaning of being Amish— that is, how they should think and behave—and they learn to view this type of life as "natural" and right. Not everyone born into an Amish community can tolerate these demands for conformity, but most members establish a coherent and satisfying personal identity (Hostetler, 1980).

Mass societies, with their characteristic diversity and rapid change, provide only shifting sands on which to build a personal identity. Left to make their own life decisions, people confront a bewildering range of options. Autonomy has little value without standards for making choices; in a tolerant mass society, one path may seem no more compelling than the next. Not surprisingly, many people shuttle from one identity to another, changing their lifestyle in search of an elusive "true self." They may join one or another social movement in search of purpose and belonging, and even experiment with various religions hoping to find a system of beliefs that "fits" them. The problem is not psychological, although it is often treated as an individual problem. More accurately, such people are suffering from the widespread "relativism" of modern societies; they have lost the security and certainty once provided by tradition.

Affluent Americans confront such a wide range of choices about how to live that they often speak of their "lifestyles" as something they shape for themselves. For most of humanity, however, tradition and lack of opportunity generate a more fixed existence and a more well-defined personal identity.

David Riesman (1970; orig. 1950) has analyzed modernization in terms of changing **social character,** *personality patterns common to members of a society.* Preindustrial societies promote a type of social character Riesman calls **tradition-directedness,** *rigid personalities based on conformity to time-honored ways of living.* Members of such societies model their lives on what has gone before so that what is "good" translates into "what has always been." Tradition-directedness is the individual correlate of Toennies's *Gemeinschaft* and Durkheim's mechanical solidarity. Tradition-directed people are culturally conservative and therefore think and act alike. Unlike their modern counterparts, this conformity is not an effort to mimic one another. Instead, their resemblance derives from everyone drawing on the same cultural foundation, which is held to be the one proper way to live. Amish women and men, for example, are tradition-directed, conforming to what they see as God's will (Hostetler, 1980).

Obviously, tradition-directed behavior is likely to be defined as deviant in a culturally diverse and rapidly changing society. Modern, industrial societies prize personal flexibility, the capacity to adapt, and sensitivity to others. Riesman calls this type of social character **other-directedness,** *variable personality patterns among people open to change and likely to imitate the behavior of others.* Because their socialization occurs in societies that are continuously in flux, other-directed people develop identities characterized by superficiality, inconsistency, and change. They try on different roles and identities, almost like so many pieces of new clothing, and engage in various "performances" as they move from setting to setting (Goffman, 1959). In a traditional society, such "shiftiness" would mark a person as untrustworthy, but in a modern society, the ability to fit in virtually anywhere can be a valuable asset (Wheelis, 1958). Put a different way, if conformity among tradition-directed people reflects unchanging morality, what passes for morality among other-directed people generally amounts to little more than conforming to changing public opinion.

In societies that value the up-to-date rather than the traditional, people look to members of their own generation as significant role models rather than looking up to their elders. Following the same reasoning, "peer pressure" may seem irresistible to people with no enduring standards to guide them. Our society urges individuals to be true to themselves. But when social surroundings change so rapidly, how can people determine to which self they should be true? This problem lies at the root of the identity crisis so widespread among Americans today. The question "Who am I?" plagues many people throughout their lives. In sociological terms, this personal problem reflects the inherent instability of modern mass society.

Class society: Problems of powerlessness.   Class-society theory paints a different picture of modernity's effects on individuals. This approach maintains that persistent inequality undermines modern society's promise of individual freedom. For some, modernity has brought great privilege; but, for the majority, life involves coping daily with powerlessness. For minorities, the problems of modern life are even greater. Nonwhites contend with various forms of prejudice and discrimination that raise poverty rates. Women enjoy increasing participation in modern societies, but continue to run up against traditional barriers of sexism. Similarly, elderly people face the impediment of ageism. In short, this approach rejects mass-society theory's claim that people suffer from too much

Mass-society theory explains weak social ties as a result of rapid social change and the erosion of tradition. Class-society theory, in contrast, suggests that social inequality diminishes the likelihood of meaningful human community.

freedom. Instead, class-society theory holds that a majority of people in American society are still denied full participation in social life.

The struggle to empower individuals therefore goes on. For example, employees seek greater power in the workplace, consumers press for more control over the marketplace, and citizens attempt to make government more responsive to their needs (Toffler, 1981).

On a global scale, as Chapter 8 ("Global Inequality") explained, the expanding scope of world capitalism has placed more of the earth's population under the influence of multinational corporations. As a result, about two-thirds of the world's income is concentrated in the richest societies, which encompass only about 15 percent of its people. Class-society theorists therefore ask: Is it any wonder that throughout the Third World people are also seeking greater power to shape their own lives?

Such problems led Herbert Marcuse (1964) to challenge Max Weber's contention that modern society has a rational foundation. Marcuse labels modern society as irrational because it fails to meet the basic needs of so many people. While modern capitalist societies produce unparalleled wealth, poverty remains the daily plight of millions and, in global terms, billions of people. Moreover, Marcuse argues, technological advances do not empower people, but often further reduce their control over their own lives. High technology generally means that specialists—not the majority of people themselves—set the agenda for a variety of public issues, from energy production for communities to health care for individuals. Defined as ill-equipped for decision making, most people are urged to defer to elites of one kind or another. And elites often have little concern for the common interest. Despite the popular view that technology *solves* the world's problems, Marcuse concludes, the truth may be that technology helps *cause* them. In sum, class-society theory asserts that people suffer because modern societies have concentrated both wealth and power in the hands of a privileged few.

SOCIAL CHANGE AND PROGRESS

In modern societies we expect social change and, generally, applaud it. People link modernity to the idea of *progress* (from Latin, meaning "a moving forward"), a

What's Happened to Honor?

Honor occupies about the same place in contemporary usage as chastity. An individual asserting it hardly invites admiration, and one who claims to have lost it is an object of amusement rather than sympathy. (Berger, Berger, & Kellner, 1974:83)

Honor is a human virtue that seems distinctly out of place in modern society. Honor means acting according to traditional cultural norms. Since traditional norms vary for different categories of people, honor also implies behaving in a way that reflects the kind of person you are: A man could never honorably behave in a feminine way, for example. Honor, then, cannot be separated from strong morality and rigid social distinctions—between males and females, nobles and serfs, one's own family and outsiders. During the Middle Ages, European nobles claimed honor when they performed their feudal obligations toward their social inferiors and displayed proper respect for their peers. Similarly, commoners acted honorably to the extent that they fulfilled their duties to their superiors and everyone else.

Honor also lies at the heart of traditional relationships between men and women. To be honorable, men must deal with women as females rather than as people; according to medieval cultural norms, men were required to take a fatherly, protective attitude toward women and under no circumstances to "take advantage" of them. For their part, women behave honorably by observing proper morals and manners in their affairs with men. Honor thus underlies a powerful system of social control; to suffer dishonor is to be stigmatized and excluded from further social contact.

With modernization, cultural norms have weakened and become more variable, while categorical distinctions among people have been challenged by drives for equality. The modern ideal holds that all people are socially alike. Therefore, though the concept of honor survives among some ethnic minorities and traditional occupations, such as the military, it has less appeal to most members of modern societies.

Modernization enhances concern for people as *individuals*, which is expressed in the concept of *dignity*. Whereas various categories of people have distinctive codes of honor, dignity is a universal human trait, origi-nating in the inherent value of everyone. We recognize the dignity of others when we acknowledge our common humanity despite any social differences.

In the spirit of modern dignity, women may object to men treating them as women rather than as individuals. The male practices of holding open a door for a woman and paying for a shared meal may be honorable by traditional standards, but are more likely to be viewed as an affront to the dignity of women by underscoring social differences based on sex.

As a result, the significance of honor is fading in modern societies. The cultural diversity and rapid social change sweeping modern societies make traditional scripts for living suspect, at best. In contrast to codes of honor that guided human interaction in the past, human beings now value individual self-worth and aspirations to self-determination. This forms the essence of dignity.

SOURCE: Based on Peter Berger, Brigitte Berger, and Hansfried Kellner, *The Homeless Mind: Modernization and Consciousness* (New York: Vintage Books, 1974), pp. 83–96.

---

state of continual improvement. By contrast, we look on stability as stagnation.

This chapter began by describing the Kaiapo of Brazil, for whom affluence has broadened opportunities but weakened traditional heritage. In examining the Kaiapo, we note that social change is too complex to be simply equated with progress. More precisely, whether or not we see a given change as progress depends on our underlying values. A rising standard of living among the Kaiapo—or, historically, among Americans—has helped make lives longer and more comfortable. But affluence has also fueled materialism at the expense of spiritual life, setting up an ambivalence towards change in the minds of many people.

Many Americans celebrate modern society's recognition of basic human rights. The concept that people have rights simply by virtue of their humanity is a distinctly modern idea reflected in the American Declaration of Independence and the United Nations' Declaration of Human Rights (Berger, Berger, & Kellner, 1974).

But at the same time, the notion of personal honor seems to have little importance in modern society. The box on page 391 explains why.

In principle, Americans support the idea that individuals should have considerable autonomy in shaping their own lives. Thus the demise of traditional conceptions of honor is widely seen as progress. Yet, as people exercise their freedom of choice, they inevitably challenge cherished social patterns. For example, people may choose not to marry, remaining single, living with someone without marrying, having children outside of marriage, or forming a partnership with a member of their own sex. To those who support individual choice, such changes symbolize progress; to those who value traditional family patterns, however, these developments are cause for despair (Wallis, 1985).

Even technological advancement generates controversy. Rapid transportation and efficient communication have improved the lives of Americans in some respects. At the same time, however, complex technology has weakened traditional attachments to hometowns and maybe even to family. Industrial technology has also unleashed an unprecedented threat to the natural environment and, in the form of nuclear weapons, imperiled the future of humanity. In short, then, because social change is uncertain, complex, and controversial, we should never assume the modern world is simply becoming better or worse.

MODERNIZATION IN GLOBAL PERSPECTIVE

Sometimes social change proceeds haphazardly, sometimes deliberately. Some change that is desperately

To some analysts, modernization is within the reach of all of the world's people; to others, the current global economy makes such improvement unlikely. Whether the majority of humanity living in the Third World is confronting a dawn of development or a dusk of dependency is a vital question likely to affect the lives of Americans as well.

needed has not occurred at all, as in much of the Third World, where almost 1 billion people struggle daily against life-threatening poverty.

Two competing views of the causes of global poverty were presented in Chapter 8 ("Global Inequality"). *Modernization theory* claims that in the past the entire world was poor and that technological change, especially the Industrial Revolution, has enhanced human productivity and raised living standards. From this point of view, the solution to global poverty is to encourage technological development elsewhere.

For reasons suggested earlier, however, global modernization may be difficult. Recall that David Riesman portrayed preindustrial people as *tradition-directed*; by embracing a way of life rooted in the past, they may resist change. According to modernization theory, the world's rich societies should deliberately intervene in poor societies to encourage productive innovation. First-World nations should export technology to the Third World, welcome students from abroad to their colleges and universities, and provide foreign aid to stimulate economic development.

The review of modernization theory in Chapter 8 suggested that the success of these policies has been limited. Even where dramatic change has occurred, resistance has complicated the process of social change. Traditional people such as Brazil's Kaiapo have gained wealth by selling their resources on world markets, but only at the cost of being drawn into the "global village" where concern for monetary gain replaces traditional values. In some societies, including Iran and Ethiopia, rapid modernization has sparked a strong backlash from powerful segments of the population who want to restore traditional culture.

A daunting problem facing advocates of modernization theory, then, is that modernity may bring higher living standards but, in the process, sweep a traditional society into the global mass culture of Western pop music, trendy clothes, and fast food. One Brazilian anthropologist expressed uncertainty about the future of the Kaiapo: "At least they quickly understood the consequences of watching television. . . . Now [they] can make a choice" (Simons, 1989:37).

But is modernization really an option? According to a second approach to global inequality, *dependency theory*, poor societies have little ability to improve, whatever their desires. From this point of view, the major barrier to economic development is not traditionalism but rather world capitalism. Initially, as Chapter 8 ex-

plained, this system took the form of colonialism whereby European societies seized much of Latin America, Africa, and Asia. Trading relationships soon enriched England, Spain, and other colonial powers, while impoverishing their colonies. Almost all societies subjected to this form of domination are now politically independent, but colonial-like ties continue in the form of multinational corporations operating throughout the world.

In effect, dependency theory asserts, rich countries achieved modernization at least partly at the expense of poor nations, which provided valuable resources and inexpensive human labor. Even today, the Third World remains locked in a one-sided economic relationship with the First World, dependent on rich societies to buy their cheap raw materials and in return provide them with whatever expensive manufactured products they can afford. Continuing ties with rich societies appears likely to perpetuate current patterns of global inequality.

Dependency theory implies that social change is not under the control of individual societies. On the contrary, the fate and fortune of individual nations worldwide is tied to their position in the global economy. Thus, change to improve the plight of people in the Third World will involve corresponding changes in First-World societies.

Whichever approach individuals find more convincing, we can no longer isolate the study of American society from the rest of the world. At the beginning of the twentieth century, a majority of people in even the richest societies lived in relatively small settlements with limited awareness of others. Now, at the threshold of the twenty-first century, people everywhere participate in a far larger human drama. The world is smaller and the lives of all its people are increasingly linked. We now discuss the relationships among nations in the same way that people a century ago talked about the expanding ties among towns and cities.

The twentieth century has witnessed unparalleled human achievement. Yet solutions to many of the timeless problems of human existence—finding meaning in life, eradicating poverty, resolving internal conflicts—remain elusive. To this list of pressing matters, new concerns have been added, such as managing the global environment and maintaining world peace. One source of optimism as we approach the twenty-first century is that we look ahead with an unprecedented understanding of human society.

SUMMARY

1. Every society changes continuously, although with varying speed and consequences. Whether social change is intentional or unplanned, it is usually controversial.

2. One cause of social change is cultural processes, including invention, discovery, and cultural diffusion from one society to another. Another cause of change is conflict within society itself. The physical environment and population dynamics are also closely linked to social change.

3. Social movements represent deliberate efforts to promote or resist change. Social movements have been explained in terms of perceived deprivation, the rootlessness of mass society, and the availability of resources. In recent decades, many social movements have become national and international in scope.

4. Modernity refers to the social consequences of industrialization. According to Peter Berger, general characteristics of modernity include the weakening of traditional communities, expanding personal choice, tolerance of more diverse beliefs, and a keener awareness of time, especially the future.

5. Ferdinand Toennies described modernization as the transition from *Gemeinschaft* to *Gesellschaft*. This process signifies the progressive loss of community amid growing individualism.

6. Émile Durkheim linked modernization to an expanding division of labor. Mechanical solidarity, based on shared activities and beliefs, gradually gives way to organic solidarity, in which specialization makes people interdependent.

7. Max Weber described the rise of modernity as the replacement of traditional thought by rationality. He feared that rational organization would dehumanize modern society.

8. According to Karl Marx, modernity amounts to the triumph of capitalism over feudalism. Viewing capitalist societies as fraught with social conflict, he sought revolutionary change to achieve a more egalitarian socialist society.

9. In the view of mass-society theorists, modernity increases the scale of life and transfers to government and other formal organizations responsibility for tasks previously performed informally by family members and neighbors. Mass-society theory explains that cultural diversity and rapid social change prevent individuals in modern societies from developing a stable identity and finding certainty and significance in their lives.

10. Class-society theory holds that capitalism underlies Western modernization. According to this approach, widespread powerlessness in modern societies stems from capitalism's propensity to concentrate wealth and power.

11. Americans commonly equate modernity with social progress. This simplistic view overlooks the fact that social change is rarely entirely good. Social change is an exceedingly complex process; from any point of view the consequences of modernization can be perceived as good and bad.

12. In a global context, modernization theory advances intentional intervention to stimulate the development of poor societies. Advocates of this view hold that global poverty primarily stems from traditionalism. Dependency theory argues that a society's potential for development depends on that society's position in the world economic system. Poor, Third-World societies are unlikely to duplicate the modernization of rich, First-World societies because they have become economically dependent on these rich societies.

KEY CONCEPTS

anomie a condition in which society provides little moral guidance to individuals

class society a capitalist society with pronounced social stratification

collective behavior relatively spontaneous activity, involving large numbers of people, that does not conform to established norms

mass society a society in which industrialization and

expanding bureaucracy have weakened traditional social bonds

modernity patterns of social life linked to industrialization

modernization the process of social change initiated by industrialization

other-directedness variable personality patterns among people open to change and likely to imitate the behavior of others

relative deprivation a perceived disadvantage based on some standard of comparison

social change the transformation of culture and social institutions over time

social character personality patterns common to members of a society

social movement organized activity that encourages or opposes some dimension of change

tradition-directedness rigid personalities based on conformity to time-honored ways of living

Glossary

absolute poverty a deprivation of resources that is life-threatening

achieved status a social position that people assume voluntarily and that reflects a significant measure of personal ability and effort

age-sex pyramid a graphic representation of the age and sex of a population

ageism prejudice and discrimination against the elderly

agriculture a way of life based on large-scale cultivation using plows drawn by animals

alienation the experience of powerlessness in social life

animism the belief that natural objects are conscious forms of life that can affect humanity

anomie a condition in which society provides little moral guidance to individuals

anticipatory socialization the process of social learning directed toward gaining a desired position

arms race a mutually reinforcing escalation of military power

ascribed status a social position attached to a person at birth or one that is involuntarily assumed later in life

assimilation the process by which minorities gradually adopt patterns of the dominant culture

authoritarianism denying the majority participation in government

authority power that is widely perceived as legitimate rather than coercive

blue-collar occupations lower-prestige work that involves mostly manual labor

bureaucracy an organizational model rationally designed to perform complex tasks efficiently

bureaucratic inertia the tendency of bureaucratic organizations to persist over time

bureaucratic ritualism a preoccupation with organizational rules and regulations as ends in themselves rather than as the means to organizational goals

capitalism an economic system in which natural resources and the means of producing goods and services are privately owned

capitalists people who own factories and other productive enterprises

caste system social stratification based on ascription

cause and effect a relationship between two variables in which change in one (the independent variable) causes change in another (the dependent variable)

charisma extraordinary personal qualities that can turn an audience into followers

charismatic authority power legitimated through extraordinary personal abilities that inspire devotion and obedience

church a formal religious organization that is well integrated into the larger society

civil religion a quasi-religious loyalty binding individuals in a basically secular society

class society a capitalist society with pronounced social stratification

class system social stratification based on individual achievement

cohabitation the sharing of a household by an unmarried couple

collective behavior relatively spontaneous activity involving large numbers of people that does not conform to established norms

colonialism the process by which some nations enrich themselves through political and economic control of other nations

communism a hypothetical economic and political system in which all people have social equality

concept an abstract idea that represents some aspect of the world, inevitably in a somewhat ideal and simplified form

concrete operational stage Piaget's term for the level of human development characterized by the use of logic to link objects or events

control the ability to neutralize the effect of one variable so that the relationships among other variables can be more precisely determined

corporation an organization with a legal existence including rights and liabilities apart from those of its members

correlation a relationship between two (or more) variables

counterculture cultural patterns that are strongly at odds with the dominant culture

credentialism evaluating people for employment on the basis of educational degrees

crime the violation of norms formally enacted into criminal law

crimes against property (property crimes) crimes that involve theft of property belonging to others

crimes against the person (violent crimes) crimes against people that involve violence or the threat of violence

criminal justice system a multifaceted system of social control that responds to alleged violations of the law through the use of police, courts, and punishment

criminal recidivism subsequent offenses committed by people previously convicted of crimes

crude birth rate the number of live births in a given year for every thousand people in a population

crude death rate the number of deaths in a given year for every thousand people in a population

cult a religious movement that is highly unconventional in terms of the surrounding society

cultural ecology a theoretical paradigm that explores the relationship of human culture and the physical environment

cultural integration the close relationship among various parts of a cultural system

cultural lag inconsistencies within a cultural system resulting from the unequal rates at which different cultural elements change

cultural relativism the practice of judging any culture by its own standards

cultural transmission the process by which culture is passed from one generation to the next

cultural universals traits found in every culture

culture the beliefs, values, behavior, and material objects shared by a particular people

culture shock the personal disorientation that may accompany exposure to an unfamiliar way of life

democracy a type of political system in which power is exercised by the people as a whole

democratic socialism a political and economic system in which free elections coexist with a market system modified by government policies to minimize social inequality

demographic transition theory the thesis that population patterns are linked to a society's level of technological development

demography the study of human population

denomination a church that recognizes religious pluralism

dependency theory an approach maintaining that global inequality stems from the exploitation of poor societies by rich ones

dependent variable a variable that is changed by another (independent) variable

descent the system by which kinship is traced over generations

deterrence the attempt to discourage criminality through punishment

deviance the recognized violation of cultural norms

direct-fee system a medical-care system in which patients pay directly for the services of physicians and hospitals

discrimination treating various categories of people unequally

dramaturgical analysis the investigation of social interaction in terms of theatrical performance

dyad a social group with two members

ecclesia a church that is formally allied with the state

economy the institutionalized system for production, distribution, and consumption of goods and services

education the various ways in which knowledge—including facts, skills, and values—is transmitted to members of society

ego Freud's designation of the conscious attempt to balance the pleasure-seeking drives of the human organism and the demands of society

empirical evidence evidence we are able to verify with our senses

endogamy marriage between people within a social group or category

ethnicity a cultural heritage shared by a category of people

ethnocentrism the practice of judging another culture by the standards of our own culture

ethnomethodology the study of the everyday, common-sense understandings that people within a culture have of the world around them

euthanasia (mercy killing) assisting in the death of a person suffering from an incurable illness

exogamy marriage between people of different social groups or categories

experiment a research method that investigates cause-and-effect relationships under highly controlled conditions

expressive leadership group leadership that emphasizes collective well-being

extended family (consanguine family) a social unit including parents, children, and other kin

faith belief that is not based on scientific evidence

family a relatively permanent social group of two or more people, who are related by blood, marriage, or adoption and who usually live together

feminism the advocacy of social equality for the sexes, in opposition to patriarchy and sexism

feminization of poverty a trend by which females represent an increasing proportion of the poor

fertility the incidence of childbearing in a society's population

First World a category of industrial societies with predominantly capitalist economies

folkways norms that have little moral significance

formal operational stage Piaget's term for the level of human development characterized by highly abstract thought and the ability to imagine alternatives to reality

formal organization a large, secondary group that is organized to achieve its goals efficiently

functional illiteracy reading and writing skills inadequate for everyday needs

Gemeinschaft a type of social organization based on tradition and enduring, personal relationships

gender human traits that are linked by culture to each sex

gender roles (sex roles) attitudes and activities that a culture links to each sex

gender stratification the unequal distribution of wealth, power, and privilege between the two sexes

generalized other George Herbert Mead's term for widespread cultural norms and values used as a reference in evaluating ourselves

genocide the systematic killing of one category of people by another

gerontocracy a form of social organization in which the elderly have the most wealth, power, and privileges

gerontology the study of aging and the elderly

Gesellschaft a type of social organization based on cultural pluralism and transitory, impersonal social relationships

government formal organization that directs a society's political life

"groupthink" a reduced capacity for critical thinking caused by group conformity

health a state of complete physical, mental, and social well-being

health maintenance organization (HMO)   an organization that provides comprehensive medical care for which subscribers pay a fixed fee

hermaphrodite   a human being with some combination of male and female internal and external genitalia

holistic medicine   an approach to health care that emphasizes prevention of illness and takes account of the whole person within a physical and social environment

homogamy   marriage between people with the same social characteristics

horticulture   a way of life based on the use of hand tools to raise crops

"humanizing" bureaucracy   fostering an organizational environment that develops human resources

hunting and gathering   a way of life based on the use of simple tools to hunt animals and gather vegetation

hypothesis   an unverified statement of a relationship between two (or more) variables

id   Freud's designation of the human being's basic needs

ideology   ideas that reflect and support the interests of some portion of a society

incest taboo   a cultural norm forbidding sexual relations or marriage between certain kin

income   occupational wages or salaries and earnings from investments

independent variable   a variable that causes change in another (dependent) variable

industrial society   a society that produces goods using sophisticated machinery powered by advanced fuels

infant mortality rate   the number of infant deaths for each thousand live births in a given year

ingroup   an esteemed social group commanding a member's loyalty

institutional discrimination   patterns of discrimination that are woven into the fabric of a society

instrumental leadership   group leadership that emphasizes the completion of tasks

intergenerational social mobility   a change in the social position of children in relation to that of their parents

interview   a series of items or questions administered personally by a researcher to respondents

intragenerational social mobility   a change in social position occurring during a person's lifetime

juvenile delinquency   the violation of legal standards that apply to the young

kinship   social relationships based on blood, marriage, or adoption

labeling theory   the assertion that deviance and conformity arise in the response of others

labor unions   organizations of workers that attempt to improve wages and working conditions through various strategies, including negotiations and strikes

language   a system of symbols with standard meanings that allows members of a society to communicate with one another

latent functions   the unrecognized and unintended consequences of any social pattern

liberation theology   a fusion of Christian principles with political activism, often Marxist in character

life expectancy   the average lifespan of a society's population

looking-glass self   Cooley's term meaning a conception of self derived from the responses of others

macro-level orientation   a concern with large-scale patterns that characterize society as a whole

magnet schools   schools that attract students through special facilities and programs promoting educational excellence

manifest functions   the recognized and intended consequences of any social pattern

marriage   a socially approved relationship that is expected to be enduring, involving economic cooperation and allowing sexual activity leading to childbearing

mass media   impersonal communications directed to a vast audience

mass society   a society in which industrialization and expanding bureaucracy have weakened traditional social bonds

master status   a status that serves as the focal point of an individual's social identity, often shaping that person's entire life

matriarchy   a form of social organization in which females dominate males

mean   the arithmetic average of a series of numbers

measurement   the process of determining the value of a variable in a specific case

mechanical solidarity   social bonds, typical of people in rural settings, based on conforming to tradition

median   the value that occurs midway in a series of numbers or, simply, the middle case

medicalization of deviance the transformation of moral and legal issues into medical matters

medicine an institutionalized system for combating disease and promoting health

megalopolis a vast urban region containing a number of cities and their surrounding suburbs

meritocracy a system linking rewards to personal merit

metropolis a large city that dominates an urban area socially and economically

micro-level orientation a concern with small-scale patterns of social interaction in specific settings

migration the movement of people into and out of a specific territory

military-industrial complex the close association between the government, the military, and defense industries

minority a category of people, defined by physical or cultural traits, who are socially disadvantaged

miscegenation the biological process of interbreeding among racial categories

mode the value that occurs most often in a series of numbers

modernity patterns of social life linked to industrialization

modernization the process of social change initiated by industrialization

modernization theory an approach maintaining that global inequality reflects differing levels of technological development among world societies

monarchy a type of political system in which power is passed from generation to generation within a single family

monogamy a form of marriage with one relationship between two partners

monopoly domination of a market by a single producer

mores norms that have great moral significance

mortality the incidence of death in a society's population

multinational corporation a large corporation that operates in many different countries

neocolonialism a new form of economic exploitation involving not formal political control but the operation of multinational corporations

network a web of social ties that links people, often with little common identity and social interaction

nonverbal communication communication using body movements, gestures, and facial expressions rather than spoken words

norms rules by which a society guides the behavior of its members

nuclear family (conjugal family) a social unit composed of one or, more commonly, two parents and children

objectivity the state of complete personal neutrality in conducting research

oligarchy the rule of the many by the few

oligopoly domination of a market by a few producers

operationalizing a variable specifying exactly what is to be measured when assigning a value to a variable

organic solidarity social bonds, typical of people in industrial cities, based on specialization and interdependence

other-directedness variable personality patterns among people open to change and likely to imitate the behavior of others

outgroup a scorned social group toward which one feels competition or opposition

participant observation a method in which researchers systematically observe people while joining in their routine activities

pastoralism a way of life based on the domestication of animals

patriarchy a form of social organization in which males dominate females

peace the absence of war

peer group people in regular interaction who share common interests and social position and are of similar age

personal space the surrounding area over which a person makes some claim to privacy

personality a person's fairly consistent pattern of thinking, feeling, and acting

plea bargaining a legal negotiation in which the prosecution reduces a defendant's charge in exchange for a guilty plea

pluralism a state in which racial and ethnic minorities are distinct but have social parity

pluralist model an analysis of politics that views power as dispersed among many competing interest groups

political action committee (PAC) an organization formed by a special-interest group, independent of political parties, to pursue specific aims by raising and spending money

politics the institutionalized system by which a society distributes power and makes decisions

polygamy a form of marriage that unites three or more people

population the people about whom a researcher seeks knowledge

positivism a path to understanding the world based on science

postindustrial economy economic activity centered on service work and high technology

power the ability to achieve desired ends despite resistance from others

power-elite model an analysis of politics that views power as concentrated among the rich

prejudice a rigid and irrational generalization about a category of people

preoperational stage Piaget's term for the level of human development in which language and other symbols are first used

presentation of self the ways in which individuals, in various settings, attempt to create specific impressions in the minds of others

primary group typically a small social group in which relationships are both personal and enduring

primary sector the segment of the economy that generates raw materials directly from the natural environment

primary sex characteristics the genitals, used to reproduce the human species

profane that which is defined as an ordinary element of everyday life

profession a prestigious, white-collar occupation that requires extensive formal education

proletariat people who provide productive labor

public opinion the attitudes of people throughout a society about one or more controversial issues

questionnaire a series of written questions or items to which subjects are asked to respond

race a category composed of men and women who share biologically transmitted traits that are defined as socially significant

racism the belief that one racial category is innately superior or inferior to another

rational-legal authority (bureaucratic authority) power legitimated by legally enacted rules and regulations

rationality deliberate, matter-of-fact calculation of the most efficient means to accomplish any particular task

rationalization Max Weber's term for the change from tradition to rationality as the dominant mode of human thought

reference group a social group that serves as a point of reference for people making evaluations and decisions

rehabilitation reforming the offender to preclude subsequent offenses

relative deprivation a perceived disadvantage based on some standard of comparison

relative poverty being deprived of social resources in relation to those who have more

reliability the quality of consistency in measurement

religion a system of beliefs and practices based on recognizing the sacred

religiosity the importance of religion in a person's life

religious fundamentalism conservative religious organizations that seek to restore what are viewed as fundamental elements of religion

research method a systematic strategy for carrying out research

resocialization deliberate socialization intended to radically alter the individual's personality

retribution subjecting an offender to suffering comparable to that caused by the offense

retrospective labeling the interpretation of someone's past consistent with present deviance

revolution the overthrow of one political system to establish another

role patterns of expected behavior attached to a particular status

role conflict incompatibility among the roles corresponding to two or more statuses

role set a number of roles attached to a single status

role strain incompatibility among roles corresponding to a single status

routinization of charisma the transformation of charismatic authority into some combination of traditional and bureaucratic authority

sacred that which is defined as extraordinary, inspiring a sense of awe, reverence, and even fear

sample a relatively small number of cases selected to be representative of an entire population

Sapir-Whorf hypothesis the assertion that people perceive the world only in terms of the symbols provided by their language

scapegoat a person or category of people unfairly blamed for the troubles of others

schooling formal instruction under the direction of specially trained teachers

science a logical system that bases knowledge on direct, systematic observation

Second World a category of industrial societies with predominantly socialist economies

secondary group typically a large and impersonal social group based on some special interest or activity

secondary sector the segment of the economy that transforms raw materials into manufactured goods

secondary sex characteristics physical traits, other than the genitals, that distinguish physiologically mature males and females

sect an informal religious organization that stands apart from the larger society

secularization the historic decline in the influence of religion

segregation the physical and social separation of categories of people

self George Herbert Mead's term for the individual's active self-awareness

sensorimotor stage Piaget's term for the level of human development in which the world is experienced only through the senses in terms of physical contact

sex the division of humanity into biological categories of male and female

sex ratio the number of males for every hundred females in a given population

sexism the belief that one sex is innately superior to the other

sexual orientation the manner in which people experience sexual arousal and achieve sexual pleasure

sick role patterns of behavior that are socially defined as appropriate for those who are ill

social change the transformation of culture and social institutions over time

social character personality patterns common to members of a society

social conflict struggle among segments of society over valued resources

social-conflict paradigm a theoretical framework based on the assumption that society is a complex system characterized by inequality and conflict that generate social change

social construction of reality the process by which individuals creatively build reality through social interaction

social control attempts by society to regulate the behavior of individuals

social dysfunction the undesirable consequences of any social pattern for the operation of society

social epidemiology the study of the distribution of health and disease in a society's population

social function the consequences of any social pattern for the operation of society

social group two or more people who identify with one another and have a distinctive pattern of interaction

social institution a major structural part of society, such as the family or the economy, that addresses one or more basic activities

social interaction the process by which people act and react in relation to others

social mobility changes in people's positions in a system of social stratification

social movement organized activity that encourages or opposes some dimension of change

social protection rendering an offender incapable of further offenses either temporarily through incarceration or permanently by execution

social stratification a system by which categories of people in a society are ranked in a hierarchy

social structure a relatively stable pattern of social behavior

socialism an economic system in which natural resources and the means of producing goods and services are collectively owned

socialization the lifelong process of social experience by which individuals develop their human potential and learn the patterns of their culture

socialized medicine a health-care system in which most medical facilities are owned and operated by the government, and most physicians are salaried government employees

society people interacting in a limited territory on the basis of shared culture

sociobiology a theoretical paradigm that seeks to explain cultural patterns as a product, at least in part, of biological forces

sociocultural evolution the historical process of cultural change that accompanies technological innovation

socioeconomic status a composite social ranking based on various dimensions of social inequality

sociology the scientific study of human social activity

special-interest group a political alliance of people with an interest in a particular economic or social issue

spurious correlation a "false" relationship between two (or more) variables not based on direct cause and effect

status a recognized social position that an individual occupies in society

status consistency consistency of ranking across various dimensions of social standing

status set all the statuses a particular person holds at a given time

stereotype a set of prejudices concerning some category of people

stigma a powerfully negative label that radically changes a person's social identity and self-concept

structural-functional paradigm a theoretical framework based on the assumption that society is a complex system whose parts work together to promote stability

structural social mobility social mobility of large numbers of people that is due primarily to changes in society and the economy rather than to the efforts of individuals

subculture a cultural pattern that differs from the dominant culture in some distinctive way

suburbs the urban area beyond the political boundaries of a city

superego Freud's designation of the presence of culture within the individual in the form of internalized values and norms

survey a research method in which subjects respond to a series of items or questions in a questionnaire or interview

symbol anything that carries a particular meaning recognized by members of a culture

symbolic-interaction paradigm a theoretical framework based on the view that society emerges from the construction of reality by individuals in everyday life

technology the application of cultural knowledge to the task of living in a physical environment

terrorism the use of violence or the threat of violence by an individual or group as a political strategy

tertiary sector the segment of the economy that generates services rather than goods

theoretical paradigm a set of fundamental assumptions that guides thinking and research

theory an explanation of the relationship between two or more specific facts

Third World a category of primarily agrarian societies in which most people are poor

Thomas theorem the assertion that situations that are defined as real are real in their consequences

total institution a setting in which individuals are isolated from the rest of society and manipulated by an administrative staff

totalitarianism denying the majority participation in a government that extensively regulates people's lives

totem an object in the natural world imbued with sacred qualities

tracking assigning students to different types of educational programs

tradition sentiments and beliefs about the world that are passed from generation to generation

tradition-directedness rigid personalities based on conformity to time-honored ways of living

traditional authority power that is legitimated through respect for long-established cultural patterns

transsexuals people who feel they are one sex though biologically they are the other

triad a social group with three members

urban ecology study of the link between the physical and social dimensions of cities

urban renewal government programs intended to revitalize cities

urbanization the concentration of humanity into cities

validity the quality of measurement gained by actually measuring what one intends to measure

values culturally defined standards of desirability, goodness, and beauty that serve as broad guidelines for social life

variable a concept with a value that changes from case to case

victimless crimes violations of law in which there are no readily apparent victims

war armed conflict among the people of various societies, formally initiated by their governments

wealth the total amount of money and valuable goods that any person or family controls

white-collar crime crimes committed by people of high social position in the course of their occupations

white-collar occupations higher-prestige work that involves mostly mental activity

zero population growth the level of reproduction that maintains population at a steady state

References

ABERLE, DAVID F. *The Peyote Religion Among the Navaho.* Chicago: Aldine, 1966.

ADORNO, T. W., ET AL. *The Authoritarian Personality.* New York: Harper and Brothers, 1950.

AKERS, RONALD L., MARVIN D. KROHN, LONN LANZA-KADUCE, AND MARCIA RADOSEVICH. "Social Learning and Deviant Behavior." *American Sociological Review.* Vol. 44, No. 4 (August 1979):636–655.

ALBA, RICHARD D. *Italian Americans: Into the Twilight of Ethnicity.* Englewood Cliffs, NJ: Prentice Hall, 1985.

ALBON, JOAN. "Retention of Cultural Values and Differential Urban Adaptation: Samoans and American Indians in a West Coast City." *Social Forces.* Vol. 49, No. 3 (March 1971):385–393.

ALEXANDER, CHARLES P. "Playing Computer Catch-Up." *Time.* Vol. 125, No. 15 (April 1985):84–85.

ALLAN, EMILIE ANDERSEN, AND DARRELL J. STEFFENSMEIER. "Youth, Underemployment, and Property Crime: Differential Effects of Job Availability and Job Quality on Juvenile and Young Adult Arrest Rates." *American Sociological Review.* Vol. 54, No. 1 (February 1989):107–123.

ALTMAN, DREW, ET AL. "Health Care for the Homeless." *Society.* Vol. 26, No. 4 (May/June 1989):4–5.

AMERICAN COUNCIL ON EDUCATION, AS REPORTED IN "NUMBER OF BLACK STUDENTS STILL FALLING, STUDY FINDS." *The Chronicle of Higher Education.* Vol. XXXIV, No. 11 (November 11, 1987):2.

AMERICAN SOCIOLOGICAL ASSOCIATION. "Code of Ethics." Washington, DC: 1984.

ANDERSON, DANIEL R., AND ELIZABETH PUGZLES LORCH. "Look at Television: Action or Reaction?" In Jennings Bryant and Daniel R. Anderson, eds., *Children's Understanding of Television: Re-search on Attention and Comprehension.* New York: Academic Press, 1983:1–33.

ANG, IEN. *Watching Dallas: Soap Opera and the Melodramatic Imagination.* London: Methuen, 1985.

ARCHER, DANE, AND ROSEMARY GARTNER. *Violence and Crime in Cross-National Perspective.* New Haven: Yale University Press, 1987.

ARENDT, HANNAH. *The Origins of Totalitarianism.* Cleveland, OH: Meridian Books, 1958.

ARIÈS, PHILIPPE. *Centuries of Childhood: A Social History of Family Life.* New York: Vintage Books, 1965.

———. *Western Attitudes Toward Death: From the Middle Ages to the Present.* Baltimore, MD: The Johns Hopkins University Press, 1974.

ASCH, SOLOMON. *Social Psychology.* Englewood Cliffs, NJ: Prentice Hall, 1952.

ATCHLEY, ROBERT C. *Aging: Continuity and Change.* Belmont, CA: Wadsworth, 1983; also 2nd ed., 1987.

AYENSU, EDWARD S. "A Worldwide Role for the Healing Powers of Plants." *Smithsonian.* Vol. 12, No. 8 (November 1981):87–97.

BACHRACH, PETER, AND MORTON S. BARATZ. *Power and Poverty.* New York: Oxford University Press, 1970.

BAILEY, WILLIAM C., AND RUTH D. PETERSON. "Murder and Capital Punishment: A Monthly Time-Series Analysis of Execution Publicity." *American Sociological Review.* Vol. 54, No. 5 (October 1989):722–743.

BAINBRIDGE, WILLIAM SIMS, AND DANIEL H. JACKSON. "The Rise and Decline of Transcendental Meditation." In Bryan Wilson, ed., *The Social Impact of New Religious Movements.* New York: The Rose of Sharon Press, 1981:135–158.

BAKER, MARY ANNE, CATHERINE WHITE BERHEIDE, FAY ROSS GRECKEL, LINDA CARSTARPHEN GUGIN, MARCIA J. LIPETZ, AND MARCIA TEXLER SEGAL. *Women Today: A Multidisciplinary Approach to Women's Studies*. Monterey, CA: Brooks/Cole, 1980.

BALES, ROBERT F. "The Equilibrium Problem in Small Groups." In Talcott Parsons et al., eds., *Working Papers in the Theory of Action*. New York: Free Press, 1953:111–115.

BALES, ROBERT F., AND PHILIP E. SLATER. "Role Differentiation in Small Decision-Making Groups." In Talcott Parsons and Robert F. Bales, eds., *Family, Socialization and Interaction Process*. New York: Free Press, 1955:259–306.

BALLANTINE, JEANNE H. *The Sociology of Education: A Systematic Analysis*. Englewood Cliffs, NJ: Prentice Hall, 1983.

BALTZELL, E. DIGBY. *The Protestant Establishment: Aristocracy and Caste in America*. New York: Vintage, 1964.

BALTZELL, E. DIGBY, ED. *The Search for Community in Modern America*. New York: Harper & Row, 1968.

BALTZELL, E. DIGBY. "The Protestant Establishment Revisited." *The American Scholar*. Vol. 45, No. 4 (Autumn 1976):499–518.

BALTZELL, E. DIGBY. *Philadelphia Gentlemen: The Making of a National Upper Class*. Philadelphia, PA: University of Pennsylvania Press, 1979; orig. 1958.

BALTZELL, E. DIGBY. *Puritan Boston and Quaker Philadelphia*. New York: Free Press, 1979.

BALTZELL, E. DIGBY. "The WASP's Last Gasp." *Philadelphia Magazine*. Vol. 79 (September 1988):104–107, 184, 186, 188.

BANFIELD, EDWARD C. *The Unheavenly City Revisited*. Boston, MA: Little, Brown, 1974.

BARASH, DAVID. *The Whispering Within*. New York: Penguin Books, 1981.

BARBERIS, MARY. "America's Elderly: Policy Implications." *Population Bulletin*. Vol. 35, No. 4 (January 1981). Population Reference Bureau.

BARKER, EILEEN. "Who'd Be a Moonie? A Comparative Study of Those Who Join the Unification Church in Britain." In Bryan Wilson, ed., *The Social Impact of New Religious Movements*. New York: The Rose of Sharon Press, 1981:59–96.

BARRY, KATHLEEN. "Feminist Theory: The Meaning of Women's Liberation." In Barbara Haber, ed., *The Women's Annual 1982–1983*. Boston, MA: G. K. Hall, 1983:35–78.

BASSUK, ELLEN J. "The Homelessness Problem." *Scientific American*. Vol. 251, No. 1 (July 1984):40–45.

BATESON, C. DANIEL, AND W. LARRY VENTIS. *The Religious Experience: A Social-Psychological Perspective*. New York: Oxford, 1982.

BAUER, P. T. *Equality, the Third World, and Economic Delusion*. Cambridge, MA: Harvard University Press, 1981.

BEATRICE COMPANY, INC. *Annual Report 1985*. Chicago: Beatrice, 1985.

BECKER, HOWARD S. *Outsiders: Studies in the Sociology of Deviance*. New York: Free Press, 1966.

BELL, ALAN P., MARTIN S. WEINBERG, AND SUE KIEFER-HAMMERSMITH. *Sexual Preference: Its Development in Men and Women*. Bloomington, IN: Indiana University Press, 1981.

BELLAH, ROBERT N. *The Broken Covenant*. New York: Seabury, 1975.

BELLAH, ROBERT N., RICHARD MADSEN, WILLIAM M. SULLIVAN, ANN SWIDLER, AND STEVEN M. TIPTON. *Habits of the Heart: Individualism and Commitment in American Life*. New York: Harper & Row, 1985.

BELSKY, JAY, RICHARD M. LERNER, AND GRAHAM B. SPANIER. *The Child in the Family*. Reading, MA: Addison-Wesley, 1984.

BEM, SANDRA LIPSITZ. "Gender Schema Theory: A Cognitive Account of Sex-Typing." *Psychological Review*. Vol. 88, No. 4 (July 1981):354–364.

BENEDICT, RUTH. "Continuities and Discontinuities in Cultural Conditioning." *Psychiatry*. Vol. 1 (May 1938):161–167.

BENEDICT, RUTH. *The Chrysanthemum and the Sword: Patterns of Japanese Culture*. New York: New American Library, 1974; orig. 1946.

BENNETT, NEIL G., DAVID E. BLOOM, AND PATRICIA H. CRAIG. "The Divergence of Black and White Marriage Patterns." *American Journal of Sociology*. Vol. 95, No. 3 (November 1989):692–722.

BENOKRAITIS, NIJOLE, AND JOE FEAGIN. *Modern Sexism: Blatant, Subtle, and Overt Discrimination*. Englewood Cliffs, NJ: Prentice Hall, 1986.

BERARDO, F. M. "Survivorship and Social Isolation: The Case of the Aged Widower." *The Family Coordinator*. Vol. 19 (January 1970):11–25.

BERGER, BRIGITTE, AND PETER L. BERGER. *The War Over the Family: Capturing the Middle Ground*. Garden City, NY: Anchor/Doubleday, 1983.

BERGER, PETER L. *Invitation to Sociology*. New York: Anchor Books, 1963.

BERGER, PETER L. *The Sacred Canopy: Elements of a Sociological Theory of Religion*. Garden City, NY: Doubleday & Company, Inc., 1967.

BERGER, PETER L. *Facing Up to Modernity: Excursions in Society, Politics, and Religion*. New York: Basic Books, 1977.

BERGER, PETER L. *The Capitalist Revolution: Fifty Propositions About Prosperity, Equality, and Liberty*. New York: Basic Books, 1986.

BERGER, PETER, BRIGITTE BERGER, AND HANSFRIED KELLNER. *The Homeless Mind: Modernization and Consciousness*. New York: Vintage Books, 1974.

BERGER, PETER L., AND THOMAS LUCKMANN. *The Social Construction of Reality: A Treatise in the Sociology of Knowledge*. Garden City, NY: Anchor, 1967.

BERGESEN, ALBERT, ED. *Crises in the World-System*. Beverly Hills, CA: Sage Publications, 1983.

BERNARD, JESSIE. *The Female World*. New York: Free Press, 1981.

BERNARD, JESSIE. *The Future of Marriage*. New Haven, CT: Yale University Press, 1982; orig. 1973.

BERNARD, LARRY CRAIG. "Multivariate Analysis of New Sex Role Formulations and Personality." *Journal of Personality and Social Psychology*. Vol. 38, No. 2 (February 1980):323–336.

BERRY, BRIAN L., AND PHILIP H. REES. "The Factorial Ecology of Calcutta." *American Journal of Sociology*. Vol. 74, No. 5 (March 1969):445–491.

BERSCHEID, ELLEN, AND ELAINE HATFIELD. *Interpersonal Attraction*. 2nd ed. Reading, MA: Addison-Wesley, 1983.

BEST, RAPHAELA. *We've All Got Scars: What Boys and Girls Learn in Elementary School*. Bloomington, IN: Indiana University Press, 1983.

Black Issues in Higher Education. "Black Graduate Students Decline." Vol. 4, No. 8 (July 1, 1987):1–2.

BLAU, JUDITH R., AND PETER M. BLAU. "The Cost of Inequality: Metropolitan Structure and Violent Crime." *American Sociological Review.* Vol. 47, No. 1 (February 1982):114–129.

BLAU, PETER M. *Exchange and Power in Social Life.* New York: Wiley, 1964.

BLAU, PETER M., AND OTIS DUDLEY DUNCAN. *The American Occupational Structure.* New York: John Wiley, 1967.

BLAUSTEIN, ALBERT P., AND ROBERT L. ZANGRANDO. *Civil Rights and the Black American.* New York: Washington Square Press, 1968.

BLOOM, LEONARD. "Familial Adjustments of Japanese-Americans to Relocation: First Phase." In Thomas F. Pettigrew, ed., *The Sociology of Race Relations.* New York: Free Press, 1980:163–167.

BLUM, ALAN, AND GARY FISHER. "Women Who Kill." In Delos H. Kelly, ed., *Criminal Behavior: Readings in Criminology.* New York: St. Martin's Press, 1980:291–301.

BLUMBERG, ABRAHAM S. *Criminal Justice.* Chicago: Quadrangle Books, 1970.

BLUMBERG, PAUL. *Inequality in an Age of Decline.* New York: Oxford University Press, 1981.

BLUMER, HERBERT G. "Collective Behavior." In Alfred McClung Lee, ed., *Principles of Sociology.* 3rd ed. New York: Barnes & Noble Books, 1969:65–121.

BLUMSTEIN, PHILIP, AND PEPPER SCHWARTZ. *American Couples.* New York: William Morrow, 1983.

BODENHEIMER, THOMAS S. "Health Care in the United States: Who Pays?" In Vicente Navarro, ed., *Health and Medical Care in the U.S.: A Critical Analysis.* Farmingdale, NY: Baywood Publishing Co., 1977:61–68.

BOFF, LEONARD AND CLODOVIS. *Salvation and Liberation: In Search of a Balance Between Faith and Politics.* Maryknoll, NY: Orbis Books, 1984.

BOGARDUS, EMORY S. "Comparing Racial Distance in Ethiopia, South Africa, and the United States." *Sociology and Social Research.* Vol. 52, No. 2 (January 1968):149–156.

BOLLOUGH, VERN, AND MARTHA VOGHT. "Women, Menstruation, and Nineteenth-Century Medicine." In Judith Walzer Leavitt, ed., *Women and Health in America.* Madison, WI: The University of Wisconsin Press, 1984:28–37.

BONNER, JANE. Research presented in "The Two Brains." Public Broadcasting System telecast, 1984.

BOOTH, ALAN, AND LYNN WHITE. "Thinking About Divorce." *Journal of Marriage and the Family.* Vol. 42, No. 3 (August 1980):605–616.

BOSWELL, TERRY E. "A Split Labor Market Analysis of Discrimination Against Chinese Immigrants, 1850–1882." *American Sociological Review.* Vol. 51, No. 3 (June 1986):352–371.

BOTT, ELIZABETH. *Family and Social Network.* New York: Free Press, 1971; orig. 1957.

BOWLES, SAMUEL, AND HERBERT GINTIS. *Schooling in Capitalist America: Educational Reform and the Contradictions of Economic Life.* New York: Basic Books, 1976.

BOYER, ERNEST L. *College: The Undergraduate Experience in America.* Prepared by The Carnegie Foundation for the Advancement of Teaching. New York: Harper & Row, 1987.

BRAITHWAITE, JOHN. "The Myth of Social Class and Criminality Reconsidered." *American Sociological Review.* Vol. 46, No. 1 (February 1981):36–57.

BRAND, DAVID. "The New Whiz Kids." *Time.* Vol. 130, No. 9 (August 31, 1987):42–46, 49, 51.

BRINTON, CRANE. *The Anatomy of Revolution.* New York: Vintage Books, 1965.

BRINTON, MARY C. "The Social-Institutional Bases of Gender Stratification: Japan as an Illustrative Case." *American Journal of Sociology.* Vol. 94, No. 2 (September 1988):300–334.

BROMLEY, DAVID G., AND ANSON D. SHUPE, JR. *New Christian Politics.* Macon, GA: Mercer University Press, 1984.

BROWN, E. RICHARD. *Rockefeller Medicine Men: Medicine and Capitalism in America.* Berkeley, CA: University of California Press, 1979.

BROWNMILLER, SUSAN. *Femininity.* New York: Linden Press, Simon and Schuster, 1984.

BROWNSTEIN, RONALD, AND NINA EASTON. *Reagan's Ruling Class: Portraits of the President's Top One Hundred Officials.* New York: Pantheon, 1983.

BROYLES, J. ALLEN. "The John Birch Society: A Movement of Social Protest of the Radical Right." In Louis E. Genevie, ed., *Collective Behavior and Social Movements.* Itasca, IL: F. E. Peacock, 1978:338–345.

BRZEZINSKI, ZBIGNIEW. *The Grand Failure: The Birth and Death of Communisim in the Twentieth Century.* New York: Charles Scribner's Sons, 1989.

BURCH, ROBERT. Testimony to House of Representatives Hearing in "Review: The World Hunger Problem." October 25, 1983, Serial 98–38.

BURNHAM, WALTER DEAN. *Democracy in the Making: American Government and Politics.* Englewood Cliffs, NJ: Prentice Hall, 1983.

BURNS, JAMES A. "Discipline: Why Does It Continue to Be a Problem? Solution Is in Changing School Culture." *National Association of Secondary School Principals Bulletin.* Vol. 69, No. 479 (March 1985):1–47.

BUSBY, LINDA J. "Sex Role Research on the Mass Media." *Journal of Communications.* Vol. 25 (Autumn 1975):107–113.

BUTTERWORTH, DOUGLAS, AND JOHN K. CHANCE. *Latin American Urbanization.* Cambridge (UK): Cambridge University Press, 1981.

"Buy America while Stocks Last." *The Economist.* Vol. 313, No. 7633 (december 16, 1989):63–66.

CALLOW, A.B., JR., ED. *American Urban History.* New York: Oxford University Press, 1969.

CALMORE, JOHN O. "National Housing Policies and Black America: Trends, Issues, and Implications." In *The State of Black America 1986.* New York: National Urban League, 1986:115–149.

CAMERON, WILLIAM BRUCE. *Modern Social Movements: A Sociological Outline.* New York: Random House, 1966.

CANTOR, MURIAL G., AND SUZANNE PINGREE. *The Soap Opera.* Beverly Hills, CA: Sage Publications, 1983.

CAPLOW, THEODORE, ET AL. *Middletown Families.* Minneapolis, MN: University of Minnesota Press, 1982.

CAPUTO, PHILIP. *A Rumor of War.* New York: Holt, Rinehart and Winston, 1977.

CARLSON, NORMAN A. "Corrections in the United States Today: A Balance Has Been Struck." *The American Criminal Law Review.* Vol. 13, No. 4 (Spring 1976):615–647.

CARLTON, ERIC. *Ideology and Social Order.* London: Routledge & Kegan Paul, 1977.

CHAGNON, NAPOLEON A. *Yanomamö.* 3rd ed. New York: Holt, Rinehart and Winston, 1983.

CHANDLER, TERTIUS, AND GERALD FOX. *3000 Years of Urban History.* New York: Academic Press, 1974.

CHANGE, KWANG-CHIH. *The Archaeology of Ancient China.* New Haven, CT: Yale University Press, 1977.

CHERLIN, ANDREW. *Marriage, Divorce, Remarriage.* Cambridge, MA: Harvard University Press, 1981.

CHERLIN, ANDREW, AND FRANK F. FURSTENBERG, JR. "The American Family in the Year 2000." *The Futurist.* Vol. 17, No. 3 (June 1983):7–14.

CHILDREN'S DEFENSE FUND. *A Children's Defense Budget: An Analysis of the President's FY 1986 Budget and Children.* Washington, DC: 1985.

CLARK, JUAN M., JOSE I. LASAGA, AND ROSE S. REGUE. *The 1980 Mariel Exodus: An Assessment and Prospect: Special Report.* Washington, DC: Council for Inter-American Security, 1981.

CLARK, THOMAS A. *Blacks in Suburbs.* New Brunswick, NJ: Rutgers University Center for Urban Policy Research, 1979.

CLINARD, MARSHALL B. *Cities with Little Crime: The Case of Switzerland.* Cambridge (UK): Cambridge University Press, 1978.

CLINARD, MARSHALL, AND DANIEL ABBOTT. *Crime in Developing Countries.* New York: Wiley, 1973.

CLOWARD, RICHARD A., AND LLOYD E. OHLIN. *Delinquency and Opportunity: A Theory of Delinquent Gangs.* New York: Free Press, 1966.

COAKLEY, JAY J. *Sport in Society: Issues and Controversies.* 3rd ed. St. Louis, MO: C. V. Mosby, 1986; also 4th ed., 1990.

COCKERHAM, WILLIAM C. *Medical Sociology.* 2nd ed. Englewood Cliffs, NJ: Prentice Hall, 1982; also 3rd ed., 1986.

COE, MICHAEL D., AND RICHARD A. DIEHL. *In the Land of the Olmec.* Austin, TX: University of Texas Press, 1980.

COHEN, ALBERT K. *Delinquent Boys: The Culture of the Gang.* New York: Free Press, 1971; orig. 1955.

COHEN, MICHAEL. "Restructuring the System." *Transaction.* Vol. 26, No. 4 (May/June 1989):40–48.

COHEN, MICHAEL, AND E. ELAINE CROE. *Early Estimates: National Estimates of Higher Education: School Year 1988–89.* Washington, DC: U.S. Government Printing Office, 1988.

COLEMAN, JAMES, ET AL. *Equality of Educational Opportunity* ("The Coleman Report"). U.S. Department of Health, Education, and Welfare. Washington, DC: U.S. Government Printing Office, 1966.

COLEMAN, JAMES S., AND THOMAS HOFFER. *Public and Private High Schools: The Impact of Communities.* New York: Basic Books, 1987.

COLEMAN, JAMES, THOMAS HOFFER, AND SALLY KILGORE. *Public and Private Schools: An Analysis of Public Schools and Beyond.* Washington, DC: National Center for Education Statistics, 1981.

COLEMAN, RICHARD P., AND BERNICE L. NEUGARTEN. *Social Status in the City.* San Francisco, CA: Jossey-Bass, 1971.

COLEMAN, RICHARD P., AND LEE RAINWATER. *Social Standing in America.* New York: Basic Books, 1978.

COLLINS, RANDALL. "A Conflict Theory of Sexual Stratification." *Social Problems.* Vol. 19, No. 1 (Summer 1971):3–21.

COLLINS, RANDALL. *The Credential Society: An Historical Sociology of Education and Stratification.* New York: Academic Press, 1979.

COLLINS, RANDALL. *Sociological Insight: An Introduction to Nonobvious Sociology.* New York: Oxford University Press, 1982.

COLLOWAY, N. O., AND PAULA L. DOLLEVOET. "Selected Tabular Material on Aging." In Caleb Finch and Leonard Hayflick, eds., *Handbook of the Biology of Aging.* New York: Van Nostrand Reinhold, 1977:666–708.

COMTE, AUGUSTE. *Auguste Comte and Positivism: The Essential Writings.* Gertrud Lenzer, ed. New York: Harper Torchbooks, 1975.

COOLEY, CHARLES HORTON. *Human Nature and the Social Order.* New York: Schocken Books, 1964; orig. 1902.

COPPOCK, MARJORIE L. "Women's Leadership Involvement in Community Volunteer Organizations." Paper presented to Southwestern Sociological Association, Dallas, Texas, 1987.

CORSARO, WILLIAM A., AND THOMAS A. RIZZO. "*Discussione* and Friendship: Socialization Processes in the Peer Culture of Italian Nursery School Children." *American Sociological Review.* Vol. 53, No. 6 (December 1988):879–894.

COTTRELL, JOHN, AND THE EDITORS OF TIME-LIFE. *The Great Cities: Mexico City.* Amsterdam: 1979.

COUNTS, G. S. "The Social Status of Occupations: A Problem in Vocational Guidance." *School Review.* Vol. 33 (January 1925):16–27.

COURTNEY, ALICE E., AND THOMAS W. WHIPPLE. *Sex Stereotyping in Advertising.* Lexington, MA: D. C. Heath, 1983.

COX, HARVEY. *The Secular City.* Rev. ed. New York: Macmillan, 1971; orig. 1965.

COX, HARVEY. *Turning East: The Promise and Peril of the New Orientalism.* New York: Simon and Schuster, 1977.

CROUSE, JAMES, AND DALE TRUSHEIM. *The Case Against the SAT.* Chicago: University of Chicago Press, 1988.

CURRIE, ELLIOTT. *Confronting Crime: An American Challenge.* New York: Pantheon, 1985.

DAHL, ROBERT A. *Who Governs?* New Haven, CT: Yale University Press, 1961.

DAHL, ROBERT A. *Dilemmas of Pluralist Democracy: Autonomy vs. Control.* New Haven, CT: Yale University Press, 1982.

DAHRENDORF, RALF. *Class and Class Conflict in Industrial Society.* Stanford, CA: Stanford University Press, 1959.

DALY, MARTIN, AND MARGO WILSON. *Homicide.* New York: Aldine De Gruyter, 1988.

DANIELS, ROGER. "The Issei Generation." In Amy Tachiki et al., eds., *Roots: An Asian American Reader.* Los Angeles: UCLA Asian American Studies Center, 1971:138–149.

DANNEFER, DALE. "Adult Development and Social Theory: A Reappraisal." *American Sociological Review.* Vol. 49, No. 1 (February 1984):100–116.

DAVIES, JAMES C. "Toward a Theory of Revolution." *American Sociological Review.* Vol. 27, No. 1 (February 1962):5–19.

DAVIES, MARK, AND DENISE B. KANDEL. "Parental and Peer Influences on Adolescents' Educational Plans: Some Further Evidence." *American Journal of Sociology.* Vol. 87, No. 2 (September 1981):363–387.

DAVIS, KINGSLEY. "Extreme Social Isolation of a Child." *American Journal of Sociology.* Vol. 45, No. 4 (January 1940):554–565.

DAVIS, KINGSLEY. "Final Note on a Case of Extreme Isolation." *American Journal of Sociology.* Vol. 52, No. 5 (March 1947):432–437.

DAVIS, KINGSLEY, AND WILBERT MOORE. "Some Principles of Stratification." *American Sociological Review.* Vol. 10, No. 2 (April 1945):242–249.

DAVIS, SHARON A., AND EMIL J. HALLER. "Tracking, Ability, and SES: Further Evidence on the 'Revisionist-Meritocratic Debate.'" *American Journal of Education.* Vol. 89 (May 1981):283–304.

DECKARD, BARBARA SINCLAIR. *The Women's Movement: Political, Socioeconomic, and Psychological Issues.* 2nd ed. New York: Harper & Row, 1979.

DEDRICK, DENNIS K. Personal communication, 1990.

DEDRICK, DENNIS K., AND RICHARD E. YINGER. "MAD, SDI, and the Nuclear Arms Race." Manuscript in development. Georgetown, KY: Georgetown College, 1990.

DEGLER, CARL. *At Odds: Women and the Family in America From the Revolution to the Present.* New York: Oxford University Press, 1980.

DELACROIX, JACQUES, AND CHARLES C. RAGIN. "Structural Blockage: A Crossnational Study of Economic Dependency, State Efficacy, and Underdevelopment." *American Journal of Sociology.* Vol. 86, No. 6 (May 1981):1311–1347.

DEVINE, JOEL A. "State and State Expenditure: Determinants of Social Investment and Social Consumption Spending in the Postwar United States." *American Sociological Review.* Vol. 50, No. 2 (April 1985):150–165.

DEWEY, JOHN. *Experience and Education.* New York: Collier Books, 1968; orig. 1938.

DIPRETE, THOMAS A. "Unemployment over the Life Cycle: Racial Differences and the Effect of Changing Economic Conditions." *American Journal of Sociology.* Vol. 87, No. 2 (September 1981):286–307.

DOBYNS, HENRY F. "An Appraisal of Techniques with a New Hemispheric Estimate." *Current Anthropology.* Vol. 7, No. 4 (October 1966):395–446.

DOLLARD, JOHN, ET AL. *Frustration and Aggression.* New Haven, CT: Yale University Press, 1939.

DOMHOFF, G. WILLIAM. *Who Rules America Now? A View of the '80s.* Englewood Cliffs, NJ: Prentice Hall, 1983.

DONOVAN, VIRGINIA K., AND RONNIE LITTENBERG. "Psychology of Women: Feminist Therapy." In Barbara Haber, ed., *The Women's Annual 1981: The Year in Review.* Boston: G. K. Hall, 1982:211–235.

DOYLE, JAMES A. *The Male Experience.* Dubuque, IA: Wm. C. Brown, 1983.

DUBOS, RENÉ. *Man Adapting.* New Haven, CT: Yale University Press, 1980; orig. 1965.

DUHL, LEONARD J. "The Social Context of Health." In Arthur C. Hastings et al., eds., *Health for the Whole Person: The Complete Guide to Holistic Medicine.* Boulder, CO: Westview Press, 1980:39–48.

DURKHEIM, EMILÉ. *The Division of Labor in Society.* New York: Free Press, 1964a; orig. 1895.

DURKHEIM, EMILE. *The Rules of Sociological Method.* New York: Free Press, 1964b; orig. 1915.

DURKHEIM, EMILE. *Suicide.* New York: Free Press, 1966; orig. 1897.

DURKHEIM, EMILE. *Selected Writings.* Anthony Giddens, ed. Cambridge (UK): Cambridge University Press, 1972.

DWORKIN, ANDREA. *Intercourse.* New York: Free Press, 1987.

DZIECH, BILLIE WRIGHT, AND LINDA WEINER. *The Lecherous Professor: Sexual Harassment on Campus.* Boston, MA: Beacon Press, 1984.

EASTERLIN, RICHARD A. "Immigration: Economic and Social Characteristics." In *Harvard Encyclopedia of American Ethnic Groups.* Cambridge, MA: Harvard University Press, 1980:476–486.

EBAUGH, HELEN ROSE FUCHS. *Becoming an EX: The Process of Role Exit.* Chicago: University of Chicago Press, 1988.

ECKHOLM, ERIK. "Malnutrition in Elderly: Widespread Health Threat." *The New York Times* (August 13, 1985):19–20.

EDMONSTON, BARRY, AND THOMAS M. GUTERBOCK. "Is Suburbanization Slowing Down? Recent Trends in Population Deconcentration in U.S. Metropolitan Areas." *Social Forces.* Vol. 62, No. 4 (June 1984):905–925.

EDWARDS, DAVID V. *The American Political Experience.* 3rd ed. Englewood Cliffs, NJ: Prentice Hall, 1985.

EDWARDS, HARRY. *Sociology of Sport.* Homewood, IL: Dorsey Press, 1973.

EDWARDS, RICHARD. *Contested Terrain: The Transformation of the Workplace in the Twentieth Century.* New York: Basic Books, 1979.

EHRENREICH, BARBARA. *The Hearts of Men: American Dreams and the Flight from Commitment.* Garden City, NY: Anchor, 1983.

EHRENREICH, JOHN. "Introduction." In John Ehrenreich, ed., *The Cultural Crisis of Modern Medicine.* New York: Monthly Review Press, 1978:1–35.

EHRLICH, PAUL R. *The Population Bomb.* New York: Ballantine Books, 1978.

EICHLER, MARGRIT. *Nonsexist Research Methods: A Practical Guide.* Winchester, MA: Unwin Hyman, 1988.

EISENSTEIN, ZILLAH R., ED. *Capitalist Patriarchy and the Case for Socialist Feminism.* New York: Monthly Review Press, 1979.

ELIAS, ROBERT. *The Politics of Victimization: Victims, Victimology and Human Rights.* New York: Oxford University Press, 1986.

EKMAN, PAUL, ET AL. "The International Language of Gestures." *Psychology Today* (May 1984):64–69.

ELKIN, FREDERICK, AND GERALD HANDEL. *The Child and Society: The Process of Socialization.* 4th ed. New York: Random House, 1984.

ELKIND, DAVID. *The Hurried Child: Growing Up Too Fast Too Soon.* Reading, MA: Addison-Wesley, 1981.

ELLIOT, DELBERT S., AND SUZANNE S. AGETON. "Reconciling Race and Class Differences in Self-Reported and Official Estimates of Delinquency." *American Sociological Review.* Vol. 45, No. 1 (February 1980):95–110.

EMBER, CAROL, AND MELVIN M. EMBER. *Anthropology.* 4th ed. Englewood Cliffs, NJ: Prentice Hall, 1985.

EMBER, MELVIN, AND CAROL R. EMBER. "The Conditions Favoring Matrilocal versus Patrilocal Residence." *American Anthropologist.* Vol. 73, No. 3 (June 1971):571–594.

EMERSON, JOAN P. "Behavior in Private Places: Sustaining Definitions of Reality in Gynecological Examinations." In H. P. Dreitzel, ed., *Recent Sociology.* Vol. 2. New York: Collier, 1970:74–97.

ENGELS, FRIEDRICH. *The Origin of the Family.* Chicago: Charles H. Kerr and Company, 1902; orig. 1884.

ERIKSON, KAI T. *Wayward Puritans: A Study in the Sociology of Deviance.* New York: John Wiley, 1966.

ERIKSON, ROBERT S., NORMAN R. LUTTBEG, AND KENT L. TEDIN. *American Public Opinion: Its Origins, Content, and Impact.* 2nd ed. New York: Wiley, 1980.

ETZIONI, AMITAI. *A Comparative Analysis of Complex Organization: On Power, Involvement, and Their Correlates.* Revised and enlarged ed. New York: Free Press, 1975.

ETZIONI-HALEVY, EVA. *Bureaucracy and Democracy: A Political Dilemma.* Rev. ed. Boston: Routledge & Kegan Paul, 1985.

EVE, SUSAN BROWN. "Age Strata Differences in Utilization of Health Care Services among Adults in the United States." *Sociological Focus.* Vol. 17, No. 2 (April 1984):105–120.

FALK, GERHARD. Personal communication, 1987.

FALLOWS, JAMES. "Immigration: How It's Affecting Us." *The Atlantic Monthly.* Vol. 252 (November 1983):45–52, 55–62, 66–68, 85–90, 94, 96, 99–106.

Family Economics Review. "Updated Estimates of the Cost of Raising a Child." Vol. 2, No. 4 (1989):30–31.

FANTINI, MARIO D. *Regaining Excellence in Education.* Columbus, OH: Merrill, 1986.

FARRELL, MICHAEL P., AND STANLEY D. ROSENBERG. *Men at Midlife.* Boston, MA: Auburn House, 1981.

FEAGIN, JOE. *The Urban Real Estate Game.* Englewood Cliffs, NJ: Prentice Hall, 1983.

FEATHERMAN, DAVID L., AND ROBERT M. HAUSER. *Opportunity and Change.* New York: Academic Press, 1978.

FERGUSON, TOM. "Medical Self-Care: Self Responsibility for Health." In Arthur C. Hastings et al., eds., *Health for the Whole Person: The Complete Guide to Holistic Medicine.* Boulder, CO: Westview Press, 1980:87–109.

FERGUSSON, D. M., L. J. HORWOOD, AND F. T. SHANNON. "A Proportional Hazards Model of Family Breakdown." *Journal of Marriage and the Family.* Vol. 46, No. 3 (August 1984): 539–549.

FINKELSTEIN, NEAL W., AND RON HASKINS. "Kindergarten Children Prefer Same-Color Peers." *Child Development.* Vol. 54, No. 2 (April 1983):502–508.

FIORENTINE, ROBERT. "Men, Women, and the Premed Persistence Gap: A Normative Alternatives Approach." *American Journal of Sociology.* Vol. 92, No. 5 (March 1987):1118–1139.

FIREBAUGH, GLENN, AND KENNETH E. DAVIS. "Trends in Antiblack Prejudice, 1972-1984: Region and Cohort Effects." *American Journal of Sociology.* Vol. 94, No. 2 (September 1988):251–272.

FISCHER, CLAUDE S., ET AL. *Networks and Places: Social Relations in the Urban Setting.* New York: Free Press, 1977.

FISHER, ELIZABETH. *Woman's Creation: Sexual Evolution and the Shaping of Society.* Garden City, NY: Anchor/Doubleday, 1979.

FISHER, ROGER, AND WILLIAM URY. "Getting to YES." In William M. Evan and Stephen Hilgartner, eds., *The Arms Race and Nuclear War.* Englewood Cliffs, NJ: Prentice Hall, 1988:261–268.

FISHMAN, PAMELA M. "Interactional Shitwork." *Heresies: A Feminist Publication on Art and Politics.* Vol. 2 (May 1977):99–101.

FISHMAN, PAMELA M. "The Work Women Do." *Social Problems.* Vol. 25, No. 4 (April 1978):397–406.

FITZPATRICK, JOSEPH P. *Puerto Rican Americans: The Meaning of Migration to the Mainland.* Englewood Cliffs, NJ: Prentice Hall, 1971.

FITZPATRICK, JOSEPH P. "Puerto Ricans." In *Harvard Encyclopedia of American Ethnic Groups.* Cambridge, MA: Harvard University Press, 1980:858–867.

FLAHERTY, MICHAEL G. "A Formal Approach to the Study of Amusement in Social Interaction." *Studies in Symbolic Interaction.* Vol. 5. New York: JAI Press, 1984:71–82.

FLAHERTY, MICHAEL G.. "Two Conceptions of the Social Situation: Some Implications of Humor." *The Sociological Quarterly.* Vol. 31, No. 1 (Spring 1990), in press.

Forbes. "The Forbes Four Hundred." Vol. 144, No. 9 (October 23, 1989):152–154.

FORD, CLELLAN S., AND FRANK A. BEACH. *Patterns of Sexual Behavior.* New York: Harper & Row, 1951.

FRANK, ANDRÉ GUNDER. *On Capitalist Underdevelopment.* Bombay: Oxford University Press, 1975.

FRANK, ANDRÉ GUNDER. *Crisis: In the World Economy.* New York: Holmes & Meier, 1980.

FRANK, ANDRÉ GUNDER. *Reflections on the World Economic Crisis.* New York: Monthly Review Press, 1981.

FRANKLIN, JOHN HOPE. *From Slavery to Freedom: A History of Negro Americans.* 3rd ed. New York: Vintage Books, 1967.

FRAZIER, E. FRANKLIN. *Black Bourgeoisie: The Rise of a New Middle Class.* New York: Free Press, 1965.

FRENCH, MARILYN. *Beyond Power: On Women, Men, and Morals.* New York: Summit Books, 1985.

FRIEDRICH, CARL J., AND ZBIGNIEW BRZEZINSKI. *Totalitarian Dictatorship and Autocracy.* 2nd ed. Cambridge, MA: Harvard University Press, 1965.

FRIEDRICH, OTTO. "Braving Scorn and Threats." *Time.* Vol. 125, No. 30 (July 23, 1984):36–37.

FRIEDRICH, OTTO. "A Proud Capital's Distress." *Time.* Vol. 124, No. 6 (August 6, 1984):26–30, 33–35.

FRIEDRICH, OTTO. "United No More." *Time.* Vol. 129, No. 18 (May 4, 1987):28–37.

FUCHS, VICTOR R. *Who Shall Live?* New York: Basic Books, 1974.

FUCHS, VICTOR R. "Sex Differences in Economic Well-Being." *Science.* Vol. 232 (April 25, 1986):459–464.

FUGITA, STEPHEN S., AND DAVID J. O'BRIEN. "Structural Assimilation, Ethnic Group Membership, and Political Participation among Japanese Americans: A Research Note." *Social Forces*. Vol. 63, No. 4 (June 1985):986–995.

FUJIMOTO, ISAO. "The Failure of Democracy in a Time of Crisis." In Amy Tachiki et al., eds., *Roots: An Asian American Reader.* Los Angeles: UCLA Asian American Studies Center, 1971:207–214.

FUMENTO, MICHAEL. *The Myth of Heterosexual AIDS.* New York: Basic Books, 1989.

FURSTENBERG, FRANK F., JR. "The New Extended Family: The Experience of Parents and Children after Remarriage." Paper presented to the Changing Family Conference XIII: The Blended Family. University of Iowa, 1984.

FURSTENBERG, FRANK F., JR., J. BROOKS-GUNN, AND S. PHILIP MORGAN. *Adolescent Mothers in Later Life.* New York: Cambridge University Press, 1987.

GAGLIANI, GIORGIO. "How Many Working Classes?" *American Journal of Sociology.* Vol. 87, No. 2 (September 1981):259–285.

GALLUP, GEORGE, JR. *Religion in America.* Princeton, NJ: Princeton Religion Research Center, 1982.

GALLUP, GEORGE, JR. *Religion in America: The Gallup Report.* Report No. 222. Princeton, NJ: Princeton Religion Research Center, March 1984.

GALLUP, GEORGE H. "The 16th Annual Gallup Poll of the Public's Attitudes toward the Public Schools." *Phi Delta Kappan.* Vol. 66 (September 1984):23–38.

GANS, HERBERT J. *People and Plans: Essays on Urban Problems and Solutions.* New York: Basic Books, 1968.

GANS, HERBERT J. *Deciding What's News: A Study of CBS Evening News, NBC Nightly News, Newsweek and Time.* New York: Vintage, 1980.

GANS, HERBERT J. *The Urban Villagers: Group and Class in the Life of Italian-Americans.* New York: Free Press, 1982; orig. 1962.

GARFINKEL, HAROLD. "Conditions of Successful Degradation Ceremonies." *American Journal of Sociology.* Vol. 61, No. 2 (March 1956):420–424.

GARFINKEL, HAROLD. *Studies in Ethnomethodology.* Cambridge (UK): Polity Press, 1967.

GEERTZ, CLIFFORD. "Common Sense as a Cultural System." *The Antioch Review.* Vol. 33, No. 1 (Spring 1975):5–26.

GEIST, WILLIAM. *Toward a Safe and Sane Halloween and Other Tales of Suburbia.* New York: Times Books, 1985.

GEORGE, SUSAN. *How the Other Half Dies: The Real Reasons for World Hunger.* Totowa, NJ: Rowman & Allanheld, 1977.

GERSTEL, NAOMI. "Divorce and Stigma." *Social Problems.* Vol. 43, No. 2 (April 1987):172–186.

GESCHWENDER, JAMES A. *Racial Stratification in America.* Dubuque, IA: Wm. C. Brown, 1978.

GIBBONS, DON C. *Delinquent Behavior.* 3rd ed. Englewood Cliffs, NJ: Prentice Hall, 1981.

GIBBONS, DON C., AND MARVIN D. KROHN. *Delinquent Behavior.* 4th ed. Englewood Cliffs, NJ: Prentice Hall, 1986.

GIDDENS, ANTHONY. *Sociology: A Brief but Critical Introduction.* New York: Harcourt Brace Jovanovich, 1982.

GIELE, JANET Z. "Gender and Sex Roles." In Neil J. Smelser, ed., *Handbook of Sociology.* Newbury Park, CA: Sage, 1988:291–323.

GIELE, JANET ZOLLINGER. "Women's Work and Family Roles." In Janet Zollinger Giele, ed., *Women in the Middle Years: Current Knowledge and Directions for Research and Policy.* New York: John Wiley and Sons, 1982:115–150.

GILBERT, ALAN, AND JOSEF GUGLER. *Cities, Poverty, and Development.* New York: Oxford University Press, 1983.

GILBERT, DENNIS, AND JOSEPH A. KAHL. *The American Class Structure: A New Synthesis.* 3rd ed. Homewood, Il: The Dorsey Press, 1987.

GILLIGAN, CAROL. *In a Different Voice: Psychological Theory and Women's Development.* Cambridge, MA: Harvard University Press, 1982.

GIMENEZ, MARTHA E. "Silence in the Classroom: Some Thoughts about Teaching in the 1980s." *Teaching Sociology.* Vol. 17, No. 2 (April 1989):184–191.

GINSBURG, PAUL B. "Market-Oriented Options in Medicare and Medicaid." In Jack B. Meyer, ed., *Market Reforms in Health Care: Current Issues, New Directions, Strategic Decisions.* Washington, DC: American Enterprise Institute for Public Policy Research, 1983:103–118.

GIOVANNINI, MAUREEN. "Female Anthropologist and Male Informant: Gender Conflict in a Sicilian Town." In John J. Macionis and Nijole V. Benokraitis, eds., *Seeing Ourselves: Classic, Contemporary, and Cross-Cultural Readings in Sociology.* Englewood Cliffs, NJ: Prentice Hall, 1989:30–35.

GLADUE, BRIAN A., RICHARD GREEN, AND RONALD E. HELLMAN. "Neuroendocrine Response to Estrogen and Sexual Orientation." *Science.* Vol. 225, No. 4669 (September 28, 1984):1496–1499.

GLAZER, NATHAN, AND DANIEL P. MOYNIHAN. *Beyond the Melting Pot.* 2nd ed. Cambridge, MA: M.I.T. Press, 1970.

GLENN, CHARLES L., AND FRANMARIE KENNEDY-KEEL. "Commentary." *Education Week.* Vol. V, No. 21 (February 5, 1986):21.

GLENN, NORVAL D., AND BETH ANN SHELTON. "Regional Differences in Divorce in the United States." *Journal of Marriage and the Family.* Vol. 47, No. 3 (August 1985):641–652.

GLUCK, PETER R., AND RICHARD J. MEISTER. *Cities in Transition.* New York: New Viewpoints, 1979.

GLUECK, SHELDON, AND ELEANOR GLUECK. *Unraveling Juvenile Delinquency.* New York: Commonwealth Fund, 1950.

GOFFMAN, ERVING. *The Presentation of Self in Everyday Life.* Garden City, NY: Anchor, 1959.

GOFFMAN, ERVING. *Asylums: Essays on the Social Situation of Mental Patients and Other Inmates.* Garden City, NY: Anchor, 1961.

GOFFMAN, ERVING. *Stigma: Notes on the Management of Spoiled Identity.* Englewood Cliffs, NJ: Prentice Hall, 1963.

GOFFMAN, ERVING. *Interactional Ritual: Essays on Face to Face Behavior.* Garden City, NY: Anchor, 1967.

GOFFMAN, ERVING. *Gender Advertisements.* New York: Harper Colophon, 1979.

GOLDBERG, STEVEN. *The Inevitability of Patriarchy.* New York: William Morrow and Co., 1974.

GOLDBERG, STEVEN. Personal communication, 1987.

GOLDFARB, JEFFREY C. *Beyond Glasnost: The Post-Totalitarian Mind.* Chicago: University of Chicago Press, 1989.

GOLDFIELD, MICHAEL. *The Decline of Organized Labor in the United States.* Chicago and London: University of Chicago Press, 1987.

GOLDSBY, RICHARD A. *Race and Races*. 2nd ed. New York: Macmillan, 1977.

GOLDSMITH, H. H. "Genetic Influences on Personality from Infancy." *Child Development*. Vol. 54, No. 2 (April 1983):331–335.

GOODE, WILLIAM J. "The Theoretical Importance of Love." *American Sociological Review*. Vol. 24, No. 1 (February 1959):38–47.

GOODE, WILLIAM J. "Why Men Resist." In Arlene S. Skolnick and Jerome H. Skolnick, eds., *Family in Transition*. 4th ed. Boston, MA: Little, Brown, 1983:201–218.

GORDON, JAMES S. "The Paradigm of Holistic Medicine." In ARTHUR C. HASTINGS ET AL., EDS., *Health for the Whole Person: The Complete Guide to Holistic Medicine*. Boulder, CO: Westview Press, 1980:3–27.

GORDON, MILTON M. *Assimilation in American Life*. New York: Oxford University Press, 1964.

GORING, CHARLES BUCKMAN. *The English Convict: A Statistical Study*. Montclair, NJ: Patterson Smith, 1972; orig. 1913.

GORTMAKER, STEVEN L. "Poverty and Infant Mortality in the United States." *American Journal of Sociology*. Vol. 44, No. 2 (April 1979):280–297.

GOTTMANN, JEAN. *Megalopolis*. New York: Twentieth Century Fund, 1961.

GOUGH, KATHLEEN. "The Origin of the Family." *Journal of Marriage and the Family*. Vol. 33, No. 4 (November 1971):760–771.

GOULDNER, ALVIN. *Enter Plato*. New York: Free Press, 1965.

GOULDNER, ALVIN. "The Sociologist as Partisan: Sociology and the Welfare State." In Larry T. Reynolds and Janice M. Reynolds, eds., *The Sociology of Sociology*. New York: McKay, 1970a:218–255.

GOULDNER, ALVIN. *The Coming Crisis of Western Sociology*. New York: Avon Books, 1970b.

GRANOVETTER, MARK. "The Strength of Weak Ties." *American Journal of Sociology*. Vol. 78, No. 6 (May 1973):1360–1380.

GRANT, KAREN R. "The Inverse Care Law in the Context of Universal Free Health Insurance in Canada: Toward Meeting Health Needs Through Public Policy." *Sociological Focus*. Vol. 17, No. 2 (April 1984):137–155.

GREELEY, ANDREW M. *Why Can't They Be Like Us? America's White Ethnic Groups*. New York: E. P. Dutton, 1971.

GREELEY, ANDREW M. *Ethnicity in the United States: A Preliminary Reconnaissance*. New York: John Wiley, 1974.

GREELEY, ANDREW M. *Religious Change in America*. Cambridge, MA: Harvard University Press, 1989.

GREENBERG, DAVID F. *The Construction of Homosexuality*. Chicago, University of Chicago Press, 1988.

GREER, SCOTT. *Urban Renewal and American Cities*. Indianapolis: Bobbs-Merrill, 1965.

GREGORY, PAUL R., AND ROBERT C. STUART. *Comparative Economic Systems*. 2nd ed. Boston, MA: Houghton Mifflin, 1985.

GRISWOLD, WENDY. "The Fabrication of Meaning: Literary Interpretation in the United States, Great Britain, and the West Indies." *American Journal of Sociology*. Vol. 92, No. 5 (March 1987):1077–1117.

GUPTE, PRANAY. *The Crowded Earth: People and the Politics of Population*. New York: W. W. Norton, 1984.

GWARTNEY-GIBBS, PATRICIA A., JEAN STOCKARD, AND SUSANNE BOHMER. "Learning Courtship Agreession: The Influence of Parents, Peers, and Personal Experiences." *Family Relations*. Vol. 36, No. 3 (July 1987):276–282.

HAAS, LINDA. "Domestic Role Sharing in Sweden." *Journal of Marriage and the Family*. Vol. 43, No. 4 (November 1981):957–967.

HABERMAS, JÜRGEN. *Toward a Rational Society: Student Protest, Science, and Politics*. Jeremy J. Shapiro, trans. Boston, MA: Beacon Press, 1970.

HACKER, HELEN MAYER. "Women as a Minority Group." *Social Forces*. Vol. 30 (October 1951):60–69.

HACKER, HELEN MAYER. "Women as a Minority Group: 20 Years Later." In Florence Denmark, ed., *Who Discriminates Against Women?* Beverly Hills, CA: Sage, 1974:124–134.

HADDEN, JEFFREY K., AND CHARLES E. SWAIN. *Prime Time Preachers: The Rising Power of Televangelism*. Reading, MA: Addison-Wesley, 1981.

HAGAN, JOHN, A. R. GILLIS, AND JOHN SIMPSON. "The Class Structure of Gender and Delinquency: Toward a Power-Control Theory of Common Delinquent Behavior." *American Journal of Sociology*. Vol. 90, No. 6 (May 1985):1151–1178.

HAGAN, JOHN, AND PATRICIA PARKER. "White-Collar Crime and Punishment: The Class Structure and Legal Sanctioning of Securities Violations." *American Sociological Review*. Vol. 50, No. 3 (June 1985):302–316.

HAGAN, JOHN, JOHN SIMPSON, AND A. R. GILLIS. "Class in the Household: A Power-Control Theory of Gender and Delinquency." *American Journal of Sociology*. Vol. 92, No. 4 (January 1987):788–816.

HALBERSTAM, DAVID. *The Reckoning*. New York: Avon, 1986.

HALLINAN, MAUREEN T., AND RICHARD A. WILLIAMS. "Interracial Friendship Choices in Secondary Schools." *American Sociological Review*. Vol. 54, No. 1 (February 1989):67–78.

HAMBLIN, DORA JANE. *The First Cities*. New York: Time-Life, 1973.

HAMMOND, PHILLIP E. "Introduction." In Phillip E. Hammond, ed., *The Sacred in a Secular Age: Toward Revision in the Scientific Study of Religion*. Berkeley, CA: University of California Press, 1985:1–6.

HAMRICK, MICHAEL H., DAVID J. ANSPAUGH, AND GENE EZELL. *Health*. Columbus OH: Merrill, 1986.

HANDLIN, OSCAR. *Boston's Immigrants 1790–1865: A Study in Acculturation*. Cambridge, MA: Harvard University Press, 1941.

HANNAN, MICHAEL T., AND GLENN R. CARROLL. "Dynamics of Formal Political Structure: An Event-History Analysis." *American Sociological Review*. Vol. 46, No. 1 (February 1981):19–35.

HARDOY, JORGE E. "Two Thousand Years of Latin American Urbanization." In Jorge E. Hardoy, ed., *Urbanization in Latin America: Approaches and Issues*. Garden City, NY: Anchor Books, 1975.

HAREVEN, TAMARA K. "The Life Course and Aging in Historical Perspective." In Tamara K. Hareven and Kathleen J. Adams, eds., *Aging and Life Course Transitions: An Interdisciplinary Perspective*. New York: Guilford Press, 1982:1–26.

HARLOW, HARRY F., AND MARGARET KUENNE HARLOW. "Social

Deprivation in Monkeys." *Scientific American.* Vol. 207 (November 1962):137–146.

HARRINGTON, MICHAEL. *The New American Poverty.* New York: Penguin Books, 1984.

HARRIS, CHAUNCEY D., AND EDWARD L. ULLMAN. "The Nature of Cities." *The Annals.* Vol. 242 (November 1945):7–17.

HARRIS, MARVIN. *Cows, Pigs, Wars and Witches: The Riddles of Culture.* New York: Vintage Books, 1975.

HARRIS, MARVIN. "Why Men Dominate Women." *New York Times Magazine* (November 13, 1977):46, 115–123.

HARRIS, MARVIN. *Good to Eat: Riddle of Food and Culture.* New York: Simon and Schuster, 1985.

HARRIS, MARVIN. *Cultural Anthropology.* 2nd ed. New York: Harper & Row, 1987.

HARRISON, PAUL. *Inside the Thrid World: The Anatomy of Poverty.* 2nd ed. New York: Penguin Books, 1984.

HARTMANN, BETSY, AND JAMES BOYCE. *Needless Hunger: Voices from a Bangladesh Village.* San Francisco: Institute for Food and Development Policy, 1982.

HAVILAND, WILLIAM A. *Anthropology.* 4th ed. New York: Holt, Rinehart and Winston, 1985.

HAYNEMAN, STEPHEN P., AND WILLIAM A. LOXLEY. "The Effect of Primary-School Quality on Academic Achievement Across Twenty-nine High- and Low-Income Countries." *American Journal of Sociology.* Vol. 88, No. 6 (May 1983):1162–1194.

HEALTH INSURANCE ASSOCIATION OF AMERICA. *Sourcebook of Health Insurance Data 1989.* Washington, DC, 1989.

HELMUTH, JOHN W. "World Hunger Amidst Plenty." *USA Today.* Vol. 117, No. 2526 (March 1989):48–50.

HENLEY, NANCY, MYKOL HAMILTON, AND BARRIE THORNE. "Womanspeak and Manspeak: Sex Differences in Communication, Verbal and Nonverbal." In John J. Macionis and Nijole V. Benokraitis, eds., *Seeing Ourselves: Classic, Contemporary, and Cross-Cultural Readings in Sociology.* Englewood Cliffs, NJ: Prentice Hall, 1989:105–111.

HERITAGE, JOHN. *Garfinkel and Ethnomethodology.* Cambridge (UK): Polity Press, 1984.

HERMAN, EDWARD S. *Corporate Control, Corporate Power: A Twentieth Century Fund Study.* New York: Cambridge University Press, 1981.

HEWLETT, SYLVIA ANN. *A Lesser Life: The Myth of Women's Liberation in America.* New York: William Morrow, 1986.

HIRSCHI, TRAVIS. *Causes of Delinquency.* Berkeley, CA: University of California Press, 1969.

HIRSCHI, TRAVIS, AND MICHAEL GOTTFREDSON. "Age and the Explanation of Crime." *American Journal of Sociology.* Vol. 89, No. 3 (November 1983):552–584.

HIRSCHMAN, CHARLES, AND MORRISON G. WONG. "Socioeconomic Gains of Asian Americans, Blacks, and Hispanics: 1960–1976." *American Journal of Sociology.* Vol. 90, No. 3 (November 1984):584–607.

HOCHSCHILD, ARLIE, WITH ANNE MACHUNG. *The Second Shift: Working Parents and the Revolution at Home.* New York: Viking, 1989.

HODGE, ROBERT W., DONALD J. TREIMAN, AND PETER H. ROSSI. "A Comparative Study of Occupational Prestige." In Reinhard Bendix and Seymour Martin Lipset, eds., *Class, Status, and Power: Social Stratification in Comparative Perspective.* 2nd ed. New York: Free Press, 1966:309–321.

HOGAN, DENNIS P., AND EVELYN M. KITAGAWA. "The Impact of Social Status and Neighborhood on the Fertility of Black Adolescents." *American Journal of Sociology.* Vol. 90, No. 4 (January 1985):825–855.

HOLLMAN, FREDERICK W. *U.S. Population Estimates, by Age, Sex, Race, and Hispanic Origin: 1989.* Washington, DC: U.S. Government Printing Office, 1990.

HOLT, THOMAS C. "Afro-Americans." In *Harvard Encyclopedia of American Ethnic Groups.* Cambridge, MA: Harvard University Press, 1980:5–23.

HONEYWELL, ROY J. *The Educational Work of Thomas Jefferson.* Cambridge, MA: Harvard University Press, 1931.

HOOK, ERNEST B. "Behavioral Implications of the XYY Genotype." *Science.* Vol. 179 (January 12, 1973):139–150.

HOSTETLER, JOHN A. *Amish Society.* 3rd ed. Baltimore: Johns Hopkins University Press, 1980.

HOUSE OF REPRESENTATIVES. *A.I.D. and Third World Women, the Unmet Potential.* Hearing held May 11, 1988. Washington, DC: U.S. Government Printing Office, 1988.

HOUT, MICHAEL, AND ANDREW M. GREELEY. "The Center Doesn't Hold: Church Attendance in the United States, 1940–1984." *American Sociological Review.* Vol. 52, No. 3 (June 1987):325–345.

HOWLETT, DEBBIE. "Cruzan's Struggle Left Imprint: 10,000 Others in Similar State." *USA Today* (December 27, 1990):3A.

HOYT, HOMER. *The Structure and Growth of Residential Neighborhoods in American Cities.* Washington, DC: Federal Housing Administration, 1939.

HSU, FRANCIS L. K. *The Challenge of the American Dream: The Chinese in the United States.* Belmont, CA: Wadsworth, 1971.

HUBER, JOAN, AND GLENNA SPITZE. "Considering Divorce: An Expansion of Becker's Theory of Marital Instability." *American Journal of Sociology.* Vol. 86, No. 1 (July 1980):75–89.

HUET-COX, ROCIO. "Medical Education: New Wine in Old Wine Skins." In Victor W. Sidel and Ruth Sidel, eds., *Reforming Medicine: Lessons of the Last Quarter Century.* New York: Pantheon Books, 1984:129–149.

HULS, GLENNA. Personal communication, 1987.

HUMPHRIES, HARRY LEROY. *The Structure and Politics of Intermediary Class Positions: An Empirical Examination of Recent Theories of Class.* Unpublished Ph.D. dissertation. Eugene, OR: University of Oregon, 1984.

HUNT, MORTON. *Sexual Behavior in the 1970s.* Chicago: Playboy Press, 1974.

HUNTER, JAMES DAVISON. *American Evangelicalism: Conservative Religion and the Quandary of Modernity.* New Brunswick, NJ: Rutgers University Press, 1983.

HUNTER, JAMES DAVISON. "Conservative Protestantism." In Phillip E. Hammond, ed., *The Sacred in a Secular Age.* Berkeley, CA: University of California Press, 1985:50–66.

HURN, CHRISTOPHER. *The Limits and Possibilities of Schooling.* Boston: Allyn and Bacon, 1978.

HWANG, SEAN-SHONG, STEVEN H. MURDOCK, BANOO PARPIA, AND RITA R. HAMM. "The Effects of Race and Socioeconomic Status on Residential Segregation in Texas, 1970–80." *Social Forces*. Vol. 63, No. 3 (March 1985):732–747.

ILLICH, IVAN. *Medical Nemesis: The Expropriation of Health*. New York: Pantheon Books, 1976.

IRWIN, JOHN. *Prison in Turmoil*. Boston, MA: Little, Brown, 1980.

ISAACSON, WALTER. "O'er the Land of the Free." *Time*. Vol. 134, No. 1 (July 3, 1989):14–15.

ISAY, RICHARD A. *Being Homosexual: Gay Men and Their Development*. New York: Farrar, Straus, Giroux, 1989.

JACOB, JOHN E. "An Overview of Black America in 1985." In James D. Williams, ed., *The State of Black America 1986*. New York: National Urban League, 1986:i-xi.

JACOBS, DAVID. "Inequality and Police Strength." *American Sociological Review*. Vol. 44, No. 6 (December 1979):913–925.

JACOBS, JANE. *The Death and Life of Great American Cities*. New York: Random House, 1961.

JACOBS, JANE. *The Economy of Cities*. New York: Vintage, 1970.

JACOBS, JANE. *Cities and the Wealth of Nations*. New York: Random House, 1984.

JACOBS, JERRY A. "Long-Term Trends in Occupational Segregation by Sex." *American Journal of Sociology*. Vol. 95, No. 1 (July 1989):160–173.

JACOBY, TAMAR. "A Fight for Old Glory." *Newsweek* (July 3, 1989):18–20.

JACQUET, CONSTANT H., JR., ED. *Yearbook of American and Canadian Churches, 1987*. Nashville, TN: Abingdon Press, 1988.

JAEGER, ART, AND ROBERT GREENSTEIN. "Poverty Rate and Household Income Stagnate as Rich-Poor Gap Hits Post-War High." Washington, DC: Center on Budget and Policy Priorities, 1989.

JAGGER, ALISON. "Political Philosophies of Women's Liberation." In Laurel Richardson and Verta Taylor, eds., *Feminist Frontiers: Rethinking Sex, Gender, and Society*. Reading, MA: Addison-Wesley, 1983.

JAMES, DAVID R. "City Limits on Racial Equality: The Effects of City-Suburb Boundaries on Public-School Desegregation, 1968–1976." *American Sociological Review*. Vol. 54, No. 6 (December 1989):963–985.

JANIS, IRVING. *Victims of Groupthink*. Boston, MA: Houghton Mifflin, 1972.

JANIS, IRVING L. *Crucial Decisions: Leadership in Policymaking and Crisis Management*. New York: Free Press, 1989.

JAYNES, GERALD DAVID, AND ROBIN M. WILLIAMS, EDS. *A Common Destiny: Blacks and American Society*. Washington, DC: National Academy Press, 1989.

JENCKS, CHRISTOPHER. "Genes and Crime." *The New York Review* (February 12, 1987):33–41.

JENCKS, CHRISTOPHER, ET AL. *Inequality: A Reassessment of the Effect of Family and Schooling in America*. New York: Basic Books, 1972.

JOHNSON, PAUL. "The Seven Deadly Sins of Terrorism." In Benjamin Netanyahu, ed., *International Terrorism*. New Brunswick, NJ: Transaction Books, 1981:12–22.

JOHNSTON, R. J. "Residential Area Characteristics." In D. T. Herbert and R. J. Johnston, eds., *Social Areas in Cities*. Vol. 1: Spatial Processes and Form. New York: Wiley, 1976:193–235.

JOHNSTONE, RONALD L. *Religion in Society: A Sociology of Religion*. 2nd ed. Englewood Cliffs, NJ: Prentice Hall, 1983.

JOINT ECONOMIC COMMITTEE. *The Concentration of Wealth in the United States: Trends in the Distribution of Wealth Among American Families*. Washington, DC: United States Congress, 1986.

JOSEPHY, ALVIN M., JR. *Now That the Buffalo's Gone: A Study of Today's American Indians*. New York: Alfred A. Knopf, 1982.

KAELBLE, HARTMUT. *Social Mobility in the 19th and 20th Centuries: Europe and America in Comparative Perspective*. New York: St. Martin's Press, 1986.

KAIN, EDWARD L. "A Note on the Integration of AIDS Into the Sociology of Human Sexuality." *Teaching Sociology*. Vol. 15, No. 4 (July 1987):320–323.

KAIN, EDWARD L., AND SHANNON HART. "AIDS and the Family: A Content Analysis of Media Coverage." Presented to National Council on Family Relations, Atlanta, 1987.

KALISH, CAROL B. "International Crime Rates." Bureau of Justice Statistics *Special Report*, May 1988. Washington, DC: U.S. Government Printing Office, 1988.

KALISH, RICHARD A. *Late Adulthood: Perspectives on Human Development*. 2nd ed. Monterey, CA: Brooks/Cole, 1982.

KALMUSS, DEBRA, AND JUDITH A. SELTZER. "Continuity of Marital Behavior in Remarriage: The Case of Spouse Abuse." Unpublished paper. November 1984.

KAMINER, WENDY. "Volunteers: Who Knows What's in It for Them." *Ms.* (December 1984):93–94, 96, 126–128.

KANTER, ROSABETH MOSS. *Men and Women of the Corporation*. New York: Basic Books, 1977.

KANTER, ROSABETH MOSS. *The Change Masters: Innovation and Entrepreneurship in the American Corporation*. New York: Simon and Schuster, 1983.

KANTER, ROSABETH MOSS. "All That Is Entrepreneurial Is Not Gold." *The Wall Street Journal* (July 22, 1985):18.

KANTER, ROSABETH MOSS. *When Giants Learn to Dance: Mastering the Challenges of Strategy, Management, and Careers in the 1990s*. New York: Simon and Schuster, 1989.

KANTER, ROSABETH MOSS, AND BARRY A. STEIN. "The Gender Pioneers: Women in an Industrial Sales Force." In R. M. Kanter and B. A. Stein, eds., *Life in Organizations*. New York: Basic Books, 1979:134–160.

KANTER, ROSABETH MOSS, AND BARRY STEIN. *A Tale of "O": On Being Different in an Organization*. New York: Harper & Row, 1980.

KANTROWITZ, BARBARA. "Mothers on Their Own." *Newsweek* (December 23, 1985):66–67.

KAPLAN, ERIC B., ET AL. "The Usefulness of Preoperative Laboratory Screening." *Journal of the American Medical Association*. Vol. 253, No. 24 (June 28, 1985):3576–3581.

KAPTCHUK, TED. "The Holistic Logic of Chinese Medicine." In Shepard Bliss et al., eds., *The New Holistic Health Handbook*. Lexington, MA: The Steven Greene Press/Penguin Books, 1985:41.

KARP, DAVID A., AND WILLIAM C. YOELS. "The College Classroom: Some Observations on the Meaning of Student Participation." *Sociology and Social Research*. Vol. 60, No. 4 (July 1976):421–439.

KASARDA, JOHN D. "Entry-Level Jobs, Mobility and Urban Minority

Employment." *Urban Affairs Quarterly*. Vol. 19, No. 1 (September 1983):21–40.

KAUFMAN, POLLY WELTS. "Women and Education." In Barbara Haber, ed., *The Women's Annual, 1981: The Year in Review*. Boston, MA: G. K. Hall and Company, 1982:24–55.

KAUFMAN, WALTER. *Religions in Four Dimensions: Existential, Aesthetic, Historical and Comparative*. New York: Reader's Digest Press, 1976.

KELLER, SUZANNE. *The Urban Neighborhood*. New York: Random House, 1968.

KEMP, ALICE ABEL, AND SHELLEY COVERMAN. "Marginal Jobs or Marginal Workers: Identifying Sex Differences in Low-Skill Occupations." *Sociological Focus*. Vol. 22, No. 1 (February 1989):19–37.

KENYON, KATHLEEN. *Digging Up Jericho*. London: Ernest Benn, 1957.

KERCKHOFF, ALAN C., RICHARD T. CAMPBELL, AND IDEE WINFIELD-LAIRD. "Social Mobility in Great Britain and the United States." *American Journal of Sociology*. Vol. 91, No. 2 (September 1985):281–308.

KILBOURNE, BROCK K. "The Conway and Siegelman Claims Against Religious Cults: An Assessment of Their Data." *Journal for the Scientific Study of Religion*. Vol. 22, No. 4 (December 1983):380–385.

KILLIAN, LEWIS M. "Organization, Rationality and Spontaneity in the Civil Rights Movement." *American Sociological Review*. Vol. 49, No. 6 (December 1984):770–783.

KING, KATHLEEN PIKER, AND DENNIS E. CLAYSON. "The Differential Perceptions of Male and Female Deviants." *Sociological Focus*. Vol. 21, No. 2 (April 1988):153–164.

KING, MARTIN LUTHER, JR. "The Montgomery Bus Boycott." In Walt Anderson, ed., *The Age of Protest*. Pacific Palisades, CA: Goodyear, 1969:81–91.

KING, PATRICIA. "When Desegregation Backfires." *Newsweek*. Vol. 144, No. 5 (July 31, 1989):56.

KINSEY, ALFRED, ET AL. *Sexual Behavior in the Human Male*. Philadelphia: W. B. Saunders, 1948.

KINSEY, ALFRED, ET AL. *Sexual Behavior in the Human Female*. Philadelphia: W. B. Saunders, 1953.

KIPP, RITA SMITH. "Have Women Always Been Unequal?" In Beth Reed, ed., *Towards a Feminist Transformation of the Academy: Proceedings of the Fifth Annual Women's Studies Conference*. Ann Arbor, MI: Great Lakes Colleges Association, 1980:12–18.

KITANO, HARRY H. L. "Japanese." In *Harvard Encyclopedia of American Ethnic Groups*. Cambridge, MA: Harvard University Press, 1980:561–571.

KITANO, HARRY H. L. *Race Relations*. 3rd ed. Englewood Cliffs, NJ: Prentice Hall, 1985.

KITSON, GAY C., AND HELEN J. RASCHKE. "Divorce Research: What We Know, What We Need to Know." *Journal of Divorce*. Vol. 4, No. 3 (Spring 1981):1–37.

KITTRIE, NICHOLAS N. *The Right to Be Different: Deviance and Enforced Therapy*. Baltimore, MD: The Johns Hopkins University Press, 1971.

KLEIN, FREDA. "Violence Against Women." In Barbara Haber, ed., *The Women's Annual, 1981: The Year in Review*. Boston, MA: G. K. Hall and Company, 1982:270–302.

KLEIN, SUSAN SHURBERG. "Education." In Sarah M. Pritchard, ed., *The Women's Annual, Number 4, 1983–1984*. Boston, MA: G. K. Hall and Company, 1984:9–30.

KLEUGEL, JAMES R., AND ELIOT R. SMITH. *Beliefs About Inequality: Americans' Views of What Is and What Ought to Be*. New York: Aldine de Gruyter, 1986.

KLUCKHOHN, CLYDE. "As An Anthropologist Views It." In Albert Deuth, ed., *Sex Habits of American Men*. Englewood Cliffs, NJ: Prentice Hall, 1948.

KNAUS, WILLIAM A. *Inside Russian Medicine: An American Doctor's First-Hand Report*. New York: Everest House, 1981.

KNOKE, DAVID, AND RICHARD B. FELSON. "Ethnic Stratification and Political Cleavage in the United States, 1952–1968." *American Journal of Sociology*. Vol. 80, No. 3 (November 1974):630–642.

KOHLBERG, LAWRENCE, AND CAROL GILLIGAN. "The Adolescent as Philosopher: The Discovery of Self in a Postconventional World." *Daedalus*. Vol. 100 (Fall 1971):1051–1086.

KOHN, MELVIN L. *Class and Conformity: A Study in Values*. 2nd ed. Homewood, IL: The Dorsey Press, 1977.

KOMAROVSKY, MIRRA. *Blue Collar Marriage*. New York: Vintage Books, 1967.

KOMAROVSKY, MIRRA. "Cultural Contradictions and Sex Roles: The Masculine Case." *American Journal of Sociology*. Vol. 78, No. 4 (January 1973):873–884.

KOMAROVSKY, MIRRA. *Dilemmas of Masculinity: A Study of College Youth*. New York: W. W. Norton, 1976.

KORNHAUSER, WILLIAM. *The Politics of Mass Society*. New York: Free Press, 1959.

KOZOL, JONATHAN. *Prisoners of Silence: Breaking the Bonds of Adult Illiteracy in the United States*. New York: Continuum, 1980.

KOZOL, JONATHAN. "A Nation's Wealth." *Publisher's Weekly* (May 24, 1985):28–30.

KOZOL, JONATHAN. *Rachel and Her Children: Homeless Families in America*. New York: Crown Publishers, 1988.

KRAMARAE, CHERIS. *Women and Men Speaking*. Rowley, MA: Newbury House, 1981.

KRAMARAE, CHERIS, BARRIE THORNE, AND NANCY HENLEY. "Sex Similarities and Differences in Language, Speech, and Nonverbal Communication: An Annotated Bibliography." In Barrie Thorne, Cheris Kramarae, and Nancy Henley, eds., *Language, Gender and Society*. Cambridge: Newbury House, 1983:150–331.

KRIESI, HANSPETER. "New Social Movements and the New Class in the Netherlands." *American Journal of Sociology*. Vol. 94, No. 5 (March 1989):1078–1116.

KRISBERG, BARRY, AND IRA SCHWARTZ. "Rethinking Juvenile Justice." *Crime and Delinquency*. Vol. 29, No. 3 (July 1983):333–364.

KROC, ELAINE. *Early Estimates, National Higher Education Statistics: Fall 1989*. Washington, DC: National Center for Education Statistics, 1989.

KÜBLER-ROSS, ELISABETH. *On Death and Dying*. New York: Macmillan, 1969.

KUHN, THOMAS. *The Structure of Scientific Revolutions*. 2nd ed. Chicago: University of Chicago Press, 1970.

KURTZ, LESTER R. *The Nuclear Cage: A Sociology of the Arms Race*. Englewood Cliffs, NJ: Prentice Hall, 1988.

KUZNETS, SIMON. "Economic Growth and Income Inequality." *The American Economic Review*. Vol. XLV, No. 1 (March 1955):1–28.

KUZNETS, SIMON, *Modern Economic Growth: Rate, Structure, and Spread*. New Haven, CT: Yale University Press, 1966.

LADD, JOHN. "The Definition of Death and the Right to Die." In John Ladd, ed., *Ethical Issues Relating to Life and Death*. New York: Oxford University Press, 1979:118–145.

LADNER, JOYCE A. "Teenage Pregnancy: The Implications for Black Americans." In James D. Williams, ed., *The State of Black America 1986*. New York: National Urban League, 1986:65–84.

LAI, H. M. "Chinese." In *Harvard Encyclopedia of American Ethnic Groups*. Cambridge MA: Harvard University Press, 1980:217–233.

LAMAR, JACOB V., JR. "Redefining the American Dilemma." *Time*. Vol. 126, No. 19 (November 11, 1985):33, 36.

LAMBERG-KARLOVSKY, C. C., AND MARTHA LAMBERG-KARLOVSKY. "An Early City in Iran." In *Cities: Their Origin, Growth, and Human Impact*. San Francisco: Freeman, 1973:28–37.

LANDERS, ANN. Syndicated column: *The Dallas Morning News* (July 8, 1984):4f.

LANE, DAVID. "Social Stratification and Class." In Erik P. Hoffman and Robbin F. Laird, eds., *The Soviet Polity in the Modern Era*. New York: Aldine, 1984:563–605.

LAPPÉ, FRANCES MOORE, AND JOSEPH COLLINS. *World Hunger: Twelve Myths*. New York: Grove Press/Food First Books, 1986.

LAPPÉ, FRANCES MOORE, JOSEPH COLLINS, AND DAVID KINLEY. *Aid as Obstacle: Twenty Questions about Our Foreign Policy and the Hungry*. San Francisco: Institute for Food and Development Policy, 1981.

LASLETT, BARBARA. "Family Membership, Past and Present." *Social Problems*. Vol. 25, No. 5 (June 1978):476–490.

LASLETT, PETER. *The World We Have Lost: England Before the Industrial Age*. 3rd ed. New York: Charles Scribner's Sons, 1984.

LEACOCK, ELEANOR. "Women's Status in Egalitarian Societies: Implications for Social Evolution." *Current Anthropology*. Vol. 19, No. 2 (June 1978):247–275.

LEAVITT, JUDITH WALZER. "Women and Health in America: An Overview." In Judith Walzer Leavitt, ed., *Women and Health in America*. Madison, WI: University of Wisconsin Press, 1984:3–7.

LEE, BARRETT A., R. S. OROPESA, BARBARA J. METCH, AND AVERY M. GUEST. "Testing the Decline of Community Thesis: Neighborhood Organization in Seattle, 1929 and 1979." *American Journal of Sociology*. Vol. 89, No. 5 (March 1984):1161–1188.

LEERHSEN, CHARLES. "Unite and Conquer." *Newsweek* (February 5, 1990):50–55.

LEMERT, EDWIN M. *Social Pathology*. New York: McGraw-Hill, 1951.

LEMERT, EDWIN M. *Human Deviance, Social Problems, and Social Control*. 2nd ed. Englewood Cliffs, NJ: Prentice Hall, 1972.

LENGERMANN, PATRICIA MADOO, AND RUTH A. WALLACE. *Gender in America: Social Control and Social Change*. Englewood Cliffs, NJ: Prentice Hall, 1985.

LENSKI, GERHARD. *Power and Privilege: A Theory of Social Stratification*. New York: McGraw-Hill, 1966.

LENSKI, GERHARD, AND JEAN LENSKI. *Human Societies: An Introduction to Macrosociology*. 3rd ed. New York: McGraw-Hill, 1978; also 4th ed., 1982; also 5th ed., 1987.

LEONARD, EILEEN B. *Women, Crime, and Society: A Critique of Theoretical Criminology*. New York: Longman, 1982.

LESLIE, GERALD R., AND SHEILA K. KORMAN. *The Family in Social Context*. 7th ed. New York: Oxford University Press, 1989.

LESTER, DAVID. *The Death Penalty: Issues and Answers*. Springfield, IL: Charles C. Thomas, 1987.

LEVER, JANET. "Sex Differences in the Complexity of Children's Play and Games." *American Sociological Review*. Vol. 43, No. 4 (August 1978):471–483.

LEVINSON, DANIEL J., WITH CHARLOTTE N. DARROW, EDWARD B. KLEIN, MARIA H. LEVINSON, AND BRAXTON MCKEE. *The Seasons of a Man's Life*. New York: Alfred A. Knopf, 1978.

LEVITAN, SAR A., AND ISAAC SHAPIRO. *Working but Poor: America's Contradiction*. Baltimore, MD: Johns Hopkins University Press, 1987.

LEVY, FRANK. *Dollars and Dreams: The Changing American Income Distribution*. New York: Russell Sage Foundation, 1987.

LEWIS, FLORA. "The Roots of Revolution." *The New York Times Magazine* (November 11, 1984):70–71, 74, 77–78, 82, 84, 86.

LEWIS, OSCAR. *The Children of Sachez*. New York: Random House, 1961.

LEWONTIN, R. C., STEVEN ROSE, AND LEON J. KAMIN. *Not In Our Genes: Biology, Ideology, and Human Nature*. New York: Pantheon, 1984.

LIAZOS, ALEXANDER. "The Poverty of the Sociology of Deviance: Nuts, Sluts and Preverts." *Social Problems*. Vol. 20, No. 1 (Summer 1972):103–120.

LICHTER, DANIEL R. "Race, Employment Hardship, and Inequality in the American Nonmetropolitan South." *American Sociological Review*. Vol. 54, No. 3 (June 1989):436–446.

LIEBERSON, STANLEY. *A Piece of the Pie: Black and White Immigrants Since 1880*. Berkeley, CA: University of California Press, 1980.

LIEBOW, ELLIOT. *Tally's Corner*. Boston, MA: Little, Brown, 1967.

LIN, NAN, WALTER M. ENSEL, AND JOHN C. VAUGHN. "Social Resources and Strength of Ties: Structural Factors in Occupational Status Attainment." *American Sociological Review*. Vol. 46, No. 4 (August 1981):393–405.

LING, PYAU. "Causes of Chinese Emigration." In Amy Tachiki et al., eds., *Roots: An Asian American Reader*. Los Angeles, CA: UCLA Asian American Studies Center, 1971:134–138.

LINK, BURCE G., FRANCIS T. CULLIN, JAMES FRANK, AND JOHN F. WOZNIAK. "The Social Rejection of Former Mental Patients: Understanding Why Labels Matter." *American Journal of Sociology*. Vol. 92, No. 6 (May 1987):1461–1500.

LINTON, RALPH. "One Hundred Percent American." *The American Mercury*. Vol. 40, No. 160 (April 1937):427–429.

LINTON, RALPH. *The Study of Man*. New York: D. Appleton-Century, 1937.

LIPSET, SEYMOUR MARTIN, AND REINHARD BENDIX. *Social Mobility in Industrial Society*. Berkeley, CA: University of California Press, 1967.

LIPSET, SEYMOUR MARTIN, MARTIN TROW, AND JAMES COLEMAN.

Union Democracy: The Inside of the International Typographical Union. New York: Free Press, 1977; orig. 1956.

LISKA, ALLEN E. *Perspectives on Deviance.* 2nd ed. Englewood Cliffs, NJ: Prentice Hall, 1987.

LISKA, ALLEN E., AND MARK TAUSIG. "Theoretical Interpretations of Social Class and Racial Differentials in Legal Decision Making for Juveniles." *Sociological Quarterly.* Vol. 20, No. 2 (Spring 1979):197–207.

LITMAN, MARK S. "Poverty in the 1980s: Are the Poor Getting Poorer?" *Monthly Labor Review.* Vol. 112, No. 6 (June 1989):13–18.

LOGAN, JOHN R., AND MARK SCHNEIDER. "Racial Segregation and Racial Change in American Suburbs, 1970–1980." *American Journal of Sociology.* Vol. 89, No. 4 (January 1984):874–888.

LOGAN, RAYFORD W. "Charles Richard Drew." In Rayford W. Logan and Michael R. Winson, eds., *Dictionary of American Negro Biography.* New York: W. W. Norton, 1982:190–192.

LONDON, BRUCE. "Structural Determinants of Third World Urban Change: An Ecological and Political Economic Analysis." *American Sociological Review.* Vol. 52, No. 1 (February 1987):28–43.

LONG, EDWARD V. *The Intruders: The Invasion of Privacy by Government and Industry.* New York: Frederick A. Praeger, 1967.

LORD, WALTER. *A Night to Remember.* Rev. ed. New York: Holt, Rinehart and Winston, 1976.

LORENZ, KONRAD. *On Aggression.* New York: Harcourt, Brace and World, 1966.

LOW, W. AUGUSTUS, AND VIRGIL A. CLIFT. "Charles Richard Drew." *Encyclopedia of Black America.* New York: McGraw-Hill, 1981:325–326.

LOY, PAMELA HEWITT, AND LEA P. STEWART. "The Extent and Effects of Sexual Harassment of Working Women." *Sociological Focus.* Vol. 17, No. 1 (January 1984):31–43.

LUBENOW, GERALD C. "A Troubling Family Affair." *Newsweek* (May 14, 1984):34.

LYND, ROBERT S. *Knowledge for What? The Place of Social Science in American Culture.* Princeton, NJ: Princeton University Press, 1967.

LYND, ROBERT S., AND HELEN MERRELL LYND. *Middletown in Transition.* New York: Harcourt, Brace & World, 1937.

MACCOBY, ELEANOR EMMONS, AND CAROL NAGY JACKLIN. *The Psychology of Sex Differences.* Palo Alto, CA: Stanford University Press, 1974.

MACE, DAVID, AND VERA MACE. *Marriage East and West.* Garden City, NY: Doubleday (Dolphin), 1960.

MACIONIS, JOHN J. "Intimacy: Structure and Process in Interpersonal Relationships." *Alternative Lifestyles.* Vol. 1, No. 1 (February 1978):113–130.

MACIONIS, JOHN J. "The Search for Community in Modern Society: An Interpretation." *Qualitative Sociology.* Vol. 1, No. 2 (September 1978):130–143.

MACIONIS, JOHN J. "A Sociological Analysis of Humor." Presentation to the Texas Junior College Teachers Association, Houston, 1987.

MACKAY, DONALD G. "Prescriptive Grammar and the Pronoun Problem." In Barrie Thorne, Cheris Kramarae, and Nancy Henley, eds., *Language, Gender and Society.* Cambridge: Newbury House, 1983:38–53.

MADSEN, AXEL. *Private Power: Multinational Corporations for the Survival of Our Planet.* New York: William Morrow, 1980.

MAJOR, BRENDA. "Gender Patterns in Touching Behavior." In Clara Mayo and Nancy M. Henley, eds., *Gender and Nonverbal Behavior.* New York: Springer Verlag, 1981:15–37.

MALTHUS, THOMAS ROBERT. *First Essay on Population 1798.* London: Macmillan, 1926; orig. 1798.

MANGAN, J. A., AND ROBERTA J. PARK. *From Fair Sex to Feminism: Sport and the Socialization of Women.* London: Frank Cass, 1987.

MARCUSE, HERBERT. *One-Dimensional Man.* Boston, MA: Beacon Press, 1964.

MARLIOS, PETER. "Interlocking Directorates and the Control of Corporations: The Theory of Bank Control." *Social Science Quarterly.* Vol. 56, No. 3 (December 1975):425–439.

MARSDEN, PETER. "Core Discussion Networks of Americans." *American Sociological Review.* Vol. 52, No. 1 (February 1987): 122–131.

MARSHALL, SUSAN E. "Ladies Against Women: Mobilization Dilemmas of Antifeminist Movements." *Social Problems.* Vol. 32, No. 4 (April 1985):348–362.

MARTIN, WILLIAM. "The Birth of a Media Myth." *The Atlantic.* Vol. 247, No. 6 (June 1981):7, 10, 11, 16.

MARULLO, SAM. "The Functions and Dysfunctions of Preparations for Fighting Nuclear War." *Sociological Focus.* Vol. 20, No. 2 (April 1987):135–153.

MARX, KARL. *Karl Marx: Selected Writings in Sociology and Social Philosophy.* T. B. Bottomore, trans. New York: McGraw-Hill, 1964.

MARX, KARL. *Capital.* Friedrich Engels, ed. New York: International Publishers, 1967; orig. 1867.

MARX, KARL. "Theses on Feuer." In Robert C. Tucker, ed., *The Marx-Engels Reader.* New York: W. W. Norton, 1972:107–109; orig. 1845.

MARX, KARL, AND FRIEDRICH ENGELS. "Manifesto of the Communist Party." In Robert C. Tucker, ed., *The Marx-Engels Reader.* New York: W. W. Norton, 1972:331–362; orig. 1848.

MARX, KARL, AND FRIEDRICH ENGELS. *The Marx-Engels Reader,* 2nd ed. Robert C. Tucker, ed. New York: W. W. Norton, 1977.

MASHEK, JOHN W., AND PATRICIA AVERY. "Women Politicians Take Off the White Gloves." *U.S. News and World Report* (August 15, 1983):41–42.

MASSEY, DOUGLAS S., AND NANCY A. DENTON. "Hypersegregation in U.S. Metropolitan Areas: Black and Hispanic Segregation Along Five Dimensions." *Demography.* Vol. 26, No. 3 (August 1989):373–391.

MASTERS, WILLIAM H., VIRGINIA E. JOHNSON, AND ROBERT C. KOLODNY. *Human Sexuality.* 3rd ed. Glenview, IL: Scott, Foresman/Little, Brown, 1988.

MATTHEWS, MERVYN. "Long Term Trends in Soviet Education." In J. J. Tomiak, ed., *Soviet Education in the 1980s.* London: Croom Helm, 1983:1–23.

MATTHIESSEN, PETER. *In the Spirit of Crazy Horse.* New York: Viking Press, 1983.

MATTHIESSEN, PETER. *Indian Country*. New York: Viking Press, 1984.

MAURO, TONY. "Cruzan's Struggle Left Imprint: Private Case Triggered Public Debate." *USA Today* (December 27, 1990):3A.

MAYO, KATHERINE. *Mother India*. New York: Harcourt, Brace and Co., 1927.

MCADAM, DOUG, JOHN D. MCCARTHY, AND MAYER N. ZALD. "Social Movements." In Neil J. Smelser, ed., *Handbook of Sociology*. Newbury Park, CA: Sage, 1988:695–737.

MCCARTHY, JOHN D., AND MAYER N. ZALD. "Resource Mobilization and Social Movements: A Partial Theory." *American Journal of Sociology*. Vol. 82, No. 6 (May 1977):1212–1241.

MCGLEN, NANCY E., AND KAREN O'CONNOR. *Women's Rights: The Struggle for Equality in the Nineteenth and Twentieth Centuries*. New York: Praeger Publishers, 1983.

MCGUIRE, MEREDITH B. *Religion: The Social Context*. 2nd ed. Belmont, CA: Wadsworth, 1987.

MCKUSICK, LEON, ET AL. "Reported Changes in the Sexual Behavior of Men at Risk for AIDS, San Francisco, 1982–84—The AIDS Behavioral Research Project." *Public Health Reports*. Vol. 100, No. 6 (November-December 1985):622–629.

MCLANAHAN, SARA. "Family Structure and the Reproduction of Poverty." *American Journal of Sociology*. Vol. 90, No. 4 (January 1985):873–901.

MCRAE, SUSAN. *Cross-Class Families: A Study of Wives' Occupational Superiority*. New York: Oxford University Press, 1986.

MCROBERTS, HUGH A., AND KEVIN SELBEE. "Trends in Occupational Mobility in Canada and the United States: A Comparison." *American Sociological Review*. Vol. 46, No. 4 (August 1981):406–421.

MEAD, GEORGE HERBERT. *Mind, Self, and Society*. Charles W. Morris, ed. Chicago: University of Chicago Press, 1962; orig. 1934.

MEAD, MARGARET. *Sex and Temperament in Three Primitive Societies*. New York: William Morrow, 1963; orig. 1935.

MECHANIC, DAVID. *Medical Sociology*. 2nd ed. New York: Free Press, 1978.

MELTZER, BERNARD N. "Mead's Social Psychology." In Jerome G. Manis and Bernard N. Meltzer, eds., *Symbolic Interaction: A Reader in Social Psychology*. 2nd ed. Boston, MA: Allyn & Bacon, 1977:15–27; also 3rd ed., 1978.

MELUCCI, ALBERTO. "The New Social Movements: A Theoretical Approach." *Social Science Information*. Vol. 19, No. 2 (May 1980):199–226.

MELUCCI, ALBERTO. *Nomads of the Present: Social Movements and Individual Needs in Contemporary Society*. Philadelphia: Temple University Press, 1989.

MELVILLE, KEITH. *Marriage and Family Today*. 3rd ed. New York: Random House, 1983.

MERTON, ROBERT K. "Social Structure and Anomie." *American Sociological Review*. Vol. 3, No. 6 (October 1938):672–682.

MERTON, ROBERT K. *Social Theory and Social Structure*. New York: Free Press, 1968.

MERTON, ROBERT K. "Discrimination and the American Creed." In *Sociological Ambivalence and Other Essays*. New York: The Free Press, 1976:189–216.

MESSNER, STEVEN R. "Economic Discrimination and Societal Homicide Rates: Further Evidence of the Cost of Inequality." *American Sociological Review*. Vol. 54, No. 4 (August 1989):597–611.

MICHELS, ROBERT. *Political Parties*. Glencoe, IL: Free Press, 1949; orig. 1911.

MILGRAM, STANLEY. "Behavioral Study of Obedience." *Journal of Abnormal and Social Psychology*. Vol. 67, No. 4 (1963):371–378.

MILGRAM, STANLEY. "Group Pressure and Action Against a Person." *Journal of Abnormal and Social Psychology*. Vol. 69, No. 2 (August 1964):137–143.

MILGRAM, STANLEY. "Some Conditions of Obedience and Disobedience to Authority." *Human Relations*. Vol. 18 (February 1965):57–76.

MILIBAND, RALPH. *The State in Capitalist Society*. London: Weidenfield and Nicolson, 1969.

MILLER, ARTHUR G. *The Obedience Experiments: A Case of Controversy in Social Science*. New York: Praeger, 1986.

MILLER, FREDERICK D. "The End of SDS and the Emergence of Weatherman: Demise Through Success." In Jo Freeman, ed., *Social Movements of the Sixties and Seventies*. New York: Longman, 1983:279–297.

MILLER, WALTER B. "Lower Class Culture as a Generating Milieu of Gang Delinquency." In Marvin E. Wolfgang, Leonard Savitz, and Norman Johnston, eds., *The Sociology of Crime and Delinquency*. 2nd ed. New York: John Wiley, 1970:351–363; orig. 1958.

MILLET, KATE. *Sexual Politics*. Garden City, NY: Doubleday, 1970.

MILLS, C. WRIGHT. *The Power Elite*. New York: Oxford University Press, 1956.

MILLS, C. WRIGHT. *The Causes of World War Three*. New York: Simon and Schuster, 1958.

MILLS, C. WRIGHT. *The Sociological Imagination*. New York: Oxford University Press, 1959.

MINTZ, BETH, AND MICHAEL SCHWARTZ. "Interlocking Directorates and Interest Group Formation." *American Sociological Review*. Vol. 46, No. 6 (December 1981):851–869.

MIROWSKY, JOHN. "The Psycho-Economics of Feeling Underpaid: Distributive Justice and the Earnings of Husbands and Wives." *American Journal of Sociology*. Vol. 92, No. 6 (May 1987):1404–1434.

MOLNAR, STEPHEN. *Human Variation: Races, Types, and Ethnic Groups*. 2nd ed. Englewood Cliffs, NJ: Prentice Hall, 1983.

MOLOTCH, HARVEY. "The City as a Growth Machine." *American Journal of Sociology*. Vol. 82, No. 2 (September 1976):309–333.

MOLOTCH, HARVEY L., AND DEIRDRE BODEN. "Talking Social Structure: Discourse, Domination, and the Watergate Hearings." *American Sociological Review*. Vol. 50, No. 3 (June 1985):273–288.

MONTAGUE, ASHLEY. *The Nature of Human Aggression*. New York: Oxford University Press, 1976.

MOORE, JOAN, AND HARRY PACHON. *Hispanics in the United States*. Englewood Cliffs, NJ: Prentice Hall, 1985.

MOORE, WILBERT E. "Modernization as Rationalization: Processes and Restraints." In Manning Nash, ed., *Essays on Economic Development and Cultural Change in Honor of Bert F. Hoselitz*. Chicago: University of Chicago Press, 1977:29–42.

MOORE, WILBERT E. *World Modernization: The Limits of Convergence.* New York: Elsevier, 1979.

MORAN, JOHN S., S. O. ARAL, W. C. JENKINS, T. A. PETERMAN, AND E. R. ALEXANDER. "The Impact of Sexually Transmitted Diseases on Minority Populations." *Public Health Reports.* Vol. 104, No. 6 (November-December 1989):560–565.

Morbidity and Mortality Weekly Report. "Abortion Surveillance: Preliminary Analysis—United States, 1986 and 1987." Vol. 38, No. 38 (September 29, 1989):662.

MULLER, THOMAS, AND THOMAS J. ESPENSHADE. *The Fourth Wave: California's Newest Immigrants.* Washington, DC: The Urban Institute Press, 1985.

MUMFORD, LEWIS. *The City in History: Its Origins, Its Transformations, and Its Prospects.* New York: Harcourt, Brace & World, 1961.

MURDOCK, GEORGE P. "Comparative Data on the Division of Labor by Sex." *Social Forces.* Vol. 15, No. 4 (May 1937):551–553.

MURDOCK, GEORGE P. "The Common Denominator of Cultures." In Ralph Linton, ed., *The Science of Man in World Crisis.* New York: Columbia University Press, 1945:123–142.

MURDOCK, GEORGE PETER. *Social Structure.* New York: Free Press, 1965; orig. 1949.

MURPHY, ROBERT F. *An Overture to Social Anthropology.* Englewood Cliffs, NJ: Prentice Hall, 1979.

MURRAY, PAULI. *Proud Shoes: The History of an American Family.* New York: Harper & Row, 1978.

MYERS, DAVID G. *Psychology.* New York: Worth, 1986.

MYERS, SHEILA, AND HAROLD G. GRASMICK. "The Social Rights and Responsibilities of Pregnant Women: An Application of Parsons' Sick Role Model." Paper presented to Southwestern Sociological Association, Little Rock, Arkansas, March 1989.

MYRDAL, GUNNAR. *An American Dilemma: The Negro Problem and Modern Democracy.* New York: Harper and Brothers, 1944.

NATIONAL CENTER FOR HEALTH STATISTICS. Press release. Washington, DC, 1990.

NATIONAL COMMISSION ON EXCELLENCE IN EDUCATION. *A Nation at Risk.* Washington, DC: U.S. Government Printing Office, 1983.

NAVARRO, VICENTE. "The Industrialization of Fetishism or the Fetishism of Industrialization: A Critique of Ivan Illich." In Vicente Navarro, ed., *Health and Medical Care in the U.S.: A Critical Analysis.* Farmingdale, NY: Baywood Publishing Co., 1977:38–58.

NEIDERT, LISA J., AND REYNOLDS FARLEY. "Assimilation in the United States: An Analysis of Ethnic and Generation Differences in Status and Achievement." *American Sociological Review.* Vol. 50, No. 6 (December 1985):840–850.

NEUHOUSER, KEVIN. "The Radicalization of the Brazilian Catholic Church in Comparative Perspective." *American Sociological Review.* Vol. 54, No. 2 (April 1989):233–244.

NEWMAN, JAMES L., AND GORDON E. MATZKE. *Population: Patterns, Dynamics, and Prospects.* Englewood Cliffs, NJ: Prentice Hall, 1984.

NEWMAN, WILLIAM M. *American Pluralism: A Study of Minority Groups and Social Theory.* New York: Harper & Row, 1973.

NISBET, ROBERT. "Sociology as an Art Form." In *Tradition and Revolt: Historical and Sociological Essays.* New York: Vintage Books, 1970.

NISBET, ROBERT A. *The Sociological Tradition.* New York: Basic Books, 1966.

NISBET, ROBERT A. *The Quest for Community.* New York: Oxford University Press, 1969.

N.O.R.C. *General Social Surveys, 1972–1983: Cumulative Codebook.* Chicago: National Opinion Research Center, 1983.

N.O.R.C. *General Social Surveys, 1972–1987: Cumulative Codebook.* Chicago: National Opinion Research Center, 1987.

N.O.R.C. *General Social Surveys, 1972–1987: Cumulative Codebook.* Chicago: National Opinion Research Center, 1989.

NUNN, CLYDE Z., HARRY J. CROCKETT, JR., AND J. ALLEN WILLIAMS, JR. *Tolerance for Nonconformity.* San Francisco, CA: Jossey-Bass Publishers, 1978.

OAKES, JEANNIE. "Classroom Social Relationships: Exploring the Bowles and Gintis Hypothesis." *Sociology of Education.* Vol. 55, No. 4 (October 1982):197–212.

OAKES, JEANNIE. *Keeping Track: How High Schools Structure Inequality.* New Haven, CT: Yale University Press, 1985.

O'DEA, THOMAS F., AND JANET O'DEA AVIAD. *The Sociology of Religion.* 2nd ed. Englewood Cliffs, NJ: Prentice Hall, 1983.

OFFIR, CAROLE WADE. *Human Sexuality.* New York: Harcourt Brace Jovanovich, 1982.

OGBURN, WILLIAM F. *On Culture and Social Change.* Chicago: University of Chicago Press, 1964.

O'HARE, WILLIAM. "In the Black." *American Demographics.* Vol. 11, No. 11 (November 1989):25–29.

OKIMOTO, DANIEL. "The Intolerance of Success." In Amy Tachiki et al., eds., *Roots: An Asian American Reader.* Los Angeles, CA: UCLA Asian American Studies Center, 1971:14–19.

OLZAK, SUSAN. "Labor Unrest, Immigration, and Ethnic Conflict in Urban America, 1880–1914." *American Journal of Sociology.* Vol. 94, No. 6 (May 1989):1303–1333.

OSTLING, RICHARD N. "Technology and the Womb." *Time.* Vol. 129, No. 12 (March 23, 1987):58–59.

OSTRANDER, SUSAN A. "Upper Class Women: The Feminine Side of Privilege." *Qualitative Sociology.* Vol. 3, No. 1 (Spring 1980):23–44.

OSTRANDER, SUSAN A. *Women of the Upper Class.* Philadelphia, PA: Temple University Press, 1984.

OUCHI, WILLIAM. *Theory Z: How American Business Can Meet the Japanese Challenge.* Reading, MA: Addison-Wesley, 1981.

OWEN, DAVID. *None of the Above: Behind the Myth of Scholastic Aptitude.* Boston, MA: Houghton Mifflin, 1985.

PAMPEL, FRED C., KENNETH C. LAND, AND MARCUS FELSON. "A Social Indicator Model of Changes in the Occupational Structure of the United States: 1947–1974." *American Sociological Review.* Vol. 42, No. 6 (December 1977):951–964.

PARCEL, TOBY L., CHARLES W. MUELLER, AND STEVEN CUVELIER. "Comparable Worth and Occupational Labor Market: Explanations of Occupational Earnings Differentials." Paper presented to the American Sociological Association, New York, 1986.

PARKINSON, C. NORTHCOTE. *Parkinson's Law and Other Studies in Administration.* New York: Ballantine Books, 1957.

Parsons, Talcott. *Essays in Sociological Theory.* New York: Free Press, 1954.

Parsons, Talcott. *The Social System.* New York: Free Press, 1964; orig. 1951.

Parsons, Talcott. *Societies: Evolutionary and Comparative Perspectives.* Englewood Cliffs, NJ: Prentice Hall, 1966.

Parsons, Talcott, and Robert F. Bales, eds. *Family, Socialization and Interaction Process.* New York: Free Press, 1955.

Patchen, Martin. "The Escalation of Inter-Nation Conflicts." *Sociological Focus.* Vol. 20, No. 2 (April 1987):95–110.

Pear, Robert. "Women Reduce Lag in Earnings, But Disparities With Men Remain." *The New York Times* (September 4, 1987):1, 7.

Perez, Lisandro. "Cubans." In *Harvard Encyclopedia of American Ethnic Groups.* Cambridge, MA: Harvard University Press, 1980: 256–260.

Persell, Caroline Hodges. *Education and Inequality: A Theoretical and Empirical Synthesis.* New York: Free Press, 1977.

Pescosolido, Bernice A., and Sharon Georgianna. "Durkheim, Suicide, and Religion: Toward a Network Theory of Suicide." *American Sociological Review.* Vol. 54, No. 1 (February 1989):33–48.

Peter, Laurence J., and Raymond Hull. *The Peter Principle: Why Things Always Go Wrong.* New York: William Morrow, 1969.

Peters, Thomas J., and Robert H. Waterman, Jr. *In Search of Excellence: Lessons From America's Best-Run Companies.* New York: Warner Books, 1982.

Physicians' Task Force On Hunger In America. "Hunger Reaches Blue-Collar America." Report issued 1987.

Pines, Maya. "The Civilization of Genie." *Psychology Today.* Vol. 15 (September 1981):28–34.

Piotrow, Phyllis T. *World Population: The Present and Future Crisis.* Headline Series 251 (October 1980). New York: Foreign Policy Association.

Pirandello, Luigi. "The Pleasure of Honesty." In *To Clothe the Naked and Two Other Plays.* New York: Dutton, 1962:143–198.

Piven, Frances Fox, and Richard A. Cloward. *Poor People's Movements: Why They Succeed, How They Fail.* New York: Pantheon, 1977.

Piven, Frances Fox, and Richard A. Cloward. *Why Americans Don't Vote.* New York: Pantheon, 1988.

Plomin, Robert, and Terryl T. Foch. "A Twin Study of Objectively Assessed Personality in Childhood." *Journal of Personality and Sociology Psychology.* Vol. 39, No. 4 (October 1980):680–688.

Polenberg, Richard. *One Nation Divisible: Class, Race, and Ethnicity in the United States Since 1938.* New York: Pelican Books, 1980.

Polsby, Nelson W. "Three Problems in the Analysis of Community Power." *American Sociological Review.* Vol. 24, No. 6 (December 1959):796–803.

Pomer, Marshall I. "Labor Market Structure, Intragenerational Mobility, and Discrimination: Black Male Advancement Out of Low-Paying Occupations, 1962–1973." *American Sociological Review.* Vol. 51, No. 5 (October 1986):650–659.

Portes, Alejandro. "The Rise of Ethnicity: Determinants of Ethnic Perceptions Among Cuban Exiles in Miami." *American Sociological Review.* Vol. 49, No. 3 (June 1984):383–397.

Portes, Alejandro, and Leif Jensen. "The Enclave and the Entrants: Patterns of Ethnic Enterprise in Miami Before and After Mariel." *American Sociological Review.* Vol. 54, No. 6 (December 1989):929–949.

Powell, Chris, and George E. C. Paton, eds. *Humour in Society: Resistance and Control.* New York: St. Martin's Press, 1988.

Queenan, Joe. "The Many Paths to Riches." *Forbes.* Vol. 144, No. 9 (October 23, 1989):149.

Quinney, Richard. *Class, State and Crime: On the Theory and Practice of Criminal Justice.* New York: David McKay, 1977.

Radin, Norma. "Primary Caregiving and Role-Sharing Fathers." In Michael E. Lamb, ed., *Nontraditional Families: Parenting and Child Development.* Hillsdale, NJ: Lawrence Erlbaum Associates, 1982:173–204.

Randall, Vicki. *Women and Politics.* London: Macmillan Press, 1982.

Raphael, Ray. *The Men from the Boys: Rites of Passage in Male America.* Lincoln and London: University of Nebraska Press, 1988.

Reckless, Walter C. "Containment Theory." In Marvin E. Wolfgang, Leonard Savitz, and Norman Johnstone, eds., *The Sociology of Crime and Delinquenc;.* 2nd ed. New York: John Wiley, 1970:401–405.

Reckless, Walter C., and Simon Dinitz. "Pioneering with Self-Concept as a Vulnerability Factor in Delinquency." *Journal of Criminal Law, Criminology, and Police Science.* Vol. 58, No. 4 (December 1967):515–523.

Reed, Rodney J. "Administrator's Advice: Causes and Remedies of School Conflict and Violence." *National Association of Secondary School Principals Bulletin.* Vol. 67, No. 462 (April 1983):75–79.

Reich, Robert B. "As the World Turns." *The New Republic* (May 1, 1989):23, 26–28.

Reid, Sue Titus. *Crime and Criminology.* 3rd ed. New York: Holt, Rinehart and Winston, 1982.

Reiman, Jeffrey. *The Rich Get Richer and the Poor Get Prison: Ideology, Class, and Criminal Justice.* 3rd ed. New York: Macmillan, 1990.

Reiman, Jeffrey H. *The Rich Get Richer and the Poor Get Prison: Ideology, Class, and Criminal Justice.* 2nd ed. New York: John Wiley & Sons, 1984.

Reimers, Cordelia W. "Sources of the Family Income Differentials Among Hispanics, Blacks, and White Non-Hispanics." *American Journal of Sociology.* Vol. 89, No. 4 (January 1984):889–903.

Remoff, Heather Trexler. *Sexual Choice: A Woman's Decision.* New York: Dutton/Lewis, 1984.

Ridgeway, Cecilia, and David Diekema. "Dominance and Collective Hierarchy Formation in Male and Female Task Groups." *American Sociological Review.* Vol. 54, No. 1 (February 1989):79–93.

Ridgeway, Cecilia L. *The Dynamics of Small Groups.* New York: St. Martin's Press, 1983.

Riesman, David. *The Lonely Crowd: A Study of the Changing American Character.* New Haven, CT: Yale University Press, 1970; orig. 1950.

RILEY, MATILDA WHITE, ANNE FONER, AND JOAN WARING. "Sociology of Age." In Neil J. Smelser, ed., *Handbook of Sociology*. Newbury Park, CA: Sage Publications, 1988:243–290.

RITZER, GEORGE. *Man and His Work: Conflict and Change*. New York: Appleton-Century-Crofts, 1972.

ROBERTS, J. DEOTIS. *Roots of a Black Future: Family and Church*. Philadelphia, PA: The Westminster Press, 1980.

ROBINSON, VERA M. "Humor and Health." In Paul E. McGhee and Jeffrey H. Goldstein, eds., *Handbook of Humor Research, Vol II, Applied Studies*. New York: Springer-Verlag, 1983:109–128.

ROESCH, ROBERTA. "Violent Families." *Parents*. Vol. 59, No. 9 (September 1984):74–76, 150–152.

ROETHLISBERGER, F. J., AND WILLIAM J. DICKSON. *Management and the Worker*. Cambridge, MA: Harvard University Press, 1939.

ROHLEN, THOMAS P. *Japan's High Schools*. Berkeley, CA: University of California Press, 1983.

ROOF, WADE CLARK. "Socioeconomic Differentials Among White Socioreligious Groups in the United States." *Social Forces*. Vol. 58, No. 1 (September 1979):280–289.

ROOF, WADE CLARK. "Unresolved Issues in the Study of Religion and the National Elite: Response to Greeley." *Social Forces*. Vol. 59, No. 3 (March 1981):831–836.

ROOS, PATRICIA. "Marriage and Women's Occupational Attainment in Cross-Cultural Perspective." *American Sociological Review*. Vol. 48, No. 6 (December 1983):852–864.

ROPER ORGANIZATION. *The Virginia Slims American Women's Public Opinion Poll*. New York, 1974.

ROSEN, ELLEN ISRAEL. *Bitter Choices: Blue-Collar Women in and out of Work*. Chicago: University of Chicago Press, 1987.

ROSENBAUM, RON. "A Tangled Web for the Supreme Court." *The New York Times Magazine* (March 12, 1989):60.

ROSENTHAL, JACK. "The Rapid Growth of Suburban Employment." In Lois H. Masotti and Jeffrey K. Hadden, eds. *Suburbia in Transition*. New York: New York Times Books, 1974:95–100.

ROSKIN, MICHAEL G. *Countries and Concepts: An Introduction to Comparative Politics*. Englewood Cliffs, NJ: Prentice Hall, 1982.

ROSS, SUSAN. "Education: A Step Ladder to Mobility." *Popline*. Vol. 7, No. 7 (July 1985):1–2.

ROSSI, ALICE S. "Gender and Parenthood." In Alice S. Rossi, ed., *Gender and the Life Course*. New York: Aldine, 1985:161–191.

ROSSIDES, DANIEL W. *Social Stratification: The American Class System in Comparative Perspective*. Englewood Cliffs, NJ: Prentice Hall, 1990.

ROSTOW, WALT W. *The World Economy: History and Prospect*. Austin, TX: University of Texas Press, 1978.

ROWE, DAVID C. "Biometrical Genetic Models of Self-Reported Delinquent Behavior: A Twin Study." *Behavior Genetics*. Vol. 13, No. 5 (1983):473–489.

ROWE, DAVID C., AND D. WAYNE OSGOOD. "Heredity and Sociological Theories of Delinquency: A Reconsideration." *American Sociological Review*. Vol. 49, No. 4 (August 1984):526–540.

RUBIN, BETH A. "Class Struggle American Style: Unions, Strikes and Wages." *American Sociological Review*. Vol. 51, No. 5 (October 1986):618–631.

RUBIN, LILLIAN B. *Intimate Strangers: Men and Women Together*. New York: Harper & Row, 1983.

RUBIN, LILLIAN BRESLOW. *Worlds of Pain: Life in the Working-Class Family*. New York: Basic Books, 1976.

RUBINSON, RICHARD. "Class Formation, Politics, and Institutions: Schooling in the United States." *American Journal of Sociology*. Vol. 92, No. 3 (November 1986):519–548.

RUDOLPH, BARBARA. "Tobacco Takes a New Road." *Time*. Vol. 126, No. 20 (November 18, 1985):70–71.

RYAN, WILLIAM. *Blaming the Victim*. Rev. ed. New York: Vintage, 1976.

RYTINA, JOAN HUBER, WILLIAM H. FORM, AND JOHN PEASE. "Income and Stratification Ideology: Beliefs About the American Opportunity Structure." *American Journal of Sociology*. Vol. 75, No. 4 (January 1970):703–716.

SABATO, LARRY J. *PAC Power: Inside the World of Political Action Committees*. New York: Norton, 1984.

SACKS, HOWARD L. Letter to the author, 1986.

SALAS, RAFAEL M. "The State of World Population 1985: Population and Women." *Popline*. Vol. 7, No. 7 (July 1985):4–5.

SALHOLZ, ELOISE. "The Future of Gay America." *Newsweek* (March 12, 1990):20–25.

SAMPSON, ANTHONY. *The Changing Anatomy of Britain*. New York: Random House, 1982.

SAMPSON, ROBERT J. "Urban Black Violence: The Effects of Male Joblessness and Family Disruption." *American Journal of Sociology*. Vol. 93, No. 2 (September 1987):348–382.

SAPIR, EDWARD. "The Status of Linguistics as a Science." *Language*. Vol. 5 (1929):207–214.

SAPIR, EDWARD. *Selected Writings of Edward Sapir in Language, Culture, and Personality*. David G. Mandelbaum, ed. Berkeley, CA: University of California Press, 1949.

SCAFF, LAWRENCE A. "Max Weber and Robert Michels." *American Journal of Sociology*. Vol. 86, No. 6 (May 1981):1269–1286.

SCHEFF, THOMAS J. *Being Mentally Ill: A Sociological Theory*. 2nd ed. New York: Aldine, 1984.

SCHLESINGER, ARTHUR. "The City in American Civilization." In A.B. Callow, Jr., ed., *American Urban History*. New York: Oxford University Press, 1969:25–41.

SCHOOLER, CARMI, JOANNE MILLER, KAREN A. MILLER, AND CAROL N. RICHTAND. "Work for the Household: Its Nature and Consequences for Husbands and Wives." *American Journal of Sociology*. Vol. 90, No. 1 (July 1984):97–124.

SCHREINER, TIM. "Your Cost to Bring Up Baby: $142,700." *USA Today* (October 19, 1984):1D.

SCHUR, EDWIN M. *Labeling Women Deviant: Gender, Stigma, and Social Control*. Philadelphia, PA: Temple University Press, 1983.

SCHUTT, RUSSELL K. "Objectivity versus Outrage." *Society*. Vol. 26, No. 4 (May/June 1989):14–16.

SCHWARTZ, JOE. "Rising Status." *American Demographics*. Vol. 11, No. 1 (January 1989):10.

SCHWARTZ, MARTIN D. "Gender and Injury in Spousal Assault." *Sociological Focus*. Vol. 20, No. 1 (January 1987):61–75.

SCHWARTZ-NOBEL, LORETTA. *Starving in the Shadow of Plenty*. New York: McGraw-Hill, 1981.

SCOTT, JOHN, AND CATHERINE GRIFF. *Directors of Industry: The*

British Corporate Network, 1904–1976. New York: Blackwell, 1985.

SCOTT, W. RICHARD. *Organizations: Rational, Natural, and Open Systems.* Englewood Cliffs, NJ: Prentice Hall, 1981.

SELIMUDDIN, ABU K. "The Selling of America." *USA Today.* Vol. 117, No. 2525 (March 1989):12–14.

SELLIN, THORSTEN. *The Penalty of Death.* Beverly Hills, CA: Sage Publications, 1980.

SENGOKU, TAMOTSU. *Willing Workers: The Work Ethics in Japan, England, and the United States.* Westport, CT: Quorum Books, 1985.

SENNETT, RICHARD, AND JONATHAN COBB. *The Hidden Injuries of Class.* New York: Vintage, 1973.

SHANAS, ETHEL. "Social Myth as Hypothesis: The Case of the Family Relations of Old People." *The Gerontologist.* Vol. 19, No. 1 (February 1979):3–9.

SHAWCROSS, WILLIAM. *Sideshow: Kissinger, Nixon and the Destruction of Cambodia.* New York: Pocket Books, 1979.

SHEEHAN, TOM. "Senior Esteem as a Factor in Socioeconomic Complexity." *The Gerontologist.* Vol. 16, No. 5 (October 1976):433–440.

SHELDON, WILLIAM H., EMIL M. HARTL, AND EUGENE McDERMOTT. *Varieties of Delinquent Youth.* New York: Harper, 1949.

SHELER, JEFFERY L. "Lobbyists Go for It." *U.S. News & World Report.* Vol. 98, No. 23 (June 17, 1985):30–34.

SHEPHARD, ROY J. *The Risks of Passive Smoking.* London: Croom Helm, 1982.

SHERRID, PAMELA. "Hot Times in the City of London." *U.S. News & World Report* (October 27, 1986):45–46.

SHEVKY, ESHREF, AND WENDELL BELL. *Social Area Analysis.* Stanford, CA: Stanford University Press, 1955.

SHIPLEY, JOSEPH T. *Dictionary of Word Origins.* Totowa, NJ: Rowman & Allanheld, 1985.

SIDEL, RUTH, AND VICTOR W. SIDEL. *A Healthy State: An International Perspective on the Crisis in United States Medical Care.* Rev. ed. New York: Pantheon, 1982a.

SIDEL, RUTH, AND VICTOR W. SIDEL. *The Health Care of China.* Boston, MA: Beacon Press, 1982b.

SILLS, DAVID L. "The Succession of Goals." In Amitai Etzioni, ed., *A Sociological Reader on Complex Organizations.* 2nd ed. New York: Holt, Rinehart and Winston, 1969:175–187.

SIMMEL, GEORG. *The Sociology of Georg Simmel.* Kurt Wolff, ed. New York: Free Press, 1950:118–169.

SIMMEL, GEORG. "The Mental Life of the Metropolis." In Kurt Wolff, ed., *The Sociology of Georg Simmel.* New York: Free Press, 1964:409–424; orig. 1905.

SIMON, DAVID R., AND D. STANLEY EITZEN. *Elite Deviance.* Boston, MA: Allyn & Bacon, 1982; also 2nd ed., 1986.

SIMONS, CAROL. "Japan's *Kyoiku* Mamas." In John J. Macionis and Nijole V. Benokraitis, eds., *Seeing Ourselves: Classic, Contemporary, and Cross-Cultural Readings in Sociology.* Englewood Cliffs, NJ: Prentice Hall, 1989:281–286.

SINGER, DOROTHY. "A Time to Reexamine the Role of Television in Our Lives." *American Psychologist.* Vol. 38, No. 7 (July 1983):815–816.

SINGER, JEROME L., AND DOROTHY G. SINGER. "Psychologists Look at Television: Cognitive, Developmental, Personality, and Social Policy Implications." *American Psychologist.* Vol. 38, No. 7 (July 1983):826–834.

SIVARD, RUTH LEGER. *World Military and Social Expenditures, 1987–88.* 12th ed. Washington, DC: World Priorities, 1988.

SIZER, THEODORE R. *Horace's Compromise: The Dilemma of the American High School.* Boston, MA: Houghton Mifflin, 1984.

SJOBERG, GIDEON. *The Preindustrial City.* New York: Free Press, 1965.

SKOCPOL, THEDA. *States and Social Revolutions: A Comparative Analysis of France, Russia, and China.* Cambridge (UK): Cambridge University Press, 1979.

SKOLNICK, ARLENE. *The Psychology of Human Development.* New York: Harcourt Brace Jovanovich, 1986.

SLATER, PHILIP. *The Pursuit of Loneliness.* Boston, MA: Beacon Press, 1976.

SLATER, PHILIP E. "Contrasting Correlates of Group Size." *Sociometry.* Vol. 21, No. 2 (June 1958):129–139.

SMITH, ADAM. *Enquiry into the Nature and Causes of the Wealth of Nations.* New York: The Modern Library, 1937; orig. 1776.

SMITH, DOUGLAS A. "Police Response to Interpersonal Violence: Defining the Parameters of Legal Control." *Social Forces.* Vol. 65, No. 3 (March 1987):767–782.

SMITH, DOUGLAS A., AND PATRICK R. GARTIN. "Specifying Specific Deterrence: The Influence of Arrest on Future Criminal Activity." *American Sociological Review.* Vol. 54, No. 1 (February 1989):94–105.

SMITH, DOUGLAS A., AND CHRISTY A. VISHER. "Street-Level Justice: Situational Determinants of Police Arrest Decisions." *Social Problems.* Vol. 29, No. 2 (December 1981):167–177.

SMITH, ROBERT ELLIS. *Privacy: How to Protect What's Left of It.* Garden City, NY: Anchor Press/Doubleday, 1979.

SMITH-LOVIN, LYNN, AND CHARLES BORDY. "Interruptions in Group Discussions: The Effects of Gender and Group Composition." *American Journal of Sociology.* Vol. 54, No. 3 (June 1989):424–435.

SMITH-ROSENBERG, CAROL, AND CHARLES ROSENBERG. "The Female Animal: Medical and Biological Views of Woman and Her Role in Nineteenth Century America." In Judith Walzer Leavitt, ed., *Women and Health in America.* Madison, WI: University of Wisconsin Press, 1984:12–27.

SNOW, DAVID A., E. BURKE ROCHFORD, JR., STEVEN K. WORDEN, AND ROBERT D. BENFORD. "Frame Alignment Processes, Micromobilization, and Movement Participation." *American Sociological Review.* Vol. 51, No. 4 (August 1986):464–481.

SNOWMAN, DANIEL. *Britain and America: An Interpretation of Their Culture 1945–1975.* New York: Harper Torchbooks, 1977.

SOWELL, THOMAS. *Ethnic America.* New York: Basic Books, 1981.

SPATES, JAMES L. "Sociological Overview." In Alan Milberg, ed., *Street Games.* New York: McGraw-Hill, 1976a:286–290.

SPATES, JAMES L. "Counterculture and Dominant Culture Values: A Cross-National Analysis of the Underground Press and Dominant Culture Magazines." *American Sociological Review.* Vol. 41, No. 5 (October 1976b):868–883.

SPATES, JAMES L. "The Sociology of Values." In Ralph Turner, ed., *Annual Review of Sociology.* Vol. 9. Palo Alto, CA: Annual Reviews, 1983:27–49.

SPATES, JAMES L., AND JOHN J. MACIONIS. *The Sociology of Cities*. 2nd ed. Belmont, CA: Wadsworth, 1987.

SPATES, JAMES L., AND H. WESLEY PERKINS. "American and English Student Values." *Comparative Social Research*. Vol. 5. Greenwich, CT: Jai Press, 1982:245–268.

SPECTOR, LEONARD S. "Nuclear Proliferation Today." In William M. Evan and Stephen Hilgartner, eds., *The Arms Race and Nuclear War*. Englewood Cliffs, NJ: Prentice Hall, 1988:25–29.

SPEIZER, JEANNE J. "Education." In Barbara Haber, ed., *The Women's Annual 1982–1983*. Boston: G. K. Hall, 1983:29–54.

SPENCER, GARY. *Projections of the Population of the United States, by Age, Sex, and Race: 1988 to 2080*. Washington, DC: U.S. Government Printing Office, 1989.

SPENDER, DALE. *Man Made Language*. London: Routledge & Kegan Paul, 1980.

SPITZER, STEVEN. "Toward a Marxian Theory of Deviance." In Delos H. Kelly, ed., *Criminal Behavior: Readings in Criminology*. New York: St. Martin's Press, 1980:175–191.

SRINIVAS, M. N. *Social Change in Modern India*. Berkeley, CA: University of California Press, 1971.

STACEY, JUDITH. *Patriarchy and Socialist Revolution in China*. Berkeley: University of California Press, 1983.

STACK, CAROL B. *All Our Kin: Strategies for Survival in a Black Community*. New York: Harper & Row, 1975.

STAHURA, JOHN M. "Suburban Development, Black Suburbanization and the Black Civil Rights Movement Since World War II." *American Sociological Review*. Vol. 51, No. 1 (February 1986):131–144.

STAPLES, BRENT. "Where Are the Black Fans?" *New York Times Magazine* (May 17, 1987):26–34, 36.

STARK, RODNEY, AND WILLIAM SIMS BAINBRIDGE. "Of Churches, Sects, and Cults: Preliminary Concepts for a Theory of Religious Movements." *Journal for the Scientific Study of Religion*. Vol. 18, No. 2 (June 1979):117–131.

STARK, RODNEY, AND WILLIAM SIMS BAINBRIDGE. "Secularization and Cult Formation in the Jazz Age." *Journal for the Scientific Study of Religion*. Vol. 20, No. 4 (December 1981):360–373.

STARK, RODNEY, AND CHARLES Y. GLOCK. *American Piety: The Nature of Religious Commitment*. Berkeley, CA: University of California Press, 1968.

STARR, PAUL. *The Social Transformation of American Medicine*. New York: Basic Books, 1982.

Statistics of Income Bulletin. Vol. 9, No. 1 (Summer 1989).

STAVRIANOS, L. S. *A Global History: The Human Heritage*. 3rd ed. Englewood Cliffs, NJ: Prentice Hall, 1983.

STEIN, MAURICE R. *The Eclipse of Community: An Interpretation of American Studies*. Princeton, NJ: Princeton University Press, 1972.

STEPHENS, JOHN D. *The Transition from Capitalism to Socialism*. Urbana, IL: University of Illinois Press, 1986.

STERNLIEB, GEORGE, AND JAMES W. HUGHES. "The Uncertain Future of the Central City." *Urban Affairs Quarterly*. Vol. 18, No. 4 (June 1983):455–472.

STEVENS, GILLIAN, AND GRAY SWICEGOOD. "The Linguistic Context of Ethnic Endogamy." *American Sociological Review*. Vol. 52, No. 1 (February 1987):73–82.

STEVENS, ROSEMARY. *American Medicine and the Public Interest*. New Haven, CT: Yale University Press, 1971.

STOCKWELL, EDWARD G., DAVID A. SWANSON, AND JERRY W. WICKS. "Trends in the Relationship Between Infant Mortality and Socioeconomic Status." *Sociological Focus*. Vol. 20, No. 4 (October 1987):319–327.

STOHL, MICHAEL, AND GEORGE A. LOPEZ, EDS. *The State as Terrorist: The Dynamics of Governmental Violence and Repression*. Westport, CT: Greenwood Press, 1984.

STONE, LAWRENCE. *The Family, Sex and Marriage in England 1500–1800*. New York: Harper & Row, 1977.

STOUFFER, SAMUEL A., ET AL. *The American Soldier: Adjustment During Army Life*. Princeton, NJ: Princeton University Press, 1949.

STRAUS, MURRAY A., AND RICHARD J. GELLES. "Societal Change and Change in Family Violence from 1975 to 1985 as Revealed by Two National Surveys." *Journal of Marriage and the Family*. Vol. 48, No. 4 (August 1986):465–479.

SUDNOW, DAVID N. *Passing On: The Social Organization of Dying*. Englewood Cliffs, NJ: Prentice Hall, 1967.

SUMNER, WILLIAM GRAHAM. *Folkways*. New York: Dover, 1959; orig. 1906.

SUNG, BETTY LEE. *Mountains of Gold: The Story of the Chinese in America*. New York: Macmillan, 1967.

SUTHERLAND, EDWIN H. "White Collar Criminality." *American Sociological Review*. Vol. 5, No. 1 (February 1940):1–12.

SUTHERLAND, EDWIN H., AND DONALD R. CRESSEY. *Criminology*. 3rd ed. Philadelphia, PA: J. B. Lippincott, 1930; 8th ed., 1970; 10th ed., 1978.

SUZUKI, DAVID, AND PETER KNUDTSON. *Genethics: The Clash Between the New Genetics and Human Values*. Cambridge, MA: Harvard University Press, 1989.

SWARTZ, STEVE. "Why Michael Milken Stands to Qualify for Guinness Book." *The Wall Street Journal*. Vol. LXX, No. 117 (March 31, 1989):1, 4.

SWEET, ELLEN. "Date Rape: The Story of an Epidemic and Those Who Deny It." *Ms./Campus Times* (October 1985):56–59, 84–85.

SYZMANSKI, ALBERT. *Class Structure: A Critical Perspective*. New York: Praeger, 1983.

SZASZ, THOMAS S. *The Manufacturer of Madness: A Comparative Study of the Inquisition and the Mental Health Movement*. New York: Dell, 1961.

SZASZ, THOMAS S. *The Myth of Mental Illness: Foundations of a Theory of Personal Conduct*. New York: Harper & Row, 1970; orig. 1961.

TAEUBER, KARL, AND ALMA TAEUBER. *Negroes in Cities*. Chicago, Aldine, 1965.

TAJFEL, HENRI. "Social Psychology of Intergroup Relations." *Annual Review of Psychology*. Palo Alto, CA: Annual Reviews, 1982:1–39.

TANNENBAUM, FRANK. *Slave and Citizen: The Negro in the Americas*. New York: Vintage Books, 1946.

TAVRIS, CAROL, AND SUSAN SADD. *The Redbook Report on Female Sexuality*. New York: Delacorte Press, 1977.

THEEN, ROLF H. W. "Party and Bureaucracy." In Erik P. Hoffmann and Robbin F. Laird, eds., *The Soviet Polity in the Modern Era*. New York: Aldine, 1984:131–165.

THOITS, PEGGY A. "Self-labeling Processes in Mental Illness: The Role of Emotional Deviance." *American Journal of Sociology*. Vol. 91, No. 2 (September 1985):221–249.

THOMAS, PIRI. *Down These Mean Streets*. New York: Signet, 1967.

THOMAS, W. I. "The Relation of Research to the Social Process." In Morris Janowitz, ed., *W. I. Thomas on Social Organization and Social Personality*. Chicago: University of Chicago Press, 1966:289–305; orig. 1931.

THORNBERRY, TERRANCE, AND MARGARET FARNSWORTH. "Social Correlates of Criminal Involvement: Further Evidence on the Relationship Between Social Status and Criminal Behavior." *American Sociological Review*. Vol 47, No. 4 (August 1982):505–518.

THORNE, BARRIE, CHERIS KRAMARAE, AND NANCY HENLEY, EDS. *Language, Gender and Society*. Cambridge: Newbury House, 1983.

THORNTON, ARLAND. "Changing Attitudes Toward Separation and Divorce: Causes and Consequences." *American Journal of Sociology*. Vol. 90, No. 4 (January 1985):856–872.

THUROW, LESTER C. "A Surge in Inequality." *Scientific American*. Vol. 256, No. 5 (May 1987):30–37.

TIENDA, MARTA, AND DING-TZANN LII. "Minority Concentration and Earnings Inequality: Blacks, Hispanics, and Asians Compared." *American Journal of Sociology*. Vol. 93, No. 1 (July 1987):141–165.

TIGER, LIONEL, AND JOSEPH SHEPHER. *Women in the Kibbutz*. New York: Harcourt Brace Jovanovich, 1975.

TILLY, CHARLES. "Does Modernization Breed Revolution?" In Jack A. Goldstone, ed., *Revolutions: Theoretical, Comparative, and Historical Studies*. New York: Harcourt Brace Jovanovich, 1986:47–57.

TITTLE, CHARLES R., AND WAYNE J. VILLEMEZ. "Social Class and Criminality." *Social Forces*. Vol. 56, No. 22 (December 1977):474–502.

TITTLE, CHARLES R., WAYNE J. VILLEMEZ, AND DOUGLAS A. SMITH. "The Myth of Social Class and Criminality: An Empirical Assessment of the Empirical Evidence." *American Sociological Review*. Vol. 43, No. 5 (October 1978):643–656.

TOBIN, GARY. "Suburbanization and the Development of Motor Transportation: Transportation Technology and the Suburbanization Process." In Barry Schwartz, ed., *The Changing Face of the Suburbs*. Chicago: University of Chicago Press, 1976.

TOCQUEVILLE, ALEXIS DE. *The Old Regime and the French Revolution*. Stuart Gilbert, trans. Garden City, NY: Doubleday Anchor Books, 1955; orig. 1856.

TOENNIES, FERDINAND. *Community and Society (Gemeinschaft und Gesellschaft)*. New York: Harper & Row, 1963; orig. 1887.

TOFFLER, ALVIN. *The Third Wave*. New York: Bantam Books, 1981.

TOMIAK, JANUSZ. "Introduction." In J. J. Tomiak, ed., *Soviet Education in the 1980s*. London: Croom Helm, 1983:vii–x.

TROELTSCH, ERNST. *The Social Teaching of the Christian Churches*. New York: Macmillan, 1931.

TROIDEN, RICHARD R. *Gay and Lesbian Identity: A Sociological Analysis*. Dix Hills, NY: General Hall, 1988.

TUMIN, MELVIN M. "Some Principles of Stratification: A Critical Analysis." *American Sociological Review*. Vol. 18, No. 4 (August 1953):387–394.

TUMIN, MELVIN M. *Social Stratification: The Forms and Functions of Inequality*. 2nd ed. Englewood Cliffs, NJ: Prentice Hall, 1985.

TYGIEL, JULES. *Baseball's Great Experiment: Jackie Robinson and His Legacy*. New York: Oxford University Press, 1983.

TYLER, S. LYMAN. *A History of Indian Policy*. Washington, DC: United States Department of the Interior, Bureau of Indian Affairs, 1973.

UNITED NATIONS. *Demographic Yearbook 1983*. New York: United Nations, 1983.

UNITED NATIONS. *World Economic Survey 1988: Current Trends and Policies in the World Economy*. New York: United Nations Publications, 1988.

UNNEVER, JAMES D., CHARLES E. FRAZIER, AND JOHN C. HENRETTA. "Race Differences in Criminal Sentencing." *The Sociological Quarterly*. Vol. 21, No. 2 (Spring 1980):197–205.

UNRUH, JOHN D., JR. *The Plains Across*. Urbana, IL: University of Illinois Press, 1979.

U.S. BUREAU OF THE CENSUS. *Statistical Abstract of the United States 1985*. 105th ed. Washington, DC: U.S. Government Printing Office, 1985.

U.S. BUREAU OF THE CENSUS. *Statistical Abstract of the United States 1987*. 107th ed. Washington, DC: U.S. Government Printing Office, 1987.

U.S. BUREAU OF THE CENSUS. *School Enrollment—Social and Economic Characteristics of Students, October 1986*. P-20, No. 429. Washington, DC: U.S. Government Printing Office, 1988.

U.S. BUREAU OF THE CENSUS. *Characteristics of Persons Receiving Benefits from Major Assistance Programs*. P-70, No. 14. Washington, DC: U.S. Government Printing Office, 1989.

U.S. BUREAU OF THE CENSUS. *Fertility of American Women: June 1988*. Washington, DC: U.S. Government Printing Office, 1989.

U.S. BUREAU OF THE CENSUS. *The Hispanic Population in the United States: March 1988*. Washington, DC: U.S. Government Printing Office, 1989.

U.S. BUREAU OF THE CENSUS. *Household and Family Characteristics: March 1988*. Washington, DC: U.S. Government Printing Office, 1989.

U.S. BUREAU OF THE CENSUS. *Households, Families, Marital Status, and Living Arrangements: March 1989* (Advance Report). Washington, DC: U.S. Government Printing Office, 1989.

U.S. BUREAU OF THE CENSUS. *Marital Status and Living Arrangements: March 1988*. Washington, DC: U.S. Government Printing Office, 1989.

U.S. BUREAU OF THE CENSUS. *Money Income and Poverty Status in the United States: 1988*. Washington, DC: U.S. Government Printing Office, 1989.

U.S. BUREAU OF THE CENSUS. *Money Income of Households, Families, and Persons in the United States, 1987*. P-60, No. 162. Washington, DC: U.S. Government Printing Office, 1989.

U.S. BUREAU OF THE CENSUS. *Patterns of Metropolitan Area and County Population Growth: 1980 to 1987*. Washington, DC: U.S. Government Printing Office, 1989.

U.S. BUREAU OF THE CENSUS. *Per Capita Income Up, Median*

Family Income and Poverty Rate Unchanged in 1988, Census Bureau Reports. (Press release) Washington, DC: U.S. Government Printing Office, 1989.

U.S. Bureau of the Census. *Poverty in the United States 1987.* P-60, No. 163. Washington, DC: U.S. Government Printing Office, 1989.

U.S. Bureau of the Census. *Projections of the Population of the United States, by Age, Sex, and Race: 1988 to 2080.* Series P-25, No. 1018. Washington, DC: U.S. Government Printing Office, 1989.

U.S. Bureau of the Census. *Public Employment in 1988.* Washington, DC: U.S. Government Printing Office, 1989.

U.S. Bureau of the Census. *Statistical Abstract of the United States 1989.* 109th ed. Washington, DC: U.S. Government Printing Office, 1989.

U.S. Bureau of the Census. *Voting and Registration in the Election of November 1988.* Washington, DC: U.S. Government Printing Office, 1989.

U.S. Bureau of the Census. *Money Income and Poverty Status in the United States: 1989.* Washington, DC: U.S. Government Printing Office, 1990.

U.S. Bureau of the Census. *Population Estimates for Metropolitan Statistical Areas, July 1, 1988, 1987, and 1986.* Washington, DC: U.S. Government Printing Office, 1990.

U.S. Bureau of the Census. *Statistical Abstract of the United States 1990.* 110th ed. Washington, DC: U.S. Government Printing Office, 1990.

U.S. Bureau of Justice Statistics. *Recidivism of Prisoners Released in 1983.* Washington, DC: U.S. Government Printing Office, 1989.

U.S. Bureau of Labor Statistics. *Employment and Earnings.* Vol. 37, No. 1 (January 1990).

U.S. Center for Education Statistics. *The Condition of Education 1989.* Washington, DC: U.S. Government Printing Office, 1989.

U.S. Commission on Civil Rights. *Twenty Years After Brown: The Shadows of the Past.* Washington, DC: U.S. Government Printing Office, 1974.

U.S. Commission on Security and Cooperation in Europe. "Staff Report of Homelessness in the United States." August 1990. Staff of the U.S. Commission on Security and Cooperation in Europe. Washington, DC: U.S. Government Printing Office.

U.S. Department of Commerce. *U.S. Industrial Outlook.* Washington, DC: U.S. Government Printing Office, 1989.

U.S. Department of Health and Human Services. *Alcohol, Drug Abuse, and Mental Health News.* Vol. 15, No. 8 (October 1989).

U.S. Department of Justice. *Criminal Victimization in the United States, 1987.* Washington, DC: U.S. Government Printing Office, 1987.

U.S. Department of Labor. *Time of Change: 1983 Handbook on Women Workers.* Bulletin 298. Washington, DC: U.S. Government Printing Office, 1983.

Useem, Michael. "Corporations and the Corporate Elite." In Alex Inkeles et al., eds., *Annual Review of Sociology.* Vol. 6. Palo Alto, CA: Annual Reviews, 1980:41–77.

U.S. Federal Bureau of Investigation. *Crime in the United States 1986.* Washington, DC: U.S. Government Printing Office, 1987.

U.S. Federal Bureau of Investigation. *Crime in the United States 1988.* Washington, DC: U.S. Government Printing Office, 1989.

U.S. Federal Bureau of Investigation. *Crime in the United States 1989.* Washington, DC: U.S. Government Printing Office, 1990.

U.S. Federal Election Commission. *FEC Final Report on 1988 Congressional Campaigns Show $459 Million Spent.* Washington, DC: The Commission, 1989a.

U.S. Federal Election Commission. *Federal Election Commission Record.* Vol. 15, No. 8 (August 1989b).

U.S. House of Representatives, Select Committee on Children, Youth, and Families. *U.S. Children and Their Families: Current Conditions and Current Trends, 1989.* Washington, DC: U.S. Government Printing Office, 1989.

U.S. National Center for Health Statistics. *Current Estimates from the National Health Survey, 1988.* Washington, DC: U.S. Government Printing Office, 1989.

U.S. National Center for Health Statistics. *Current Estimates from the National Health Survey, 1989.* Washington, DC: U.S. Government Printing Office, 1990.

U.S. Office of Educational Research and Improvement. *The Condition of Education 1990.* Vol. 1, *Elementary and Secondary Education.* Washington, DC: U.S. Government Printing Office, 1990.

Van De Kaa, Dirk J. "Europe's Second Demographic Transition." *Population Bulletin.* Vol. 42, No. 1 (March 1987). Washington, DC: Population Reference Bureau.

Van Den Haag, Ernest, and John P. Conrad. *The Death Penalty: A Debate.* New York: Plenum Press, 1983.

Van Valey, T. L., W. C. Roof, and J. E. Wilcox. "Trends in Residential Segregation." *American Journal of Sociology.* Vol. 82, No. 4 (January 1977):826–844.

Vatz, Richard E., and Lee S. Weinberg. *Thomas Szasz: Primary Values and Major Contentions.* Buffalo, NY: Prometheus Books, 1983.

Vaughan, Mary Kay. "Multinational Corporations: The World as a Company Town." In Ahamed Idris-Soven et al., eds., *The World as a Company Town: Multinational Corporations and Social Change.* The Hague: Mouton Publishers, 1978:15–35.

Vayda, Eugene, and Raisa B. Deber. "The Canadian Health Care System: An Overview." *Social Science and Medicine.* Vol. 18, No. 3 (1984):191–197.

Vines, Gail. "Whose Baby Is It Anyway?" *New Scientist.* No. 1515 (July 3, 1986):26–27.

Vinovskis, Maris A. "Have Social Historians Lost the Civil War? Some Preliminary Demographic Speculations." *Journal of American History.* Vol. 76, No. 1 (June 1989):34–58.

Vogel, Ezra F. *Japan as Number One: Lessons for America.* Cambridge, MA: Harvard University Press, 1979.

Vogel, Lise. *Marxism and the Oppression of Women: Toward a Unitary Theory.* New Brunswick, NJ: Rutgers University Press, 1983.

Vold, George B., and Thomas J. Bernard. *Theoretical Criminology.* 3rd ed. New York: Oxford University Press, 1986.

VON HIRSH, ANDREW. *Past or Future Crimes: Deservedness and Dangerousness in the Sentencing of Criminals.* New Brunswick, NJ: Rutgers University Press, 1986.

WALL, THOMAS F. *Medical Ethics: Basic Moral Issues.* Washington, DC: University Press of America, 1980.

WALLERSTEIN, IMMANUEL. *The Modern World-System: Capitalist Agriculture and the Origins of the European World-Economy in the Sixteenth Century.* New York: Academic Press, 1974.

WALLERSTEIN, IMMANUEL. *The Capitalist World-Economy.* New York: Cambridge University Press, 1979.

WALLERSTEIN, IMMANUEL. "Crises: The World Economy, the Movements, and the Ideologies." In Albert Bergesen, ed., *Crises in the World-System.* Beverly Hills, CA: Sage Publications, 1983:21–36.

WALLERSTEIN, IMMANUEL. *The Politics of the World Economy: The States, the Movements, and the Civilizations.* Cambridge (UK): Cambridge University Press, 1984.

WALLERSTEIN, JUDITH S., AND SANDRA BLAKESLEE. *Second Chances: Men, Women, and Children a Decade After Divorce.* New York: Ticknor & Fields, 1989.

WALLIS, CLAUDIA. "Stress: Can We Cope?" *Time.* Vol. 121, No. 23 (June 6, 1983):48–54.

WALLIS, CLAUDIA. "Children Having Children." *Time.* Vol. 126, No. 23 (December 9, 1985):78–82, 84, 87, 89–90.

WARNER, SAM BASS, JR. *Streetcar Suburbs.* Cambridge, MA: Harvard University and M.I.T. Presses, 1962.

WARNER, W. LLOYD, AND J. O. LOW. *The Social System of the Modern Factory.* Yankee City Series, Vol. 4. New Haven, CT: Yale University Press, 1947.

WARNER, W. LLOYD, AND PAUL S. LUNT. *The Social Life of a Modern Community.* New Haven, CT: Yale University Press, 1941.

WATSON, RUSSELL. "Riding the Tiger." *Newsweek.* Vol. CXIV, No. 23 (December 4, 1989):40–42, 44.

WATTEL, H. "Levittown: A Suburban Community." In William Dobriner, ed., *The Suburban Community.* New York: G. P. Putnam's Sons, 1958:287–313.

WAXMAN, CHAIM I. *The Stigma of Poverty: A Critique of Poverty Theories and Policies.* 2nd ed. New York: Pergamon Press, 1983.

WEBER, ADNA FERRIN. *The Growth of Cities.* New York: Columbia University Press, 1963; orig. 1899.

WEBER, MAX. *The Protestant Ethic and the Spirit of Capitalism.* New York: Charles Scribner's Sons, 1958; orig. 1904–1905.

WEBER, MAX. *Economy and Society.* G. Roth and C. Wittich, eds. Berkeley, CA: University of California Press, 1978.

WEINBERG, GEORGE. *Society and the Healthy Homosexual.* Garden City, NY: Anchor Books, 1973.

WEINRICH, JAMES D. *Sexual Landscapes: Why We Are What We Are, Why We Love Whom We Love.* New York: Charles Scribner's Sons, 1987.

WEINTRAUB, SIDNEY, AND STANLEY R. ROSS. *"Temporary" Alien Workers in the United States: Designing Policy from Fact and Opinion.* Boulder, CO: Westview Press, 1982.

WEISNER, THOMAS S., AND BERNICE T. EIDUSON. "The Children of the '60s as Parents." *Psychology Today* (January 1986):60–66.

WEITZMAN, LENORE J. *The Divorce Revolution: The Unexpected Social and Economic Consequences for Women and Children in America.* New York: Free Press, 1985.

WEITZMAN, LENORE J., DEBORAH EIFLER, ELIZABETH HODAKA, AND CATHERINE ROSS. "Sex-Role Socialization in Picture Books for Preschool Children." *American Journal of Sociology.* Vol. 77, No. 6 (May 1972):1125–1150.

WELCH, KEVIN. "Community Development and Metropolitan Religious Commitment: A Test of Two Competing Models." *Journal for the Scientific Study of Religion.* Vol. 22, No. 2 (June 1983):167–181.

WELLFORD, CHARLES. "Labeling Theory and Criminology: An Assessment." In Delos H. Kelly, ed., *Criminal Behavior: Readings in Criminology.* New York: St. Martin's Press, 1980:234–247.

WELLMAN, BARRY. "The Community Question: Intimate Networks of East Yorkers." *American Journal of Sociology.* Vol. 84, No. 5 (March 1979):1201–1231.

WENKE, ROBERT J. *Patterns of Prehistory.* New York: Oxford University Press, 1980.

WERMAN, JILL. "Who Makes What?" *Working Woman* (January 1989):72–76, 80.

WESTERMAN, MARTY. "Death of the Frito Bandito." *American Demographics.* Vol. 11, No. 3 (March 1989):28–32.

WESTOFF, CHARLES F., AND ELISE F. JONES. "The Secularization of U.S. Catholic Birth Control Practices." *Family Planning Perspective.* Vol. X, No. 5 (September/October 1977):203–207.

WHEELIS, ALLEN. *The Quest for Identity.* New York: W. W. Norton, 1958.

WHITAKER, MARK. "Ten Ways to Fight Terrorism." *Newsweek* (July 1, 1985):26–29.

WHITE, RALPH, AND RONALD LIPPITT. "Leader Behavior and Member Reaction in Three Social Climates.'" In Dorwin Cartwright and Alvin Zander, eds., *Group Dynamics.* Evanston, IL: Row, Peterson, 1953:586–611.

WHITMAN, DAVID. "Shattering Myths about the Homeless." *U.S. News & World Report* (March 20, 1989):26, 28.

WHORF, BENJAMIN LEE. "The Relation of Habitual Thought and Behavior to Language." In *Language, Thought, and Reality.* Cambridge, MA: The Technology Press of M.I.T./New York: Wiley, 1956:134–159; orig. 1941.

WHYTE, WILLIAM H., JR. *The Organization Man.* Garden City, NY: Anchor, 1957.

WIARDA, HOWARD J. "Ethnocentrism and Third World Development." *Society.* Vol. 24, No. 6 (September-October 1987):55–64.

WIATROWSKI, MICHAEL A., DAVID B. GRISWOLD, AND MARY K. ROBERTS. "Social Control Theory and Delinquency." *American Sociological Review.* Vol. 46, No. 5 (October 1981):525–541.

WILL, GEORGE F. "No Psycho-Socio Babble Lessens the Fact That Evil Was the Crux of Central Park Rape." *The Philadelphia Inquirer* (May 1, 1989).

WILLIAMS, ROBIN M., JR. *American Society: A Sociological Interpretation.* 3rd ed. New York: Alfred A. Knopf, 1970.

WILSON, CLINTY C., II, AND FÉLIX GUTIÉRREZ. *Minorities and Media: Diversity and the End of Mass Communication.* Beverly Hills, CA: Sage Publications, 1985.

WILSON, EDWARD O. *Sociobiology: The New Synthesis.* Cambridge, MA: Belknap Press of the Harvard University Press, 1975.

426   References

WILSON, EDWARD O. *On Human Nature*. New York: Bantam Books, 1978.

WILSON, JAMES Q., AND RICHARD J. HERRNSTEIN. *Crime and Human Nature*. New York: Simon and Schuster, 1985.

WILSON, THOMAS C. "Urbanism and Tolerance: A Test of Some Hypotheses Drawn from Wirth and Stouffer." *American Sociological Review*. Vol. 50, No. 1 (February 1985):117–123.

WILSON, WILLIAM JULIUS. "The Black Underclass." *The Wilson Quarterly*. Vol. 8 (Spring 1984):88–99.

WINN, MARIE. *Children Without Childhood*. New York: Pantheon Books, 1983.

WIRTH, LOUIS. "Urbanism As a Way of Life." *American Journal of Sociology*. Vol. 44, No. 1 (July 1938):1–24.

WITKIN-LANOIL, GEORGIA. *The Female Stress Syndrome: How to Recognize and Live with It*. New York: Newmarket Press, 1984.

WOLFGANG, MARVIN E., AND FRANCO FERRACUTI. *The Subculture of Violence: Towards an Integrated Theory in Criminology*. Beverly Hills, CA: Sage Publications, 1982.

WOLFGANG, MARVIN E., ROBERT M. FIGLIO, AND THORSTEN SELLIN. *Delinquency in a Birth Cohort*. Chicago: University of Chicago Press, 1972.

WOLFGANG, MARVIN E., TERRENCE P. THORNBERRY, AND ROBERT M. FIGLIO. *From Boy to Man, From Delinquency to Crime*. Chicago: University of Chicago Press, 1987.

WOLFINGER, RAYMOND E., AND STEVEN J. ROSENSTONE. *Who Votes?* New Haven, CT: Yale University Press, 1980.

WOLFINGER, RAYMOND E., MARTIN SHAPIRO, AND FRED J. GREENSTEIN. *Dynamics of American Politics*. 2nd ed. Englewood Cliffs, NJ: Prentice Hall, 1980.

WONG, BUCK. "Need for Awareness: An Essay on Chinatown, San Francisco." In Amy Tachiki et al., eds., *Roots: An Asian American Reader*. Los Angeles, CA: UCLA Asian American Studies Center, 1971:265–273.

WOODWARD, C. VANN. *The Strange Career of Jim Crow*. 3rd rev. ed. New York: Oxford University Press, 1974.

WOODWARD, KENNETH L. "Feminism and the Churches." *Newsweek*. Vol. 13, No. 7 (February 13, 1989):58–61.

THE WORLD BANK. *World Development Report 1984*. New York: Oxford University Press, 1984.

WORLD HEALTH ORGANIZATION. *Constitution of the World Health Organization*. New York: World Health Organization Interim Commission, 1946.

WRIGHT, ERIK OLIN, AND BILL MARTIN. "The Transformation of the American Class Structure, 1960–1980." *American Journal of Sociology*. Vol. 93, No. 1 (July 1987):1–29.

WRIGHT, JAMES D. "Address Unknown: Homelessness in Contemporary America." *Society*. Vol. 26, No. 6 (September/October 1989):45–53.

WRIGHT, QUINCY. "Causes of War in the Atomic Age." In William M. Evan and Steven Hilgartner, eds., *The Arms Race and Nuclear War*. Englewood Cliffs, NJ: Prentice Hall, 1987:7–10.

WRONG, DENNIS H. "The Oversocialized Conception of Man in Modern Sociology." *American Sociological Review*. Vol. 26, No. 2 (April 1961):183–193.

YODER, JAN D., AND ROBERT C. NICHOLS. "A Life Perspective: Comparison of Married and Divorced Persons." *Journal of Marriage and the Family*. Vol. 42, No. 2 (May 1980):413–419.

ZASLAVSKY, VICTOR. *The Neo-Stalinist State: Class, Ethnicity, and Consensus in Soviet Society*. Armonk, NY: M. E. Sharpe, 1982.

ZHOU, MIN, AND JOHN R. LOGAN. "Returns of Human Capital in Ethnic Enclaves: New York City's Chinatown." *American Sociological Review*. Vol. 54, No. 5 (October 1989):809–820.

ZIPP, JOHN F. "Perceived Representativeness and Voting: An Assessment of the Impact of 'Choices' vs. 'Echoes.'" *The American Political Science Review*. Vol. 79, No. 1 (March 1985):50–61.

ZIPP, JOHN F., AND JOEL SMITH. "A Structural Analysis of Class Voting." *Social Forces*. Vol. 60, No. 3 (March 1982):738–759.

ZOLA, IRVING KENNETH. "Medicine as an Institution of Social Control." In John Ehrenreich, ed., *The Cultural Crisis of Modern Medicine*. New York: Monthly Review Press, 1978:80–100.

Photo Credits

CHAPTER 7 Paul Liebhardt, 150; Ted Spiegel/Black Star, 153; William Campbell/*Time* Magazine, 154; Peter Turnley/Black Star, 157; Art Resource, 158; Henry Gris/FPG International, 160; The Granger Collection, 161; Michael Grecco/Stock, Boston, 169; Henry Gris/FPG International, 171; FPG International, 175; Bettmann Archive, 176.

CHAPTER 8 Bruce Gordon/Photo Researchers, 181; Paul Liebhardt, 182; J. Langevin/Sygma, 186; Collection, The Museum of Modern Art, New York. Gift of Edward M. M. Warburg, 187; Paul Liebhardt, 190; Paul Liebhardt, 191; ARCHIV/Photo Researchers, 193; Paul Liebhardt, 195; The Granger Collection, 197; C. Carrion/Sygma, 198; Paul Liebhardt, 201.

CHAPTER 9 Richard Hutchings/Photo Researchers, 204; Paul Liebhardt, 206; Patricia Upchurch, 212; Raymond Depardon/Magnum Photos, 214; Wally McNamee/Woodfin Camp & Associates, 214; Woolaroc Museum, Bartlesville, Oklahoma, 216; UPI/Bettmann Newsphotos, 217; Bob Adelman, 217; Joanna Pinneo/Black Star, 219; Sepp Seitz/Woodfin Camp & Associates, 221; Randy Taylor/Sygma, 225.

CHAPTER 10 Herman Kokojan/Black Star, 228; Michel Tcherevkoff/The Image Bank, 230; Paul Liebhardt, 232; The Pennsylvania State University, 236; Filman/FPG International, 237; Jim Weiner/Photo Researchers, 237; Courtesy of Revlon, 239; Library of Congress, 241; Steve McCuny/Magnum Photos, 242; Courtesy of the National Organization of Women, 247; Sylvia Johnson/Woodfin Camp & Associates, 249; Library of Congress, 251.

CHAPTER 11 Gad Gross/JB Pictures, 254; The Granger Collection, 257; Museum of American Textile History, 258; Marcello Bertinetti/Photo Researchers, 261; Gilda Schiff/Photo Researchers, 261; Collection of Whitney Museum of American Art. Purchase 37.44. Photo by Geoffrey Clements, N.Y., 265; Gamma-Liaison, 267; JB Pictures, 268; David Becker/Photoreporters, 271; Bettye Lane/Photo Researchers, 274; Reuters/Bettmann Newsphotos, 280.

CHAPTER 12 Collection of Marilyn Lanfear; photograph courtesy of Bernice Steinbaum Gallery, NYC, 286; Farrel Grehan/Photo Researchers, 288; Barry King/Gamma-Liaison, 291; Wolfgang Dietze, 295; Will & Deni McIntyre/Photo Researchers, 298; Sygma, 299; Petit-Format/Nestle/Science Source/Photo Researchers, 301; Paul Liebhardt, 302; Ira Wyman/Sygma, 304; Sepp Seitz/Woodfin Camp & Associates, 307; Anthony Suau/Black Star, 307; From the collection of the New Britain Museum of American Art, Connecticut. Harriet Russell Stanley Fund, 312.

CHAPTER 13 Paul Liebhardt, 316; TVA, Hine/Photo Researchers, 318; Jeffrey Agronson, 320; G. B. Trudeau, 326; Erich Hartmann/Magnum Photos, 329; Paul Fetters, 333; P. P. O. W. Gallery, New York, 335: The Granger Collection, 337; Anthony Suau/Black Star, 338; Howard Sochurek/Woodfin Camp & Associates, 341; Lauros-Giraudon/Art Resource, 343.

CHAPTER 14 Kim Newton/Woodfin Camp & Associates, 346; Hella Hammid/Photo Researchers, 348; Bruce Brander/Photo Researchers, 352; N. Maceschal/The Image Bank, 353; Anderson/Gamma-Liaison, 355; Monkmeyer Press, 357; George Hall/Woodfin Camp & Associates, 361; Collection, The Museum of Modern Art, N. Y. Mrs. Simon Guggenheim Fund, 363; Courtauld Institute, London/Four by Five, 363; The University of Chicago Library, 366; Allan Tannenbaum/Sygma, 369.

CHAPTER 15 James Willis/Tony Stone Worldwide, 372; Mauri Rautkari/W. W. F.-Photolibrary, 374; Louie Psihoyos/Matrix, 376; J. L. Turpin/Sygma, 379; Art Institute of Chicago, 380; Bildarchiv Preussischer Kulturbesitz, 381; Stephanie Maze/Woodfin Camp & Associates, 383; Paul Liebhardt, 389; Andrew Holbrooke/Black Star, 390; Paul Liebhardt, 392.

Index

Name Index

Subject Index

Democratic socialism, 260
Demographic transition theory, 352–53
Demography, 348–51, 356
Denmark, 264, 269, 299, 349
Denomination, 306
Dependency theory, 196–200, 201, 393
Dependent variable, 18
Descent, 290
Deterrence, 147
Deviance, 122–49
  biological causes, 125–26
  psychological causes, 126
  social foundations, 126–27
Differential association theory, Sutherland's, 134–35, 148
Direct-fee medical system, 339
Discrimination, 211–12
  in sports, 14
Division of labor, 382
Divorce, 297
Dominican Republic, 278
Dramaturgical analysis, 13, 85–92
Dyad, 107–8

Eastern Europe, 157, 161, 164, 183, 260, 270, 271, 277, 338, 384
Ecclesia, 306
Economics, 256–68
Education, 318–29 (see also Schooling)
  achievement in U.S., 319
  gender and, 244
  lifetime earnings and, 324
  mainstreaming, 324
  public vs. private, 322–23
Ego, 57
Egypt, 31, 349
Elderly, 7 (see also Old Age, Death and dying, Aging)
Electronic church, 313
Embarrassment, 91
Empirical evidence, 16
Enclosure Movement, 10
Endogamy, 153, 289
England, 10, 11, 148, 256 (see also Great Britain)
Equal Rights Amendment (ERA), 248–49, 273
Ethics, in research, 20–21
Ethiopia, 187, 349
Ethnicity, 204–27
  composition of United States, 208
  defined, 207–8
  educational achievement and, 325
  family life and, 295

poverty and, 175
  religious affiliation and, 311
  social stratification and, 168
Ethnocentrism, 43–45, 107
Ethnomethodology, 84–85
Euthanasia, 336
Exogamy, 289
Experiment, 21, 24
Expressive leadership, 103
Extended family, 288, 289

Faith, 302
Family, 288–301
  alternative forms, 298–300
  defined, 289
  gender roles and, 103
  gender socialization and, 235–36
  social class and, 172
  socialization and, 62–63
  stages of family life, 292–94
  in twenty-first century, 300–301
  violence in, 297–98
Females, 230–31 (see also Women)
  gender roles and, 232–33
  patriarchy and, 233–35
  socialization and, 235–39
Feminine traits, 235
Feminism, 248–51
  resistance to, 250–51
  variations of, 250
Feminization of poverty, 175
Fertility, 348–49
First World, 183–85
Folkways, 36
Formal operational stage, 59
France, 10, 11, 262, 281, 349, 353
Freedom, human:
  changes in Eastern Europe and, 271
  culture and, 49–50
  socialization and, 73
French Revolution, 10, 11, 277
Functional illiteracy, 327
Funeral rites, 46

Game stage (Mead), 60–61
Gays (see Homosexuality)
Gemeinschaft, 364, 381–82
Gender, 6–7, 16, 232–53
  crime and, 5
  cultural variability, 232–33
  defined, 232
  deviance and, 138–39
  education and, 244
  family life and, 295–96
  in formal organizations, 116, 117
  group leadership and, 103
  homicide rates and, 3–4
  language and, 92–93

networking and, 109
  patriarchy and, 290
  personal performances and, 88–90
  research and, 20
  social inequality and, 37, 39
  socialization and, 235–39
  social stratification and, 239–46
  sports and, 14
  suicide rates and, 6
  in twenty-first century, 251–52
Gender roles, 235
Generalized other, 62
Genocide, 214
Germany, 11, 260, 261, 262, 270
Gerontocracy, 69
Gerontology, 68
Gesellschaft, 364, 381–82
Gestures, 91
Government, 269
Graying of America, 68–71
Great Britain, 84, 155–56, 158, 194, 260, 262, 264, 269, 272, 273, 281, 319
  medical system in, 339
Great Depression, 7–8, 265
Greece, 31, 261, 262, 357
Grenada, 278
"Groupthink," 105
Gun control, 143, 145

Haiti, 268, 270
Health, 329–45
  cross-cultural perspective, 330–31
  defined, 329
  old age and, 68–69, 70–71
  society and, 329–30
  in the U.S., 331–36
Health maintenance organization (HMO), 340
Hermaphrodite, 231
Heterosexuality, 231
Hidden curriculum, 63, 321
Hidden injury of class, 177
Hispanic Americans, 223–25, 295
Holistic medicine, 337–38
Homelessness, 177
Homicide, 139
  statistics, 3–4
Homogamy, 293
Homophobia, 231
Homosexuality, 231
  family life and, 299
Hong Kong, 201
Honor, 391
Horticultural society, 37–38, 164 (see also Preindustrial society)
  religion and, 308

Housework, 241–42
"Humanizing" bureaucracy, 116–17
Humor, 46, 93–96
Hungary, 260, 262
Hunting and gathering society, 37 (see also Preindustrial society)
  religion and, 308
  social stratification and, 164
"Hurried child," 66–67
Hypothesis, 21

Id, 57, 62
Idealism, 46
Idealization, 90–91
Identity, modernity and, 388–89
Ideology, 158
Illiteracy (see also Functional illiteracy):
  in U.S., 34
Incest taboo, 291
Income, 165
  college attendance and, 324
  gender and, 242–44
  health and, 332
  world comparisons, 188, 189
Independent variable, 18
India, 31, 33, 47, 79, 153–54, 158, 281, 292, 349
  poverty in, 191
Individuality, 4–6, 34, 35, 380
Indonesia, 31
Industrialization, 196
Industrial Revolution, 10, 39, 156, 158, 256–67, 308, 330, 358
Industrial society, 39
  aging and, 69
  education and, 318
  family groups and, 288
  health and, 330
  population growth and, 353–54
  rational world view and, 111
  religion and, 308
  social groups and, 102
  social inequality in, 154–56, 163, 164
Inequality, 152, 158–59 (see also Social-conflict paradigm)
  family life and, 294–96
  global, 180–203, 268
  health and, 330
  medicine and, 342
  modernity and, 387–88
  religion and, 304–5
  schooling and, 321–25
  social change and, 376
Infant mortality rate, 349
Information Revolution, 258
Ingroup, 106–7

Innovation, 128
Instincts, 32
Institutional discrimination, 211
Instrumental leadership, 103
Intelligence, culture and, 32
Intergenerational social mobility, 172
Interlocking directorate, 266
Interview, 21
Intragenerational social mobility, 172
Iran, 31, 33, 105, 306
Iran-contra affair, 105
Iraq, 278, 279, 281
Israel, 349
Italy, 260, 262

Japan, 7, 32, 33, 117–20, 160, 261, 262, 264, 267, 302, 318, 319, 349
medical system in, 339
Japanese Americans, 222–23
Juvenile delinquency, 124, 126, 130

Kaiapo, 374
Kenya, 31
Kibbutz, 232–33
Kinship, 288–89 (see also Family)
Ku Klux Klan, 41
Kuznets Curve, 164, 165

Labeling theory, 131–35, 138–39
Labor unions, 264
Laissez-faire leader, 103
Language, 33–34
gender and, 92–93
Latent function, 12
Leadership, group, 102–3
in formal organizations, 112–13
Lebanon, 278, 331
Lesbians, 231, 299
Liberation theology, 305–6
Libya, 281, 331
Life expectancy, 332, 349
Looking-glass self, 61
Lower class, 171
Lying, 88–89

Macro-level orientation, 13
Magnet schools, 328
Malaysia, 209
Males, 230–31 (see also Men and masculinity)
dominance of, 233–35 (see also Patriarchy)
gender roles and, 232–33
socialization and, 235–39

Malthusian theory, 351–52
Mandatory education laws, 318
Manifest function, 12
Marriage, 17, 289, 293
Masculine traits, 235
Mass-society theory of modernity, 378, 384–87, 388–89
Master status, 80–81
stigma as, 133
Material culture, 30
Materialism, 47
Matriarchy, 233
Matrilocality, 290
Mean, 18
Measurement, 17
Mechanical solidarity, 364, 382
Media, mass, 64–65
adolescent development and, 67
childhood development and, 66
gender socialization and, 238
Median, 18
Medicalization of deviance, 134
Medicine, 329–45
defined, 329
economics and, 338–39
scientific, 336–37
in the U.S., 339–40
Megalopolis, 363
Men and masculinity, 234 (see also Males; various topics)
family and, 290, 294, 297, 300
feminism and, 248
masculine traits, 235
masculinity as contest, 237
networking and, 109
sexism and, 233–34
stratification and, 239–41, 244
Mental illness, 133–34
Meritocracy, 159
Metaphysical stage, 9
Metropolis, 360
Metropolitan statistical area (MSA), 363
Mexican Americans, 223, 224
Mexico, 348, 349
Micro-level orientation, 13
Middle Ages, 10, 147, 155–56, 158, 160, 192, 358
Middle class, 170
"middle-class slide," 173–74
Migration, 350
Military, 279–81
Military-industrial complex, 281
Minority, 208
educational achievement of, 325
hundred-year perspective, 226
women as, 245–46
Miscegenation, 213
Mode, 18
Modernity, 379–95

Modernization, 379–81
in global perspective, 392–93
Modernization theory, 192–96, 201, 267–68, 393
"Mommy-track" controversy, 242–43
Monarchy, 269
Monogamy, 289
Monopoly, 266
Mores, 36
Mormonism, 307–8
Mortality, 349
Multinational corporations, 192, 267–68

Names, changes in, 4
Native Americans, 17, 215–17
Nature vs. nurture, 49, 54–55
Nazi Germany, 214, 270
Neocolonialism, 192
Neolocality, 290
Netherlands, 269, 273
Network, 108–9
New social movements theory, 378–79
Nicaragua, 105, 116, 349
Nigeria, 349
Nonmaterial culture, 30
Nonverbal communication, 87–89
Norms, 36
North Korea, 270
Nuclear family, 289
Nuclear power, 332–33
Nuclear weapons, 281
Norway, 269

Objectivity, in scientific research, 19–20
Occupations, 166–67
gender and, 240–41
Old age, 68–71
poverty and, 70
Oligarchy, 116
Oligopoly, 266–67
One-parent families, 298–99
Operationalizing a variable, 17
Organic solidarity, 364, 382
Organization, 109–20
bureaucracy in, 110–20
in Japan, 117–20
Other-directedness, 389
Outgroup, 106–7

Pakistan, 281, 306, 357
Panama, 270, 278, 279
Paradigm (see Theoretical paradigm)
Parkinson's Law, 114

Participant observation, 23, 24
Pastoralism, 37 (see also Preindustrial society)
religion and, 308
Patriarchy, 290
defined, 233
religion and, 304–5
sexism and, 233–35
Patrilocality, 290
Peace, 278, 282–83
Peer group, 63–64
gender socialization and, 236
Perestroika, 256, 263, 320
Performance, 85–87, 101
Personality, 54
deviant behavior and, 126
Freud's model, 57–58
Personal space, 90
Peru, 31
Peter Principle, 114–15
Philippines, 32, 37, 116, 270
Physical disability:
education and, 328
as master status, 80, 133
Physicians, 86–87, 90–91, 340–41
Pink-collar jobs, 166
Play, 60, 237
"play stage" (Mead), 61
Plea bargaining, 146
Pluralism, cultural, 212–13
Pluralism, political, 275, 276
Poland, 260, 262, 271
Police, 143, 145–46
Political action committee, 274
Politics, 268–85
American, 272–75
defined, 268
gender and, 245
party identification, 273
social class and, 172
Pollution, 332–33
Polygamy, 289
Population, 348–56, 359
growth, 350, 351–56, 358, 360
in research, 21
social change and, 377
Third-World poverty and, 190
Positivism, 9
Postindustrial economy, 257–58
work in, 263–66
Poverty:
in the U.S., 174–78
Third-World, 182, 187–92
Power, 163, 268
Power-elite, 275–76
Powerlessness, modernity and, 389–90
Preindustrial society:
aging and, 69, 70
conformity and, 380
economy of, 256